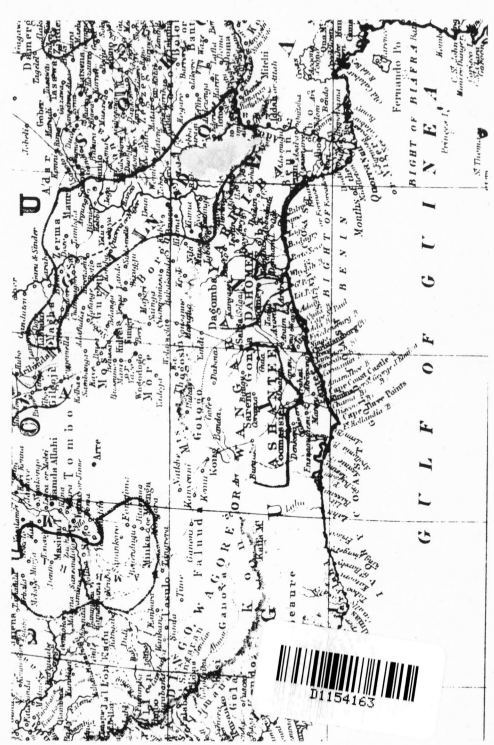

The Trade Makers

Elder Dempster in West Africa
1852-1972

BY

P. N. DAVIES
M.A., Ph.D., F.R.S.A.

Lecturer in Economic History in the
University of Liverpool

WITH A FOREWORD BY
LORD COLE

London
GEORGE ALLEN & UNWIN LTD
Ruskin House   Museum Street

First published in 1973

© George Allen & Unwin Ltd, 1973

ISBN 0 04 387003 1

To 'Old Tom'

Printed in Great Britain
in 12 point Barbou type
by W & J Mackay Limited, Chatham

Foreword

It is fifty years since my introduction to the business scene in West Africa, and I was particularly fortunate to have been throughout my career fairly close to where the action was taking place. My first appointment was as the second male member (there were 19 girl clerks) of the newly formed Statistical Department in The Niger Company when efforts were being made to bring order and system into the newly acquired group of companies. From there I became personal assistant to the Vice Chairman who was in effect the Managing Director. From the beginning, therefore, I was able to see Elder Dempster in its rightful position as an important element in West African Trade—as the mainstay of ocean carriage and, consequently, as an arbiter of that most important cost element to the trader, freight. At the lower end of the scale my own timetable was governed by the fortnightly sailing of the mailboat which had to be caught. Born and brought up in a seaport, I was fascinated by ships and shipping but it was something entirely new to hear these subjects discussed at a top managerial level. My subsequent promotion was to lead me to become Chairman of Palm Line (Unilever's shipping fleet), and eventually at the end of my career, Chairman of Unilever Limited.

My first voyage in an Elder Dempster vessel was in September, 1926, when I accompanied the Vice Chairman of The Niger Company on a visit which extended throughout West Africa, and it was largely that experience which enabled me to appreciate the opposing points of view when the two Companies were set on a collision course. But even though events must have been extremely painful to both sides (more so for Elder Dempster than for the United Africa Company, who had a fairy godmother in Unilever), there was within the rank and file of both Companies a great bond of sympathy, no doubt partly based on a common Merseyside origin. Part of the difficulty arose from Elders' determination not to give the larger firms more favourable terms than the smaller ones—a civilised creed more acceptable now than then. Dr Davies says that, even in the darkest period, the conversations went on. This is correct, and on the merchants side they went on too between themselves and the U.A.C.—with perhaps more acrimonious feelings. But all were blessed with great leaders, among whom none did more than Frank Samuel to promote a better understanding. I well remember the occasion when the leading merchants were first able to laugh about their 'secret' meetings and the exaggerated steps they then took to conceal them. That was the foundation for paving the way for a better understanding between Elders and Unilever—that, and the understanding which Elders showed (and I have always believed myself that only a bank-connected chairman could have appreciated it) when a monetary crisis in January, 1934, led to the increase in, and building up of, the U.A.C. fleet. Fortunately, trade was increasing and when the war came these ships were under the right flag.

Earlier negotiations between Elders and U.A.C. had broken down because of the U.A.C. demand that Elder Dempster's should hand over to them their lighterage interests. Apart from the fact that no shipping company in the conditions which existed in West Africa could so expose itself at that time, both parties must have known that lighterage had no worthwhile long term future; but it was a subject charged with emotion and the service a source of great pride. This relatively unimportant issue over-rode more important ones. Incidentally, lighterage in the Gold Coast was, so far as I am aware, the only operation in which the labour was paid the full cost of its work in advance—and never failed to carry out its contract. On another occasion the two managements were close to agreement over a luncheon in a London hotel when Leonard Cripps, who had been ill, was ushered into the room in a wheel chair, swathed in blankets, and fatally interrupted the proceedings! But it was only a matter of time before better understanding was reached.

Dr Davies has written a magnificent and accurate account of the events. So often when I read a report of things of which I have first hand knowledge it appears to bear little relation to the facts—not so these pages. This is a history about the management and the men—not about the ships. As such, it deserves to be read far beyond the confines of the West African trade. I can commend it to all who would have some knowledge of how such matters are ordered and the events which influence men in momentous decisions.

COLE

Contents

CONTENTS

Illustrations

ILLUSTRATIONS

Preface

Members of the public who recognise the name of 'Elder Dempster' might link its activities with West Africa. Amongst these people there may, at best, be an awareness of its role as a large and progressive shipping company; at worst there could be an unfounded suspicion that in some way it had its antecedents in the slave trade. Until now there has been no single authoritative source to which reference could be made, although the need for one had been clearly recognised:—'The history of the way in which Elder Dempster and Company acquired control of the West African carrying trade is still to be written. The glimpse of their activities which appears in the merchants' records suggest that it will be, when it is told, as much a story of "cut-throat competition" as theirs.'[1]

The work of Charlotte Leubuscher did shed some light on certain aspects of West African shipping and but for her untimely death she would undoubtedly have contributed a great deal more.[2] Nevertheless, serious gaps in our knowledge remained and it is the purpose of the present work to attempt to remedy these omissions so far as it is possible in the space of a single volume.

The scope of this book, therefore, is to describe and analyse the economic history of Elder Dempster and its predecessors. It aims to provide a guide to the Company's business affairs and this necessarily involves the reader in some aspects of shipping and trading practices down the years, together with an account of the economic background both in West Africa and in the United Kingdom. It is in no sense a 'Romance of the Sea'. Ships are discussed but, apart from the periods of war, are regarded as the tools of the trade and are only significant in so far as they contribute to profitability. Individuals, too, receive rather less attention than might be expected. The author is firmly of the belief

[1] Cherry Gertzel, 'A British Merchant in West Africa in the Era of Imperialism'. Unpublished Ph.D. thesis in the Bodleian Library, Oxford, 1959.

[2] Miss Leubuscher died in 1961 and her unrevised manuscript was published as *The West African Shipping Trade, 1909-1959*, by A. W. Sythoff of Leyden, in 1963.

that the personnel and management of a firm are its prime assets and that whatever progress is made rests ultimately on their efforts, but he also feels that the difficulties of evaluation are so great that only the really exceptional character can be given any prominence. The criteria of a commercial undertaking's success or failure is essentially a financial one and this is the yardstick which is applied, with some reservations, to Elder Dempster achievements during the past one hundred and twenty years.

The author is well aware of the many imperfections of this work in spite of the long period spent in research and composition. One major difficulty has been that few records cover such a long time-span in a single format. Consequently it is not claimed that the sources which have been consulted were in any sense complete or comprehensive. In practice, therefore, many short series, or fragments, have had to be used—not because they were considered ideal but because, in many cases, they alone were available. With advantage, several additional years could have been spent on the interpretation of the source material but the paucity of existing works have convinced him that publication must not be further delayed. This view has been strongly confirmed by the demands for information both by scholars and by members of the public. As a result, this study is offered in its present form with the thought that it may provide a basis for the criticism and further researches of other academics. This, of course, is the true path to a fuller understanding in this field as in all others.

Any academic study which attempts to deal with the history or economic development of a business or industry is necessarily heavily dependent upon the willing co-operation of members of the trade. In this examination of Elder Dempster Lines and its predecessors, in the period from 1852 to the present day, I have been extremely fortunate in securing the help of many men who have spent the whole of their working lives in the shipping, finance or trade of the Coast. In effect, therefore, this work has been in the nature of a joint effort between a member of the Department of Economic History in the University of Liverpool and many of the senior executives of the principal companies engaged in the shipping and commerce of West Africa.

I am especially indebted to the late Sir Alan Tod, formerly a senior partner in Baring Brothers, a former chairman of Elder Dempster Lines Holdings Limited (now Liner Holdings Limited), and a past director of Elder Dempster Lines Limited. He granted me the rare privilege of several stimulating interviews at which he discussed the theoretical as well as the practical problems posed by the collapse of the Royal Mail group. He was also kind enough to read the section of this work which deals with the reconstruction of Elder Dempster from 1932 to 1936, and a number of his suggestions proved to be extremely useful.

My sincere thanks are due to Mr F. L. Lane, chairman of Elder Dempster Lines from 1963 to 1972, and to a number of his fellow directors including Mr G. J. Ellerton—the present chairman—Mr P. F. Earlam and Mr J. D. Robertson, all of whom have helped to give me an insight into the current workings and policies of the firm. I owe a special debt to Mr J. H. Joyce, chairman from 1945 to 1963 and a former chairman of the West African Lines Conference. Mr Joyce's vast experience of the West African shipping trade has been made freely available to me and has provided an essential background to my study of post-war reconstruction. I would also like to acknowledge the invaluable assistance supplied by former directors of the Company including Mr A. M. Bennett, Mr M. B. Glasier, Mr A. E. Muirhead and Brigadier P. J. D. Toosey. I am also indebted to Mr H. J. Bowers for his assistance with technical matters, to Mr S. A. Cotton for his kindness in the early stages of this work, to Mr F. Grayson for the provision of statistical support, to Mr C. A. C. Hamilton for his help in preparing for publication, to Mr T. Kennan for his clarification of accountancy conventions, to Mr M. H. Smye for giving me the benefit of his previous research and to Mr A. J. White, Secretary of Ocean Transport and Trading Limited, for his helpful guidance on many occasions.

The present staff of Elder Dempster Lines have given me every possible assistance with my research, and my visit to West Africa in 1969 brought me into contact with a large number of extremely kind people who did everything possible to ensure that my trip was both comfortable and profitable. I feel it would be unfair to single out particular individuals for praise but would just like to mention Captain J. C. Gibson (M.V. *Falaba*) and Captain J. Morris (M.V. *Daru*) who together with their crews made sure that my journey was especially instructive and pleasant. The Company's pensioners proved to be an invaluable mine of information and I would like to offer my sincere thanks to Messrs. H. Ambler, T. D. Anderson, R. H. Chalcroft, the late Ade Lewis-Coker, T. H. Cowley, A. S. Glendinning, W. L. Leinster,

J. C. Lucas, G. H. Neville, F. E. Ogley, William Toe, E. T. Wheeler and A. C. Wyness. My thanks are also due to Mr John Gordon and Mr F. T. Griffiths of Ocean Management Services' Publicity Department. Without their constant aid and encouragement this work would have been much the poorer.

I am especially indebted to Lord Cole, the former chairman of Unilever Limited, on two counts: firstly for agreeing to write a Foreword to this study and, secondly, for a most informative interview. His first-hand evidence in respect of the break between the United Africa Company and the West African Lines Conference, and of their subsequent relations in the thirties is of the utmost importance to this study and I am grateful for his permission to include it here. Sir Frederick Pedler, a former managing director of the United Africa Company, is currently working on a history of that firm and has given me much valuable assistance on matters of common concern. Mr A. I. Anderson and Mr J. D. Keir, the present chairman and secretary of the U.A.C. have also made a significant contribution to my understanding by ensuring that the records of their Company were placed at my disposal. The late Mr W. K. Findlay, a former chairman of the Niger Company, gave me a unique picture of West African affairs in the eighties and nineties of the last century and I owe him an important debt. To Mr R. H. Muir, a former director with special responsibility for transport, to Mr A. C. Geake, a former Liverpool shipping manager and to Mr T. C. Catherall, the present Liverpool manager, I offer my sincere thanks.

I would also like to express my thanks to Mr A. E. Hoffman, a former chairman of the Palm Line Limited, and to his colleagues, Mr J. C. McNeil, Mr J. G. W. Tilby and Mr H. W. Turner, all of whom took considerable pains to assist my understanding of their firm and its history. The then manager of Palm Line's Liverpool Office, M J. Merriweather and the late Captain G. G. Astbury, master of the Niger Company's first ocean-going ship, also gave me substantial aid in their own particular spheres. Henry Tyrer and Company were managers of the U.A.C.'s shipping division before this was reorganised as the Palm Line in 1950. The late Mr Frederick Cutts spent seventy-two years with Tyrer's, and in spite of heavy commitments in the running of this business while in his eighties he generously made a great deal of his time available to me. The present chairman, Mr C. W. Harrison, has continued the friendly relationship developed with Mr Cutts and has given considerable help in the more recent affairs of his Company.

I am exceedingly grateful to the late Mr Cecil Holt, formerly a senior partner of John Holt and Company (Liverpool) Limited, and to Mr Douglas Mather, a past chairman of the Guinea Gulf Line Limited. Both of these gentlemen took time and trouble to explain the policies and attitudes of their companies and were able to clarify many difficult issues. It was particularly useful for me to be able to consult the John Holt archives and for this privilege I would like to thank, amongst others, Mr Ian Holt. My gratitude is also due to the late Captain Harry Fuller, one of John Holt's longest serving officers, who provided some much appreciated information on the sailings of the Line's early vessels.

Elder Dempster's relationships with other shipping lines form an important part of this study and I would like to acknowledge the friendly assistance given by M. Paul Vereecke and Commodore J. C. Bernaerts of the Compagnie Maritime Belge; by Mr A. McCrae and Mr R. Borland of the Henderson Line; Mr J. D. Wilson and Mr G. Walker of the Mountwood Shipping Company; Mr B. Whittingham of the Nigerian National Shipping Line: Mr J. J. Gawne of the Pacific Steam Navigation Company; Mr W. R. Barlow of Royal Mail Lines and Mr L. Bohlen and Mr K. Lindenberg of the Woermann Line.

I am also greatly indebted to the following who, in various ways, have made information available to me or have aided my understanding of topics on the fringe of the main study: Mr S. S. Anagnostis, formerly of Paterson, Zochonis; Mr W. H. Cotterell, grandson of Harry Cotterell; the late Mr D. E. Erlebach of Erlebach and Company (Ship Charterers); Mr J. W. Evans of the Survey Office, Kano; Mr J. Griffiths, Secretary of the Chamber of Mines, Jos, Nigeria; Mr Redfern Halsall, formerly a West African merchant; Mrs Fisher Hoch, eldest daughter of Lord Kylsant; Mr K. Hopkins of the Commercial Library, Liverpool; Mr Harding F. Hunt of J. T. Fletcher and Company; Mr D. J. Leacock, a banana grower in Grand Canary; Miss A. Lythgoe of the Arts Reading Room, University of Liverpool; Mr J. McCormick, Secretary of United Kingdom/West Africa Lines Joint Services; Mr Gerald Miller of Las Palmas; Mrs F. N. Mocatta, a grand-niece of Sir Alfred Jones; Chief Ben Oluwole of West African Steel and Wire Limited; Mr A. E. Orme, formerly a West African merchant; Mr D. J. T. Owens, Secretary of the West African Shippers Association; Mr E. V. Pavillard of Elder Dempster (Canary Isles) Limited; Commander F. W. Skutil, the last director of the Nigerian Marine; Mr F. R. Stuart, whose family were connected with Stuart and Douglas and the African Association; Sir Eric Tansley, formerly director of the West African Produce Control Board and Mr E. W. Paget-Tomlinson, a former Keeper of Shipping at the City of Liverpool Museum.

I am also most anxious to express my gratitude to my colleagues (and former colleagues) in the School of Economics, at the University of Liverpool. In particular, Professor A. M. Bourn, now Director of Liverpool University's Business School, gave considerable assistance with the interpretation of company accounts; Dr J. R. Harris, now Professor of Economic History at the University of Birmingham, and Dr Sheila Marriner made their considerable experience in shipping matters available to me; Mr W. T. Osborn, now with the Ministry of Housing, gave me his willing help with the statistical sections and Dr S. B. Saul, now Professor of Economic History at the University of Edinburgh, provided much stimulating advice. I am also indebted to many other members of the academic community who have guided me with their specialised knowledge and would especially like to offer my thanks to Professor K. Burley (University of London, Ontario), Dr Dennis Chapman (University of Liverpool), Mr Robin Craig (University College, London), Dr P. E. H. Hair (University of Liverpool) and Dr A. G. Hopkins (University of Birmingham).

My thanks are also due to Miss Valerie Dodd and Mrs E. Harris who were responsible for the typing of the text. Their unflagging interest in what must eventually have been an arduous task did much to sustain me and I am truly grateful for their help.

Finally, I wish to acknowledge that whatever merit this work might have as scholarship it owes to the constant example and sympathetic encouragement given to me by Professor F. E. Hyde, Chaddock Professor of Economic History in the University of Liverpool. For this, and for permission to quote from his published work, I am deeply grateful and offer my sincere thanks.

P. N. Davies
Department of Economic History,
University of Liverpool   *August, 1972*

Abbreviations Used in the Footnotes

A.S.P.	*African Steam Ship Company Papers*
C.O.	*Colonial Office Papers*
D.N.B.	*Dictionary of National Biography*
E.D.P.	*Elder Dempster Papers*
E.D.L.P.	*Elder Dempster Lines Papers*
E.M.P.	*E. D. Morel Papers*
E.&O.P.N.&S.C.	*Report of the Committee on Edible and Oil Producing Nuts and Seeds*
F.O.	*Foreign Office Papers*
G.G.L.MSS.	*Guinea Gulf Line Mss.*
HOLT MSS.	*Alfred Holt and Company Mss.*
I.S.C.	*Final Report of the Imperial Shipping Committee on the Deferred Rebate System*
J.H.P.	*John Holt Papers*
LEVER MSS.	*Lever Brothers Limited, Mss.*
R.C.S.R.	*Royal Commission on Shipping Rings*
R.M.S.P. MINUTES	*Minutes of the Royal Mail Steam Packet Company*
R.N.C.P.	*Royal Niger Company Papers*
HENRY TYRER MSS.	*Henry Tyrer and Company Mss.*
U.A.C.MSS.	*United Africa Company Mss.*

Note: Full details of these abbreviations and of all others works cited in the footnotes are given in the Bibliography, pp. 497–506.

Acknowledgments

The photographs and pictures utilised in this work were included with the kind permission of Dr A. S. Davidson, Mr G. J. Ellerton, Mr C. W. Harrison, Mrs Fisher-Hoch, the Misses Howie, Mr Harding F. Hunt, Mr. F. L. Lane, Lady H. M. Tod and Mr. J. H. Joyce.

Quotations and references are all fully documented in the text. The author also wishes to thank the following for permission to quote extensive extracts from their published works or archives:

Chamber of Shipping of the United Kingdom.

Fairplay Publications Limited.

John Holt and Company (Liverpool) Limited.

The Federal Government of Nigeria's Ministry of Information.

Thomas Skinner (West African) Directories.

The magazine 'West Africa'.

United Africa Company.

United Nations.

Extracts from Her Majesty's Stationery Office publications are used with the permission of the Controller of Her Majesty's Stationery Office.

The maps used in the end papers are produced by kind permission of Geographia Ltd and are taken from the map prepared for WALCON in 1962.

Introduction

The coastline of West Africa lies between Cape Verde and Mount Cameroon. This is a distance of approximately 2,400 miles, but it only contains two good natural harbours—those at Dakar and Freetown. Both of these are situated in the extreme west of the region, while the remainder of the seaboard provides few satisfactory port sites because of the presence of esturine bars, heavy surf, shallow lagoons, marshes or mangrove swamps.[1] The land behind the coast consists mainly of tropical rain forests or savannah and these diverse areas have naturally developed two different cultures. The inhabitants of the forest lands near the coast, where the climate is hot and moist, have tended to live in small, inward-looking communities, with a subsistence economy based on a limited technology; whereas those who lived in the hot, dry climate of the savannah have more commonly joined together in larger societies which have enjoyed a more advanced economy and technology. Moreover, the existence of a coastal forest belt to the south, allied with the activities in the forest of the tsetse fly, has meant that the savannah areas of the interior were virtually isolated from the western seaboard. In these circumstances the trade that was undertaken tended to be relatively small and came overland from either the north or east of Africa.[2]

Europe first came into contact with West Africa as a result of the voyages organised by Prince Henry of Portugal in the middle of the fifteenth century.[3] The prime objective of these explorations was to find a new route to India but a small trade slowly evolved along the West African coastline. This activity assumed a new significance with the discovery of the Gold Coast and in 1482 a fort was established on the site of what is now Elmina. Gold, ivory, pepper, civet, palm oil, palm mats, ambergris, wax, hides, skins, cotton, rice, wooden bowls and

[1] H. P. White, 'The Ports of West Africa', *Tijdschrift voor Economische en Sociale Geographie* (1959), Vol. L, No. 1, pp. 1–8.

[2] Roland Oliver and J. D. Fage, *A Short History of Africa* (Penguin, 1962), pp. 102–11.

[3] John W. Blake, *European Beginnings in West Africa, 1454–1578* (London: Longmans, 1937).

millet were then exported in increasing quantities in exchange for imports of cloth, brass bracelets, corals, wine, shells and beads. Profits from these transactions proved to be extremely high, but the heavy mortality from tropical diseases tended to inhibit the growth of the trade.[1]

Until about 1530 the Portuguese enjoyed a near monopoly in West Africa, but then French privateers and merchants started to take an ever-increasing interest. Twenty years later the British also began to take a share in the business and in 1562 John Hawkins of Plymouth inaugurated English participation in the transatlantic slave trade. The trade in slaves was not, of course, a European innovation. Domestic slavery was a common feature of African society, and for many thousands of years black slaves had been brought down the Nile into the Mediterranean, and from the east coast of Africa to the nearer lands of the Indian Ocean. Moreover, since at least 1000 A.D., slaves had been brought from West Africa, across the Sahara, to the Arab lands of North Africa and the Middle East, where they were employed as soldiers and guards as well as in more mundane occupations. There was also an internal demand within West Africa, but this varied from time to time and from place to place as circumstances changed. The Portuguese found that slaves were cheap at Benin owing to its numerous wars with its neighbours, but dear at Elmina, where external trade was stimulating fresh activities. Consequently they entered into this remunerative business and acted as intermediaries between the African groups along the coast. The Portuguese, therefore, became well acquainted with the idea of slavery and were only continuing what was regarded as the normal practice when they sent a small number of slaves to work in Portugal and Spain. The demand for labour in the 'new world' then transformed this situation and from modest beginnings in the sixteenth century the transatlantic slave trade grew rapidly and dominated West African economic development until the early nineteenth century.[2]

Throughout the sixteenth century, in spite of increasing competition from France and Britain, the Portuguese not only retained their power in West Africa but also built up a predominant position in the slave trade. The intervention of the Dutch gradually altered this situation and by 1642 the Portuguese had been permanently ejected from the

---

[1] S. Daniel Neumark, *Foreign Trade and Economic Development in Africa* (Food Research Institute, Stanford University, 1963), pp. 34-7.

[2] S. Daniel Neumark, op. cit., p. 50.

Gold Coast. The Dutch also seized a substantial share of the transatlantic slave trade from the Portuguese but, in turn, lost their ascendancy in this field to the French and British. By the middle of the eighteenth century British firms had largely ousted French ones and by 1800 British ships were carrying the vast majority of all slaves exported to America and the Caribbean. But British pre-eminence in the slave trade did not necessitate the establishment of formal colonies. The native rulers were not only prepared to deal with European merchants but also insisted that all commerce, including slaves, must pass through their hands. African middlemen thus became intermediaries between the sources of supply in the interior and the expatriate firms on the seaboard. Some of the coastal chiefs then developed their territories into slave-trading kingdoms such as Lagos, Dahomey, Bonny, and many others owed their origin and greatness to the rise of the slave trade.'[1]

From its earliest days British trade with West Africa was organised by chartered companies. These attempted to give a monopoly of British trade to exclusive groups who banded together for mutual advantage and protection. The trade was therefore illegal for all other British nationals, but this did not deter the activities of many interlopers, or indeed the commerce enjoyed by other European powers. The most successful of the chartered firms was the Royal African Company.[2] This was formed in 1672 but lost its monopoly in 1697 after continual pressure from other interested parties. Thereafter the trade was open to all, but the competition which followed and which led ultimately to the supremacy of Liverpool over London and Bristol led to a demand for some controlling authority. In 1750, therefore, the Company of Merchants Trading to Africa was established by Act of Parliament. This provided that all British subjects having business in West Africa were entitled to join the Company on demand. The only obligation was that members had to contribute a small annual sum to help pay for the upkeep of the forts it was proposed to maintain on the coast. In practice this meant that the trade remained 'open' to all British firms and this proved to be a significant factor in increasing British participation in West African affairs.

The profitability of slave trading to both African middleman and

[1] K. Onwuka Dike, *Trade and Politics in the Niger Delta, 1830–1885* (London: Oxford University Press, 1956), p. 13.
[2] K. G. Davies, *The Royal African Company* (London: Longmans, 1957).

European merchant was so high that in many areas it retarded the growth of other commercial activities. Nevertheless, the export of traditional commodities did continue and it should not be assumed that concentration on slave trading was the only factor to limit its development. Tropical fevers and extremes of climate attacked merchants irrespective of their type of business, but the difficulties of inland transport and of shipping bore more heavily on legitimate trade, particularly where bulky items were concerned. Slaves, on the other hand, could not only walk to the coast but were also, in a sense, self-stowing on board ship, so the lack of satisfactory roads or waterways, or of loading facilities, was seldom a serious drawback to those engaged in the slave trade.

In the early days of trade with West Africa a ship would anchor at a convenient point in a creek or river. The topmasts would be removed and grass mats be placed in position to roof over the deck. The vessel, in effect, then became a shop. During the trading period, which could be a lengthy one, many of the crew might become ill owing to the terrible climate and the insanitary conditions. As a means of reducing the high mortality rate, the 'relay system' then came to be adopted. This arranged for the ships to be run in pairs with only one crew—the ship remaining off the coast being left with only a small trading staff. From this method to the use of an old hulk permanently moored in a suitable place was only a small transition, and this had an agent on board instead of a captain. At situations where it was considered safe, a shore trading station or 'beach' then developed and the hulks were gradually abandoned. In other places where the political position ashore was dangerous, casual trading direct from ships continued to a much later date.

Trading conditions in the Bight of Benin, now part of Nigeria, were typical of those in many other parts of West Africa. Trade was almost entirely in the hands of the native chiefs of the coastal areas and their main currencies were manillas, or rods of copper and brass. A deal would begin with an exchange of visits at which time a present called a 'handshake' would be given by the trader to the native ruler. Credit was sometimes arranged and was calculated in puncheons of palm oil—the usual rate of interest was 25 per cent and was known as 'topside'. For each transaction the chief received a present called 'gentlemen's dash', and his followers received 'boys' dash'. An export tax known as 'comey' was levied in some places in addition to the 'dashes' and this was supposed to be for the benefit of the whole tribe. The British merchants made much use of African agents to trade with places in the interior which it would not have been safe for them to visit, and even when Europeans were able to move some distance inland there were always large areas still further afield where the African middlemen could do useful work. The system commonly used was for the merchant to advance credit to the African by supplying him with a quantity of trade goods. The latter would then go up country and exchange these goods for local produce (or promises of local produce) and on his return to the coast would settle his account with his supplier. The grave disadvantage of this system was that it meant giving large credits to itinerant Africans who thus had a strong incentive to become dishonest. Unfortunately it was not possible to end this type of trading without universal agreement between all the merchants—hardly a practical proposition—and it did enable goods to reach areas which would otherwise have been untouched by trade.

The last English slaver, the *Kitty's Amelia* sailed from Liverpool on 27 July 1807.[1] Thereafter trading in slaves, as distinct from the owning of slaves, was illegal for British subjects. Denmark had already taken this step and the United States, Sweden, the Netherlands, France and Brazil had all followed suit by 1825. In addition, by 1817 Portugal and Spain had agreed to limit their activities to the seas south of the Equator, so that theoretically they were no longer active in West Africa. Unfortunately, however, this did not mean an end to the transatlantic slave trade for it was not until 1888 that all nations finally abolished slave owning. In the meanwhile, an active trade continued to flourish in spite of the activities of the British naval blockade,[2] for the growing of slave-produced sugar in Cuba and Brazil and of slave-produced cotton in the United States was an extremely profitable undertaking.[3]

The legal ending of the slave trade, however ineffective in practice, did mark the beginning of a new commercial era in West Africa. The staple exports were no longer subjected to the same degree of competition, and the palm oil industry gradually began to expand. Difficulties of internal transport prevented rapid growth but the quantity of palm

[1] Christopher Lloyd, *The Navy and the Slave Trade* (London: Longmans, 1949), p. 3.
[2] S. Daniel Neumark, op. cit., p. 58.
[3] Christopher Lloyd, op. cit., Appendix A, 'Exports and Captures'.

oil imported into Liverpool rose from 55 tons in 1785 to 1,000 tons in 1810 and to 30,000 tons in 1851.[1] In spite of the development of this trade the oil proved to be a poor substitute for slaves and the ensuing problems led to a reorganisation of British commerce. In 1821 the Company of Merchants Trading to Africa ended its activities and after that date the trade was completely free of all restrictions. This did little, however, to encourage the growth of legitimate trade because the reluctance of the British government to undertake direct responsibilities in West Africa, allied to the terribly high rates of mortality from tropical diseases, was a strong limiting factor. In addition, trade could not be significantly increased until the merchants or their agents penetrated to the interior and this could not be achieved until the outlet of the Niger was discovered.

At the beginning of the nineteenth century it was still not understood that the 'Oil Rivers' were, in fact, the delta of the River Niger. Mungo Park had seen that the Niger flowed to the east and not west into Senegal as previously assumed, but had been killed while attempting to sail down the river to the coast. In 1825 Clapperton and Lander also failed when the former died of fever, but in 1830 Lander and his brother finally managed to follow the course of the river to its mouth. At one stroke this appeared to open the interior to European trade for it offered a means of bypassing the native middlemen on the seaboard as well as providing a highway for the cheap carriage of imports and exports. Macgregor Laird was convinced that this was the case, but an expedition organised by him and Richard Lander was not only a financial disaster but also resulted in the deaths of almost all who took part.[2] Several other parties shared the same fate and it became clear to Laird that the Niger would only be of real value to commerce when medicine could provide an answer to tropical diseases. He accordingly turned his attention to other matters and it was not until 1849 that he was again actively concerned with West Africa. He then directed all of his energies towards the provision of regular shipping services to that coast and these reached fruition in 1852 with the formation of the African Steam Ship Company.[3]

[1] Allan McPhee, *The Economic Revolution in British West Africa* (London: George Routledge, 1926), p. 32.

[2] Christopher Lloyd, op. cit., p. 21.

[3] P. N. Davies, 'The African Steam Ship Company', in J. R. Harris, Ed., *Liverpool and Merseyside* (London: Frank Cass, 1969).

As previously indicated, neither the slave trade nor the rise in legitimate business required the establishment of formal British colonies in West Africa. Nevertheless, British interests had gradually acquired a number of footholds along the coastline and these were to form the centres from which colonial territories were ultimately to be created. The Gambia had been settled on a permanent basis in 1816 after several centuries of fluctuating trade in beeswax, ivory, hides, gold and slaves. The ending of the slave trade left the economy at a low ebb and this continued until the ground-nut industry began to develop. The first few baskets of nuts were exported in 1830 and by 1848 exports had risen to 8,600 tons valued at £104,000.[1] The existence of a modest harbour at Bathurst and the communications provided by the Gambia River, navigable for ocean-going vessels for 150 miles, were obvious advantages in promoting the growth of trade. Sierra Leone had been founded in 1787 as a centre for emancipated slaves who could not be returned to their former homes. At first it was organised by the Sierra Leone Company but in 1807 the Crown assumed direct control. The colony was fortunate in having an excellent harbour at Freetown and a number of small but navigable rivers which assisted in the bringing of produce to the coast. In the earlier period, timber, ground-nuts, ginger and a little coffee were the main exports, but by 1850 palm kernels and palm oil were of paramount importance.

The Gold Coast '. . . was the special preserve of the successive African Companies from the days of James I to the times of George IV.'[2] The Crown took over the government in 1821, but bad relations with the merchants, the terrible effects of the climate and an unsuccessful war against the Ashanti led the home government to decide to withdraw in 1828. This evoked so many protests from the British traders that a compromise was reached. A subsidy of £4,000 a year was granted for the merchants to man and maintain the coastal forts, and it was with this pitiful sum that George Maclean, appointed Governor in 1830, did so much. Under his guidance, trade and British influence increased to such an extent that in 1843 the Crown resumed direct control. From 1820 onwards palm-oil exports grew rapidly and were the largest item when the Gold Coast became a separate colony in 1850.

[1] Sir Alan Pim, *The Financial and Economic History of the African Tropical Territories* (Oxford: Clarendon Press, 1940), p. 34.
[2] Allan McPhee, op. cit., p. 10.

The fourth region of British influence in West Africa was in what we now know as Nigeria. In 1850 this still remained a purely trading area and the British government was not involved in its administration.[1] The export of palm oil had by then become quite important and the Liverpool merchants were very active in this trade. They operated only in the coastal areas, receiving the oil from Africans at various points near the sea or on the 'Oil Rivers'. By and large they were antagonistic to attempts to open up the Niger for they felt that if this were successful it would tend to divert much of their business. The Liverpool merchants therefore had a common interest with many African middlemen and together they resisted all efforts to change the pattern of trade. Medical advances made sailing up the Niger a practical proposition after 1854 but the opposition of European and African vested interests meant that little commercial progress was achieved until the formation of the United African Company (the forerunner of the Royal Niger Company) in 1879.[2]

In the second half of the nineteenth century British interests in West Africa were gradually increased. A brief survey of political events might suggest that Britain was following a policy of dynamic expansion, but this is a misleading impression. In 1850 all the Danish interests in the Gold Coast were purchased for £10,000. In 1861 Lagos was annexed and in 1872 came the cessation of the Dutch forts. These gains were confirmed by the defeat of the Ashantis in 1874 but many influential people in England were against any expansion and in 1865 a Parliamentary Committee had advised almost complete withdrawal from West Africa.[3] While this was not acted upon the government was quick to end its occupation of Ashanti and funds for West African projects became even more difficult to obtain. At the Congress of Berlin in 1884, however, the British government began to appreciate that if it took no action France and Germany would reap a considerable benefit. A policy was then evolved to extend British sovereignty to inland areas. This was partly designed to increase trade but its primary object was to prevent the French and Germans from cutting off the coastal settlements from the interior. But the British government believed that the

[1] Sir Alan Burns, *History of Nigeria* (London: Allen & Unwin, 1942).

[2] J. E. Flint, *Sir George Goldie and the Making of Nigeria* (London: Oxford University Press, 1960).

[3] Parliamentary Papers, 1865, v. (412), p. iii.

public would not support the undertaking of vast new expenses and responsibilities in West Africa, and so it adopted the expedient of creating a chartered company to do its work for it.[1]

Thus, in 1886 the Royal Niger Company came into being and was given the duty of ruling as well as the privilege of exclusive trading in enormous areas of the Niger basin. A gradual change in public opinion was then reflected by changes within the British government and these were confirmed by the advent of Joseph Chamberlain to the Colonial Office in 1895. Chamberlain was known to be in favour of a more vigorous colonial policy and one aspect of his work came to fruition in 1900 when the Royal Niger Company was replaced by the Crown—having played a large part in laying the foundations of modern Nigeria.

The main exports of British West Africa after the introduction of regular steam-shipping services in 1852 continued to be palm oil and palm kernels. Added together these formed from 43 to 76 per cent of the annual totals.[2] The enlarged demand was due to two factors. Larger quantities of edible oils and fats had to be imported into England merely to maintain existing standards, because of the rise in the population. At the same time a new demand was growing for oils to be used in the manufacture of soap and candles, and for use in lubricating the machinery called into being by the industrial revolution. Later in the century the discovery that kernels could be used instead of animal fats in the manufacture of margarine gave this export a tremendous impetus. From 1855 to 1900 the average amount of palm oil exported from British West Africa was about 50,000 tons each year. It would undoubtedly have been more, but the African producer was very sensitive to falling prices and the average price was halved in the period from 1850 to 1900.[3] Consequently many producers abandoned cash crops at times and returned to the growing of food for their own consumption.

The discovery that palm-kernel oil possessed valuable keeping qualities led to a rapid increase in its export during the eighteen-sixties. These qualities—not shared by palm oil—made it particularly useful in the manufacture of margarine and up to 1914 it found a ready market in

[1] J. D. Hargreaves, *Prelude to the Partition of West Africa* (London: MacMillan, 1963), p. 253.

[2] See Appendix, p. 397, Table 1.

[3] *Annual Abstract of the United Kingdom,* quoted by A. McPhee, op. cit., footnote to p. 33. Note that as shipping charges were also falling during this period the producer in Africa did not have to bear the full weight of the decline of prices in the U.K.

Germany. Ground-nut production was greatly stimulated by the demands of French soap-makers. As a result production rose from 12,000 tons in 1851 to an average of between 15,000 and 20,000 tons per annum during the latter part of the nineteenth century.[1] Cocoa began to be grown commercially in the eighties under the supervision of the local government. The industry expanded at a tremendous rate and by 1914 exports amounted to 52,888 tons—the Gold Coast proving to be the most suitable area for the production of cocoa.[2] Cotton was also encouraged and exports rose significantly during the American Civil War. It then went into a decline until 1902 when the British Cotton Growing Association was able to find new export markets. As a result production increased, especially in Nigeria, but the crop remained extremely small when compared with that of either the United States or the Sudan.[3] The export of rubber began in the seventies and reached a peak towards the end of the century. The plantations of Malaya then produced rubber at a far cheaper rate than it could be collected from West Africa forests, and so the industry failed to make progress. In more recent years there has been a trend towards more intensive development and the export figures have again risen. Timber, especially teak and mahogany, had been exported for several centuries. After 1850 it continued to be an important item but its relative value has declined owing to the expansion of other commodities.

A great deal of gold was found by the pioneer traders in West Africa but this proved to be the accumulation of many years of production. The amount actually mined was only small and the value of exports fell from £3,500,000 in 1700 to £400,000 in 1800. There was little attempt to introduce large-scale mining until about 1878 and the attempts then made by European firms failed because of the high costs of transport from the sea or river to the mines. It was not until the railways were extended to reach the goldfields that output could be increased, but then the 71,000 ounces mined in 1903 rose quickly to become 462,000 ounces in 1915.[4] Like gold, the tin and coal industries required rail transport before they could become efficient producers. Since this has

---

[1] J. R. McCulloch, *Dictionary of Commerce* (1883), p. 965.

[2] *Annual Reports for the Gold Coast*, H.M.S.O. (Relevant years).

[3] P. N. Davies, 'Sir Alfred Jones and the Development of West African Trade' (Unpublished M.A. thesis, University of Liverpool, 1964), p. 161.

[4] W. Page, *Commerce and Industry*, Vol. II, p. 199.

been provided great strides have been made and with the aid of modern technology many other minerals are now being exploited.

In 1787 British imports into West Africa consisted of the following main items: textiles (£408,000), metal goods (£97,000), spirits (£40,000) and arms and ammunition (£39,000).[1] During the nineteenth century imports rose both in volume and value but the chief commodities and their proportions of the total trade remained fairly constant until about 1880 when the growth of cash crops led to a large increase in the quantity of food imported. The Convention of Brussels in 1890 forbade the importation of all arms except flint-locks and smooth-bore weapons. Continuous attempts were also made to control the quality and quantity of spirits, but apart from these two items practically everything else was brought in without restriction. The range of imports gradually expanded to cover the numerous items necessary to maintain a European standard of living for the expatriate merchants and government officials. Towards the end of the nineteenth century the rise in the numbers of Europeans resident on the coast caused these commodities to assume a new importance and this was further enhanced as Western tastes and customs spread amongst members of the African community.

The inauguration of regular steam-shipping services in 1852 led to a number of significant changes in the organisation of West African trade. Until then the merchants operating on the coast had of necessity to own or charter a vessel in order to provide transport. This could, of course, be done in co-operation with other traders but in practice it meant that only firms with substantial resources took part in the trade. Once the African Steam Ship Company began to provide frequent sailings, the established merchants gradually utilised its services to supplement their own vessels and in time most came to rely entirely upon them. More important, however, was the large increase in the number of small traders. For the first time these individuals could order and receive goods from Britain quickly and cheaply, and could also transport the produce received in exchange in a convenient manner. The more successful of these were able to return to the United Kingdom after only a few years' hard work. They could then build up their business still further through the contacts they had acquired while on the Coast, the ease of communication enabling a satisfactory control to be maintained.

[1] A. Anderson, *Annals of Commerce*, Vol. IV, p. 154.

John Holt of Liverpool was an outstanding example of a merchant who developed his business in this way.[1]

The commercial system which became common towards the end of the nineteenth century was for British merchants to create their own branches in West Africa. These had the dual function of selling the goods sent out from Britain and purchasing the local products for transmission home. This fitted in quite naturally with the increase in the size of many firms which was consequent on the enlargement of the total trade, and many amalgamations hastened this process. The development of commerce ran concurrently with the growth in the use of a standardised currency, although barter and the employment of traditional measures of value also continued. Practically the entire trade of British West Africa was in the hands of English business houses until the eighties and even then the nationals of other European countries took only a minor part. Africans gradually came to take a fuller part in trade but their relative importance was very small at this time. The partnership was the customary method of organisation and it was only when a firm reached very large proportions that it became a joint-stock company. The size of the typical concern rose steadily, as did the employed capital, but as the partnerships did not make their accounts public, exact figures are not available. It is very clear, however, that most of the capital invested in British West Africa up to 1914 was of external origin, and that an overwhelming proportion of this came from Britain.

The provision of a satisfactory shipping service by the African Steam Ship Company in 1852 and of a second by the British and African Steam Navigation Company in 1869 was an important factor in the economic development of British West Africa. The really crucial event, however, came when these two lines were effectively merged into one operating entity under the auspices of Elder Dempster and Company, for this resulted in substantial investments being made in the facilities so essential for the expansion of trade.[2] In the absence of similar capital outlay by the British government these investments exerted a disproportionate influence when the 'scramble for Africa' began in 1884. Without them certain areas of West Africa might never have come under British

---

[1] *Merchant Adventure,* (Liverpool: John Holt, 1948).

[2] P. N. Davies, 'British Shipping and the Growth of the West African Economy, 1910–1950' (Unpublished Ph.D. thesis, University of Liverpool, 1967).

protection and in others the pace of development would inevitably have been far slower. Shipping lines, of course, have a vested interest in the promotion of trade—in the case of West Africa the activities of Elder Dempster in the nineteenth century were so comprehensive that the suggestion that they 'made' the trade has more than a grain of truth. It is not claimed that the Company's motives were ever altruistic, for commercial considerations were obviously paramount. Nevertheless, it can be argued with much justification that the policies adopted by Elder Dempster in its own self-interest not only had a significant impact on the shaping of British West Africa but also had a beneficial and lasting effect on the economic well-being of its population.

Macgregor Laird.

Alexander Elder.

PLATE I

John Dempster.

Sir Alfred Lewis Jones.

Lord Pirrie.

Lord Kylsant.

PLATE 2

Sir Richard Durning Holt.

Mr and Mrs Henry Tyrer.

PART ONE

The Pioneers

Chapter 1

Macgregor Laird

The Penetration of the Niger

Macgregor Laird was in many ways the most important of the early pioneers of West African trade. He was a grandson of the John Laird who had been born into a farming community in Kilmacolm, Renfrewshire in the middle of the eighteenth century. This was the same John Laird who established a firm of ropemakers at Greenock and eventually became Provost of that Burgh. He was said to be a friend of Wesley and 'a very handsome man, somewhat stern in his manner and kept his family at a great distance'.[1]

One of John Laird's ten children was William, born in 1780. William married Agnes, the daughter of Gregor Macgregor who at one time commanded a ship which traded between Greenock and the West Indies, and their family included John, Macgregor, William, Henry and Hamilton. In 1822 William Laird left Greenock where he had become a partner in his father's rope-works and moved to Merseyside. He acquired land at Birkenhead from the Lord of the Manor, Mr F. R. Price, and in 1824 developed a boiler-works and shipyard. His eldest son, John, joined the firm in 1828 and the concern became known as William Laird and Son. The successors of this establishment are, of course, the present shipbuilding firm of Cammell Laird and Company.

Macgregor, born in October 1809, was the second son of William Laird. He was educated at Edinburgh University where he excelled at mental arithmetic and mathematics. While at college Macgregor Laird experienced a severe attack of typhus. His survival was largely due to the devoted nursing given by his parents and by Thomas Briggs, a

[1] *Dictionary of National Biography*, Vol. XXXI, 1892, p. 406 (John Laird Jn.).

doctor who was later to accompany him up the Niger. After leaving Edinburgh, Macgregor joined his father and brother in the family firm at Birkenhead and it was while engaged in shipbuilding that he heard of the discovery of the outlet of the River Niger.

The importance of the discovery cannot be over-emphasised for although West Africa can be divided into two distinct zones—the tropical rain forests near the seaboard and the savannah in the interior—both suffered from a lack of adequate communications. Draught animals could not be used in many places because of the presence of the tsetse fly, while only the Gambia River and the coastal creeks provided suitable channels for waterborne commerce. In these circumstances the trade of the forest regions was restricted to areas near the sea, and the savannah districts were almost completely isolated from the western seaboard. The peoples of the interior, in fact, found it easier to establish trade links with the Mediterranean and Red Seas than with the Atlantic Ocean, although the caravans which regularly crossed the Sahara Desert were very limited in the amount of goods they could carry.

Even on the Atlantic coast legitimate trade was slow to develop. This was partly because of the reluctance of the British government to undertake direct responsibilities, and expense, in West Africa and partly because of the terribly high rates of mortality from tropical disease. The essence of the difficulty, however, was that when produce did percolate to the sea it was heavily taxed by the coastal chiefs as it passed through their territories. These middlemen, in fact, were the real barrier to the expansion of trade for they were extremely successful in preventing the tribes of the interior from gaining access to the sea, and in discouraging the European merchants from penetrating much beyond the coastline. The importance of finding a way into the interior was, therefore, quite obvious and many attempts were made to find the outlet of the great river which was known to exist in the interior. All of these failed until 1830 when it was learned that the 'Oil Rivers' were branches of the Niger. This resulted from the expedition organised by the Lander Brothers in which they made their way overland to the known upper reaches of the river and then followed its course by canoe to the delta on the coast.

Macgregor Laird was delighted to learn that the Niger promised a satisfactory highway into Central Africa. In his own words:

'To the merchant it offered a boundless field for enterprise; to the manufacturer, an extensive market for his goods; and to the energy and ardour of youth, it presented the irresistible charms of novelty, danger and adventure.'[1]

These, however, were not the only motives which persuaded Laird and several of his friends to take action:

'By introducing legitimate commerce with all its attendant blessings into the centre of the country, they knew that they were striking a mortal blow to that debasing and demoralising traffic which has for centuries cursed that unhappy land, and rendered some of the loveliest tracts on the face of the globe the habitation of wild beasts and noxious reptiles, or of man in a condition more disgusting and degraded than either. Under Providence, they aspired to become the means of rescuing millions of their fellowmen from the miseries of a religion characterised by violence and blood, by imparting to them the truths of Christianity. . . .'[2]

Urged by such considerations the African Inland Commercial Company was formed in Liverpool with the objects of opening direct communications with the interior and of establishing a permanent trading settlement at the Confluence of the Niger and the Tchadda.[3] An approach was then made to Richard Lander and he agreed to lead the proposed expedition.

Macgregor Laird took a large share in the Company and, as might be expected, concerned himself with the design, construction and fitting out of the ships. At first it was not intended that he would go up the Niger, but gradually his enthusiasm overcame his reluctance to displease his parents. This is clearly shown in a letter written to his father at the beginning of 1832:

'I cannot be a hypocrite any longer, and much as I know my determination will grieve you and my mother, yet I do hope I am acting for the best. I made have up my mind to accompany the African Expedition, and nothing will change it; it is the only chance I may ever have of distinguishing myself, and a nobler one I shall never have. . . . With regard to the personal risk, I feel assured that I shall run more by remaining at home, and the only thing that annoys me now is that you will think me ungrateful for all the kindness you have heaped upon me. I have now relieved my mind, and do hope upon consideration you will agree with me that it is the best for us all that I should go. It is a sure name, and a probable

[1] Macgregor Laird and R. A. K. Oldfield. *Narrative of an Expedition into the Interior of Africa by the River Niger in the Steam vessels* Quorra *and* Alburkah *in 1832, 1833 and 1834* (London: Richard Bentley, 1837), Vol. I, p. 3.
[2] Ibid., pp. 3–4.
[3] Now known as the River Benue. This is the present site of Lokoja.

fortune, and I would sooner earn such a name than live in splendour and ease at home....'[1]

On Lander's advice it was decided that the expedition should employ two steamers of light draught to ascend the Niger and that a sailing vessel should be used as a floating depot at the mouth of the river. The Company was able to purchase a satisfactory sailing ship, *Columbine*—a six-year-old brig of two hundred tons—but the paddle steamers had to be specially built.

The *Quorra*, constructed of wood, was the larger of the two vessels measuring 112 by 16 by 8 feet and was equipped with a single-cylinder engine of forty horse-power manufactured by Messrs Fawcett and Preston of Liverpool. *Alburkah* was much smaller, being only 70 by 13 by 6½ feet.[2] Apart from her deck she was made entirely of wrought iron and was fitted with a sixteen horse-power engine. She was the first sea-going vessel to be constructed of iron and many people considered her to be rather impractical.

'It was gravely asserted that the working in a sea-way would shake the rivets out of the iron of which she was composed: the heat of a tropical sun would bake alive her unhappy crew as if they were in an oven; and the first tornado she might encounter would hurl its lightnings upon a conductor evidently sent forth to brave its power.'[3]

In fact *Alburkah* turned out to be extremely successful. Her iron hull was completely watertight on the voyage to West Africa and proved to be strong enough to withstand many groundings in the Niger without damage. She was no hotter than a comparable wooden ship and lightning was never a problem. The engines of both vessels worked well and gave little trouble although operated for long periods without the benefit of skilled engineers or proper lubricants. Similarly, the navigation of the Niger did not present any special problems for the river proved to be eminently suitable for this type of steamship and the expedition was able to reach a number of previously inaccessible regions. Many difficulties were encountered, however, and all could be attributed to a single factor—the lack of adequate medical knowledge to combat the attacks of tropical disease.

When the party left Liverpool it consisted of forty-eight picked men,

[1] D. N. B. Vol. XXXI, 1892, p. 407 (Macgregor Laird).
[2] For further details of these vessels see Appendix, p. 404, Table 9.
[3] Laird and Oldfield, op. cit., Vol. I, p. 7.

including two doctors. Thirty-nine of these died in West Africa, mainly from fever or dysentry. No precautions were taken against mosquitoes and it was seldom considered necessary to boil drinking-water, so it is, perhaps, surprising that anyone survived. The bewilderment of the doctors seems all the more ironic when it is realised that had they used quinine, a supply of which was actually on board,[1] as a prophylactic and taken more care with the water supply their problems would have been greatly diminished. In the event, the heavy mortality and the prolonged sickness suffered by even the least affected seriously impaired the efficiency of the enterprise. As a result the expedition was unable to achieve all that had been hoped for and was a commercial failure.[2] Nevertheless, it proved that the Niger was navigable for moderately sized steam vessels as far as Rabbah, several hundred miles above the confluence with the Benue, and the expedition penetrated the latter river, previously unexplored, for a distance of 104 miles.

Macgregor Laird was up the Niger from October 1832 to August 1833, and his health suffered severely. In consequence it was necessary for him to spend two months in convalescence at Fernando Po. The governor of the island, Colonel Nicolls, did everything possible to restore him to fitness and Laird then sailed *Columbine* to Liverpool, arriving on 1 January 1834. Continuing ill-health prevented him from pursuing an active career for a while but in 1837 he helped to promote the British and North American Steam Navigation Company. In the same year he married Ellen Nicolls, the daughter of General Sir Edward Nicolls—the former governor of Fernando Po.[3] For the next seven years Laird worked as secretary for the British and North American, operating ships such as *Sirius, British Queen* and *President* between Liverpool and New York. He then re-joined the family firm at Birkenhead and spent four years helping to develop its shipbuilding activities. The Lairds enjoyed a happy family life during this period; they eventually had eight children, but Macgregor never really settled, for his interest and enthusiasm continued to be inspired only by matters which concerned West Africa.

[1] Ibid., p. 352.

[2] Laird also attributed the failure to the neglect of the palm oil trade, their ignorance of conditions in the interior and the fact that they were the first Europeans to communicate with the natives. Ibid., Vol. II, p. 402.

[3] Plumb and Howard, *West African Explorers* (London: Oxford University Press 1955), pp. 465–483.

By 1849 Macgregor Laird was convinced that he ought to take a more active part in West African affairs. He therefore resigned from his position in Birkenhead and moved to London, establishing himself as a merchant at 3, Mincing Lane. The reasons for this decision are not difficult to discover. Since his return to England, Laird had kept closely in touch with developments in West Africa, and it was against his advice that a large expedition was sent to complete the exploration of the Niger in 1841. This had the full support of the British government, but the dreadful deathrate—48 out of 145 Europeans died—seemed to end all hope that a large and legitimate commerce could be developed with the interior.[1] On the other hand Laird knew that in spite of all difficulties trade with the coastal regions was growing each year, and it was easy to see that an improvement in communications would further accelerate its development. In addition, Laird's personal knowledge of the coast and his experience in operating a steamship service across the Atlantic gave him a special insight into the advantages which a power-driven vessel possessed over a sailing-ship in the particular conditions prevailing in West African waters. It was thus obvious to Laird that scope must soon exist for a regular steamship service, and it became his aim in life to see it established.

In 1850 the registered tonnage employed in the trade between England and West Africa amounted to 40,410 tons outward and to 42,057 tons inward and by 1851 the importation of palm oil alone amounted to over 31,000 tons.[2] These cargoes were transported by sailing-ships at an average outward rate of £3 per ton and at a homeward average of £4 per ton. In Laird's opinion these quantities and rates were quite sufficient to justify the formation of a steamship line. He therefore approached the government and after long negotiations was successful in obtaining a ten-year mail contract, together with a subsidy which amounted to an average of £21,250 per annum.[3] He then issued a prospectus in which he stated his case for the use of steam in the West African shipping trade:

[1] Ibid., pp. 465–483.

[2] African Steam Ship Company papers in the author's possession—hereinafter referred to as A.S.P. Statement of the Trade between England and the West Coast of Africa (attached to the Prospectus).

[3] A.S.P. Prospectus, p. 4. See also: C. W. Newbury, *British Policy Towards West Africa. Select Documents*, 1786-1874 (London: Oxford University Press, 1965). Letter from Macgregor Laird to Earl Grey, 'Steam Communication with Africa', 25 March 1851.

'From the peculiar character of the winds upon the coast, and the great detention unavoidably experienced by sailing vessels from constant calms and currents, the length of the voyage out and home for a sailing vessel varies from five to eight months, while by steam communication the voyage from London to the various ports on the coast would not average more than 35 days on the outward voyage, and the same number of days on the homeward voyage; there cannot, therefore, be any doubt that at the same rate of freight, screw steamers would command the entire tonnage that they were capable of carrying—the shortness of the passage, and the superior facility and lowness of insurance, would be sufficient inducement to shippers to give them the preference'.[1]

As a result of these arguments, the known expansion of the trade and, no doubt, the annual subsidy and limited liability, the proposal received substantial support and led to the organisation of the African Steam Ship Company in 1852.

The Formation of the African Steam Ship Company
The African Steam Ship Company was incorporated by Royal Charter on 7 August 1852, and it is from this date that the history of Elder Dempster rightly begins. The chairman of the new firm was Sir John Campbell and Macgregor Laird became its first managing director. Also on the board were James Hartley, a director of the Peninsular and Oriental Company, and Henry William Currie who represented the firm's bankers.[2] The Company was

'. . . formed to carry out a Contract with Her Majesty's Government for the monthly conveyance of the mails to Madeira, Teneriffe, and the principal ports and places on the West Coast of Africa.'[3]

Shares in the new company were quickly taken up, and the report of the directors at the First Ordinary Meeting of the Proprietors on 11 June 1853, showed that 11,008 shares of £20 each had been issued.[4] The capital account was then as follows:

[1] A.S.P. 'Statement of the Trade . . .', op. cit.
[2] A.S.P. The other members of the board were Henry William Schneider (Deputy-Chairman), John Black, Charles William Gregory and William Law Ogilby.
[3] A.S.P., Prospectus, p. 4.
[4] Investment in the African Steam Ship Company was undoubtedly encouraged by the limited liability status conferred by its Royal Charter. This was an uncommon form of commercial organisation until the Limited Liability Acts of 1855 and 1856.

Deposit on 11,008 shares at £5   = £55,040 os od
First call of £5 on 11,008 shares = £55,040 os od
Amount paid in anticipation of calls = £19,712 10s od

£129,792 10s od[1]

It was arranged that London would be the Company's terminal port in England but that each vessel would call at Plymouth on each leg of its voyage in order to expedite the mails. To further this end special plans were made with the Great Western Railway who agreed to co-ordinate their services with those of the Company. Provisional arrangements were also made for coaling facilities to be provided at Sierra Leone so that bunkers could be replenished on both the outward and homeward trips.

In order to establish the service, the Company had previously placed an order for five iron-screw steamships with Mr John Laird of Birkenhead.[2] These were *Forerunner* of 400 tons, *Faith* and *Hope* of 922 tons and *Charity* and *Northern Light* of 1,062 tons. In accordance with the terms of the mail contract *Forerunner* was ready to sail at the beginning of September 1852, but at the request of the Board of Admiralty her departure was delayed to the 24th of that month. The first voyage of *Forerunner* suffered a second setback when she was dismasted in the Bay of Biscay during a violent gale. Repairs were satisfactorily completed at Gibraltar, however, and she then concluded her journey without further incident.[3] Delays in the construction of the other vessels ordered from Laird's resulted in a loss for the Company, because the compensation received from the builders did not altogether offset the cost of chartering alternative steamers. However, the delivery of *Faith* in January, and *Hope* in April 1853, ended these initial difficulties.

Details of the maiden voyage of *Faith* still survive.[4] She left London under the command of James Parsons on 27 January 1853, and arrived

[1] A.S.P. First Ordinary General Meeting of the Proprietors of the African Steam Ship Company. 11 June 1853, Directors Report, p. 12.

[2] John Laird was the elder brother of Macgregor Laird and both were sons of William Laird who founded the Birkenhead ship-building firm in 1824. See above, p. 35.

[3] An account of an outward voyage in *Forerunner* is given in W. B. Baikie's *Narrative of an Exploring Voyage up the Rivers Kwo're and Bi'nue in 1854* (London: John Murray, 1856), Chapter 2.

[4] A.S.P. Abstract of log of S.S. *Faith*: London to Fernando Po and return. January to April, 1853.

at Plymouth on the 29th. It took less than ten hours to collect her passengers and mail, and to top up her bunkers, and then she was off. Unfortunately on the next day she 'broke air pump rod and cap of Larboard Engine', so was forced to put about and go into Falmouth. Repairs took until 1 February but at 7.00 p.m. she weighed her anchor and stood out to sea. At 8.00 p.m. the pilot left the ship and her voyage to West Africa had really begun.

On *Faith*'s first outward journey she called at Madeira, Tenerife, Goree, Bathurst, Sierra Leone, Monrovia, Cape Coast Castle, Accra, Ouidah, Badagri and Fernando Po, and it took her twenty-eight days and twenty hours to complete the outward voyage. The actual time under way amounted to twenty-one days, six hours for the 4,855 miles trip and this works out at 228 miles a day or nine and a half knots per hour.

The ship remained at Fernando Po for just over three days before beginning her homeward journey. In this time she discharged the balance of her cargo, shifted the remaining coal from the holds to the bunkers, took on 2,000 gallons of water and loaded 151 casks of palm oil and 65 ounces of gold-dust. Other cargo collected on the voyage back to England included gold-dust and gum from Cape Coast; gold-dust, gum, ginger, camwood, pepper, arrowroot, ivory and palm oil and nuts from Sierra Leone; bees-wax and ivory from Bathurst; cochineal and wine from Tenerife and seventy-six boxes of lemons from Madeira.

The *Faith* returned to Plymouth on 13 April after a homeward voyage in which the steaming time was seven days more than on the outward trip. This was largely because the wind gave more assistance on the southern journey as the prevailing breeze was in this direction. As a result of this the consumption of coal was 352 tons from Plymouth to Fernando Po, but 533 tons for the return to England. All of the African Steam Ship Company's vessels carried sails but the extent to which these were used for propulsion—as distinct from steadying—is not altogether clear. The log of *Faith* occasionally refers to the setting of sails and the disconnecting of the screw, but was the wind merely used to supplement or replace steam when it happened to be blowing in the right direction, or was the vessel to be navigated as a sailing-ship using power only when absolutely necessary? Records of *Faith*'s first voyage show that coal was consumed on every single day outward and homeward, but on the other hand they contain the following reference:

'Blowing hard gale from E. to E.N.E.—very heavy sea on—ship going thro' it beautifully close reefed Fore and Main topsails unable to head it out so close hauled on Starboard tack.

do. do—sea running very high increasing gale all day, passed two vessels outward bound under close reefed topsails.

do. do—gale moderated—out reefs and set jib. Strong breeze—fore and aft sails set going 8 and 9 knots close by the wind.

Breeze ahead—steaming head to breeze 9¾ knots smooth water. 4.00 a.m. arrival by Plymouth.'[1]

The way in which sail was used by *Faith* is not necessarily typical of the fleet as a whole and the only general guide to Company policy is inconclusive. This is in the form of a letter written by Macgregor Laird to Captain Andrew McIntosh of the *Hope*:

September 19, 1856

'Dear Sir, I beg your acceptance of a book from the perusal of which I have received great pleasure and I hope profit.

As the valuable commerce of the world will soon be carried altogether by vessels with auxiliary screws you will find the accounts of the winds and currents of the Ocean collected from so many sources by Captain Maury a most useful and instructive study. I particularly desire your attention to it with reference to the trade between Liverpool and the Bights direct—using steam power only in calms, going into and out of Port and getting clear of the Guinea current on the homward voyage.'[2]

Maury's book, *The Physical Geography of the Sea*, had as its essential thesis the suggestion that a scientific knowledge of prevailing winds and currents would assist the master of a sailing-vessel to cut down the times of his voyages.[3] The value of this work to the captain of a steamship is not clear, but it would have been of value in cases where, after engine failure, it was desirable to bring a vessel home under canvas. Pictures of the early vessels of the African Steam Ship Company show that their lines and rig made this a feasible proposition. It may also have been considered that Maury would be useful in finding favourable routes where the employment of sails could help to reduce fuel consumption, but the adoption of super heaters and of compound engines in the 1860s would seem to lessen the force of this argument.

The vessels of the African Steam Ship Company made only five

[1] A.S.P. Log of *Faith* op. cit., p. 13.

[2] Supplement to the *West African Review*, 1939, p. 43.

[3] The copy of this work given by Macgregor Laird to Captain McIntosh is now in the author's possession. See: M. F. Maury, *The Physical Geography of the Sea*, 6th edn. (London: Samson Low, Son & Co., 1856).

voyages in the first financial year, the other three being undertaken by chartered steamers at heavy expense.[1] In spite of this the working account was in a very satisfactory state and largely justified the Company's expectations:

Receipts:	£11,041 1s 9d
Plus Mail Contract:	8,259 4s 8d
	19,300 6s 5d
Less Disbursements:	13,228 7s 10d
	6,071 18s 7d
Less Depreciation on *Forerunner* & *Faith*	2,584 1s 10d
Balance to Profit & Loss a/c	£ 3,486 19s 9d[2]

Perhaps of even more importance was the fact that not a single man was lost by accident or from tropical disease during the Company's first financial year. This may have been a reflection of the careful way in which the Company was organised, as can clearly be seen from the documentation carried by the ships. A typical sailing-vessel of the time would carry only a log and a manifest, while her captain might or might not write a letter or report to the owners at the end of each voyage. Yet even the earliest of the African Steam Ship Company's vessels carried a set of documents and returns that was almost equal to those carried by a modern cargo liner.[3]

In the African Steam Ship Company's second year it was found that, while receipts increased steadily, the increase was more than offset by the rise in wages, coal, oil, stores and provisions (amounting to nearly 35 per cent) engendered by the onset of the Crimean War. As a result the directors thought it prudent to dispose of their two larger ships, *Charity* and *Northern Light* (the latter still on the stocks) and these were sold at a profit to the Canadian Steam Navigation Company. The rise in costs was also partially offset by *Hope* and, later, *Faith* being chartered to the government's Commissariat Service. While these activities proved to be financially rewarding to the Company its West African activities

[1] The Company's operations did not begin until September 1852, but under the Deed of Settlement the Annual General Meeting had to be held in June each year.
[2] A.S.P. First Ordinary General Meeting, op. cit., pp. 12-13.
[3] P. N. Davies, 'The African Steam Ship Company', in J. R. Harris, Ed., *Liverpool and Merseyside* (London: Frank Cass, 1969), p. 235.

naturally suffered and had to be maintained by chartered vessels. The *Candace* and *Ethiope*, both of 675 tons, were therefore built but both proved to be subject to frequent mechanical failures and the postal service was not carried out as efficiently as the directors would have wished.

The Company's difficulties were further increased by the loss of *Forerunner* after striking a sunken rock off Madeira. Many lives were lost and the subsequent investigation held under the Mercantile Marine Act returned a verdict of gross negligence on the part of the master. The line was therefore forced to pay over £5,000 into the Court of Chancery:

'. . . to stop and bar the numerous actions commenced by different parties against the Company for amounts far exceeding in the aggregate, the limit of the Company's liability, which by the ninth section of the Mercantile Marine Act, is confined to the value of the ship, freight and passage money.'[1]

The loss of *Forerunner* could not be absorbed by the depleted fleet, so an immediate search was made for a replacement. The best available ship, *Retriever* of 440 tons, was therefore purchased and proved to be a sound investment.

The following year, 1856, was a very important one for the African Steam Ship Company. The ending of the Crimean War released *Hope* and *Faith* from the transport service and they joined *Candace* and *Ethiope*, (both fitted with new geared engines of 120 h.p. and improved boilers) *Retriever* and the newly built *Gambia* and *Niger*. It was not possible to keep all of these vessels fully employed in the difficult days which followed the closing of hostilities, so *Hope*, which was considered to be inefficient, was laid up and *Faith* was sold to the Turkish government. The problems engendered by the decline in West African trade at this time meant that even the reduced fleet had to be operated below capacity, and they were all the more acute because the Company was no longer under the guidance of Macgregor Laird.

The progress of the African Steam Ship Company
The African Steam Ship Company had made satisfactory progress under Macgregor Laird until he resigned his position as managing director in October 1855. After this date, however, although Laird remained a member of the board the effective control of the Company was in

[1] A.S.P. Third Ordinary General Meeting, 20 June 1855. Directors report; p. 5.

other hands. Laird's motives in leaving at this time were concerned with further attempts which he was making to open the Niger to commerce. These had recommenced in 1854 when he had made a contract with the Admiralty under which he was to build a steamer and pay all the expenses of a voyage of exploration in return for a payment of £5,000.[1] *Pleiad*, a screw steamship of forty horse-power measuring 107 by 23 by 7½ feet, was then constructed by John Laird at Birkenhead.[2] It was arranged that Governor Beecroft of Fernando Po would lead the expedition but when the vessel arrived on the West African Coast Beecroft had died so the senior admiralty officer took his place.[3]

Under the command of Dr Baikie[4] the expedition explored the Benue for a distance of 300 miles above the point previously reached, and although *Pleiad* was in the river for 118 days not a man was lost. This was due, in part, to the regular use of quinine as a preventative, but it was also because only twelve of the crew of sixty-six were Europeans.[5] The commercial results were satisfactory but in Laird's view it was essential that the government provide assistance until the trade could become self-supporting. After much discussion, therefore, the Admiralty reluctantly entered into a five-year contract under which Laird was to organise annual sailings up the Niger and its tributaries. To do this he formed the Central African Company Limited,[6] and this began its work in 1857 when *Dayspring* ascended the river.[7] Unfortunately this vessel was wrecked at Jebba,[8] but her crew was rescued by *Sunbeam* in 1858. The following year *Sunbeam* and *Rainbow* made successful voyages up the Niger and trading posts were maintained at Ebo, Lairdspoint (now Onitsha) and Lairdstown (opposite what is now Lokoja). These

[1] T. J. Hutchinson, *Narrative of the Niger, Tshadda and Benue Exploration* (London, 1855), p. 9. (Reprinted in 1966 by Frank Cass, London).

[2] List of Iron, Steel and Wood Vessels built at the Birkenhead Iron Works, Birkenhead (Willmer Brothers, Birkenhead, 1894), No. 110.

[3] T. J. Hutchinson, op. cit., p. 36.

[4] E. W. Marwick, *William Balfour Baikie* (Kirkwall: W. R. Mackintosh, 1965), pp. 8–9.

[5] T. J. Hutchinson, op. cit., pp. 191–239.

[6] See the Articles of Association of the Central Africa Co. Ltd.

[7] A. C. G. Hastings, *The Voyage of the Dayspring* (London: John Lane, The Bodley Head Ltd, 1926).

[8] The engines of *Dayspring* were subsequently discovered during the construction of the railway bridge at Jebba in 1915 and they are now permanently on show at Jebba Station. H. B. Hermon-Hodge, *Gazetteer of Ilorin Province* (London: George Allen & Unwin, 1929), p. 20.

activities were viewed by the Delta chiefs as 'an encroachment on their privileges, as they had been accustomed to levy heavy exactions on all goods passing up and down the river.'[1] The hostility of these natives resulted in the ships being fired on and, after two members of the crew of *Rainbow* had been killed, Laird asked for naval support. Orders were then given that a warship should escort the annual expedition up the river and in 1861 H.M.S. *Espoir* ascended the Niger.[2] The death of Macgregor Laird, also in 1861, removed much of the pressure that had forced the British government to take an active part in assisting the development of the Niger trade. Nevertheless Laird's work on the river was not to be wasted, for a number of firms followed in his footsteps and these were eventually amalgamated by Sir George Goldie into what ultimately became the Royal Niger Company.[3]

When Macgregor Laird turned his attention back to the Niger at the end of 1855 the direction of the African Steam Ship Company was undertaken by the secretary, Benjamin Fisher, under the supervision of a committee of the Board.[4] His period of authority, however, was only shortlived, for the ending of the Crimean War and the poorness of West African trade led the directors to consider winding up the entire business.[5] The Liverpool agents then recommended that direct sailings from the Mersey be given a trial before a final decision was reached. These voyages began in July 1856, and from that time the control of the Company was centred in Liverpool. The new sailing arrangements proved to be an improvement, but in spite of this the level of trade was poor and, as only four of the Company's six vessels could be regularly employed, no dividend could be paid. The following half-year, from July to December 1857, saw the Company in a better financial position and a dividend was paid in spite of *Niger* being lost at Santa Cruz. No dividend was paid for the next half-year period because of a further chapter of accidents.

Gambia broke her main shaft at Bathurst and was six weeks late in

---

[1] H. S. Goldsmith, C.M.G. 'Macgregor Laird and the Niger', *Journal of the African Society*, Vol. XXXI, No. CXXV (October, 1932), p. 391.

[2] Sir Alan Burns, *History of Nigeria* (London: Allen & Unwin, 1942), pp. 148–51.

[3] J. E. Flint, *Sir George Goldie and the Making of Nigeria* (London: Oxford University Press, 1960).

[4] A.S.P. Directors report for the year ending 30 April 1856, p. 6.

[5] A.S.P. Pamphlet sent to the shareholders of the African Steam Ship Company by Messrs Fletcher & Parr, 24 June 1875, p. 2.

getting home, while *Armenian* (acquired in 1857) lost over a fortnight by getting stranded in the River Cameroons, and *Candace* was lost after a collision. These difficulties were followed by the commercial crisis of 1857 and 1858 which restricted trade to such an extent that freight receipts declined by over £1,600.[1] The second half of 1858 was much more favourable for the African Steam Ship Company. No losses were reported and, while revenue fell slightly, the fall in expenses was far greater and resulted in a net gain. A new seven-year postal contract was entered into and this gave rise to certain economies, for Liverpool was recognised as the centre of the trade and became the mail port. It was then no longer necessary to call at Plymouth and costs were accordingly reduced. The payment under the mail contract was increased to £30,000 per annum and as no losses were experienced in 1859 the Company made substantial progress. It was in this year that *Cleopatra* was purchased to replace *Candace*, lost in 1858. *Cleopatra* was the first of the Line's ships to be fitted with a super heater, and the success of this apparatus in reducing fuel consumption was such that it became standard fitting throughout the fleet. *Gambia*, of 650 tons, was found to be too small to operate the new mail contract and she was sold in 1860.[2] All the sailings for that year were completed satisfactorily with one exception—that of *Cleopatra*. This ship broke her propeller shaft at Sierra Leone and, as it was impossible to repair it on the spot, she was brought home under canvas by her captain.

Macgregor Laird's death in 1861 was followed by an examination of the Company's financial position. This was in accordance with a Deed of Covenant under which Laird was to receive one-fifth of the profits available for distribution during the first ten years of the Line's existence.[3] The accounts then showed a very satisfactory state of affairs:

Statement Showing the Financial Position of the Company on 31 August 1862

Liabilities

First & Second Calls of £5 each on 11,008 shares =	£110,080	0s 0d
Amount paid in advance of Calls =	21,962	10s 0d
Outstandings due by the Company =	6,615	7s 10d

£138,657 17s 10d

---

[1] A.S.P. Directors report for the year ending 29 June 1858, p. 5.
[2] A.S.P. Directors report for the year ending 5 June 1860, p. 4.
[3] A.S.P. Directors report for the half-year ending 31 October 1862, p. 4.

Assets

Five Steamers, measuring 4,019 tons gross	= £	79,359 3s 1d
Two hulks	=	3,304 17s 9d
Coals at Stations	=	7,201 8s 4d
Cash and Bills	=	5,324 4s 3d
East India Stock	=	14,887 1s 7d
Out-standings due to the Company	=	33,770 13s 2d
		£143,847 8s 2d
Surplus Profit		£ 5,189 10s 4d[1]

Macgregor Laird's executors were then paid the sum of £1,000 in settlement of the agreement and this ended his financial connection with the African Steam Ship Company. In memory of their founder the directors named a new ship *Macgregor Laird* and this came into service in 1862. During the same year *Cleopatra* was chartered by the government and sailed to Canada with troops and stores.[2] She then returned to the West African run but became a total loss at Shebar on 19 August. There was only one casualty, the chief engineer, but the mails, cargo and passengers' luggage were all lost.[3]

The period from 1863 to 1868 was one of increasing trade, and the vessels provided by the African Steam Ship Company were insufficient to bring home all the cargo that was offered. Their Liverpool agents made strong and repeated representations for additional ships but the fleet was increased only very slowly:

Fleet of The African Steam Ship Company, 1862–1869

OCTOBER 1862–5 ships totalling 4,116 tons

1863–5	4,116
1864–6	5,324
1865–5	4,346
1866–7	6,914
1867–6	6,474
1868–6	7,085
1869–7	8,565[4]

[1] A.S.P. Directors report for the half-year ending 31 October 1862, p. 6.
[2] A.S.P. Directors report for the half-year ending 30 April 1862, p. 5.
[3] A.S.P. Directors report for the half-year ending 31 October 1862, p. 5.
[4] A.S.P. Details from the Directors reports for the relevant years.

The failure to expand the fleet at a rapid rate was quite deliberate, for although the resources of the Company were comparatively small it would have been quite easy for it to have raised extra capital, as it did at a later date. The basic reason for the directors' reluctance to accept further responsibilities was the uncertainty of the trade. Their heritage of past disappointments and their reliance on the certain but limited returns offered by the mail contract were in direct contrast to the views of their agents, who were paid on a commission basis and naturally wished to see an expanding business. This is not to suggest that the directors of the African Steam Ship Company were completely inflexible on this point. The revision of the mail contract in 1866 forced them to consider changes in the services they provided to West Africa, but it should be noted that these were to be made without enlarging the size of the fleet:

'Your Directors have to report that their Tender accepted by the Postmaster-General was for a single Service per month. They had offered to perform a fortnightly Service, but their offer was declined. They have for a considerable period had their serious attention drawn to the propriety of providing more accommodation for the increasing traffic on the Coast of Africa, and while regretting the decision of Her Majesty's Government, they have thought it expedient to make arrangements for an experimental additional line, which the modifications introduced into the New Contract have enabled them to do, without increasing the present fleet.' [1]

The new services made reasonable progress but the directors still refused to develop their fleet sufficiently in spite of almost continuous requests by their Liverpool agents. This failure to expand, however defended, had the unwelcome result that it led to the intervention of a second line in the West African shipping trade. This was the British and African Steam Navigation Company and its entry was an especially bitter pill for the Liverpool agents because the promoters of the new line were their own ex-employees—John Dempster and Alexander Elder.

[1] A.S.P. Directors report for the half-year ending 31 October 1866, p. 5.

Chapter 2

Alexander Elder
and
John Dempster

The Liverpool Agency

William and Hamilton Laird had been in business together as coal merchants for many years, but when the African Steam Ship Company was formed in 1852 they readily agreed to their brother Macgregor's suggestion and became its Liverpool agents. Until 1856 the agency formed only a small part of their work, but once Liverpool replaced London as the terminal port their responsibilities grew rapidly. This was not only because of the additional effort required to ensure an efficient turnround together with the staffing, victualling and repairing problems which this involved, but also because the control of the Company— formerly undertaken by Macgregor Laird—was placed in their hands. The death of Hamilton Laird in 1860 did not change this situation but after William Laird had taken Mr J. T. Fletcher into partnership the name of the agency was altered to Messrs Laird and Fletcher.[1] In 1863 William Laird retired and Mr L. H. Parr joined the business—the firm being subsequently known as Fletcher and Parr.[2] The retirement of William Laird had, however, a more significant meaning than the mere

[1] Mr Joseph Taylor Fletcher was born on 29 September 1826, and baptised in St Nicholas's Church, Liverpool, on 18 October 1826. He was the tenth child of James and Frances Fletcher and died on 20 February 1893, at the age of sixty-six. He is buried at Anfield Cemetery, Liverpool.

[2] Mr Lawrence Hodson Parr lived at Beach-Lawn, Waterloo. He died on 6 November 1885 at the age of fifty-one. See his obituary in the *Liverpool Courier* 9 November 1885.

loss of his name would suggest. Instead of being the organisers of the African Steam Ship Company, the Liverpool agents became solely its representatives and the control passed back to London.[1] In theory this change ought to have placed the board of directors in a better position to guide the Company but in practice the real power was quickly assumed by its secretary, Mr Duncan Campbell.[2]

The year 1863 was also important for the fact that the Liverpool agents formed a new firm, Messrs Fletcher, Parr and Company which opened an office in London. This establishment was under the control of two new partners—W. S. Partridge and J. P. Higginson—but it would appear that it was mainly concerned with coal factoring and chartering and was not directly concerned with the West African trade.[3] The Liverpool office remained very small, having only thirteen employees at this time,[4] but the staff included four members whose future work, power and influence were to change the whole of Britain's shipping and commercial relationship with West Africa. These were Alexander Elder, John Dempster, John Holt (who left in 1862) and Alfred Jones.

Alexander Elder was born in Glasgow in 1834 and was the son of David Elder, who for many years was manager of Robert Napier and Sons, the engine-and ship-builders.[5] One of his older brothers, John Elder, served an apprenticeship with Napier and became his chief draughtsman when only twenty-four years of age. Four years later he formed a partnership with Charles Randolph and founded a firm at Govan which was first known as Randolph, Elder and Company, then as John Elder and Company and, eventually, as the Fairfield Shipbuilding and Engineering Company.[6] In 1853 Randolph and Elder took out a patent for a compound engine and the following year they fitted the first practical machinery of this type to the *Brandon*, an iron, screw vessel of

[1] A.S.P., Directors report for the half-year ending 31 October 1863, p. 5, and pamphlet sent to the shareholders of the African Steam Ship Company by Messrs Fletcher and Parr, 24 June 1875, p. 2.

[2] Campbell had been employed as company secretary since the death of Mr Fisher in 1857.

[3] See Appendix p. 424, Table 31, for full details of these arrangements.

[4] A.S.P. Private Journal of Fletcher and Parr, No. 1.

[5] C. Wilson and W. Reader, *Men and Machines. A history of D. Napier and Son, Engineers, Limited* (London: Weidenfeld and Nicolson, 1958). This is not an account of the marine engineering firm but it contains many references to it as the principals were related.

[6] E. C. Smith. *A Short History of Naval and Marine Engineering* (Cambridge University Press, 1937), p. 178.

764 tons.[1] *Brandon* was built for the American trade and when she completed her maiden voyage in 1854 she was the first ship fitted with compound engines to cross the Atlantic. Newspaper reports say that Alexander Elder was the chief engineer on this trip,[2] but if this were the case one can only assume that it was largely because of his brother's influence, because he was only twenty at the time. On the other hand, marine engineering was still in its infancy and, as men specifically trained for this work were hard to find, locomotive engineers, millwrights and many other craftsmen were frequently employed. It also seems probable that Alexander Elder would have gained extensive knowledge of this particular engine during his apprenticeship, and this experience would naturally have strengthened his claims for the job. Alexander Elder then served as chief engineer of *Columbian*, an iron barque of 2,189 tons fitted with a 400 horse-power auxiliary engine.[3] This vessel, built for the Australian run, was chartered by the French in 1855 and saw service in the Crimean War—Elder spending some hours in Sebastopol on the day of its fall.[4]

John Dempster was born in 1837 in Penport, Thornhill, Dumfriesshire where his father, William Dempster, was builder to the Duke of Buccleuch. The Dempster family moved to Birkenhead in the 1840s and John joined W. & H. Laird as a clerk in 1851 when he was aged fourteen. In 1856 Alexander Elder also became a member of Laird's staff. This was in order to act as superintendent engineer for the African Steam Ship Company which, as previously noted, had transferred their sailings to the Mersey at that time. Elder's position in the firm was very much superior to that of Dempster who was still a junior clerk, but the smallness of the office and the nearness of their ages—Elder being twenty-two and Dempster nineteen—helped to ensure a growing friendship. The fact that both originated in Scotland provided a further bond, but there is no evidence to suggest that in the early years of their acquaintanceship they ever envisaged the common future which fate had in store for them.

John Holt was another of the staff of the Liverpool agents who was

---

[1] *Lloyds Register of Shipping*, 1857. Entry No. B.349. For a discussion of the advantages and problems of compound engines see F. E. Hyde, *Blue Funnel*, (Liverpool University Press, 1957), pp. 13–16.

[2] *Journal of Commerce*, Obituary of Alexander Elder, 26 January 1915.

[3] Lloyds Register of Shipping, 1857. Entry No. C.616.

[4] Journal of Commerce, 26 January 1915, op. cit.

to make his mark in West Africa. The son of an inn-keeper, he was born in 1841 in the village of Garthorpe, Lincolnshire.[1] After leaving the local school at the age of fourteen, Holt took a job on the *Thomas Holt*, a coastal schooner owned by his grandfather. He soon realised the limitations of this occupation, however, and with the assistance of his father obtained an apprenticeship with William Laird in Liverpool. This was for a five-year period beginning in July, 1857, and was designed to teach him the business of a coal dealer.[2] Laird's increasing interest in West African shipping meant that in practice much of Holt's time was concerned with that particular trade, so it is not surprising that when he completed his apprenticeship he determined to seek his fortune on the Coast. Having made this decision Holt first considered taking a job as purser on one of the vessels of the African Steam Ship Company, but before he had committed himself he was offered a position as assistant to James Lynslager—an African merchant with premises at Fernando Po—and this he decided to accept.[3]

John Holt sailed from Liverpool in *Cleopatra* in June 1862,[4] on a venture which was ultimately to grow into a large and lasting firm of African merchants.[5] The ending of his apprenticeship also involved the interruption of a friendship which had been developing with a young Welshman who had joined the Liverpool agents of the African Steam Ship Company in 1860. This was Alfred Lewis Jones—a man who, as will be seen later, was to play a vital role in the West African shipping trade. At this stage in his career Jones was a junior clerk, aged seventeen, and although the ability which was to carry him to great heights was already manifesting itself he was confined to the more elementary tasks. This was naturally irksome but even at this early age he

'. . . was always active and intelligent, and always at work, early and late. He never lost a chance of doing a good turn.'[6]

[1] *Merchant Adventure* (Liverpool: John Holt, 1948), p. 13.

[2] Ibid. The indenture between John Holt and William Laird is reproduced on page 12.

[3] C. R. Holt (Editor), *The Diary of John Holt* (Liverpool: Henry Young & Sons, 1948), pp. xii–xvii.

[4] Ibid. pp. 3–22. This gives an extensive account of the outward voyage and of life in an early vessel of the African Steam Ship Company.

[5] The best guide to John Holt's merchanting activities is in the unpublished Ph.D. thesis by Cherry Gertzel, 'A British Merchant in West Africa in the Era of Imperialism'. In the Bodleian Library, Oxford, 1959.

[6] *Journal of Commerce*, 13 June 1895. Speech by John Holt at the Adelphi Hotel, Liverpool, on the occasion of the presentation to Alfred Jones on his fiftieth birthday.

Thus this tiny office contained four men who were to play a major role in shaping the economic future of British West Africa. Much of this present work is therefore concerned with their lives and with their impact on the British West African shipping trade in general and on Elder Dempster in particular.

The Formation of the British and African Steam Navigation Company
Alexander Elder resigned from Messrs Fletcher and Parr in 1866 and brought to a temporary end the close association which he had developed with John Dempster. It is not clear why Elder decided to leave at this time for his salary had been raised from £300 to the not inconsiderable sum of £400 per annum in 1865[1] and there is no evidence to suggest that he had any serious disagreements with the partners. It may be that the failure of the African Steam Ship Company to expand its fleet in accordance with the needs of the trade led him to believe that the Company's prospects were not particularly bright. A more likely explanation is that his position as superintendent engineer brought him into frequent contact with the Company secretary, Duncan Campbell, and he may have wished to end what to his mind was a potentially dangerous situation.[2] The deciding factor, however, was undoubtedly the offer of a responsible post as engineer and shipwright surveyor to the Liverpool Board of Trade. The security of government service was, no doubt, a great inducement to a canny Scot! John Dempster remained with Fletcher and Parr, and with the departure of Elder was the highest-paid member of the staff. He earned £297 10s od in 1866 and this rose to £350 the following year.[3] There is little doubt that Dempster's salary would have continued to rise had he remained with the Liverpool agents for, as chief clerk, he was a valuable asset to the firm, but his position and, in fact, the whole of the trade was to be dramatically altered by the advent of a new steamship company which was to compete on the West African route.

The new line was the British and African Steam Navigation Company and it was registered in Edinburgh in 1868 with a nominal capital of £200,000 made up of 400 shares of £500 each. The issued capital consisted of 192 'A' shares on which £275 had been called up, and 130

[1] A.S.P., Private Journal of Fletcher and Parr, No. 1.
[2] See below p. 63.
[3] A.S.P., Private Journal of Fletcher and Parr, No. 1.

'B' shares on which £120 had been paid.[1] These 322 shares gave the company £68,400 in cash, contributed by what has been described as a number of 'Glasgow Businessmen.'[2] A glance at the list of subscribers, however, shows that the shareholders covered many occupations although the main geographical centres were Glasgow and Merseyside. The principal investors were Thomas Coats, the thread manufacturer of Paisley; Peter Brush, a merchant of Leith; S. R. Wilson, a merchant of Liverpool; and Charles Randolph and James B. Mirrlees, both engineers of Glasgow.[3]

It was decided that the new line should run from Glasgow via Liverpool to the West Coast of Africa. A suitable agent to handle the Liverpool side of the business was therefore a necessity. The only experienced firm was Messrs Fletcher and Parr and they could not be approached because they already represented the African Steam Ship Company. In view of this, contact was made with John Dempster to see if he would consent to be the Liverpool agent for the new concern and after due consideration he agreed to do so. Dempster was obviously a good choice for he had spent his entire career in the West African trade, and when he decided to seek a partner he also chose an experienced man. This was Alexander Elder, still employed at the Liverpool branch of the Board of Trade, and when he accepted Dempster's offer it brought into being the firm of Elder Dempster and Company. It should be appreciated that the appointment of an efficient Liverpool agent was crucial to the success of the British and African Steam Navigation Company. The trade between Glasgow and West Africa was growing[4] and it was to suit the convenience of this traffic that the line was contemplated, but Liverpool was at the centre of the trade and it was there that the shortage of cargo space was most apparent. Without Dempster's help, therefore, it is quite possible that the projected shipping line would not have been a viable proposition, and it is conceivable that it might not even have commenced operations. In the event, of course, both Dempster and Elder were so convinced of the potential of the West African trade and of their ability to obtain cargoes

[1] File E.67206 at Companies Registration Office, 102, George Street, Edinburgh.
[2] Supplement to the *West African Review* (1939), p. 35.
[3] See Appendix p. 427, Table 34.
[4] See: 'Glasgow and Africa, Connexions and Attitudes, 1870–1900'. This is an unpublished Ph.D. thesis presented to the University of Strathclyde by W. Thompson in 1970.

that they were well content to associate their future prosperity with that of the British and African. Proof of their whole-hearted confidence in the venture is the fact that they invested in the company at its inception and took every opportunity of increasing their shareholdings.[1]

Elder Dempster and Company began its commercial activities on 1 October 1868, when John Dempster made it his business to circularise all potential customers:

> 'I beg to inform you that this Company intend to dispatch, early in January next, the first of their line of Steamers, at present being constructed on the Clyde for trading between Glasgow, Liverpool and the West Coast of Africa.
>
> The Steamers are to sail monthly, and the ports which it is intended shall be called at are Sierra Leone, Cape Palmas, Cape Coast Castle, Accra, Lagos, Benin, Bonny, Old Calabar and Fernando Po, but should sufficient inducement offer, arrangements will be made for their calling at other ports, either on the outward or homeward voyages.
>
> The Steamers are being specially built for the African Trade and, besides being comfortably fitted up for passengers, they will have extensive cargo space, which will enable them to carry rough goods at moderate rates.'[2]

Dempster also wrote many letters to prospective clients on a more personal basis:

> 'Knowing that you are large importers of cochineal I take the liberty of writing to ask your opinion with respect to our steamers calling at Grand Canary or Teneriffe during the cochineal season. My idea of rate would be $\frac{1}{2}$d. per lb., and if we thought there was any likelihood of our getting cochineal in any quantity at that rate, we might arrange for to call at one or both ports on the homeward voyage.'[3]

The British and African began its monthly service between Glasgow, Liverpool and the West Coast of Africa in January 1869.[4] The first sailing was undertaken by *Bonny* which had been built for the new line by John Elder and Company at Glasgow. She was an iron screw vessel and like her sister ships, *Roquelle* and *Congo*—also constructed by John Elder—was of approximately 1,280 gross tons and measured 261 by 30 by 23 feet. Each of these ships possessed a direct-acting, surface-

[1] See Appendix, p. 429, Table 35.

[2] A.S.P., Circular letter, dated 1 October 1868, signed by John Dempster on behalf of Elder Dempster and Company.

[3] A.S.P., Letter from John Dempster to Messrs Lemaitre and Buckle, Paris, 7 October 1868.

[4] Note that the direct Glasgow service was discontinued in 1874.

condensing engine fitted with two inverted cylinders of 38 and 68 inches respectively and a 33-inch stroke. These produced 200 horse-power, enough to give a speed of about 11 knots and, in addition, *Congo* was rigged as a schooner and her sister ships as brigs.[1] The early sailings were extremely successful and the British and African made such rapid progress that it was decided to order three additional vessels. Accordingly *Liberia*, *Loanda* and *Volta* were built by John Elder and they came into service in 1870. These ships were slightly larger than the original trio and averaged 1,475 gross tons. They were also a little more powerful, their engines producing 250 horse-power, and all three were rigged as brigs.[2] In addition, *Rio Formoso*, a small steamship of 163 gross tons was purchased for use on the West African coast.[3]

Competition between the African Steam Ship Company and the British and African Steam Navigation Company
The first public reaction of the African Steam Ship Company to the activities of its new rival can be seen by reference to a letter sent by its secretary to their shippers on 9 January 1869:

> 'I am desired by the Directors of this Company to state that their attention has been drawn to an advertisement and a List of Rates of Freight, issued by a new Company, called the "British and African Steam Navigation Company", which has been established to meet the alleged requirements of the trade between Glasgow, Liverpool and the West Coast of Africa. Under these circumstances, and in view of the interests of this Company, which was the first to establish Steam Communication with the West Coast of Africa, the Directors have resolved on making very considerable reductions in their Rates of Freight. These new Rates will be in your hands in the course of a few days, and will come into operation on the 24th inst.
>
> The Directors have at all times endeavoured to meet the requirements of the Trade, and, looking to the superior class of vessels belonging to this Company, and the manner in which the service has hitherto been, and will in future be conducted, they hope to retain your support.'[4]

[1] Liverpool Underwriters Registry for Iron Vessels. Sept. 1872 p. 156, p. 180 and p. 342. Each of these vessels had identical hulls and two masts, but *Congo* is classed as a schooner because she was equipped with fore and aft sails. Her sister ships are described as brigs because they were fitted with square sails.
[2] Liverpool Underwriters Registry for Iron Vessels. Sept. 1872, p. 272, p. 275 and p. 395.
[3] Liverpool Underwriters Registry for Iron Vessels. Sept. 1872, p. 287. This, in fact, shows her to be still registered in the name of Mr G. F. Fisher.
[4] A.S.P., Letter from the African Steam Ship Company to its shippers, 9 January 1869.

The new competition also appears to have forced the African Steam Ship Company to take a more active interest in the complaints of their shippers:

'The attention of the Directors of the African Steam Ship Company has been called to certain injurious rumours which have lately been circulated amongst the shippers and consigners of goods to and from the West Coast of Africa, to the effect that the captains of the Company's vessels are in the habit at the various places on the Coast and more especially at Benin of showing a preference to certain shippers over others—and it is even suggested, as the Directors understand, that in thus acting the captains are carrying out the instructions they receive in this Country.

So far from this latter suggestion having any foundation, such preference is not only opposed to the wishes of the Directors, but is in direct contravention of the instructions to the Captains, and the Directors believe that no such preference has in reality been shown.

The Directors however have instructed me at once to assure you that being desirous of preventing any preference whatever in conveyance of the goods of shippers, they trust they may rely upon the co-operation of shippers and consignees immediately to bring to their knowledge any cases which may from this time occur.'[1]

A third reaction to the sailings of the British and African vessels was the raising of fresh capital by the African Steam Ship Company. This had remained unaltered since 1853[2] but in June 1869 the Directors recommended that all unallotted shares should be issued to the proprietors in the proportion of three shares to every twenty-two held.[3] The additional 1,492 shares were quickly taken up and resulted in the Company obtaining a further £15,000. Thus by the end of 1869 the capital account of the African Steam Ship Company was as follows:

First and Second Calls on 12,500 shares =	£122,874
Cash paid in anticipation of Calls =	£ 21,962
Balance =	£ 47,536
	£192,372[4]

With the aid of this extra capital the Company increased its fleet from the 7,085 tons of 1868 to 8,565 tons in 1869 and to 11,244 tons in 1870.

[1] A.S.P., Circular letter, dated 19 March 1869, signed by the Secretary, Duncan Campbell, on behalf of the African Steam Ship Company.
[2] See Chapter 1, p. 42 above.
[3] A.S.P., Director's Report for the half-year ending June 1869, p. 5.
[4] A.S.P., Directors Report for the half-year ending December 1869, p. 6.

In addition, two steamships *Don* and *Norway* were chartered on a temporary basis during the second half of 1869 and the first half of 1870.[1] Unfortunately the revenue earned by the Company did not keep pace with its increased fleet:

*Receipts from Freight, Passage
Money and Postal Subsidies*

Half-year ending 31 October	1868	£88,253
30 April	1869	£91,768
31 October	1869	£92,835
30 April	1870	£78,690
31 October	1870	£84,831[2]

This is particularly noticeable when it is realised that the figure for the second half of 1869 includes an unspecified amount received as premium on the new share issue.[3] The basic reason for the fall in revenue was, of course, the activities of the British and African Steam Navigation Company:

'Owing to competition which has existed since January last, your Directors have deemed it necessary to make important reductions in the Rates of Freight and Passage Money, and also to increase the number of sailings; the profits of the Half-year just ended have consequently been diminished.'[4]

In turn the reduction in receipts led to a decline in profits so, although dividends were maintained at their previous levels, the balance of the revenue account began to fall:

Half-year ending 31 October	1868	£6,887
30 April	1869	£6,570
31 October	1869	£6,299
30 April	1870	£5,218
31 October	1870	£5,456[5]

It was obvious, therefore, that this situation could not be allowed to continue for long and after a twelve months' struggle the directors of

[1] A.S.P., Directors Report for the half-year ending June 1870, p. 5. According to Lloyds Register for 1867, *Don* (D.238) was an iron screw steamship of 331 tons built in 1863. *Norway*, according to Lloyds 1872 Register (N.222), was an iron screw steamship built in 1868.

[2] A.S.P., Directors reports for the relevant years.

[3] A.S.P., Directors report for the half-year ending 31 October 1869. Abstract of Accounts.

[4] A.S.P., Directors report for the half-year ending 31 October 1869, p. 5.

[5] A.S.P., Directors reports for the revelant years.

the African Steam Ship Company resolved to come to terms with their rival. This decision was communicated to the shareholders as follows:

> 'The proprietors are aware from previous reports, that active competition with the Company, in the carrying trade by steam, to and from the West Coast of Africa, has for some time existed; which, added to the stoppage of trade at Bonny and other places, caused by serious local disturbances, has been prejudicial to the half-year's working. An agreement, however, has been concluded between your Directors and those of the British and African Steam Navigation Company, which it is expected will be profitable to both Companies, and advantageous to the trade generally. In conformity with this agreement, the Directors are at present dispatching two of the Company's steamers per month, and they are happy to report that the business of the Company is assuming a more favourable appearance.'[1]

The Growth of Co-operation

The agreement made between the African Steam Ship Company and the British and African Steam Navigation Company was for a three-year period beginning on 4 January 1870. It provided for rates to be agreed for both goods and passengers and for sailing dates to be fixed. The British and African also agreed not to compete with the African Steam Ship Company for the renewal of the mail contract.[2] During the early months of 1870 both lines had sailings every fortnight but then—by arrangement between the rival firms—the African increased its sailings to three per month while the British and African kept to its original schedule.[3]

In spite of this co-operation the directors of the African Steam Ship Company appear to have regarded their agreement with the British and African as a temporary truce that might be broken at any time. Feeling it necessary to have more capital at their disposal, they called up an additional £2 per share and, having applied to the government for the requisite authority, issued debentures to the value of £83,000 (a third of the subscribed capital).[4] The strengthening of the Company's financial base placed it in a good position to face the future, and there was a small

[1] A.S.P., Directors report for the half-year ending 30 April 1870, p. 5.
[2] 'African Steam Ship Company (Shareholders Meeting)', *Railway News*, 18 June 1870, pp. 675–6.
[3] 'African Steam Ship Company (Shareholders Meetings)', *Railway News*, 17 December 1870.
[4] A.S.P., Directors report for the half-year ending 31 October 1870, p. 5.

increase in the size of the fleet during 1871 and 1872. The trading position of the line also remained satisfactory but two events in 1872 precluded any possibility of the development of a complacent attitude. The first of these concerned the secretary, Mr Duncan Campbell, for it was discovered that he had embezzled a large sum of money. Much of this was subsequently recovered by Messrs Fletcher and Parr but the loss remained considerable and confidence was badly affected.[1]

The second event of 1872 that ended any complacency still remaining in the minds of the directors of the African Steam Ship Company was the termination of the mail contract. Negotiations to renew the 1865 contract were begun in 1870,[2] but it quickly became clear that the Post Office was not prepared to extend the existing system whereby the Company was paid a flat annual subsidy.[3] The Post Office decision was, no doubt, influenced by the sailings of the British and African because for the first time these appeared a satisfactory alternative. The reaction of the African Steam Ship Company was to approach its now friendly competitor:

'Our Mr. Dempster had a long conversation yesterday respecting the Mail Contract. The African Company having received official intimation that the existing contract will not be renewed, and knowing that it would be useless going to the Post Office Authorities to ask for any new contract, unless application was made conjointly with this Company, Mr. Fletcher is desirous that we should join them in making such application . . .

'Our own opinion in the matter is that we should join them in endeavouring to get a contract for the conveyance of mails, and we fancy a combination between the two Companies on this point would compel the Government to give us a subsidy. They *must* send the mails, and if we would not carry them on other terms the Government would have no option. We think although we combined to get a subsidy, it will be necessary to have separate contracts with the Post Office. Our notion is that we should ask £12,000 and the other Company, £18,000.'[4]

Further information must then have reached Alexander Elder, for less than a week later he wrote to the British and African suggesting it

[1] P. N. Davies, 'The African Steam Ship Company', in J. R. Harris, Ed., *Liverpool and Merseyside* (London: Frank Cass, 1969), pp. 236–7.
[2] A.S.P., Directors report for the half-year ending 31 October 1870, p. 5.
[3] This had amounted to £20,000 in 1868. *Money Market Review*, 6 June 1868.
[4] Elder Dempster Papers, (hereinafter referred to as E.D.P.) Letter from Elder Dempster and Company to R. S. Cunliffe, Esq., (Managing Director of the British and African Steam Navigation Company), 2 November 1871.

was unlikely that the Post Office would accept the contract proposed by Mr Fletcher and that it would be unwise to attempt to coerce a settlement. Elder thought that a better line of attack would be to dispense with the subsidy but to obtain a higher rate for the items carried. In support of this argument he stated:

> 'You will observe the Pacific Company are paid 2s. 6d. per ounce for letters, although the Post Office only receive 2s. per ounce, or portion of an ounce, from the public. This contrasts favourably with our 8½d. per ounce—as the Post Office charge the public 1/- and ought therefore to pay us something like 1s. 6d. to put us on equally good terms . . .'[1]

Elder made it quite clear, however, that any prospect of success depended on joint action being taken by the two lines. Lengthy negotiations then followed, but the old mail contract expired before these could be finalised. Thus after October, 1872, all correspondence had to be sent to West Africa via 'Ship Letter Mails',[2] which was a most unsatisfactory arrangement for the public and the Post Office, as well as for the shipping lines.[3]

The African Steam Ship Company were naturally upset at the loss of their subsidy and determined to press the postal authorities for an arrangement whereby they would at least obtain a special rate of 'Sea Postage' on all correspondence carried by their vessels. They therefore approached Elder Dempster for a second time:

> 'It is very humble pie for African Company to bear, after all their boasting, to come and ask us to help them to get a new contract and allow us a fair share.'[4]

By this time, the inconvenience of the situation had modified the attitude of the Post Office and a new contract was made on 15 March 1873. Under the new agreement both the African and British and African Companies were to receive £1,200 a year for calling at Bathurst. This was the only direct subsidy—the main provision was for the Postmaster General to pay 'a sum per ounce equal to the sea postage calculated at 4d. per half ounce letter'.[5] In practice it was found 'that

[1] E.D.P., Letter from Alexander Elder to R. S. Cunliffe, 7 November 1871.

[2] Under this system the Captain (or Company) received a proportion of the sea postage charged by the Ship-Letter Office. Howard Robinson, *Carrying British Mails Overseas* (London: George Allen & Unwin, 1964), pp. 111–13 *et seq.*

[3] A.S.P., Directors report for the half-year ending 31 October 1872, p. 5.

[4] E.D.P., Letter from John Dempster to R. S. Cunliffe, 2 November 1872.

[5] E.D.P., Letter from the General Post Office, London, to the British and African Steam Navigation Company, 15 March 1873.

Sir Alan Tod.

J. H. Joyce Esq.

PLATE 3

F. L. Lane Esq.

G. J. Ellerton Esq.

PLATE 4 Members of the African Association, c. 1890.

the rate of payment for ordinary letters should be 1/- per ounce, that being found to be on average the equivalent of 4d. per single letter'.[1]

The effect of the new postal contract was to increase the profitability of the British and African Steam Navigation Company, for previously it had received no payment for the carriage of mail. As far as the African Steam Ship Company was concerned, the loss of the original postal subsidy was not an unmitigated disaster, for the Company still received a reasonable remuneration for whatever it carried and was relieved of the responsibility of running unprofitable services. What it did mean was that a new approach had to be made to the trade and proof that the directors recognised this fact can be seen by their fleet policy. Three of the older, less efficient ships, *Mandingo, Lagos* and *Calabar*, were sold and replaced by the newly constructed *Eithiopia, Monrovia* and *Elmina*. The loss of *Macgregor Laird*[2] and *Yoruba* was balanced by the purchase of *Ambritz* (formerly *Asiatic*) and *Nigretia* (formerly *Bentinck*),[3] but the subsequent sinking of the latter in 1875 meant that the fleet showed only a small increase:

Fleet of the African Steam Ship Company
1870–1873

October 1870 9 ships totalling 11,244 tons
1871 9 ,, ,, 11,804
1872 9 ,, ,, 12,648
1873 9 ,, ,, 12,951[4]

During the same period the British and African also made steady, if limited, progress but the only addition to the original fleet came in 1872 when *Senegal* was ordered from the Glasgow firm of Cunliffe and Dunlop. The line suffered no serious casualties during its early years, so in 1873 its vessels totalled just over 10,000 tons—still significantly less than those of its competitor. The reasons for this apparent near stagnation are not altogether clear, but much responsibility must rest with Alexander Elder and John Dempster. As managers of the Line, Elder Dempster and Company were in a strong position to influence policy and they appear to have placed more emphasis on consolidation than

[1] E.D.P., Letter from the General Post Office, London, to the British and African Steam Navigation Company, 25 August 1873.

[2] An extensive account of the loss of *Macgregor Laird* is given in the *Liverpool Courier*, 26 January 1872.

[3] Note that *Bentinck* had formerly been used on the West African Coast. See: *Cox and the JuJu Coast* (Journal kept on H.M.S. *Fly*) (St Helier: Ellison & Co., 1968).

[4] A.S.P., Details from the Directors reports for the relevant years.

expansion. Of course, the shipping company had to take ultimate decisions, but it was unlikely lightly to disregard advice given by people it had appointed for their expertise in West African shipping affairs. The relationship between Elder Dempster and R. S. Cunliffe, (the managing director of the British and African), seems, in fact, to have been a close and cordial one—quite unlike that between Messrs Fletcher and Parr and the African Steam Ship Company.

A new agreement was made between the African Steam Ship Company and the British and African Steam Navigation Company and came into effect in 1873.[1] This provided that a steamer of each line should sail every alternate week and illustrated the increasing harmony between the two firms as well as the acceptance by the African of the equal status of its rival. The basic reason for the success of these agreements was the fear of competition from outside firms; both concerns accepted the principle that co-operation with a friendly rival was preferable to unrestricted competition with innumerable interlopers.

The African Steam Ship Company made a further agreement at this time—one which concerned their relationship with Messrs Fletcher and Parr. The Liverpool agents were the largest shareholders of the Company and it was customary for them to advance it large amounts. They were anxious, therefore, to prevent a repetition of the secretary's embezzlement and wished to see the business completely reorganised. The directors, still shaken by Duncan Campbell's depredations, agreed to Fletcher and Parr's proposals, stipulating, however, that their agents must deposit £10,000 of Company stock as security. Under this arrangement Fletcher and Parr were to receive 5 per cent on the gross receipts (excluding all postal monies), provided the net profits would admit of the payment of 7½ per cent dividend to the shareholders and the carrying over of a surplus of not less than £500; otherwise they were to contribute to the extent of 1 per cent of their commission towards any deficiency. Except on the first half-year, profits, in fact, did not admit of such dividends. It followed, therefore, that their remuneration did not exceed 4 per cent. Fletcher and Parr were also to receive 3 per cent on the premiums of insurance for transacting that branch of the Company's business. These were the total payments received by the Liverpool agents and out of them:

'. . . we defrayed all office and other expenses of the Agency in Liverpool,

[1] A.S.P., Directors report for the half-year ending 31 October 1873, p. 6.

including Clerks and salaries of the Marine and Engineer Superintendents and Wharfinger. The other Company (the British and African) was at the same time paying its Agents (Elder Dempster) a considerably larger amount and higher scale or remuneration . . .'[1]

During the period 1871–5 the commission earned by Fletcher and Parr was as follows:

$$1871 = \pounds\ 8,000$$
$$1872 = \pounds 10,588$$
$$1873 = \pounds 11,506$$
$$1874 = \pounds\ 9,681$$
$$1875 = \pounds\ 4,694[2]$$

Thus the immediate effect of the new arrangement was to give a substantial rise to the Liverpool firm but, thereafter, there was a decline which accelerated in 1875.[3] The reasons for this rapid reduction originated in 1874 when the secretary of the African Steam Ship Company asked Fletcher and Parr if it were possible for them to consider a reduction in their commission. They had replied that they would give the matter their serious attention, but that in view of the increasing expenses of the agency they thought it unlikely that anything could be done. In addition they '. . . hoped that the projected economy was not to be limited to the Liverpool Agency', a comment which the chairman apparently resented as being a slur on the board.[4] Then in February, 1875, the secretary reminded them of this conversation by sending a note to enquire if they had reached any conclusions. Fletcher and Parr replied to this as follows:

Liverpool, 25th February, 1875

Dear Sir,

Agency

We looked upon this matter as put aside for the present by the loss of the *Soudan* and the indisposition of the Directors to replace her. A steamer more or less in the trade makes a very material difference in our commission, though it does not in any degree admit of our reducing our working expenses. We trust the Directors will not think it objectionable to let this question rest until the result of their offer for the Portuguese service is ascertained. They will then be able to decide what arrangements can be made for West Coast sailings, and what proportion of them the Directors will be prepared to take up. We may deem it

---

[1] A.S.P., Pamphlet issued by Fletcher & Parr, 24 June 1875, pp. 7–8.

[2] A.S.P., Fletcher & Parr's Private Journals, Nos. 1 and 2.

[3] Not all of this commission came from the African Steam Ship Company. See below, p. 69.

[4] A.S.P., Fletcher and Parr's Pamphlet, op. cit., p. 8.

to our interest to offer, with permission of the Directors, to take up and hold on our own account any of the sailings the Directors may prefer to miss rather than buy or charter vessels to maintain. Any place the Company vacates in the West Coast trade will otherwise be eagerly filled by the other Company, to the mutual detriment both of ourselves and of our Company. Having regard to the recent additional misfortunes of the Company, we may say that we shall not be found unwilling to contribute, by a reasonable concession, towards putting the receipts of the Company into a more satisfactory position.'[1]

The loss of *Soudan* was a very serious matter for the Liverpool agents because it had been one of the largest vessels in the fleet and meant a reduction of about 15 per cent in their commission. It is also likely that this could not be offset by a significant reduction in expenses as these tended to be fixed and would not vary with the number of ships employed. To this extent Fletcher and Parr had a reasonable case for asking that any changes in their rate of commission be deferred and it came as a great shock, therefore, when the secretary replied to their letter by return of post to say, '. . . that the Directors had unanimously decided to open an office of their own in Liverpool, with a Manager who would be under the more immediate control of the Board'.[2] Fletcher and Parr's reaction to this message was to issue a pamphlet and circulate it amongst the shareholders of the African Steam Ship Company in an unsuccessful attempt to persuade them to get the decision reversed. In this they detailed their near twenty years of service to the Company and itemised their disputes with the directors. It shows that, as they were completely dependent upon commission for their income, they were naturally eager to expand trade while the London office was mainly concerned with reducing risks and cutting costs. With two such divergent viewpoints it is not surprising that antagonism developed between Liverpool and London, but the abrupt ending of the agency was an unfortunate way to end such a long and mutually beneficial association.

The loss of the agency of the African Steam Ship Company meant less work for Fletcher and Parr, and their commission fell from £3,268 in the first half of 1875 to only £1,426 in the second half.[3] This was in spite of great efforts that were made to develop the firm's other agen-

---

[1] A.S.P., Letter from Fletcher and Parr to the African Steam Ship Company, 25 February 1875.
[2] A.S.P., Fletcher and Parr's Pamphlet, op. cit., p. 9.
[3] A.S.P., Extracted from Fletcher & Parr's Private Journal, No. 2.

cies, which included the Liverpool and Antwerp Steamers and the Peninsular and Oriental Steam Navigation Company. As a result there was obviously less scope for one of Fletcher and Parr's most able and ambitious employees, Alfred Lewis Jones, and when he decided to leave them his action was to have a momentous effect on the entire structure of the West African shipping trade.[1]

[1] This ended Fletcher & Parr's connection with the West African trade but they continue as steamship agents to this day (1972) under the title of J. T. Fletcher (Shipping) Limited.

PART TWO

Elder Dempster
and Company

Chapter 3

Alfred Lewis Jones

His Early Life

Alfred Lewis Jones was born in Picton Place, Carmarthen, on 24 February 1845, of what can best be described as respectable, middle-class Welsh parents.[1] Alfred's father was Daniel Jones, a currier or leather-worker by trade, and also the reputed owner of the Carmarthen newspaper *The Welshman*. His grandfather was Charles Jones, also a currier, who at one time had been an alderman of Carmarthen, and his great-grandfather was John Lewis who had kept the Half Moon Hotel in Carmarthen at the beginning of the nineteenth century.[2] Mary Jean Jones, Alfred's mother, was the eldest daughter of the Revd. Henry Williams, the Rector of Llanedi, and other near relatives included many clergy, a doctor, a wine merchant and a barrister. Thus it would not be true to state that Alfred Jones came from a very poor family although this has been suggested on many occasions. The truth of the matter is that as Daniel and Mary Jones had ten children it was unlikely that they could provide them with all the luxuries of life. At the same time there is no reason to suppose that Alfred or his brothers and sisters were ever short of necessities—especially as seven of these children died while very young.

When Alfred was three years old his father decided to move to Merseyside and from then on his home was to be in Liverpool. His own description of his childhood was that it was 'happy and uneventful'.[3] He could not remember '. . . any amusing escapades or stirring

[1] Picton Place appears to be little changed from the time of Jones's birth, but there is considerable local controversy as to the exact house where he was born.

[2] This was only demolished in the late 1950s.

[3] A. L. Jones, 'Autobiography'. This appeared in the magazine *M.A.P.* dated 28 December 1901.

adventures'. He was quite content to go to school, where he was looked on as a studious pupil. Having a good head for figures he excelled at arithmetic, and apart from this natural ability he was greatly helped by a fine constitution. Even during his schooldays Alfred possessed a keen ambition to do well, and he was usually to be found near the top of his class. Although he was said to have '. . . preferred work to play', his life also had its lighter side. He was very fond of swimming and keen on sailing, and he developed an interest in dogs which remained with him all his life. It was also at this time that a lasting affection grew up between Alfred and his sister, Mary Isabel. She became his constant companion and her friendship was to be a major influence for the remainder of his life.

At the age of fourteen Alfred Jones decided to strike out for himself. He found that in the Liverpool of 1859 the prospects of employment for a youth without influence and but a simple education were strictly limited. After due consideration he came to the conclusion that the sea offered him his best opportunity for a worthwhile career, and he began to make frequent visits to the city docks. Alfred spoke to the masters of numerous ships and received many rebuffs because of his youth and inexperience. Yet he refused to be discouraged and was finally successful in persuading the captain of a steamer of the African Steam Ship Company into giving him a job as a cabin-boy. It speaks well for his powers of persuasion that he secured this appointment; West Africa's reputation as the 'white man's grave' no doubt reduced the number of applicants but it made the captain extremely reluctant to take an inexperienced boy to such a bad climate.

Jones was only to make one journey to West Africa.[1] No records of this particular voyage have survived, but it must have been typical of many made by the vessels of the African Steam Ship Company at that date. In 1859 the Company possessed seven steamers and as these ranged from *Cleopatra* of 1,280 tons down to *Retriever* of only 440 tons, Jones must have sailed in what would now be regarded as a very small craft. The route from Liverpool to West Africa was via St George's Channel and then across the Bay of Biscay. Then, while coal was loaded at Lisbon or Dakar, Jones got his first glimpse of a foreign port. His first introduction to British West Africa came a little later, probably at

[1] In later life he travelled extensively on the Continent and visited the Canary Islands and the West Indies, but he never returned to West Africa.

ALFRED LEWIS JONES

Bathurst at the mouth of the Gambia.[1] The next part of the trip was along the coastline of West Africa where every little river and creek had its own small port, so the routine of stopping and unloading a few pieces of cargo quickly became familiar.[2] Jones also witnessed the difficulties experienced in getting the ship away from each petty port, as the local boatmen—in spite of frequent warnings—hung on till the last possible moment.[3] At every stop he saw something new to attract his attention. So he had gained a real knowledge of West Africa by the time his ship arrived at Fernando Po—the Spanish island that was the southernmost point of the voyage.

After a brief stay the journey home began. This took less than the five or six weeks of the outward trip because fewer calls were made at the minor ports. The vessel averaged nine knots for the 10,000-mile round voyage, so Jones was away from Liverpool for under three months, but this brief period was to shape the whole of his future life. In his sister's words: 'the sad state of things so impressed him he determined no effort should be wanting to better the condition of the natives.'[4] Jones must have made a very favourable impression on his captain while on board. When the vessel returned to Liverpool he made a point of recommending the boy to the ship's agents and as a result Jones obtained a position as junior clerk with them.

The office of W. & H. Laird was a small one but, as previously mentioned, the staff included several members who were destined to make important contributions to the development of West Africa. Apart from Elder, Dempster, and Holt, Jones was associated at an impressionable age with William and Hamilton Laird and also met Macgregor Laird on several occasions:

'. . . Mr. (Macgregor) Laird had a great idea of the future of West Africa and I have taken my ideas from him. When I was a very small boy I used to carry the tea to Mr. Laird, and Mr. Laird used very often to give me half-a-crown. That

[1] The African Steam Ship Company's mail steamers made the following calls at this time: Madeira, Tenerife, Bathurst, Sierra Leone, Cape Palmas, Cape Coast Castle, Accra, Lagos, Benin, Nun, Brass, Bonny, Fernando Po, Cameroons and Old Calabar. A.S.P. Notice issued by Messrs Laird & Fletcher on 30 January 1860.

[2] This was usually in the nature of an open beach without any facilities except, perhaps, a number of surf boats.

[3] E. D. Morel Papers at the British Library of Political and Economic Science, Houghton Street, Aldwych, London, (hereinafter referred to as E.M.P.) Box F.8/1. Letter from Jones to Morel, 9 September 1901.

[4] Unpublished biographical notes on Jones by his sister, Mary Isabel Pinnock.

half crown was put away and I have it still. I did not lose it and it has yielded me very good interest.'[1]

The death of Hamilton and retirement of William Laird brought Fletcher and Parr together as partners and the latter took a strong liking to Alfred Jones. He gave him much encouragement and advice and paid for him to attend night-school. In addition, Jones spent a lot of his spare time at Mr Parr's house and this was an invaluable help in strengthening his social background. At this early stage in his career Jones lived in Freehold Street, West Derby, some four miles from Fletcher and Parr's office.[2] The pay was very poor—he started at half-a-crown a week, and even by the time he was twenty he was only earning a pound —so he carried his lunch and usually walked to and from his work to save the fare charged on the horse-drawn buses of that era. This meant that he left home early in the morning and arrived home late at night, particularly on those occasions when he went straight to an evening class at the Liverpool College in Shaw Street.[3]

Alfred Jones remained with Fletcher and Parr throughout the eighteen-sixties, gradually gaining in status and salary. The departure of Holt in 1862, the resignation of Elder in 1866, and the exit of Dempster in 1868 assisted his progress, and by 1870 he was in a relatively senior position and earning £125 a year.[4] By this time he was making a name for himself by his shrewd decisions and smart business acumen and he played an important part in negotiating the truce between the African and the British and African lines. His progress was marred, however, to some extent by the death of his father, Daniel Jones, in February 1869. This blow made his relationship with his mother even closer and he continued to live with her and his sister, Mary Isabel, at the family house in Freehold Street, West Derby. The following year saw Isabel married to John Pinnock, but as he was an African merchant and spent much time abroad, she continued to live with her mother and brother.

During the early seventies Jones continued to make progress in the employ of Fletcher and Parr and his salary rose to £137 10s in 1871,

[1] *The Times*, 20 August 1902. Speech by A. L. Jones at a banquet given in his honour by the inhabitants of West Africa.

[2] Note that this house was destroyed by bombing in 1941 but that the street is otherwise little changed.

[3] Unpublished biographical notes on Jones by his sister, Mary Isabel Pinnock.

[4] A.S.P., Fletcher and Parr Private Journal, No. 1.

£150 in 1872 and £175 in 1873 and 1874.[1] It was at this time that he made many suggestions for extending the business, but 'his colossal charter-schemes, as they were then thought, fairly appalled his old-fashioned employers . . .'[2] As a result of this attitude Jones was unable to institute any changes in agency policy but he did obtain permission to organise a small amount of chartering and for this he received a commission which in 1875 amounted to £26 15s 3d. Thus his total remuneration for that year amounted to just over £201—the most he had ever earned—but any satisfaction he may have felt was rapidly dissipated by the loss of the agency of the African Steam Ship Company. It was obvious to Jones that the loss of their key agency would mean less work for Fletcher and Parr and consequently there would be less scope within the firm. He was aware of Elder and Dempster's successful venture and he knew of John Holt's return from West Africa after having laid the foundations of a profitable and lasting concern. It seemed to him, therefore, that in spite of his achievements within Fletcher and Parr's he was in danger of being left behind by his more progressive and adventurous former associates. The loss of the African Steam Ship Company's agency was the final straw to this ambitious man and he decided to open up in business on his own account.

Alfred Jones remained with Fletcher and Parr for a further period of two years while he finalised his plans and accumulated capital. In 1876 he received £175 in salary which with his commission on chartering of £57 9s 7d gave him an income of £232 9s 7d and in 1877 he earned a total of £247 8s 4d.[3] Then, during the critical period when making his final arrangements to set up on his own, came a shock which destroyed much of Jones's contentment with life. This was the death of his mother in January 1877, and it was perhaps this event which made him concentrate all his energies on a successful business career to the exclusion of all other interests. Following the death of his mother, Alfred's sister, Mary Isabel, kept house for him and when her husband died in 1878 this arrangement became permanent.

On 1 January 1878, Jones established the firm of Alfred L. Jones and Company and acquired offices at the North Western Bank Building, 6 Dale Street, Liverpool. At first the business was concerned only with

[1] A.S.P., Fletcher and Parr's Private Journals, Nos. 1 & 2.
[2] *Shipping World*, 22 December 1909. Obituary of Alfred Jones.
[3] A.S.P., Fletcher and Parr's Private Journal, No. 2.

shipping and insurance broking, so the experience gained with Fletcher and Parr stood him in good stead and, in fact, he received commission from his former employers to the amount of £115 12s 6d during 1878. By working long hours, paying great attention to detail and taking only short holidays, he was able gradually to increase the number of his clients and the firm prospered. In his own words:

> 'Any anxiety experienced at the start was more than compensated for by the independence of my new position, and the knowledge that success depended on my own exertions.'[1]

Jones later claimed that he made more money in his first year on his own than during the whole time he was with Fletcher and Parr. As this only amounted to just over £2,000 during the entire period his statement may well be true[2] and together with his savings and credit this profit enabled him to begin a new facet of his enterprise in the second year.

Early in 1879 Jones purchased a number of small sailing-vessels which he had been chartering to carry goods to West Africa. The success of these sailing-ship voyages was a key factor in his progress but he did not allow this to alter his opinion that the future of the carrying trade lay with the steamship. When, therefore, an advantageous moment arrived he disposed of his little fleet and made arrangements to charter a small steamship. This had immediate repercussions. The established lines, the African Steam Ship Company and the British and African Steam Navigation Company, were represented in Liverpool by a branch office[3] and Elder Dempster and Company. The latter recognised that in Jones they had a dangerous rival who, though small, was efficient. With this in mind they decided to avert future difficulties by offering him a junior partnership. No doubt their previous liaison in Fletcher and Parr's office enabled them to make a correct assessment of his potential. On the other hand, Jones's personal knowledge of Alexander Elder and John Dempster was an important factor in making his decision, but perhaps the most essential single consideration was that after trading on his own account for eighteen months he was in an excellent position to judge the possibilities of his own business. In comparing the advantages of a small but independent position with a partnership in a much larger firm, Jones decided that he could not

[1] A. L. Jones, op. cit.
[2] A.S.P., Fletcher and Parr's Private Journals, Nos. 1 and 2.
[3] See p. 80.

afford to ignore the scope and challenge that the situation with Elder
Dempster offered him. He therefore gave up his steamship charter and
dissolved the firm of Alfred L. Jones and Company. Then on 1 October
1879, he joined his former colleagues in Messrs Elder Dempster and
Company.

Junior Partner with Elder Dempster and Company
At the time that Alfred Jones was made a partner of Elder and Dempster, a further partner was admitted. This was Mr W. J. Davey and,
like Jones, he was not a native of Liverpool. He was born in Cornwall
in 1853 and lived in that county until 1871. He then moved to Liverpool and obtained employment in Elder Dempster's office.[1] His progress thereafter was steady, if unspectacular, and culminated in the offer
of a partnership in 1879. But although his advancement was entirely due
to the favourable opinion of Alexander Elder and John Dempster, he
appears to have fallen quickly and completely under the new partner's
influence, and he was to become Jones's right-hand man for the rest of
his life.

Alfred Jones was to be a junior partner with Elder Dempster and
Company until 1884, and at first he did little but learn thoroughly every
aspect of the business:

'Until one has made himself practically acquainted with every detail of the business which he is called upon to direct, it is impossible to gauge its possibilities
or properly carry out the duties of a director, therefore my first object was to
become thoroughly acquainted with each branch of the work the firm was
engaged in, a thing not to be done in a moment.'[2]

The decisions made by Elder Dempster at this time cannot be traced
to any single partner, but there is little doubt that Jones played an increasingly important role. The strengthening of ties between the two
British lines, the smashing of rival companies, and the early agreements
with German shipping interests all bear his stamp. But he was content at
this stage to feel his way and although his name appears, with that of
Davey, amongst the list of shareholders of the British and African Steam
Navigation Company, he made no attempt to gain control.[3] It was dur-

[1] *Journal of Commerce*, 2 November 1900.
[2] A. L. Jones, op. cit.
[3] See Appendix p. 429, Table 35, for list of shareholders in the British and African
Steam Navigation Company.

ing the time that Jones was a junior partner that his firm became the managers of the British and African. This meant that Elder Dempster henceforth controlled all their vessels and organised many aspects of the shipping company which then became, in effect, only a financial body. Here, too, one can deduce Jones's influence, for until this time there had been no basic change in the relationship between the British and African and Elder Dempster since they had started in business together in 1868.

Alfred Jones's influence also appears to have been a decisive factor in the financial reconstruction of the British and African which began in 1881 and which was to pay for the expansion of the fleet. The effect of this was to raise the nominal capital from £200,000 to £250,000 and the issued capital was increased from £200,000 to £210,960.[1] Then on 23 April 1883, the British and African changed its status and became a limited company. At the same time the nominal capital was increased to £750,000 and the issued capital was more than doubled to £492,240.[2] The issued capital was further increased in 1884 and 1885 and by the latter year it had reached £546,000 which, in fact, proved to be its highest point.[3]

While Elder Dempster and Company took over the management of the British and African and also remained its Liverpool agents, the African Steam Ship Company was developing on different lines. The sacking of Fletcher and Parr in 1875 was followed by the opening of a Company office on Merseyside. Alexander Sinclair was appointed as manager and,

> 'The Directors are happy to state that the change in the Liverpool management has worked to their satisfaction, and their expectations as to the economy likely to arise therefrom are being fully realised.'[4]

The sinking of *Soudan* in February 1875 was not a disaster, for all but £3,000 (the amount carried by the African Steam Ship Company) was covered by outside insurance. When, however, this was combined with a poorness of trade which resulted in losses of £4,606 and £2,769

[1] In 1881 the issued capital was altered from 320 shares of £625 to 2,500 (less 156 unissued) shares of £100 (£90 called).

[2] 15,000 shares of £50 = £750,000; 11,720 shares taken up (£42 called up) = £492,240.

[3] In 1884 1,280 new shares were issued on which £25 was called up. In 1885 these 'new' shares had a further £17 called making them equal to the 'old shares'. The total share issue was then 13,000 of £42 = £546,000. See Appendix p. 426, Table 33.

[4] A.S.P., Directors report for the half-year ending 31 October 1875.

for the half-years ending April and October 1875, the directors were justifiably concerned. Their reaction, unlike that of the British and African which continued to expand, was one of retrenchment. Head office was moved to less expensive quarters in Great St Helens and they reduced their own remuneration from £1,200 to £600 per annum. In 1876, *Monrovia* of 1,019 tons was lost off Sierra Leone and this entailed a loss of £3,000—the amount of insurance cover carried by the Company[1]—but as there had been some improvement in trade it was possible to absorb this item. This increase in trade was maintained the following year and was assisted by an agreement made with the British and African in respect of sailings to the south-west coast of Africa.[2]

During the next few years the African Steam Ship Company made only slow progress. The emphasis was on retrenchment and the debenture issue of £82,000 in 1875 was reduced to £58,000 in 1876 and progressively to £30,000 in 1880.[3] Behind this conservative policy lay the fluctuations which characterised the trade and also the opposition of rival lines, including that of the West African Steam Navigation Company, which ensured that freight rates were kept at a very low level.[4] On the other hand a joint service from Hamburg to West Africa was begun in March 1879, in co-operation with the British and African and this proved to be an immediate success. Partly owing to the demands for additional tonnage on this route and perhaps influenced by the example of the British and African, the African Steam Ship Company then began to expand its fleet. (See table on page 82.)

New vessels constructed for the African Steam Ship Company included *Winnebah* and *Akassa* in 1881, *Mandingo* in 1882 and *Benin* in 1884. To pay for this expansion the debenture issue was increased by £25,000 to £55,000, but even so its capital and fleet remained much smaller than that of the British and African. Furthermore, the results achieved by the African during this period continued to be poor although the enlarged fleet was almost fully employed—largely owing

[1] In consequence of a general rise in insurance rates the African Steam Ship Company created its own Insurance Fund in 1874. It was intended that the Company should limit its risk to £3,000 per steamer, although this was sometime exceeded, as this enabled the fleet to be covered for very moderate premiums. A.S.P., Directors reports for the half-years ending 16 December 1874, p. 5 and 31 October 1875, p. 6.

[2] A.S.P., Directors report for the half-year ending 30 April 1877, p. 5.

[3] A.S.P., See Directors reports for the relevant years.

[4] A.S.P., Directors reports for the half-years ending 30 April and 31 October 1879.

Fleets Engaged in the West African Shipping Trade

	African Steam Ship Company		British & African S.N. Company	
Year	Ships	Total	Ships	Total
1874	10	13,605 tons	10	12,760 tons
1875	8	11,305	9	12,597
1876	7	10,051	12	16,782
1877	8	10,236	12	16,782
1878	7	9,218	15	20,728
1879	8	11,175	16	21,259
1880	10	14,298	18	24,298
1881	11	15,550	18	24,298
1882	12	17,250	18	25,069
1883	11	16,069	20	28,669
1884	12	18,284	24	35,245[1]

to the activities of the Anglo-African Steam Ship Company. This line began operating early in 1883, so freight rates had to be reduced and losses were incurred in chartering vessels in conjunction with the British and African to make special voyages against the new competitor. These measures proved to be successful—the Anglo-African was wound up by order of the Court of Chancery in 1884—but the cost to both the established lines was a heavy one.[2]

This was a typical example of the increasing co-operation between the African Steam Ship Company and the British and African Steam Navigation Company Ltd. and, incidentally, of the growing importance of Elder Dempster and Company. The British and African had its head office in Glasgow while the African was controlled from London, so the close liaison between the two firms was greatly assisted by the proximity of Elder Dempster and Alexander Sinclair in Liverpool. In fact, most of the working arrangements and agreements were the result of their consultations and together the two lines were able to resist the opposition of the many companies and tramp steamers that attempted to enter the trade. In this connection it should be appreciated that, even when no rival line was seeking to enter the trade, many single interlopers continuously sought to find an opening and, from June 1884 to June 1885, no less than fifteen outside vessels sailed from Hamburg and Liverpool

[1] Details of the African Steam Ship Company from the Directors reports; the British and African figures have been calculated from the firms fleet list.

[2] A.S.P., Directors report for the half-year ending 30 April 1884, p. 6.

to West Africa. The reaction of the directors to this particular on-slaught was to reduce their tariff still further:

'Owing to the extremely depressed state of the Steam Shipping Trade there are a large number of steamers of a similar class seeking employment, many of the owners of which would rather face loss than have their vessels laid up. At the rates now charged by our (the African Steam Ship) Company and the British and African Company it is not possible for outside steamers to compete success-fully with our vessels.'[1]

Thus by 1884 the two established lines continued to maintain their position in the trade but as this was frequently only achieved by un-remunerative freight rates there seemed to be little prospect of lasting progress. This, however, was not to be the case, for it was at this stage that Alfred Jones took a decisive step. By 1884 Jones was ready to run Elder Dempster and Company, but the senior partners were not men who would lightly give him the control he desired. Yet they did so, and ended their association with the firm they had created. The secrecy which surrounded the departure of Alexander Elder and John Demp-ster has never been dispelled. In his autobiography Jones merely stated that:

'My opportunity came soon after when on the retirement of Mr. Elder and Mr. Dempster, I rose to be the senior partner of Elder Dempster and Company.'[2]

A. H. Milne, in his *Sir Alfred Lewis Jones* wrote:

'A few years after this, Mr. Elder and Mr. Dempster retired from the business. It was then carried on by Mr. Jones and Mr. Davey. . . .'[3]

But it is unlikely that the two senior partners just retired. Both were comparatively young men—Elder being fifty and Dempster forty-seven —and both were to remain actively in business in Liverpool for another sixteen years.

The *Dundee Advertiser* of 14 December 1909, in its obituary of Jones, writing of the time he agreed to join Elder Dempster states:

'On condition of receiving a certain proportion of the Company's shares he agreed to join the firm. He then gradually bought up the shares till he controlled the concern.'

[1] A.S.P., Directors report for the half-year ending April 1885, p. 7.
[2] A. L. Jones op. cit.
[3] A. H. Milne *Sir Alfred Lewis Jones, K.C.M.G.* (Liverpool: Henry Young & Sons, 1914).

This view of the events leading to Jones becoming senior partner does not agree with the popular account given in many of his obituary notices,[1] and *The Times* of 13 December 1909, is typical of these:

> 'The story runs that when a young man he had risen to a responsible position in the office of Elder Dempster and Company, he went to the heads of the concern and told them he saw his way to an immense development of their business if they would put the control of it in his hands, and that he was prepared to buy them out on terms to be agreed upon if they were not prepared to carry out his views. They replied that the purchase of the concern was far beyond his resources at the time, and that they were not prepared to entertain his proposals. He then asked for six months to obtain the money required, and at the end of that time, so good was his credit in Liverpool, and so high was his reputation for business capacity and enterprise, that he returned to the partners and told them he had raised the amount required and was prepared to advance it on terms which would give him complete control of the business.'

John Holt, in a letter to James Knott dated 13 May 1891, put the matter in a nutshell:

> 'Fletcher and Parr were the trainers of the West African (Steam) trade. Elder and Dempster started the British and African S.S.Co. in opposition to Fletcher and Parr, and later Jones came on the scene with a couple of tramps which he took off in order to get into a partnership with E.D. & Co. which ended in Elder and Dempster leaving Jones and their Correspondent Clerk Davey as their successors.'[2]

In a letter to Elder dated June 1895, Holt also wrote:

> '. . . as a ship's agent pure and simple as you and Mr. Dempster used to be in bygone days in Liverpool,—when nobody had a thought of your giving up the interests of your shipping and against whom, rates being equal, no opposition would have had ever started.'[3]

Thus Elder and Dempster were well thought of, their business was prospering, and yet they handed it over to Jones. What was the explanation for this remarkable action? As Elder Dempster and Company remained unlimited until 1910 they were under no obligation to forward returns under the Company Acts of 1856 and 1862.[4] It is therefore not

---

[1] It is likely that this version is based on an interview given by Jones to Rudolph de Cordova in 1903. An account of this appears in *The Sunday Strand*, November 1903, entitled 'The New Gospel of Wealth', but it is written in very general terms, so does not really help.

[2] *John Holt Papers*, (hereinafter referred to as J.H.P.). Letter from John Holt to James Knott, 13 May 1891.

[3] J.H.P. Letter from John Holt to Alexander Elder, June 1895.

[4] Legally Elder Dempster and Company was a partnership.

possible to verify the suggestion that Jones gradually acquired sufficient shares to gain a controlling interest and was then able to push out the senior partners. In any case, the shares of a private company such as this were customarily held by the principals, their families and close friends, so it would have been difficult for Jones to buy enough shares, even assuming he had sufficient money to pay for them.

The story put forward by *The Times* seems improbable and would need documentary evidence before it could be accepted, but it does appear to possess a germ of truth. If we consider that it would have been impossible for Jones to have slowly obtained a controlling number of shares—the only reasonable viewpoint—then we are left with the alternative that he offered Elder and Dempster such a large sum of money for their interest that they found it convenient to accept. But it is almost certain that this is only half the story. Jones undoubtedly received some shares when he joined the firm, and he probably purchased a few more in his five years as a junior partner. His fellow junior partner, Mr W. J. Davey, could be relied upon to support him, but in comparison with the shares held by Elder and Dempster their combined holdings were very small. To counteract this unfavourable share distribution, Jones had two possible courses of action, and it is to be expected that he carried these out simultaneously. He ingratiated himself with any shareholder he could by holding out the promise of higher dividends if he were in control. In this task his tremendous reputation stood him in good stead, and he was able to threaten Elder and Dempster with the possibility of his persuading an adequate number of shareholders to change their allegiance. Jones also suggested, both to the shareholders and the senior partners, that if he were not allowed to buy control of the company then he would leave it at an opportune moment. In this event the rival concern he would start must certainly reduce the profitability of Elder Dempster, if it did not end its existence altogether.

In this way Jones could have maintained a heavy pressure on Elder and Dempster. By making their position appear to be insecure—however slightly—and by threatening to start a rival company, Jones would be able to make his offer to buy them out the more attractive. Apart from the pressure to sell caused by these actions and the great financial inducements, Elder and Dempster also had to contend with the man himself. Alfred Jones's forceful personality; his large capacity for work; his enormous knowledge of the trade; and his drive and initiative, all made him a very formidable character. The close daily contact of the partners must have resulted in friction and at these times the strength of purpose possessed by Jones must have been of immense value in wearing down his seniors. In due course it seemed to Elder and Dempster that they had to decide either to accept the generous terms offered by their subordinate or be prepared to fight him. Realising that a struggle would be financially disastrous for their interests, and having such a rewarding alternative, they therefore allowed Jones to buy them out, and gave him the control he desired.

Senior Partner with Elder Dempster and Company

When Alfred Jones obtained control of Elder Dempster and Company in 1884 it was but the first step towards his domination of the West African shipping business. Elder Dempster at this date was still only a tiny firm of shipping agents with a precarious hold on the trade, and if this were to be expanded many serious problems had to be overcome. Perhaps the two most important of these were the maintenance of friendly relations between the established lines, and the elimination of interlopers. Individually these were quite substantial difficulties but fortunately for Jones they tended to cancel one another out. By keeping on the closest terms the two regular lines were able to put up a solid barrier against any outside interest and both realised not only how much could be gained by co-operation but also how disastrous rivalry would be. Thus Jones's task was made easier in both ways; the possibility of a rift was lessened, competing steamers got short shrift, and the two companies were enabled to maintain their place in the trade. It was, therefore, of paramount importance to Jones that he continued the friendly connection between the two firms, and his success in achieving this objective were to be the basis for his entire strategy and plans for the future.

Another factor of prime importance to Jones was the relationship between Elder Dempster and the British lines sailing to West Africa. It was essential that he retained the goodwill and co-operation of both these companies but the way in which this was maintained differed in each case. Jones did not feel it was necessary for him to invest in the shares of the British and African Steam Navigation Company at this stage, for Elder Dempster already had an almost exclusive say in the running of this line 'Practically they have no accounts with anyone except through their Liverpool Agents.'[1]

Alexander Elder and John Dempster, however, not only increased their already considerable holdings but also became directors of the firm.[2] On the other hand Jones had no say in the policy of the African Steam Ship Company, so he made it his business to buy their shares whenever they came on to the market. Details of the share distribution of this line are not available,[3] but as Jones gained control by 1900 it is likely that he had collected their shares from an early date. In the short term every share meant a vote in his favour at annual general meetings and as his holdings increased so did the ineffectiveness of any opposition. Jones continued to expand his interests in the African Steam Ship Company till his death in 1909, and he then owned 26,328 shares of £20 each, fully paid.[4] By this date the issued capital of the Company amounted to 33,732 shares,[5] so Jones held over 75 per cent of the total.

A final, crucial, problem which faced Jones throughout his period as senior partner of Elder Dempster was the satisfaction of the trading firms who provided the bulk of his cargoes. As late as the mid-eighties it was still quite customary for many merchants to own sailing-vessels, although most of their goods were carried by the regular lines. In addition, a few of the traders would sometimes join together to charter sailing- (and occasionally) steamships, but this naturally depended on the level of freight rates. Some of the larger merchants also thought it would be of advantage to establish their own independent line, but as this would necessarily involve co-operation with other trading firms— frequently deadly rivals—the difficulties are obvious. Nevertheless the possibility that merchants might acquire or charter vessels, might utilise the services of an outside line or interloper, or even start their own line was a tremendous source of worry to Jones and, as will be seen later,[6] required constant effort to be overcome.

[1] Petition of the British and African Steam Navigation Company Limited, unto the Rt. Hon. the Lords of Council and Sessions, Section 8, 26 February 1891.
[2] See Appendix p. 429, Table 35, for details of these shareholdings.
[3] The African Steam Ship Company being established by Royal Charter did not come within the provisions of the Company Acts of the 1850s and was not required to submit returns of shareholders to the Registrar of Companies.
[4] Agreements relating to the formation of Elder Dempster and Company Limited, in 1910. Third Schedule, p. 13. *See* Appendix, p. 455, Table 49.
[5] A.S.P., Directors report for the twelve months ending 31 December 1909, p. 7.
[6] See below, Chapter 4, p. 95.

The period from 1884 to 1895 was a very difficult one for Alfred Jones, yet he succeeded in achieving all his main objectives. Elder Dempster remained on friendly terms with the two British lines and cordial relations were maintained between the shipping companies. Indeed, after 1891, the relationship between the three firms became even closer, for in that year Elder Dempster became the managing agents for the African Steam Ship Company as well as for the British and African Steam Navigation Company. It was fortunate for the established lines that this close co-operation existed, as several other shipping companies tried to enter the trade. All these attempts were defeated, with one exception—the Woermann Line of Hamburg. This German firm could not be easily disposed of because it possessed certain natural advantages, and so Jones made an arrangement whereby it agreed to restrict itself to particular areas on the coast and not to enter the United Kingdom trade to West Africa.[1] The established lines were also attacked during this period by the Royal Niger Company—the largest firm in West Africa—and by the African Association[2]—an amalgamation created by a number of merchants. It took all of Jones's skill to defend his position in the short run but ultimately he was able to make satisfactory arrangements with both of these opponents.[3]

Prior to 1887 Elder Dempster had been ships' agents and ships' managers but never shipowners. This situation was rectified in that year when Jones bought *Clare* of 2,034 tons.[4] In the next few years the Elder Dempster fleet grew rapidly and by 1890 it possessed eleven vessels totalling 28,373 gross tons. This fleet was transferred to the African Steam Ship Company the following year as part of the arrangement whereby Elder Dempster became the Company's managing agents and marked another important milestone in Jones's career. Ever since he had become the senior partner of Elder Dempster, Jones had worked for the closest possible relationship with the African Steam Ship Company. He had constantly worried in case their understanding was broken, for he regarded it as the foundation of his position in the West African carrying trade. Accordingly he had taken every opportunity to ingratiate himself with the Company and his efforts bore fruit when he

[1] See below, Chapter 4, p. 109.
[2] See below, Chapter 4, p. 94, and Appendix, p. 425, Table 32.
[3] See below, Chapter 4, p. 108, et. seq.
[4] *Lloyds Register* 1889–90 C.825.

secured the management of the concern for his own firm. Jones's own holdings in the African Steam Ship Company at this time were still relatively small, so the decision to make Elder Dempster managing agents was made purely on grounds of increased efficiency. In his dealings with the Royal Niger Company and the African Association, Jones had conclusively demonstrated to the directors of the African Steam Ship Company that their interests were safe in his hands. They therefore placed the management of their line in his keeping with the sole proviso that Alexander Sinclair—former manager of their Liverpool office which was now closed—should be appointed a partner in Elder Dempster and Company.

The result of this activity was that for the first time Jones could really control and integrate the fleets of both the regular British shipping lines. These had made considerable progress in the decade which followed Jones's rise to power in 1884, but the growth of the African Steam Ship Company's fleet was by far the more marked even when allowance is made for the transfer of the Elder Dempster vessels. Thus, as will be seen from the following table, while the African's tonnage increased from 18,299 to 90,862 tons, the British and African fleet only rose from 34,956 to 50,194 tons.

Fleets Engaged in the West African Shipping Trade

Year	African Steam Ship Company		British & African S.N. Co.	
	Ships	Total	Ships	Total
1885	12	18,299 tons	23	34,956 tons
1886	12	19,830	23	34,956
1887	12	19,830	23	34,956
1888	12	19,831	23	34,956
1889	14	24,468	24	38,615
1890	19	41,181	22	35,260
1891	31	69,087	24	41,889
1892	33	80,526	24	41,889
1893	31	77,544	24	46,466
1894	36	86,593	25	51,340
1895	36	90,862	25	50,194[1]

The change in the relative sizes of these fleets was reflected in alterations in the capital structure of the two companies. Thus the British and

[1] Details of the African Steam Ship Company from the Directors reports; the British and African figures have been calculated from the firms fleet list.

African reduced its issued capital from a peak of £546,000 in 1885 to £390,000 in 1888[1] at which it remained throughout the nineties—while the African Steam Ship Company increased its issued capital and debentures as follows:

	Ordinary Shares Issued	Debentures Issued
1885	12,500 @ £16 = £200,000	£ 56,152
1890	12,500 @ £16 = £200,000	£ 83,000
1891	26,500 @ £16 = £424,000	£ 83,000
1892	28,270 @ £16 = £452,320	£188,466
1896	33,731 @ £16 = £539,696	£212,786
1900	33,731 @ £16 = £539,696	£207,486[2]

The largest increase in the capital of the African Steam Ship Company took place in 1891 when it was necessary to finance the purchase of the Elder Dempster tonnage,[3] but even without an incentive of this type in other years the Company continued a policy of steady expansion. This is not surprising when it is realised that trade between British West Africa and the United Kingdom more than doubled in monetary terms between 1884 and 1900[4] and, as this was a period of falling prices, in real terms the increase was much greater.[5]

Why, then, should the British and African—formerly the more progressive of the two lines—fail to keep pace with the African Steam Ship Company? Both had the benefit of Elder Dempster's advice but while the London-organised firm expanded, the Glasgow-financed company allowed its interests to suffer a relative decline. It may have been Scottish caution! In general, world trade in this period was developing more slowly than had been anticipated[6] and consequently there was much surplus tonnage. This depressed freight rates and the few buoyant routes attracted much attention from shipowners anxious at least to earn their depreciation. The West African trade was subjected to many attacks of this nature[7] and it is possible, therefore, that these persuaded the directors of the British and African that it would be unwise to in-

[1] See Appendix p. 426, Table 33.
[2] A.S.P., Directors reports for the relevant years.
[3] A.S.P., Directors report for the year ending 31 December 1891, p. 5.
[4] See Appendix p. 397, Table 1.
[5] Alan McPhee, op. cit., Footnote to p. 33.
[6] William Ashworth, *An Economic History of England, 1870–1939* (London: Methuen, 1960), Table VIII, p. 148. A. W. Kirkaldy, *British Shipping* (London: Kegan Paul, 1914), Appendix XVI, pp. 619–32.
[7] See below, Chapter 4, p. 101, et. seq.

crease an already large investment in what might not be a virtual duopoly for much longer.

From the time Alfred Jones achieved control of Elder Dempster in
1884 all his energies were directed to making the firm supreme in the
West African trade. The close co-operation of the two regular British
lines, aided by the agreement with the Woermann Line of Hamburg,
enabled Jones to prevent the merchants from taking up chartering or
shipowning on a significant scale. Great as these victories were, however, they did not satisfy Jones, for he was well aware that his position
was based on a very insecure footing. The reasons for his disquiet were
threefold: there was the growth in the number of attacks by organised
lines and the increase in tramps attempting to obtain cargoes, and there
was the nagging doubt about the attitude of the larger firms of merchants. Average world freight rates declined by 40 per cent between
1889 and 1895[1] and this forced more and more shipping companies and
tramps to look enviously at the relatively busy trade organised by Elder
Dempster. Simultaneously the low rates made chartering a very attractive proposition and stimulated the Royal Niger Company, the African
Association and other large firms to press for preferential rates.

Alfred Jones had succeeded in preventing an amalgamation between
the Royal Niger Company and the African Association in 1888,[2] and
thereafter had favoured first one and then the other, but it was unlikely
that he could continue to satisfy both concerns. In fact, it appeared to
be only a question of time before demands were made upon him that he
could not meet. It was also quite conceivable that these two concerns—
the largest in the West African trade—would one day end their disagreements, in which case they would be able to combine their cargoes and be in a position either to dictate freight rates or to establish
their own line. With these possibilities in mind and, no doubt, seeking
and end to the unremunerative levels to which unrestricted competition
was forcing freight rates, Jones consulted the Woermann Line and
with their agreement decided to create a conference system to regulate
the West African shipping trade.

[1] A. W. Kirkaldy, op. cit., p. 630.
[2] See below, Chapter 4, p. 97, et. seq.

The West African Shipping Conference

The West African Merchants

A vital prerequisite for any understanding of the West African shipping trade is a knowledge of the West African merchants. Three major groupings of merchants developed during the nineteenth and twentieth centuries. These were the Niger Company, the Miller-Swanzy group, and the African Association, all of whom were in turn the result of previous amalgamations. There were also many other smaller firms which operated on the coast. These were usually quite small concerns, but a few reached a significant size and the most important of these was the firm which later took the title of John Holt and Company (Liverpool) Limited.

The Niger Company had originally been formed in 1879[1] when Captain Goldie-Taubman, (later Sir George Goldie) had amalgamated the Niger interests of four British firms.[2] Soon after it was established, the Company applied to the British Government for a charter to enable it to govern as well as trade in those parts of the Niger basin where it had made suitable treaties with the local chiefs. This application was refused, as was a second attempt in 1882. The lack of a charter, plus the presence of two rival French companies,[3] threatened the ultimate

[1] This was first called the *United African Company,* and had a capital of £125,000. In 1882 it changed its name to the National African Company, and increased its capital to £1,000,000.

[2] The Central African Trading Company Limited (of London); Messrs Alexander Miller, Brother and Company (of Glasgow); The West African Company Limited (of Manchester); Messrs James Pinnock and Company (of Liverpool)

[3] These were the Societé Française de l'Afrique Equatoriale and the Cie de Senegal.

supremacy of the British firm when the 'scramble for Africa' began in 1884. Fortunately the Niger Company was able to purchase both of these French firms[1] as well as a new English competitor[2] before the Berlin conference got under way.[3] As a result the Niger area was accepted as a British sphere of influence, and in 1886 a charter was granted to the firm which changed its title to the Royal Niger Company, Chartered and Limited.

The charter contained many clauses which attempted to limit the monopoly of the Company, but in practice other traders quickly found that it was impossible to compete successfully.[4] In spite of this the Royal Niger Company returned only 6 per cent on its paid-up capital, with the exception of a single year when 7 per cent was paid. It did, however, continuously extend the area of its operations, and in 1897 its forces under Goldie were successful in defeating the northern Emirs who had challenged its authority for many years. The charter came to an end on the 1 January 1900. The firm was then renamed the Niger Company Limited, and the loss of its administrative duties seems to have enhanced its profitability, for until 1918 there was only one year when it failed to pay a 10 per cent dividend.[5]

Alexander Miller, Brother and Company were a Glasgow firm with large interests in the Niger basin, the 'Oil Rivers', and the Gold Coast. When the Niger Company was formed in 1879 it included Miller's Niger basin business and Alexander Miller became a joint managing director of the new concern. Alexander Miller also continued to look after the Gold Coast side of his firm's remaining affairs while his brother George took care of the Oil Rivers department. In 1904, Millers Limited was established to deal with the Gold Coast and, in 1907, Miller Brothers (of Liverpool) Limited was formed to take over their Oil River trade.[6]

---

[1] This was largely because the British firm had been so successful in making treaties with the local rulers that little scope remained for its rivals. The death of Lambetta, the Prime Minister who had provided much support, also had a discouraging effect on the French companies.

[2] The Manchester Trading Company.

[3] J. D. Hargreaves, Prelude to the Partition of West Africa (London: Macmillan, 1963), p. 253 et. seq.

[4] *The History of the United Africa Company to 1938.* Circulated privately by the Company, London 1938. See: *Niger Government's Revenue from Import and Export Duties,* p. 21.

[5] This was on a smaller capital, but shareholders received mining royalties in addition to those dividends.

[6] The old firm of Messrs Alexander Miller, Brother and Company then came to an end.

Another firm which had been trading with West Africa for many years was that of Messrs F. and A. Swanzy.[1] They specialised in the United States–West African business and were prosperous for a long period, but in 1902 they found themselves to be in financial difficulties. This embarrassment forced Swanzys to turn for help to Millers, their chief rivals on the Gold Coast. The generous terms on which this was given led to very close co-operation between the two firms, and after 1904 their actions were those of a single, joint concern.

The African Association Limited was formed by a number of firms whose business lay in the delta of the Niger—the region known as the 'Oil Rivers'.[2] These firms were normally in violent competition with one another but the 'Ja Ja' affair drew them together,[3] and the example of the amalgamation that had resulted in the formation of the Royal Niger Company suggested a profitable form of collaboration. Alexander Miller, Brother and Company refused to join the proposed merger, but in spite of this the plan went forward and the African Association Limited was incorporated in 1889.[4] Attempts were quickly made to secure a charter to cover the Oil Rivers on the same lines as the Royal Niger Company's charter for the Niger basin. These attempts were a failure, but on the other hand the efforts of the Royal Niger Company to extend its territory to include the 'Oil Rivers' were also unsuccessful.[5]

The formation of the African Association led to a tremendous fight with Millers in the Oil Rivers. The African Association set up trading stations in the interior of the delta instead of waiting for native traders to bring produce to the coast. Millers were forced to do the same but both found these posts to be unprofitable and they were withdrawn in 1893. Partly as a result of these activities the African Association made very little profit in its early days and this led to a rift amongst its board of directors. One section, led by John Holt, was prepared to continue to fight its rivals but the other, led by Harry Cotterell,[6] believed it would

[1] In 1789 one of the brothers went out to the Coast as a surgeon for the Company of Merchants Trading to Africa.

[2] The African Association (unlimited) was originally founded in 1843 and membership was open to any partner in a firm of West African merchants.

[3] Ja Ja was the chief of the Opobo who was deported following a disagreement with the European merchants. Millers were the only firm to support him.

[4] Details of the constituent firms are given in the Appendix, Table 32, p. 425

[5] See below, pp. 100.

[6] Harry Cotterell, 'Reminiscences of one connected with the West African Trade from 1863 to 1910', Private MS. in the author's possession.

be better if co-operation could replace the existing state of cut-throat competition. Cotterell was able to persuade the board to sell those of its inland stations which lay within the sphere of the Royal Niger Company and so re-established good relations with that firm. Cotterell also wished to make peace with Millers, but could not get the board to make the necessary concessions and when John Holt became the chairman of the African Association in 1894 this signified the ascendency of his opponents. Cotterell therefore resigned his position as a manager, although he retained his seat on the Board, and became manager of the Sierra Leone Coaling Company—a private trading concern organised by Alfred Jones.[1]

By 1896 the 'peace' party was back in power owing to a dispute between John Holt and Alfred Jones over the sale of the fleet of the African Association to Elder Dempster.[2] This had the effect of forcing Holt to resign his chairmanship and, after a few months, Cotterell was re-appointed a manager.[3] The differences with Millers were then quickly resolved so that in 1899, when the Royal Niger Company was about to lose its charter, the two groups felt themselves able to take part in the formation of the 'Niger Pool'[4] and this in turn resulted in the growing prosperity of the African Association. It then expanded and purchased several other firms[5] and, in 1905, it helped to create the 'Gold Coast Pool' whereby it shared its profits in this area with the Miller-Swanzy group.[6]

Attempts to Enter the Shipping Trade
It is clear, therefore, that the West African merchants—although highly competitive and deeply divided—could coalesce into sufficiently large groups to enable them to charter on a substantial scale or even to organise their own shipping line. Indeed, there were many attempts to achieve

[1] See below Chapter 7, pp. 182.

[2] See below pp. 112.

[3] H. Cotterell, op. cit. p. 42. Once John Holt was no longer connected with the African Association he gradually renewed his old friendship with Harry Cotterell.

[4] Under this arrangement the following companies engaged in trade in Nigeria agreed to pool their profits: The Niger Company, The African Association, Alexander Miller, Brother and Company and the Company of African Merchants.

[5] The African Association purchased D. Jones and Company and Hutton and Osborne, and in conjunction with Millers it acquired Messrs Pinnock Limited.

[6] The African Association's interest in the Gold Coast dated from 1896 when it had bought the business of Taylor, Laughland and Company—one of its founder members.

independence from the regular shipping companies and George Miller and John Holt were prominent in this respect from as early as 1884:

> 'For your guidance, I may mention that someone you have communicated your ideas has not attended to your request to keep the matter strictly private and I have reason to believe that Elder Dempster and Company have got wind of it. It is not Stuart and Douglas who have originated the report, but the result will be seen immediately in the lower rates that will be quoted outwards and homewards to the few merchants who, in the river trade, can united[ly] command so much freight as to enable them easily to run a line of their own, if so minded.'[1]

Many of the other merchants, however, were not anxious to support action of this kind:

> 'I enclose reply from Messrs. Thomas Harrison and Company which is not favourable to our proposal as far as they are concerned. The fact that an arrangement exists between them and the companies which precluded them from considering the matter may lead to the inference that preferential rates are given to certain parties.'[2]

The lack of general backing, assiduously discouraged by Alfred Jones, prevented Holt and Miller from proceeding with an independent line and they turned their attention to chartering. The economics of chartering at this time can best be understood by reference to an actual case, that of *Beeswing*,[3] a steel screw steamship of 1,119 gross tons.

This indicated a profit of nearly £600 over a three-month voyage.[4] George Miller discussed the calculations with Alfred Jones who agreed that *Beeswing* might be run without loss—although he doubted if it would prove to be as profitable as the figures indicated. And even if it had, chartering was not so attractive a proposition as might first appear for it was better for a merchant to be able to send a regular parcel of items to the coast rather than one large cargo. For while a cargo would probably be insured, its non-arrival might bankrupt a merchant, as his contacts with the native middlemen would be interrupted and his business ruined. It seems, therefore, that it was the threat of action rather than the actual chartering that merchants like Holt and Miller found so valuable. On one occasion, in fact, Holt maintained that it was uneconomic for him to charter but nevertheless he proposed to hire a

[1] J.H.P. 26/3A. Letter from John Holt to George Miller, 29 February 1884.
[2] J.H.P. 4/1. Letter from George Miller to John Holt, 12 March 1884.
[3] *Lloyds Register of Shipping*, 1884. Entry No. B.199.
[4] Full details are given in the Appendix, p. 404, Table 10.

RATES OF FREIGHT,

BY THE

AFRICAN STEAM SHIP COMPANY'S

MAIL STEAMERS,

Leaving LONDON on the Morning of the 21st, and from PLYMOUTH at 8 p.m. of the 24th of every Month.

Freight Outwards must be prepaid.	Teneriffe.	Africa.	HOMEWARDS.	Africa.	Teneriffe & Madeira.
	All with 10 per cent. Primage.			All with 10 per cent. Primage.	
BALES, CASES, & CASKS, ℔ Ton of 40 cubic feet	80/.	£5	ARROWROOT & COFFEE, ℔ ton gross	£5	
BAGGAGE, per cubic foot...	2/6.	3/0	COPPER ORE, CAMWOOD, & PALM OIL, ℔ Ton of 20 cwt. gross	£5	
IRON, CHAINS, NAILS, & Heavy Goods	60/.	£5	COTTON, pressed, gross weight, ℔ lb..	1d.	
BOTTLED WINES and SPIRITS, per dozen	3/0.	5/0	GINGER, PEPPER, ℔ Ton of 20 cwt. gross	£5	
BOTTLED ALE & BEER, per Dozen..	2/6	3/6	GUM, per lb.	1d.	
WINE & SPIRITS, per Tun of 2 pipes.	60/.	£5	BEES' WAX, ℔ Ton of 20 cwt. gross.	£5	
TOBACCO, per Ton of 40 cubic feet ...	60/.	£5	IVORY, ℔ lb.	1d.	
COFFEE do. of 20 cwt. gross	60/.	£5	INDIA RUBBER.........................	£6	
GUNPOWDER, per Barrel of 100 lbs.	....	10/	FRUIT, in Cases or Baskets, per 40 cubic feet......................	£5	£3.
HORSES, each, owner providing box & food	10 Guineas......	12 Guineas.	PLANTS OR TREES, ditto	£5	£4.
DOGS, do. do.	2 Guineas......	2 Guineas.	TURTLE, per cwt.	15/	
BIRDS, do. do.	½ Guinea ℔ cu. ft.	½ Guinea ℔ cu. ft	GOLD DUST & SPECIE, per ct.....	£1	15/
PUBLICATIONS and PAMPHLETS ...	for 1-lb. and	under, 1/	From beyond Sierra Leone	1½	
Ditto ditto	.. for 2-lbs. and	under, 2/	COCHINEAL, per lb. in full		1d.
SPECIE	12/6 per cent	......	SMALL ANIMALS, owner to provide cage & food	2 Guineas each.	2 Guineas each
Do. to Goree, Bathurst, & Sierra Leone	......	£1 per cent			
Do. Elsewhere	....	£1½ "	SMALL BIRDS, ditto, per foot	5/	5/
TEA, per lb.	....	2d.	WINE, per Ton of 2 Pipes, or 4 Hhds. ..	....	50/.
BEADS .... per lb.	....	1d.			
CORAL & AMBER , or value	....	£1 per cent.			

The weight of Tea, Beads, and the value of Coral and Amber, must be declared on the Bills of Lading.

COARSE GOODS, AND GOODS OF SMALL VALUE, SUBJECT TO AGREEMENT.

TABLE OF FREIGHT on Small Parcels and Packages, to which is to be added Ten per Cent. Primage.

	£ s. d		£ s. d		£ s. d		£ s. d
½ cubic foot and under..	0 5 6	2½ cubic feet and under ..	0 12 6	4½ cubic feet and under..	1 2 6	8 cubic feet and under..	1 10 0
1 ditto ditto ..	0 5 0	3 ditto ditto ..	0 15 0	5 ditto ditto ...	1 4 0	9 ditto ditto ...	1 12 6
1½ ditto ditto ..	0 7 6	3½ ditto ditto ..	0 17 6	6 ditto ditto ...	1 6 0	10 ditto ditto	1 15 0
2 ditto ditto ..	0 10 0	4 ditto ditto ..	1 0 0	7 ditto ditto	1 8 0		

Packages exceeding 10 feet will be charged 2s. 6d. per foot additional.

INSURANCES EFFECTED BY THESE VESSELS AT VERY MODERATE RATES.

FREIGHT MUST BE PRE-PAID.

NO GOODS WILL BE RECEIVED WITHOUT AN ORDER FROM THE AGENTS.

Bills of Lading, according to the Company's form, are to be had at 12, East Front, Royal Exchange, London.

NOTICE IS HEREBY GIVEN, That no Goods or Property will be conveyed as Cargo in this Vessel, except under Bills of Lading, in the form adopted by the Company, for the time being. And if from any cause whatever Goods or Property shall be shipped as Cargo, without a Bill of Lading, the Company only agrees that the same shall be conveyed and delivered on the terms of the Bill of Lading adopted by the Company, namely:—That the Company's Ships have leave to tow and assist Vessels in all situations, and to sail with or without a Pilot ; and that the Company are not liable for Leakage or breakage, Contents, or weight of Packages, nor for the incorrect delivery of Goods from insufficiency of Marks or Numbers, nor for any Accident, Loss, or Damage, arising from the Act of God, the Queen's Enemies, Pirates, Restraint of Princes, Rulers, and People, Vermin, Jettisons, Barratry, and Collision, Fire on Board in Hulk or Craft, or on shore, nor for any Accident, Loss, or Damage whatsoever, from Machinery, Boilers, and Steam, and Steam Navigation, nor for any Perils of the Seas, and Rivers, nor for any Act, Neglect, or Default whatsoever of the Pilot Master or Mariners in Navigating the Ship, nor for any consequences of the causes above stated ; and the Company shall not be under any other liability whatever than the liability incurred by them by the terms of the Bills of Lading.

The destination, in letters Two Inches in length, must be marked on every Package.

For further information, apply in **Liverpool** to **W. LAIRD & Co.** and in **London** to

OGILBY, MOORES, GREGORY & CO.

3, INGRAM COURT, FENCHURCH STREET.

LONDON,—*January 1st*, 1855.

E. COLYER, Printer, 17, Fenchurch Street.

PLATE 5   A.S.S. Co. Rates of Freight, 1855.

MAIL STEAMERS

FROM

LIVERPOOL TO MADEIRA, TENERIFFE,

AND THE

WEST COAST OF AFRICA,

(CALLING AT PLYMOUTH.)

◆

The African Steam-Ship Company's

POWERFUL AND FIRST-CLASS SCREW STEAM-SHIPS

ARMENIAN . . G. Corbett, Commander.		ETHIOPE . . . A. J. M. Croft, Commander.	
HOPE . . . . . . A. M'Intosh,	„	GAMBIA . . . . C. Tutt,	„
ATHENIAN . . H. Dring,	„	RETRIEVER . J. Phillips,	„
CANDACE . . . J. H. Rolt, .	„		

LEAVE LIVERPOOL ON THE 21ST OF EVERY MONTH,

EMBARKING THE ROYAL MAILS AND PASSENGERS AT PLYMOUTH, ON THE 24TH.

These Steamers convey Goods and Passengers to the undermentioned Ports :—

Madeira, Teneriffe, Goree, Sierra Leone, Monrovia, Cape Coast Castle, Accra, Lagos, Bonny, Old Calabar, Camaroons, and Fernando Po.

And Passengers only for Bathurst (Gambia.)

THE STEAM SHIP

HOPE,

CAPTAIN A. MCINTOSH,

WILL LEAVE LIVERPOOL ON WEDNESDAY, THE 21st APRIL, AT 4 A.M.

This Vessel is now ready to receive Cargo, and all Goods must be alongside by noon on the 20th. Parcels and Specie only will be received at Plymouth up to the 23rd. No Cargo can be shipped at Plymouth.

Goods forwarded by Railway to Liverpool should be sent to the Waterloo Station, to save extra Cartage.

Goods for **SIERRA LEONE** will be landed there at the Company's expense but Shippers' risk, and Bills of Lading must contain a clause to this effect.

Bills of Lading, according to the Company's form, are to be had of *Messrs. Whitehead and Morris*, 1, *Philpot-lane, Fenchurch-street, London*, and of *Messrs. Turner and Dunnett, James-street, Liverpool.* The destination, in letters two inches in length, must be marked on two sides of every package.

ALL FREIGHT MUST BE PREPAID.

☞ NOTICE IS HEREBY GIVEN, That no Goods or Property will be conveyed as Cargo in these Vessels, except under Bills of Lading, in the form adopted by the Company for the time being. And, if from any cause whatever, Goods or Property shall be shipped as Cargo, without a Bill of Lading, the Company only agrees that the same shall be conveyed and delivered on the terms of the Bill of Lading adopted by the Company, namely :— That the Company's Ships have leave to touch and stay at all intermediate ports and places whatever, particularly in connexion with their employment in Her Majesty's Mail service, with liberty to tow and assist Vessels in all situations, and to sail with or without a Pilot ; and that the Company are not liable for Leakage and Breakage, Contents, or Weight of Packages, nor for the incorrect delivery of Goods from insufficiency of Marks or Numbers, nor for any Accident, Loss, or Damage, arising from the Act of God, the Queen's Enemies, Pirates, Restraints of Princes, Rulers, and People, Vermin, Jetison, Barratry, and Collision, Fire on Board, in Hulk, or Craft, or on Shore, nor for any Accident, Loss, or Damage whatsoever, from Machinery, Boilers, and Steam, and Steam Navigation, nor for any Perils of the Seas, and Rivers, nor for any Act, Neglect, or Default whatsoever of the Pilot, Master, or Mariners, in Navigating the Ship, nor any consequences of the causes above stated; and the Company shall not be under any other liability whatever than the liability incurred by them by the terms of the Bills of Lading.

For further information apply in Plymouth to H. J. WARING, Octagon; or to

LAIRD, FLETCHER & CO.

23, CASTLE STREET, LIVERPOOL, AND
49, LIME STREET, LONDON.

Liverpool, 14th April, 1858.

PLATE 6   A.S.S. Co. *Hope* Sailing Notice.

ship called the *Vats*.[1] Most of Holt's schemes never matured but for a short time he did use the vessels owned by Messrs Waldorf and Company of Antwerp. Holt, however, was dissatisfied with their service and the arrangement came to an end in 1887 when they failed to settle an outstanding insurance claim.[2] He then came to the conclusion that it would be a better proposition for him to develop his interest in the British and African Steam Navigation Company[3] and his shareholding rose from 40 shares in 1883 to 200 shares in 1888 and to 357 shares in 1891.[4] This number of shares was insufficient to influence the policy of the British and African, but at least it was a highly profitable venture for him.

The failure of Holt's arrangements with Waldorf and the relatively moderate amounts of chartering undertaken by the merchants were pleasing to Alfred Jones, but his satisfaction was soon to be ended by the activities of the Royal Niger Company. When this firm received its charter in 1886 its territory was the enormous basin of the Niger, but after only a short time it became interested in acquiring the Niger delta. This area was the preserve of the African Association and a number of small independent traders and so negotiations were started to see if a grand amalgamation could be arranged. Jones was suspicious of these developments because in his view they would have the effect of making the Royal Niger Company so large that it would be profitable for it to run its own line of steamships. He accordingly used every means within his power to prevent the Company's charter from being extended.

John Holt, a member of the African Association by virtue of his partnership in Holt and Cotterell, was well to the forefront in the negotiations with the Royal Niger Company, and in a letter to Sir George Goldie he wrote:

'Of course they will move all they can to prevent a coalition of interests where they have all to gain by our divisions. If it be true that Jones knows more than I think he does, you have no reason longer to defer calling us all to a meeting to discuss matters . . . If the merchants be agreed I don't think the government will hesitate to extend the charter in spite of the opposition of the steamship companies. . . .'[5]

[1] J.H.P. 26/3A. Letter from John Holt to Mr Watts, 23 February 1886.
[2] J.H.P. 26/3A. Letter from John Holt to Waldorf and Company, 31 March 1887.
[3] J.H.P. 26/3A. Letter from John Holt to Alexander Elder, 8 September 1888.
[4] See Appendix p. 429, Table 35, for details of Holt's shareholding in the British and African.
[5] J.H.P. 26/3A. Letter from John Holt to Sir George Goldie, 6 April 1888.

Holt was afraid that if Goldie delayed matters it would give Jones time to organise an effective opposition:

'. . . I hear that Jones is agitating amongst the shippers and commission houses in this city (Liverpool) and in Manchester. His object will be to induce people outside the Association to support his views at the Foreign Office and to go into the River Trade, possibly on promise of support. He will not sit still, you may depend upon it and the longer we delay uniting the greater will our difficulties become. It is necessary that we should at once come to a decision or we may miss our opportunity.'[1]

In fact, Jones had already exerted much pressure on the government. On 27 February 1888, Mr Bond, the chairman of the African Steam Ship Company had written a letter of protest to the Foreign Office. This suggested that a better alternative would be for the Lagos government to take over the Oil Rivers part of the coast. Mr John Dempster, the managing director of the British and African endorsed this letter.[2] Jones was also very busy lobbying his friends in the House of Commons and Mr J. A. Baird M.P. wrote to the Foreign Office asking that the steamship companies be consulted before any changes were made.[3] The shipping firms wrote a second joint letter to the Foreign Office in March 1888.[4] In this it was pointed out that if Goldie obtained exclusive rights in the Oil Rivers it would mean that native and European traders alike would be dependent upon the one firm which would consequently give the lowest of prices and exports would fall. The Foreign Office comments on this letter are worth noting:

'This is a sound line of argument. . . . The Shipping Companies are carriers only—consequently their interest is in extension of trade to get an extension of their business.'

The letter from Bond, plus the Foreign Office memo giving its comments, was then sent with a private letter to Sir George Goldie.[5] In this letter Lister had given his opinion that the shipping companies would oppose the extension of the charter to 'the uttermost'. This belief was further strengthened by a letter that had just arrived at the Foreign

[1] J.H.P. 26/3A. Letter from John Holt to Sir George Goldie, 24 April 1888.
[2] Foreign Office Papers in the Public Record Office, London, (hereinafter referred to as F.O.) 84–1916. Letter from African S.S.Co. & British and African to Foreign Office 27 March 1888.
[3] F.O. 84–1917. Letter from J. A. Baird, M.P., to Foreign Office, 9 March 1888.
[4] F.O. 84–1917. Letter from Bond to Foreign Office, 23 March 1888.
[5] F.O. 84–1919. Letter from T. V. Lister to Sir George Goldie, 29 March 1888.

Office from Thomas Sutherland M.P., the chairman of the Peninsular and Oriental Steamship Company and the leader of the shipping lobby in the Commons, which stated, 'There will therefore be a very strong opposition in the House of Commons, if this idea is allowed to be carried out. . . .'[1]

As the opposition organised by Alfred Jones increased its activities, it forced the Royal Niger Company to take action, and it terminated its agreements with the shipping lines. Elder Dempster then sat tight, and did not comment on this matter. As a result, Goldie sent the following telegram to Jones on 9 April, 'Jones c/o Elder Liverpool Before rupture final suggest meeting here Wednesday 12 to 2 will suit us if convenient to you' Jones refused to attend and a lengthy correspondence ensued.[2]

The dispute between Alfred Jones and Sir George Goldie was an embarrassment to the Foreign Office and Lord Salisbury decided to try direct conciliation. The Prime Minister therefore received a deputation headed by Jones. The meeting was inconclusive, but when Jones returned to Liverpool he gave the impression that he had won a great victory. This was of great value to him in his object of organising all the merchants who were not members of the African Association, and the opposition to the Royal Niger Company was intensified.[3] Lord Salisbury was forced by this activity to look even deeper into the affair and it was realised that if the Royal Niger Company received the extension it wanted it would be able to eliminate its rivals.

Yet the government did not feel it was expedient to establish direct control of the Oil Rivers as it was considered to be politically undesirable to sanction the spending of further large sums of public money on the colonies. Consequently it was decided to suggest an apparent compromise.

The Royal Niger Company was to be allowed to extend its charter, but only if it could end the hostility of the shipping interests, and also secure the approval of the Africans who lived in the region.[4] These were impossible conditions and public opinion—influenced by Jones—began to demand a parliamentary committee of inquiry. Goldie then wrote

[1] F.O. 84-1917. Letter from T. Sutherland to Foreign Office, 23 March 1888.

[2] F.O. 84-1919. Letter from Elder Dempster and Company to Foreign Office, 5 April 1888. Attached to this is the correspondence referred to above.

[3] J.H.P. 3/6. Letters from John Holt to Sir George Goldie, 23 & 24 April 1888.

[4] J. E. Flint, *Sir George Goldie and the Making of Nigeria* (London: Oxford University Press, 1960), p. 126, et. seq.

a letter to *The Times* in which he referred to the inhabitants of the Niger delta as 'barbarians'.[1] He also suggested that it was the Liverpool merchants who had wanted his company to expand in order that they could escape the higher taxation that a Crown Colony would have imposed. The effect of this letter was to cause both John Holt and the Miller Brothers to end their support for an extension of the charter. They realised that the African chiefs would never voluntarily agree (as required by the government) and that their own trade would be jeopardised if they continued to help Goldie. A final series of blows then fell on the Royal Niger Company. The Chambers of Commerce of Liverpool, Manchester, Glasgow, Belfast and London sent resolutions of opposition. Twenty-one West African firms signed a petition against the new charter and Lord Hartington[2] promised his support if the issue reached Parliament. Goldie then dropped the matter and, as he could not afford to upset the shipping interests if he did not have the assistance of the Liverpool merchants, continued to ship his goods and produce by the regular lines.

Alfred Jones had good cause for satisfaction from his victory over Sir George Goldie, but this success was not to be the end of his troubles in the Niger Delta. In the June of 1889 the old African Association was reorganised as the African Association Limited, and this had as its main objective the obtaining of a separate charter for the Oil Rivers. In fact, however, the agitation against the extension of the charter of the Royal Niger Company had already precluded the possibility of a separate one for the African Association, and in 1891 the Oil Rivers became the Niger Coast Protectorate. Jones had much to do with the establishment of this colony, for he encouraged the British government to think that the costs of administration could be met from revenue. In an interview which Jones had with Lister at the Foreign Office, the following conversation was reported:

'I asked Mr. Jones what he reckoned the revenue of the Oil Rivers would be from spirits alone at 6d. a gallon. He said "£150,000, but to be safe let us call it £100,000". "But", he added, "I tell you what I would do with pleasure. I would pay you £100,000 a year to be allowed to farm the duty on spirits, not to exceed 1s a gallon, and I am certain I should make £100,000 out of it."[3]

[1] *The Times*. 4 January 1889.

[2] Lord Hartington (Spenser Compton Cavendish) was a prominent Whig politician. He became the eighth Duke of Devonshire in 1891.

[3] F.O. 84-2094 Memo. from Sir T. V. Lister to Foreign Office, 1 November 1890.

There is little doubt that Jones was only guessing at these figures and knew there was little chance of his offer being accepted. Nevertheless, it showed his confidence in the trade and in the long term his assumptions were sound enough.[1]

In spite of their failure to obtain a charter, the African Association Limited felt strong enough to oppose the shipping lines when it considered that their freights were too high. After a freight-rate dispute in 1890, the Association threatened to start its own line, and this galvanised Alfred Jones into action. In the early months of 1891 he sent Mr G. W. Neville from Lagos to select suitable positions for a series of trading posts in the delta area. Mr Neville visited Nana at Benin and was well received and obtained an option on a site there. He also received options on sites at Brass, Ogeba Beach, Goshawk Point, Warne, Escardos River, New Calabar and Bonny.[2] Jones also had the objects of the British and African Steam Navigation Company Limited altered ostentatiously so as to '. . . carry on the business of merchants and to acquire such trading rights, concessions and privileges as may be necessary therefore . . .'[3] The success of these manoeuvres will be seen by reference to a letter from Jones to Major MacDonald, the first Administrator of the Oil Rivers:

'For your private information, the (African) Association have agreed to support our Shipping Companies, so we are friends again for a time at least. I will tell you all about it when we meet . . .'[4]

Although Alfred Jones was successful in preventing the Royal Niger Company and the African Association from setting up in opposition to the established shipping companies this was not to be the end of his difficulties. Prominent amongst the opponents of the regular lines was a Liverpool shipping agent named Henry Tyrer.[5] Tyrer failed to see why Elder Dempster should act for the entire West African carrying trade

[1] Actual importation of British and French (but not German) spirits in 1891 were 372,361 galls. i.e. £18,600 at 1s. per gallon.

[2] F.O. 84-2157. Letter from Bond to Foreign Office, 18 February 1891. This encloses copies of three letters from G. W. Neville to Elder Dempster and Company.

[3] Company resolution passed 4 February 1891. Section 1.

[4] F.O. 84-2157. Letter from Jones to MacDonald, 18 February 1891.

[5] Henry Tyrer, born in 1856, gained experience with Grant, Murdoch & Co., one of the pioneer houses in the 'Oil Rivers' area of West Africa. Tyrer commenced business on his own account as a general merchant and shipbroker in Liverpool in 1878. See Shipping, 1 April 1895, p. 534.

and he decided to interest other shipping firms in the business in the hope of becoming their Liverpool representative. His first success came when he persuaded James Knott, the controller of the Prince Line, to enter the trade. Jones at once attempted to discourage Knott from starting his sailings, but only succeeded in provoking him to go ahead with his plans.[1] Knott then proposed to build between twelve and twenty ships of advanced design, and he asked John Holt to be one of the seven contributors to the company. Holt agreed and in the early part of 1891 he received many enthusiastic letters from Knott. Unfortunately it was not possible for his plans to be implemented at once and he began to find some of the snags in opposing Alfred Jones. Thus he found it difficult to obtain cargo from the Crown Agents for the Colonies[2] and, after he had fallen out with Henry Tyrer,[3] found it hard to replace him by the man he wanted. This was Captain Thompson, formerly with Messrs Hatton and Cookson, and he appeared to be interested, but before arrangements could be finalised he accepted a position with Elder Dempster.[4] The firm of Messrs Japp and Kirby was eventually appointed as Liverpool agents of the Prince Line and appears to have been moderately successful but it lacked the specialised knowledge so important in this particular trade.

During the remainder of 1891 Knott continued to run his steamships to West Africa. Some of these vessels belonged to him and some were chartered, but he had not so far made specific arrangements for a company to operate exclusively to the coast. This aspect began to occupy his attention in November 1891, and he asked Holt if he could suggest a good man to be the secretary of the new firm. Holt thereupon recommended a Mr Charlton, but he refused to leave his existing job as chief clerk with Elder Dempster, even though it would have meant a substantial rise in his salary.[5] Of more importance was the treatment which Knott's vessels received in the Oil Rivers:

'. . . while writing you I would wish to name the detention suffered at the Rivers, and the Rivers only, part of this is explained by the African Association's Agents systematically giving the preference to what they call the Mail Boats, even when our ships had been there some time, immediately the others arrived

[1] J.H.P. Letter from James Knott to Henry Tyrer, 14 February 1891.
[2] J.H.P. Letter from James Knott to John Holt, 12 May 1891.
[3] J.H.P. Telegram from James Knott to John Holt, 9 June 1891.
[4] J.H.P. 26/3A. Letter from John Holt to James Knott, 22 October 1891.
[5] J.H.P. 26/3A. Letter from John Holt to James Knott, 13 November 1891.

work was either stopped on ours altogether or practically and all the energy and interest centred on the others to get them away . . . consequently our ships with their present appliances on board could easily discharge and load in twelve days, then why should they be there regularly six and eight weeks. . . .'[1]

James Knott's new company was never formed. Instead he suspended the existing sailings in 1892 and diverted his ships to more profitable routes. The reasons for this change of policy are clear, for apart from the very important question of detention on the coast—no doubt assiduously prompted by Jones's agent—the Prince Line lacked the bulk cargoes for the outward run which the Crown Agents alone could supply. Knott's ships were not so well suited for the job, nor were his crews so experienced as those of the regular lines. Knott's contacts in West Africa were through the merchants and these did not give him the backing he had been led to expect. This lack of support may be explained by the merchants' lack of cohesion. On the other hand, Jones was in control of some ninety per cent of the carrying trade and so was in a position to intimidate or offer special rates to enough merchants to render the activities of the remainder abortive. Jones was also busily buying out many of the boating companies whose craft were used to land and load the cargoes of the deep-sea ships. In 1892 this was not a decisive factor, but it at least made Knott's attempts to enter the trade more difficult than they would otherwise have been.

The defeat of the Prince Line gave Jones little respite, because of the struggle which had developed between the Royal Niger Company and the African Association. Once Sir George Goldie realised that his plan for extending the charter to include the Oil Rivers had failed, he quickly adopted another course of action. The boundaries of the new Niger Coast Protectorate were not clearly defined, and so Goldie advanced his outposts as rapidly as he could. Then, when his claim to the Oguta Lake was accepted by the government it meant that much of the produce obtained by the African Association from this area was diverted to the Royal Niger Company. The resulting outcry led to a meeting between Goldie and the African Association in December, 1892, but no agreement was possible. Both sides wanted the help of the shipping interests but until March 1893 this was given to the African Association. In that month the offer of a long-term contract persuaded the shipping companies to change sides. Jones appears to have been reluctant to make

[1] J.H.P. Letter from James Knott to John Holt.

the change, probably because he was thankful for the assistance given by some of the members of the Association in defeating the Prince Line. In this instance, however, he felt obliged to put his firm's interest before his own inclination and in the circumstances he decided to resign his chairmanship of the African Trade Section of the Liverpool Chamber of Commerce. This was because this body was in direct opposition to the Royal Niger Company—an attitude which he had formerly encouraged at every opportunity.[1] Jones could not be friendly with both of the rivals at the same time, but his period of friendship with the Royal Niger Company (which lasted until 1896) was at first regarded as having been forced on him by the directors of the shipping lines. The sympathy felt for Jones in this respect gradually evaported as he pursued a relentless policy of expansion, and as their relationship deteriorated the African Association began to increase its fleet.

Still more problems followed for Alfred Jones and Elder Dempster. In 1894, a London firm, the General Steam Navigation Company, began a service in opposition to the established lines. Mr Henry Tyrer became the Liverpool agent for the Company's new venture and doubtless it was his favourable reports that influenced the directors to enter the West African trade. In an attempt to bolster up their trade the General Steam Navigation introduced a service up the newly-opened Manchester Ship Canal,[2] but in spite of this and the assistance of John Holt[3] it failed to secure enough support. This was, of course, due to the activities of Alfred Jones, who continued to monopolise the shipment of goods for the Crown Agents. His influence with many of the merchants prevented his rival from securing cargoes when it was convenient, and made them available when the ships were full. By cutting rates to the bone he made it unattractive for the General Steam to compete, for he was quite prepared to run at such uneconomic prices that the more the General shipped the more it lost. In addition, Jones's control of the West African boating companies was by now a significant factor. He acquired these in most cases from the merchants, who were frequently pleased to be rid of the expense, and it meant that Jones alone could load and unload on a particular beach. Jones's energy in establishing the Bank of British West Africa[4] was also beginning to bear

---

[1] *Liverpool Daily Post*, 8 March 1893.   [2] *Journal of Commerce*, 10 October 1894.
[3] J.H.P. 26/3A. Letter from John Holt to George Miller, 18 January 1895.
[4] See below, pp. 118.

fruit. A loan could easily be made on the unofficial understanding that the goods purchased were to be shipped by one of the regular lines.

The result of Jones's activities was seen when the General Steam Navigation Company announced its trading figures in the *Financial News* dated 19 February 1895. No dividend could be paid and the lengthy report was full of the difficulties caused by the actions of Elder Dempster. John Holt attempted to persuade George Miller to join with himself and the African Association to save the struggling company.[1] Miller was not prepared to join Holt on this occasion because he wished to keep his trading on the Coast separate from that of the African Association. As a result the General Steam Navigation Company lost its last hope of being able to stay in the West African business and it withdrew its ships in the June of 1895.[2]

Henry Tyrer, the Liverpool agent of the General Steam Navigation Company, was out of business as soon as his principals terminated their sailings to West Africa. He knew the trade, and was still convinced that if a new firm were properly organised on a sufficient scale it could break the monopoly being established by Jones. Tyrer was shrewd enough to have benefited from the mistakes of the past, and he realised that without the help of the merchants a new company would have little chance of success. When, therefore, he approached and gained the interest of Sir Christopher Furness, of the shipbuilding firm of Furness Withy, he got in touch with John Holt to solicit his support.[3] At first Holt welcomed the new line, and he urged Miller to back it.[4] Furness, Withy then proceeded to plan the capital structure of the new firm, which it was decided to call the West African Traders Company, but when Holt and Miller realised that they were expected to subscribe £50,000 each for ordinary shares they lost interest.[5] Furness, Withy subsequently suggested that if Holt and Miller would find £25,000 each they would find the balance, and when this offer was refused the shipbuilders decided not to proceed with their plans.[6]

---

[1] J.H.P. 26/3A. Letter from John Holt to George Miller, 10 May 1895.
[2] *Journal of Commerce*, 11 June 1895. Circular from the General Steam Navigation Company. The West African venture of this firm was, of course, only one of its many activities and it continued to operate in other areas.
[3] J.H.P. 22/5. Letter from Henry Tyrer to John Holt, 24 July 1895.
[4] J.H.P. 26/3A. Letter from John Holt to George Miller, 29 August 1895.
[5] J.H.P. 26/3A. Letter from John Holt to Sir Christopher Furness, 17 October 1895.
[6] J.H.P. 26/3A. Letter from John Holt to Furness, Withy, 2 December 1895.

While Alfred Jones had been occupied with the actual intervention of the General Steam Navigation Company and the proposed opposition of Furness Withy, the African Association had been quietly building up its fleet. This had become a definite aspect of the Association's policy following Elder Dempster's support of the Royal Niger Company in 1893, but to some extent it was a device to obtain preferential rates and treatment. An indication of the attitude of the African Association can be seen in the position they adopted in August 1894, when they asked for tenders for their goods to be carried to and from West Africa. This action caused Jones to ask Holt, the chairman of the Association, for an interview. In fact, Jones and Dempster met Holt twice, and after the first meeting Jones wrote:

'. . . Our Directors, at their meeting yesterday, carefully considered the whole question and we are instructed to say that they regret they cannot see their way to fall in with the views you expressed, namely to give special advantages to the Association as against our other large shippers, but as they are very desirous to receive the carrying of your goods and produce they are prepared to quote very low rates. In the meantime, competitive rates will continue.'[1]

Holt replied to this letter the following day, saying that he had not asked for better rates than those charged to other large shippers, only that the rates he paid might be as low as those paid by his competitors.[2] The result of this correspondence was a second meeting between Jones, Dempster and Holt. At this, certain concessions were offered to the African Association but these would still have meant that chartering was cheaper,[3] and so they were not accepted. A desultory correspondence then ensued but terms could not be agreed.[4] The failure of the African Association to obtain sufficient concessions left it free to make what arrangements it wished for the carriage of its cargoes. Most continued to be carried by the regular lines, but at least 20,000 tons a year were transported by chartered vessels.[5] In addition, the Association's resolve to build up a fleet of its own received further impetus.

[1] J.H.P. 6/6. Letter from Alfred Jones to John Holt, 6 September 1894.
[2] J.H.P. 6/6. Letter from John Holt to Alfred Jones, 7 September 1894.
[3] J.H.P. 6/6. Rough memo made by John Holt, 2 October 1894.
[4] J.H.P. 6/6. Three letters between Holt and John Dempster, 2, 3 and 4 November 1894.
[5] J.H.P. 6/6. Memorandum of interview between Dempster, Jones and Holt at the Liverpool Club on Tuesday evening, 28 August 1894.

It was clear, therefore, that unless Alfred Jones could make suitable arrangements to deal with the African Association the situation would develop into a serious problem. Until June 1895, Jones was occupied with the activities of the General Steam Navigation Company, but once these ended he was able to devote more of his time to evolving a scheme to prevent future competitors from entering the trade. There can be no doubt that such a scheme had been in Jones's mind since he gained control of Elder Dempster, but he had had to wait for the correct opportunity. With the elimination of the General Steam Navigation Company, Elder Dempster held a commanding position in the trade and Jones, worried by the growing threat from the African Association and the possibility of intervention by Furness Withy, apparently decided that his time had come. Consequently he consulted his only possible competitor, the Woermann Line of Hamburg, and with their agreement proceeded to establish a conference system which would regulate the shipping trade on a more stable basis.

The Establishment of the Conference
A shipping conference is a combination of shipping companies that has been formed to regulate and restrict competition in the carrying trade on a given route. It has two main aims. The first is to regulate rivalry between the regular companies themselves so as to obtain and maintain reasonable rates of freight. To this end unified rates are charged and the trade is divided either by fixing the number of sailings for each line during a specific period, allotting certain ports to each company, or by pooling an agreed proportion of the freight receipts. The second aim is to restrict the entry of outside interests and this is normally achieved by the use of a deferred rebate system.[1]

It is probable that the system was first worked out by John Samuel Swire on the River Yangtse in the early eighteen-seventies,[2] but the first deep-sea conference was not established until 1875.[3] This was designed to regulate the Calcutta trade and, after a deferred rebate system was introduced in September 1877, it proved to be a workable proposi-

[1] A. W. Kirkaldy, op. cit., pp. 183–4. See also, Daniel Marx, Jr., *International Shipping Cartels* (New Jersey: Princeton U. P., 1953), p. 3.

[2] S. Marriner and F. E. Hyde, *The Senior, John Samuel Swire* (Liverpool University Press, 1967), pp. 61–73.

[3] F. E. Hyde, *Shipping Enterprise and Management—Harrisons of Liverpool* (Liverpool University Press, 1967), pp. 69–74.

tion and many other shipping lines decided to follow this example. Thus the China conference was formed in 1879[1] and this was followed by the Australian in 1884, the South African in 1886 and the North Brazilian in 1895. Later conferences were established to deal with the River Plate, South Brazil and west coast of South American trades, and by 1904 they had achieved almost world-wide coverage. In these circumstances it is not surprising that Alfred Jones should wish to follow what was becoming the common practice, and so when an opportune moment arose in 1895 he decided to introduce regulation into the West African shipping trade.

The technique adopted by Alfred Jones to inaugurate the West African shipping conference was an efficient one, and was well described by George Miller while giving evidence before the Royal Commission on Shipping Rings. Miller stated that he received a rebate circular through the post and this was the first intimation he had had that a shipping ring was being established.[2] The circular was signed by the British and African Steam Navigation Company, the African Steam Ship Company and the Woermann Line and informed him that a conference had been set up with a 10 per cent deferred rebate. The circular also asked him, like all other West African merchants, to sign an agreement giving his whole carrying to the conference lines. He had less than a month in which to do this and, in the absence of a satisfactory alternative, he decided to sign. He could have provided his own ships, but this would have been expensive, and more trouble than he cared to take.[3] Miller appears to have been typical of the West African merchants. None wished to join the scheme, yet all did so, and once they had shipped with the conference lines the deferred rebate ensured their continued support.

In practice the conference operated as the original circular had laid down. All freights were increased by 10 per cent—the additional amount being known as primage. Freight was only accepted from merchants who signed a declaration to the effect that all their shipments would be made via the conference lines for the succeeding six months. Once the six-month period had elapsed the rebate due could be claimed by the

[1] F. E. Hyde, *Blue Funnel* (Liverpool University Press, 1956).
[2] See Appendix p. 474, Table 76, for copy of a rebate circular.
[3] *Royal Commission on Shipping Rings* (H.M.S.O., CMD.4668–70, 1909), (hereinafter referred to as R.C.S.R.). Evidence of George Miller. Q. 4311–4314.

shipper for all outward cargo, and for palm oil and kernels for the home-ward journey. This claim would not be paid until a further period of six months' exclusive shipment had taken place.

Thus Elder Dempster always had in their possession a sum equal to 10 per cent of nine months' freight receipts. This gave them an interest-free loan which was a valuable addition to their working capital for although it was continually being repaid it was simultaneously being re-placed by fresh payments of primage. To a merchant like John Holt this meant that deferred rebate owing to him, perhaps approaching £10,000, was always being held on behalf of the shipping companies, and so this was an almost irresistible incentive for him to continue to use their services. Smaller merchants had proportionately smaller sums held by the conference lines, but the general effect was the same. Under these circumstances it is not surprising that other shipping companies were wary of entering the trade and, in fact, only one British firm began a rival service between the setting up of the conference in 1895 and the death of Jones in December, 1909.[1]

When Jones came to terms with Woermann and established the con-ference, certain rules were laid down which were to guide the future activities of the firms concerned. The Woermann Line was prohibited from calling at British ports, but the two British lines were allowed to load and unload at all continental ports. These included Hamburg which was the home-port of the German line. It was also agreed at this time that the through rate for freight from New York to West Africa should be the same as that charged from Liverpool to West Africa. This meant that cargo from the United States would be carried across the Atlantic, trans-shipped at Liverpool and then delivered to its desti-nation on the Coast for the same cost as freight that was merely carried from the Mersey to West Africa. The results of this arrangement were two fold. Firstly, the conference lines were insulated against the compe-tition of any rival American shipping firm, but American goods were marketed in West Africa at a very cheap rate. This naturally provoked the hostility of many British manufacturers who found American pro-ducts more highly competitive than would otherwise have been the case. Secondly, it annoyed those British merchants who used ports other than Liverpool. The conference system prevented these merchants from sending their goods direct to the coast. They were therefore forced

[1] See below, Chapter 5, p. 132.

to ship to Liverpool and trans-ship at that port, and, unlike their American competitors, they had to pay the full cost of this handling.

All the merchants and shippers concerned agreed to accept the terms which led to the establishment of the conference because there was little time for alternative arrangements to be made. Having once begun, the deferred rebate made it difficult to break away, and this was as true for the Crown Agents for the colonies as for the ordinary traders. The Crown Agents were treated as principals right from the start of the new system. This meant that they were entitled to rebate, but would lose it if they chartered or shipped by an outside line. Elder Dempster interpreted this to mean that if the Crown Agents broke the rules of the conference on a single item then they would forfeit the entire rebate for all their shipments. The Crown Agents undoubtedly objected to this arrangement but, probably in return for some concessions and, perhaps, to suit their own convenience, they continued to support the conference loyally. While the larger firms of merchants were strongly against the deferred-rebate system from its inception, many smaller firms like Paterson, Zochonis praised the conference for providing speedy and regular services. These welcomed the equal treatment of large and small merchants which suited them, so that they were quite content to support the shipping ring. The commission houses which sent goods to West Africa against specific orders were also strong upholders of the conference. This was because as a general rule they did not find it necessary to refund the rebate to their clients. They were thus able to pocket the rebate when it was returned and this gave them every incentive to hope for the perpetuation of the system.

As a result of the establishment of the conference, private chartering came to an end and those merchants who possessed ocean-going sailing vessels found it best to dispose of them. The Royal Niger Company and the African Association then remained as the sole owners of small fleets and Jones determined to remove these as soon as the opportunity presented itself. In 1895 Jones was on friendly terms with the Royal Niger Company, but his relations with the African Association remained somewhat strained. In November of that year his fear of an end to the rivalries between the two largest firms came to a head. John Holt then invited him to attend a meeting with Sir George Goldie in London and this he agreed to do. Jones and Bond (the chairman of the African Steam Ship Company) duly met Goldie and Holt and after their discussions reported what had taken place to C. M. MacDonald at the Foreign Office.[1] According to Jones, Goldie wanted the Royal Niger Company to extend its charter and take over the administration of the coastal region. All trading in this area would be left to the African Association and all shipping was to be placed in the hands of Elder Dempster. Jones told Goldie that this plan was not acceptable to the shipping interests he represented, and that he would have to inform his directors of what was proposed. Goldie then replied:

'. . . If you do you will spoil the whole thing and remember there are rumours of an opposition line of steamers and it is now for the Niger Company to decide which course they will take.'

Mr Jones said:

'That will not weigh with me at all. If you are in it I shall be glad to oppose you.'[2]

In fact, this struggle did not materialise. The Royal Niger Company's monopoly of trade had led to trouble with the inhabitants of Brass. An official inquiry was then made by Sir John Kirk, and he recommended that a customs union be made between the Niger Company and the Niger Coast Protectorate.[3] This proposal was accepted by Goldie, and it seemed to have a good chance of being approved by Parliament. In June 1895, however, there had been a change of government and it was known that Joseph Chamberlain favoured a policy of vigorous colonial expansion. Goldie therefore feared that he would oppose any scheme that prolonged the rule of a chartered company and so he tried to get the Kirk plan adopted before the new Colonial Secretary had found his feet. He was put off, so he tried to force the government into action by gaining the support of the merchants and shipping interests. The merchants, mainly members of the African Association, favoured the plan, because they did not relish paying the taxes which Crown control necessitated, but Goldie was not able to obtain the assistance of the British shipping lines. Then in January 1896, Goldie learned that the Kirk scheme was unacceptable to the government and that the charter of his company was not to be allowed to run for very much longer. In the circumstances he had less incentive to fight the shipping companies

[1] J. E. Flint, op. cit., p. 129, gives details of MacDonald's career.
[2] F.O. 2/85. Confidential memorandum, MacDonald to F.O., 8 November 1895.
[3] F.O. 83/1382. Report by Sir John Kirk to Foreign Office, 25 August 1895.

and accordingly he continued to ship via the conference on the best terms he could obtain.[1]

This development left the African Association as the only concern with its own ships on the West African run. Jones was consequently very anxious to come to a suitable arrangement and he accordingly began a fresh series of negotiations with John Holt, the chairman of the Association. These were finalised in December, 1896, and the vessels of the African Association were handed over.[2] The arrangement was a verbal one and when it came to be set down Jones and Holt disagreed over the precise terms:

'At the time of making the agreement, not a word was mentioned about any guaranteed minimum freight. That was not mooted by you until a much later date. You undertook to pay £70,000 for the company's named fleet and in return you were to have its entire carrying for a limited term at rates terms and conditions neither better nor worse than the best given to any other person or persons.'[3]

As Jones had the ships in his possession Holt was in a difficult position. This was made worse by the lack of unity on the board of the African Association which failed to approve of his actions. If Holt had been backed by a united board he would have stood a far better chance of repudiating Jones's action, but in the circumstances he could only end his problems by resigning.[4] With Holt out of the way Jones proceeded to deal directly with the African Association, and the original arrangement was adhered to with the addition of a compromise clause in respect of a guaranteed minimum freight.[5] Holt then issued a pamphlet which gave his side of the dispute and this was sent to the Company's shareholders with a letter which asked for their votes at the forthcoming annual general meeting.[6] This took place on 4 March 1897, and after Holt had explained his actions and the new chairman, Mr Rogerson, had announced the agreement with Elder Dempster, Alfred Jones[7] found it convenient to say a few words:

[1] See also J. E. Flint, op. cit., pp. 214-5.

[2] The vessels concerned were the steamships *Ebani* (1093 net tons) and *Erasmus* (713 net tons), and the sailing ships *Eboe* (305 net tons), *Luke Bruce* (310 net tons), *Charlotte Young* (302 net tons) and *Montezuma* (326 net tons). The s.s. *Christopher Thomas* (91 net tons) was retained by the African Association.

[3] J.H.P. 6/6. Letter from John Holt to Alfred Jones, 5 January 1897.

[4] J.H.P. 6/3. Letter from John Holt to the African Association, 11 December 1896.

[5] J.H.P. 6/3. Letter from Alfred Jones to the African Association, 11 January 1897.

[6] J.H.P. 6/6. Letter from John Holt to the African Association, 11 January 1897.

[7] Alfred Jones was a shareholder in the African Association Ltd.

'There is no doubt that our worthy friends Mr. Cookson and Mr. Holt are well versed in this trade, but I think the time has come, seeing that they have retired from the Board, when we can fairly ask to have the Board elected reduced as it is in a way that is likely to work harmoniously together for the future. There is no doubt that Mr. Holt's policy has done a great deal for the Company: he is a very shrewd, hardworking fellow and drives a hard bargain, but sometimes these people don't get the best of it. However, he has done well.'[1]

At the end of the meeting the board received 24,710 votes in support of their policy, while Holt and Cookson obtained only 2,258 and 1,514 respectively. A resolution proposing that Holt and Cookson be re-elected to the board was then made, but it was not put to the vote as both men refused to stand.[2]

From this time onward, Elder Dempster possessed an almost complete monopoly of the British West African carrying trade. In addition, in conjunction with the Woermann Line of Hamburg, they had almost complete control of the continental West African carrying trade. The power of this position was such that Elder Dempster were able to resist all external competitors, enlarge their fleets, strengthen their position in West Africa and diversify into other activities and trades.

[1] J.H.P. 6/6. Notes on A.G.M. of the African Association Ltd., 4 March 1897.
[2] H. Cotterell. op. cit., p. 92.

Chapter 5

Expansion and Diversification

Extension of Elder Dempster's Interests

The establishment of the West African shipping conference in 1895 and the subsequent acquisition of the fleet of the African Association placed Alfred Jones in a position to control the external communications of British West Africa. The way in which Jones extended this power and the limitations on his authority must now be examined.

From the start of his association with Elder Dempster Jones had felt that if he could control or own the ancillary services on the coast it would be both profitable and prudent. He therefore made every effort to acquire the boating companies belonging to the merchants; he developed a series of branch lines to facilitate the movement of cargo to the better loading-ports; he invested in innumerable projects designed to provide essential services; and he created a credit and banking structure that allowed trade to expand without undue hindrance.

The boating companies were a prime objective. These had sprung up because of the difficulties experienced by deep-sea ships in landing their cargoes on the almost harbourless coast of West Africa. In many places the 'port' was nothing more than an open roadstead,[1] and cargo and passengers had to be carried through the surf by small boats manned by the local natives. These local boats proved to be inadequate in many instances and so the loading and unloading of cargo was a very slow process. Accordingly it became profitable for merchants to set up their

[1] H. P. White, 'The Ports of West Africa', *Tijdschrift voor Economische en Sociale Geografie* (1959), Vol. L, No. I, pp. 1–8.

own boating concerns, and they built or purchased suitable surf-boats and provided men to crew them. In other places the shipping companies themselves established boating organisations and Jones was quick to see the advantages of obtaining control of as many of the merchants' facilities as he could. He realised that a series of integrated boating companies would not only assist in the rapid loading and discharging of his ships, but it would also be an ideal method of preventing competitors from gaining a foothold in the trade. The majority of the merchants appear to have been quite content to sell their boats to Elder Dempster quite content to sell their boats to Elder Dempster so long as they were assured of an efficient service. Even those who were not too keen to relinquish control of their boats gradually found it convenient to do so, and these included large firms like Millers.[1]

In the event of a merchant deciding not to sell his boats, Jones devised a simple system which ensured that he changed his mind. An example of the way in which this worked was given by Mr J. H. Batty in respect of a small 'port' called Saltpond.[2] Elder Dempster had taken over most of the surf-boats there and wished to acquire the remainder, but one firm of traders refused to let theirs go. Jones therefore increased the freight rate from Liverpool to Saltpond by 5s per ton, and announced that in future the charge would include the landing of the goods in West Africa. At the same time the normal discharging fee of 5s per ton was withdrawn. This meant that the Saltpond merchants were paying for the unloading service whether they used it or not, and although they objected strongly there was nothing they could do but accept the new arrangement. Jones gained a high proportion of the surf-boats by the use, or threatened use, of such measures, and was then able to control the loading and unloading along most of the coast-line. It should be remembered, however, that in many districts produce was embarked directly in the rivers and creeks, and it was impossible for Jones to attempt to control all of this activity.

The existence of these rivers and creeks in certain parts of West Africa enabled ships to penetrate some way into the interior, but obviously the larger sea-going vessels were at a disadvantage in this respect. Accordingly Jones instituted a number of branch-line services which had the task of feeding the ocean-going ships. Some of these branch-line boats delivered and collected cargo from the inland river ports

[1] R.C.S.R., Q.4532.   [2] R.C.S.R., Q.6934.

and trans-shipped to the larger vessels at convenient places on or near the coast. Others were employed to move goods along the coast itself so that the sea-going ships could reduce the number of calls they had to make. The most important port was Lagos and, by 1906, its inward and outward freight amounted to some 200,000 tons. This was almost ten times greater than any other West African port at this time.[1] Yet the bar which separated the harbour from the open sea possessed only ten feet of water at high tide, so the larger ships could not enter. These merely stood off the bar and loaded and unloaded by means of surf-boats. In bad weather much cargo was lost, so the practice of trans-shipping at Forcados gradually developed. This enabled the transfer to take place in the quiet and safety of a wide river from where branch-boats of up to 1,000 tons were used to carry the goods to and from Lagos. After 1900 almost all cargo was moved in and out of the port by this means, and very little was trans-shipped at the bar.[2]

Apart from the expansion and amalgamation of the boating companies under his direct control, and the development of branch lines, Jones created a number of other subsidiary firms. These had the task of sup-plying steam tugs, lighters, barges and river craft and were intended to supplement and support the activities of the external communication system. Other subsidiary companies provided hotels, cold-storage and victualling facilities and, in time, Jones created a complete network of integrated concerns that helped to channel the produce of West Africa to his main-line ships. After his death it was considered desirable to amalgamate all these companies into one concern. This resulted in the establishment of the West African Lighterage and Transport Company Limited in 1910—in each case Elder Dempster owned all the issued shares of the firms taken over.[3]

Banking formed another field in which Jones was to become vitally interested. At first most of the internal and external trade of West Africa had utilised some form of barter, but cowries, manillas and brass

---

[1] R.C.S.R., Q.5096.　　[2] R.C.S.R., Q.4876.

[3] These companies were: the Saltpond Boating Company; the Winnebah Boating Company; the West African Cold Storage Company; the Calabar Lighterage and Trans-port Department; the Cameroon Lighterage Department; the Accra Boating Company; the Cape Coast Boating Company Limited; the Sekondi Lighterage and Hotel Company Limited.

Source: West African Lighterage and Transport Co. Ltd. Statement of Consideration. (File 112584 at Companies House, City Road, London.)

rods gradually gained general acceptance as common currencies. The cowries were small shells about half an inch in length which were fastened together in strings of forty or one hundred. They were imported from the East Indies—the rate of exchange being usually fixed at one pound sterling to a bag of cowries. As the bag would have contained approximately 80,000 shells it was an inconvenient form of money[1] and died out as better forms of currency became available. The use of brass rods also tended to diminish during the nineteenth century. This was because the cost of their metal content rose above their face value and it therefore paid the local craftsmen to use them instead of purchasing copper and zinc. This left the manilla as the remaining native currency. This was in the form of a small copper horseshoe of about four inches in circumference. It was usually valued at a few pence, sometimes rising to sixpence, but a few larger manillas of greater value were also used. The manilla was used extensively throughout the nineteenth century and was so popular that it remained in regular use until 1948.[2]

Many foreign coins also circulated in West Africa and in time their value was fixed by the local governments. Thus in 1875 the silver dollar was worth 4s 2d; the French 5-franc, 3s 10½d; the doubloon, 64s; the French napoleon, 15s 10d and the U.S. eagle, 41s.[3] British coins, circulated freely and were supposed to be accepted at their face value, but the natives preferred silver to copper and shiny, new coins exchanged at a higher rate than old, worn ones. As the trade of West Africa increased the local currencies proved more and more inadequate and so the supply of British silver coin was steadily increased. This was introduced into the economy as payment for government employees and for railway construction workers. At the same time the system of taxation that was introduced in some areas also tended to compel the natives to accumulate silver, and so encouraged them to work for the government or to produce cash crops. This resulted in a tremendous rise in the demand for silver:

[1] A silver 3d piece was worth 1,000 cowries—25 strings of 40 shells.
[2] For obvious reasons the governments of the British West African colonies disliked the circulation of a currency which rivalled the official coin and finally decided that the only way to remove it was by a redemption scheme. Nearly 33 million manillas were then withdrawn at a cost of £400,000. The scrap metal obtained amounted to 2,460 tons and when this was sold it reduced the cost of the operation to £284,000.
[3] Nigeria Handbook (London: Crown Agents for the Colonies, 1953). p. 69.

British Sterling Silver Issued for West Africa[1]

Average for 1886–1890	£24,426
1891–1895	£116,323
1896–1900	£257,090
1901–1905	£262,786
1906–1910	£666,190

Once the silver began to circulate freely, a bank became a necessity in order to economise the use of the coin, to help in the settlement of accounts, and to regularise the imports from the Mint in England. The answer to these needs came in 1891 when the West African Bank Limited was established.[2] This received a monopoly under which it alone could obtain new silver from the Mint, and in return it guaranteed to repatriate any that became redundant. In spite of this very valuable concession, however, the bank did not pay and it failed. The failure of the West African Bank did not suit Alfred Jones, for he recognised that trade would be stifled if reasonable banking facilities were not provided. He therefore decided to establish his own bank. In his own words:

'When this idea of introducing banks into Africa came up he went to some people interested and induced them to make arrangements to go into the West African trade. They worked for about two years and lost £3,000 and the directors saw me once or twice on the matter. The result was we said the bank must stay there, but they said they were going to withdraw. We said they must not do that, and that we would give them £1,000 towards their loss, and take the bank over ourselves and form a company . . .'[3]

As a result, the African Banking Corporation was formed and this was granted the same privileges in respect of new silver as had been enjoyed by its predecessor.[4] In due course Alfred Jones decided to form a limited company with a wider base and was able to persuade the government to give this their approval.[5]

The new company was the Bank of British West Africa Limited, and it was formed on 30 March 1894. Jones owned 1,733 of the 3,000 shares,

[1] Report of the West African Currency Committee, 1912 (Cd.6426), p. 6.

[2] See Appendix p. 434, Table 37, for details of the West African Bank Limited.

[3] Committee on the Currency of the West African Colonies. Evidence given by Alfred Jones. Q.1081.

[4] M. F. Ommanney (Crown Agents) to the African Banking Corporation, 28 January, 1892. See C. W. Newbury, *British Policy towards West Africa, Selected Documents 1875–1914* (London: Oxford University Press, 1971), p. 385.

[5] Ibid., Colonial Office to A. L. Jones, 14 March 1894.

while his partners in Elder Dempster (Davey and Sinclair) had 433 each.[1] The bank was thus the preserve of the shipping companies and this was reflected in the composition of the first board of directors. Jones was the chairman and his fellow directors were F. W. Bond (chairman of the African Steam Ship Company), O. Harrison Williams (who was married to Jones's niece), and Henry Coke, a merchant. Mr G. W. Neville (an ex-employee of Elder Dempster) was the first manager of the bank, which had a nominal capital of £100,000,[2] and it undertook to transact all types of business including the opening of current accounts, dealings in bills of exchange, the cabling of remittances and the receiving of deposits.

The result of the first year's working was highly satisfactory but a dividend was not paid, as it was considered desirable to build up the strength of the new concern. This suggests a cautious approach and is confirmed by the speech made by Jones at the first annual general meeting of the bank:

'The Bank has as much business as it cares to do at present, and the directors have no wish to extend it too rapidly, although there is an unlimited demand for money on the coast, with good security. In addition, the directors are very pleased at the success of the banking system in West Africa which has been the means of conferring a very great benefit on the people of that country. There is no doubt that the country which introduces its coinage and its language into a new territory succeeds in a great measure in securing the trade of the place.'[3]

The second year's working of the bank was even more satisfactory than the first, and a dividend of 8 per cent was paid. Bills purchased were valued at £430,544—an increase of £172,982 over the previous year, while £151,520 in new silver was shipped to West Africa as against £64,800.[4] The success of the Lagos business then persuaded Jones to extend the activities of the bank, and new branches were opened at Accra and at Old Calabar. This progress was, of course, based on the privilege of being the sole supplier of new silver coins.

[1] See Appendix p. 436, Table 39, for list of shareholders in the Bank of British West Africa.

[2] See Appendix p. 435, Table 38, for details of the capital structure of the Bank of British West Africa Limited.

[3] *Journal of Commerce*, 17 July 1895. Report on the First Annual General Meeting of the Bank of British West Africa Limited.

[4] *Liverpool Mercury*, 17 June 1896. Report on the Second Annual General Meeting of the Bank of British West Africa Limited.

All traders could import silver from Britain without restriction, but as the Africans preferred new coins and as only the bank could obtain these from the Mint, it meant that it enjoyed a virtual monopoly. The bank's concession was still further enhanced by the fact that silver was legal tender to any amount, whilst gold was not universally acceptable. In practice, therefore, everyone requiring currency was forced to obtain silver via the bank and so it received a commission on every transaction which took place. The commission on the silver was usually 1 per cent but it could be reduced by half if the annual requirements of a firm were ordered in advance. Miller Brothers were one firm that benefited under this special arrangement.[1]

The success enjoyed by the bank led to many objections from its detractors. These were based on two separate grounds. It was suggested firstly that as the bank and the shipping firms were controlled by the same man, advances were made conditional upon goods being shipped by the conference lines. This suggestion cannot be substantiated because any such request would hardly be put in writing and, in any case, the merchants already had to ship via the conference because they had no immediate alternative. The second criticism was that as all new silver had to be obtained from the bank it had the power to delay or withhold supplies and consequently it could exert pressure on its customers.[2] The Colonial Office however, was convinced that these charges were without foundation and the evidence given before the Royal Commission on Shipping Rings would appear to confirm that the bank did not in practice restrict or delay the supply of silver to the opponents of Elder Dempster.

A further confirmation of the satisfactory nature of the system may be seen by reference to the Manchester Chamber of Commerce. This body was naturally anxious about the exclusive right of importing new coins which the bank had inherited from its predecessor, and in a letter to the Colonial Office dated the 18 July 1895 it asked what were the terms on which this privilege rested. In its reply the Colonial Office stated that Clause 10, relating to the importation of silver '. . . is in accordance

---

[1] R.C.S.R., Q.9145.

[2] Colonial Office Papers (hereinafter referred to as C.O.) 147/102, Lagos, 13531. Letter from G. L. Gaiser and Company to the Colonial Office, 3 August 1895, and reply by the Colonial Office. Note that these papers are kept at the Public Record Office, London, but that Colonial Office Confidential Print, Africa West: No. 616 referred to on succeeding pages is held at the Colonial Office Library, London.

with the usual practice in Colonies where public banks are established . . .'[1] However much this arrangement may have worried the members of the Chamber in 1895 they were quick to appreciate the advantages offered by the bank and later stated that they did not wish to see the system changed in any way.[2]

It might seem, therefore, that the British and Colonial governments were quite happy with the arrangements made for banking in West Africa, but this was only true to a limited extent. This was made clear when the Bank of British West Africa sought the power to issue notes to the value of £20,000, for the official comment on the application stated:

> 'This must be declined. If notes are wanted at Lagos they must be a government issue, and in sending the (Colonial) government a copy of the correspondence ask if there is any real necessity, for without it it will be undesirable to introduce a cumbersome and troublesome system. The bank is not of the character to be allowed to issue notes.'[3]

If Alfred Jones was not to be allowed to issue his own notes in British West Africa at least he could protect his control of the silver currency, and in 1899 he wrote to the Colonial Office as follows:

> 'I understand that you are pursuing the question of a currency for West Africa. Now as one largely connected with that part of the world, and as Chairman of the Bank of British West Africa, I beg to suggest that no change be made. I am certain that any departure from the present currency would be attended with very serious results. It might on the face of it appear an advantage but I view with very great alarm any restriction as to the currency. i.e. If a man has 5/- in Africa I would like it to be of the same value at any place—Great Britain and all settlements in West Africa.
> My directors are strongly of the same opinion.'[4]

Jones was also instrumental in persuading the African trade section of the Liverpool Chamber of Commerce to send a resolution to the Colonial Office:

---

[1] C.O. 147/102. C.O. 12593. Letter (and reply) from the Manchester Chamber of Commerce to Colonial Office, 18 July 1895.

[2] R.C.S.R., Q.13260. Evidence given by G. B. Zochonis of Paterson, Zochonis and Co., and J. H. Hutton—the representatives of the Manchester Chamber of Commerce.

[3] Colonial Office 147/102. C.O. 15343. Comments written on letter from the Bank of British West Africa to the Colonial Office, 30 August 1895.

[4] Colonial Office, Africa, West No. 616. Appendix VI Letter from Liverpool Chamber of Commerce to Colonial Office, 5 December 1899.

'Resolved, That in the event of the government thinking it desirable to provide British West Africa with a special currency in order to give the colonies the benefit of the profit on the coinage, the Committee of the West African Trade Section of the Incorporated Chamber of Commerce of Liverpool would consider such a change from the present Imperial Currency as retrograde and injurious which would not provide for the redemption of the special currency to an unlimited amount in the Imperial Sterling Gold Coinage at its face value'.[1]

In his evidence before the Committee on the Currency of the West African Colonies, Jones continued to maintain that it would be a mistake to introduce a separate silver currency.[2] His view carried considerable weight but in addition (and of more importance) the government was swayed by the opposition of the Treasury. The latter disliked the possibility of sharing its profit from minting the coins with the colonial governments and so preferred to keep the existing system. The report of the Committee was not acted upon, therefore, and no change was made until 1912.

Jones's monopoly of new silver and the resulting prosperity of the Bank of British West Africa led to the formation of the Bank of Nigeria Limited in 1899. This was first known as the Anglo-African Bank and it had a nominal capital of £150,000. It was established by representatives of the leading merchant houses and these included the Royal Niger Company, the African Association Limited and Messrs Alexander Miller, Brother and Company. Branches were set up at Calabar, Burutu and Lokoja, but they were handicapped by having to pay the 1 per cent premium for any new silver they required.[3] This disability appears to have prevented the Bank of Nigeria from developing satisfactorily and in 1912 it was taken over by the Bank of British West Africa. The latter concern then had no competitors until 1917, when the Colonial Bank began activities in West Africa.

Even the acquisition of the boating companies, the development of the branch-lines and the control of the credit structure of British West Africa did not satisfy Alfred Jones. Nothing was too small to be beneath his attention, and nothing was too large to be tackled. Whenever

[1] Colonial Office, Africa, West No. 616. Appendix VI. Letter from Bank of British West Africa to Colonial Office, 16 November 1899.
[2] Committee on the Currency of the West African Colonies, Colonial Office, Africa, West No. 616. Minutes of evidence 1067 to 1229.
[3] R.C.S.R., Q.11732. Evidence given by Mr Clifford Edgar, a director of the Bank of Nigeria Limited.

possible he trained the pilots and buoyed the channels so that the ways into the ports, creeks and rivers would be known only to his employees. He also purchased and ran a few plantations with the dual object of encouraging new ways and methods and, it must be admitted, of benefiting from the appreciation of land values.[1] An example of this was concerned with the growing of cotton in West Africa, for Jones was largely responsible for the founding of the British Cotton Growing Association in 1902.[2] There can be little doubt that he was motivated in this activity by a desire to make Britain independent of American cotton as well as by a wish to enlarge the number of West African exports. In 1901 Jones obtained an expert from New Orleans to instruct on cotton production[3] and later wrote to the Colonial Office on the need to promote its growth in West Africa. This letter was forwarded on to Kew Gardens and, in his reply, the curator agreed it would be possible to grow the crop on the Coast.[4]

To help get the cotton established in West Africa Jones offered to have it carried to the United Kingdom without charge. This was done but it proved to be necessary for only a short period and he then reaped a substantial reward in the form of a new trade for his vessels to carry.[5] This was, in fact, a just reward, for many merchants had doubted the wisdom of developing a British cotton-growing scheme because of the large crops being produced in the United States. Jones was convinced, however, that, because of the cost advantage possessed by West Africa, it could always be marketed at an economic price.[6] The result of Jones's work in promoting cotton growing in West Africa was that a small crop was produced for export and this was gradually increased. To this extent it was successful, but it completely failed to provide an alternative to the imports from the United States, although the growth of the Egyptian crop was encouraged by the British Cotton Growing Association:

[1] Note that in many parts of West Africa land could not actually be bought, but even so speculation could and did take place.

[2] W. F. Tewson, *The British Cotton Growing Association, Golden Jubilee, 1904–1954.* Issued by the Association in 1954.

[3] C.O. 45686/01. Letter from Elder Dempster and Company to the Colonial Office, 1 April 1901.

[4] C.O. 45696/01. Letter from Elder Dempster and Company to the Colonial Office, 24 February 1902.

[5] R.C.S.R., Q.7294–7297. Evidence given by Sir Ralph Moor.

[6] *Liverpool Daily Post*, 19 December 1904. American and British grown cotton.

Raw Cotton Imports into the United Kingdom[1]

Year	British West Africa	Unites States	Egypt	Total
1896	£ —	£ 27 million	£ 6 million	£ 36 million
1900	938	30	9	40
1904	15,099	40	11	54
1908	66,780	39	13	55
1912	122,092	55	20	80
1916	259,451	60	19	84
1919	554,053	125	50	190

Alfred Jones was also interested in the possibility of mineral wealth being discovered in West Africa. He believed that a rich harvest was waiting to be uncovered as the inland areas were opened up. He refused to be discouraged by the poorness of the internal communications, and was convinced that in time these would be improved so that economic development would become profitable. To further these ideas he formed the Liverpool West Africa Syndicate Limited, in 1901. This had a nominal capital of £10,000 and its ostensible objects were to acquire concessions, rights and properties. Its interests grew to include mines, quarries, mills, timber, factories, railways and tramlines, and it was frequently used to hold properties and options which did not conveniently belong to any other body in the huge Elder Dempster organisation. It was through this company that Jones shared to some extent in the gold finds of 1904 and would have benefited from the tin boom of 1909 but for his death. The real gain, however, was in the increased demand for his ships that the new industries eventually generated.

So far we have been examining the network of activities that Elder Dempster built up in West Africa, but Alfred Jones was far from idle in creating an integrated system in the United Kingdom that was complementary to his other interests.[2] In Liverpool he was the Master Porter and Stevedore for his main-line shipping firms and as the Liverpool Cartage Company he was responsible for the movement of cargo belonging to most of the shippers or consignees. Jones (together with Elder and Dempster) privately owned the Sefton Street Stores where

[1] Compiled from Annual Statements of the Trade of the United Kingdom, H.M.S.O., relevant years.

[2] The best indication of Alfred Jones's many interests is seen in the three schedules attached to the formation documents of Elder Dempster & Co. Ltd. See Appendix pp. 450–6, Tables 48 and 49.

palm oil could be warehoused, while Elder Dempster and Company rented the remaining spaces on Coburg Dock quay, where they charged high rates once the permitted time for goods to be removed had elapsed. This may have been simply in order to keep the space clear for incoming and outgoing cargo but, according to John Holt, it was to force produce into the nearby store at Sefton Street.[1]

As previously noted, any cartage that was required was performed by the Liverpool Cartage Company in which Jones had large holdings. He was also one of the first to see the promise of mechanical road transport and was associated with the trials organised in 1898, 1899 and 1901 when hill-climbing tests were undertaken up Everton Brow. Later he was connected with the Liverpool Self Propelled Traffic Association and invested in the Road Carrying Company.[2]

Another of Jones's aims was to encourage the development of an oil-crushing industry in Liverpoool. In the 1890s most of West Africa's palm kernels were crushed in Europe, but Jones wished to divert at least some of this profitable trade from the Continent to Britain. Accordingly he helped to found the African Oil Mills Company, and invested heavily in it. The new mill was completed in 1894 and its machinery and equipment were then considered to be of the latest design.[3] Jones does not appear to have taken an active interest in the running of this company but, at times, he was severely criticised for the policies it adopted.[4]

The vast majority of the ships controlled by Elder Dempster were run on coal.[5] Alfred Jones therefore created two subsidiary companies to provide for their needs and to sell coal to other lines if required. These were the Sierra Leone Coaling Company and the Grand Canary Coaling Company. Jones also supplied much fuel to the colonial governments of British West Africa and so it was very much to his advantage to possess a cheap and reliable source of coal. He found this at Garth, Maesteg, in Glamorgan, and proceeded to purchase the colliery. He then formed Elders Navigation Colliery Limited and sold the mine to it. From the inception of this company in 1900 till his death

---

[1] J.H.P. Rough memo written by John Holt in 1897.
[2] *The Motor Trader*, 22 December 1909.
[3] *Journal of Commerce*, 23 October 1894 and 15 June 1896.
[4] *Journal of Commerce*, 1 December 1904.
[5] This was before the advent of oil burners or motor ships.

in 1909 Alfred Jones held practically all of its ordinary shares and debentures.[1]

An important effect of Jones's interest in the coal trade was on the economy of the Canary Islands:

'Before Sir Alfred established the Grand Canary Coaling station at Puerto de la Luz in 1884, the port of Las Palmas was only an open roadstead and about twenty ships per month called there, but four years later the monthly average had increased to a hundred and Grand Canary became one of the most important centres for the coaling of steamers trading to and from South America, Australia, New Zealand and South and West Africa.'[2]

Once Jones had made up his mind to establish a coaling station in the Canaries other activities soon followed. In his own words:

'I visited the Islands for the purpose of deciding on the feasibility or otherwise of establishing a coaling station for our African steamers. I was much struck by the poverty of the old Spaniards, who form the bulk of the population. They formerly existed by producing cochineal, and on the substitution of the aniline dyes the community was practically ruined. The cohineal had fallen from 10/- to 2/- a pound; the land was lying waste and the people sunk in an apathy of despair. Well, observing the prolific character of the soil, I bought up what land I could and grew fruit on it. Then, as I knew that that was not nearly enough for the trade I could foresee, I went round to the farms and offered so much for all the fruit they could grow, and where necessary, made them advances and financed them generally. The consequence is that land has now gone up to £1,000 per acre, the Islands receive a million a year for fruit, and the people are prosperous and comparatively speaking contented for they more than pay their way.'[3]

Alfred Jones made numerous visits to the Canary Islands and always received an enthusiastic reception.[4] In time he extended his activities by forming the Interinsular Steamship Company to provide communications between the main islands; he established a large marine engineering workshop and built a patent slip at the port of La Luz, and owned and operated a cold-storage plant and two hotels.[5] The extent to which Jones helped to revitalise the economy of the Canary Islands will be seen by the following table:

[1] See Appendix 437–8, Tables 40 and 41, for full details of the capital structure and list of shareholders in Elders Navigation Colliery Limited.

[2] *Weekly Courier*, Obituary of Alfred Jones, 18 November 1909.

[3] 'A Napoleon of Commerce', *Great Thoughts*, 18 June 1898.

[4] *El Liberal* (Newspaper of Grand Canary), translated and reproduced in *Journal of Commerce*, 16 March 1892.

[5] See also *Journal of Commerce*, 26 April 1892, *Liverpool Echo*, 17 April 1894 and *The Times*, Obituary of Alfred Jones, 14 December 1909

Imports from the Canary Islands to the United Kingdom[1]

Average for	Cochineal	Bananas	Tomatoes	Total
1885–1889	£64,579	£ —	£ —	£ 99,179
1890–1894	36,184	—	—	255,757
1895–1899	29,805	—	—	612,307
1900–1904	14,186	785,559	312,849	1,246,361
1905–1909	19,147	863,120	440,675	1,542,217
1910–1914	13,388	727,396	546,254	1,494,108
1915–1916	85,248	1,077,596	729,660	2,068,928
1917–1918	No figures available			
1919–1920	33,223	2,529,420	1,339,525	4,048,975

Thus it will be seen that as the sale of cochineal declined, the sale of bananas and tomatoes rose and stimulated the economy. The rise in the export of these fruits is not shown in the figures till 1900, as before that date they were not shown separately. An example of the lengths that Jones was prepared to go to ensure the success of this project will be seen by the following extract from his obituary:

'When Jones first began to import Canary bananas in his African ships he encountered great difficulties in obtaining a market for them—difficulties of transport and difficulties of retail sale. But he was not to be beaten. Finding that the retailers would not help him, and that even the carters put difficulties in his way, he engaged a number of coster-mongers, bringing some of them, it is said, from London and loading up their barrows from one of his ships, he told the carters to go and sell them in the streets of Liverpool for what they would fetch, and that he did not want to be paid for them. By this means he popularised the consumption of the banana first in Liverpool and afterwards throughout Lancashire and the North of England.'[2]

Jones's success in marketing bananas and other fruit from the Canary Islands led in 1901 to a further extension of his interests. This was in Jamaica where activity was at a low ebb.[3] The island's main products were sugar, cocoa, rum and cotton, while bananas were also grown in large quantities. Prices for the last were especially poor as the United Fruit Company of America was the sole buyer. Sir Daniel Morris, the Imperial Commissioner of Agriculture in the West Indies, thought that if some of this fruit could be exported to Britain it would help to raise prices, and he therefore asked Jones for his assistance.

[1] Compiled from the *Annual Statements of the Trade of the United Kingdom,* H.M.S.O.
[2] *The Times,* 13 December 1909, Obituary of Alfred Jones.
[3] S. B. Saul, 'The Economic Significance of Constructive Imperialism', *Journal of Economic History* (June 1957) and 'The British West Indies in Depression', *Journal of Inter-American Economic Affairs* (1958), Vol. XII, No. III.

After due consideration, and encouraged by Joseph Chamberlain, Jones agreed to help and he joined with Messrs Fyffe, Hudson and Company Limited—a firm of London fruit merchants—to form Messrs Elder and Fyffes Limited. This handled the purchase and sale of the bananas while the responsibility for shipment was placed in the hands of another new firm organised by Jones—the Imperial Direct West India Mail Service Company Limited. This did not completely meet the need of Elder and Fyffes, partially because of its interest in mail and passengers, and so in April 1902 a new firm was formed to ship their bananas. This was Elder and Fyffes (Shipping) Limited, but it had only a short life and was wound up in 1907.[1] To ensure an adequate supply of fruit, Jones made an agreement with the United Fruit Company which undertook to purchase and load bananas on all his steamships. As his critics were quick to point out, this still left the Jamaican growers with only a single outlet for their crop, and so in spite of increased demand prices did not rise.[2] However, the importation of bananas from Jamaica to the United Kingdom rose from £874 in 1900 to an average of over £200,000 for the years 1906 to 1910.[3]

The establishment of the Imperial Direct West India Mail Service Company Limited had little effect on Jones's main activities in West Africa. Once set up it did not require his constant attention, as the fleet remained relatively constant. From 1901 to 1909 the Company had four or five ships always engaged on the West Indian run and few changes were necessary. The average size of these vessels was about 4,000 tons. Another interest outside the main stream of Alfred Jones's West African affairs was the Ocean Transport Company Limited which was formed by Messrs Harland and Wolff in August 1894. Elder Dempster managed this line until 1902 when C. F. Torrey and Company took over. During this period neither Jones nor any of his subsidiary companies held any shares in this firm, and it appears it was purely a Harland and Wolff concern.[4]

An extremely profitable venture for Elder Dempster was the purchase and sale of the Canada Shipping Company—better known as the

[1] See Appendix pp. 439–45, Tables 42, 43 and 44, for details of the capital structure and shareholdings of Messrs Elder & Fyffes Ltd, the Imperial Direct West India Mail Service Co. Ltd and Elder & Fyffes (Shipping) Ltd.

[2] *Manchester City News,* 13 December 1902, gives a good description of this problem.

[3] Compiled from the *Annual Statements of the Trade of the United Kingdom,* H.M.S.O.

[4] File 41742 (Dissolved) at Companies House, London.

AFRICAN ROYAL MAIL STEAMERS.

RULES

TO BE OBSERVED BY PASSENGERS.

LIGHTS to be extinguished in the Saloon and Cabin at 10.30 P.M. unless in cases of necessity, such as arrival at port of Destination during the night, or of illness.

MEALS.—Breakfast will be prepared at Half-past 8, Luncheon at Noon, Dinner at 4 P.M., and Tea at 7 P.M. Passengers are requested not to assemble in the Saloon while the Servants are preparing the Tables. No Passengers can be allowed to take Meals in their Cabins.

WINES.—It is requested that orders for Wine will be given to the Steward as early in the day as possible, so as to allow time for Cooling in the Ice-house.

SMOKING is strictly prohibited in the Saloon or Cabins.

GAMBLING not allowed in the Saloon.

BEDS will be made up by the Servants after Breakfast, and only once during the twenty-four hours. Bed Linen will be changed every eighth day, and Five Towels per week will be allowed to each Passenger.

WATER.—A Quart of Water will be served out to each Person every Morning, for washing purposes, Drinking Water may always be had from the Steward.

SEATS.—Passengers will have their places pointed out at Table by the Commander, which must be considered as arranged for the voyage.

As a sufficient number of Clothes-hooks have been placed in each Cabin, Passengers will be held accountable for any Damage done to the Bulkheads or Panels, by fixing Hooks, &c.

SERVANTS.—Any neglect or annoyance on the part of the Servants having been once represented to the Purser, any repetition of the same must be laid before the Commander, who will take every means to promote the happiness and comfort of all on board.

FLETCHER & PARR,
MANAGING AGENTS,
23, Castle Street, Liverpool.

PLATE 7   A.S.S. Co. Rules for Passengers, c. 1860.

African Steam Ship Company.

Regulations for Engineers' Mess.

THE FIRST, SECOND, THIRD, AND FOURTH ENGINEERS MESS TOGETHER.

The following Scale is to be adhered to as far as possible :—

BREAD ....1 lb. of soft Bread or Captain's Biscuit, or half of each per man per day.

MEAT ....1½ lb. per man per day, either all fresh or half fresh and half salted; also, ½ lb. each of Pickled Pork, Beef, or Bacon, at breakfast.

VEGETABLES ....A sufficient suppply of Potatoes or Yams.

PUDDINGS ....Plum Puddings on Sundays, plain twice a-week.

SUGAR......................1 lb. per man per week.

CHEESE....................½ lb.   do.   do.

BUTTER....................1 lb.   do.   do.

TEA..........................3½ oz. of Tea per man per week, or 1¾ oz. of Tea and 3½ oz. of Coffee.

THE MESS SERVANT TO BE PAID BY THE COMPANY, BUT TO BE RATIONED AFTER THE SCALE LAID DOWN IN THE SHIP'S ARTICLES FOR CREW.

Chief Engineer is allowed 1s. 2d. per diem; other Engineers, 1s. per diem, in lieu of a liquor allowance.

PLATE 8   A.S.S. Co. Regulations for Engineers' Mess, *c.* 1860.

EXPANSION AND DIVERSIFICATION

Beaver Line.[1] Elder Dempster had first entered the Canadian trade in 1894 when it took over the Bristol service formerly operated by the Dominion Line. In 1898 the Beaver Line was known to be in dire financial straits, so although it was acquired as a going concern the price paid was a small one. A regular service between Liverpool and Canada[2] was maintained by the Beaver Line after its purchase and this led to a conflict with the Beaver Line Associated Steamers Limited who were run by Messrs D. & C. McIver. The difficulty arose because Jones had only bought the former company, so it was brought into opposition with what had previously been its partner. As Jones was in a position to give the Beaver Line a sound financial backing it was able to defeat its rival and the Beaver Line Associated Steamers Limited went into voluntary liquidation. Jones then continued to build up the Beaver Line and it made good profits during the Boer War, but when he learned that the Canadian Pacific Railway Company[3] had decided to establish a service from Liverpool to Canada he sold the firm to it for £1,417,500.[4]

Of more direct concern to Alfred Jones was the trade between Belgium and the Congo. Leopold II had taken full advantage of the major powers' lack of interest (and failure to agree) in this area and following the Congress of Berlin had succeeded in establishing the Congo Free State. Belgium possessed few merchant ships and Leopold's other commitments made it inconvenient to spend large sums on new tonnage and so at first he depended upon chartered vessels or on casual calls made by the regular West African lines. In 1891, however, a syndicate was formed by Elder Dempster and Woermann so that a monthly service was established between Antwerp and Matadi. Initially this provided an adequate means of communication but with the growth of the trade it became desirable to put the arrangement on a more formal basis and to make more provision for Belgian participation. To this end Elder Dempster formed the Compagnie Belge Maritime du Congo, and Woerman established the Société Maritime du Congo.

[1] F. C. Bowen, *History of the Canadian Pacific Line* (London: Sampson Low, 1928), pp. 68–84.
[2] Elder Dempster established a service from Capetown to Canada in 1901. This was not part of the Beaver Line's operations and it continued after the Beaver Line was sold.
[3] H. A. Innis, *A History of the Canadian Pacific Railway* (London: P. S. King and Son, 1923), pp. 169–70.
[4] See Appendix, p. 407, Table 14.

Both of these new lines were registered in Antwerp and came into operation in 1895. Each was based on the idea that the expatriate firms would provide the ships while the Belgian interests would ensure full cargoes. The capital of the Compagnie Belge Maritime du Congo was fixed at 2,100,000 francs. Elder Dempster contributed two ships, *Coomassie* and *Leopoldville*, whose estimated value was 2,075,000 francs, so the Belgian side had little actual cash to contribute.[1] On the other hand the guarantee[2] of a high load factor made certain the profitability of the Company and so in spite of the disproportionate investment the profits were divided so that Elder Dempster received only a modest return.[3] As anticipated, the arrangement proved to be an advantageous one for both Elder Dempster and its Belgian friends and during the next decade the fleet was increased slightly so that it usually consisted of three or four vessels totalling about 9,000 net tons. Throughout this period the 1895 agreement remained in force with only minor modifications, but it was terminated by mutual consent in 1911.[4]

Limitations on Elder Dempster's Power

Alfred Jones's control of the West African shipping trade after 1895 was extensive and enabled him to extend his authority in many fields, but it should not be thought that there were no restrictions on his power. It is true that, after the fleet of the African Association was acquired in 1897, only the Royal Niger Company was permitted to charter independent steamships. By then there were few vessels engaged in the trade that were under private ownership and even these were gradually eliminated. A typical case of this was in June 1897 when *Koningin Wilhelmina* was purchased from Messrs De Nieume Afrikaansche Handels, of Rotterdam.[5] But it was impossible for Jones to remove every small craft, and a few sailing-vessels persisted throughout this period and there was always the danger of tramp intervention.

The deferred rebate system was normally too strong for tramp

[1] House History of the Compagnie Maritime Belge (Lloyd Royal) Antwerp, 1948, pp. 39–40. Note that the change in name occurred in 1930.

[2] At this time the Congo was the private concern of the Belgian Crown so almost all cargoes were carried on its behalf and would come under the agreement with Elders and Woerman.

[3] The author is greatly indebted to M. Paul Vereecke, Chairman of Associated Central West Africa Lines, and Commodore J. C. Bernaerts (late of the Compagnie Maritime Belge) for this assistance with the early history of the Company.

[4] See below, Chapter 7, p. 183.   [5] *Journal of Commerce*, 18 June 1897.

steamships to overcome, and after Jones had purchased the boating companies it made intervention practically impossible. But the details of at least one successful venture have survived. This concerned the steamer *Prestonian* which was managed by Henry Tyrer and Company Limited. The vessel, of 1,152 gross tons, was usually employed to carry salt from Fleetwood to Denmark, returning with cargoes of Baltic wood pulp for Preston. In 1906, however, she made two trips to West Africa carrying salt, stockfish and general groceries outward, and returning with mahogany for the account of W. B. MacIver and Company. The shallow draught of *Prestonian* enabled her to go up river and she used her own gear to load the logs. This naturally took time, so after a lengthy delay Henry Tyrer telegraphed to her captain:

'You must move heaven and earth to sail Saturday.'

To which her master, Captain William Kerr, replied:

'Heaven and earth immovable am raising hell.'[1]

In spite of the success of these two voyages they were not repeated the following year, probably because of pressure brought to bear by Alfred Jones. The shipping companies did not particularly wish to ship the logs themselves as this type of cargo was difficult to handle and easy to obtain. On the other hand they felt it unwise to allow a precedent to be established. Jones had £3,000 invested in MacIver's and while this could not affect their policy its sudden withdrawal might have caused a temporary embarrassment. Jones could also threaten to withhold the rebate held to MacIver's credit from the shipment of their other cargoes. In the event, a compromise was reached. MacIvers agreed not to charter again, and they continued to receive their rebate in the normal way. The importance of these voyages lies in the fact that MacIvers were subsequently taken over by Lever Brothers, and the experience gained with *Prestonian* was passed on and later was to influence Lever's decision to enter the West African shipping business.[2]

[1] Story told by Mr Frederick Cutts, the late chairman of Henry Tyrer and Company. In 1906 he had already been with the firm for nine years. He died in 1968, aged 87, and was still actively in control of the firm till his death. The author of this work is greatly indebted to Mr Cutts for his invaluable help and is deeply sorry that he could not have lived to see its publication.

[2] This was particularly true because Mr W. K. Findlay, the organiser of MacIvers, joined Levers when the company was taken over and he was able to guide their development on the Coast. He subsequently became chairman of the Niger Company, and died in December 1966, at the age of 99. He had given the author of this work considerable help in his research.

Alfred Jones was equally successful in preventing other lines from obtaining a foothold in the trade and for many years no rival shipping company sent its vessels to West Africa. Then in 1906 the Sun Line was organised by the Gold Coast mining companies. It owned no vessels of its own, but used chartered ships to carry coal and machinery out to West Africa. The line was naturally anxious to obtain return cargoes of produce but the deferred rebate system proved to be too powerful to permit any merchants to take advantage of its services. Consequently the only return cargo was the gold produced by the mining companies and when this proved to be insufficient, the line left the trade after running for two years at a loss.[1]

Of more serious consequence was the opposition of the Hamburg-Bremen Africa Line which began sailing to West Africa in 1907. The reaction of the conference to this intruder was to reduce its rates:

'By desire of our numerous shippers we are compelled to concede the following safeguard against the underbidding of freights by the Hamburg-Bremen Africa Line: withdrawal of the circular published in December, 1906, for some districts and of same published 25th of February for the S.S. *EDWARD BOHLEN* we are prepared to allow those of our shippers who consider it their interest to make use for the future exclusively of our lines for their shipments from and to the West Coast of Africa always the same rates of freight as those obtained by other shippers from the competing line.'[2]

In effect this meant a reduction of 40 per cent on the tariff rates of the time to all merchants who would bind themselves to ship exclusively by the conference for a five-year period.[3] This apparently had the desired effect on the new competitors for they agreed to come to terms and an agreement was made between the Woerman Line and the Hamburg-Bremen Africa Line. Under this arrangement the new concern purchased eight steamships from Woerman who in return arranged for it to be accepted into the conference.[4] This was the beginning, in fact, of a complete reorganisation of the German side of the West African shipping trade.[5] But the need to take the Hamburg-Bremen Africa Line into the conference shows that its position was not so strong as to

[1] R.C.S.R. Appendixes Part II, p. 196. Letter to the Colonial Office from John Rodger, Governor of the Gold Coast, 21 June 1907.

[2] Circular issued by the Woerman Line, Hamburg, 1 March 1907.

[3] R.C.S.R. Evidence of George Miller, Q.4374.

[4] R.C.S.R. Evidence of J. H. Batty, Q.6834.

[5] See below, Chapter 6, p. 159.

be able to ignore a really powerful competitor—even though an apparently high fee was charged as an admittance fee.

Once the new German firm had been taken care of Jones reduced the 40 per cent reduction in tariff rates to 10 per cent, and after April 1907 he adjusted the transit rates so that even this 10 per cent was offset by a rise in handling charges.[1] The reason that Jones was able to disregard the activities of the Sun Line—and a strong factor in persuading the Hamburg-Bremen Africa Line to come to terms—was the attitude of the merchants. The Sun Line, for example, failed to secure the backing of a single important trader. This, of course, was largely due to the power which Jones held over his shippers by means of the deferred rebate system. Yet it did provide an alternative and if Jones had attempted to extort the last penny from the merchants they could have used its services. Jones fully appreciated that this was the case and he was prepared to go to great lengths to placate the merchants so long as this did not interfere with his essential interests. The co-operation of the merchants was, in fact, a virtual necessity to the operation of the conference, so within the structure of its framework it was politic for Jones to be as accommodating as possible.

Of great annoyance to the merchants was the habit of the shipping firms in trading on their own account. This took two forms. The ships carried bulky cargoes such as coal and cement for the owners, while the crews engaged in extensive petty trading. Both these activities were especially irksome in the West African trade, as the deferred rebate prevented any effective retaliation by the individual merchants. Their reaction was to set up an association to defend their collective interests —George Miller and John Holt being largely responsible for calling the body of traders together. Miller had called to see Elder Dempster on 2 December 1896, and had discussed the question of the trading carried out by the shipping firms and their crews. He then received an assurance that this would stop, but as nothing was apparently done he wrote to Elder Dempster and informed them that he intended to call a meeting of the merchants to consider what further action should be taken.[2] In reply Miller received a note from Alexander Elder written on behalf of the British and African Steam Navigation Company:

[1] R.C.S.R. Evidence of J. H. Batty, Q.6959.
[2] J.H.P. 6/4. Letter from George Miller to Elder Dempster. 15 January 1897.

'I have just returned from Glasgow where I have had an opportunity of consider-ing your letter re trading. I am very sorry that any misunderstandings should arise on this subject as my colleagues and myself are desirous to stop, by all means in their power, any trading by the Company's servants.'[1]

In spite of this communication a meeting of West African merchants was held on 27 January 1897, and shippers were present from Rotter-dam, Hamburg, France, Bristol, London, Glasgow, Manchester and Liverpool. Miller addressed the assembly and gave details of a dis-cussion with Alfred Jones in which the latter had made light of the problem.[2] The meeting therefore approved a memorial that was to be sent to Elder Dempster and a committee was set up to deal with the matter. Both Miller and Holt were elected to this body and it would appear that the protests of such a combination of traders could not be ignored so easily as earlier individual complaints had been. At any rate the trading carried out by crew members appears to have been pro-hibited, although the carriage of bulky goods on ship's account was not immediately affected.

The success of this activity led Miller to decide to put the *ad hoc* committee on a more permanent basis. In November 1897 he sent Holt a copy of a letter which he proposed to send to all shippers engaged in the West African trade. This letter asked for everyone concerned to attend a meeting at which the setting up of a properly constituted body would be considered. Once Holt had agreed to the draft the letter was printed and then distributed.[3] When the meeting took place it was agreed that a formal organisation was desirable and it was decided to call it the West African Traders Association. It was stated at this time that the trading by ships' crews, previously complained of, '. . . had been almost entirely stopped'.[4] The constitution of the West African Traders Association was finalised in February 1898, and thereafter it continually harassed the shipping companies when the interests of its members were threatened. It could not exert much pressure on the major issues on which Jones was not prepared to co-operate, but it could and did rectify many smaller matters which caused irritation to the merchants. It has been suggested that it was largely the activity of the Association

[1] J.H.P. 6/4. Letter from Alexander Elder to George Miller, 23 January 1897.
[2] J.H.P. 6/4. Report of meeting held 27 January 1897.
[3] J.H.P. 6/4. Printed letter addressed to West African merchants and signed by George Miller, 6 November 1897.
[4] J.H.P. 6/4. Report of meeting held on 1 December 1897.

which led to the setting up of the Royal Commission on Shipping Rings in 1907,[1] but this is questionable. It was certainly a factor in the forces which led to the inquiry being made, but it is doubtful if it was the main consideration of the government at that time.

The importance of the West African Traders Association lay not so much in what it actually achieved as in its potential. If Jones had allowed his relations with the merchants to deteriorate, the discontent would have been focused and magnified by the Association. In fact, Jones was careful not to push the larger firms too far and he therefore prevented the natural leaders of the group from having too many personal grievances. He was particularly anxious not to antagonise the Niger Company, for he realised that if a split developed the firm could well afford to run its own line of steamships. The Niger Company had lost its 'Royal' prefix in 1900 when its charter was revoked and thereafter it was purely a trading concern.[2] After the West African Shipping Conference was set up in 1895 all the Company's goods and produce were carried by Elder Dempster vessels, with the exception of four ships per year which it was entitled to charter. The latter were used at the height of the season to help move the surplus produce that accumulated at that time of the year. A further concession obtained by the Niger Company as the price of their continued support was a promise that Elder Dempster's vessels would keep out of the Niger river. Ocean-going ships could ascend the river towards the end of the rainy season and the smaller branch-line vessels could travel along many of the larger tributaries, but the Niger Company wished to retain a monopoly of the traffic. Jones agreed to this in his own interest, but Elder Dempster ships were occasionally still discovered in the river[3] and the Niger Company sometimes chartered in defiance of the agreement.[4]

Another bone of contention between Lord Scarborough (the chairman of the Niger Company) and Alfred Jones was the freight rates

[1] C. Gertzel, A British Merchant in West Africa in the Era of Imperialism, Ph.D. thesis in Bodleian Library, Oxford: 1959, p. 565.

[2] J. E. Flint, Sir George Goldie and the Making of Nigeria (London: Oxford University Press, 1960). See chapters 12 and 13 for a good description of the background to this event.

[3] Royal Niger Company Misc. Papers (Hereinafter referred to as R.N.C.P.) 1904-5. Vol. XI, Mss. Afr. S.95, p. 517.

[4] R.N.C.P. Vol. XII, p. 116. Letter from Jones to Scarborough, 9 July 1906.

charged by Elder Dempster. Jones refused to reduce the general level
and would not be budged.[1] He also refused to reduce specific rates even
though it was argued that he was stifling trade and thus limiting the
amount of cargo available for his vessels.[2] Both Jones and Scarborough
desired to keep to their verbal understanding, as it suited them to do so.
The former wished to keep his exclusive control of ocean carriage
while the latter wanted to retain the Niger for his own vessels. Thus,
however much they might bicker, their mutual interests prevented any
breakdown in their arrangements. Jones was pressed on many occasions
to make a formal agreement with the Niger Company but until 1907 he
always refused. Then in that year the question arose of how the material
to build the new Southern Nigerian railway was to be delivered to
Jebba up the Niger. The normal procedure would have been that Elder
Dempster would carry it to the Niger delta where it would have been
trans-shipped, and then the Niger Company would have taken it up
river to the inland port. The amount of material required to build the
railway, however, was so great that it was desirable to make special
plans for its carriage.[3]

Jones and Scarborough met in August 1907, to discuss these arrangements and took the opportunity to place their relationship on a proper
business-like footing. The result of this meeting was a written agreement which gave the Niger Company exclusive rights on the river and
Elder Dempster the ocean carriage of all its cargoes. The Company's
right of charter was to be curtailed to two each year but Elder Dempster were to supply it with all its coal requirements at a special rate. It
was also arranged that future freight rates between Britain and places
on the Niger would be fixed by joint consultation and that Elder
Dempster would charter the branch boat *Oshogbo* at a reasonable rate,
while the Southern Nigerian railway was being constructed.[4] This was
not, however, to mark the beginning of a period of harmony between
Elder Dempster and the Niger Company for no decision was made in
respect of existing agreements. The problem lay in the rates which Jones
had already negotiated for the carriage of the railway material to Jebba.

[1] R.N.C.P. Vol. XI, p. 147. Letter from Jones to Scarborough, 20 April 1904.
[2] R.N.C.P. Vol. XII, p. 74. Letter from Niger Company to Elder Dempster, 16 March 1906.
[3] R.N.C.P. Vol. VII, p. 181.
[4] R.N.C.P. Vol. VII, p. 160. Memorandum of interview between Sir Alfred Jones and Lord Scarborough, 21 August 1907.

These were very low, but, as Jones pointed out, if he had not quoted a very low figure for delivering this cargo the railway might not have been built for many years.[1]

Lord Scarborough felt so strongly about these rates that he complained to the Crown Agents for the Colonies who eventually gave him some assistance.[2] In return he made great efforts to have the contract fulfilled and most of the season's railway material was delivered before the coming of the dry months caused the river to fall. The real cost of this to the Niger Company was in the amount of produce it was forced to leave behind on the Benue. The existing fleet, even with the help of *Oshogbo*, just could not cope with its normal task and the additional work, so from the Company's point of view the season was a failure.[3] During this period Jones did what he could to help and in January 1908 an agreement was made whereby nine Elder Dempster branch steamers were to work for the Niger Company in the coming season.[4] A further agreement was reached in April the same year when provision was made for the charter of an additional eight steamships.[5] Even then, however, disagreements continued to disrupt the relationship between Jones and Scarborough. One of the ships chartered to the Niger Company was *Bassa* which was stranded in the river and had to wait for many months until the water rose sufficiently to free her. During this time Jones not only refused to replace her with another vessel, but also charged the Niger Company for her retention.[6] Jones's policy towards the Niger Company thus resulted in a compromise. He kept the ocean-carriage and allowed it to keep the river transport as its own preserve. At times he threatened to re-enter the Niger trade and although Scarborough believed this to be a bluff[7] it was a useful device to help retain his position. It is clear, too, that if Jones had pushed Scarborough much

[1] R.N C.P. Vol. XII, p. 353. Letter from Jones to Scarborough, 13 September 1907.

[2] R.N.C.P. Vol. VII, p. 184. Correspondence between Blake and Scarborough.

[3] R.N.C.P. Vol. XII, p. 424. Letter from R. Lenthall, Agent General in the Niger area to the Niger Company in London, 24 October 1907.

[4] R.N.C.P. Vol. VII, p. 220. Agreement between Jones and Scarborough, 21 January 1908.

[5] R.N.C.P., op. cit., Vol. XIII, p. 146. Agreement between Jones and Scarborough, 29 April 1908.

[6] R.N.C.P. Vol. XII, p. 226. Correspondence between Elder Dempster and the Niger Company.

[7] J.H.P. 17-3. Letter from Scarborough to John Holt, 10 July 1909

harder he could easily have gone too far and destroyed the balance he was anxious to maintain.[1]

Alfred Jones's need to placate the West African Traders Association and his arrangements with the African Association and the Niger Company show that while his authority was great it was not unlimited. It was also necessary for him to keep individual merchants like George Miller and John Holt reasonably content with the service and conditions he provided. His relationship with Miller was a serene one and the two were usually on a friendly, if business-like, footing. This was probably not unconnected with the arrangements between Elder Dempster and the Miller firms whereby the latter received various agencies from the shipping firm.

John Holt was, of course, an early friend of Alfred Jones. They had worked together in Fletcher and Parr's office when they were boys and had remained in contact throughout their lives. Holt was instrumental in organising a testimonial to Jones on the occasion of his fiftieth birthday in 1895. A banquet was held at the (old) Adelphi Hotel in Liverpool and a silver cup was presented on behalf of the West African merchants.[2] Jones was equally friendly with Holt at this time and took his son into Elder Dempster's Hamburg office and provided him with a sound training.[3] As previously described, Jones and Holt were the principals in the negotiations for the sale of the fleet of the African Association to Elder Dempster in 1896 and when Jones broke his verbal agreement he also broke his friendship with Holt.[4] In the course of time they appear to have patched up their differences—at any rate Holt spoke very highly of Jones when the shipowner received his knighthood in November 1901.[5] Their relationship was subsequently subjected to further heavy strain by Holt's disapproval of Jones's attitude to affairs in the Congo. Nevertheless, they maintained some semblance of friendly terms, and Holt appears to have been genuinely sorry when Jones died in 1909.[6]

In spite of his more or less amicable relations with these two pre-

---

[1] J.H.P. 17–3. Letter from Scarborough to John Holt, 15 July 1909.

[2] J.H.P. 6–7. Note that Alexander Elder and John Dempster refused to contribute to the presentation.

[3] J.H.P. 6–5. Letter from Jones to Holt, 16 September 1895.

[4] See above, Chapter 4, pp. 112–3.

[5] *Liverpool Mercury*, 12 November 1901. Speech by John Holt.

[6] E.M.P. Letter from Holt to Morel, 14 December 1909.

eminent merchants, Jones could not rely on their support unless their interests were safeguarded. Fortunately for him, however, Holt and Miller were usually in conflict on the Coast and as a result they seldom found it practicable to join together, even though it would have been to their mutual advantage. This was a major reason for the failure of the General Steam Navigation Company in the West African trade in 1895. Holt had wanted Miller to ship all his cargo by this outside line, but Miller felt he could not agree to combining his shipments while he was competing with Holt in West Africa.[1] Yet on at least one occasion Miller approached Holt with a view to setting up their own shipping company. Holt's reply showed that he needed little urging[2] but their grand schemes came to nothing as Jones succeeded in mollifying each of the firms concerned in turn by removing the more serious of their outstanding grievances. Jones also made it very clear that he was prepared to fight very strongly to uphold his position and the merchants decided to continue to ship via the conference. A later attempt to interest Holt in the formation of a new line also failed[3] but it is obvious that his co-operation with the shipping lines was only achieved by the use of suitable incentives.

Jones was thus able to prevent the larger firms of merchants from combining against him and he recognised that in part this was due to the natural reluctance of merchants to become shipowners. The men concerned were too busy with the running of their own businesses to wish to take on added responsibilities if they could possibly avoid it. John Holt, in fact, was convinced that the merchants would do almost anything to avoid having to combine together to run their own line.[4] There was also a personal element that tended to prevent merchants from becoming shipowners in the West African trade. In spite of the many hard things said about Jones, most of the traders had a grudging admiration for him and, although they put their own interest first, they were reluctant to harm his affairs if it could be helped. The evidence given by George Miller to the Royal Commission on Shipping Rings makes this very clear.[5] Jones sometimes encouraged this sympathy by looking the other way when his essential interests were not involved. An

[1] See above, Chapter 4, p. 105.
[2] J.H.P. 26/30. Letter from John Holt to George Miller, 3 October 1900.
[3] J.H.P. 26/30. Letter from John Holt to Major Cecil Pownoy, 16 October 1903.
[4] R.C.S.R. Evidence of John Holt, Q.4913–4916.
[5] R.C.S.R. Evidence of George Miller. Q.4473–4475.

example of this was to be seen in his application of the rules of the rebate system. These specifically forbade merchants to ship from the
French ports in West Africa to the United Kingdom or the Continent,
but in practice they did send much produce to Marseilles and le Havre,
and yet did not lose their rebate.[1] Tact may not have been Jones's
strongest feature, but he knew how to use it at the appropriate moment!

The near duopoly established by Jones in West Africa was also limited to some extent by the official inquiries which were held whilst his
power was at its peak. The first of these was held by the Committee on
the Currency of the West African Colonies and Jones gave his evidence in public. In this instance the inquiry was restricted to banking
and the financial background, though mention was made of Elder
Dempster's many other interests, and Jones was able to present a strong
case in favour of the existing system.[2] The second official inquiry was
the Royal Commission on Shipping Rings. The terms of reference of this
body were very wide and all of Elder Dempster's activities in West
Africa came under careful scrutiny. The evidence was heard in 1907—
towards the end of Jones's life—and so it provides an admirable commentary on the development of his vast commercial empire.

The Royal Commission heard evidence in respect of several shipping conferences, but that relating to West Africa was particularly
extensive.[3] The main witnesses who were questioned on this conference
included John Holt, James Henry Batty and George Miller on behalf of
the larger merchants; J. H. Hutton and G. B. Zochonis on behalf of the
smaller traders; Sir Walter Couper for the Bank of British West Africa;
Clifford Edgar for the Bank of Nigeria; and Sir Ralph Moor—a former
High Commissioner of Southern Nigeria, but currently a director of the
African Steam Ship Company. Both Alfred Jones (who appeared on
behalf of the shipping companies) and John Holt gave their evidence in
private but later Holt agreed that his examination be published. Unfortunately Jones's evidence—the most important of all—was not released (and does not seem to have been preserved)[4] but its effects can

[1] R.C.S.R. Evidence of John Holt. Q.4922-4. Note that the rebate circulars of Woerman and Elder Dempster differed slightly in this respect.

[2] Committee on the Currency of the West African Colonies. Minutes of evidence given
by Alfred Jones, Q.1067-1229, 1 December 1899.

[3] C. Leubuscher, *The West African Shipping Trade, 1909-59* (Leyden: A. W. Sythoff,
1963), pp. 13-28.

[4] The author has contacted the libraries of the House of Commons, the House of

be ascertained by reference to the majority and minority reports issued by the Commission. The majority of the members recommended that an association be formed in each trade so that the merchants could present a solid front to the shipowners and thus make bargaining a more realistic feature of the system. They also suggested a compulsory publication of tariff rates that would include every item. A minority of the Commission members wanted the Board of Trade to establish a system of limited supervision over the conference. They also wanted a comprehensive tariff to be published and circulated to all shippers, but neither the majority nor minority reports made any proposal for ending the deferred rebate system and were apparently quite content to see the conference perpetuated.[1]

It is impossible to say to what extent Alfred Jones was able to influence the Commission. It would seem, however, that he was able to prove that the creation of the West African Conference had enabled him to establish and maintain regular services at reasonable and steady rates. The Commission may then have been persuaded that, as these were of such vital importance to the development of the British colonies, and in the absence of a satisfactory alternative, it was advisable to leave the system intact in spite of its many imperfections. This is not to say that even in well-informed circles there was not much adverse criticism of Elder Dempster but fortunately for Jones he had his admirers as well as detractors in high places. Typical of many questions asked in the House of Commons was that put forward by Mr Cathcart Mason in May 1907, when attention was drawn to the Conference freight rates,[2] and those asked by Mr Wedgewood in 1906.

'Mr. Wedgewood asked if government freight could be carried to West Africa other than by Elder Dempster Liners, and if so would they lose their rebate. Mr. W. S. Churchill said other ships could be used, but might be dearer taking into account the loss of rebate: in 1903 to 1905 this averaged £4,500 per annum. Mr. Wedgewood then asked if it would not be best if the rebate system were ended as soon as possible, but Mr. Churchill refused to give an answer as it concerned policy.'[3]

Lords, the Board of Trade, the Public Record Office and the Colonial Office without success

[1] R.C.S.R. Vol. I, 'The Report'.

[2] *Liverpool Daily Post*, 24 May 1907, 'West African Freights'.

[3] Houses of Parliament: Notices of Motions and Orders of the Day, Thursday 19 July 1906, Question 57.

Jones feared press criticism and would go to great lengths to prevent hostile comment. He was remarkably successful, in fact, in presenting himself to the nation as a shrewd but honest shipowner whose chief desire and pleasure were to help the spread of the flag in West Africa. As a result few personal criticisms of Jones were ever printed and those that were seem to have been largely discounted by their readers. In part, this was due to his genuine efforts to meet complaints—especially when they did not conflict with his own vital interests. As he wrote in a letter to E. D. Morel, 'It is not in our interest to treat people badly.'[1]

Jones, however, did have one weak point in his public relations. The establishment of the Compagnie Belge Maritime du Congo had led to his appointment as honorary Consul for the Congo and this was to prove an embarrassment. Jones was, of course, obliged to maintain friendly relations with the Belgian government if he wished to continue to carry all their cargoes. Yet round the beginning of the twentieth century public opinion was being wakened to the way in which the Congo was being developed. King Leopold's desire for rubber at any price was being achieved at what was believed to be an appalling cost in misery, and the Congo Reform Association was formed in England to get matters altered. The secretary of this Association was E. D. Morel, who had worked for Elder Dempster from 1890 to 1900. Morel had left his employment under Jones to start a newspaper that was to deal exclusively with West Africa.[2] He started this venture with Jones's blessing and at one point the shipowner offered to lend him £1,000 to extend the business.[3] Thereafter their relationship deteriorated, particularly after Morel became interested in the Congo reform movement and his newspaper had failed. Morel subsequently led this agitation for many years and eventually became a Member of Parliament. His views on the Congo were shared by John Holt who gave him much encouragement, and a lengthy correspondence took place between Morel and Holt on the one hand, and Morel and Jones on the other.[4]

As Morel had worked for Elder Dempster he was well briefed on Jones's business in West Africa. He was consequently well able to decide when Jones was being strictly accurate and when he was white-

---

[1] E.M.P. Box F.8. Letter from Jones to Morel, 7 September 1901.
[2] E.M.P. Box F.8. Letter from Jones to Morel, 30 December 1907.
[3] E.M.P. Box F.8. Letter from Jones to Morel, 19 October 1902.
[4] The Morel Collection of Mss. is now kept at the London School of Economics.

washing events in the Congo. Some of their letters became quite heated as their opposing positions drove them apart. Yet as late as 1903 Jones was keeping on friendly terms and wrote to Morel '. . . I am glad to hear your book is selling well. Don't be hurt by anything Mr. Ellis Edwards or myself say, because we don't mean it . . .'[1]

It was at this time that Jones sent two representatives to the Congo to investigate Morel's charges. These were Mr John Henderson and Mrs French Sheldon. Henderson's mission was to '. . . write about the Congo from the Congo State part . . .'[2] while Mrs Sheldon was to see '. . . everything which is to the credit of the Congo .[3] This lady duly produced a report which showed Belgian activities in the Congo in a favourable light and it was when Morel refused to accept it as a true picture that he and Jones finally fell out. Jones then attempted to minimise the hardships of the natives in the public mind and to this end sought to influence the judgment of any missionaries returning from the Congo. These normally obtained much publicity for their exposures and so Jones was anxious to ensure that they were fully aware of the other side of the story.[4]

Thus Jones's power, though great, was not absolute. He could not afford to upset the merchants in case they combined against him, and he could not fix freight rates at too high a level in case he encouraged an interloper to enter the trade. The need to keep the tacit approval of the British and Colonial governments meant that he had to act in a reasonable manner at all times, and made sure that he did not alienate public opinion. This, in fact, was the ultimate factor in limiting his authority, because he knew that if he lost the respect and confidence of the general public its reaction could have caused Parliament to take action. And in that event the government always held the whip hand—for it could have ended his regulation of the West African carrying trade which was the basis of his position.

[1] E.M.P. Box F.8. Letter from Jones to Morel, 18 January 1903.
[2] E.M.P. Box F.8. Letter from Jones to Captain Tubbs, his Marine Superintendent at Banana, 10 June 1903.
[3] E.M.P. Box F.8. Letter from Jones to Tubbs, 3 October 1903.
[4] E.M.P. Box F.8-1. Letter from Holt to Morel, 29 November 1906.

Chapter 6

The Effects of the
Conference System

Sir Alfred Jones

Alfred Jones's success in promoting Elder Dempster's interests led almost inevitably to an enhancement of his own personal situation, and ultimately to a knighthood. When he gained control of Elder Dempster in 1884 the Company managed the British and African Steam Navigation Company, but had only a working arrangement with its principal competitor, the African Steam Ship Company. By 1890 Jones had secured the management of the latter firm and from that time onward the two British shipping firms worked as a single integrated unit under his leadership. This achievement, however, was not sufficient to satisfy his ambitions. It was possible, though highly unlikely, that at some future date one or other of these companies might wish to change its manager. To guard against this eventuality, and also to share in the prosperity he was striving to ensure, Jones decided to seek power within the two lines. By 1900 his efforts had begun to bear fruit.

In the case of the African Steam Ship Company Jones pursued a policy of systematically buying its shares when they came on to the market. At the turn of the century he owned sufficient stock to preclude the possibility of any change being made[1] and by the time of his death in 1909 he owned 26,328 of the Company's £20 ordinary shares.[2] (i.e. 75 per cent of the issued capital).

[1] Committee on the Currency of the West African Colonies, 1899, evidence of A. L. Jones, Q.1071.

[2] Elder Dempster & Co. Ltd, Formation Documents, Third Schedule. File 108502, p. 13. See Appendix, p. 455, Table 49.

Jones handled the British and African Steam Navigation Company in a different way. He made no attempt to buy their shares and from 1884 to 1900 his holdings in the Company were purely nominal.[1] Then in 1900 he bought the firm, complete with its fleet, for £800,000. Jones did not possess anything like this amount of cash, but Elder Dempster did own many ships, and he used these to give him the capital he required. His method of operation is very interesting, and well worth revealing. Acting through Elder Dempster he made an agreement to buy the British and African Steam Navigation Company Limited. He then set up a new concern, calling it the British and African Steam Navigation Company (1900) Limited and the new firm offered $4\frac{1}{2}$ per cent debentures to the public to the value of £800,000. As the book value of the fleet was certified at £1,438,300 by Messrs H. E. Moss and Company, and was aided by the association of Jones's name, the issue was quickly taken up.[2] This money was then used to buy out the shareholders in the original firm, and these were content to accept Jones's offer as the company provided only 5 per cent dividends.

Jones then made two agreements between Elder Dempster and the British and African Steam Navigation company (1900) Limited. These were dated 26 November and the 15 December 1900. Both provided for the transfer to the new company of ships owned by Elder Dempster. The first exchanged the steamships *Monmouth, Priam, Lake Megantic* and *Sangara* for 21,440 ordinary £10 shares in the new firm. The second exchanged the steamships *Montezuma, Montreal, Lake Erie, Lake Champlain* and *Montauk* for 41,560 ordinary £10 shares. These gave Jones a total of 63,000 ordinary shares and as only 63,276 were issued it meant that he had absolute control.[3] This position was then substantially maintained till Jones died in 1909, and, together with his holdings in the African Steam Ship Company, they assured his continued control of the West African carrying trade, besides being a very profitable manoeuvre.

In addition to the acquisition of the two main shipping companies engaged in the West African trade, Jones also bought many ships on behalf of Elder Dempster and Company. The first of these was purchased in 1887, and thereafter several ships a year were either built or

[1] See Appendix p. 429–30, Table 35, for details of Jones's holdings in the British & African.

[2] *Journal of Commerce*, 23 October 1900.

[3] See Appendix p. 431–2, Table 35, for list of shareholders in the British and African Steam Navigation Company (1900) Limited.

acquired from other firms. These ships were seldom kept for long and it would appear that Jones transferred them from Elder Dempster to the operating companies to suit his own convenience. A few were run directly by Elder Dempster but these formed only a small percentage of the total.[1] On 3 May 1899, Jones formed another company to look after his shipping interests. This was Elder Dempster Shipping Limited, and it was basically designed to obtain capital from the public. In this instance Jones floated the firm with a nominal capital of £1,000,000 made up of 100,000 ordinary shares of £10 each.[2] Then on 18 May 1899 he offered £600,000 of 4½ per cent debenture stock to the public. This was quickly taken up, but Jones did not allow any of the ordinary shares to be sold. Instead he made an agreement with the new firm and sold it seventeen ships—the late property of Elder Dempster and Company. These ships were then paid for by the £600,000 received for the debentures, plus 50,000 shares at £10 each, making a total of £1,100,000. Thus Jones in his capacity as senior partner of Elder Dempster and Company received the vast bulk of the money for the sale of their ships, and in addition received the entire ordinary share issue of the new firm.[3] The ships continued to work for Elder Dempster and Company as before, so the net result of the exercise was a loan of £600,000 on advantageous terms.[4]

Elder Dempster Shipping Limited did much work on the North Atlantic routes, but its ships could and did go to West Africa, whilst other vessels under Jones's control were used on the Atlantic run at times.[5] Jones's control of the West African carrying trade provided employment for the vast majority of Elder Dempster ships irrespective of their flag. His activities on the North Atlantic and in the West Indies were at all times subsidiary to his main interests, but he tried to use his vessels to best advantage no matter what part of the fleet they represented. Thus, when the opportunity presented itself he inaugurated a service to New Orleans for the cotton trade, and vessels from all his

[1] See Appendix p. 405, Table 11.
[2] See Appendix pp. 446–8, Tables 45 and 46. for details of the capital structure of Elder Dempster Shipping Limited.
[3] Until 1904 all the ordinary shares of the company were held by Jones. Their distribution was then widened, but until 1909 Jones maintained his controlling interest. See Appendix p. 448, Table 46.
[4] For full details see File 61912 (dissolved) Public Record Office, London.
[5] See Appendix, Table 84, p. 481.

associated companies partook in this activity as he did not consider it necessary to establish a separate line. A similar situation existed in the Canadian service before the Beaver Line was acquired in 1898.[1] This demonstrates the flexibility which was an important feature of Elder Dempster's success but, of course, the basic reason for its continued expansion rested on the growth of West African trade[2] and the increase in its services to the Coast:

Expansion of Elder Dempster Services to West Africa[3]

Route	1895	1904
Liverpool to West Africa	Every Saturday and alternate Wednesday	Every Saturday, Wednesday and alternate Thursdays
Liverpool to South-West Africa	Every four weeks	Fortnightly
London to West Africa	—	Monthly
Hamburg to West Africa	Every ten days	Three times a month
Rotterdam to West Africa	Every ten days	Three times a month
Hamburg to South-West Africa	Every month	—
Antwerp to South-West Africa	Every month	Operated by the C.M.B.
Hamburg to Lagos (Direct)	—	Three weekly

A measure of Elder Dempster's increasing activity is in the size of its fleet, which more than doubled between 1895, when the West African Conference was established, and 1909, when Jones died.[4] During this period the number of vessels owned or managed which had no connection with the West African trade also rose considerably.[5] Furthermore, Elder Dempster owned shares in Elder and Fyffes Limited, which in turn owned stock in Elder and Fyffes (Shipping) Limited.[6] Both of these companies operated vessels during this period, but they are not included as they were not managed by Elder Dempster. Conversely, the fleet of the Ocean Transport Company Limited, which was wholly owned by Harland and Wolff, Limited is included as Elder Dempster managed them at this time.

The financing of the Elder Dempster fleet expansion must next be examined. As previously noted Elder Dempster Shipping Limited was floated in 1899 and obtained £600,000 by the issue of debentures. The

[1] See above, Chapter 5, p. 128.   [2] See Appendix p. 397, Table 1.
[3] E.D.P. Pamphlets issued by Elder Dempster and Company in October 1895, and April 1904.
[4] See Appendix p. 405, Table 11.   [5] See Appendix p. 405, Table 12.
[6] See Appendix pp. 439–441 and 444–5, Tables 42 and 44.

reorganisation of the British and African Steam Navigation Company in 1900 resulted in the issue of a further £800,000's worth of debentures and in 1902 the Imperial Direct Line issued £250,000 of debentures. These were real additions to the capital stock of the group, but against this must be placed the reduction of the African Steam Ship Company's issued debentures from £212,786 in 1895 to £154,030 in 1909. The ordinary share issue of the British and African—39,000 at £10 in 1895—was increased to 63,276 at £10 and remained at this figure until 1909. The African Steam Ship Company had an issue of 33,731 ordinary shares at £16 in 1896. It was not altered until 1908 when £4 per shares was called up, raising the issued capital from £539,696 to £674,620.[1] Elder Dempster Shipping Limited issued 50,000 £10 shares when it was formed in 1899 and the Imperial Direct West India Mail Service Company Limited issued 25,000 £10 shares when it was formed in 1901. As Alfred Jones retained the whole of both these issues it is doubtful whether this indicated more than a redistribution of existing assets. This was also the case when the British and African ordinary share issue was increased at the time of the reorganisation of this company in 1900.

Elder Dempster and Company, being a private firm—or partnership —provided no information about its financial situation until it acquired 'limited' status in 1910. Before then it is clear that it acted almost entirely as a kind of holding company for Alfred Jones's interests, but it did have the function of providing the initial capital for new ventures. Thus Elder Dempster and Company financed the establishment of the Compagnie Maritime Belge and the purchase of the Beaver Line, and helped the formation of Elder and Fyffes Limited. It also financed the purchase of many new ships, most of which were subsequently transferred to other members of the group, but a small number were retained in the Company's own name. Of more importance, however, was the backing which Elder Dempster provided for whatever enterprises Alfred Jones decided to support.

Precise details of sources and amounts of income are not available, but it is certain that most was derived from holdings in the other firms in the group rather than from its own activities. Elder Dempster's managerial functions were self-financing, each line under its auspices paying *pro rata* for the services it received, so that administration was

[1] A.S.P. Directors Report for the year ending December 1907, p. 6. The effect of this was less than indicated as many shareholders had already paid in advance of the call.

not a large expense. It is true that Jones lived well while senior partner, but his mode of living could hardly be described as either wasteful or extravagant and his companies paid only moderate dividends and interest to their shareholders and debenture holders.[1] In the absence of large outgoings most income was perforce retained by Elder Dempster and was available to be ploughed back as required. It should also be remembered that the Company always had in its possession large sums of deferred rebate which were being replenished as quickly as they were being repaid. In these circumstances any attempt to estimate the true profitability of the concern can only be meaningful if the assets are calculated at two points in time and the new accretion will represent the gain. If we take as our starting point 1884 when Jones became senior partner and 1909, when Jones died, as our finish, then it will be seen that he transformed the value of the firm from, at most, £50,000[2] to such an extent that when the new limited company took over it required a capital of £1,910,000.[3] Such a measure is by its nature an arbitrary and general one, but in the present context it would appear to be of value in confirming not only that large profits were made, but also that they were retained in the business.

The Sources of Profit

Jones's control of the West African shipping trade did not of itself guarantee large profits. The tariff freight rates were a little higher than those charged for comparable voyages to other areas but, taking into account the difficulties of the route, they were not altogether unjust. The items on which large sums were made, in fact, were silver, coal and cement, and the carriage of any unclassified goods.

As previously noted, the profits made by the Bank of British West

[1] A typical example of this is provided by the African Steam Ship Company which paid an average dividend of 4.3 per cent in the period 1890 to 1899, and an average 4.8 per cent in the years from 1900 to 1909. During the two decades debenture payments tended to fall from an average of 5 per cent to an average of 4 per cent; this no doubt reflecting the security engendered by the working of the conference system.

For a comparison with other investments available at this time see: R. J. Irving, 'British Railway Investment and Innovation, 1900–1914', *Business History*, Vol. XIII, No. I (January 1971), pp. 52–3.

[2] This is the author's outside estimate of the value of goodwill, agency agreements and physical assets of Elder Dempster and Company in 1884.

[3] Elder Dempster and Co. Ltd, File 108502, dissolved at Company House, London. See below Chapter 7, p. 172.

Africa were partly due to its position as sole importer of freshly minted silver coin,[1] although it is certain that it also earned substantial sums from normal banking activities. Coal was rather a different case, for shipowners traditionally regarded it as a cargo that could be utilised to fill any empty spaces. They considered it was far better to carry coal at very low prices than to carry nothing and, in addition, it formed a useful ballast if the ship was light. There was no demand for coal in West Africa from the local inhabitants but stocks were needed by the government for the railways, and the mining companies also required large amounts. When the rebate system was introduced the Crown Agents asked Elder Dempster if they could import coal in chartered vessels without losing their rebate. Elder Dempster refused to allow this and so the Crown Agents suggested that the colonial governments should ask locally for tenders for the supply of coal. When this was done Elder Dempster took up the contract.[2]

From 1895 to 1905 Elder Dempster supplied nearly all the coal required in British West Africa.[3] The fact that the tenders were advertised only on the Coast and not in Britain helped Jones to keep the monopoly, but the basis for his power lay in the high freight rate which was charged to carry coal out from home. All tenders included provision for this charge, but when Elder Dempster supplied the coal it could charge itself just enough to cover the true cost of carriage. In effect, this ensured that merchants or colliery owners could not compete.

The high price of coal in Lagos led eventually to the governor, Sir William Macgregor, asking for a tender to be published in England.[4] This asked for 15,000 tons of coal to be delivered in Lagos, and at that time the current price was 45s per ton. Miller Brothers then tendered at 35s per ton, and intended to get round the rebate problem by getting the colliery owners to supply directly to West Africa with the aid of chartered steamships. Unfortunately for Millers their bid became known to Elder Dempster who then bid 32s 6d per ton. Later an officer was discharged from the telegraph office, but by then Elder Dempster had

---

[1] See above, Chapter 5, pp. 119.

[2] R.C.S.R. Evidence of Sir Ernest Blake, Q.10793.

[3] Elder's Navigation Collieries Limited produced approximately 250,000 tons of coal per year—the balance was obtained from the market. See 'Ocean Highways' (An illustrated souvenir of Elder Dempster and Company) Published by the *Shipping Gazette & Lloyds List* (Liverpool, 1902), pp. 58–64.

[4] R.C.S.R. Evidence of John Holt, Q.5541 and *Journal of Commerce*, 3 June 1907.

secured the contract.[1] The fact that Elder Dempster found it worth their while to supply coal at 12s 6d per ton below their original figure shows the tremendous profit previously enjoyed by them. In this particular case their profit was reduced by £8,000 (15,000 × 12s 6d) yet they were still able to complete a worthwhile deal.[2]

Elder Dempster's right to fill their ships with coal (or cement) when cargo was short was strongly disputed by John Holt:

> *Mr. J. Barry:* 'I was thinking there might be cases a shipowner might legitimately fill up his hold by goods on ship's account or for himself?' 'He may fill it up, but if he does he fills it up at the expense of his shippers. That has been Sir Alfred Jones's plea to me over and over again— "I must fill my steamers". But he is constantly building bigger steamers, and so he has more and more space to occupy. I have pointed out to him over and over again: "You cannot do that without depriving your shippers of a similar amount of freight; you do not create any greater consumption because you put your stuff into your ship when she is empty".'[3]

Cement was another item which Jones supplied in bulk to the colonial governments of British West Africa.[4] John Holt was particularly bitter about this and maintained that before the deferred rebate system was introduced he was able to export cement to the coast.[5] A copy of Holt's evidence before the Royal Commission was sent to the Crown Agents for the Colonies who commented:

> 'The statements made by Mr. Holt in his evidence as to a monopoly in connection with the Burham brand of cement being established by the Crown Agents are without foundation. The statements refer apparently to some business arrangements between Messrs. Elder Dempster and Company and the Burham Company of which the Crown Agents have no knowledge. The Crown Agents have never in their contracts for cement specified any particular brand, but have always required the supply to conform to the requirements of their standard specification'.[6]

In the discussion which followed the reading of the above statement it became clear that Jones had secured the whole supply of Burham cement and this was the only make he was prepared to ship to West Africa. Consequently, when cement was purchased on the Coast it was

---

[1] R.C.S.R. Evidence of George Miller, Q.4328.
[2] Note Jones's activities as a coal mine owner: See above, Chapter 5, p. 125.
[3] R.C.S.R. Evidence of John Holt, Q.5260.
[4] C.O. 147/136. It was illegal for government departments to buy cement locally.
[5] R.C.S.R. Evidence of John Holt, Q.5043.
[6] R.C.S.R. Statement by Sir Ernest Blake, p. 380.

automatically Burham cement, and any supplied by the Crown Agents was also of the same make because it was the only brand available.[1] As a result of the publicity which the Royal Commission brought to shipping matters a change was made in the method of supplying cement, and this ended Elder Dempster's practice of supplying it to Lagos at a price which included cost, insurance and freight. It substituted instead a system whereby merchants could ship it themselves at the normal freight rate. Elder Dempster continued to stress, however, that the cement must be of the Burham brand.[2] The precise nature of the agreement which Jones had made with the cement ring has never been revealed, but it certainly gave him the exclusive right to the brand, and in return he guaranteed that only this would be shipped to West Africa. No doubt a commission was payable to Elder Dempster—the amount depending on the quantity sold—and in addition their shipping lines received the normal profit from carrying the cement.[3]

Apart from carrying coal and cement on ships' account, it was alleged by John Holt that Elder Dempster carried at special rates for the Sierra Leone Coaling Company, the Grand Canary Coaling Company, and other firms in which Jones had an interest:

'The shipowners, for example, or a trading firm in which they are interested, can sell cement at 9/- a barrel, whereas the ordinary merchant could not charge less than 10/6d. The Sierra Leone Trading Company, he said, can undersell merchants in all cheap goods such as iron pots or rice, on which the tariff rate is high in relation to the value of the goods, They cannot, however, do so in cases where, as in the case of cotton goods, the freight bears a very small proportion of the value.'[4]

Holt regarded this as proof that these firms received differential rates of freight, but Jones denied that this was the case. The essential point of these arguments about Jones's trading companies was that as Elder Dempster had a near monopoly of the carrying trade he had an unfair advantage over legitimate merchants. This was because he could always charge his own firms less freight than he charged their competitors, and hence they could have lower costs. Furthermore, it would be a simple matter for a man in Jones's situation to arrange for preferential treatment for cargoes in which he was financially interested. Conversely, he could

[1] R.C.S.R. Evidence of Sir Ernest Blake, Q. 10696.
[2] R.C.S.R. Evidence of John Holt, Q.5041.
[3] R.C.S.R. Vol. I, p. 70. Para 248–252.   [4] R.C.S.R. Vol. I, p. 70, Para 253.

delay the delivery of stocks to rival concerns at the most opportune moments. The evidence given before the Royal Commission on this point is inconclusive, and the Commission returned a verdict of 'not proven'. This would appear to be a correct interpretation of the matter. Jones undoubtedly did trade on occasion, but he was too clever to press it too far in case he forced the merchants to retaliate.

The freight rates charged by Elder Dempster were high, but do not seem to have been excessive in view of the difficulties of the trade. It was when goods had to be carried that were in some way out of the ordinary that special charges were levied. Such goods as petrol and dynamite were charged very heavy rates, and these could be arbitrarily increased at any time. Bulky items such as boats were also rated extremely highly, and were assessed individually at the time of shipment. There was no redress. The shipper had either to pay the freight or do without the goods.

An example of the way in which any unusual cargo was made to enhance Elder Dempster's profits was given to the Royal Commission by Sir Walter Egerton, the governor of Southern Nigeria. The government wished to ship two boilers of twenty tons each out to Lagos. The Crown Agents therefore approached Elder Dempster and were told the cost would be between £600 and £700. This fantastically high cost of over £15 per ton included transhipment at Forcados, but did not include a further charge of £10 per boiler for the branch-steamer to land them on the quay at Lagos. The vessel which took out these boilers also carried a normal cargo out to the Coast.[1] The following extract shows the charges made by Elder Dempster for other heavy cargo and makes it clear just how great was the rate for unclassified items:

Rates of Freight Outward—Liverpool or Hamburg to Lagos[2]
(1900 to 1906)

Iron	£1 12s 6d per ton
Timber	£1 12s 6d per ton
Machinery	£1 15s 0d per ton
Pipes	£1 15s 0d per ton
Brass Rods	£2 6s 0d per ton

The ordinary tariff rates charged by Elder Dempster also came in for some criticism. The rate for shipping salt to Lagos was 20s per ton, while

[1] R.C.S.R. Evidence of Sir Walter Egerton, Q.11430 & 11515.
[2] R.C.S.R. Evidence of John Holt, Q.4823, p. 3.

to America and Calcutta it was 4s 6d per ton; to South America it was 11s 3d and to Yokohama it was 15s per ton. Flour cost 7s 6d per ton to ship from New York to Liverpool, but from Liverpool to the Gold Coast it cost 35s per ton, although the distances were nearly the same. Timber cost 35s for 40 cubic feet from West Africa to the Mersey, while from the United States it cost only 20s for the same quantity. The rate for cotton from West Africa was ¼d per pound—the equivalent of 45s per ton—compared with the North American rate of 7s 6d per ton.

These very damaging comparisons can, however, be excused to some extent by the fact that few southbound cargoes to West Africa consisted of one exclusive item, whereas many of the cargoes to or from other areas were made up of a single commodity. Also, some goods such as salt were carried on many routes at a ballast rate on their outward journey, the ships carrying a good paying cargo on their homeward voyage. This argument has been frequently put forward in defence of high rates, but in the present instance it may be discounted to some extent by the attitude of Elder Dempster towards rubber and cocoa. Rubber cost 70s per ton and cocoa 50s per ton when both were being transported to Britain in very small quantities. These may then have been reasonable rates, but it was unjust to keep them at the same level once they had developed into major items of trade.

A more convincing explanation for higher rates was given to the Royal Commission by Sir Walter Egerton who was no lover of the conference lines:

Professor Gonner: 'With regard to the high level of the rates, do you think that there is anything in West Africa which tends to justify a higher level?'

'Yes, certainly'

'What?'

'The extreme unhealthiness and the difficulty of landing and shipping at many ports. I think it would be reasonable for West African freights to be probably 50% higher than for the same distance elsewhere'.

'When you speak of the great unhealthiness of the country, does that mean that they have to pay higher wages to the people engaged on board the ships?'

'They certainly have to pay more. A man who can command a certain salary in the American trade would want a great deal more to go into the West African trade'.

'I doubt if they get the men from the American trade?'

'No, they do not. I mean that a man who commands a certain salary on a healthier line would not accept a ship to West Africa unless he got more'.[1]

[1] R.C.S.R. Evidence of Sir Walter Egerton, Q.11647-50.

According to John Holt the effect of the deferred rebate system was not to make the normal tariff rates any higher, but it kept them at their previous peak and did not permit of any reductions which normal competition would have ensured.[1] In fact a few reductions did take place from time to time. These included timber (from 35s to 25s per 40 cubic feet), ground-nuts (50s to 40s per ton) and ginger (from 45s to 35s per ton). These items formed only a small percentage of the total traffic, and there is no doubt that normal profits were made from the carriage of goods at the tariff rates. This does not invalidate the theory of Sir Walter Egerton that expenses were greater in West Africa than in other places. It means that as Elder Dempster were a highly efficient organisation the slightly higher tariff in the West African trade was sufficient to compensate for the extra expenses.

The effect of this efficiency was apparent to many travellers to West Africa, who praised Elder Dempster for the greatly improved standard of their vessels. The Crown Agents noticed this particularly because the number of complaints from their passengers dropped considerably after the deferred rebate system had been adopted.[2] In fact, the Crown Agents thought that the ships might be too good for their purpose. John Holt also thought that the vessels were too fine for the trade, and stated that in his view this was a direct result of the monopoly profits enjoyed by the shipowners.[3] Sir Walter Egerton agreed that the class of vessel had been greatly improved but thought that this was because of the increase in the number of passengers, the volume of freight and the competition of the Woermann Line.[4]

In the main it was only the larger merchants who were dissatisfied with the conference system. This was because the deferred rebate prevented them from chartering outside steamships and at certain times of the season this facility would have been of advantage to them.[5] They were permitted to charter a complete ship from any of the firms within the conference, but the charge for this was appreciably above the open market rate. On the other hand the smaller merchants welcomed the conference. It secured for them the advantage of equal opportunities

[1] R.C.S.R. Evidence of John Holt, Q.5125 and 5354.
[2] R.C.S.R. Evidence of Sir Ernest Blake. Q.10952.
[3] R.C.S.R. Evidence of John Holt, Q.5109.
[4] R.C.S.R. Minutes. Section 7, p. 199. Letter from Sir Walter Egerton to the Colonial Office, 31 March 1907.
[5] R.C.S.R. Evidence of J. H. Batty, Q.6753.

with the larger traders, because all shippers were charged—at least nominally—the tariff rate. This had also been the case before the conference was established but, in fact, there had been many instances of the more important firms receiving preferential rates. Even under the rebate system there were still many allegations of favouritism, but either there was much less manipulation of rates, or it was better concealed.

The smaller traders did not feel the disadvantage of not being able to charter, because they did not have enough goods or produce to make it viable. Holt maintained that even without the conference the little firm would still be able to compete, because the West African trade had few aspects to which economies of scale could be applied.[1] This view was opposed by both J. H. Hutton and G. B. Zochonis who stated that regular sailings were of greater importance than the level of freight rates, and these had been made possible by the adoption of the rebate system. They were sure that the small man was enormously assisted by the fact that tariff rates were applied equally to all merchants, and they thought the freight charges were not unreasonable. They also believed that the impartiality of the Bank of British West Africa was of much significance to the smaller traders.[2]

One type of firm trading to West Africa found the deferred rebate system to be very much in their interest. These were the commission agents who sent goods out to the coast in response to specific orders. Many of these catered for African buyers who normally sent a remittance to cover the cost, the freight and the agency fee of $2\frac{1}{2}$ per cent. After the agents had sent the goods they seldom ever heard from the African merchant again. This was because the African companies were in a fluid state of development, and so their business associations were quickly formed and dissolved. It would, therefore, have been difficult in many cases to have returned the rebate but the problem seldom, if ever, arose and the agents were quite prepared to pocket the money when it was returned by the shipping lines.[3] Thus these firms has a great incentive to see the system perpetuated. Apart from their African clients many of their customers were foreign merchants or people without contacts in England. These were unlikely to be able to understand the complicated

[1] R.C.S.R. Evidence of John Holt, Q.5312.
[2] R.C.S.R. Evidence of J. H. Hutton and G. B. Zochonis, Q.13260.
[3] R.C.S.R. Evidence of J. H. Batty, Q.6893.

procedure for obtaining a refund of 10 per cent of the freight charge they had paid twelve months earlier, unless it was specially explained to them.[1] The commission agents, of course, took great care to keep the matter dark and their success can be judged by the following letter written by the Secretary of the Kissy Road Traders Association of Freetown:

'I have to acknowledge the receipt of your letter No. 1639/919/1907, enquiring whether the small traders of this colony received rebate on their shipping charges for goods shipped by any of the line of steamers that call at this port. I have the honour to respectfully inform you, for His Excellency the Governor's information, that after due enquiry, I find that not one of the native traders ever received rebate from any shipping companies, not even such large importers as J. H. Thomas, Esq., Messrs. T. C. Bishop, F. A. Noah and J. Galba Bright, etc. etc.'[2]

The Growth of the Woermann Line

To some extent Elder Dempster's success was only gained by allowing the Woermann Line of Hamburg to grow under the aegis of the West African Conference. The rapid expansion of the German company was the price which Jones had to pay for its co-operation but had he tried to exclude it, it is unlikely that he would have succeeded. Woermann had the advantage of a steady trade with the German colonies on the Coast, and many of the trade goods used by the British merchants were obtained from German sources or via German ports. Apart from this, West African produce found a ready sale in Hamburg, from where it was distributed to many parts of the Continent. This was especially true of palm kernels, for three-quarters of the amount exported from British West Africa were crushed in Germany.[3] In this case the early start enjoyed by the German firm of Gaisers was an important factor, but the decisive influence was the lack of demand in England for cattle cake made from the residue of the crushed kernels. This enabled the German firms to undercut their British rivals, so that little of this commodity came to Britain until after the outbreak of the First World War.[4] Thus even if Elder Dempster had been prepared to face a serious struggle with Woermann it would have been difficult to have won a final victory.

[1] R.C.S.R., Evidence of John Holt, Q.5178.
[2] R.C.S.R., Appendices Part II, pp. 197–8.
[3] Report of the Committee on Edible and Oil Producing Nuts and Seeds (Hereinafter referred to as E.&O.P.N.&S.C.) (H.M.S.O., 1916), CD. 8248, Table 1, p. 5.
[4] See below, Chapter 8, pp. 197.

The economic advantages of a German-based firm were such that if Woermann could have been defeated, a new competitor would soon have arisen.

John Holt was convinced, however, that the setting up of the conference was a prime factor in the rapid growth of the Woermann Line and submitted the following table to the Royal Commission:

Growth of British and German Shipping Firms Engaged
In the West African Trade[1]

	1892–3	1906–7
Woermann Line:	13 steamships of 15,741 tons	47 steamships of 71,957 tons
British & African S.N.Co. & The African S.S.Co.:	50 steamships of 67,125 tons	61 steamships of 97,646 tons

This table, although correct in so far as it goes, is misleading. Lloyd's Register of Shipping for 1896 shows that Woermann then had a fleet of fourteen steamships totalling 15,709 net tons. The African Steam Ship Company (50,315) and the British and African (29,304) then had a combined fleet of 79,619 net tons. Lloyd's Register for 1906 shows that by then Woermann had indeed increased their tonnage to 71,966 net tons while the combined African, and British and African, fleet had risen to only 95,631 net tons—substantially as recorded by John Holt. From our previous examination of the expansion of the Elder Dempster fleet it is clear that while the African and British and African tonnage may only have increased at a moderate rate, the other fleets they controlled rose substantially.[2] Thus the total tonnage of the Elder Dempster fleets in 1896 was 89,380 net tons, but by 1906 it amounted to 164,843 net tons and it is this figure which ought, more properly, to be compared with that of the Woermann fleet.[3]

It can be argued, of course, that a proportion of the Elder Dempster fleet was not always employed in the West African trade. This is true, but while it is difficult to calculate even an approximate estimate of the tonnage employed on other routes, it is certain that it represented only a small percentage of the whole. It must also be remembered that the Woermann fleet likewise was not engaged exclusively on the West African run. In 1904, for example, it operated two main-line services—

[1] R.C.S.R.　　[2] See Appendix, p. 405, Table 11.
[3] See Appendix, p. 406, Table 13.

one to the west coast and the other to South West Africa.[1] Many of the vessels on the latter route may have deviated to West African ports but, as in the Elder Dempster case, the only certainty is that the whole tonnage was not employed entirely in the West African trade.

The situation became further complicated in 1907 when the Woermann Line made an agreement with the Hamburg America Line whereby the latter arranged to operate 25 per cent of the German services to Africa. In the same year the German East Africa Line joined in this joint operation, and in 1908 the Hamburg-Bremen Africa Line (after providing a brief opposition)[2] also agreed to provide a combined service to Africa. Thereafter all of the German shipping companies engaged in the African trade operated as a single smoothly functioning unit. The fleet of the Woermann Line continued to be shown in Lloyd's Register as a separate entity, but its vessels were liable to be used anywhere the combine dictated and other, non-Woermann ships, could be used on the West African route if necessary.

During the period from 1890 to 1914 Germany made a serious challenge to British maritime superiority and this was reflected in both the naval and mercantile spheres. The commercial effort was based on the through-rate system operated by the state-owned railways which provided a substantial secret subsidy.[3] This was supported by an arrangement amongst the shipowners which allocated routes to specific companies or groups, and did much to ensure that German lines competed against foreign companies rather than with one another. In these circumstances it was fortunate for the British lines engaged in the West African shipping trade that they were able to present a united front to the German threat, for without it Woermann may well have made even greater progress than he actually achieved. It would appear, therefore, that while the establishment of the West African Conference in 1895 did assist the development of the Woermann Line it also strengthened Elder Dempster and the British firms who were then in a much stronger position to resist German advances. Had the conference not been formed it seems probable that, in common with nearly all German shipping companies at this time, the Woermann Line would still have expanded at a great rate—perhaps even more rapidly than was actually the case.

[1] A Short History of the German Africa Lines. Published privately by the Deutsche Afrika-Linien, Hamburg, 1967.
[2] See above Chapter 5, pp. 132–3.
[3] H. Hausea, *Germany's Commercial Grip on the World* (London: Eveligh Nash, 1917).

The Development of British West Africa

The pace of the development of British West Africa during the second half of the nineteenth century was conditional on the overcoming of its geographical disadvantages. The invention of the steamship and the advance of medical science provided the technical means for doing this, but without large-scale investment, viable economic growth could not have taken place. This investment was encouraged by the rising demand for the products of West Africa, and the ever increasing need for the traditional exports such as palm oil and palm kernels was reinforced by the demand for the newer articles of trade such as cocoa, rubber and tin ore.[1] Yet the existing organisation on the Coast was just not capable of significantly increasing supplies of produce. This was not a matter of production, for the most important items, i.e. palm oil and kernels, were merely collected. The real problem lay in getting these products from the interior to places from where they could be shipped to Europe. This was primarily a transport difficulty but, of course, the provision of credit and the right financial atmosphere were almost as important.

The overcoming of the geographical disadvantages obviously required large amounts of capital. The merchant firms were relatively small and were engaged in intense competition with one another and so were in no position to make significant investments in the country. Even if the firms had possessed large financial reserves it is unlikely that they could have agreed how to employ them, for mutual suspicions and jealousies continuously prevented co-operative action even when it would have been most beneficial to all concerned. Such native firms of traders as existed tended to be small and usually enjoyed only a short life. Some leaders, such as Ja Ja, organised trade on a large scale but even their resources were tiny when compared with what was required and they were in any case constantly being eroded by petty wars and unnecessary expenses.

Like the trading firms, the British government was in no position to proceed with large-scale investment in West Africa because it felt that the British public would object to the expense. The local governments had originally been established to regulate the activities of the merchants and to end the slave trade. They maintained an extremely nominal authority over the seaboard and rivers, but the interior was scarcely

[1] See Appendix, p. 397, Table 1.

AFRICAN
STEAM SHIP COMPANY.

PRICES OF WINES, &c.
TO OFFICERS AND ENGINEERS.

	Quart.		Pint.	
	s.	d.	s.	d.
PORT	3	6	1	9
SHERRY	3	6	1	9
HOCK	4	6	.	..
MOSELLE	5	0	2	6
CLARET	4	0	2	0
CHAMPAGNE	4	6	2	3
BRANDY	4	0	2	0
GENEVA	1	6	.	..
WHISKEY	1	6	.	..
GIN	1	6	.	..
SELTZER WATER, per Bottle	.	..	0	6
SODA WATER, do. .	.	..	0	6
LEMONADE, do. .	.	..	0	6
PALE ALE	0	9	.	..
LONDON PORTER . . .	0	9	.	..

CIGARS . . Os. 3d. each.

TOBACCO . . 2s. 6d. per lb.

By order of the Board of Directors,

14, LEADENHALL STREET, LONDON,   DUNCAN CAMPBELL, Sec.
29th November, 1866.

PLATE 9   A.S.S. Co. Prices of Wines . . . 1866.

British and African Steam Navigation Company.

Under Contract with the Postmaster-General for the Conveyance of Her Majesty's Mails between Liverpool and the West Coast of Africa.

The Steamers will be despatched from Liverpool to West Coast ports, as far as Old Calabar, every alternate Saturday. Those of 14th February and 11th April will proceed as far South as St. Paul de Loanda, after which it is intended to sail the South Coast Steamers as a separate Line, to leave Liverpool on the 15th of every alternate month.

RATES OF PASSAGE MONEY.

	1st Class.	2nd Class.		1st Class.	2nd Class.
Madeira	£17 10 6	£13 5 0	Bonny	£40 10 6	£28 5 0
Teneriffe	19 10 6	14 5 0	Fernando Po	41 10 6	29 5 0
Bathurst	27 10 6	19 5 0	Old Calabar	41 10 6	30 5 0
Sierra Leone	28 10 6	20 5 0	Gaboon	43 10 6	31 5 0
Monrovia	31 10 6	21 5 0	Black Point	46 10 6	32 5 0
Cape Palmas	32 10 6	22 5 0	Landana	47 10 6	32 15 0
Half Jack	33 10 6	23 5 0	Congo	48 10 6	33 5 0
Cape Coast Castle	34 10 6	23 5 0	Ambrizette	50 10 6	35 5 0
Accra	35 10 6	24 5 0	Kinsembo	50 10 6	35 5 0
Jellah Coffee	36 10 6	25 5 0	Ambriz	50 10 6	35 5 0
Lagos	37 10 6	26 5 0	Loanda	50 10 6	35 5 0
Benin	38 10 6	27 5 0			

CONDITIONS AND REGULATIONS.

Children of Passengers, under twelve years of age, half-fare; under eight years of age, quarter-fare, but not entitled to separate berths. One child of a family under three years carried free.

Passengers' Male Servants to pay Second Cabin Rate.

Female Servants two-thirds of Chief Cabin Rates.

In cases where Chief Cabin Passengers are obliged to have beds made up for them in the Saloon, a deduction of one-fifth of the rates will be made.

To secure a berth, a deposit of Half Passage Money must be made, the balance to be paid before embarkation.

These rates include Provisions and the use of Bedding and Linen, but without Wines, Spirits, Malt Liquors, &c., which will be supplied on board at moderate prices.

Each Chief Cabin Adult Passenger is allowed to carry luggage free of charge to the extent of twenty cubic feet, and Second Cabin Passengers ten cubic feet; Children and Servants in proportion. All extra luggage to be charged freight at the Fine Goods rate.

No Ladies travelling alone can be taken in the Second Cabin.

Passengers will embark by Steam Tender from the Prince's Landing Stage on the day of sailing, but heavy luggage must be sent to the loading berth two days before.

Homeward-bound Passengers to pay their Passage Money to the Captain or Purser on board.

Passengers not embarking after engaging a berth to forfeit Half Passage Money.

Merchandise, Specie, Bullion, Jewellery, or other Treasure cannot be carried as luggage, but must be shipped as cargo, paying the established rate of freight.

The attention of Passengers by the Company's Steamers is requested to the Conditions endorsed on their Passage Ticket; and particularly to the necessity of causing their Luggage to be distinctly marked with the Owner's Name and Port of Destination, in PAINT; and the word "Wanted" to be on all Packages to which they may wish to have access during the voyage. The attention of Passengers is also specially directed to the following clause in the Merchant Shipping Act, 1854, sec. 329, relative to articles of a dangerous or damaging character: "No person shall be entitled to carry in any ship, or to require the master or owner of any ship to carry therein, any aquafortis, oil of vitriol, gunpowder, or any other goods which, in the judgment of such master or owner, are of a dangerous nature; and if any person carries or sends by any ship any goods of a dangerous nature, without distinctly marking their nature on the outside of the package containing the same, or otherwise giving notice in writing to the master or owner, at or before the time of carrying or sending the same to be shipped, he shall for every such offence incur a penalty not exceeding £100; and the master or owner of any ship may refuse to take on board any parcel that he suspects to contain goods of a dangerous nature, and may require them to be opened to ascertain the fact.

Passengers must bear the risk of quarantine, and if they cannot, in consequence, be landed on the vessel's arrival at the port booked for, they must pay 10s. per day for victualling for such further time they may have to remain on board.

Passengers will only be received on board these Vessels on the express condition and agreement on their part that the Company are not liable for the detention or delay of Passengers, arising from accidents or from extraordinary or unavoidable circumstances, nor for any loss or damage arising from perils of the seas, or accidents from machinery, boilers, or steam; nor from any act, neglect, or default whatsoever of the pilot, master, or mariners.

For further information apply in London to MALCOLM HUTTON & Co., 5, Crosby Square; in Glasgow, to TAYLOR, LAUGHLAND & Co., 24, Oswald Street; and in Liverpool, to

PLATE 10   B. & A. Rates of Passage Money, c. 1870.

touched. Successive British governments regarded these colonies as an embarrassment and considered them to be more trouble than they were worth. The slow expansion of trade in the nineteenth century was speeded up when the steamship service was inaugurated in 1852, but the interest of the government did not keep pace with this development of the economy. In 1865 there were even suggestions that the British might withdraw altogether.[1] Then as trade became more and more extensive and profitable, the government began to appreciate the value of its West African connection, but it still did little to assist its merchants or to protect the valuable hinterland that lay behind its coastal settlements.

A third possible source of finance to develop the resources lay in the steamship companies. The co-operation between the British lines gave them stability which they would otherwise have lacked, and put them on a permanently profitable basis. This permitted them to borrow on very favourable terms and much of this money was ultimately invested in the extension of shipping services or in subsidiaries on the coast.[2] As we have seen, Jones used part of these funds to establish the Bank of British West Africa. This had the effect of putting both the currency and the control of credit on a sound footing, and had the extra advantage of being highly profitable, owing to its monopoly of the importation of new silver coin from the Mint. Jones also organised the boating companies on the coastline and a system of branch-line steamers that channelled the produce to his deep-sea vessels. He also created numerous companies to help in the development of the Coast itself, and was a constant agitator for the building of railways. These usually provided highly profitable cargoes but in the case of the Southern Nigerian Railway, at least, he was prepared to ship at cost in order to get the line completed.[3]

Jones's activities gave a strong impetus to trade. This gave the colonial governments a larger revenue and allowed them to take stronger action against foreign penetration, besides enhancing their value in the eyes of the imperial government. This was of immense importance because of the growing interest being shown in the coast by other European nations. The extent of this interest was demonstrated in 1884 when a meeting was held in Berlin by the principal colonial powers. The aspirations of France, Germany, Belgium and Portugal were then made abundantly

[1] *Parliamentary Papers* V. 1865 (Adderley's Committee).
[2] See above, this Chapter, pp. 145–8.   [3] See above, Chapter 5, p. 136.

clear to the British government and faced it with a difficult dilemma. It wished to protect its interests now that they were promising a useful return, but it did not believe that public opinion was prepared for it to assume what would be considered fresh liabilities and expenses. Accordingly it adopted the expediant of chartering the Royal Niger Company which was given the right to administer the upper reaches of the Niger basin in return for a virtual monopoly of trade in that region.

The threat of foreign intervention also reacted on the other British settlements on the coast. They were gradually revitalised and their areas enlarged—the process being accelerated as time went on. More funds were made available, larger staffs were employed, and many new services were introduced. These took the form of medical,[1] educational and welfare activities, while trade was encouraged by the beginnings of harbour, road and rail construction and by the increased security of the interior. The increased activity within West Africa then reacted favourably on the profits of Elder Dempster's subsidiary firms. The more activity, the greater was the need for coal and cement, and both these commodities were extensively supplied by Jones. The increased tempo also meant extra work for the Elder Dempster fleet in the form of additional cargo and passengers. Government agencies were then largely instrumental in promoting the growth of new crops such as cocoa, and this too helped to fill the ships of the conference members. Jones was personally responsible (at some cost to himself) for the expansion of cotton growing, but eventually his vessels benefited from the

---

[1] In 1898 Joseph Chamberlain, then Colonial Secretary, began a correspondence with the General Medical Council which was to lead to the formation of the London School of Tropical Medicine. An unexpected side-effect was the establishment of a similar institution at Liverpool. This was mainly due to the efforts of Sir Alfred Jones who started the project with an offer of £350 p.a. for three years and who, over a twelve-year period, was able to secure some £120,000 from the business community. Largely because of Jones' insistence, Major (later Sir) Ronald Ross was appointed to lead the new school. At this time Ross's work on mosquito-borne diseases was not universally recognised—he did not receive the Novel prize until 1902—so many people were doubtful of his capabilities. However, within a few months of coming to Liverpool he organised the first of a series of expeditions to West Africa which were to play a vital role in the reduction of malaria and other diseases. The provision of free passages by Elder Dempster, and the assistance given by many firms of merchants on the Coast were, of course, important factors in the success of these expeditions. A. H. Milne, in his *Sir Alfred Lewis Jones, K.C.M.G.* (Liverpool: Henry Young, 1914), tends to exaggerate Jones' role in the formation and development of the School but Ronald Ross in his *Memoirs* (London: John Murray, 1923) may not give it the importance it deserves.

additional cargo. Then, as the railways were completed, they not only only brought new areas of traditional produce into closer touch with the Coast, but also made possible the production of new items for export. Typical of the latter were tin ore and gold, and later—after Jones's death—coal.

In turn, the quickened pace of economic development and of government activity had decisive effects on the lives of the native population. When commerce began the African's only requirements were beads, mirrors, knives and other 'trade goods'.[1] During the eighteenth century and most of the nineteenth the staple imports into West Africa consisted of spirits, guns and cloth, but as the standard of living rose in response to the intensified activity, the demands became more varied. This was particularly true in the 1890s when the use of coins became more widespread—partly because of the railway construction and partly owing to the demand for taxes to be paid in cash. Thus the natives became accustomed to the handling of money and became more discriminating in their purchases. They tended to imitate the tastes of the European merchants and civil servants who resided in their country, and this practice gradually spread downwards so that in the towns, at least, the local inhabitants acquired the trappings of western civilisation. So far as the shipping companies were concerned this was a welcome trend. Not only did the increased imports help to fill their ships, but also the natives themselves began to form a valuable proportion of their passengers.[2] In addition, with the spread in the growing of cocoa and other cash crops, the local population was unable to produce sufficient food to feed itself and so large imports of food took place, and again Elder Dempster benefited from the increased shipments.

Thus the investments made by Elder Dempster and the shipping companies had a most important effect on the economic development of British West Africa. By 'priming the pump' they increased the tempo

[1] For a good description of these see Mary Kingsley's *West African Studies* (London: 1899), Appendix III.

[2] *Elder Dempster Circular* (Sent to all Captains). 'We are particularly anxious that every consideration should be shown to natives travelling by our vessels. There is no question whatever in making these natives travel more frequently and that making them more comfortable is of great importance to West Africa and the shipping interests. We trust you will go out of your way when an opportunity occurs to make these natives happy on board our ships . . .' This circular was reproduced in the *Sierra Leone Weekly News* dated 22 November 1902, and in its editorial comment it was stated with obvious satisfaction that Elder Dempster refused to consider any form of colour bar.

of change and accelerated a process which, since the ending of the slave trade, had been very gradually expanding the growth of legitimate business. If Elder Dempster had not initiated these investments, development might not have been stifled but it would certainly have been retarded, and this could have had important political, as well as economic, effects on the future of these colonies. Once the French and German governments had decided on a policy of expansion it required very vigorous action if Britain's possessions were not to become merely isolated settlements on the West African seaboard. If these colonies had not promised an adequate return in the future—and without the investment instigated by Alfred Jones they might not have done so—it is problematical is such a great effort would have been made.

This point of view, however, may be criticised on two counts. Firstly, although steamship services were provided in 1852 it was not until 1879 that Alfred Jones became associated with Elder Dempster. It was not until after this date that the shipping companies became prosperous enough to have any significant impact on the growth of the economy, and this was only five years before the British government had to make its crucial decision at Berlin. If, therefore, we take the view that Elder Demptser's activities were sufficient to influence the policy of the government, we may have to add the rider that it was the way in which they were organising matters—their potential, in fact—rather than what they had actually achieved, that was important.

Secondly, it can be argued that in spite of its reluctance to accept new colonial responsibilities the British government could not have stood by and allowed other nations to develop the West African hinterland.[1] If this be true the government would have acted on political grounds without the need for economic justification and then the work of Alfred Jones and Elder Dempster cannot be regarded as the prime factor in securing West Africa for the British Empire. Yet even if this suggestion is accepted it in no way invalidates the proposition that, without the services and investment provided by the Elder Dempster shipping companies, serious West African economic development

[1] R. E. Robinson and J. Gallagher with Alice Denny's *Africa and the Victorians*, published by Macmillan in 1961, discusses Britain's failure to establish formal colonies in West Africa and suggests a theory as to why this policy changed in the 1880s. For a well-balanced criticism of this work see, A. G. Hopkins, 'Economic Imperialism in West Africa: Lagos 1880-1892', *Economic History Review*, Vol. XXI, No. III (December 1968).

would have begun much later and would have been far slower in gathering momentum.

On any comparison, British West Africa made great economic advances between 1852 and 1910. Some progress would naturally be expected, but the absence of any substantial government support and the lack of large merchanting firms—when compared with the size of the area—plus the relative poverty of the region, left only the shipping lines to provide sufficient capital resources. With a competitive system of shipping, profits would have been lower and the service provided would have been more irregular and inadequate. It is unlikely that dividends would have been very different from those actually paid, owing to the need to attract fresh capital, but the decline in retained profits would undoubtedly have slowed down the rate of investment and hence the development of West Africa. The theoretical criticism of monopoly is a valid one in that it objects to the consumer paying an extra and unnecessary increment of profit. Elder Dempster's 'monopoly' gains, however, meant in practical terms that the inhabitants of the area were making an involuntary investment in the expansion of their own trade, on which any hopes for the future must ultimately rest. This investment, whether in West Africa itself, or in ships, or in England, facilitated the trade and was a powerful leavening influence and stimulated both government and private sources of additional funds.

PART THREE

Elder Dempster and Company Limited

Chapter 7

Lord Kylsant

The Formation of Elder Dempster and Company Limited
Alfred Jones's success in organising the West African trade ought not to
detract from the achievements of other British shipowners. Sir Donald
Currie (Union Castle Line) Sir John Ellerman (Ellerman, Hall, City,
Leyland and Bucknall Lines) Alfred Holt (Blue Funnel Line) and Lord
Inchcape (Peninsular and Oriental) are but a few of the more pro-
minent names which spring to mind. One of the younger members of
this eminent group was Owen Cosby Philipps, better known as Lord
Kylsant, who was to play a decisive part in the history of Elder
Dempster.[1]

Philipps was born at Warminster in 1863[2] and served an apprenticeship with a shipowning and broking concern at Newcastle-upon-Tyne.
He moved to Glasgow in 1886 and the following-year, at the age of
twenty-five he founded his own firm, Philipps, Philipps and Company
and established the King Line. In 1897 Philipps formed the London
Maritime Investment Company and in 1898 became chairman of London
and Thameshaven Oil Wharves Limited. In January 1903, Philipps became a director of the Royal Mail Steam Packet Company and within
three months had become its chairman.[3] This action cemented the close
relationship that already existed between the Royal Mail and the Pacific

[1] P. N. Davies and A. M. Bourn, 'Lord Kylsant and the Royal Mail', *Business History*,
Vol. XIV, No. II (July 1972), pp. 103–123.

[2] Sir James Erasmus Philipps, the twelfth baronet, was Vicar of Warminster and later
became Prebendary of Salisbury Cathedral. Owen Philipps was the third of his six sons
being the younger brother of Sir John Wynford Phillips (later the first Viscount St
Davids) and Major-General Sir Ivor Philipps. *Source*: D.N.B. 1931–1940. pp. 696–7.

[3] The Royal Mail Steam Packet Company had already enjoyed a long and distinguished
history. See T. A. Bushell, *Royal Mail* (London, 1939).

Steam Navigation Company, for Philipps had also secured a large interest in the latter concern.

The Royal Mail Group subsequently extended its interests still further.[1] It acquired the Shire Line in 1907 and the Forwood Line in 1908 and when Alfred Jones died in 1909 its attention was turned towards Elder Dempster. This was not the first contact between the two companies, for Philipps had crossed swords with Jones on several occasions. In 1905 the West Indian mail contract expired. The Royal Mail confidently expected to renew their long-standing agreement but, instead, the Colonial Office announced that a new contract had been provisionally granted to Elder Dempster and Company.[2] Philipps then used his influence with a number of the West Indian Legislatures to prevent the contract being confirmed, but it took him until 1907 to regain even a moderate subsidy for his own vessels.[3]

Philipps's success in business led to a demand that he enter Parliament and in 1906 he became Liberal member for Pembroke and Haverfordwest. Almost immediately he was invited to join the Royal Commission on Shipping Rings where he proved to be one of its more knowledgeable and searching members.[4] Philipps asked many pertinent questions when the West African trade was under discussion and it seems likely that the information he gained at this time greatly stimulated his interest in Elder Dempster. On the death of Jones on 13 December 1909, this interest quickly turned to action and within a few days Philipps had obtained an option to his estate.

In view of the sudden nature of Jones's fatal illness the speed with which the option was granted requires some explanation. The roots of this lie in the fact that Jones had drawn up his will in 1902, selecting as executors his solicitor (Mr Augustus Frederick Warr), his partner (Mr William John Davey) and his eldest niece's husband—Mr Owen Harrison Williams. As both Mr Davey and Mr Warr had predeceased Jones, the whole responsibility for the estate fell upon Mr Williams.

[1] Davies and Bourn, op. cit. The growth of the Royal Mail Group is shown in Table 1, p. 108.

[2] T. A. Bushell, op. cit., p. 188.

[3] Royal Mail Steam Packet Co., Directors report, 13 May 1905, pp. 9–11. A more detailed account of this is given in R. G. Greenhill, 'The State under Pressure—the West Indian Mail Contract 1905', Business History, Vol. XI, No. II (July 1969), pp. 120–127.

[4] The Royal Commission on Shipping Rings sat from 1906 to 1909. See above, Chapter 5, p. 140.

This was to prove a very heavy burden, for although Williams had been a director of the Bank of British West Africa since 1894 he had only a limited knowledge of the other aspects of Jones's commercial affairs. Williams's task as sole executor was to dispose of the estate in such a way as best to enable him to fulfill the provisions of the will,[1] and he was faced with several possible courses of action. These included the sale of the whole of the commercial side to a single buyer or its piecemeal disposal. The advantages of the former course are obvious, so when a favourable offer was made Williams decided to accept. This undoubtedy had the effect of lessening the executor's burden, but financially it was probably a mistake.[2]

The offer was made jointly by Sir Owen Philipps[3] and Lord Pirrie, the Chairman of Messrs Harland and Wolff Limited, the Belfast firm of shipbuilders.[4] It is not known precisely when their bid was made but it must have been very soon after the death of Jones, for other interested parties also acted quickly. The African Association, for example, wrote to the Niger Company on 28 December 1909,[5] suggesting that they join with the other members of the 'Niger Pool' to buy Jones's West African shipping interests.[6] This was quickly agreed to, and with the further support of the members of the 'Gold Coast Pool'[7] an approach was made to Mr Williams, but they were told that an option had already been granted. Lord Scarborough (of the Niger Company) subsequently met Lord Pirrie in the House of Lords and was asked to what extent he

[1] See Appendix, p. 449, Table 47.

[2] The minutes of the Royal Mail Steam Packet Company (hereinafter referred to as R.M.S.P. Minutes) Vol. XVI, p. 63, 23 February 1910, states that the new firm—Elder Dempster and Company, Limited—would take over the business at cost price without any additions whatsoever. This part of the Royal Mail Mss. is currently kept at the Head Office of Royal Mail Lines Limited in London.

[3] He was made Knight Commander of the Order of St Michael and St George in 1909.

[4] Lord Pirrie had been a director of the African Steam Ship Company since 1891, and had been its chairman since 1901. He also owned 7,000 of the 50,000 ordinary shares of Elder Dempster Shipping Limited, and 8,000 of the 63,276 ordinary shares of the British and African Steam Navigation Company (1900) Limited. As Messrs Harland and Wolff built a large number of vessels for the Elder Dempster group of companies each year this connection is not altogether surprising.

[5] R.N.C.P. S.95, Vol. VII, Transport. p. 363 et. seq.

[6] In addition to the Niger Company and the African Association the 'Niger Pool' also included Miller Brothers (of Liverpool) Limited, and the Company of African Merchants.

[7] The 'Gold Coast Pool' consisted of the African Association, Millers Limited and Messrs F. & A. Swanzy.

and his friends were interested. On being told of their limited interest, Pirrie suggested that, as he was in negotiation with the executors for the whole estate, it would be better if Lord Scarborough would leave the matter to him and he undertook to produce a scheme which would suit everyone. With this in mind, the 'Niger Pool' agreed to stand aside and Lord Pirrie and Sir Owen Philipps purchased the company. After a while, the Committee of Control of the Niger Pool thought that there was undue delay in Lord Pirrie's proposed scheme of division. They therefore pressed him for it, but when it was produced its terms were extremely unsatisfactory. The Committee at once protested and various meetings took place. Sir George Goldie acted as a go-between on several occasions, but little was accomplished and eventually the Committee of Control allowed the matter to drop.[1]

As a first step towards taking up their option, Philipps and Pirrie formed Elder Dempster and Company Limited on 31 March 1910. The new firm then issued 500,000 £1 cumulative preference shares, 400,000 £1 ordinary shares and 10,000 £1 management shares. With the addition of £1,000,000 5 per cent debenture stock this gave the new concern a capital of £1,910,000. A formal agreement was then entered into by Williams, Pirrie and Philipps, and this provided for the:

'Sale to the company of the business and goodwill of Elder Dempster and Company, The Grand Canary Coaling Company, The Tenerife Coaling Company and the Sierra Leone Coaling Company, and of the profits and assets mentioned in an agreement dated the 2nd of April, 1910.'[2]

This arrangement also provided for the following payments to be made to the estate of Alfred Jones. £200,000 was to be paid in cash, and this, together with £200,000 in debenture stock and £100,000 in cumulative preference shares, was to make up the total purchase price of £500,000.[3]

In return the new firm received many assets. These included land,

1 *History of the United Africa Company to 1938*, pp. 88 & 89. The only firm proposal was that the Royal Mail Steam Packet Company would give up a *pro rata* number of ordinary shares in Elder Dempster and Company Limited, if other ordinary shareholders were prepared to do likewise. See R.M.S.P. Minutes, Vol. XVI, p. 77, 4 April 1910.

2 Formation Documents of Elder Dempster and Company Limited. File No. 108502 (Dissolved) at Companies House, City Road, London.

3 A description of how Elder Dempster was fitted into the financial structure of the Royal Mail Group is given in Chapter 10, pp. 251–4. See also: Davies and Bourn, op. cit., pp. 109–112.

cottages, stables, warehouses and offices (including Colonial House) in Liverpool, and land and buildings in Bristol. In the island of Grand Canary the property consisted of two hotels, several estates, warehouses, stores, stables, offices, a coal depot, a ship-building yard, and a slipway and jetty. In Tenerife the company acquired a hotel, land, offices, stores, water-tanks and a slipway. In Jamaica it obtained two wharves besides a large piece of urban land, and a steam laundry. Land and buildings were also secured at many places in West Africa, sites being situated at Banana Creek, Saltpond, Ilaro, Calabar and Freetown.[1]

Elder Dempster and Company Limited, also received a large number of shares in other companies[2] but the main consideration was a fleet of 109 vessels which totalled more than 300,000 gross tons. At the beginning of 1910 these steamships were registered as follows:

British and African Steam Navigation Company	36
Elder Dempster Shipping Limited	26
African Steam Ship Company	24
Elder Dempster and Company	15
Imperial Direct West India Mail Service	5
Compagnie Belge Maritime du Congo	3
	109 ships

To some extent the ships were interchangeable so that they could be used on a variety of routes according to the needs of trade. Apart from the special arrangements made for the West Indies, however, the main emphasis continued to be in the provision of services to West Africa.[3]

John Holt's Enter the Shipping Trade

As the agreement between Philipps, Williams and Pirrie kept all the investments and assets under a single control, the shipping conference established by Alfred Jones was not affected. Thus the British companies continued to work in close co-operation with the three German firms, the Woermann Line, the Hamburg America-Line and the Hamburg-Bremen Africa Line. There was, however, one significant change in the situation. This concerned the Liverpool firm of John Holt and Company which operated a large merchanting business on the coast. Holt's, founded in 1867, had always utilised the services provided by the regular

[1] See Appendix p. 450, Table 48, for full details of these properties.
[2] See Appendix, p. 455, Table 49. [3] See Appendix, p. 456, Table 50.

steamship lines, but in 1907 they had purchased the S.S. *Balmore* of 1,920 tons dead-weight. This vessel was mainly intended to act as a tender for their fleet of river craft, but it did carry occasional cargoes to and from West Africa.

When Alfred Jones died in 1909, Holt's decided that the time was ripe for them to extend their shipping interests and they ordered two new ships of 2,350 tons deadweight capacity from Messrs William Hamilton and Company Limited. These were the S.S. *Jonathan Holt* and the S.S. *Thomas Holt,* and both were delivered in 1910. Under the terms of the deferred rebate circular which governed the Wext African shipping trade, this action ought to have cost Holts the rebate due to them for their previous nine month's working—a sum approaching £10,000. By agreement with Philipps and Pirrie they did not, in fact, lose this money but in return had to promise to use their ships exclusively for their own trade. They were not to build any more vessels, and the balance of their goods was to be shipped by the regular lines. So long as these conditions were fulfilled, it was agreed that Holt's would continue to receive rebates on all cargoes shipped by the conference lines.

During the period from 1910 to 1914, therefore, John Holt's own vessels were able to carry a substantial proportion of their cargoes both southbound and northbound.[1] It is clear that Philipps and Pirrie quickly regretted their agreement with John Holt and wished to bring it to an end. It is equally clear that Holts, having discovered the profitability of owning their own vessels, wished to expand rather than contract their activities. At the same time Holts appreciated that the existing situation gave them the best of two worlds. On the one hand they were always able to keep their ships full, both outwards and homewards, whereas with a larger fleet their load factor might well have fallen significantly, with a consequent rise in expense.[2] This was of particular importance in a trade where at this time the homeward cargoes were considerably larger than the outward ones. On the other hand the balance of their goods and produce was carried by the conference at rates equal to those paid by their competitors. They thus enjoyed all the advantages of a regular service on about half their shipments, without penalty, and carried

[1] See Appendix, p. 468, Table 64.
[2] The cargoes available at this time would have permitted a 50 per cent increase in the fleet without causing a fall in the load factor, but if more ships had been purchased or chartered the conference would have undoutedly withdrawn its concessions.

the remainder themselves at what was really a preferential rate. This was not immediately apparent to the casual observer because, in accordance with their agreement with Philipps and Pirrie, Holt's freight rates were the same as those charged by the conference lines.

The cost of working the Holt ships in March 1914, was calculated to be 20s per ton.[1] This figure included 1s 9d per ton for depreciation, 1s 9d per ton for interest and 9d per ton for management charges. Returns from passengers worked out at 1s 4d from fares and 4d from sales. Thus if Holts were prepared to deduct the passenger items the net cost would be 18s 4d per ton. If depreciation, interest and management fees were ignored, the cost of working would be further reduced to 14s 1d per ton. Obviously it is not possible to neglect the last three amounts, but they were fixed in an arbitrary manner and reference to John Holt's accounts would suggest that they were over-generous as far as depreciation was concerned.

In this respect the Holt's profit on the *Jonathan Holt* was largely due to their receiving her replacement value at a time when wartime prices were very high.[2] This advantage was lost by her successor, the *Clematis*, which was purchased in 1920 for £153,718 but which was subsequently sold in 1926 for only £8,500. On balance, however, the depreciation charged can be seen to have more than adequate, and it is probable that the management fees were also overestimated, as much of this work could be carried out by the existing staff. But whether the true cost of carriage by Holt's ships should be regarded as 20s, 18s 4d or some smaller figure per ton, it was certainly much less than the rates charged by the conference lines.[3] As a result the earnings of the Holt vessels were extremely large. The *Balmore* made a profit of £59,839 in her thirteen years of service; the *Jonathan Holt* made £65,000 in seven years and the *Thomas Holt* made £141,886 in nineteen years.[4]

In addition to these financial considerations it was found that, as the shipments remained under Holt's direct control, delivery was more certain, while damage and pilferage were less than with the regular lines. In these circumstances it is not surprising that they wished to continue to carry at least some of their cargoes in their own ships, and perhaps, even, to expand.

[1] Guinea Gulf Line Mss., (Hereinafter referred to as G.G.L.Mss.) Con/2A.
[2] See Appendix, p. 469, Table 65.   [3] See Appendix, p. 476, Table 77.
[4] G.G.L.Mss., Con/2A.

By 1914, however, other events were forcing Holts to reappraise their position. The African Association, Alexander Miller Brother and Company and the Company of African Merchants—all firms involved in the 'Niger Pool'—were attempting to negotiate an amalgamation under which their assets would be acquired by the Niger Company in return for an allocation of its shares.[1]

Negotiations were also under way for both Holts and MacIvers (the firm controlled by Levers)[2] to join in with this combination. This could have meant that the Holt vessels would have formed the nucleus of an enlarged fleet that would have carried the new group's cargoes outside the conference system. More likely, however, was the prospect that if Holts joined the scheme they would be asked to give up their sailings.[3] Holts, therefore, had to decide whether the potential advantages of joining the combination were going to outweigh the known disadvantages of ending their private shipping service. The Holt directors then agreed that little could be determined without a full knowledge of the terms on which they could end their sailings, so a meeting with Elder Dempster was arranged for 27 February 1914. During the discussion it was agreed that Holts would consider the terms offered to them and would then communicate their reply to the shipping company. While these deliberations were going on a telegram arrived from John Holt and this said: 'Fear not. Rely on yourself, Keep a good heart. (signed) Father.'[4]

Partly because of this intervention, the manager of the shipping department, Mr Robert L. Holt, was emboldened to send the following answer to Elder Dempster and Co. Ltd.:

'In reference to your interview with us on the 27th ultimo, when you suggested we should sell our steamers to you at a "fair valuation", with no other proviso, we regret such a suggestion is not acceptable to us. If you have any clear and definite proposals to put before us, we shall be pleased to examine same.

We are not fighting or opposing anyone, but carrying on our business in way

[1] *Liverpool Echo*, 13 March 1914. Under the heading of 'Liverpool Shares', this stated that the shares of the African Association had risen to 43s 3d (an improvement of 3s 6d) on rumours of an amalgamation with the Niger Company.

[2] See below, p. 178.

[3] G.G.L.Mss., Con/2A. Letters from Joseph E. Trigge (a director of the Niger Company) to John Holt, 5 and 14 March 1914, and letter from John Holt to Trigge dated 15 March 1914.

[4] G.G.L.Mss., Con/2A.

best suited to ourselves. If you can show us how you can work our business better than we can do it ourselves, we shall be glad to hear from you.'[1]

To some extent this letter was a bluff, for Holts had not, at that time, made up their minds as to their best course of action. In an effort to discover the true interest of the firm, Mr R. L. Holt drew up a memorandum on 2 March. This gave details of the Company's past record in respect of cost per ton and tonnage carried, and also suggested four possible ways in which future development might take place. The first suggestion was for the firm to carry all its cargo in its own ships. If the conference lines were to be ignored, however, it would be necessary to establish a fortnightly service. This would require six or seven vessels instead of the three owned at present, and while these could be filled for the homeward journey, the Company's outward cargo could only amount to about 50 per cent of the capacity provided. This could be overcome, in part, by a policy of direct sales, ex ship, in those parts of West Africa where the company did not normally trade, but this might involve retaliation from other interested parties.

A second possibility was for Holts to join with Millers and operate a joint steamship company. This would also be subject to the problems outlined above, but the increased size of the fleet could be expected to give added flexibility and strength to the operations. A third proposal was for the firm to sell its three ships for the best price obtainable. Holts would then be free to encourage an outside steamship company to enter the trade by promising it the exclusive carriage of all its cargoes. The final proposition put forward was for Holts to withdraw from the West African shipping trade and come to an arrangement with Elder Dempster. This would be in return for a good price for the ships, plus heavy compensation, but would mean that all future shipments would have to be by the conference lines.

This memorandum was then circulated to the directors of the firm with the request that the matter be given urgent consideration. The comments of one of these directors are still available, and though unsigned their force and authority would suggest that they were those of John Holt. This is quite a realistic assumption, for although Holt was an invalid and semi-retired, he was still very keen and quite able to keep a watchful eye on his company's affairs. Partly as a result of these

[1] G.G.L.Mss., Con/2A.

comments,[1] but also because arrangements for the amalgamation were delayed,[2] Holts decided to continue the sailings of their existing ships but not to increase the size of their fleet. Holts therefore maintained their policy so that about half of their cargoes were carried in their own vessels. The balance continued to be shipped by the conference at normal rates in the usual way, and Holts received the customary rebate on these shipments.

Lever Brothers Enter the West African Trade

Another change in the post-Alfred Jones era concerned the development of the Lever interest in West Africa.[3] William Hesketh Lever, later the first Lord Leverhulme, was naturally interested in the area as a source of palm products that were vital to the manufacture of both soap and margarine. In 1896 he had invested privately in the Oil Rivers and Exploration Company Limited, but had sold his shares in 1904. In 1903 a trusted employee, Mr H. R. Greenhalgh, visited the Coast and gave a favourable report, but it was not until 1910 that Lever Brothers actually entered the trade. In that year the old-established firm of W. B. MacIver and Company Limited was bought and this was followed by the purchase of Messrs Peter Ratcliffe and Company Limited and the Cavella River Company Limited, in 1912. The acquisition of MacIvers was of special importance in two ways. It secured the services of Mr W. K. Findlay who had been concerned with West Africa since 1889 and who possessed the experience necessary to guide Lever's future development on the Coast.[4] It also gave Levers a unique insight into West African shipping conditions, for MacIvers was one of the very few firms with recent knowledge of successful chartering in this region.[5]

Lever's purchase of MacIvers, Ratcliffes and the Cavalla River Company was to be only the start of his interest in West Africa. He quickly realised that the traditional method of trading goods for crudely produced palm oil, based on the collection of wild fruit, was a most inefficient method of organisation. He therefore proposed that mills be established so that modern machinery could improve both the yield and

[1] G.G.L.Mss., Con/2A. Comments by John Holt on memorandum drawn up by R. L. Holt, 2 March 1914.

[2] See below, Chapter 9, pp. 211–2.

[3] C. Leubuscher, *The West African Shipping Trade, 1909–1959* (Leyden: A. W. Sythoff, 1963), p. 30.

[4] See above, Chapter 5, p. 131.   [5] See above, Chapter 5, p. 131.

the quality of the oil, and that, where conditions permitted, plantations be developed so that the fruit could be improved and a steady supply ensured. The palm fruit produces two valuable oils. Palm oil comes from the juicy pericarp which forms the outer covering of the nut, while palm-kernel oil is obtained from the kernel found inside the hard shell in the centre of the fruit. A separate and distinct process is required to deal with each type of oil. Thus the kernel-crushing mills erected in 1910 at Opobo and Apapa in Nigeria, and at Adjuiah in the Gold Coast were based on wild fruit and were solely for extracting kernel oil. In 1912, however, a mill was built at Yonnibannal in Sierra Leone where 300 square miles of territory had been leased, and this was designed to obtain palm oil from the pericarp as well as to crush the kernels.[1]

Lever's problems began at once. The mills, dependent upon local gatherers, soon found that supplies were deliberately held up when stocks were low, in order to cause prices to rise. This was not a difficulty where land was leased and the gathering organised by the mill itself, but in the one area where this arrangement was made the fruit proved to be of low quality. It was also found that local labour was of a poor standard, and it proved expensive to employ Europeans. Another factor which added to the cost of production was that it proved impossible to sell the crushed residue of the kernels. A similar situation existed in England before 1914, but at least the English residue could be sold in Germany where it supplemented the very large quantities produced by German mills from West African produce. It was not until after the outbreak of the Great War that British farmers began to use this type of oil cake, and started to appreciate its qualities as a valuable feeding-stuff.

The major problem, however, which faced Lever was concerned with the carriage of the oil. The usual method of shipment was by cask, but the net effect of back-loading was to double the freight. The alternative of breaking down the casks into shooks[2] was helpful in that it greatly reduced the freight charged on the return journey, but native coopers were inefficient and European ones were expensive, so little was gained.

As a result of these problems, Lever's organisation—West African Oils Limited—lost over £50,000 in 1913. It was then agreed that the

[1] C. Wilson, *The History of Unilever* (London: Cassell, 1954), Book 1, p. 181.
[2] A shook is a cask that has been broken down into its component staves and packed into the smallest possible bundle.

only way substantially to reduce the deficit was by the chartering of a tank steamship. Unfortunately Elder Dempster refused to permit this, and with the aid of the deferred rebate system were able to have the project ended. Lever Brothers' resentment at this treatment was clearly expressed by their representative, Mr C. C. Knowles, when he was giving evidence before the Committee on Edible and Oil Producing Nuts and Seeds in September 1915. Speaking of primage (or deferred rebate) he said that one of the chief reasons for closing the mills was the inability to charter tank steamships,[1] and that they were essential if factories on the coast were to pay.[2]

Answering Sir Frederick Lugard, Mr Knowles stated that the difficulties of the West African mills were caused by the lack of a regular supply of fruit, the primage system, the problem of European supervision and, to some extent, the shortage of fuel.

Sir Frederick Lugard then asked:

Q.2645. 'As regards the second reason, that is, the primage system, you said you thought that ought to be got round by the merchants combining, or by individual large merchants chartering vessels, such, for instance, as the Niger Company and Millers?'

'I do not think I said it ought to be got round in that way; I said it could be got round in that way.'

Q.2646. 'Has your firm ever done anything in that direction?'

'Yes, we thought we would see whether we could save money to enable us to keep the mills open at Opobo and Lagos. We found packages cost us very heavily. We had, first of all, to buy the casks and barrels in this country, send them out to Opobo and Lagos, pay a very heavy freight on them, and then we had to get coopers; black coopers are very difficult to get out there, and very careless, and the casks were so badly coopered that when we brought the oil home in casks there was tremendous leakage; so it was very costly, and the loss very costly. Then we said "This proposition cannot pay unless we have a tank steamer." So we chartered a tank steamer, and in the different tanks we arranged different systems of heating, and said we would experiment by bringing home palm oil in bulk; because there is, no doubt, tremendous wastage in bringing the oil home in the other way. We chartered a steamer and then we got into serious trouble with Messrs. Elder Dempster and Co. We carried out the experiment, but then we had to stop at that.'

Q.2647. 'I cannot understand why you should stop at that if Elder Dempster and Co. make a profit on their ocean-going vessels. Have you sufficient freight for them both ways?'

[1] Committee on Edible and Oil Producing Nuts and Seeds (hereinafter called E.&O.P.N.&S.), 1916, CD.8248, Q.2584.
[2] Ibid., Q.2596.

'We pay a rate of freight outwards on soap and other goods in large quantities through MacIver and Co., and MacIver's bring home large quantities of palm kernels. When we pay the freight Elder Dempster and Co., say: "We will return you so much per ton at the end of twelve months if you continue to ship by our line, but if you do not ship by our line, and if you charter a boat, you will have to forfeit the whole of that rebate.'[1]

Thus, as a result of Elder Dempster's action, Levers decided that it was not a viable proposition to run the mills on the coast, and early in 1914 they were closed down. It is interesting to note at this point that while the West African mills were being closed, those belonging to the Huileries du Congo Belge (also a Lever Company) were able to continue in production, although they shipped their oil in casks. Knowles attributed this to the lower cost of collection in the Congo, where the fall in the price of rubber had greatly reduced the demand for labour.[2]

Comparison with the Alfred Jones Era
The brief survey, so far undertaken, of the period from 1910 to 1914 has shown that Philipps and Pirrie were remarkably successful in keeping Alfred Jones's empire together. The West African Conference continued to operate in much the same way as when he was alive, and, although some small concessions had been made to John Holts, the Lever organisation had been firmly put in its place. Yet if the main structure erected by Jones remained untouched, certain changes in detail were gradually made. It must be realised that Lord Pirrie was primarily concerned with his ship-building activities, and that his connection with West Africa and its shipping companies was basically as a means of ensuring the continuing sale of his vessels. Sir Owen Philipps was interested in the shipping lines themselves, but they were of no more importance to him than his other shipping concerns, and he had no special interest in West Africa. Philipps's interests were large and growing quickly and it was not possible for him to exercise personal control over every aspect of his organisation.[3] This, of course, was in direct contrast to Alfred Jones whose whole world revolved around the West Coast of Africa. Jones made it his business to keep in close touch with everyone connected with West Africa. This applied particularly to the merchants, who were his most important customers, and even the smallest had

[1] Ibid., Q.2645–2647. [2] Ibid., Q.2498.
[3] By 1915 Philipps directed 295 steamships totalling 1,520,060 gross tons. (E.&O.P.N. &S.C., Section 1, p. 206).

181

ready access to him.[1] He always kept his ear to the ground for possible difficulties and was thus able to deal with them before they reached significant proportions. The secret of his success was not the establishment of the conference or even the deferred rebate system; it was his intimate knowledge of the trade and its leaders. Philipps's other responsibilities effectively precluded him from continuing this aspect of Jones's policy, and the daily running of Elder Dempster was left in other hands. At the same time this enforced aloofness did not mean that Philipps would not attempt to satisfy the merchants when he felt this could be done with safety. The following extract from his evidence before the Committee on Edible and Oil Producing Nuts and Seeds shows this clearly:

> 'With reference to the other part of your question about the merchants owning steamers, I would like to inform the Committee that when I became Chairman of Elder Dempster and Company I had strong pressure put upon me by the trade to be no longer connected with merchant's business. Sir Alfred Jones was interested in a merchant's business. At the request of the trade we sold that merchant's business to the West African trade. Therefore, if the shipowner should not carry on trade, it appears to me it ought to work both ways to the benefit of everybody.'[2]

The company referred to was the Sierra Leone Coaling Company—sometimes referred to as the 'Old' Company—which operated in many parts of the Coast and which dealt with many items besides coal.[3]

Alfred Jones's other main coaling firm, the Grand Canary Coaling Company, was based at Las Palmas. As previously noted,[4] this company had been established in 1884 in order to supply coal to his own vessels and, incidentally, to sell it to other passing ships. The situation of Las Palmas at a crossroad of world trade led to an immense growth of its bunkering facilities and by 1910 these were quite considerable. The Grand Canary Coaling Company had benefited from this development so that in addition to providing for the ever-increasing Elder Dempster fleet it shared in the enlarged agency business. When Philipps acquired the Company he thought it should have a bigger proportion of the 'Coal

---

[1] All sources are agreed that Alfred Jones was prepared to listen to anyone with a reasonable complaint or suggestion. However, once he offered the caller a banana from the bowl on his desk this was recognised to be an indication that the interview was at an end.

[2] E.&O.P.N.&S.C. Q.5992.

[3] See copy of this firm's advertisement dated 17 October 1891. Appendix, p. 433, Table 36.

[4] See above, Chapter 5, p. 126.

Pool'. The other six members disagreed and in October 1910 a price-war broke out. This continued for several years and at one time the Las Palmas price dropped to equal the Cardiff price. During this time Philipps's opponents imported Newcastle coal in hired Danish ships— tomatoes being backloaded for the return voyage. Eventually, however, the situation was regularised the setting up of the Atlantic Isles Depot Agreement.[1]

Jones had also been responsible for the establishment of the Bank of British West Africa in 1894.[2] For many years he and his partners in Elder Dempster and Company held a controlling interest in the firm, and it is probable that Jones exercised a personal control. His shares were transferred to Pirrie and Philipps after his death, but the Bank was divorced from the shipping interest and gradually developed a separate existence.

The setting up of the Compagnie Belge Maritime was yet another of Jones's innovations which did not survive his death. As previously noted,[3] the partnership between Elder Dempster and the Belgian Crown had enjoyed a profitable existence from 1895 to 1911. The arrangement was then terminated by mutual consent, but it would appear that this was due to changed circumstances rather than to the fact that both Jones and King Leopold were dead. By 1910 the Belgians were ready for and capable of financing and organising their own shipping line, so after the completion of negotiations which lasted intermittently from July to December, the Company was reorganised and, thereafter, both Elder Dempster and the Woermann Line took a much less active part in Belgian affairs.[4]

Since that time Elder Dempster's financial interest in the Compagnie Maritime du Belge[5] has gradually declined. It still owns the 51,078 shares which it possessed on the formation of Elder Dempster Lines Holdings Limited in 1936 but these now represent a small percentage of the firm's shareholdings. At that date these shares amounted to $33\frac{1}{3}$ per

---

[1] Information based on author's interview with Mr Gerald Miller in Las Palmas during September 1967. Mr Miller's grandfather was Thomas Miller who with John Swanson had established Swanson and Miller in 1860. This firm of general agents built the original breakwater at the port. In 1885 Miller & Co. was formed and entered the coal trade—Thomas's son James being a prominent member of this firm.

[2] See above, Chapter 5, p. 118.   [3] See above, Chapter 5, pp. 129–30.

[4] House History of the Compagnie Maritime du Belge (Antwerp, 1948), p. 55.

[5] The name of the Company was transposed in 1930.

cent of the issued capital, but as a result of exchange control difficulties, amalgamations and mergers, the same holding declined to 15.7 per cent in 1960 and to 11 per cent in 1961—this is the current (1972) situation.[1]

In spite of this diminished financial stake, Elder Dempster and the Compagnie Maritime du Belge continue to enjoy the friendliest of relations—commercial interests having been deeply cemented by co-operation during two world wars.

Pirrie and Philipps also acquired Jones's West Indian interests. These had been created after Jones's success in selling bananas and other fruit from the Canary Islands, for he had then been asked by the Colonial Secretary, Joseph Chamberlain, if he would to market Jamaican bananas in England. He therefore joined with Messrs Fyffe, Hudson and Company Limited—a London firm of fruit merchants—to form Messrs Elder and Fyffes Limited. This company handled the purchase and sale of the fruit, and was partly responsible for its carriage to the United Kingdom. The Imperial Direct West India Mail Service Company Limited was also started by Jones in 1901, and, apart from mail and passengers, it carried large quantities of fruit for Elder and Fyffes. In addition, the development of satisfactory communications between the two countries was of some importance in promoting the growth of general trade.[2] For many years, however, it had been suspected that the Imperial Direct Mail Service was run at a loss in spite of an annual Mail subsidy of £40,000. The ten-year agreement made between Jones and Chamberlain expired in 1911, and there was a difference of £13,000 between the terms offered for its renewal, and those required. Whether the failure to reach a compromise was the fault of the British and Jamaican governments or the shipping company is not clear; at any rate the service ended in January 1911.[3] Once the obligations of the Imperial Direct Line had been disposed of,[4] Philipps and Pirrie must have decided that their shares in Messrs Elder and Fyffes Limited were not an essential part of their interests. In October 1913 they allowed the United Fruit Company of New Jersey to take up the whole of a new issue

[1] The author is indebted to M. Paul Vereecke, Chairman of Associated Central West African Lines, and to Mr T. Kennan, former Chief Accountant of Elder Dempster Lines, for their help in interpreting the statistics given above. Full details of Elder Dempster participation in the C.M.B. are held as part of E.D.L. Papers.

[2] See above, Chapter 5, pp. 127–8.

[3] *The Times*, January 1911. 'The West Indian Mail Service'.

[4] It was not actually wound up until 1937. See file 72110, dissolved at Company House.

of £550,000, and then sold their entire holding to Mr A. Preston on[1] advantageous terms.

Having thus divested themselves of certain sections of their inheritance from Alfred Jones, Philipps and Pirrie may have anticipated a period in which the trade would settle down and require less of their attention. But the whole nature of the West African business was against stability, as the traders were in a constant fight amongst themselves. In this situation there was an insistent demand for special freight rates, particularly by the bigger merchants, for any advantage in shipment would enable a firm to undercut its rivals. The claim of the conference that extra rebates were not given to the larger shippers was a main factor in the support given to it by the smaller concerns. Not only did each individual merchant try to ensure that his opponents received no preferential treatment, but also each looked with disfavour on any concessions which might improve the other's competitive position. The Niger Company's arrangement whereby they were allowed to charter several steamships per year,[2] and the small fleet operated by John Holts were always bones of contention.

Alfred Jones, however, had been extremely adept in preventing the merchants from either rebelling or combining against the regular lines. Apart from the deferred rebate system, it is likely that he also used special rebates and exclusive agencies as means of ensuring loyalty. Philipps and Pirrie had continued this policy, but lacked either Jones's remarkable skill or else his tremendous attention to detail. A consequence of this was seen in 1913 and 1914 when Millers chartered two sister ships, the *Stalheim* and the *Standford*; 1470 gross registered tons.[3] It seems that Miller's intention was merely to attempt to secure the same conditions as those under which the Niger Company was operating, but the steamship companies regarded the matter as virtual opposition.

The question of Miller's chartering, like that of the shipping companies' attitude to the proposed combination in the Nigerian trade, was

[1] See File 70123, live, at Company House and Appendix, p. 441, Table 42. (Mr Preston was a nominee of the United Fruit Company.)

[2] The basis for this understanding originated in 1907 following a meeting between Sir Alfred Jones and the then Lord Scarborough. See above, Chapter 5, p. 136.

[3] These vessels were built in 1912 by Fredrikstad Mek Vaerks at Fredrikstad, for Akties Standard of Christiania, Norway. Their dimensions were 243 by 39 by 17 feet and they were fitted with triple expansion engines of 150 n.h.p. (*Source*: Lloyds Register of Shipping, 1913–1914, Vol. 1.)

significantly modified by the outbreak of war in August 1914. At this time the Woermann Line and its associated companies (the Hamburg—America Line and the Hamburg—Bremen-Africa Line) possessed twenty-nine vessels of 128,000 gross tons, a large number of which were used exclusively in the West African service.[1] The Royal Navy immediately ended the activities of these ships, and most were either sunk or took permanent refuge in neutral harbours. A few were captured, but these only counterbalanced the loss of the three Elder Dempster steamers which were detained in Hamburg. As the German fleet provided a substantial proportion of the carrying capacity in the trade, its loss was of the utmost importance, and the remaining vessels found it impossible to cope with the volume of cargoes available for shipment, even though these were below that of normal times.[2] Under these circumstances the conference was ended, the rebate system was abolished and all merchants were free to charter without any financial loss. Unfortunately this newly-found freedom came at a time when chartering was both difficult and expensive, and so in the early days of the war Elder Dempster continued to carry nearly all of the cargoes to and from West Africa.

Thus the commencement of hostilities ended the West African shipping conference that had been established by Alfred Jones in 1895. In the period between his death in December 1909 and the start of the war in August 1914, the system created by him had ostensibly continued with only minor modifications. But this was more apparent than real, for the sailings of the John Holt vessels and the chartering of the Niger Company were developing frictions and jealousies which were not easily controlled. Even more important than this, however, was the growth of the interest of Lever Brothers. For the first time, an organisation which could really rival the power and authority of the shipping companies was concerning itself with West Africa, and Lever was not the man to forget Elder Dempster's refusal to allow him to charter a tanker. It is now clear that Levers were, in fact, only waiting for a suitable opportunity before making more favourable arrangements for the carriage of their goods and produce. This was not fully appreciated at the time, but the sense of uncertainty and feeling of unrest—which was a normal feature of the West African trade—was found to be especially strong in 1914.

[1] *Fairplay*, 29 August 1935, p. 398.
[2] E.&O.P.N.&S.C., Evidence of Sir Owen Philipps, p. 206.

Chapter 8

The Great War

The Effect of the War on British Shipping

All shipping companies had become increasingly apprehensive as the crisis developed, and the seriousness of the position was recognised when all charters to the Black Sea were suspended after the Austrian ultimatum to Serbia on 23 July. Within a week all tramp chartering had ended, and as soon as war was declared almost all of the regular lines cancelled their sailings. Thus for a time, all ports were full of vessels awaiting instructions from their owners, and the trade of the nation was at a standstill. Fortunately, this state of affairs was not to last for very long. The arrangements made by the Navy, plus the cover provided by the rapidly organised State Insurance Scheme[1] quickly encouraged a return to normal activity. The failure of the Germans to mount a significant attack on the British mercantile marine at this time further increased the confidence of the shipowners, and by the end of August most routes had been re-opened.

This is not to imply, however, that services were back to normal. It took many months for the shipping industry to recover from the dislocation created by the war. The shipowners' gradual recovery of confidence was only one aspect of this problem. The ending of trade with Germany and Austria, and the closure of the Baltic and Black Seas led to a tremendous change in the traditional pattern of voyages.[2] In general this rearrangement meant a change to longer ocean journeys. Thus the million and a half tons of sugar purchased by Britain from Europe

---

[1] C. Ernest Fayle, *The War and the Shipping Industry* (London: Oxford University Press, 1927), pp. 49–67. This gives a very full account of the development of plans to deal with war risk insurance.

[2] Ibid., p. 37. Over 3000 British ships took cargoes to German ports each year.

before the war had to be replaced from Java, Mauritius, the West Indies and South America.[1] Not only did the sources of supply tend to be further off, but also the routes recommended by the Admiralty frequently added many miles to the voyages. The complex system of international credit also took time to adjust itself to the changed circumstances. In Argentine, for example, 400,000 tons of shipping lay idle in the Plate ports for several weeks until the German Houses, who normally financed the maize trade, could be replaced.

The general disruption of shipping and credit was worsened by the congestion at many of the ports.[2] Some British ones including Dover, Southampton and Newhaven were completely closed to commercial services, while many others, notably London and Liverpool, lost the use of a large part of their facilities. This naturally put a tremendous strain on the remaining capacity and lengthened the process of turnround. In April 1915 Liverpool had over seventy vessels waiting for berths, and many steamers that had previously been allocated places found they were still full of cargoes discharged from earlier ships.[3] The resulting delays, plus the difficulties of manning[4], added to the enormous shock which the finely balanced mechanism of international trade had received at the beginning of the war. There was a consequent increase in the proportion of voyages in ballast—a sure sign of dislocation—and a serious decrease in the efficiency of the vessels concerned. In addition, the British mercantile marine was depleted by nearly half a million tons of shipping that had been immobilised in the Baltic, and by the four million gross tons that were quickly requisitioned for the government service.

In the circumstances it was fortunate that the years from 1911 to 1913 had been a period of boom conditions, for these had resulted in an extra six and a half million gross tons being added to the fleets of the world. Thus in July 1914 the United Kingdom, its dominions and colonies possessed 10,123 steamers of over 100 tons. These had a total tonnage of 20,524,000 gross and represented 45.2 per cent of world capacity. Many of these ships, however, were too small to be considered useful

[1] Ibid., p. 114.
[2] C. Ernest Fayle, *Seaborne Trade*, Vol. 1 (London: John Murray, 1920), pp. 401–404.
[3] J. Russell Smith, *Influence of the Great War Upon Shipping* (New York: Oxford University Press, 1919), p. 35.
[4] 8,000 merchant seamen joined the Colours within 48 hours of the declaration of war. C. Ernest Fayle, *The War and the Shipping Industry*, op. cit., p. 40.

for ocean traffic and it was the 4,000 vessels of over 1,000 tons that were of real significance. There were also many sailing ships on the British and colonial registers. These amounted to 522,000 net tons, but were of relatively little importance.

In spite of all the difficulties mentioned above, shipping services recovered so quickly that at first sufficient cargoes could not be found. This was due to the diverting of trade from its normal courses and to the disruption of the financial structure. Thus in September 1914 tramp freights fell rapidly, but as demand increased the rate began to rise and by October it was back to the July figure. After this date there was an insatiable demand for tonnage to meet the requirements of the naval and military authorities, and also to provide the food and materials needed for the civilian population. The full utilisation of the excess capacity that had existed after the 1911–13 boom, and the partial withdrawal of ships from routes between foreign ports helped to fill the gap. The conversion of passenger accommodation into cargo space, and the use of every nook and cranny, resulted in a net gain of 25 per cent in the carrying power per voyage. In these ways it was hoped it would be possible for British shipping to meet the needs of the authorities, as well as attempt to supply the country with all the food and raw materials necessary for the successful prosecution of the war.

In the early days of the war the freight market possessed three distinct sections and these reflected the tremendous changes that were taking place. The first dealt with those trades that had previously been unregulated; the second covered those routes where a conference system had been in operation before the war; and the third concerned the requisitioned ships that were becoming an increasingly important proportion of the whole as the conflict progressed. In the unregulated segment of the market, freight rates rose rapidly after October 1914. There was a certain amount of justification for this because, apart from the expense caused by the dislocation of trade, there was a sharp rise in running-costs. The increase of wages, stores and bunkers, plus the premiums for war-risk insurance added significantly to the owners' outgoings, and but for the weak state of the market they would have raised their rates at an earlier date.[1] This, in fact, was the action taken by the

---

[1] C. Ernest Fayle, *The War and the Shipping Industry*, op. cit., p. 11. Estimates of the rise in running expenses by January 1915, ranged from 3s 9d to 6s per ton for the Plate voyage.

liner companies in the regulated trades and as early as 15 August the following surcharges had been announced:

India	+ 20% on the pre-war rate
Australia	+ 25%
South & East Africa	+ 33⅓%
West Africa	+ 50%
Plate & Barzil	+ 50%
Pacific	+ 33⅓% to 50%
Mediterranean	+ 50% [1]

Many of these surcharges were subsequently reduced as the war-time situation became clearer, and by March 1915 the average surcharge was only 15 to 25 per cent. At the same date the unregulated rate had advanced by at least 100 per cent.

In the remaining sector of the market, the freights were fixed by what became known as the 'Blue Book' rates. The decision to requisition rather than charter, as in the South African War, was taken basically because of the time element. The speed of events in France made the transporting of the Expeditionary Force a matter of such urgency that even a day's delay might have proved harmful. At first these vessels were used '. . . as Transports and Auxiliaries for the convenience of the Fleet and similar services'.[2] Very quickly, however, an increasing proportion of the rising numbers of requisitioned ships was being used to carry commercial cargoes on government account. This was simply to avoid paying the market rates of freight, but it enlarged the problem of fixing the remuneration for the vessels concerned. The Admiralty Transport Arbitration Board was accordingly set up, and on 22 October this issued a number of reports which established the basis for payment. The rates suggested in the 'Blue Books'[3] were above those ruling before the war but below current ones, and according to Sir Owen Philipps they represented '. . . a fair compromise between national interests and justice to shipowners'.[4]

The possibility of gaining large returns in the open market on the

[1] C. Ernest Fayle, *Seaborne Trade*, op. cit., p. 191.
[2] Proclamation 1247, 3 August 1914, Manual of Emergency Legislation, p. 386.
[3] Troopships = 13s 6d to 17s 6d per gross ton
   Cargo liners = 12s 3d to 15s 3d per gross ton ⎱ + 6d after 2 months service
   Tramps = 9s 6d to 12s   per gross ton ⎰ + 1s after 2 months service
[4] Lloyd's List, 13 May 1915, Speech of Sir Owen Philipps to the A.G.M. of the Royal Mail Steam Packet Company.

unrequisitioned portions of their fleets may well have helped ship-owners to have accepted the government action with good grace. Difficulties then arose owing to the unequal incidence of the Admiralty's requirements, and while some fleets lost as little as 21 per cent, others had nearly 60 per cent requisitioned.[1]

In the circumstances the Director of Transports met a representative body of tramp-owners, and it was agreed that the rates by increased by 1s 6d per gross ton. This amounted to a rise of only 16 per cent (com-pared with the 100 per cent of the free market), but the Admiralty also undertook to be responsible for any rise in wages above the rates being paid at the beginning of the war. The liner companies had not been included in this agreement, and neither asked for nor received an in-crease in their remuneration. They were, however, placed under the same arrangement as the tramps for excess wages, and this went some way towards paying their increased costs. After March 1915 there was a slight drop in freight rates on the free market. The original wartime dislocation had been overcome and trade had adapted itself to the new circumstances. The better organisation of the requisitioned ships had reduced waste and they had been reinforced by the gradual introduction of the 700,000 tons of German shipping captured at the commencement of hostilities. There had also been an actual decline in the volume of imports—wheat in particular falling by 21 per cent when compared with 1914.

During the summer of 1915 freight rates began a new and even greater rise. Only half of the tonnage destroyed by the enemy was re-placed by new construction,[2] and port congestion handicapped attempts to improve the annual carrying-power of the available shipping. These increasing difficulties enforced further government action and in November 1915 authority was obtained to requisition ships to carry food or any other necessary item. At the same time a strict system of licensing was introduced to control ships trading between ports outside the British Empire. These arrangements worked reasonably well, but with demand constantly increasing and the supply of ships falling, an even stronger arrangement was required. The immensity of the

[1] *Hansard, Mr Macnamara, Parliamentary Secretary to the Admiralty*, 27 January 1916. Note that after February 1915, a system of 'proportionate requisitioning' was gradually evolved.

[2] The concentration on naval construction meant that the merchant ships completed in 1915 and 1916 amount to only a third of the 1914 tonnage.

problem was finally recognised, and early in 1916 a Shipping Control Committee was appointed with Lord Curzon as its chairman.[1] The difficulties of the British mercantile marine in the first eighteen months of the war have now been examined in sufficient detail for this present work, but to obtain a balanced picture it is also necessary to consider its achievements. Over thirty-seven million net tons of shipping engaged in foreign trade entered and cleared British ports in the six months ending on 31 January 1915. The loss on this huge tonnage amounted to only $\frac{1}{3}$ per cent[2] and only seventy-one British steamers of 275,566 gross tons were sunk.[3] Thus while Germany's overseas trade came to an almost complete standstill Britain was able to continue its normal activities. British losses during 1915 rose to 856,000 gross tons, but not only was an increasingly large war effort supported, but also the volume of imports from August 1914 to December 1915 was maintained to within 12 per cent of its pre-war quantities.[4]

The following year, 1916, saw a dramatic change in the number of sinkings, and losses rose to over 1,238,000 gross tons. As these losses tended to be concentrated in the last four months of the year it was clear that the situation was rapidly becoming intolerable. Lloyd George's new administration recognised this fact, and one of its first steps was to amalgamate into the Ministry of Shipping all the committees attempting to deal with the problem. Sir Joseph Maclay was placed in charge of the new authority, being appointed Shipping Controller in December, 1916.[5] He was soon made aware of the immensity of his task by the report produced for the Shipping Control Committee which indicated the probable tonnage deficiency for 1917. It seemed that the only way the demand for cargo space could be equated with supply was by the limitation of non-essential imports. Accordingly a large number of items were prohibited, while many others could only be imported under licence, and altogether six million tons a year were saved.

The value of these measures was quickly appreciated, for on 1 February 1917 the Germans began their policy of unrestricted submarine warfare. Shipping losses mounted quickly and reached a peak in April, when 545,000 gross tons were sunk. This made a total of over

[1] J. A. Salter, *Allied Shipping Control* (London: Oxford University Press, 1921), p. 64. (Part II of this work gives a detailed account of the extension of shipping control).

[2] C. Ernest Fayle *Seaborne Trade*, op. cit., pp. 388-9.   [3] Ibid., p. 412.

[4] C. Ernest Fayle, *The War and the Shipping Industry*, op. cit., p. 103.

[5] J. Russell Smith, op. cit., p. 167.

Laird & Fletcher's Office, *c.* 1858.

PLATE II

Elder Dempster's First Office, 1870.

PLATE 12

Colonial House, Liverpool.
Decorated on visit of King
Queen for opening of Glad
stone Dock in 1927.

India Building, Liverpool.

1,200,000 gross tons in only three months, which was more than the most optimistic estimates of construction for the entire year.[1] Thus the policies of the Ministry of Shipping had to be further intensified, and a Liner Requisitioning Scheme was organised. This was in full working order by May 1917, and thereafter all vessels were effectively requisitioned by the State.[2]

The indiscriminate attacking of merchant ships was a prime factor in deciding the United States to enter the war on the allied side. When this took place on 2 May 1917, its long-term effects were to be enormous, but in the short run it made little difference to the desperate situation which existed at sea. In fact, the position in some respects became worse, for the American government immediately requisitioned 160 steamers that were being built to British order.[3] Under these conditions the British Government redoubled its efforts to reduce the number of enemy sinkings, to increase the carrying power of the existing fleet, and to build as many new vessels as possible. The policy of concentrating our shipping resources on the shortest possible routes was also carried to its logical conclusions and nearly half of our requirements were obtained from North America.

There was no certain answer to the submarine menace but it was thought that a convoy system might help to reduce the number of casualties. A few experimental convoys were therefore run in May, and it was found that many of the anticipated difficulties had been exaggerated and that losses were light.[4] The success of the system was such that it was rapidly developed, and during the latter months of 1917 over half of the total overseas trade of the United Kingdom was protected in this way. By the end of the war this proportion had reached 90 per cent and losses were reduced as follows:

February to July 1917   = 2,305,000 gross tons
August to January 1918 = 1,400,000 gross tons
February to July 1918   = 1,150,000 gross tons[5]

The main difficulty caused by the convoy system was that it tended to increase the average length of the round voyage by 25 per cent. This

---

[1] C. Ernest Fayle, *The War and the Shipping Industry*, op. cit., p. 245.
[2] Ibid., p. 228–38.   [3] Ibid., p. 251.
[4] J. A. Salter, op. cit., pp. 117–130. This provides an excellent guide to the success of the Convoy System.
[5] C. Ernest Fayle, *The War and the Shipping Industry*, op. cit., p. 287.

was a factor of immense importance on the Atlantic run where tonnage was being concentrated, owing to the large number of voyages per year. Tremendous efforts were, therefore, made to reduce delays, and by 1918 the system had become so efficient that turn-round was back to its pre-convoy standards.

Great steps were also taken to increase the output of the British shipyards. Those employed in the industry were exempted from national service, and a few specialists were released from the forces. Really significant progress, however, only came after long negotiations with the trade unions had resulted in the adoption of increased mechanisation, payment by results, and the use of unskilled, largely female, labour. The increased supplies of steel and the emphasis on merchant instead of naval vessels aided these factors, and launchings in 1917 and 1918 were double those of 1916, although still considerably below those of pre-war days. The concentration upon five, later twelve, standard types of vessel also facilitated construction, and the final push was given in May 1918, when Lord Pirrie was appointed Controller General of Merchant Shipbuilding with a seat on the Board of Admiralty and the right of direct access to the Cabinet.[1] The tremendous growth of United States construction was also beginning to affect the situation by the summer of 1918, but to a large extent it was counterbalanced by the need to transport the American Expeditionary Force, and to maintain it in the field. The net effect, however, of reduced sinkings and increased construction was to enlarge allied tonnage so considerably that it was able to complete all its tasks without too much difficulty—although not without a great deal of danger.

The West African Trade during the War
After the outbreak of war the West African shipping business followed the pattern of other British trades. There was a brief lull while the shipowners and merchants took stock of the new position, but then the sailings were resumed on a rapidly increasing scale. This process was hardly affected by the activities of the *Kaiser Wilhelm der Grosse* which sank the Elder line's *Nyanga* on 16 August, because the German raider was herself destroyed ten days later.[2] Before the war there had been

[1] Ibid., pp. 214–54.
[2] In fact the *Kaiser Wilhelm Der Grosse* only sank one other steamship besides the *Nyanga*. See C. Ernest Fayle, *Seaborne Trade*, op. cit., pp. 78–82, 242–3.

ninety-two British vessels totalling 274,000 tons on the West African run. Although these had been more than adequate to deal with their commitments they were insufficient to cover the withdrawal of the 133,000 tons of German vessels:

'. . . They had 51 steamers. I believe the Government took twelve of them at the Cameroons, and another was captured at Sierra Leone. But the great mass of them, I should think about thirty, are lying in neutral harbours, and a good many went across to Pernambuco to avoid our cruisers at the beginning of the war.'[1]

German commerce with West Africa had thus ended abruptly in August 1914, but as this had merely increased the potential British trade, the amount of shipping required did not change. Once the original shock and dislocation were over, the West African trade found that there was a serious shortage of cargo space. Apart from the three ships belonging to Jonn Holt's, Elder Dempster found themselves to be responsible for all other shipments. In the circumstances they could have followed the example of other free trades and permitted the price mechanism to select the goods for shipment. In fact they decided to '. . . apportion the space to shippers pro rata to their average shipments over a period of twelve months'.[2] This decision was relatively easy to carry out as, unlike most other trades, all the ships were controlled by a single concern. In addition, the regular meetings between Elder Dempster, the Colonial Office and the West African merchants also helped to smooth away any difficulties as they arose. The reasons why Elder Dempster adopted this particular course of action are more complex. Ostensibly it was in line with the general principle of 'uniform rates of freight and equality of opportunity for large and small shippers'. This, however, could have been ignored on the grounds of wartime expediency, and it seems likely that Elder Dempster were taking the long view and hoping that this action would assist in the retention of their position in the post-war world. It is also probable that Pirrie and Philipps considered that any line which abused its situation would lay itself open to government intervention, and they no doubt felt that any firm which possessed a near monopoly, however temporarily, would be especially vulnerable to uninformed criticism.

[1] E.O.P.N. & S.C. Evidence of Sir Owen Philipps, Q.6076. Note that although Philipps speaks of 51 ships, he states in Q.6027 that these totalled 133,000 gross tons and this approximates to the *Fairplay* figure quoted in Chapter 7, p. 186.
[2] E. & O.P.N. & S.C. Evidence of Sir Owen Philipps, Precis. p. 207(e).

In spite of the development of this system of allocating cargo space, freight rates did show a steady rise throughout the war period.[1] In the outward trade the rise was at first quite moderate, and even at its highest represented only a 100 per cent increase. This comparatively small growth may be explained by the fact that in the West African trade at that time the outward cargoes amounted to only 50 per cent of the homeward ones. It is therefore on the return journey that the pressure on space would really be at a premium. In fact, the records[2] show quite clearly that in the first eighteen months of the war the rise in homeward freight rates was very small, although rather more than the increase in outward charges over the same period. This is the more remarkable when it is compared with other trades where, in some cases, the increase had been over 300 per cent by the end of 1915.[3] But although the rates to and from West Africa were well below current market prices for other routes, the existing fleet could not cope with the cargoes available for shipment.[4]

The shortage of cargo space was caused initially by the withdrawal of the German ships but this was rectified to some extent by the eleven Woermann liners that were secured when Douala in the Cameroons was captured at the end of 1914. Furthermore, losses from normal maritime hazards and war risks were low during the first three years of hostilities and by making the fullest use of every available space, 25 per cent more produce was brought home by Elder Dempster vessels in 1915 than in 1913, and a further 7 per cent increase over the 1915 figure was achieved in 1916.[5]

Although valuable, these increased shipments by the regular lines represented only part of the produce which formerly went to Germany. In an attempt to move the excess quantities, Elder Dempster undertook to charter as many additional vessels as might prove necessary. When they attempted to do this, however, they found that even at extortionate rates it was almost impossible.

'The merchants had a meeting with me a short time ago when they pointed out the difficulties that might occur and I then told them that I was prepared to go into the market and charter whatever steamers may be necessary to carry the West African cargo to England, but that one could not possibly do it at the pres-

---

[1] See Appendix, p. 477, Table 78.   [2] See Appendix, p. 477, Table 79.
[3] See Appendix, p. 478, Table 80.   [4] See Appendix, p. 408, Table 15.
[5] *Fairplay*, 15 June 1916, p. 940 and 31 May 1917, p. 906.

ent rates. The British Government take up our cargo steamers under requisition—
I am not making any complaint about that because they require them—and they
pay us about 7s per ton per month on the dead-weight of the steamers on time
charter. We began by paying 12s 6d. We then paid 16s per ton dead-weight per
month on time charter. We then paid 17s 6d. We have now paid 20s 6d. Last
Friday we offered 22s 6d per ton deadweight per month on time charter, and we
lost the steamer which was chartered elsewhere at 25s. At the present tariff rates
for an average cargo outwards and an average cargo homewards on the basis of
20s we should lose on this one boat, £15,426. I have had it worked out this
morning to see what the rate on kernels would have to be, not to make a profit,
but so that we should not lose money and I find that, whilst our present rate for
palm kernels is 25s per ton of 40 cubic feet or per scale ton of 13 cwts, if we had
to charter a boat at 25s it would take, (assuming the outward rates were according to the present tariff), a rate on kernels of 80s 6d per ton of 40 cubic feet or 13
cwts., to just clear the cost of the charter, and we would make £15 at that
figure.'[1]

The high cost of chartering was, of course, a symptom of the shipping
shortage. In the West African trade, however, the decline in the tonnage available was not caused by either maritime hazards or enemy
sinkings and, in fact, the main difficulties were caused by the demands
of the Admiralty Transport Department. This body requisitioned many
Elder Dempster ships and diverted them to other routes, in addition to
purchasing three vessels from the Line in the early days of the war. On
the other hand the government temporarily released other vessels when
they could be spared, for West African produce was essential to the war
effort, but even with this aid it was not always possible to ship every
item of cargo. This situation worsened rapidly in 1917 as Elder Dempster's losses rose sharply, but 1918 saw relatively few casualties and
matters were greatly improved.[2]

The most important exports from West Africa before the war were
palm kernels and palm oil. In 1913, 181,305 tons of kernels went to
Germany, but only 35,175 tons came to the United Kingdom. On the
other hand 72,237 tons of oil came to the U.K. while only 10,426 tons
went to Germany.[3] The diversion of this trade from Germany to
Britain during the war naturally created many problems. The shortage
of cargo space was intensified by the congestion at Liverpool. The
inadequacy of the facilities at that port then encouraged firms in other

[1] E. & O.P.N. & S.C. Evidence of Sir Owen Philipps, Q.6016.
[2] See Appendix. p. 408, Table 16.
[3] E. & O.P.N. & S.C. Table 1, p. 5.

areas to import palm kernels for the first time, and a new palm-kernel crushing centre developed at Hull. This process was greatly assisted by Elder Dempster who arranged to deliver the kernels to Hull at the Liverpool rate. At first this meant that they themselves paid for the carriage from Liverpool, but early in 1915 a direct service was established between West Africa and Hull. As a result, fifteen Elder Dempster ships delivered their cargoes to Hull during 1915, and a further three vessels landed palm kernels at London where crushing had also been commenced.

Palm Kernel Imports from West Africa to the United Kingdom[1]

Year	London	Hull	Liverpool	Total
1913	—	—	36,012	36,012 tons
1914	—	—	73,187	74,797
1915	8,729	42,549	178,060	233,249

The table above shows that as far as palm kernels were concerned the quantity imported into the United Kingdom in 1915 (233,249 tons), was greater than the combined amount exported from West Africa to the U.K. and Germany in 1913, (35,175 tons plus 181,305 tons making a total of 216,480 tons).[2] As palm kernels were the main item that needed to be diverted from Germany, this is a good indication of the tremendous efforts that were made by Elder Dempster.

Elder Dempster's financial results reflected their increased, almost frantic, activity. It is clear that their policy of approximating freight increases to the rise in costs, while not attempting to wring the last penny out of the shippers, prevented extortionate profits from being made. Nevertheless, in monetary terms they consistently secured adequate returns even after all previously non-requisitioned ships were taken over at 'Blue Book' rates at the beginning of 1917.[3]

On the other hand, after allowing for the rise in the issued capital and for the depreciation in the value of money, the returns in real terms were quite moderate. The other British shipping companies associated with Elder Dempster in the West Africa trade possess very similar records. All took the opportunity of strengthening their financial posi-

[1] E. & O.P.N. & S.C. Report. pp. 20–21.
[2] E. & O.P.N. & S.C. Report. p. 5 (Note the slight discrepancy with the figures for 1913 quoted above.)
[3] See Appendix, p. 457, Table 51.

tions during the war,[1] but none appears to have been unduly excessive in its freight charges. In fact, it was the proud boast of the African Steam ship Company at the end of hostilities that it had never had to pay a penny in excess profit duty.[2]

Elder Dempster's achievements were all the greater because they were accomplished at a time when most of their regular office and dock staffs had volunteered for military or naval service. Fortunately they also had a number of factors in their favour, for the ending of German competition not only left a clear field, but also permitted Elder Dempster to purchase their former rivals' facilities on the coast at favourable prices.

It must also be appreciated that Elder Dempster's position was not without its detractors even in face of its wartime record. Prominent amongst these was Mr T. Wiles, M.P., who alone refused to sign the Report of the Committee on Edible and Oil Producing Nuts and Seeds. Instead he issued a Minority Report in which he strongly attacked, amongst other things, a system which in normal times precluded the competition of tramp steamers.[3] Another member of the Committee was Mr C. C. Knowles who represented Lever Brothers. Although critical of the shipping companies, he signed the Majority Report, but there is little significance in this for the Committee was basically concerned with produce and shipping matters tended to be a side issue.

Mr Knowles also appeared as a witness before the Committee[4] and part of his evidence concerned the shipping services. He said he thought that freight was paying for passengers and that the industry was considerably restricted by the policies of the shipping companies. He considered that unless the merchants were permitted to charter in normal times the only satisfactory solution would be for the producers to combine and arrange their own carriage, even if this meant the loss of their rebate.[5]

The most important disclosures made by Mr Knowles, however, came later in his evidence:

[1] *Fairplay*, 23 May 1918, p. 882 and 6 June 1918, p. 969. Note that both the Imperial Direct Line Limited and the British and African Steam Navigation Company Limited paid off all their debentures during the war.

[2] *Fairplay*, 8 May 1919, p. 967.   [3] E. & O.P.N. & S.C. p. 25(d).

[4] Mr Knowles evidence in respect of other matters is dealt with above in Chapter 7, p. 180.

[5] E. & O.P.N. & S.C. Q. 2419–2423.

Q.2648 '. . . It was always our intention that when the quantity got sufficient—and it is still our intention—to have steamers of our own from the Congo, and then we shall arrange for tank steamers or whatever suits us best.'

Q.2649 '. . . And you do not anticipate you would have sufficient trade in British West Africa to make it worth your while to do the same there, or to combine with some other Congo firm, such as Miller Brothers or the Niger Company ?'

'I am not speaking as Lever Brothers because I do not wish to do so on this point, but I may say I personally certainly think it could be arranged with British West Africa equally well as with the Congo, but there is this difficulty that where you are big merchants and are constantly shipping goods, you want to utilise the regular lines at times, and I think if you went into competition with them in the way suggested you would find you would have great difficulty in getting your stuff over by the regular lines, because if anybody's goods had to be left out of a ship, yours would be the goods left out.'

Q.2650 'But would you not depend on your own boats ?'

'Yes, but if you chartered boats you would not run them quite so often as the regular lines run, and there would be times when you would want to ship by those lines.'[1]

Mr Knowles gave his evidence on 22 September 1915, and on 19 April 1916 the Bromport Steamship Company Limited was formed by Lever Brothers. Lever's desire to undertake their own carrying had laid dormant since 1913 when Elder Dempster had refused to give them permission to charter a tanker.[2] The collapse of the conference at the beginning of the war had removed one problem, for it ended the rebate system. At the same time, the shortage of shipping space, allied to the high profits to be made on produce, gave a real economic basis for an independent shipping line. The discussion engendered by the Committee on Edible Oils may then have been partly responsible for Lever's entry into the West African shipping trade, for it had the effect of rationalising their thoughts on the matter in the particular context of the time.

A further important aspect was that Lever had reopened the mills on the Coast early in 1916. This was done to ensure an adequate supply of raw materials, but it soon became clear that sea transport and not production was the limiting factor.[3] In these circumstances Lever's decided it was essential that they purchase sufficient vessels to carry their own cargoes. The long order-books of the shipbuilders encouraged the purchase of a ready-made fleet, although it is likely that the high cost of

[1] E. & O.P.N. & S.C. Evidence of C. C. Knowles, p. 100.
[2] See above, Chapter 7, p. 180.
[3] C. Wilson, *The History of Unilever*, Vol. I (London: Cassell, 1954), p. 237.

new tonnage may also have been a deterrent.[1] A search for suitable ships was then commenced and it was discovered that Herbert Watson and Company of Manchester were willing to sell their six steamers, plus their option on one nearing completion.[2]

The firm of Henry Tyrer and Company Limited managed the ships of the Bromport Steamship Company from the time they were acquired, and also looked after the *Kulambangra* of 2,005 gross tons which had been built in 1910 for Lever's Pacific Plantations Limited.[3] At first this arrangement was only tentative, but after twelve months a formal agreement was signed. This provided for the payment of £100 p.a. for each vessel, plus 1 per cent commission on all freight, deadfreight and demurrage earned by the steamers.[4] Tyrers thus became responsible for many aspects of the Bromport Lines business. This arrangement proved to be so satisfactory that in future years they were to perform similar duties for another Lever concern—the Southern Whaling and Sealing Company Limited.

The six ships purchased from Watson's gave Levers an annual cargo capacity of 80,000 tons, but their current requirements were only 8,675 tons outward and 43,000 tons homeward.[5] The taking of Watsons' option on the *Eskmere*, and the purchase of another new vessel, the *Rabymere*, plus the *Kulambangra* home from the Pacific all further increased the size of the fleet. In spite of this enlarged capacity, Levers never found their tonnage to be too large for their requirements. They had expected that any loss on the outward leg would be balanced by the high freights that could be earned by any spare space on the homeward run, but the loss of four ships by enemy action kept capacity at a premium.[6] This was particularly unfortunate at a time when Lever's requirements were rapidly expanding.[7] In addition, two of the ships

[1] Details of the 'Cost of a new, ready steamship of 7,500 gross tons' are given annually in *Fairplay*. These refer specifically to tramp construction, but the liner trend was very similar.

[2] *Fairplay*, 20 April 1916, p. 644. Details of the arrangement which was finalised in April 1916, are given in the Appendix, p. 471, Table 69.

[3] C. Wilson, op. cit., Vol. 1, p. 163.

[4] The papers of Henry Tyrer and Company (hereinafter referred to as *Henry Tyrer Mss.*) are held at the firm's head office in Liverpool. See Agreement dated 11 June 1917.

[5] C. Wilson, op. cit., Vol. 1, pp. 237–8.

[6] These were the *Colemere, Delamere, Eskmere,* and *Redesmere.*

[7] Lever purchased *John Walkden's,* the *Bathurst Trading Co.* and *Kings of Bristol* during the war.

were already under government requisition when they were purchased by Levers, and the remainder of the fleet came under state control in May 1917, although they remained on the West African run. There was, consequently, no difficulty in filling the remaining vessels at any time, and according to Mr Knowles, speaking in October, 1917:

'Our fleet had enabled us to bring from West Africa large quantities of produce that would not otherwise have come forward and that helped our markets generally for raw materials. MacIver's warehouses had been blocked at the time we entered into shipping, but with our ships MacIvers were able to go ahead and buy produce that they would not have been able to buy if we had not had the ships. It had further to be borne in mind that todays' prices for the steamers would show a big profit, and in a word, good results had been more real than apparent. On broad principles the steamers' purchase had been a great success.'[1]

Elder Dempster naturally disliked Lever's action in organising their own shipping service to West Africa, but with the shortage of tonnage there was nothing they could do to prevent its success. Relations between Elder Dempster and John Holts remained friendly, and part of both Lever's and Holt's homeward cargoes was shipped by the regular line. The co-operation between the three firms became even closer in May 1917, for at that time, at the government's 'request', they formed an owners' committee that was designed to ensure that all the tonnage engaged in the trade was allocated in the national interest. All vessels not previously requisitioned were then taken over by the Ministry of Shipping at 'Blue Book' rates for the duration of the war, and thereafter all freights were decided by the government.[2] At about the same time, Elder Dempster changed their arrangements for the allocation of cargo space. The policy of providing capacity in proportion to the quantity shipped before the war had worked well in the early days, but the large number of new shippers and the rise in the number of ports to be served had meant so many modifications that the old system had become un-workable. Accordingly a new arrangement had been decided upon and after this had been approved by the Ministry of Shipping all cargo space was allocated on the basis of the stocks available for shipment.[3]

As we have seen, both Elder Dempster and the Bromport Line lost many fine ships in 1917 and 1918. John Holt and Company, the only

[1] C. C. Knowles. Quoted by C. Wilson, op. cit., Vol. 1, pp. 238–9.
[2] *Fairplay*, 31 May 1917, p. 906 (A.G.M. of Elder Dempster & Co. Ltd).
[3] *Fairplay*, 13 June 1918, p. 102–8 (A.G.M. of Elder Dempster & Co. Ltd).

other British firm with ships on the run, had purchased the *Ussa* in 1916 and thus increased their fleet to four vessels. The loss of this steamer in May 1917, and the subsequent loss of the *Jonathan Holt* the following month left the line with only the *Balmore* and the *Thomas Holt*. Thus Holts, like Levers, were always short of cargo space. A further similarity between the two firms was that, despite the large profits to be made by importing produce, neither thought it desirable to purchase replacement ships for those sunk in 1917. The fantastically high costs of construction, allied to the fear of further sinkings and the possibility of government diversion to other trades, convinced both firms that it was best to delay new orders until more settled times.

The introduction of the convoy system was a partial answer to this problem but it was probably too late to influence the policies adopted by John Holts and Lever Brothers. In fact, it was not until the summer of 1918 that West Africa was completely integrated into the system, but by then a ten-knot fleet was leaving Sierra Leone for Britain every eight days.[1] The average number of ships in each convoy was only eight, but a frequent sailing of small numbers was ideal for this route with its lack of major ports.

Wartime Losses and Incidents

Elder Dempster's great effort during the war cannot be adequately conveyed by the bare statistics of cargo carried and financial results. The cost of maintaining the link with West Africa was a high one, both in men and ships, and deserves a more detailed examination than has so far been possible.

Elder Dempster lost 487 of their employees during the Great War. Of these, 67 were killed on active service. The remaining 420 men died when their ships were damaged or sunk.[2] In token of their service and gallantry forty-seven employees received awards or were mentioned in despatches—four received the O.B.E., two the M.B.E., three the M.C., seven the M.M., five the D.S.C., four the D.S.O. and two the D.S.M.[3]

In the years between August 1914 and November 1918, Elder

---

[1] C. Ernest Fayle, *The War and the Shipping Industry*, op. cit., Table 18, p. 431.

[2] *The Elder Dempster Fleet in the War*, (Published privately by the Company, Liverpool, 1921), pp. 55–66.

[3] Ibid., pp. 70–73.

Dempster lost 13 ships from normal maritime hazards and 29 from enemy action.[1] The Company's first casualty was *Nyanga* which was sunk off North-West Africa on 16 August 1914. There was no loss of life, for her crew were taken on board her captor—the armed merchant cruiser, *Kaiser Wilhelm der Grosse*. Within a few days H.M.S. *Highflyer* caught up with this vessel while she was coaling. *Nyana's* crew was transferred to a collier which succeeded in reaching Las Palmas, but the German cruiser was sunk.

Ashanti nearly suffered a like fate. She had left Hamburg for West Africa twenty-four hours before the war started and reached the Canary Islands without incident. There she was warned that the *Karlsruhe* was in the vicinity, so when she sailed for Dakar an extra special look out was kept. At midnight on 30 August a large three-funnelled vessel was sighted. It passed within half a mile of *Ashanti* without signalling and those on board were just congratulating themselves on a remarkable let-off when the stranger turned round and headed towards them. Captain Evans turned his vessel several times and each time it appeared that the cruiser followed him. Then a second vessel was seen and the *Karlsruhe* apparently spoke to it before it turned off and headed south. The cruiser proceeded north and *Ashanti* was left to make her way into port—a surprising escape that has never been explained.

Elder Dempster lost four vessels by enemy action in 1915, amongst them the *Falaba* which had the doubtful distinction of being the first unarmed passenger ship to be sunk by German submarine. She had left Liverpool on 27 March and the following day was sixty miles west of St Ann's Head when a submarine was sighted on the surface. After a brief chase *Falaba* was stopped and informed that the ship was to be sunk in five minutes. It was impossible for all the boats to be got away in that period but, nevertheless, the torpedo struck at the appointed time, and within eight minutes the vessel went down. A drifter, the *Eileen Emma*, was able to pick up many who would otherwise have died, but in spite of all efforts forty-nine of the one hundred and forty-seven passengers and fifty-three of the crew of ninety-five were killed.

No Elder Dempster vessel was lost by enemy action during 1916 but the year began badly. The R.M.S. *Appam* left Dakar for Liverpool on 11 January. Her non-arrival on the 22nd gave great cause for concern

[1] See Appendix, pp. 408-9, Table 16.

and when she was a week overdue the worst was feared. In fact, *Appam* had been captured by the German cruiser *Moewe* three days after leaving Dakar. It soon became clear that the Germans did not intend to sink their captive, for one hundred and forty-three men from sunken ships were transferred to the Elder Dempster liner while thirty passengers (mainly military officers) with stores and food were moved to the cruiser. A prize crew then sailed *Appam* to Newport News in the United States where she arrived on 1 February. The authorities immediately interned the vessel and after months of legal proceedings she was returned to her rightful owners. It was thought that the Germans might make special efforts to sink her, so she spent the remainder of the war under the name of *Mandingo*.

From the point of view of British shipping, 1917 was the worst year of the war. Nearly four million gross tons were sunk as a result of enemy action[1] and Elder Dempster lost more than their fair share of even this enormous total. During the year twenty-one vessels totalling 86,983 gross tons became war casualties, while a further three, totalling 11,794 gross tons, were lost by normal hazards. Some of these vessels were merely listed as missing, for their end is not accurately known. Typical of these is the *Yola* which sailed from New York for London on 26 January and was never heard of again. Others were technically victims of 'normal maritime hazards' but it is probable that without the restrictions imposed by wartime necessity many of these losses may never have occurred. The sinking of the *Mendi* is an example of this latter case. The vessel was sailing from Plymouth for Havre with an African labour battalion which *Mendi* had already transported from Capetown. No lights or signals were permitted, although the night was extremely foggy and at 5 a.m. on the morning of 21 February a collision occurred with the R.M.S.P. *Darro*. Within twenty minutes *Mendi* had disappeared and 656 men, including thirty-one crew members, were dead or dying.

[1] War losses of British shipping were as follows:

1914 = 241,000 gross tons   1917 = 3,730,000 gross tons
1915 = 856,000 gross tons   1918 = 1,695,000 gross tons
1916 = 1,238,000 gross tons

GRAND TOTAL 7,760,000

(C. Ernest Fayle, *The War and the Shipping Industry*, op. cit., Table 4, p. 417).

Most of Elder Dempster's war casualties in 1917 were caused by torpedoes fired by submerged U-boats. 'Unrestricted submarine warfare' meant in practice that warning of an attack was seldom given and crews sailed with the knowledge that a torpedo might strike at any moment. One of the many fine vessels lost in this manner was *Abosso*. She had left Bathurst for Liverpool on 14 April with 127 passengers and a crew of 134. Ten days later she was off Bantry Bay when, at about 9 p.m. in the evening, she was hit in the engine room. Owing to the nature of the damage it was not possible to stop the ship and a hour after the attack she was still circling at a considerable pace although getting progressively lower in the water. Eventually the boats were released but three were upset because of the way still on the vessel and twenty-five crew members lost their lives. Approximately forty passengers also died in the loss of *Abosso*—the survivors being picked up by a British destroyer.

By 1917 most of the Elder Dempster vessels had been fitted with some form of defensive armament and the value of even a single gun was seen on many occasions. The escape of *Akabo* in June is a case in point for, after a torpedo attack had failed, two submarines chased the vessel for many hours. The gunners were able to keep the German ships submerged and by slowing them down prevented their reaching an attacking position.

There was a less fortunate outcome when *Addah* was struck by a torpedo while steaming off Brest. The vessel settled on an even keel and while the boats were being got away the submarine surfaced. Captain Clarke and his gunner then opened fire on the enemy and the action continued until *Addah*'s gun was destroyed. The two men then jumped overboard and were picked up by one of the lifeboats. The submarine promptly ran down this particular boat and fired on the men in the water, killing nine. A French destroyed, attracted by the firing, then appeared on the scene and the submarine dived and left the area.

Thus the possession of a weapon proved to be a mixed blessing in some instances. The fitting of a gun gave a feeling of confidence to a crew but, of course, it was of little value against the surprise attack of a submerged submarine. Indeed, in one case where two Elder Dempster vessels were travelling together for safety the *Obuasi*, which possessed a gun, was sunk, while her consort, the *Onitsha*, which was not armed, managed to escape.

It was only when a vessel survived the initial attack that a gun proved to be useful, but the first warning in most incidents proved to be the explosion of the torpedo as it crashed into the side of the ship. Thus during the morning of 16 July, *Tamele* was attacked by a submarine when off the south-west coast of Ireland. She managed to escape but at 8.40 p.m. that evening she was struck by a torpedo amidships, although no enemy had been sighted. On this occasion only one out of a crew of fifty-nine was lost, but in the case of *Eloby* the death-rate was very much higher. This vessel was sailing through the Mediterranean with a cargo of high explosives. A torpedo from an unseen submarine caused a tremendous explosion and within a few minutes the ship had gone down together with fifty-seven members of her crew. There were only three survivors. The *Sapele* sank under similar circumstances. She was off south-west Ireland on 25 October and the weather was so bad that it was thought to be impossible for a submarine to make a useful attack. At 4 p.m., however, she was torpedoed—nothing being seen of the attacker. In spite of the terrible conditions, the boats were got away and made a successful landfall. Ten crew members died, mainly owing to exposure in the boats.

The sinking of the R.M.S. *Apapa* in November 1917 also occurred without any sight of the enemy. She was within two miles of Point Lynas when she was torpedoed—a particularly tragic incident, as she had been escorted until a few hours before the attack took place. Further tragedy was still to come. The first torpedo stopped *Apapa* and she was sinking slowly enough to permit the boats to be launched without difficulty. Then a second torpedo struck and she keeled over to starboard and sank quite quickly. The funnel took one lifeboat down with it and others were smashed by falling masts or entangled in the wireless aerials. As a result of the second, unnecessary, attack thirty-nine Elder Dempster men and many passengers were killed.

The year 1918 was a much better one for Elder Dempster, only three vessels being lost by enemy action. The worst event, in fact, was the loss of *Burutu* by collision. This was made the more poignant by the nearness of peace and by the charmed life which the vessel had hitherto enjoyed. In November 1917 *Burutu* had been attacked by a submarine, but had managed to escape. The following April she was attacked again. It seems that a submarine was shelling Monrovia when smoke was sighted on the horizon. The U-boat submerged but when she saw

it was a merchant ship she came to the surface and began to shell the
Elder Dempster liner. The fire was returned for over an hour and a
quarter before the onset of darkness enabled the pursuer to be eluded.
This came none too soon for when night fell the merchantman had only
five shells remaining in her ammunition locker.

For the next five months *Burutu* continued her service on the West
African route and she left Sierra Leone for Liverpool on 19 September.
She travelled in convoy and by 10.50 p.m. on 3 October had reached a
position about twenty-five miles south-west of Bardsey. It was a dark
night with many rain squalls and it was, perhaps, for this reason that
City of Calcutta was not seen until it was too late to avoid her. The
collision caused *Burutu* to list heavily so that only the port lifeboats could
be lowered. Number one boat got away safely but a rope snapped as
number two descended and she upset her passengers into the water.
The speed with which *Burutu* was sinking prevented any other boats
being launched and by 10.59 p.m. she had gone. This disaster resulted
in the loss of one hundred and forty-eight lives of whom seventy-seven
were members of the crew. There were only fifty survivors.

Elder Dempster's many losses during the First World War must not
disguise the fact that their service to West Africa was maintained without interruption. In addition, Elder Dempster vessels were engaged on
government service in many remote ports of the world including
Northern Russia, the Middle East and India. *Ebani*, for example,
served as a hospital ship for five years, steaming for 200,000 miles and
carrying 50,000 sick and wounded. Elder Dempster also managed over
four hundred other ships at various times during the war and this was
in spite of the loss of nearly six hundred members of the Company's
clerical staff who had joined the services.

Chapter 9

Reconstruction and Change

The Transition from War to Peace

The official attitude towards decontrol was expressed by the Shipping
Controller on the day after the armistice was signed, and this made it
clear that requisitioning was to be ended as quickly as was compatible
with the maintenance of essential services.[1] The removal of restrictions
on navigation and the ending of the convoy system gave an immediate
increase to the efficiency of the existing ships, and new tonnage was
rapidly replacing the 7,759,000 gross tons lost during the war. It was
arranged that after 1 March 1919 those privately owned ships that were
not required for special purposes would be released from requisition as
soon as they returned to the United Kingdom, and the transfer from
war duty to the import service proceeded quite quickly although the
obligations to our allies remained high.[2] The ending of the Liner Requisition Scheme on 15 February 1919 was a further step towards commercial freedom, but all vessels remained subject to licence and the
government retained a certain amount of cargo space. The difficulties
of re-starting normal trade with Europe meant that most sources of
supply continued to require lengthy voyages. To this must be added the
problems caused by port congestion and railway dislocation, and altogether the annual carrying power of the existing tonnage fell by 30 to
40 per cent as compared with 1913.[3] All of these difficulties were, of
course, to be anticipated and were gradually overcome, but their immediate effect was to inflate freight rates—and thus shipping prices—to
still higher levels.

[1] *The Times*, 12 November 1918.
[2] C. Ernest Fayle, *The War and the Shipping Industry*, op. cit., p. 366.
[3] Chamber of Shipping, Annual Report, 1919–20, p. 21.

Unfortunately for British owners, most of their vessels were subject throughout 1919 to the limited rates permitted by the Shipping Controller. They did not therefore enjoy the huge increases obtained by many neutral owners although the free space on the liner routes did receive the market rate. Freights continued to rise until March 1920, when the Budget increased Excess Profits Duty from 40 per cent to 60 per cent. Rates then commenced to decline and with the construction of surplus tonnage and the ending of port, railway and financial bottlenecks, the fall became catastrophic. The government was then able to secure ships on the open market at less than the 'limited' rates they had formerly paid, and all licences and freight restrictions were ended in July. The following month saw the finish to any remaining obligations of the liner companies, and they were free to pursue whatever policies suited them best.

In the West African shipping trade the pattern was similar to that of British shipping in general. Throughout 1919 the produce available for shipment was greater than the available tonnage, although by the end of the year all of Elder Dempster's wartime losses had been restored.[1] The West African merchants also chartered a number of ships, but much cargo continued to be shut out. By June 1920, however, the situation had been reversed:

> 'The stocks of produce that had accumulated at the various ports in West Africa have now been shipped, and it is no longer a case of goods waiting for shipment, but rather of vessels seeking for cargoes.'[2]

Changes in the Post-War Situation
The post-war situation differed in a number of significant ways from that of 1914. One of these basic changes occurred when Lever Brothers acquired the Niger Company. This deal was completed in January 1920, but financial control was not obtained until the following July. Levers then '. . . carried a responsibility which was almost completely divorced from authority',[3] and they could not dictate policy for several critical months. Thus the action taken by the Niger Company in supporting the produce market after prices had collapsed in April was not

---

[1] *Fairplay*, 4 December 1919, p. 1297, Extraordinary General Meeting of Elder Dempster and Company Limited.
[2] *Fairplay*, 10 June 1920, p. 823, A.G.M. of Elder Dempster and Company Limited.
[3] *History of the United Africa Co. Ltd* to 1938, p. 59.

in line with the policy which Levers wished to see carried out. In effect, this transformed the Company from one with large cash reserves and a small stock of produce to one with small reserves and an enormous quantity of African products. As these items had been purchased on a falling market they were priced far above their true value, and were consequently a grave embarrassment for Levers at a time when competition in the soap and margarine trades was desperately keen. In addition, the difficulties of raising the capital for the deal in the new circumstances almost crippled Levers, and in the long run ended the family control of the Lever empire.[1] An important side-effect for the West African shipping trade was on the Bromport Steamship Company. This line had deferred the purchase of new vessels in 1919 owing to the high cost of construction, but it was intended to replace its wartime losses as soon as prices returned to normal. The break in prices, however, did not come until after the disastrous Niger Company arrangement, and Levers were then in no position to consider the necessary investment.

A second change in the organisation of the West African merchants concerned the African Association. Following a dispute between the Niger Company and the other members, the 'Niger Pool' ended in violent disagreements in 1917, and it became necessary to make new arrangements. Wartime difficulties precluded any immediate action, but in 1919 the African and Eastern Trade Corporation Limited was established. The surplus of assets over liabilities of the four companies which joined together to form the new amalgamation were as follows:

African Association	£1,833,438	19s	7d
Miller Brothers	1,205,184	3s	1d
F. & A. Swanzy	946,400	2s	8d
Millers	803,340	2s	3d[2]

The first year was a great financial success and in October 1920 it became known that Lever was seeking to combine all his West African

[1] This was not only due to the fall in the produce market. Lever had been out of England for most of the year and had left his directors to buy the Niger Company. This was a task entirely outside their previous experience for Lever normally gave them little opportunity to exercise their authority, but even so they ought not to have proceeded without '. . . instructing the Company's Auditors to make a full investigation to the Niger Company's books before completing the deal'. C. Wilson, The History of Unilever, Vol. I (London: Cassell, 1954), pp. 252–9.

[2] History of the United Africa Co. Ltd., op. cit., p. 93.

interests with those of the Corporation. Although there was some opposition to the scheme it was welcomed by the vast majority of shareholders, and it was formally approved by the African and Eastern Trade Corporation in November 1920. Unfortunately the financial difficulties of the Lever group and the general slump in world trade prevented the arrangement from being finalised and in April 1921 it was announced that the scheme was being abandoned. Nevertheless, the two concerns remained friendly and it was hoped that a working agreement could be negotiated when more stable conditions prevailed.

Another change in the post-war situation concerned the shipping companies engaged on the West African route for, while Britain had been engaged in her struggle for survival, other nations were able to take advantage of her absence from the trade routes of the world. Japan was able to increase her tonnage by 50 per cent during the war but, as this was mainly employed in the Far Eastern and Indian trades, it need not concern us here. Similarly we need not investigate the activities of the United States before she entered the conflict, because these were largely concerned with South America and the Pacific.[1] The progress of the Dutch, however, was a different matter, for it was very relevant to the West African trade.

It is clear that the Dutch were able to put both their shipping and shipbuilding industries into a very strong financial situation during the war. The advantages of neutrality enabled many Dutch firms to make substantial profits and while these were reflected in increased dividends a large proportion was retained.[2] This placed the shipping companies registered in Holland in an extremely favourable position to expand once hostilities had ended, and in the West African shipping trade it was to mean the permanent addition of an extra line.[3] The 'Blue Book' rates earned by British firms were significantly improved in May 1918, but in comparison with the free market they remained very low. In most cases the British companies were able to secure reasonable re-

[1] S. G. Sturmey, *British Shipping and World Competition* (University of London, Athlone Press, 1962), p. 54.

[2] *Fairplay*, 21 September 1916, p. 403 (Report of the Rotterdam Chamber of Commerce for 1915).

[3] This was the Holland West Africa Line which had been organised by the Holland Steamship Company on behalf of the Groote Ahcht—a combination of prominent Dutch shipping firms. See C. Leubuscher, *The West African Shipping Trade 1909-1959* (Leyden: A. W. Sythoff, 1963), pp. 32-3.

turns, but they were not able to build up their reserves in the same way as neutral owners. The signing of the armistice in November 1918 saw a number of neutral countries not only determined to expand their shipping services, but also with the resources to do so, and the first twelve months of peace enabled them further to strengthen their position while British companies were still partly controlled.

A further difference in the pre- and post-war situations was reflected in the capital structure of Elder Dempster and Company Limited. The capital had increased substantially, but, although the ships and investments had grown from under five million to over twelve million pounds, the declared profit had only risen from £307,379 to £573,941 and the dividends had fallen from 8 to 5 per cent.[1] It should be noted, however, that as the growth of capital had taken place almost exclusively in the non-voting preference share section, control of the Company had remained with Philips and Pirrie.[2]

The Slump in World Trade

The fall in the price of West African produce after April 1920 was part of a world-wide trend. The cost of produce on the London market included the charge for ocean transport and it was essential, therefore that the freight rate for West African produce was kept in line with the rates from other areas. In fact, the Chamber of Shipping's general index of world freight rates fell sharply during the twenties,[3] but as this takes a boom year as its base, the subsequent falls appear to be exaggerated. While this is undoubtedly true, the index does show the trend very clearly and the ten-year fall to less than 30 per cent of the 1920 figure is of the utmost importance to any study of the period. Elder Dempster recognised that in their own interest it was vital to keep West Africa competitive with other areas, and they accordingly reduced their homeward freights by 40 per cent as from 1 January 1921.[4] At the time this reduction appeared to be a tremendous concession, but it soon proved to be insufficient and further falls had to be announced in July 1921 and in March 1922.[5]

The reduction of freight rates does not appear to have been forced

[1] See Appendix, p. 457, Table 52.　　[2] See below, Chapter 10, p. 253.
[3] See the general index supplied in the Annual Reports of the Chamber of Shipping of the United Kingdom.
[4] *Fairplay*, 23 June 1921, p. 1020, A.G.M. of Elder Dempster & Co. Ltd.
[5] *Fairplay*, 25 May 1922, p. 573, A.G.M. of Elder Dempster & Co. Ltd.

by the amalgamation movement amongst the West African merchants. Elder Dempster naturally viewed these developments with suspicion, but at first did not seem to expect that they would affect the good relations that existed between shipowners and shippers. By 1922, however, the shipping line was seeing the position in a different light. Both the Niger Company and the African and Eastern Trade Corporation were chartering ships to cover a small part of their requirements, and it was feared that they might evolve a system, either jointly or separately, which would enable them to do their own carrying. Sir Owen Philipps dealt with this problem in a speech during May 1922, when he warned the merchants that if they intended to carry their own cargoes it would be necessary for the steamship owners to become merchants.[1] He also pointed out that if one compared the dividends paid by the merchants and carriers over the previous ten years it would be seen to be greatly to the advantage of the shipping companies to take this action. Nevertheless, Philipps urged that each should stick to its own business and this, in fact, was what occurred. The Niger Company and the African and Eastern Trade Corporation were both heavily committed in West Africa and did not wish to undertake fresh capital investments unless they were absolutely vital. The freight reductions offered by Elder Dempster showed that the carriers were prepared to be reasonable and in addition there was no penalty for chartering, although it was understood that this was not to be increased. In the circumstances the merchants took no action to participate a crisis, and the changes that were ultimately made were the results of the policies of the shipping lines.

Elder Dempster's difficulties at this time can easily be imagined. Costly tonnage ordered during the boom was coming into service when it could no longer be fully utilised and the fall in running expenses was lagging far behind the rapid fall in freight and passenger receipts. During the same period the other British lines in the trade were also experiencing difficulties. The John Holt fleet ended the war with only two vessels,[2] but the *Clematis* of 5,717 gross tons was purchased in 1920. This was an old ship, built in 1898, but nevertheless she cost the company £153,718. Following the onset of the slump the cost of running their own fleet could only be justified if each vessel maintained a very high load factor. With the decline in the amount of freight being brought

---

[1] *Fairplay*, 25 May 1922, p. 573, A.G.M. of Elder Dempster & Co. Ltd.
[2] See above, Chapter 8, p. 203.

home by Holts it became progressively more difficult to operate three steamers at a high load factor and it was therefore decided to sell the *Balmore*. Thus after 1922 the Holt fleet consisted of only two vessels, and the company continued to rely on the regular lines for the shipment of the balance of their cargoes.

The Bromport Line completed the war with only four vessels, but as we have seen it was not possible to restore it to its former size. This was purely for financial reasons, because the enlargement of Lever's interests in West Africa would have made it quite easy to have kept a larger fleet fully occupied.

On the other hand the foreign shipping companies engaged in the trade were able to make steady progress. The Holland West Africa Line doubled its sailings between 1920 and 1921,[1] and the Woermann Line recommenced its services in 1921.[2] The Dutch not only benefited from their neutrality during the war, but also were able to develop their trade during the boom conditions of 1919 and 1920. The German Line, however, did not re-enter the trade until the slump was having an important effect on freight rates but it was still able to recapture a large amount of its former cargoes. There were several reasons for this German success:

'Foreign ships are, without exception, operating at a very small margin of profit, or sometimes at a loss, but German ships have shown very good results. This is, I think, chiefly accountable for two reasons, i.e. the abundant cargo and the depreciation of the mark. As to the first reason, although the German imports and exports amounted in 1921 and 1922 only to 40 per cent and 30 per cent respectively of pre-war, this was sufficient to foster the German tonnage, which was also comparatively small as against pre-war. The effects of depreciation of marks were subject to interruption. For instance, the operating expenses of ships at the present time are almost as high as foreign ships as commented on in *Fairplay* on 22 February. In 1921 and 1922, however, the mark had depreciated so progressively and violently that inland prices and wages were always behind the changed international value of marks, the German competitive power being thus considerably strengthened, and enormous profits attained.'[3]

In addition, most of these profits were not distributed but were retained to assist in the building up of the companies concerned. The

[1] See Appendix, p. 411, Table 18.

[2] It should be pointed out that the Woermann Line was associated with the Deutsche Ost-Afrika Line in many of its activities, and that both ran joint sailings with the Hamburg-Amerika Line and the Nord Deutscher Lloyd.

[3] *Fairplay*, 5 April 1923, p. 4, German Shipping News.

early stages of the depreciation of the mark helped many lines to obtain cheap ships, but contracts on a fixed-price basis became unacceptable to builders as inflation continued. Both shipowners and shipbuilders, however, took advantage of this favourable opportunity to redeem many outstanding loans and debentures at far below their true value.

The position of Elder Dempster was in direct contrast to that of the German lines. The insurance payments received as compensation for war losses had been insufficient to pay for their replacement in the boom conditions which followed the ending of hostilities. The Company had thus been forced to double its issued capital and debentures in order to assist in covering the cost of these new vessels.[1] If inflation had continued in England, as in Germany, the burden of this debt would, of course, have been lightened. In fact, the onset of the slump added greatly to the difficulty of servicing this debt. The fall in the value of shipping then meant that these vessels stood in the Company's books at figures far in excess of their true worth, and by 1922 new ships could be purchased for only 25 per cent of the 1920 figure.[2]

Thus the success of the Elder Dempster's policy in replacing their wartime losses[3] proved to be a handicap which was to have severe repercussions through the twenties. But it may be unreasonable to be too critical of Sir Owen Philipps in this matter. Although the growth of steam shipping had been subject to various fluctuations, there had been an overall expansion for over fifty years and, in common with virtually all other British and foreign shipowners, Philipps was convinced that this trend would continue. It must also be pointed out that had Philips not been prepared to acquire capacity at the earliest possible moment, his companies would have been unable to fulfil all their obligations and this could have opened many trades to foreign competition.[4] Nevertheless, it is certain that there was little or no critical analysis of future

---

[1] See Appendix, p. 457, Table 51.   [2] See Chapter 8, p. 201, f/n 1.

[3] 'Since 1 January 1919, twenty-five new steamers representing 214,076 tons deadweight have been delivered and placed in the Company's various services.' (*Fairplay*, 3 June 1920, p. 752, A.G.M. of Elder Dempster and Company Limited.)

[4] Philipps' arrangement with Lord Inchcape to buy all surplus Government merchant vessels (and later German ships) was prompted equally by a desire to prevent the Government from operating them on its own account. S. G. Sturmey, op. cit., pp. 57–8. Philipps' own account of the purchase of these ships was given at the 89th Annual Meeting of the Royal Mail Steam Packet Company on the 18 June 1930. See also: Hector Bolitho, *Lord Inchcape* (London: John Murray, 1936), pp. 138–144.

prospects and Philipps's blind faith in the future was to begin a chain of events which was ultimately to lead to his disgrace and imprisonment.

To a large extent, therefore, Elder Dempster were in a cleft stick. On the one hand the surplus of world shipping and the competition of the Dutch and German lines was forcing rates down to an unremunerative level which had to be matched or the merchants would either use the foreign lines or provide their own shipping facilities. On the other hand running expenses were falling only slowly, and the heavy capital cost of the fleet required expensive servicing. The Company was thus drifting into an untenable situation where outgoings were exceeding receipts. In these circumstances it was inevitable that the period before 1914 would be regarded as a kind of golden age, and this led to a desire to reintroduce the conference system.

The re-establishment of the West African Lines Conference

A step towards the re-establishment of a conference system was taken when a deferred rebate was re-introduced for outward cargoes in January 1922. This obviously suited the shipowners very well, but they maintained that this action had been taken at the request of between fifty and a hundred small traders.[1] These were experiencing strong competition from a large group which was in a position to charter full cargoes at 10s to 12s 6d per ton less than the liner rate, and which was using the regular services, without penalty, when convenient. The small traders then hoped that the reimposition of the system would help to restore a position of equality.[2]

Elder Dempster's action in the West African trade was fully investigated by a government inquiry during 1922. In the 'Final Report of the Imperial Shipping Committee on the Deferred Rebate System' it was stated that the shippers ought to have the choice of an 'agreement system' as an alternative to a 'deferred rebate system', and also advised that every route should form a representative association of traders. It did not, however, recommend any government action against the existing situation, and this was taken by the shipping companies to imply tacit approval.

[1] Final Report of the Imperial Shipping Committee on the Deferred Rebate System, CMD. 1902 (H.M.S.O., 1923) (hereinafter referred to as I.S.C.), p. 36.
[2] Ibid., p. 12.

Negotiations were then begun between Elder Dempster, the Woermann Line and the Holland West Africa Line. These were designed to end the period of cut-throat competition which had existed since the freight market had slumped in April 1920, and each line had its own reasons for seeking a satisfactory solution. Elder Dempster wished to end a ruinous rate-war which had led to some freights being lower in 1923 than in 1914, although the cost of running a service with British vessels was nearly double that of pre-war days.[1] So far as the Holland West Africa Line was concerned, its main aim was to secure the position it had obtained in the post-war boom. Apart from certain expensive cottons and gins which were well received on the coast the Dutch had no particular advantage in the trade and, without the special circumstances prevailing at the end of the war, it is unlikely that they could have obtained sufficient cargo. Large financial reserves, supplemented by its earnings during the boom, then enabled it to persist, but after 1920 it experienced Elder Dempster's problems and it welcomed any suggestion for making the trade more lucrative.

The German lines engaged in the West African trade were also anxious to come to terms with their competitors. In spite of the loss of the German colonies which were the basis of their business, the lines had made very good progress in the early years after the war. As we have seen,[2] this was largely because of domestic inflation and the favourable ratio between the size of fleet and the available cargo. By the end of 1923, however, German shipping had grown from the 700,000 gross tons that had been retained in 1919, to near 2,750,000 gross tons. This was only about half the pre-war size but it was almost sufficient to carry the reduced volume of cargo. Thus one important advantage had been gradually, and inevitably, whittled away. This process also applied in some measure to the German West African Trade which then possessed the following vessels:

Fleets of German Lines Engaged in the West African Trade,[3]
December 1923

Woermann Linie, Hamburg	9 ships totalling	38,878 gross tons
Hamburg-Bremen Afrika Linie, Bremen	8 ships totalling	24,797 gross tons
Deutsche Ost-Africa Linie, Hamburg	6 ships totalling	41,078 gross tons
Hamburg Amerika Linie, Hamburg	79 ships totalling	339,400 gross tons

[1] *Fairplay*, 14 June 1923, p. 674, A.G.M. of Elder Dempster & Co. Ltd.
[2] See above, pp. 215–6.
[3] *Fairplay*, 3 January 1924, p. 96, 'German Shipping in 1923'.

The difficulty with these figures is that this tonnage was used to serve many areas. This was particularly so in the case of the Hamburg Amerika Line, but even the African services of the German shipping companies covered seven routes, and these included East, South, South-West as well as West Africa. A relevant comparison can, however, be made if an examination is made of the pre-war fleets of these companies.

Fleets of German Lines Engaged in the West African Trade, 1913.[1]

Woermann Linie, Hamburg	42 ships totalling	113,028 gross tons
Hamburg-Bremen Afrika Linie	13 ships totalling	42,934 gross tons
Deutsche Ost-Afrika Linie	31 ships totalling	103,613 gross tons
Hamburg-Amerika Linie		
(including Deutsche Levante Linie)	216 ships totalling	1,102,053 gross tons

Thus the 1,361,628 gross tons of 1913 had fallen to 444,153 gross tons. This reduction amounted to two-thirds of the pre-war tonnage, but of course there had been a comparable decline in the demand for its services. Of more importance than the gradual equalisation of German cargoes and tonnage, however, was the stabilisation of the mark in November 1923, for this removed the main advantage which the German lines had enjoyed over their rivals.

'The transformation of the inland prices and wages, which are now stipulated in gold, has done away with the advantage which the German shipowners were able to draw from the low value of the currency, and which enabled them to make a profit where foreign vessels did not cover their expenses.'[2]

Other factors were also making themselves felt at about the same time:

'In addition, the occupation and separation of the Ruhr territory has resulted in a considerable quantity of goods no longer sent via the German ports. German shipbuilding has become dependent on foreign steel, and German shipping on foreign coal. What gave the German vessels a certain advantage over the other flags, has therefore, disappeared in the course of the past year (1923). What has remained is but a slight tension between the foreign and the German crews' wages; the latter have not yet reached their pre-war standard—an advantage which is offset by the prices of some articles of equipment that are above the international prices and by the purchase of expensive foreign coal. Taking it all together, German shipping has to bear the same depression as that from which international shipping is at present suffering, and there are no prospects of making profits which might permit the maintenance of the former rate of enlargement. [3]

[1] *Fairplay* 24 May 1923, p. 498, 'German Shipping News'.
[2] *Fairplay*, 3 January 1924, p. 96, 'German Shipping in 1923'.   [3] Ibid., loc. cit.

The stabilisation of the mark also had other adverse effects on the German shipping companies. In the case of the Woermann Line the dividends paid in 1913 amounted to £1,600,000 marks, or the equivalent of U.S. $400,000. In 1922 8,100,000 marks were paid out, but these were only the equivalent of U.S. $405. Thus the shareholders received only a minute return on their capital, but shares continued to be attractive as they formed a valuable hedge against inflation.

Purchase Price of Woermann Line Shares per 100 Marks in 1923

24 January	30 April	3 August	26 November
26,500 marks	44,000 marks	2,800,000 marks	37 billion marks

Once the mark was stabilised, however, this consideration lost its validity. It was then apparent that the financial structure of the Company would have to be reconstituted, or the real cost of servicing its capital would become a serious burden. In fact, all the leading shipping companies reduced their capital during 1924, the Woermann Line cutting the value of its ordinary shares from twenty million to four million marks.[1]

In these circumstances it is easy to understand why the German lines were anxious to co-operate with their former rivals and attempt to consolidate their position. Preliminary discussions between Elder Dempster and the Dutch and German interests then followed, but it was agreed that little could be achieved unless terms could be arranged with Lever Brothers, owing to their predominant share of the trade. Lever's financial difficulties, engendered by the purchase of the Niger Company, still persisted in 1923. As a result they were prepared to consider an arrangement with the shipping companies, although many directors felt that the best long-term policy would be to develop the Bromport Line. The four surviving vessels of this line had continued to carry a portion of Lever's cargoes after the war, and with a high load-factor had proved to be a good investment. The low level of freight rates since 1920, however, had removed most of the financial incentive for the owning of ships, and with their chronic shortage of capital it was felt that the investment could be more profitably utilised in some other aspect of the group's activities. Thus Levers were quite amicable to the approaches made to them, and stated that if their requirements were met they

[1] *Fairplay*, 25 December 1924, p. 622, 'German Shipping News'.

would be prepared to end their own sailings. Under these conditions agreement was quickly reached. In return for an exclusive freight arrangement the shipping companies undertook to carry Lever's cargoes at a rate which was to be no higher than that paid by their rivals. They also promised to dispose of the vessels of the Bromport Steamship Company and, in fact, three of their fleet were purchased by MacAndrews Limited, and the fourth was bought by James Moss and Company. The significance of this will be seen when it is realised that both MacAndrews and James Moss were part of Lord Kylsant's Royal Mail Group of which Elder Dempster and its associated lines were all members.[1]

The agreement with Levers left the way clear for Elder Dempster to re-establish the conference, especially as they already enjoyed the support of the smaller merchants. It was not found possible to reach an understanding with the African and Eastern Trade Corporation, whose directors thought that the volume of their cargo warranted special treatment, but this was not considered to be of sufficient importance to alter the arrangements that had been made. The need for urgency was apparent when Kylsant[2] spoke in June 1924 of the '. . . severe, and in some cases, reckless competition of foreign steamship companies . . .'[3] This, however, was not a reference to the Dutch and German lines, with whom agreement had already been reached. It referred to Danish, American, French and Italian companies who were attempting to obtain a share in the trade at almost any cost. In these circumstances it seemed to be folly to hesitate any further, and Elder Dempster, the Holland West Africa Line and the West African services of the German shipping companies joined together to form the West African Lines Conference.

The working of the Conference in the Twenties
The conference was limited to Elder Dempster, the Holland West Africa Line and the Woermann Line of Hamburg, and its object was to reserve the U.K. and continental routes to West Africa for the exclusive benefit of its members. The loyalty of the shippers was to be enforced by a 10 per cent deferred rebate on southbound cargoes, and in addi-

---

[1] See Appendix, p. 459, Table 54.
[2] Sir Owen Cosby Philipps was made Lord Kylsant in 1923.
[3] *Fairplay*, 19 June 1924, p. 741, A.G.M. of Elder Dempster & Co. Ltd.

tion, each had to contract to ship all his return cargoes via conference vessels.

The agreement also defined the rights of the shipping lines within the conference. Thus although Elder Dempster were permitted to call at the continental ports, the Dutch and Germans were not to enter the cargo service between the United Kingdom and West Africa. Other clauses determined the proportion of voyages to be undertaken by each line and the ports they could serve. Finally it was agreed that the freight rates from the Continent would be identical with those from Britain. Elder Dempster hoped that these arrangements would keep other lines and tramps out of the West African trade, and also enable the companies within the conference to obtain a reasonable return for their services.

These expectations, however, were not to be fully realised. Conditions of trade were still governed by the adverse forces created by an uncertain post-war environment and by an equally uncertain situation for future trading prospects. Thus the conference could give only a limited protection to the routes it was designed to defend. Reference has already been made to the fall in freight rates and to the decline in the cost of new tonnage. A further, very relevant, factor was the existence of a large amount of surplus capacity in the shipping industry, for it is clear that throughout the twenties a significant proportion of the British mercantile marine was continuously laid up. The amount of tonnage involved varied from year to year, but was always of sufficient importance to depress the freight market, which in turn affected the value of ships and the profits of shipping companies. Aggregate United Kingdom tonnage in commission actually rose during this period, but so did the overall size of the mercantile marine, so that there was no improvement in the situation.[1]

In the second place, although the fleets of other countries were also hard hit, the British owners were especially vulnerable because of the unfortunate cost structure of their vessels. Apart from their high capital cost and consequent high interest and depreciation charges, this was particularly reflected in wages, many British rates being double those paid on foreign-owned vessels.[2]

[1] Details of tonnage owned, laid-up and in commission are provided in the Annual Reports of the Chamber of Shipping of the United Kingdom.

[2] *Fairplay*, 23 July 1925, p. 192.

The combination of low freight rates and high wages made it impossible for all but the most efficient British lines to show a profit on current working, and those companies which had purchased more than a small proportion of their fleets during the post-war boom found themselves unable even to cover their depreciation. Unfortunately Elder Dempster, like the other members of the Royal Mail group,[1] fell into this last category, for they had been most assiduous in replacing their wartime losses—96,858 gross tons were acquired in 1919; 61,838 gross tons in 1920 and 12,776 gross tons in 1921—a grand total of 171,472 gross tons.[2]

In addition to the difficulties caused by excess capacity and an unfavourable cost structure Elder Dempster had other reasons for apprehension. In particular, although the conference included the three main shipping interests trading to West Africa, there was still competition from several lines which remained outside its structure. These included the American Bull Line, which provided a service from Manchester to the West Coast of Africa, and several French and Italian companies operating on the Mediterranean run. Individually these lines did not constitute a significant threat, but the possibility of joint action on their part could not be ignored. It was also feared that the use of chartered vessels by the larger firms of merchants was familiarising tramp steamers with the trade and thus adding to the problems of the future.

The conference was very successful in its prime object of limiting outside competition, and no new lines were able to enter the trade. In addition, the Bull Line—although backed by the United States government—was forced to end its Manchester service, and then concentrated its activities on the West Africa to North America run, which was outside the scope of the conference agreement.

The French and Italian lines were the only other companies serving West Africa and these confined their activities to the Mediterranean and the French Atlantic coast. They did not, therefore, constitute a direct threat to the conference, but nevertheless their progress was discouraged as far as possible. The Italian lines eventually ended their regular sailings to West Africa, but the French were able to maintain

---

[1] The Royal Mail group acquired 77 vessels from the British Government at a cost of £15 million at the end of the Great War. See Marischal Murray, *Union-Castle Chronicle, 1853–1953* (London: Longmans 1953), p. 178.

[2] See Appendix, p. 410, Table 17.

their position. This was in part because of their strong financial foundations, and in part because they could rely on the trade of their own West African colonies.

But the difficulties which had led Elder Dempster to decide to re-establish a conference system were paralleled in the French-West African services, and attempts to find a solution followed a similar pattern. In 1926, the Société Navale de l'Ouest, the Chargeurs Réunis and the Compagnie de Navigation Africaine agreed to combine their sailings and give exclusive shippers a 10 per cent rebate.[1] The success of this combination may have been impaired by the failure to enlist the support of the Compagnie Française de Navigation Vapeur (the Fraissinet Line), but this need not concern us here, for the French lines did not compete on the main routes of the West African Lines conference.

If the conference had to meet and overcome serious difficulties at its inception, there were signs that, with the prospect of increasing trade, order and regulation might replace the previous state of unrestricted competition. There was, however, one other serious source of competition. This sprang from the activities of three powerful groups of West African merchants; Messrs Lever Brothers, the African and Eastern Trade Corporation, and John Holt and Company. It was necessary for the shipping lines to take notice of the individual demands of these concerns in order to attempt to secure their loyalty, but in this keenly competitive atmosphere it was not possible to satisfy every request. We have already seen that Lever Brothers' financial difficulties had encouraged them to sell the Bromport Line and accept the favourable terms offered by Elder Dempster[2] when it was proposed to reconstitute the conference. The position of the African and Eastern Trade Corporation was quite different. Although second in size only to the Lever interests in West Africa, it was unable to secure what it considered to be essential concessions from Elder Dempster. The keen trading situation on the coast meant that the Corporation could not afford to ignore the arrangements made by the Niger Company, but it is probable that if no outside intervention had occurred they would have eventually achieved a compromise with the conference.

In the event, however, the firm of Henry Tyrer and Company took a hand. Tyrers, long associated with the West African shipping trade, had acted as managing agents for the Bromport Steamship Company

[1] *West Africa*, 20 February 1926, Vol. X, p. 159.   [2] See above, p. 220.

A typical surf boat and crew.

PLATE 13

Unloading into surf boats.

Alongside the ship.
PLATE 14
Returning to the shore.

throughout its active life. Lever's decision to dispose of this fleet came as a great shock to Tyrers, for they had regarded the venture as most successful from every point of view. An approach was then made to the African and Eastern Trade Corporation to see if they would be interested in running their own vessels, and in the circumstances the suggestion did not fall on deaf ears. At first the Corporation was very cautious and only utilised chartered vessels, but once it realised the advantages of possessing its own service it accepted Tyrer's advice and became shipowners. Most of the chartered vessels employed on this work belonged to the Svenska Lloyd, but one which proved to be especially suitable was the *Fordefjord*, a Norwegian shelter decker of 2,116 gross tons. This steamer, built in 1916, was therefore purchased by the Corporation and became the first of their fleet after being renamed the *Ashantian*. The *Commodore*, built in 1900, of 2,739 gross tons, was then obtained from Messrs T. & J. Harrison and renamed the *Ethiopian*.

The immediate success of these two vessels encouraged the Corporation to consider a further expansion of the fleet, and in 1925 a new ship was ordered from Barclay Curle and Company of Glasgow. This was the *Nigerian* of 3,543 gross tons, and she possessed passenger accommodation for twelve persons. Another addition to the fleet in 1925 was the *Woodville*, of 2,505 gross tons. Although somewhat elderly, (she was built in 1892), the *Woodville* gave satisfactory service until 1928. She was then replaced by the *Lafian* of 3,832 gross tons, which had been specially constructed for the Corporation by Barclay Curle and Company.

Thus during the period from 1925 to 1929, the African and Eastern Trade Corporation possessed four vessels: *Ashantian*, *Ethiopian*, *Nigerian* and either *Woodville* or *Lafian*, and these were sufficient to carry most of their cargo. A few urgently required items were shipped by the conference for the Corporation during these years, and at first these were carried at the tariff rate with no rebate, secret or normal. Later a special discount was paid by the conference,[1] but the Corporation continued to send nearly all of its goods and produce in its own vessels, or chartered additional tonnage when this proved to be necessary. The financial justification of this policy will be examined later,[2]

---

[1] *History of the United Africa Co. Ltd* to 1938, op. cit., p. 117. See below, p. 228 and Chapter 10, p. 262.

[2] See below, Chapter 10, p. 239.

and all that needs to be said at this point is that it proved to be eminently satisfactory.

The position of John Holt and Company was different from that of either Lever Brothers or the African and Eastern Trade Corporation. Holts had been willing to see the conference re-established, for it did not challenge their authority as shipowners in any way, and as merchants they welcomed the introduction of a period of stable rates. Consequently they continued their policy of owning a small number of vessels, and shipped the balance of their cargoes without penalty. This, of course, gave them the advantage of a regular service by the conference lines when it was required, without loss of rebate, and at the same time enabled them to make good profits from their own steamers because they were always fully loaded.

We have already seen that when Holts sold the *Balmore* in 1922 their fleet consisted of only two ships, the *Thomas Holt*, and the *Clematis*. These two vessels continued the service until 1926, when it was decided that the increase in trade justified an expansion of the firm's shipping capacity. Three new steamers were, therefore, ordered from Smith's Dock Company, of Middlesbrough. These were the *John Holt*, *Robert L. Holt* and the *Jonathan C. Holt* and each was of 2,920 gross tons. At the same time the *Clematis* was sold to Italian owners, so, in effect, the size of the fleet was effectively doubled. Even this increase, however, proved to be inadequate to deal with the increasing demands of the trade, and two further vessels were ordered in 1928. These were the *Godfrey B. Holt* and the *Thomas Holt* (2) and both were of 3,580 gross tons. The first *Thomas Holt* was then sold, so the fleet then comprised five ships and these maintained the service until 1938.

The *Clematis* was the only one of these vessels which failed to make a good profit. In this case it was the high original cost which caused the difficulty, for the firm paid £153,718 for her in 1920, but only received £8,500 when she was sold in 1926. Thus the penalty for buying at the top of the boom and selling during a shipping slump amounted to a loss of £52,819 but, according to the Company's records the 'loss was recovered by (the) price of produce when tonnage homeward was short.'[1] The financial achievements of the three vessels constructed in 1926 were extremely good, the *John Holt*, *Jonathan C. Holt* and *Robert L. Holt* returning respectively 17.89 per cent, 17.6 per cent and 25.7 per

[1] G.G.L. Mss., Con/2A(1), History.

cent per annum on first cost. In addition, the depreciation account was also in credit, thus showing that the profits were not obtained at the expense of insufficient provision for the future.[1]

The very high return on the original investment in these ships is the more remarkable because it was achieved at a time when world shipping was passing through a severe recession. Even when this return is discounted by the rate of interest which the Company could have obtained for its employed capital in the market, a substantial margin still remains and this can only be explained by reference to the fact that as John Holts were basically merchants engaged in carrying their own cargoes they were able to achieve very good load factors. Figures in the Company's records indicate that there was a load factor of 96.5 per cent in 1927, 83.6 per cent in 1930 and 71.2 per cent in 1938. These are very high figures, so they go a long way towards explaining the profitability of the fleet, but the limitations of the statistics should be borne in mind.[2]

The support of Levers and John Holts, plus the backing of a large number of the smaller merchants, enabled the conference to ignore the activities of the African and Eastern. The minor firms had anticipated that large and small traders would all receive equal treatment once the conference was re-formed, but the presence of secret rebates and special arrangements prevented this from being achieved. Nevertheless, it is probably true to say that the regulation of the trade helped to narrow rather than widen the gap between the rates paid by the major and minor concerns. In this context it must always be kept in mind that with so many tramp steamers desperately searching the world for cargo any unjustified increase in conference rates was impossible, and any trader who felt sufficiently aggrieved could always have recourse to chartered vessels, although this would have been at the expense of any outstanding rebate.[3]

In spite of these factors the existence of the conference prevented West African freight rates from remaining at the abysmally low level that prevailed in some other trades. The Chamber of Shipping's general index shows that rates averaged only 26 per cent of the 1920 figure during the period from 1925 to 1929[4] but Elder Dempster were able to

[1] See Appendix, p. 470, Table 66.   [2] G.G.L. Mss., JGD/KS, January 1955.

[3] It would appear that apart from the vessels chartered by the African and Eastern, few tramps were able to enter the trade.

[4] See the general index supplied in the Annual Reports of the Chamber of Shipping of the United Kingdom.

maintain their rates at a more economic level. These were increased by 50 per cent in 1924, soon after the conference was re-established but, in fact, this represented a rise of 70 per cent over the previous tariff:

'At first sight it would seem that the rates have been increased by 50 per cent, but further examination shows that by charging for services before rendered free (that is formerly included in the freight rate) the advance is more like 70 per cent.'[1]

This increase, however, is not so significant as might at first appear. Rates had been cut in January and July 1921, and again in March 1922, and were not sufficient to support a regular service. The rise in 1924 restored some revenue to the shipping companies but it cannot be considered either to be excessive or to constitute an unjust burden on the merchants. The return to a more economic rate was not the subject of great criticism, for it was generally recognised that even the new tariff was a reasonable one. The special concessions enjoyed by Lever Brothers and John Holts precluded any action by them, and left only the African and Eastern Trade Corporation as the potential leaders of any opposition. In fact, after failing to obtain suitable extra rebates the Corporation decided not to pursue the matter. Instead, as we have seen, they decided to opt out of the situation, and chose to run their own fleet. Later an agreement was reached so that the limited cargo carried by the conference for the Corporation was given 'most favoured' terms. Ultimately this agreement became known to Levers after the formation of the U.A.C. and resulted in the payment of substantial damages by the shipping companies.[2]

Elder Dempster's Financial Position

Elder Dempster's profitability after the conference had been re-established in 1924 was enhanced by the rise in its tariff, but this may give a misleading impression, because of the large number of cargoes that were subject to special discounts. Of more importance was the development of better trading conditions which were engendered by an expanding demand for West African products.[3] Thus the volume of exports from Nigeria and the Gold Coast rose substantially in the ten years between the 1919-21 period and the 1929-31 period. The rise was not a steady and continuous one, but the overall trend was almost to double

---

[1] *West Africa*, 6 December 1924, p. 1379 (Letter to the Editor).
[2] See Chapter 10, p. 262.   [3] See Appendix, p. 398. Table 2.

cargo-space requirements during the decade. Imports into both of these countries also increased significantly during this time, but it should be noted that because of falling prices these rises are reflected in volume rather than in value.

The results achieved by Elder Dempster in these circumstances must now be examined.[1] From 1925 to 1929 the capital remained almost constant. Many of the other items in the accounts also remained stable during this period, but although the declared profit in any one year was maintained at above £500,000 this was, in fact, insufficient to pay the dividends, and regular transfers had to be made from the reserves. It may be argued, however, that as Elder Dempster relied for a large part of their income on investments in shipping companies not concerned with West Africa it might be better to examine the accounts of the lines actually engaged in the trade. Furthermore, if these accounts are then compared with those of other shipping companies, a true appreciation of the state of the West African shipping trade may be deduced.

The dividends paid by the African Steam Ship Company on their total paid-up capital amounted to 5.2 per cent for each of the years from 1925 to 1929. The dividends paid by the British and African Steam Navigation Company varied a little during this period, but averaged out at 5.195 per cent per year. For convenience, therefore, it can be said that the combined dividends of the two British lines engaged in the West African trade amounted to 5.2. per cent. Other British liner companies show a very wide range of results, but this may reflect many factors apart from the efficiency and profitability of the undertaking concerned. In particular, the lack of information on retained profits at a time when few bonus issues were made, plus the great differences in capital structure and gearing, makes many of the figures of only limited value.[2]

Some of these difficulties may be dealt with by averaging out the dividends paid by all the British liner and cargo-liner companies from 1925 to 1929. The average for the period is 5.81 per cent which is marginally higher than the 5.2. per cent of the two British lines engaged in the West African trade.[3] The dividend position of the Elder Dempster companies would, therefore, appear to be slightly worse than the dividend position of the 'average' British shipping firm, but in view of the

[1] See Appendix, p. 458. Table 53.
[2] See *Fairplay's* annual list of results of British liner companies.
[3] *Fairplay*, 9 January, 1930, p. 748.

fact that their fleets included such a high proportion of vessels that were purchased at the height of the boom,[1] this really indicates a very satisfactory situation.

Unfortunately it is not possible to rely on these statistics. The process of averaging such a large set of diverse and intricate figures may well have the net effect of distorting more than it clarifies. Apart from this general objection to the combined percentages, it is also very easy to suggest specific criticisms of the dividends paid by the African, and British and African companies. The most obvious of these is the arrangement whereby Lord Kylsant was to receive $\frac{1}{2}$ per cent of the gross takings of the Royal Mail Steam Packet Company whenever it paid a dividend of 5 per cent or more.[2] The Royal Mail Company owned 433,444 ordinary shares in Elder Dempster, who held nearly all the ordinary stock and 700,000 preference shares in the African, and British and African Companies. Although this holding was only one of several possessed by the Royal Mail Steam Packet Company, Elder Dempster's contribution played a significant role in the results it achieved, and there was constant pressure, therefore, to maintain the dividends at a desired level. Whether or not these dividends were, in fact, earned or justified is therefore extremely uncertain, and it would seem to be unprofitable to use them as a serious basis for economic arguments. Further doubts concerning the accuracy of any figures produced by the companies under the control of Lord Kylsant in the twenties will be examined later in this work,[3] and it will then be seen that their inadequacy was to form the basis of the prosecution brought against Kylsant in 1931.

If the view is taken that these figures do not adequately convey the financial situation of the British shipping firms engaged in the West African trade at this time, they must be supported or refuted from other sources. There are three other indicators which are relevant to this discussion: changes in the size of the Elder Dempster fleet, changes in the proportion of the trade carried by this fleet, and changes in the trade itself.

Like so many other British shipping companies, Elder Dempster increased their tonnage in the immediate post-war period. This was

[1] See Appendix, p. 410, Table 17.

[2] Collin Brooks, *The Royal Mail Case* (Edinburgh and London: William Hodge, 1933), p. 10. See also: Special General Meeting of the Royal Mail Steam Packet Company, 15 May 1907. This gives full details of the remuneration of the Managing Director.

[3] See below, Chapter 10, p. 260.

effected by purchase and an extensive new building programme. It had been anticipated that as the newer ships were taken into the fleet the older ones would have been scrapped or sold. With the collapse of shipping prices after 1920, however, it became extremely difficult to dispose of older ships and, in Elder Dempster's case, these were retained as operational units until a more favourable opportunity for sale should occur. Thus, in 1924, Elder Dempster's fleet comprised a total of 368,000 gross tons but from then until 1929 there was an annual reduction of about 2 per cent as the older vessels were taken out of service.[1] By the end of the 1920s, therefore, Elder Dempster had a reasonably up-to-date fleet of ships totalling 324,028 gross tons, that was capable of meeting all the requirements of the rising trend in West African trade. The fact that Elder Dempster was able to maintain its fleet at this level is some indication of its commercial success and shows that it had survived the catastrophic fall in shipping values in which most of the capital raised after the war had been invested.

On the other hand the British proportion of arrivals and clearances at the ports of the British West African colonies had declined from the artificially high position it occupied in 1919. Conversely, foreign shipping lines—both conference and non-conference—had grown steadily.[2]

As we have seen, the re-entry of German shipping lines into the West African trade had been one of the main causes of the revival of the conference in 1924. In this year, British lines controlled 63 per cent of the total carrying trade, while foreign companies were responsible for the remainder: a division almost identical with that of 1913. From 1924 to 1929 the percentage share of the British lines declined by 6.1 per cent to 56.9 per cent of the total.[3] This, however, does not represent a fall in Elder Dempster's share of the trade from North Europe to West Africa. It was, in fact, caused by the increasing activities of two-non-conference foreign concerns, the Bull Line and the Chargeurs Réunis group.[4] As these companies operated only on the United States and Mediterranean routes to West Africa, they did not compete with the services arranged by the West African Lines Conference. As far as

[1] Lloyds Register of Shipping for the relevant years.
[2] See Appendix, p. 412, Table 19.
[3] 'British lines' in this context largely means Elder Dempster. The only other British vessels were those owned or chartered by the West African merchants.
[4] There were also a number of other foreign lines which operated in a small way during this period. See Appendix, p. 411, Table 18.

conference tonnage was concerned, the proportions of the trade carried by the British, German and Dutch lines remained relatively stable.

Finally, if the above facts are put into relation with the growth of West African trade as a whole, a number of interesting conclusions emerge. In the period from 1924 to 1929, in monetary terms, West African exports increased by 14.75 per cent while imports rose by 8.5 per cent. If the totals of exports and imports are expressed in real terms by allowing for changes in the price level, the percentage increases become 36.4 and 25.8 respectively.[1] Thus there was a substantial increase in trade and this was largely shared out by the members of the conference.

These various shreds of evidence give weight and background to the insufficiency and unreliability of data relating to Elder Dempster's financial position.[2] It is clear that the conference freight rates (even when discounted by secret rebates) had fallen less than the national average. To a certain extent this was the direct result of the conference agreement for it permitted marginally higher rates to be charged, while preventing other lines from entering the trade. But the extent to which it could do this was strictly limited by the existence of so much surplus shipping capacity, and it is probable that the position could not have been held without the stimulus of a growing demand for West African produce.

There is, therefore, justification for the view that all the conference lines, not least Elder Dempster, profited from the regulation of the trade. Against the background of an increasing trend in both the volume and value of the trade, freight rates were increased or maintained. Thus, earning capacity was assured and the employed capital of the shipping lines was protected. The relative share of the trade, as between one shipping line and another, was also maintained. But the beneficial effects of the conference were not confined to the shipping companies, for it brought stability to the whole organisation of interests engaged in carrying and trading goods to and from the Coast. This great benefit might well be contrasted with other less successful episodes in other trades during the same period. For example, the South African Con-

[1] See Appendix, p. 398, Table 3.

[2] Few papers of Elder Dempster & Co. Ltd's Accounts Department survived the move from Colonial House to India Building, and the war-time fire. Hence the dependence on other sources for the period up to 1932.

ference was subjected to ruthless competition from tramp steamships in 1926 and 1927.[1] Such competition not only caused financial loss to the South African Conference lines, but also led to great confusion in the organisation of the trade itself. To have established stability in the freight market, to have provided regularity of service, and to have eliminated the harmful effects of cut-throat competition must stand greatly to the credit of the West African Lines Conference, particularly as it was achieved at a time when overseas trade in general was becoming increasingly subject to severe dislocation.

From the point of view of Elder Dempster's trading position, therefore, there would seem to have been little cause for apprehension at the beginning of 1929. In fact, this year was to see the first of two disasters which were to fall upon the Company in quick succession. Whether or not these could have been averted or minimised by the prompt action of the board of directors are problems which will form an important part of the subject-matter which will be discussed in the next chapter.

[1] F. E. Hyde, *Shipping Enterprise and Management* 1830–1939 (Liverpool University Press, 1967), pp. 138–143.

Chapter 10

The END of the Royal Mail Group

The Depression Deepens

The relatively rosy expectations for West African trade that existed at the beginning of 1929 were soon to be disappointed. The onset of a slump in world trade in 1929 and the deepening of this depression in 1930 and 1931 led to a sharp decline in shipping activity throughout the world. In common with other shipping companies, the West African lines suffered severely, for commerce fell to disastrously low levels. The magnitude of the fall is illustrated by the fact that aggregate net tonnage entered and cleared from the British West African ports showed a decline of 18 per cent in 1931 and 32 per cent in 1932 when compared with the 1928 figure.[1]

A more precise indicator of the impact of the depression is to be seen in the decline in imports and exports. Thus imports fell from £29,858,000 in 1928 to only £12,184,000 in 1931 and exports were reduced from £32,593,000 to £16,167,000 during the same period.[2] When these figures are expressed in real terms, however, the extent of the fluctuation was considerably less, because of the steep decline in the price level.[3] Measured in monetary terms, therefore, imports fell to 41 per cent and exports to 50 per cent of the 1928 figures. If account is taken of changes in the price level it will be seen that in real terms the decline was less marked, imports falling to 59.2 per cent and exports to 60.1 per cent.

[1] Statistical Abstract for the British Empire, Cmd. 4819, 1935, Table 84.
[2] Compiled from Cmd. 4819, Table 100.   [3] See Appendix, p. 399, Table 4.

The course of the depression after 1929 was such that every shipping route in the world was adversely affected and shipping companies generally suffered enormous losses. In the case of West Africa, however, the decline in trade from economic causes was aggravated by other factors. These included, firstly, a change in the competitive structure of the trade, and secondly, a breakdown in the financial organisation of the Royal Mail Group. Largely as a result of these difficulties the share of British tonnage on the route tended to fall:

Share of British Shipping in the Trade of
British West Africa

1928 = 56.2%	1930 = 56.5%	1932 = 54.3%
1929 = 56.9%	1931 = 51.0%	1933 = 52.3%[1]

Although the failure of the Royal Mail Group was ultimately to have serious repercussions for Elder Dempster, a more immediate and direct threat to its well-being was caused by the creation of the United Africa Company in 1929.

The Formation of the United Africa Company

As we have already seen, Lever Brothers purchased several firms of West African merchants in 1910 and 1912. The experience gained with these companies, plus the increasing demand for palm produce that could be utilised in the manufacture of soap and margarine, then persuaded Levers that they should extend their interests on the coast. More small firms were therefore acquired, and in 1919 it was decided to purchase the Niger Company. The West African firms already owned by Lever Brothers, and those subsequently acquired in the twenties, were all vested in the Niger Company,[2] and after 1925 this made moderate profits.[3] Thus Lever's interests on the coast were all contained within

---

[1] Calculated from the Statistical Abstract for the British Empire, (Relevant years).

[2] See the *History of the United Africa Co. Ltd to 1938*, p. 103.

[3] The authorised capital of the Niger Company was £3,000,000 of which £500,000 of 6 per cent Cumulative Preference Shares, and £1,250,000 of Ordinary Shares had been issued. Levers, however, had paid approximately £8,000,000 for about 98 per cent of the Ordinary stock in 1920. Profits made after 1925 were as follows:

1926 = £201,659	1928 = £140,722
1927 = £205,748	1929 = £212,189

Source: History of the United Africa Co. Ltd to 1938, p. 58 and p. 103.

the Niger Company,[1] and by 1928 this probably constituted the largest firm of merchants in West Africa.[2]

In 1919 the African and Eastern Trade Corporation Limited was formed by the amalgamation of the African Association, the two Miller firms, and Swanzys.[3] During its first year the Corporation acquired many West African firms as well as a large number of companies based in Britain.[4] Businesses were also established in Morocco, in East Africa and in Singapore.

The African and Eastern Trade Corporation experienced heavy losses in 1921, but moderate profits were then achieved in every year up to 1928;

Results of the African and Eastern Trade Corporation Limited

1921	£1,794,796	(Loss)
1922	£ 539,774	(Profit before tax)
1923	£ 382,353	(Tax paid profit)
1924	£ 403,549	(Tax paid profit)
1925	£ 410,815	(Tax paid profit)
1926 (9 months)	£ 264,698	(Tax paid profit)
1927	£ 382,612	(Tax paid profit)
1928	£ 96,953	(Loss)[5]

Thus in spite of many early problems the Corporation had apparently survived the economic difficulties of the twenties, and during this period many additional companies were acquired or established.[6] In fact, however, once it made a loss its financial equilibrium was upset. This was because the deficit of 1928 resulted in a loss of confidence by those banks and credit houses who normally supplied it with its day-to-day requirements. Indeed, limited financial aid was only continued on the understanding that a nominee of the banks' choice would be installed as the Corporation's chairman.

[1] The only important exception was that the Huileries du Congo Belge were not in the Niger group.

[2] The assets of the African & Eastern Trade Corporation had a greater book value than those of the Niger group, and the Corporation was the only firm that counted in the Gold Coast.

[3] See above p. 211.

[4] See the *History of the United Africa Co. Ltd to 1938*, pp. 95–6.

[5] In 1920 the African and Eastern Trade Corporation had a total issued capital in Preference and Ordinary shares of £4,504,216. *Source: History of the United Africa Co. Ltd to 1938*, p. 94 and pp. 105–8.

[6] See the *History of the United Africa Co. Ltd to 1938*, p. 106.

The new chairman, appointed in December, 1928, was Sir Robert Waley Cohen,[1] and it soon became clear to him that only a merger with the Niger Company could save the Corporation from liquidation. Negotiations between Sir Robert Waley Cohen and Mr D'Arcy Cooper started almost at once and by March 1929 they had reached a compromise agreement. This provided for the Niger Company and the African and Eastern Trade Corporation to cease their activities as trading concerns. Instead, in return for the transfer of their fixed and floating assets, each became an equal holding company in a new trading firm—the United Africa Company Limited.[2]

The Break between the Conference Lines and the United Africa Company
Sir Robert Waley Cohen became the first chairman of the United Africa Company—Mr D'Arcy Cooper joining the board—and so was responsible for many of the decisions that were necessary to create a single, uniform organisation. One aspect of this work concerned the negotiation of fresh freight rates with the shipping companies, as the individual agreements that had been made by the Niger Company and the African and Eastern Trade Corporation were due to expire at the end of 1929. A preliminary meeting between Waley Cohen and Lord Kylsant took place on 14 May 1929 and a second—at which D'Arcy Cooper was also present—was held on 18 June. Little progress was made during these discussions or at a further meeting held on 7 August, so a lengthy dialogue developed in which both sides made many proposals and counter-proposals.

Waley Cohen argued his case for a substantial reduction in freight rates on the size of the shipments which had been made by the Niger Company and the African and Eastern in 1928. These consisted of 653,000 tons, out and home, and included 60 per cent of the palm oil, 45 per cent of the palm kernels, 60 per cent of the ground-nuts and 50 per cent of the cocoa exported from West Africa. Of this total, 530,000 tons were lifted by the conference lines, the balance being carried in

[1] Sir Robert Waley Cohen, (1877–1952) had a strong business background. Amongst his many positions was that of Managing Director of the Shell Transport & Trading Co. Ltd, and at one time he was Petroleum Adviser to the Army Council. (See: *Who Was Who*, 1951–1960, p. 226).

[2] This had a capital of £13,000,000 in fully paid Ordinary Shares, but was increased to £14,200,000 almost immediately. *Source: History of the United Africa Co. Ltd to 1938*, p. 112.

the two firms' own vessels. The facts which lay behind Waley Cohen's demands were that while the conference had charged a freight rate which averaged out at 45s per ton, cargo shipped on company-owned vessels cost only an average of 25s 6d per ton. It is relevant to bear in mind that rebates and other payments amounting to £265,000 were received during the year by the two Companies but, even so, there remained a substantial difference between what they actually paid for the carriage of their cargoes and what it would have cost if they had possessed sufficient tonnage of their own. This knowledge convinced Waley Cohen that the conference lines could afford to reduce their rates drastically and, in consequence, he approached the negotiations with a great deal of determination.

Mr Sharrock of Elder Dempster, acting for the conference and Lord Kylsant, recognised that the formation of the United Africa Company, together with the economic difficulties of the trade, created a situation in which major reductions in freight rates would have to be conceded. He therefore suggested concessions which would have cost the shipping companies £478,000 each year. As the U.A.C. provided some 40 per cent of all conference cargoes this would have meant a saving to them of £219,000 per annum, but Waley Cohen maintained that this was insufficient to offset the financial advantages of operating his own fleet. However, he did agree that the sacrifice of nearly half a million pounds annually by the lines was a realistic figure and he did not seriously quarrel with this amount. His dispute arose over the manner in which it was to be distributed and, at first, he was adamant that the whole sum should go to the U.A.C. and none to its competitors.

This claim may appear to be somewhat extravagant but to Waley Cohen the situation was absolutely clear. He was quite prepared to give the conference lines all his cargoes and he had no objection to them making a reasonable profit. On the other hand he was not willing to pay much more than what he felt, based on his experience with company-owned vessels, were the true costs of shipment. He appreciated the value of regular conference sailings and would have agreed to pay a little for their convenience, but he maintained that the U.A.C. could not afford the luxury of this service if it were to cost significantly more than the expense of doing it for themselves.

There is little doubt that Elder Dempster and the other lines fully understood Waley Cohen's point of view and in their own interest made strenuous attempts to meet his terms. Unfortunately there was a serious misunderstanding for which both sides must bear some responsibility as to exactly what constituted realistic freight rates. At the time of the amalgamation of U.A.C. took over five ships which had been previously owned by the Niger Company, and the African and Eastern.[1] The running of these vessels had been highly lucrative when compared with those owned and operated by the conference; but this was, perhaps, a false analogy. The margin of profit to the Niger Company and African and Eastern from ships which had involved a very small capital investment was far greater than that which Elder Dempster could earn from their ships, many of which had been originally bought at the high prices ruling during the post-war boom. In addition, the obligation to maintain regular services meant that conference vessels were forced to sail whether full or empty, so their average load factor was inevitably far below that of the company-owned ships on whose performance Waley Cohen based so many of his arguments. For example *Ethiopian*, which cost the African and Eastern only £7,442 in 1925, made a net profit of £5,857 on a single voyage in 1927.[2] Even *Nigerian*, which was built specially for the African and Eastern in 1925, cost only £70,299, and she made a net profit of £9,332 on one of her early trips.[3]

In fact, the very success of the African and Eastern's ship-owning activities had been so marked that the Niger Company had decided to follow their example and in 1928 had purchased the *Ars*. This proved to be a highly profitable investment and she paid for herself in less than two voyages to West Africa.[4] The Niger Company was so impressed with the results that it decided to acquire three additional vessels, but the amalgamation came before the policy could be

[1]Name	Gross Tons	Dead Weight	Built	Purchased	Cost	Owner
Ashantian	2,116	3,950	1916	1924	£ —	A. & E.
Ethiopian	2,739	4,270	1902	1925	£ 7,442	A. & E.
Nigerian	3,543	4,684	1925	NEW	£70,299	A. & E.
Lafian	3,832	4,895	1928	NEW	£80,588	A. & E.
Ars	2,936	4,465	1897	1928	£ 8,000	N.C.

[2] Henry Tyrer Mss., *Ethiopian*, Voyage 6.   [3] Ibid., *Nigerian*, Voyage 4.

[4] Captain G. G. Astbury, D.S.C., the first master of *Ars* when she was bought by the Niger Company, informed the author that although she was an old vessel, built in 1897, she was reliable and never missed a day through mechanical breakdown. See also, 'The Master Remembers', *Palm Bulletin*, Vol. V, No. II (1964), pp. 16–18 and No. III, pp. 13–15.

implemented.[1] Nevertheless, the ship-owning experience of both the African and Eastern and the Niger Company convinced a strong faction in the newly formed U.A.C. that it should carry its own goods, and their pressure further strengthened their chairman's resolve to secure substantial concessions or proceed independently.

Waley Cohen's main proposal was for a differential tariff for homeward cargo. Under this arrangement the first 100,000 tons shipped by any merchant in any year would be charged at the normal rate—he suggested 44s 1d per ton—but any excess over this amount would only be charged 10s per ton. It was anticipated that only the U.A.C. would benefit from this scheme, but on its projected 380,000 tons homeward the expected saving, together with a concession on outward freight rates, was equal to the £478,000 by which the conference lines had already agreed they were prepared to reduce their receipts.

From their point of view Elder Dempster and the other shipping companies disliked this proposal intensely. Their offer of nearly half a million pounds' reduction per year was as far as they could go and still remain in business, so they could not increase the total amount. If they gave all, or most, of the reduction to the U.A.C. they felt it would inevitably strengthen what they regarded as their chief rival at the expense of their main supporters. The loyalty of the unorganised 60 per cent of the trade had to be balanced against the potential support of the 40 per cent organised by the U.A.C. It was a difficult decision to make and one which might have gone either way but, in fact, the other claims made by Waley Cohen at this time effectively put the matter out of court. Many of these, possibly all, were 'window-dressing', whose chief function may have been to act as bargaining counters at the negotiating table,[2] but at least three were regarded seriously by the members of the conference.

[1] These were to be named the *Jus, Pak,* and *Lord Lugard. Source*: Author's interview with Lord Cole, the chairman of Unilever Limited, on 21 April 1965.

[2] The only comprehensive guide to the wranglings of the interested parties is to be found in the pages of the magazine *West Africa*, e.g.

9 Nov. 1929 p. 1517	4 Jan. 1930 pp. 1807–8
16 Nov. 1929 p. 1533	22 Feb. 1930 p. 174
16 Nov. 1929 pp. 1555–6	22 Mar. 1930 p. 321
23 Nov. 1929 p. 1584	29 Mar. 1930 p. 333
30 Nov. 1929 pp. 1618–20	5 Jul. 1930 p. 845
21 Dec. 1929 p. 1721	23 Aug. 1930 p. 1140
28 Dec. 1929 p. 1762	30 Aug. 1930 pp. 1184–5
	4 Oct. 1930 pp. 1370–2

Firstly, a special rate was demanded for palm oil loaded in bulk. The U.A.C. controlled some 60 per cent of the palm oil exported from the coast and possessed the only three installations for the bulk loading of this commodity. A corollary to this demand was the insistence that the shipping companies must not provide any of these facilities themselves and it was also stipulated that increased rates should be charged for the carriage of palm oil in casks. If the conference lines had accepted these suggestions it would have placed an intolerable burden on the rest of the traders who lacked bulk loading installations.[1] If this had been adopted with the intention of forcing them to construct similar facilities there could be no complaint, but the condition that the shipping companies were not to erect or operate any such machinery at any time in the future meant, in practice, that the U.A.C. would gradually have secured the whole trade in this commodity.

The second demand was that the shipping companies were required to guarantee preference over rival merchants for cargo space. In this case it was possible that some amicable arrangement might have been worked out, but the fact that an option on all space had to be actually guaranteed presented the conference lines with an almost impossible situation. However, it was the third and final claim which really upset Elder Dempster, for it was required to hand over all its West Coast agencies and lighterage companies.[2]

Taken together, the three demands were looked on as evidence that the U.A.C. was seeking to obtain a virtual monopoly of the main export commodities which, in time, would have meant the elimination of all other expatriate merchants. The conference lines feared that in this event the next step would be for the U.A.C. to develop its own transport services and in the absence of independent shippers there would be little that they could do to fight back. These fears may have been quite unjustified, for Waley Cohen always insisted that he was not anxious to become a shipowner and that each should stick to his own business.[3] Nevertheless if the U.A.C. had achieved an undue preponderance in the trade it could have been tempted to force freight rates down to

[1] In practice the United Africa Company was prepared to offer the use of these facilities to other exporters and two firms did use them.

[2] *West Africa*, 4 January 1930, pp. 1807-8. These points were confirmed by the author during discussions with Lord Cole.

[3] Papers of the United Africa Company (hereinafter referred to as U.A.C.Mss.), Letter from Sir Robert Waley Cohen to Lord Kylsant, 8 August 1929.

unremunerative levels or even to carry all its own cargoes. The chance of this happening may have been quite slight,[1] but the conference lines —especially Elder Dempster—were not prepared to take the risk, and their attitude hardened accordingly.

The net effect of the pressures on the two sides was that no appreciable progress was made towards a settlement and negotiations were broken off several times. However, it was agreed that a final attempt to find a solution ought to be made and it was arranged that this should take place at the U.A.C.'s Head Office on 1 November 1929. Both sides appreciated the importance of what was to prove the last full assembly of the interested parties and therefore sent their strongest delegations. On the one side were Sir Robert Waley Cohen, (Chairman of the U.A.C.) Mr D'Arcy Cooper (Chairman of Lever Brothers), Mr Anton Jurgens and Mr P. Rykens (of the Margarine Union) and Col. Nicholl and Mr R. H. Muir (Directors of the U.A.C. with special responsibility for shipping). On the other side were Mr David Jones and Mr Sharrock (of Elder Dempster) Mr Bicker Caarten (of the African Steam Ship Company) Mr Hudig and Mr Arriens (of the Holland West Africa Line) and Mr Bohlen and Mr Amsinck (who represented the Woermann Line).

Waley Cohen took the chair and opened the proceedings by referring to the failure of the negotiations. He said that he was anxious that each side's views should be known and understood by the other so that the possibility of misunderstandings could be eliminated. He then went on to say,

'. . . that he understood the Conference Lines were prepared to diminish their total freight charges in the West African trade by about £500,000 but that they wished to make the greater part of this reduction to all traders, not only to those who were prepared to enter into organised arrangements but also to casual traders who insisted on maintaining promiscuous competition. He stated that The United Africa Co. had always made it clear that anything they might receive from the Conference in the way of a rebate freight would be shared by them with any other firms or companies who were prepared to co-operate with them in making organised arrangements for conducting the West African trade and that the United Africa Co. would be prepared to accept the £500,000 offered as an adequate reduction of freight on that condition and provided it were used to

[1] Ibid., Letter from Sir Robert Waley Cohen to Major C. R. Bates, D.S.O., 1 November 1929. Bates was a Director of the African & Eastern who was employed by the U.A.C. to prepare and put into operation a plan for the reorganisation of its affairs in Nigeria.

promote organisation and not to perpetuate disorganisation in the West African trade. In his opinion the West African trade has suffered for years from cut-throat competition which has rendered it weak and ineffective and the issue at stake seemed to him whether that condition was to be perpetuated or whether the present opportunity was to be taken to put the trade on a sound footing.'

He further emphasised that '. . . all genuine merchants trading in West Africa would be welcome to join in the organisation irrespective of nationality.'

The leader of the conference lines representatives, Mr David Jones, then replied. He stated that: 'The sum they had in view was nearer £450,000 than £500,000, but on principle they were prepared to reduce their existing freight charges by this amount provided the United Africa Co. ceased to engage in the Ocean freight business and sold their existing fleet, but the Conference must insist upon applying the rebates to all traders whether forming part of an organised trade or not.'

A general discussion followed and then the shipping delegates withdrew to hold separate talks. On the resumption Waley Cohen made what was, in effect, the U.A.C.'s final offer:

'He said that calling the sum which the Shipping Lines were prepared to concede £450,000, the United Africa Company's proposal was that of this amount, after deducting the £125,000 which it had been agreed should be paid to them as compensation for giving up their ships, there should then be paid to The United Africa Co. £175,000 as their share of the Rebate of Freight and that the balance of £150,000 should be allocated for The United Africa Co. to divide proportionally to all other merchants who were prepared to co-operate in organised trade arrangements in the same proportion that the £175,000 bore to the 600,000 tons which were carried for The United Africa Co. in 1928.'

Further discussion followed but, eventually, Mr David Jones said that the conference would not accept such an arrangement as they believed in free competition. Both Mr D'Arcy Cooper and Mr Anton Jurgens then spoke and indicated that Lever Brothers and the Margarine Union fully supported the stand taken by the U.A.C. and that

'. . . they had both come to the definite conclusion that the West African trade as well as the public interest would best be served by using every effort to bring the trade to an organised basis on the lines that had been suggested and that they were both of them entirely opposed to any arrangement which would maintain the cut-throat competition which had already done so much harm to the development of the West African trade.'

Mr David Jones then repeated his refusal to accept the proposal and the meeting was terminated.[1]

This marked the end of formal negotiations. The U.A.C. then proceeded with the making of arrangements for the carriage of their cargoes, while the conference lines finalised their plans for the future. Almost immediately Elder Dempster made it clear that they would not allow the U.A.C. to continue to use their lighterage facilities. The U.A.C. was therefore forced to make arrangements at considerable expense to extend its own services at Lagos, Calabar, Douala, Abonema, Eket and in Sierra Leone. In spite of this added cause for dissension, efforts to heal the breach continued to be made right up to the deadline at the end of the year. The failure of these final attempts at a reconciliation then led to U.A.C. to divert its shipments to its own or chartered vessels. Nevertheless, contact between the two parties was maintained throughout the early months of 1930 and, in fact, hopes of a settlement persisted, in some respects, until the formation of Elder Dempster Lines Holdings Limited in 1936.

Action Taken by the United Africa Company to Secure Shipping Space
Although the break between the United Africa Company and the conference lines occurred with the expiration of their shipping agreements on 31 December 1929, the course of the dispute must be antedated to 1928. The fundamental cause of this earlier disagreement centred upon the bulk carriage of palm oil, particularly between West Africa and the Atlantic ports of the United States. This route was not subject to the terms of the West African Lines Conference agreement and, consequently, the trade was not regulated to anything like the same extent as that between West Africa and Northern Europe. The Niger Company was anxious to increase the carriage of palm oil in bulk, especially after it had provided bulk loading facilities at three West African ports,[2] but in the Report of its Annual General Meeting held in March 1929, it was stated that Elder Dempster had not provided sufficient capacity in the previous year:

'The bulk shipments of oil to the United States', stated the Chairman of the

[1] U.A.C.Mss., Minutes of Meeting held at Africa House, Kingsway, W.C.2. on Friday 1 November 1929, at 11.30 a.m. between a committee of the Board of United Africa and members of the West African Shipping Conference.
[2] These were situated at Burutu, Apapa and at Port Harcourt.

Company, 'have been made without major difficulties, except in regard to the provision of bulk space in steamers. The established lines running in this trade have shown a regrettable lack of enterprise in this respect, in that they failed to find space for more than 50% of our requirements in 1928. This has driven us to look to outside steamers, and has given rise to the recent attempt on the part of these lines to prevent such steamers obtaining outward cargo from the States to the Coast. This, in view of their own failure, is, in my opinion, quite unwarranted.'[1]

This was a fairly strong expression of opinion, and one not likely to encourage the continuance of a harmonious relationship between Elder Dempster and the Niger Company. During 1929 this cause of friction increased. Elder Dempster were still unable to provide sufficient bulk capacity for the American trade, so the Niger Company arranged to charter enough tonnage to carry the balance of its requirements to the United States. The evidence shows that the Niger Company contracted to provide a minimum quantity of 32,000 tons of palm oil for shipment across the Atlantic within the period 1 March 1929 to 30 June 1930.[2] This quantity was far beyond Elder Dempster's capacity at this time,[3] so the necessity for chartering additional vessels had become more urgent. Furthermore, when it became obvious towards the end of 1929 that a break with the conference lines was inevitable, the Niger Company (now amalgamated with the African and Eastern Trade Corporation as the United Africa Company) was forced to find new sources of shipping.

An agreement to replace the Elder Dempster tonnage on the West Africa to United States route was signed on 21 November 1929. Under the terms of this arrangement,[4] the American West Africa Line Incorporated (the Barber Line) was to carry all of the United Africa Company's cargoes to and from New York, Boston, Philadelphia and New Orleans. The United Africa Company promised to provide a minimum of 20,000 tons of cargo each year to the above-mentioned ports, and, in addition, undertook to give the Barber Line first refusal on cargo to and from other United States ports. Schedules of freight rates were also agreed with the proviso that should a new shipping company enter the

---

[1] *West Africa*, 23 February 1929, p. 208. (48th Ordinary General Meeting of the Niger Co.)

[2] U.A.C.Mss., Reference 114, Charter Party between Rederiaktie-Bolaget Transatlantic of Gothenburg and the Niger Company, 21 December 1928.

[3] See below, p. 248.

[4] U.A.C.Mss., Reference 559, The Barber Line Agreement, 21 November 1929.

trade, the Barber Line would reduce its charges from what amounted to the Elder Dempster tariff rates, to the level of those fixed by the new competitor.

The United Africa Company was clearly in a very strong bargaining position at this time, so it seems somewhat surprising that it agreed to allow the Barber Line the right to sub-contract up to 50 per cent of its cargoes to Elder Dempster. It is probable, however, that this freedom of action was granted in spite of the tremendous surplus of shipping because at any given moment there might be a shortage of suitable shallow-draught vessels fitted with bulk tanks, and Elder Dempster, of course, possessed a number of ships specifically designed for the trade.

Thus the United Africa Company was able to make satisfactory arrangements for its American trade, but rather different action was necessary to deal with the carriage of its cargoes between West Africa and Britain. The firm of Henry Tyrer and Company Limited had acted as managing agents for the ships of both the African and Eastern Trade Corporation and the Niger Company, and had continued this work when the United Africa Company was formed. Consequently, when Waley Cohen was negotiating with the conference lines he turned to Tyrers for guidance and as early as August 1929 they submitted a report which showed the feasibility of independent action:

> 'You will observe that with one or two exceptions the whole of your traffic can be handled without the assistance of any liner company, and in the event of your decision to charter rather than build the additional craft needed to support your own tonnage it will not be necessary for you to incur any large capital expenditure, whilst the new system of carriage need not entail any material change in your own organisation.'[1]

As we have already seen, before the break with the conference a part of the United Africa Company's cargoes was already being dealt with by the fleet of five ships which had been taken over from the Niger Company and the African and Eastern Trade Corporation. In the new circumstances it was decided to build up the competitive strength of the fleet, but financial considerations precluded the possibility of providing enough company-owned vessels to establish a comprehensive service. In fact, only two additional ships were purchased during 1930. These were the *Mendian* of 3,752 gross tons, and the *Zarian* of 3,815 gross tons.

---

[1] Henry Tyrer Mss., Henry Tyrer & Co. Ltd to the United Africa Co. Ltd, 26 August 1929, 'Carriage of Merchandise and Produce to and from West Africa'.

Both were very old steamships, having been built in 1903 and 1907 respectively, and both were quite inexpensive—the *Mendian* costing only £11,250.[1] As the *Ars* was sold during 1930, this meant a net addition to the fleet of only 4,631 gross tons. Obviously six vessels totalling 19,797 gross tons could not cope with all the requirements of the United Africa Company,[2] and it was therefore necessary to make other arrangements to carry the balance of its freight.

It was Tyrer's responsibility to ensure that adequate tonnage was available for the carriage of produce and merchandise and they, in fact, fixed the sailings of the chartered vessels that were required to supplement the services provided by the company-owned ships.[3] By the end of January 1930, the U.A.C. had thirty-seven ships on charter and although these could not be fully loaded on the outward voyage it was claimed that they were carrying its cargoes at 1s per ton less than the new reduced rates offered by the conference lines.[4]

It was also found necessary to reorganise the United Africa Company's shipping department in Liverpool. Following the amalgamation of the Niger Company and the African and Eastern Trade Corporation, their shipping departments had been joined together in name but, in fact, two separate organisations continued to exist. This duplication was both expensive and inefficient and in November 1929, Mr A. C. Geake was appointed Liverpool shipping manager with the particular task of merging the two bodies into a single unit.[5]

The United Africa Company's Liverpool office also contained a produce department for selling items received from abroad and a buying department for purchasing goods required for export. It was the shipping department's job to obtain copies of all invoices showing items ordered by the buying department. It then got in touch with the manufacturers or agents for the goods concerned, and arranged for them to

[1] U.A.C.Mss., These were formerly the *Laurel Branch* and the *Cambrian Empress*.

[2] The *Kumasian* of 3,400 gross tons was purchased in 1931, but as the *Ashantian* of 2,116 gross tons was then sold, the net gain was only 1,284 gross tons.

[3] The chartering agents who obtained the vessels for Tyrers were Messrs Erlebach and Company who were members of the Baltic Exchange. Many of the later vessels chartered by Erlebachs for Tyrers were owned by John Morrisons, of Newcastle. *Source*: Author's interview with Mr Donald E. Erlebach, March 1966.

[4] Papers of Lever Brothers (hereinafter referred to as Lever Mss.) M.D.C., 30 January 1930.

[5] Mr A. C. Geake had previously been the London Shipping Manager of the African and Eastern Trade Corporation. *Source*: Author's interview with Mr Geake in May 1965.

be delivered for shipment at a pre-arranged time.[1] Finally the shipping department notified Henry Tyrer and Company of the quantities to be expected, and Tyrers ensured that the necessary tonnage was available.

The break with the conference lines at the end of 1929 made little difference to the work of the shipping department. If anything, in fact, it simplified matters, for Tyrers were now informed of all cargo available for shipment and it was no longer necessary to consult Elder Dempster. It should be appreciated, however, that most of Lever Brothers' refrigerated items and all of its soap continued to be sent via Elder Dempster,[2] but the organisation of these shipments was the responsibility of a separate office—Lever Brothers shipping department.[3]

It is obvious, therefore, that the United Africa Company was reasonably well prepared for any eventuality when the break came with the conference lines. Their interests in the American trade were adequately safeguarded and they had, as far as was possible, minimised their risks in the trade between West Africa and the United Kingdom. It now remains for us to make an examination of Elder Dempster's reaction to these changes.

It is clear that Elder Dempster regarded as unfair the charge made by the United Africa Company that they had been slow in providing sufficient capacity to meet the requirements of their trade in palm oil in bulk. The first installation for loading this commodity in bulk was not erected until 1927,[4] but by 1928, when a second installation came into operation, Elder Dempster were already supplying enough tonnage fitted with suitable tanks to carry half of the output. By the end of 1929 when a third facility had become operational, Elder Dempster had equipped fourteen vessels with tanks and these could carry a total of 9,000 tons of oil. A further five ships were converted by the middle of 1930 and these added an extra 4,000 tons to the bulk capacity of the fleet. In addition, three new vessels were under construction at this date and as these had a tank capacity of 1,000 tons each, the total bulk carriage amounted to

[1] A more detailed description of these functions is given in 'The House on Mersey Street', *Unilever House Magazine*, Oct.–Nov. 1956 pp. 3–5 and 14.

[2] Author's interview with Mr A. E. Muirhead, Director of Elder Dempster Lines Limited, in June 1965.

[3] The Shipping Departments of Lever Brothers and the U.A.C. were amalgamated in 1935.

[4] *West Africa*, 23 February 1929, p. 207, '48th General Meeting of the Niger Company Ltd'.

16,000 tons.[1] Thus in the period of six months from January to July, 1930, Elder Dempster increased their bulk oil carrying capacity by approximately 80 per cent. Unfortunately, however, the fact that Elder Dempster had made a sustained effort to provide sufficient bulk capacity in no way invalidates the criticism that they had, in fact, failed to keep pace with the changing demands of the trade.[2] Furthermore, some of the steps which Elder Dempster took to safeguard their position obviously created suspicion and generated ill feeling. The attempt, mentioned above, made in 1928 to prevent the chartered ships of the Niger Company from obtaining back cargoes in the United States, is a case in point.

The Reaction of the Conference and Traders

When it became clear that a break with the United Africa Company was inevitable, the conference lines took drastic action to secure the loyalty of their other shippers. A new circular was issued on 14 December 1929, and while this did not alter the basic freight rates, it nevertheless made substantial changes in the structure of disbursements. Under the terms of this circular,[3] a 20 per cent primage charge was introduced on all cargoes to West African ports.[4] Provided that the shippers had complied with the regulations laid down by the conference, half of this charge was refunded immediately and the remainder after the expiration of seven months. In addition a considerable increase in rebates was announced. These amounted to 40 per cent on salt and 25 per cent on cement and galvanised sheeting for outward cargoes; 45 per cent on palm kernels and ground-nuts, 40 per cent on cocoa, 30 per cent on palm oil, 20 per cent on tin ore and 10 per cent on timber for homewards cargoes. Though subject to stringent regulations, these rebates, by comparison with those offered previously[5] and those currently allowed by other conferences, were substantial. They had the effect of securing a reduction of between 10 and 40 per cent on the earlier tariff,[6]

[1] *West Africa*, 5 July 1930, pp. 843–9, 'A.G.M. of Elder Dempster & Co. Ltd'.

[2] It could be argued that it was relatively easy and cheap to install bulk loading equipment, but difficult and expensive to alter existing ships.

[3] *West Africa*, 21 December 1929, p. 1721. 'Ocean Transport and the West African Trade'.

[4] Except on outward through shipments.

[5] These already amounted to 10 per cent on outward cargoes.

[6] *Fairplay*, 6 February 1930, p. 406, 'West African Freight Overhaul'.

and were a direct challenge to the new activities of the United Africa Company.

The Conference Circular announcing the reductions caused much annoyance to the U.A.C. Speaking early in 1930, Waley Cohen, after complaining that freight rates had previously been maintained at too high a level, objected that rates were now far too low: '". . . the level to which freights have now been reduced is not an economic one . . ." he stated.'[1] There was, however, something of a conciliatory note in his concluding remarks:

> ' "I feel sure," he added, "we shall reach friendly co-operation with them (i.e. the Conference Lines), and we shall persuade them not to return to the somewhat extravagant freights of the past." '

The annoyance was quite intense because of the feeling that it had largely been the action of the U.A.C. which had caused the conference to lower its rates. Yet far from benefiting from these charges, the only real effect was that the opposition of their rivals on the Coast was being appreciably strengthened. It should be remembered that the U.A.C. was primarily a merchanting organisation and could not, in the circumstances of the time, afford a prolonged price-cutting war with other West African merchants. They were just as vulnerable as other traders to the effects of keen competition and feared that the new conference rates would reduce the advantage they held over their opponents.

On the other hand the West African merchants who were not part of the U.A.C. regarded its formation as a direct threat. Many thought that there was a real danger that the growth of the Lever interest would ultimately lead to a destruction of most of the other traders.[2] The break between the conference lines and the U.A.C. then brought matters to a head and in March 1930 the 'unorganised' sections of the trade took steps to protect themselves and formed the West African Merchants Freight Association.

In previous years there had been several attempts to create an effec-

[1] Ibid., 'Report of the A.G.M. of the African and Eastern Trade Corporation'.
[2] Author's interview with Mr A. E. Orme on 15 December 1966. Mr Orme was in business on his own account from 1929 to 1947 in Nwaniba, Calabar Province, Nigeria. As a West African merchant he was in direct competition with the U.A.C. and like other similar traders had to fight hard not to be pushed out. He was usually quite satisfied with E.D. service and freight rates.

tive and representative association of merchants, but these efforts had always failed. This was partly because of the opposition of the shipping companies and partly because of the fear of the smaller merchants that they would be dominated by the larger groups.[1] By 1930, however, circumstances had changed, and Elder Dempster, while not giving open support to the formation of the Association, did not oppose it. As a result, the merchant body outside the United Africa Company gained strength by the possibility of taking concerted action. They were thus in a much better position to maintain their independence against pressures from the ship-owners on the one hand and the monopolistic tendencies of the United Africa Company on the other. Under the somewhat abnormal conditions ruling in 1930 the merchants, in fact, found a greater identity of interest with the shipowners and together, as organised groups, they were able to present a formidable front to the United Africa Company.

Elder Dempster's Position as a Member of the Royal Mail Group
Whatever might have been the outcome of the course of events outlined above is a matter of only academic interest, for a dramatic change in the situation transformed the relative strength of the main contestants in the struggle. Towards the end of October, 1929, it was noted that, within a period of six months, the shares of the Royal Mail Group had fallen by sixteen million pounds. The following table shows that the key figure in the Royal Mail Steam Packet Company was, of course, Lord Kylsant:

Principal Ordinary Shareholders in the Royal Mail Steam Packet Company

Lord Kylsant	£18,500
Lord Kylsant (B a/c)	30,000
Lord Kylsant and another	500,000
Lord Kylsant and E. H. Bicker Caarten	200,000
Lord Kylsant and G. Dodd (K a/c)	150,000
Lord Kylsant and G. Dodd (S a/c)	75,000
Lord Kylsant and G. H. Melly	50,000
Lord Kylsant (survivor in joint a/c)	650,000
	1,673,500

[1] The Liverpool Chamber of Commerce contained a West African section, but this was dominated by the shipping companies. This was also true of the London and Manchester Chambers of Commerce.

The Association of West African Merchants was dominated by the larger firms and these usually made their own individual arrangements with the Conference.

Elder Dempster & Co. Ltd	135,000
King Line Ltd	34,002
Lamport & Holt Ltd	64,000
Liverpool, Brazil & River Plate S.N. Co. Ltd	650,000
Union Castle Mail Steamship Company	506,000
	3,062,502
Balance held by outside interests	1,937,498
Total Ordinary Stock	£5,000,000[1]

It is clear, therefore, that Lord Kylsant's personal holdings, together with those held by his other lines, were quite sufficient to give him complete authority in the Royal Mail Steam Packet Company. This automatically made him supreme in all the companies which the Royal Mail either owned or controlled.[2] Kylsant's aim had been to reorganise companies so that they had a relatively small number of ordinary shares (which carried voting rights) and a relatively large number of preference shares and debentures (which carried only restricted voting rights).[3] The Debenture Trust Deeds placed some limitation on the extent of this capital gearing but Kylsant was able to conceal it to some extent by the development of a network of cross-holdings in ordinary shares. In 1930, just before the collapse of the Royal Mail Group, its capital comprised £45,060,946 in ordinary shares and £26,385,375 in preference shares; debentures worth £19,932,082 had also been issued. The relationship of 'voting' capital (£45m.) to 'non-voting' capital and debentures (£26m. + £20m. = £46m.) does not appear to be exceptional until it is remembered that because of the use of extensive cross-shareholdings many of the ordinary shares were just paper. Any attempt to evaluate the equity of the total ordinary shareholding necessarily involves a great number of arbitrary decisions, but Kylsant himself stated that of the whole of the preference and ordinary share capital (£26m. + £45m. = £71m.) the Group itself 'owned' no less than £50m.[4]

[1] Based on *Fairplay*'s Annual Summary of British Shipping Finance, 1927.

[2] See Appendix, p. 459, Table 54.

[3] P. N. Davies and A. M. Bourn, 'Lord Kylsant and the Royal Mail', *Business History*, Vol. XIV, No. II (July 1972), pp. 110–12.

[4] A.G.M. of the Royal Mail Steam Packet Company, June 1930. Statement made by Lord Kylsant.

Elder Dempster and Company Limited had been part of the Royal Mail Group since 1910[1] and Kylsant, or the companies he controlled, was its principal ordinary shareholder.

Principal Ordinary Shareholders in Elder Dempster & Co. Ltd

Lord Kylsant	596,040
Royal Mail Steam Packet Co.	433,444
Estate of Lord Pirrie	436,534
	1,466,018
Ocean Transport Company	62,500
Warden Investment Company	100,000
London Maritime Investment Company	64,390
	1,692,908
Other shareholders	117,092
Total ordinary shares	£1,810,000[2]

In addition, by controlling Elder Dempster, Kylsant possessed absolute authority over its wide range of subsidiary and associated companies. Investments in the subsidiary firms included the whole of the ordinary capital of the British and African Steam Navigation Company Limited, which in turn held all the ordinary stock of the Imperial Direct Line Limited. Elder Dempster also possessed 85 per cent of the ordinary shares of the African Steam Ship Company, which in turn held all the ordinary capital of the Elder Line Limited.

Furthermore, Elder Dempster owned the whole of the capital of many concerns that were only interested in the West African trade. These included Elders Insurance Co. Ltd, Elder Dempster (Grand Canary) Ltd, Elder Dempster (Tenerife) Ltd, the West African Lighterage and Transport Co. Ltd, and the Atlantic Coaling Co. Ltd. Their general investments included 12 per cent of the ordinary capital of Messrs Harland and Wolff Limited and seven and a half per cent of the ordinary capital of David Colville and Sons Limited.[3]

In many ways, therefore, Elder Dempster may be regarded at this time as a holding company for Kylsant's West African shipping interests.

[1] See above, Chapter 7, pp. 171–3.
[2] Based on *Fairplay*'s Annual Summary of British Shipping Finance, 1927.
[3] *Fairplay*, 3 July 1930, A.G.M. of Elder Dempster & Co. Ltd, p. 62.

They organised the activities of the four British lines concerned in the trade, and also supplied much of the infra-structure without which a profitable trade could not have been continued. Only a small part of Elder Dempster's income was earned by these managerial functions, and they seldom operated many ships of their own. The bulk of their receipts came from their investments, and as these were almost entirely with the Royal Mail their welfare was inevitably bound up with that of Kylsant's wider interests.[1]

The Collapse of the Kylsant Empire

The decline in the value of Royal Mail shares in 1929 was to be expected, for trade was depressed and in consequence the shares of most British shipping companies showed falls of various magnitudes.[2] The loss of confidence in the Royal Mail shares, however, was unusually great and gave rise to much disquiet and rumour. On the surface there was a number of possible reasons why the market value of these shares should have been so adversely affected. In the first place, the collapse of the Hatry organisation in September 1929[3] had made the City nervous of similarly structured financial groupings, amongst which Lord Kylsant's vast shipping interests were a prime example. In the second place, depression in the Atlantic, Australian and Brazilian trades had led to a sharp fall in the earning capacity of some of the Royal Mail associates. Thirdly, the position was aggravated by the news of disagreement between Lord Kylsant and his brother Lord St Davids, (trustee for the second debentures of the Royal Mail Steam Packet Company)—the implication being that there was a divergence of opinion on the manage-

[1] See Appendix, p. 460, Table 55.

[2] During the previous six months, the shares of other British shipping companies had fallen as follows:—

P. & O.:   69s 3d to 53s 6d
Cunard: 34s   to 23s 6d
Furness Withy: 44s   to 37s

(This represented a depreciation in the market value of the ordinary shares of these three Companies of £7,630,000). *Fairplay*, 24 October 1929, p. 161.

[3] Clarence Hatry and his associates were arrested on 19 September 1929. Hatry was later sentenced to fourteen years' imprisonment for false pretences and for issuing fraudulent share certificates.

See: C. Brooks, *The Royal Mail Case*, (Edinburgh & London: William Hodge, 1933), pp. xviii–xix and xlii, and H. Montgomery Hyde, *Norman Birkett*, (London: Hamish Hamilton, 1964), pp. 276–86.

ment and policy of the Group.[1] Furthermore, the growing uneasiness was not allayed when it was remembered that earlier in the year the auditor of the Royal Mail accounts stated that his certificate was given, '. . . subject to the values under present conditions of the investments in allied shipping Companies', and that, '. . . the provision for depreciation of the fleet in the accounts of the year had been calculated at a lower rate than hitherto.'[2]

Despite a growing volume of criticism there was, as yet, no real sign that a large-scale disaster might ensue. Nevertheless, the unpropitious atmosphere added to the difficulties of the Royal Mail Group and in December 1929 they found it necessary to issue a statement to the public. This emphasised that the undue publicity to which the organisation had been subjected had prevented the raising of fresh finance. In consequence, the directors had instructed their accountants, Messrs Price, Waterhouse and Company, to make a full investigation of their position. After a detailed examination of the relevant accounts it was claimed that:

'. . . the profits of the shipping Companies for the year 1928, after paying debenture and other interest, but before providing for depreciation on the fleets and preference dividends, amounted to over £3,400,000.'

It was further stated that: '. . . The results of the groups for the present year are expected to be very similar.' (i.e. as those for 1928.)[3]

Such an expression, however, was no real evaluation of the state of the Group's affairs. Although Price, Waterhouse also stated that adequate

[1] Lord St Davids was Kylsant's eldest brother. He studied law and entered politics, but after his marriage to a wealthy heiress (Leonora, daughter of Isidor Gerstenberg, the Chairman of the Council of Foreign Bondholders) he concerned himself more and more with the City. His specialities were investment trusts and he ultimately became chairman of twelve of these bodies. These included the '69 Old Broad Street Group' (subsequently renamed the '117 Old Broad Street Group') an organisation which was formed prior to 1914 and which expanded during the second half of the 1920s. It was the largest group of investment trusts with a common management in the City. Lord St Davids had used both a high level of leverage and cross-shareholdings in promoting the growth of these interests and it is tempting to assume that it was this example which encouraged Kylsant to follow a similar path. I am indebted to Mr P. L. Cottrell, University of Leicester, for this information; he is currently working on the International Financial Society which in its later days became a constituent part of the '117 Old Broad Street' Group. See also:— H. Burton and D. C. Corner, *Investment and Unit Trusts in Britain and America* (London: Elek Books, 1968).

[2] *Fairplay*, 24 October 1929, p. 161.   [3] *Fairplay*, 19 December 1929, p. 617.

provision had been made for depreciation, and more, in fact, had been set aside than the level permitted for income-tax purposes, it was not, perhaps, universally realised that this figure fell considerably short of that usually allowed by the more prudent shipping lines. Thus on a fleet costing over £100 million, depreciation at 5 per cent (the normal amount) would have cost the Royal Mail Group £5 million per annum. Even at 4 per cent, which Kylsant maintained was adequate, the cost was greater than the entire estimated trading profit for 1929.

Whatever ameliorating influence this statement may have achieved in other circumstances is not clear. In this instance, however, any beneficial effects were quickly dissipated by the simultaneous announcement that, as it was impossible to raise new capital, the Trade Facilities Acts loans could not be repaid.[1] The directors further stated that as a result of these difficulties they had decided that no half-year dividend be paid on the Royal Mail Steam Packet Company's preference shares, and no interim dividend be paid on the ordinary stock. The net effect of the Company's statement, therefore, was to create additional suspicion in the minds of its shareholders, and the market for its securities declined to still lower levels.

Apart from Elder Dempster's failure to reach agreement with the United Africa Company it was not until March 1930 that new and ominous cracks began to appear in the financial edifice of the Royal Mail. These were first seen in the accounts of Messrs Lamport and Holt, and it came as a great shock to shipping and financial opinion to find that there was a discrepancy of 50 per cent between the book and market values of the Company's reserve investments.[2] This state of affairs was all the more disconcerting to the Royal Mail Group as it suggested to the public that the Company could not extricate itself from its difficulties unless a large-scale reconstruction was effected. Such a reconstruction would have involved the calling up of the balance due on the partly paid ordinary shares, but the £560,000 involved could not have been

[1] A number of Trade Facilities Acts and Irish Loan Guaranty Acts were passed between 1921 and 1926. These provided for the State to guarantee loans from private sources (and thus to reduce interest rates) to firms willing to place orders with industries which possessed high levels of unemployment. A total of £29 million was guaranteed for ships built for British owners, and of this £13 million went to member companies of the Royal Mail Group.

See: S. G. Sturmey, *British Shipping and World Competition* (University of London: Athlone Press, 1962), pp. 106-7.

[2] *Fairplay*, 13 March 1930, p. 712.

Elder Dempster Agencies, Freetown.

PLATE 15

Elder Dempster Lines, Port Harcourt.

Elder Dempster wharf, Lagos, *c.* 1920.

PLATE 16

Elder Dempster Office, Lagos, 1972.

of assistance to the Group as a whole because all the ordinary shares were held by its own members. In short, the inter-connections of any scheme of reconstruction might have caused a chain reaction which would certainly have undermined the already precarious financial structure which had been created by Lord Kylsant.

The damaging effects of the disclosures about Lamport and Holt's position was a presage to further disaster involving the stability of the Royal Mail Group as a whole, and events were to follow a mounting and catastrophic sequence. In mid-April, Lord St Davids was replaced by the Law Union and Rock Insurance Company Limited as trustee of the 5 per cent second debenture holders of the Royal Mail Steam Packet Company.[1] The obvious conclusion to be drawn from this by outsiders was that the Group was in a serious financial position and that there was the probability that drastic measures would have to be taken to remedy the situation. Furthermore, it was well known in shipping circles that the Royal Mail Group had to meet many liabilities in the near future from assets which were already subject to considerable strain. These liabilities included the repayment of the £2,550,000 borrowed by the Royal Mail Steam Packet Meat Transports, which was due at the end of September 1930; the overdue amount of £1,485,000 by the White Star line to the Australian Government which was in part payment for the purchase of the Commonwealth Line; an unspecified amount in respect of the shares of the Shaw, Savill and Albion Company; and the sum of £2,350,000 which was to be paid to the International Mercantile Marine Company of New Jersey before 1936 to complete the acquisition of the White Star Line.[2] As the available assets were not sufficient to meet these liabilities, and as it was not possible to raise new capital, the only inference which the shareholders could draw was that these commitments would have to be met from funds created by the surpluses from trading receipts. In times of normal trade it might have been possible to have achieved this result. In 1930, however, there was no prospect of realising this solution to the problem, for even the most optimistic anticipation of a trading profit did not exceed £3,400,000 and this was not enough to provide for normal depreciation, let alone allow for outstanding commitments.[3] It was in an atmosphere of

[1] *Fairplay*, 17 April 1930, p. 132.   [2] *Fairplay*, 3 April 1930, p. 1.
[3] The depreciation need not have been charged in the short run but, even so, the cash flow would have been insufficient to have met the Group's obligations.

mounting crisis, therefore, that Lord Kylsant's statement to the annual general meeting of the Royal Mail Steam Packet Company was awaited.[1]

A week before this meeting was due to take place, the directors of the Royal Mail Steam Packet Company took a significant action— probably to try to retain the continued support of the financial institutions. A committee was established to confer with the directors on the problems of the Group and this consisted of Mr F. Hyde, Managing Director of the Midland Bank; General A. Maxwell, Managing Partner of Glyn, Mills and Company; and Sir William McLintock, who represented the Treasury and the Government of Northern Ireland.[2] It was then agreed that this body would remain in being until the end of 1930 and in the meantime arrangements were approved for the banks and discount houses to continue their accommodation and for the Trade Facilities Acts Advisory Committee and the Government of Northern Ireland to do the same.[3] The Rt Hon. Walter Runciman, M.P. was then invited to join the boards of all the companies associated with the Group and he became deputy chairman of the Royal Mail Steam Packet Company on 16 June 1930.[4] On that date he, together with Maxwell and McLintock, was appointed to act as voting trustee with voting control of the Company, pending the report of the Committee of Inquiry and until such time as a final solution could be devised.[5] A statement was then issued by the Company to explain the actions which had been

[1] It was during this period that Lord Kylsant attempted to improve the Group's liquidity by the sale of non-essential assets. These included some of Elder Dempster's properties in the Canary Islands—many had previously been disposed of in 1911—but only very poor prices could be obtained because of the world wide economic depression. See Appendix, p. 464, Table 61.

[2] Sir William McLintock, (1873–1947) was Senior Partner of Thomson, McLintock and Company, an eminent firm of Chartered Accountants. He had previously served as financial adviser on many government committees and enquiries. (*Who Was Who*, Vol. IV.)

[3] R.M.S.P., Minutes, Vol. XX, p. 147, 16 June 1930.

[4] Walter Runciman (1870–1949) had been an M.P. since 1899 and had held many important posts in the Government including that of President of the Board of Trade (1914–16). He had a strong shipping background. (His father was the senior partner of Walter Runciman and Company, and the chairman of the Moor Line, and had been President of the Chamber of Shipping in the years 1926–7.) He resigned from the board of the R.M.S.P. Company in 1931 when he became President of the Board of Trade. He became Baron Runciman of Shoreston in 1933 and was made 1st Viscount Runciman of Doxford in 1937. (*Who Was Who*, Vol. V.)

[5] R.M.S.P. Minutes, Vol. XX, p. 147, 16 June 1930.

taken,[1] and this achieved a limited success in restoring confidence.[2] Of more importance, however, was the implication that a major limitation had been placed on Lord Kylsant's personal prestige and power.

The annual general meeting of the Royal Mail Steam Packet Company took place at the end of June 1930, and it needed all the skill which Kylsant had gained in his lifetime's experience as a shipowner to convince the shareholders that the Company possessed secure financial foundations. Unfortunately, his statement was far too general to carry lasting weight, and he added little to that already known to the public. It is perhaps easy to criticise in retrospect, but it now appears to be obvious that many of the shrewder shareholders at the meeting realised that Kylsant had underestimated the extent of the decline in trade and that his estimate of future prospects was far too complacent. His observations on levels of depreciation, though valid if one accepted his premises, were not relevant when viewed against the hard facts of the financial position. To have claimed that a fleet costing £106 million had been written down to £52 million was no real answer to the vital point that these assets had a realisable value of, perhaps, only £30 million.

In fact, the annual general meeting of the Royal Mail Steam Packet Company passed off without serious incident, but there is little doubt that Lord Kylsant had lost control of the situation. Thus in September 1930 Lamport and Holt Limited were put into the hands of the official receiver,[3] and in the following November Lord Kylsant was granted leave of absence from all his directorships.[4] At the same time the committee set up to inquire into the affairs of the Group had its term of office extended for a year and Mr Walter Runciman, already deputy chairman of the Royal Mail Steam Packet Company, was appointed

[1] *Fairplay*, 19 June 1930, p. 722.

[2] The Ordinary stock of the Royal Mail Steam Packet Company rose from 15 to 17½; the 5 per cent preference from 29 to 31; the 6½ per cent preference from 25 to 27; the 4½ per cent debentures from 70 to 72½ and the 5 per cent debentures from 55 to 62. *Source*: *Fairplay*, 19 June 1930, p. 722.

[3] The irony of this will be appreciated when it is realised that this came about as a result of an application by the London Maritime Investment Co. Ltd., of which Kylsant was still Chairman, acting as Trustee for the debenture holders. *Fairplay*, 4 September 1930, pp. 558–60.

[4] All his executive functions were then suspended and he was not allowed to attend the Company's office or contact the managers or staff. R.M.S.P. Minutes, Vol. XX, p. 199, 19 November 1930.

deputy chairman of its thirteen principal associated companies.[1]

The voting trustees, no doubt influenced by the continuing fall in trading receipts, then suspended the payments of all dividends and debenture interest.[2] This was followed by an appeal to the High Court and on 27 January 1931 it was announced that, subject to agreement by the first and second debenture holders of the Royal Mail Steam Packet Company and the preference shareholders of the White Star Line Limited, authority had been given for a moratorium to be declared until 30 June 1931 on any action for recovery.[3] This arrangement was subsequently agreed to by the debenture and preference shareholders, and was approved by the Court in April.[4]

Against this background of rapidly depreciating assets came a further blow, '. . . which resulted in even the giving away of $6\frac{1}{2}$ per cent preference stock and deferred stock'.[5] This was because of a legal opinion which suggested that in the event of the Royal Mail Steam Packet Company going into liquidation, liability might be unlimited. Although denied immediately by the voting trustees,[6] the net effect was to reduce still more the market value of the Company's securities, and those of other British shipping firms fell in sympathy. Confidence continued to remain at a low level despite the pronouncements that the trustees were preparing a scheme of wholesale reconstruction. The culmination of this unhappy chapter of events then came with the news that Lord Kylsant had been served with a summons to face charges of publishing accounts which, '. . . you knew to be false.'[7] A subsequent charge also accused him of having issued a false prospectus, and thus a long career was about to end in tragic circumstances. The collapse of a vast shipping empire at a time when world trade had reached unprecedented depths was to cause havoc and confusion amongst many shipping companies.[8] It is remarkable, therefore, that the recovery of Elder Dempster from this disaster took place on such a sound financial basis that future growth and expansion were to be actively promoted.

Elder Dempster's New Relationship with the United Africa Company
It is not relevant here to follow the course of the Royal Mail disclosures,

[1] *Fairplay*, 4 December 1930, p. 521.   [2] *Fairplay*, 8 January 1931, p. 77.
[3] *Fairplay*, 5 February 1931, p. 389.   [4] *Fairplay*, 23 April 1931, p. 177.
[5] *Fairplay*, 12 February 1931, p. 443.   [6] *Fairplay*, 5 February 1931, p. 390.
[7] *Fairplay*, 21 May 1931, p. 436.   [8] Davies and Bourn, op. cit., p. 121.

nor to make any significant reference to Lord Kylsant's trial and subsequent conviction.[1] We are only concerned with the effects of these events upon the position of Elder Dempster and on its relationship with the United Africa Company. In the short term the impact of the collapse on the day-to-day running of the Company's business was less serious than might have been supposed. The voting trustees maintained regular shipping services on Elder Dempster's usual routes, and saw to it that all its essential activities were continued.[2] The working arrangements with the other members of the conference also continued to function normally and it must be added that it was to the lasting credit of these partners that they took no advantage of Elder Dempster's precarious situation.[3] Thus the conference structure held fast, and competition from outside lines, which would have assuredly arisen if this co-operation had been lacking, was not allowed to develop. The basic dangers inherent in the situation as a whole were, therefore, obviated. The remaining difficulty, which was common to all shipping companies at this time, arose from the continuing low level of trade, and the consequent paucity of earning capacity.

There was, however, a gradual change in Elder Dempster's attitude towards the U.A.C. At first this may just have been a reaction to changing circumstances but it was undoubtedly strengthened by the fact that the voting trustees were not willing to sustain uneconomic freight rates as a long-term weapon. Accordingly negotiations, which had never really stopped, were continued and there was a constant exchange of views. David Jones, of Elder Dempster, acted for the shipping lines until the middle of 1930 but then his responsibility was assumed by

[1] Lord Kylsant was found not guilty on two counts of issuing misleading accounts for the Royal Mail Steam Packet Company in 1926 and 1927, but he was found guilty of issuing a fraudulent prospectus in connection with an issue of £2 million of second debentures made in June 1928. A detailed account of the court proceedings is given by C. Brooks, op. cit., and a commentary on this is provided by Sir Patrick Hastings, 'The Case of the Royal Mail', W. T. Baxter and S. Davidson, Eds. *Studies in Accounting Theory* (London: Sweet & Maxwell, 1962), pp. 452–461. A guide to the rather limited sources on Lord Kylsant's life and career is provided in Davies and Bourn, op. cit., pp. 103–105.

[2] It should be understood that the Voting Trustees were only able to keep the services going by making no long run provision for the future; by not meeting the Group's financial obligations as they arose and by following the moratorium on the debts as at April 1931.

[3] This was in spite of the fact that German harbours were described as 'Ship Cemeteries' —many newly completed vessels joining older tonnage to lie idle, 'A Short History of the German Africa Lines', Hamburg, 1967.

Walter Runciman who had recently joined the Board of the Royal Mail and its subsidiary firms.[1] Mr R. D. Holt and Major L. H. Cripps, both partners in Alfred Holt and Company,[2] also joined in the discussions at this stage but little, or nothing, was actually achieved.

The U.A.C. still felt that the size of its shipments entitled it to special treatment. It also remained reluctant to pay freight rates that were significantly higher than the cost of shipping in its own or chartered vessels. A third factor further strengthened its position in that its shipping department, aided by Henry Tyrer's, had been relatively successful in coping with the loss of the conference facilities. An express service from Liverpool to the Coast had been established by three company-owned ships,[3] while time-and-voyage chartered vessels had maintained a connection between West Africa and other United Kingdom and Continental ports. Nevertheless, although the U.A.C. was now carrying a very high proportion of its own cargoes quite profitably, losses were being sustained through its inability to match the previous regularity of service. With a small number of ships this was, of course, inevitable as it led to the holding of larger stocks with consequently greater expense and tying up of capital.[4]

From its point of view Elder Dempster, faced with the loss of 40 per cent of its trade, was very anxious to reach an amicable agreement. The realities of the situation may well have caused it to lower its sights but it still objected to any system of differential freight rates. Furthermore, a new complication had arisen in the form of the West African Merchants Freight Association, for the co-operating firms had

'. . . requested that they should be regarded as one unit for all purposes of freight and it will, therefore, be necessary for any further negotiations to be considered in conjunction with these new circumstances'.[5]

Another disturbing factor was the claim made by the U.A.C. on behalf of the African and Eastern, against the conference. This alleged a breach of the 1924 Agreement under which the shipping lines had arranged to give 'most favoured' terms to several firms. The establish-

[1] See above, p. 258.   [2] See below, Chapter 11, p. 270.
[3] Henry Tyrer Mss. Henry Tyrer & Co. Ltd to the U.A.C. Ltd 14 August 1931 'Report of activities from April 1929, to August 1931.' These ships were *Lafian*, *Nigerian* and *Zarian*.
[4] Based on the author's interview with Lord Cole, 21 April 1965.
[5] U.A.C.Mss. Letter from West African Lines Conference to Anton Jurgens of the Margarine Union, Ltd, 12 March 1930.

ment of the U.A.C. had indicated that some companies had not received their full entitlement and Elder Dempster were asked to pay the sum of £230,000 as their proportion. The affair was eventually settled by the payment of one-third of the claim in 1931,[1] but in the interim it was an additional problem which tended to embitter relations and thus lessened the possibility of a compromise.

Yet another bone of contention was the sale of Thomas Hedley and Company to Procter and Gamble in September 1930. This time, how- ever, it was Lever Brothers who felt they were the aggrieved party, for the transaction had the effect of opening the British market to their chief American rivals. In fact they did not have any real cause for complaint on this particular issue, for Elder Dempster[2] had offered Hedley's to them on several earlier occasions. Thus in 1923 Lord Lever- hulme had the opportunity of acquiring the business for £20,000 plus the buildings, plant and stocks at valuation.[3] The offer was declined at this time and when it was repeated in 1925, Levers again decided not to proceed with its purchase.[4] In September 1929, when negotiations for the renewal of the agreements with the conference lines had reached a crucial stage, the question of Hedley's was raised once more but Levers refused to consider the matter at that time.[5] The subsequent failure of the discussions between the conference and the U.A.C. then left Elder Dempster free to sell to the highest bidder and their controll- ing interest passed into the hands of the giant American soap combine. According to Charles Wilson[6] this was the most decisive new factor which was to affect the soap trade in the thirties. Procter and Gamble had been under severe pressure from Lever Brothers in North America, but with the acquisition of Hedleys they were able to counter-attack, and with the building of additional factories at Manchester and Pur- fleet they quickly obtained a substantial share of the home market. This

[1] Lever Mss., M.D.C., 12 May 1931.

[2] Lord Kylsant, then Owen Philipps, first took an interest in Thomas Hedley and Company in 1905. At that time his family controlled the firm but his own holding was quite modest. Over the years he built up his share of the firm and in 1921 he persuaded Elder Dempster to take a large interest. Thereafter Elder Dempster controlled the Com- pany, though there is no evidence to suggest that it ever took an active part in the manage- ment. (See file 83758 at Companies Registration Office, London.)

[3] Lever Mss., M.D.C. 55/1925, 3 June 1925.

[4] Ibid., M.D.C. 61/1925 (10 June 1925) and M.D.C. 189/1926 (30 June 1926).

[5] Ibid., M.D.C. 243/1929, 26 September 1929.

[6] Charles Wilson, The History of Unilever (London: Cassell, 1954), Vol. II, pp. 343–4.

is not to suggest that the purchase of Hedleys was essential for this action to succeed—but at the very least it enabled the operation to go forward with a minimum of difficulty.

In spite of all these disruptive happenings, discussions between Elder Dempster and the United Africa Company persisted and many constructive suggestions were put forward by both sides. One such proposal was for the formation of a new company into which both sides would put their ships in return for shares.[1] Elder Dempster agreed to consider this, subject to the approval of the other lines, but the U.A.C. had anticipated additional consideration for the trade they brought in and this appears to have been a serious snag. Consequently the idea was not pursued and, in 1932, R. D. Holt made it clear that in his view the basis of any agreement must be the restriction of the U.A.C. to a small fleet with the balance of its cargoes carried by the conference lines at normal rates.[2] This, of course, did not commend itself to the U.A.C. but further discussions continued and the possibility of a joint charter-ing pool was considered before being rejected. Finally there was a suggestion that the U.A.C. should either take over the Elder Dempster fleet or join up with it on terms that would have given it outright con-trol.[3] However valid this proposal may have been when it was made in 1935, it was quickly overtaken by events, for the formation of Elder Dempster Lines Holdings Limited in 1936 effectively re-established Elder Dempster Lines on a sound financial footing.[4]

It was unfortunate that when the dispute originated in 1929 the two main negotiators—Lord Kylsant and Sir Robert Waley Cohen—had substantial differences in outlook and personality. Lord Kylsant, of course, was preoccupied with organisational and financial problems affecting his shipping empire and could not, therefore, give the matter the full attention it deserved. As the controller of the world's largest fleet of merchant vessels his authority was virtually unchallenged in shipping affairs, and he found it distasteful to have to justify his policies to an outsider. Sir Robert, on the other hand, was more interested in profit and loss accounts than in ships, and Kylsant found it hard to un-bend and convince him of the gulf between running a regular public service and organising a few, privately loaded vessels. Waley Cohen found it difficult to see beyond his immediate balance-sheets and would

---

[1] Lever Mss., M.D.C., 23 April 1931.   [2] Ibid., M.D.C., 18 August 1932.
[3] Ibid., M.D.C., 14 February 1935.   [4] See below, Chapter 11, p. 273.

not take a long view of the situation. In the circumstances, therefore, the two men were bound to have a very different approach to the dispute and consequently were unable to appreciate fully each other's point of view. It would seem to have been in both parties' interest to have reached a compromise whereby most, if not all, of the U.A.C.'s cargoes were carried by the conference lines at freight rates which were fair to each side. The consequences of the disagreement meant no more than inconvenience for the U.A.C. and this it was able to overcome by a combination of hard work and extensive capital investment which effectively duplicated the services formerly provided by the conference. For Elder Dempster, however, it was such a severe blow that it was to exert a serious long-term influence on the Company's prospects and policy.

PART FOUR

Elder Dempster Lines Limited

Chapter 11

The Reorganisation of the Company

The Establishment of Elder Dempster Lines Limited

The collapse of the Royal Mail Group left its voting trustees with the task of maintaining its various companies as going concerns until such time as they could be sold. The depth of the depression in trade made any question of the realisation of assets quite pointless, so it was decided that the best solution was to create a number of new, independent companies to acquire the assets of the old. Shares in the new firms could then be distributed on a *pro rata* basis so as to provide some compensation for the creditors and debenture holders. These, of course, took precedence over the ordinary and preference shareholders who could expect no return before all other accounts in their respective companies were settled. In fact, as the table on page 270 shows, so much capital was lost that the ordinary and preference shareholders received nothing. The only exception to this was in the case of the Union Castle Mail Steam Ship Company Limited, for as it had issued no debentures its cumulative preference shareholders were able to take control and ultimately they restored the Company to independence and prosperity without the loss of any capital.[1]

The scheme of reorganisation proposed by the voting trustees was effective from 1 January 1932, although it was not finally approved by the debenture stockholders and sanctioned by the High Court until later in 1932.[2] Under the terms of the reconstruction agreement, two

[1] See M. Murray, *Union Castle Chronicle, 1853–1953* (London: Longmans, 1953), pp. 191–8, and also *Fairplay*, 8 November 1934, p. 226, and 29 November 1934, p. 385.

[2] The Debenture Stockholders' meeting was held in March and the order of the High Court of Justice was dated 24 June 1932.

Capital Losses of the Royal Mail Group

Name of Company	Amount of Capital	Amount Lost
Royal Mail Steam Packet Company	£8,800,000	£8,800,000
African Steam Ship Company	2,500,000	2,500,000
Nelson Steam Navigation Company	2,000,000	1,300,000
Elder Line	1,000,000	800,000
Elder Dempster and Company	8,485,000	8,485,000
Lamport and Holt	4,680,071	4,680,071
British and African Steam Navigation Company	2,350,000	2,000,000
White Star Line	9,000,000	9,000,000
Totals:	38,815,071	37,565,071[1]

new firms were to be formed to continue existing services. These were the Royal Mail Lines Company and the West African Lines Company, and it is the second of these with which we are now concerned. To all intents and purposes this was made up of the West African interests of Elder Dempster and its associates.

Richard (later Sir Richard) Durning Holt, a partner in Alfred Holt and Company, then began an active association with the West African shipping trade for he was:

> . . . invited by the Governor of the Bank of England on behalf of the Governments of Great Britain and Northern Ireland to undertake the chairmanship of the Elder Dempster branch of the Royal Mail combination'.[2]

The choice of Richard Holt was a wise one, for he was a man of great ability and experience, and his record as a shipowner over a period of more than forty years had given him an unassailable reputation.[3] The managers of the Ocean Steam Ship Company agreed that Holt should accept this position and he began his new duties in March 1932. At the same time the Hon. Leonard Harrison Cripps, C.B.E., also a partner in Alfred Holt, joined what was to be the new Elder Dempster and under Holt was to be responsible, together with the other directors, for the day-to-day working of the Company for many years.

In August, 1932, the West African Lines Company came to an end

---

[1] *Fairplay*, 14 December 1944, p. 474.

[2] Papers of Alfred Holt and Company (hereinafter referred to as Holt Mss.) Minutes of Ocean Steam Ship Company, 68th Annual Meeting, 8 February 1933.

[3] F. E. Hyde, *Blue Funnel* (Liverpool University Press, 1957).

and Elder Dempster Lines Limited was inaugurated. The objects of this new concern were:

'To acquire and amalgamate the undertakings or parts of the undertakings and in particular the fleets of vessels and all or any of the other assets of the shipping undertakings of the following companies, namely, Elder Dempster and Company Limited, the African Steam Ship Company, Elder Line Limited, the British and African Steam Navigation Company Limited and Imperial Direct Line Limited . . .'[1]

Elder Dempster Lines Limited then took possession of most of the ships which had formerly operated on the West African routes. It was specifically arranged that these vessels should be free of all liabilities[2] and, in return, the companies who provided the ships received the whole of the issued capital of the new firm:

Issued Capital of Elder Dempster Lines Limited
(£1 Ordinary Shares)

African Steam Ship Company	807,762
Elder Line Limited	110,241
British & African S.N. Co. Ltd.	1,449,891
Imperial Direct Line Limited	104,774
Elder Dempster & Co. Ltd.	27,332
	2,500,000[3]

The part of the fleet not covered by this arrangement consisted of the eight ships of the 'Explorer' class. These were retained by the mortgagers but operated on their account by Elder Dempster Lines. The Company subsequently purchased these vessels, free of all charges, in 1935.

The scheme of reorganisation also safeguarded the interests of the debenture stockholders and creditors in the former companies for it laid down that:

'. . . before any dividends are paid on the preference and ordinary shares, the debenture stockholders are to receive their principal and interest and the holders

[1] File 267738 (live at Companies House, City Road, London). Formation documents of Elder Dempster Lines Limited 15 August 1932.

[2] See Appendix, p. 413, Table 20, for full details of these vessels.

[3] See Appendix, p. 461, Table 57 (List of Shareholders in Elder Dempster Lines Limited), and p. 462, Table 58 (List of shareholders in Elder Dempster Lines Holdings Limited).

of deferred creditors' certificates the principal and interest in respect of the amounts due to them.'[1]

Certain other assets of Elder Dempster and Company Limited, essential ancillaries to the working of the steamships, were also taken over by the new company and were paid for by unsecured three-year notes.

It is necessary to give only a brief account of the complicated pattern of developments which followed the creation of Elder Dempster Lines Limited. Until the end of 1934 two Elder Dempster companies existed side by side. As we have seen, the new company—Elder Dempster Lines Limited—had become either owners or managers of the ships formerly owned by the previous operating lines. It had also inherited the goodwill and connections of Elder Dempster and Company Limited, and continued to provide comprehensive services to the Coast.

At the same time the original firm—Elder Dempster and Company Limited—remained in being but its sole function was as a holding company and it retained an accumulated deficiency of over £8,400,000.[2]

The original moratorium had ended on 30 June 1931,[3] but had subsequently been extended to 31 December 1934. The approach of this date then led to important changes in the situation. A circular sent by the secretary of Elder Dempster and Company, Limited, to the debenture stockholders on 22 December proposed a scheme of arrangement under which the assets of the firm were to be transferred to a new concern to be called the E.D. Realisation Company Limited.[4] This scheme was quickly approved by the debenture stockholders and after it had been sanctioned by the High Court in February 1935, Elder Dempster and Company Limited came to a formal end.[5]

A similar scheme of arrangement was also approved at this time for the Royal Mail Steam Packet Company and this established the R.M. Realisation Company Limited. The lines whose assets were taken over then ceased to exist, with the exception of the chartered firms (the Royal Mail Steam Packet Company and the African Steam Ship Company), for their affairs had to be wound up by a liquidator.[6]

[1] 22nd A.G.M. of Elder Dempster & Co. Ltd, October 1932.
[2] Details of these losses are given in the Appendix, p. 460, Table 56.
[3] See above, Chapter 10, p. 260.   [4] *Fairplay*, 27 December 1934, p. 557.
[5] *Fairplay*, 14 February 1935, p. 351.
[6] *West Africa*, 19 September 1936, p. 1305. Statutory first meeting of creditors and shareholders under the liquidation of the African Steam Ship Company.

The prime object of the E.D. Realisation Company Limited was, of course, to sell the assets of Elder Dempster & Company Limited (and its subsidiaries) and thus repay its debenture stockholders and other creditors.[1] It was appreciated that this could only be achieved over a period of time, but an important step forward was taken in June 1936, with the formation of Elder Dempster Lines Holdings Limited. The new company had an authorised capital of £3,000,000 in shares of £1 each, of which 1,596,000 were issued at once as follows: 1,506,133 were placed privately for cash at 22s 3d per share; 28,867 were allocated to the E.D. Realisation Company as consideration for the purchase of 27,332 Elder Dempster Lines Limited shares, and 55,000 were allocated to the British and African Steam Navigation Company Limited, and 6,000 to the African Steam Ship Company in part payment for their assets.[2]

The balance of 1,404,000 shares was reserved to meet the conversion rights attached to a new debenture stock. This consisted of £1,560,000 of 3 per cent convertible non-cumulative income debentures which Elder Dempster Lines Holdings Limited were to issue and allocate to the holders of the African Steam Ship Company debenture stock on the basis of £100 of new stock for every £100 of African debenture stock held.

The reason for the establishment of Elder Dempster Lines Holdings Limited was to provide the necessary finance to purchase the ordinary shares of Elder Dempster Lines Limited which as we have seen were owned by the former operating lines.

The previous companies were then to use this cash to settle the claims of their creditors, and it was utilised as follows:

Amount in Cash, Shares or Debentures
Payable to Each Separate Vendor

1. *African Steam Ship Company:* 6,000 shares at £1 each and the discharge of a Bank Loan amounting to £66,791, and the satisfaction of £1,560,000 6 per cent Debenture Stock with all arrears of interest thereon and sundry liabilities estimated at £1,400.

[1] Many assets were, in fact, sold quite quickly but it took until May 1946, for the E.D. Realisation Company Limited to complete its tasks. As a result of these sales the debenture holders, but not the other creditors, were paid in full. *Fairplay*, 16 May 1946, pp. 933–4.

[2] Formation Documents of Elder Dempster Lines Holdings Ltd, Certificate 314709, 29 July 1936.

2. *British & African Steam Navigation Company Limited:* 55,000 shares of £1 each and the discharge of debts aggregating £1,663,000 (estimated).

3. *E.D. Realisation Company Limited:* 28,867 shares of £1 each.[1]

The total price, therefore, which Elder Dempster Lines Holdings Limited paid for the shares (in fact, the assets) of the old concerns amounted to £3,391,157. This was made up of £1,731,191 in cash, £1,560,000 in debenture stock and shares valued at £99,966.[2]

The original concept of this vast operation was the idea of Baring Brothers,[3] and as it was guaranteed by them in association with Morgan, Grenfells it would have stood a good chance of being accepted by potential investors.[4] The deciding factor, however, was the commitment of Alfred Holt and Company to purchase 675,000 ordinary shares at a cost of £750,957.[5]

As previously noted, Elder Dempster came under the active direction of Richard Holt and L. H. Cripps, in 1932. Major G. F. Torrey, nominated by the voting trustees, and Picton Hughes Jones, formerly with Elder Dempster and Company Limited were the other members of the board and together they had begun to put Elder Dempster Lines Limited on the road to a satisfactory financial position.[6] The establishment of the 'Holdings' Company then further strengthened the Alfred Holt connection with Elder Dempster. Holt's investment made the Ocean Steam Ship Company the largest ordinary shareholder in the new firm and by virtue of the fact that the 'Holding' Company owned all the ordinary stock of Elder Dempster Lines Limited they were consequently in a position to control its policies.[7]

In practice, Richard Holt and his fellow directors appear to have enjoyed a great deal of autonomy even though the links between Alfred Holt and Elder Dempster became even stronger as a result of a seven-year agreement under which the former were to act as managers of the Elder Dempster fleet.[8] The effects of these arrangements meant that,

---

[1] Formation Documents of Elder Dempster Lines Holdings Ltd, Statement in Lieu of Prospectus, 3 June 1936.

[2] Ibid.

[3] Author's interview with Sir Alan Tod of Baring Brothers, 15 November 1966.

[4] *Fairplay*, 28 May 1936, p. 348.

[5] Holt Mss., Minutes of Ocean Steam Ship Company 72nd Annual Meeting, 4 February 1937.

[6] See below, pp. 278–9.   [7] *Fairplay*, 4 April 1935, p. 10 and 1 July 1937, p. 4.

[8] Holt Mss., Minutes of Ocean Steam Ship Company, 72nd Annual Meeting, 4 February 1937.

henceforth, Elder Dempster had not only emerged from their financial entanglements with the Royal Mail group and had been freed from all liabilities, but had also been given new strength to play a full part in their traditional trade.

The management agreement with Alfred Holt's lasted until the end of 1943 and then Elder Dempster were left to manage their own affairs.[1]

Progress in the Thirties

The fluctuations in West African imports and exports during the nineteen thirties were a reflection of the economic depression and subsequent recovery in world trade. In 1931 there was a catastrophic fall and, although matters were a little better in 1932, further reductions occurred in both 1933 and 1934. From then until 1937 there was a sharp rise, but this was not maintained and the last two years of the decade produced very poor results. This general picture—typical in most but not all respects of other trades—is translated by the following table so that the import/export statistics are clarified by the use of constant prices:

Trade of British West Africa, 1930–1939[2]

Year	Imports At Constant Prices	Exports At Constant Prices
1930	100	100
1931	65.7	70.7
1932	81.1	78.7
1933	75.8	72.9
1934	62.6	69.4
1935	93.6	89.2
1936	113.3	117.5
1937	135.9	142.5
1938	88.9	72.9
1939	76.9	76.3

As might be expected, fluctuations in the volume of the West African

[1] It should be noted, however, that the Ocean Steam Ship Company continued to be the largest single ordinary shareholder in Elder Dempster Lines Holdings Limited (later Liner Holdings Limited) and in 1965 became the sole ordinary shareholder.

[2] Based on the *Statistical Abstract for the British Empire*, 1935, CMD. 4819, Tables 96 and 100; *Statistical Abstract for the British Empire*, 1939, CMD. 6140, *British Commonwealth* 1950, CMD. 8051, Summaries 3 and 8. The constant prices were obtained from the current prices by applying the *Average Value Index of Imports and Exports* for the relevant years. Source of this index is the *London & Cambridge Economic Service* Bulletin II. May 1949. p. 72.

trade led to somewhat comparable changes in the level of shipping activity. The shipping statistics, however, do not follow an exactly similar pattern to the trade figures because the load factor of the vessels concerned varied from year to year. It will be seen[1] that the total tonnage entering the ports of British West Africa declined by 24 per cent between 1930 and 1933, and then rose steadily up to 1937, by when it was 11 per cent higher than in 1930. The British share of this tonnage remained fairly consistent throughout the period, falling from the 56.9 per cent in 1930 to 50.9 per cent in 1931 and then rising to a maximum of 58.3 per cent in 1939. The relative strengths of the fleets belonging to the British companies engaged on this route also changed during the thirties, but although this led to a redistribution of the trade it did not change its fundamental character.

The total tonnage owned by Elder Dempster during the transitional period is given by Lloyd's as follows:

1929	324,028 gross tons[2]
1930	318,241
1931	328,362
1932	325,158

Unfortunately these figures do not convey an accurate picture, for after 1929 they include many ships that were either redundant or temporarily or permanently out of commission. The records of Elder Dempster and Company Limited suffered from the effects of the wartime blitz in 1941; consequently few have survived and cannot remedy these defects. For the years after 1932, however, the records of the new company, Elder Dempster Lines, are available, so the size of the fleet can be precisely stated.[3]

Thus at the beginning of 1933 Elder Dempster owned 46 ships totalling 268,516 gross tons, but of these 15, totalling 84,335 gross tons, must be eliminated as they were redundant, never commissioned, and were sold during 1933 and 1934.[4] Subsequent changes in the size of the operational fleet during the thirties are shown on the page opposite.

These two tables make it clear that Elder Dempster's tonnage had declined by nearly 50 per cent in the period between 1929 and 1933,

[1] See Appendix, p. 416, Table 22.
[2] Lloyds Register of Shipping for the relevant years.
[3] Elder Dempster Lines Papers (hereinafter referred to as E.D.L.P.).
[4] Details of these vessels are given in the Appendix, p. 415, Table 21.

Size of the Elder Dempster Fleet, 1933–1939[1]

1933	=	176,647 gross tons (Average)
1934	=	169,112
1935	=	190,857
1936	=	208,694
1937	=	210,773
1938	=	211,896
1939	=	213,423

and that in spite of some growth after 1934 the average annual tonnage settled down at approximately two-thirds of the comparative figure for the twenties. The decline in trade and break with the United Africa Company were, of course, responsible for this calamity but it should not be overstated. The proportion of vessels laid up in 1929 is not known, and the tonnages before 1935 do not include the eight 'Explorer' vessels (32,160 gross tons) which were being operated, but were not owned by, the Company. In spite of these mitigating factors, it is certain that Elder Dempster had suffered a serious reverse—even if its magnitude cannot be precisely determined.

Although the size of its fleet is important, perhaps a better indication of Elder Dempster's success or failure in the thirties is to be found in its financial results. As we have already seen, trade began to revive after 1934 and by 1937 there had been a rise of 60 per cent in exports and 45 per cent in imports. This in turn led to an enlarged demand for cargo space and total shipping entered rose by 11 per cent. As the British share of the trade increased from 56.3 per cent in 1935 to 57.2 per cent in 1937, this represented an additional activity on the part of the British Lines of approximately 17 per cent. To some extent this can be accounted for by a slight rise in the tonnage of the John Holt vessels and a somewhat larger increase in the fleet owned, or chartered, by the United Africa Company. In the absence of any corresponding increase in Elder Dempster tonnage, however, the conclusion must be reached that load factors became higher. Working their ships to fuller capacity, together with increases in the levels of freight rates on some categories of goods in January 1937,[2] resulted in substantially improved profit margins in Elder Dempster Lines voyage accounts:

[1] E.D.L.P., Accounts Department, Black Books. The average is calculated by adding the tonnage at the beginning and end of the year and dividing by two.
[2] West Africa, 19 December 1936, p. 179.

Annual Net Voyage Profits 1933–1939[1]

Year	Voyage Profits	Administrative Costs	Net	Depreciation	Net
1933	516,955	194,523	322,432	240,000	82,432
1934	515,205	183,140	322,065	240,000	92,065
1935	611,334	154,785	456,549	275,000	181,549
1936	595,643	153,936	441,707	275,000	166,707
1937	1,028,224	193,378	834,846	300,000	534,846
1938	772,766	176,478	596,288	300,000	296,288
1939	797,441	183,438	614,003	300,000	314,003

The size of the fleet may then be taken into account in order to calculate the net earnings per gross ton:

Net Earnings per Gross Ton, 1933–1939[2]

Year	Net Voyage Profits	Gross Tonnage	Net Earnings Per Gross Ton
1933	94,349	176,647	.53
1934	94,316	169,112	.56
1935	181,549	190,857	.95
1936	166,707	208,694	.80
1937	534,846	210,773	2.54
1938	296,288	211,896	1.40
1939	314,003	213,423	1.47

It should be noted that the fifteen redundant vessels have been eliminated from the gross tonnage in 1933 and 1934. This makes it necessary to add back the lying-up costs which had previously been deducted from the net voyage profits for these years. As a result these show rises of £11,917 (for 1933) and £2,251 (for 1934) when compared with the figures given in the earlier table.

If we now compare Elder Dempster's net voyage profits per gross ton of ships employed with those of two representative shipping firms some interesting and significant facts emerge. The table on page 279 shows that Elder Dempster's earnings, ton for ton, were very little behind—and occasionally ahead of—those of two highly successful and well-managed concerns. In view of Elder Dempster's recent emergence from near disaster this might be considered to be quite surprising. In fact, it was a reflection of both the peculiar characteristics of the West African shipping business and the soundness of its reconstruction.

[1] E.D.L.P. Accounts Department, Black Books.   [2] Ibid.

Comparison of the Net Earnings Per Gross Ton
of Elder Dempster's, Harrison's and Alfred Holt's[1]

Year	Harrisons (Charente S.S. Co.)	Alfred Holt (Ocean S.S. Co. & China Mutual S.N. Co.)	Elder Dempster Lines, Limited
1933	0.86	0.96	0.53
1934	0.90	0.75	0.56
1935	1.11	0.64	0.95
1936	1.33	1.01	0.80
1937	2.43	1.79	2.54
1938	1.79	2.09	1.40
1939	1.26	1.74	1.47

Elder Dempster were engaged almost exclusively in trade to a single geographic area[2] and when this was prosperous it carried them with it but, conversely, in times of depression they were apt to suffer with it. In addition, most of Elder Dempster's voyages terminated in the United Kingdom, so a close watch could be kept on operating costs. On the other hand, the Company operated on what were relatively short sea-routes and this meant that its vessels spent a higher proportion of their time unprofitably in port than those owned by either Harrisons or Alfred Holts. Harrisons were engaged in trades with long sea-routes to India, South and East Africa, the Gulf, Mexico, Brazil and the West Indies; Alfred Holts had an even longer voyage-pattern to the Far East and to Australia. These two companies, therefore, were concerned in a number of trades which were not strictly comparable with that of West Africa and, while some did become busy after the middle thirties, others remained unremunerative throughout the whole of this period. Furthermore, Harrisons and Holts chose to provide many services which, in the short run, were uneconomic and not justified by the level of trade whereas, as we have seen, Elder Dempster was able to increase its load factor quite significantly. It is also clear that while the Harrisons and Holt fleet were maintained at dimensions which were too great for the cargo being offered at this time, the reconstruction of Elder Dempster had reduced its tonnage by approximately a third of the 1930 figure and

[1] The figures for Harrisons and Holts are quoted from: F. E. Hyde, *Shipping Enterprise and Management* (Liverpool University Press, 1967), Table 14, p. 171.

[2] Elder Dempster also operated Canada–South Africa and U.S.A.–West Africa services. These were reasonably buoyant during this period and undoubtedly made some contribution to the Company's success.

it thus possessed an optimum capacity for its share of the West African trade.

In addition, the strength of the West African Lines Conference and the special relationships and agreements with the Merchants Freight Association and Messrs John Holts also had important results. These enabled the trade to be confined to a small number of lines which were consequently able to maintain and even increase freight rates at a time when competition on many of the Harrison and Holt routes was forcing their charges down to very low levels. In short, Elder Dempster's speedy recovery after its drastic reconstruction was, in part, a reflection of the special circumstances and prosperity of the West African trade itself.

From the foregoing it seems certain that the measures taken to reorganise Elder Dempster after the crash of the Royal Mail Group were highly successful. Elder Dempster could, naturally, take no credit for the improvement in trade during the thirties, but the strength of its new management enabled it to take full advantage of the changing economic conditions. The Company's progress was reflected in its net voyage profits which ran at a high level, particularly after 1936, and its economy was demonstrated by the fact that administrative costs for 1934 and 1939 were almost identical although the size of the fleet was greatly enlarged during this period.[1]

Thus the close relationship with Alfred Holt and Company had led to a revival of the efficiency which had previously characterised Elder Dempster's business activities and had encouraged it to grasp whatever opportunities were available. In particular, the direction of Sir Richard Holt and the constant attention given by L. H. Cripps should be noted, for they played a vital part in producing these results. With an increasing income and a financial structure devoid of former liabilities, Elder Dempster was then able to accumulate reserves which soon permitted its policy to be freed from the restraints imposed by consideration of financial stringency.

The Growth of Rival Lines
There was no change in the membership of the West African Lines Conference during the nineteen-thirties and what new competition there was came from isolated and sporadic attempts by French, Italian

[1] See above, p. 278.

and Japanese lines to break into the trade. These were rarely successful and did not usually affect the routes between West Africa and the United Kingdom and Northern European ports.[1]

The United Africa Company, however, was able to increase both its strength and its effectiveness for, following the reconstruction of its financial structure in 1931, it was in a better position to employ its resources on a really efficient basis.[2] Added to this, the steady rise in receipts from the improvement of trade which, of course, the United Africa Company shared with the other West African merchants and shipping lines, enabled them to promote the formation of many new firms and to acquire and control a further number of established companies on the coast.[3] The powerful backing which the United Africa Company received from Lever Brothers and Unilever[4] was a significant factor in this expansion, but the adoption of 'new principles of management and new methods of control'[5] were also important. Many unprofitable trades were shed at this time, so the merchanting position of the U.A.C. was greatly improved. In turn this strengthened the hand of the Company in its dealings with the conference lines. An excellent example of this changing relationship was in the acquisition by the United Africa Company of the old established firm of G. B. Ollivant & Co. Ltd. This concern had been a staunch supporter of Elder Dempster for many years and, in fact, part of its funds had been provided by the shipping lines.[6] When Elder Dempster and Company Ltd. was placed in the hands of the official receiver its loan to Ollivants became part of its realisable assets and had to be withdrawn on behalf of its creditors. As the new shipping firm, Elder Dempster Lines Ltd. was not prepared to replace this money, the only practicable course open to Ollivants was to turn to the United Africa Company. When this action was taken, new capital was quickly made available, but it was only provided on the

[1] The West African Lines Conference had a freight understanding with those French lines which operated from Northern French ports and similar arrangements with the members of the Mediterranean Conference. However, some competition with these lines did develop in the coastal shipping services.

[2] See Appendix, p. 472, Table 70.

[3] See the *History of the United Africa Company Ltd to 1938*, pp. 133–4.

[4] Lever Brothers and Unilever amalgamated as one concern in 1937, taking the name of Lever Brothers and Unilever Ltd.

[5] F. J. Pedler, *The United Africa Company*, to be published in 1973.

[6] This was in the nature of a loan of £80,000 which Ollivants used to develop their interests in the Gold Coast.

condition that control of the firm passed to the Lever interests.[1]

On the shipping side, the United Africa Company also increased its relative strength. As we have seen, Elder Dempster was able to accommodate an increasing volume of trade after 1934 with only a small addition to the size of its fleet.[2] On the other hand, the United Africa Company possessed only 23,000 gross tons in 1931 and these had to be supplemented by a number of chartered vessels, according to the demands of their business. It is noticeable, however, that in each successive year after 1934, the United Africa Company increased the tonnage under its direct control and by 1939 it owned a total of over 81,000 gross tons:

Growth of the U.A.C. Fleet, 1929–1939[3]

1929	15,166 gross tons	1935	28,935 gross tons
1930	19,797	1936	56,391
1931	23,197	1937	77,045
1932	22,679	1938	81,916
1933	29,781	1939	81,916
1934	29,871		

The reasons for a growth in tonnage of nearly 300 per cent in only four years are not difficult to find. In the first place there was, as has been seen,[4] a substantial increase in trade after 1934. Secondly, the United Africa Company obtained a slightly larger share of both imports and exports by its policy of acquiring established firms and by forming new ones. Neither of these factors, however, appears sufficient to justify so big an increase in the size of its fleet and, in fact, it was the replacement of chartered vessels by company-owned ships which provides the main explanation.

In view of the events of 1929 it might be wondered if the expansion of the United Africa Company's fleet between 1935 and 1938 was a further stage in a continuing struggle with Elder Dempster. This was not the case. Conversations with the new Elder Dempster management had been held in June 1932, and although it was not possible to reach an agreement a friendlier atmosphere began to develop.[5] This was helped when Elder Dempster gave the U.A.C. the first option on a

---

[1] U.A.C. Executive Committee Minutes No. 2, pp. 229, 239, 244 and 318. See also, P. T. Bauer, *West African Trade* (Cambridge University Press, 1954), p. 108.

[2] See above, p. 277.   [3] U.A.C. Mss.   [4] See above, p. 275.

[5] U.A.C. Mss., Executive Committee Minutes (No. 2), p. 356, 26 June, 1932.

valuable site which it was selling at Opobo.[1] As noted earlier,[2] many other meetings and discussions followed but the two sides still could not settle their differences. Nevertheless the U.A.C. were sufficiently interested to support Elder Dempster Lines Holdings Limited, when it was formed in 1936, by purchasing 200,000 of its shares.

The United Africa Company's new shipping policy sprang to some extent from the interests of their parent company, Lever Brothers and Unilever Limited, for it was to the benefit of the group as a whole that the United Africa Company should acquire a number of new ships. The underlying factor which tended to dictate this policy was concerned with the pattern of Lever's trade with Germany, for this had resulted in the building up of substantial balances of blocked marks. Under the prescriptions imposed by the government of the Third Reich these balances could only be used inside Germany. Levers used part of these funds to purchase a wide variety of firms and part went into government loans, but there were still embarrassingly large accumulations which could be neither profitably invested nor withdrawn. The further tightening of control which followed Schacht's 'New Plan' in July, 1934, together with the revival in trade which began at this time, emphasised the need for realistic plans to transfer at least some of this capital.

One solution which was suggested was to turn these resources into ships which could then be exported from Germany and either sold or used by the companies within the Lever group.[3] Accordingly negotiations were concluded for the laying down of 300,000 gross tons of trawlers, tramps, tankers and whale-catchers,[4] which were to be constructed in German shipyards over a four-year period. All these vessels were supplied at an economic price which was financed entirely from blocked marks. There was no additional premium and no payment of any other currency, so the ships represented a real transfer of resources from within Germany. During 1936 and 1937 eight vessels totalling 42,524 gross tons were built in Germany for the United Africa Company.[5] These ships proved to be adequate for the needs of the West African trade, but tended to be slow and under-powered. It

[1] F. J. Pedler, op. cit., Chapter 16.   [2] See above, Chapter 10, pp. 261-4.
[3] The original idea was first put forward by Mr R. H. Muir (Managing Director of the U.A.C. responsible for shipping).
[4] C. Wilson, *The History of Unilever* (London: Cassell, 1954), pp. 370-372.
[5] See Appendix, p. 473, Table 72.

should be noted that the new construction was not only utilised to increase the size of the fleet, for the opportunity was taken to replace most of the United Africa Company's older vessels, four ships totalling 19,204 gross tons being sold in 1935 and 1936.[1]

The purchase of German ships at a time when many British yards were idle aroused some criticism and questions were asked in Parliament as to the political and economic implications of this policy, bearing in mind the high level of unemployment. The United Africa Company had, in fact, ordered two new vessels in Britain before the decision to build in Germany was finalised. A further four vessels were subsequently built in the United Kingdom—making a total of 28,735 gross tons—and these were delivered between 1936 and 1938.[2] The addition of new construction from Germany and Britain, less those sold, meant that the U.A.C. fleet was increased from seven ships totalling 29,871 gross tons in 1934, to sixteen vessels of 81,916 gross tons in 1939.[3] The enlargement of the U.A.C. fleet does not appear to have been the result of a direct attempt by Levers to improve the relative strength of their West African shipping interests, but nevertheless it is clear that the United Africa Company was not averse to operating a larger fleet. As early as August 1934, they had discussed proposed new itineraries which would have required the services of at least nine or ten vessels,[4] and the additional ships would only have been built if U.A.C. cargoes were sufficient to keep them fully employed. In fact there was ample cargo to justify the new tonnage, while the U.A.C. was also anxious to lessen its dependence on the charter market. In spite of these factors, however, it seems likely that so many new ships would not have been built without the incentive of utilising the balances blocked in Germany.[5]

There was one other agreement relating to the division of the trade which needs to be mentioned. It will be remembered[6] that John Holt and Company (Liverpool) Limited had a long-standing arrangement with Elder Dempster whereby they were able to use their own ships to carry part of their own cargoes. Any requirements surplus to this capacity were met by the conference lines which carried these cargoes

[1] See Appendix, p. 473, Table 73.   [2] See Appendix, p. 473, Table 74.
[3] See Appendix, p. 474, Table 75.
[4] Henry Tyrer Mss., Letter from Mr T. Wilson of Henry Tyrer & Co. Ltd, to Mr T. B. Bragg, Manager of the U.A.C. Shipping Department, 2 August 1934.
[5] Author's interview with Lord Cole.   [6] See above, Chapter 9, p. 226.

at conference rates and gave Holts the benefit of the normal deferred rebate. This arrangement continued to work throughout the nineteen-thirties with only minor variations.[1] Holts continued to operate a small fleet as specified in the understanding, but as the older ships were replaced by new ones of larger capacity, its total tonnage was gradually enlarged from the 15,940 gross tons of 1930 to 20,045 gross tons in 1939.[2]

This increase in size was held not to infringe the terms of the agreement, as trade was rising and required additional carrying capacity. The net effect was that Holts continued to enjoy an advantage over the other West African merchants. As a result, Holt's net profits rose during this period, but it would be unwise to compare these with those earned by Elder Dempster because they included merchanting as well as shipping activities.[3] A comparison with the net profits of the U.A.C. might be considered more apt, but the financial reconstruction of this firm in 1931—in particular the reduction of its capital[4]—renders such an examination of little value.[5] A more precise guide to the success of the U.A.C.'s ship-owning activities is provided by the following table:

U.A.C. Steamers Voyage Results[6]

Year ended 30 April	1930	£110,505
30 April	1931	£115,188
30 April	1932	£180,856
30 September	1932	£ —
30 September	1933	£248,618
30 September	1934	£209,423
30 September	1935	£227,243
30 September	1936	£259,021
30 September	1937	£297,264
30 September	1938	£290,064
31 August	1939	£273,185

The U.A.C. charged itself the '. . . net rates after rebate which

---

[1] At a meeting held in April 1930, John Holts had suggested that if the U.A.C. was prepared to build another five vessels and thus increase its fleet to ten, then they would be prepared to consider including their own ships in a common 'pool'. This would have resulted in substantial economies in management and operation, but the U.A.C. did not respond and the plan was abandoned. Lever Mss., M.D.C. 3.4.1930.

[2] See Appendix, p. 470, Table 67.   [3] See Appendix, p. 471, Table 68.

[4] See Appendix, p. 472, Table 70.   [5] See Appendix, p. 472, Table 71.

[6] U.A.C. Mss. Extract from Descriptive Profit and Loss Accounts, AB/VAE, 12 November 1969.

would be payable by Conference Shippers',[1] so the results given above represent the savings which were made by using company-owned or chartered tonnage. In the accounts the company-owned vessels were debited with 5 per cent depreciation and the chartered ships with the cost of hire. Both also bore their own running and administrative costs for the voyage, but did not contribute to head office expenses. Consequently they are not directly comparable with Elder Dempster's results and any attempted comparison would be unjustified.

The voyage profits indicated above are, of course, in addition to the amount by which the conference rates were above the true cost of shipping. It would appear, therefore, that the U.A.C.'s policy of breaking with the conference had paid handsome dividends, but is this really the case? It will be remembered that Elder Dempster and the other lines had offered substantial concessions during the negotiations and when these are taken into account it may be thought that the financial grounds for the break were barely adequate.[2]

The working of the Conference System

During the nineteen-thirties the relative strengths of the constituent companies engaged in the West African trade remained fairly stable. Despite the collapse of the Royal Mail Group and the entry of the United Africa Company into shipping, either of which might have had catastrophic effects on Elder Dempster's power to retain its preponderant position in the trade, there was little alteration in the relative shares of the conference lines. It must again be emphasised that the German and Dutch lines did not attempt to take advantage of Elder Dempster's difficulties, but it should also be pointed out that it was only the maintenance of the conference structure which prevented the effective competition of external lines. The growth of the Lever interest in West Africa and the rising tonnage under the direct control of the United Africa Company also presented a potential challenge to the authority of the conference. In practice, however, the United Africa Company mainly shipped its own cargoes and did not attempt to become common carriers at this time.[3]

[1] U.A.C. No. 1 Minute Book, p. 133, 31 December 1929.

[2] See above, Chapter 10, p. 238 et. seq.

[3] The U.A.C.'s ships occasionally carried palm oil for third parties and may have obtained a little produce from the Delta ports but these were isolated incidents of small significance. Nevertheless the Board recorded the following view when it was offered

With the more general recovery in trade after 1934 the conference was in a better position to maintain its regulatory functions. It continued to resist the attempts of outside lines to enter its sphere of influence and was able to keep freight rates at levels which gave the shipowners a reasonable return on their employed capital. It is possible to argue that freight rates could have been lower, but this implied criticism is scarcely valid. In the particular circumstances of the early thirties the shipowner was especially anxious to protect his capital as well as to earn a reasonable remuneration and without the encouragement of a conference system it is unlikely that fresh capital could have been obtained on reasonable terms.

The merchant, moreover, was more concerned with regularity of service and stable shipping costs than with grinding rates down to a level which could only be maintained for short periods. Freight rates usually form only a minor part of the landed cost of a commodity, but in a fiercely competitive trade—such as this—even small changes could be quite important. Thus if the shipping services had not been regulated and if carriage charges had varied substantially, the merchants would have been constantly revising their prices—which was commercially undesirable—or would have been forced to absorb the fluctuations themselves. Either of these courses would have meant the introduction of further uncertainty into the trade and would have made forward planning and the holding of stocks extremely difficult.

This is not to suggest that there were no rate changes in the West African trade in the thirties—rather that there were fewer than might otherwise have been the case.[1] In fact, after the conference had failed to come to terms with the United Africa Company, freight rates rose by between 10 per cent and $17\frac{1}{2}$ per cent[2] and they were again raised— this time by 10 per cent to $12\frac{1}{2}$ per cent—in June 1932.[3] Certain items paid reduced rates after August 1935,[4] but the general tariff was in-

---

freight by a mining company:—'Whilst not deliberately seeking it, if such business should be offered to the Company of sufficient bulk and of sufficiently long duration to make it worth while, it should be accepted.'

U.A.C. Mss., Board Executive Committee, Para 9, of the minutes of the meeting held 2 January 1934.

[1] S. G. Sturmey, *British Shipping and World Competition* (University of London, Athlone Press, 1962), pp. 343–350.

[2] *West Africa*, 19 December 1931, p. 1576 and 24 October 1931, p. 1295.

[3] *West Africa*, 28 May 1932, p. 537.   [4] *West Africa*, 3 August 1935, p. 877.

creased by 10 per cent to 20 per cent from the beginning of January
1937.[1] During this period the General Index of Shipping Freights varied
as follows:

Index Numbers of Shipping Freights 1930–1937[2]

	1920 = 100	1930 = 100
1930	19.11	—
1931	19.88	104.0
1932	18.76	98.2
1933	18.13	94.9
1934	18.86	98.7
1935	18.97	99.3
1936	22.58	118.2
1937	34.93	182.8

An examination of these two sets of figures indicates that the level of
West African freight rates was above that of the general index up to
1936, but below it in 1937. It must be remembered, however, that the
West African charges had been drastically reduced in 1930—much more
than in other trades—so the increase in 1931 and 1932 had done little
more than restore the previous position. If this factor is taken into
account it is clear that West African freight rates were only a little above
the general level in the first half of the thirties, although they were
significantly below this level in the boom year of 1937.

Thus the regulation of the trade, based on the agreements between
Elder Dempster and the Merchants Freight Association, and Elder
Dempster and John Holts was an arrangement between free agents and
it derived its strength from the self-interest of all parties. It had the
effect of reducing cut-throat competition, apart from that with the
U.A.C., and of securing an equitable distribution of the trade that was
based on consent rather than rivalry. As a result, all the participants
were able to take advantage of the good years when the demand for
West African products was rising and thus offset the losses of the bad
years when the trade had been in the depths of the depression.

The outbreak of war in 1939 and more particularly the conditions
of the immediate post-war period brought fundamental changes to the
trade and to the relationship of those engaged in it. The closely-knit
structure of the nineteen-thirties, which was, in some respects, still part

[1] *West Africa*, 19 December 1936, p. 1791.
[2] Chamber of Shipping, *Annual Year Book* (1938), p. 130.

King Tom office and works, Freetown, *c.* 1940.

PLATE 17

King Tom covered slipway, Freetown, *c.* 1940.

Wilmot Point Works, Lagos, *c.* 1940.

PLATE 18

Slipway at Wilmot Point, Lagos, *c.* 1940.

of the legacy of Sir Alfred Jones, was to be replaced by a more flexible system in which traditional concepts were to give way to new ideas. The age of economic paternalism begun by Jones some fifty years earlier was coming to an end.

Elder's Colonial Airways

Typical of Elder Dempster's new approach to the changing conditions of the thirties was their entry into commercial aviation. As early as 1930 Mr A. C. Wyness spent a month with Imperial Airways in London.[1] There he examined the workings of each department before returning to West Africa, where he took up the position of Company's Representative at Kano. The R.A.F. had flown from Cairo to Kano in 1925 and had made occasional flights thereafter. In 1930 an Air Ministry survey was made by W. A. Campbell and the importance of the city as a potential air-link of the future was clearly recognised. For both technical and economic reasons, however, no steps were taken to inaugurate a service at that time and it was not until 1936 that further progress was made on this route.[2]

In the meanwhile, however, Elder Dempster and Imperial Airways entered into discussions in respect of a proposed air service between Nigeria and the Gold Coast. These negotiations resulted in a demand for additional information and in 1934 Mr L. E. Webb visited the Coast on behalf of Imperial Airways and produced a report which was then submitted to Elder Dempster.[3] During his visit an outline of the scheme was submitted to the Government in Lagos:

'I have the honour to refer to my interview with you on Monday last, at which Mr. L. E. Webb of Messrs. Imperial Airways Ltd., was present when I informed you that my Company is contemplating the establishment of an inter-colonial air service between Nigeria and the Gold Coast, with a view to improving and accelerating mail, passenger and freight connections between these colonies. It is proposed to make a commencement by operating a service between Takoradi,

[1] Wyness was selected for this job primarily because of his previous experience—he had served as a pilot with the Royal Flying Corps during the First World War. *Source:* Author's interview with Mr A. C. Wyness, 14 May 1969.

[2] Note that when the United Africa Company was approached by the Aircraft Operating Company Limited, in 1929, it refused to take a substantial interest in its activities. (U.A.C. No. 1 Minute Book, p. 50, 9 July 1929.)

[3] E.D.L.P. Imperial Airways Limited. *A Report to Elder Dempster Lines Limited on the operation and commercial possibilities of an air service in British West Africa.* (Hereinafter referred to as 'Air Report'.)

Accra and Lagos, in conjunction with the arrival and departure of our express service vessels at Takoradi.

The aircraft operating this service will be of a type recommended by Messrs. Imperial Airways for passenger and mail transport in this country.

The Imperial Airways will be responsible for the provision of competent pilots, licensed ground engineers and the maintenance of the aircraft and engines under precisely the same standards obtaining in their Continental, Indian and African routes.

You will appreciate that an undertaking of this description will involve my Company in considerable expenditure with little possibility of a commensurate return in the near future. Nevertheless, it is not our intention to ask Government for a subsidy, but we trust we may rely on Government assistance and support in other directions, the most important of which is the provision and maintenance of an aerodrome and the question of granting a mail contract, will also, I trust, be favourably considered.'[1]

The underlying assumption was that businessmen and government officials in a hurry, together with urgent items of mail and freight, would leave the southbound express vessel at Takoradi. Thus there would be a saving of six or seven hours on the journey to Accra and of between thirty-six and forty hours to Lagos. It was appreciated, however, that this would not generate enough business to put the airline on a viable basis, so other suggestions were considered:

'The present homeward schedule is for the mail vessel to leave Lagos ten days after the arrival of the outward (southbound) vessel, which means that the public have ten days in which to deal with their homeward mail, leaving nothing for the air mail leaving a day later, but if the homeward mail schedule was altered so that it left Lagos the same day as the outward vessel, or even a day before, mails will be forced onto the air service in order to catch the return mail homeward at Takoradi, or be faced with the alternative of waiting thirteen or fourteen days . . .'[2]

It is doubtful if Elder Dempster would, or could, have implemented this recommendation but, in fact, the Report came to the conclusion that it would not be a practical proposition to attempt to run a local service in association with the mail steamers. It suggested, instead, that it would be much better to provide an air link with Khartoum from where passengers and letters could be carried to Britain by the aircraft already being operated by Imperial Airways on the London–Johannesburg service:

[1] E.D.L.P., *Air Report*, p. 42, Letter from H. S. Feggetter (Nigerian Manager) to the Chief Secretary of the government, 8 November 1934.
[2] E.D.L.P., *Air Report*, p. 57a.

As a result of this investigation, we consider that the local service proposed cannot hope to pay its way by itself, unless an aircraft of small size and low safety factor were employed, which we cannot recommend. Its prospects might be better if it were extended to Sierra Leone in order to connect with the mail steamers there. The gain in time, however, by this extension is in our view not sufficiently large to warrant the great increase in mileage involved, particularly as permission would have to be obtained to fly over and land in foreign territory. We recommend, therefore, that this local service should be regarded simply as "staking the claim" for the company running it and as a part of a weekly air service connecting the West Coasts of Africa with the main Africa service at Khartoum. By this means letters and passengers could travel from London to Lagos and Takoradi in 5½ and 6 days respectively on the schedules at present in operation for the main African air service.

We suggest that in any approach to the Governments in West Africa a statement to this effect would be likely to arouse more interest and assistance than a proposal to start a purely intercolonial service without any idea of a through service, when ground organisation permits.'[1]

The Report was completed in March 1935 and after careful consideration was accepted by the Elder Dempster Board. It was then decided to form a new company to be known as Elders Colonial Airways Limited. The new concern was to have a capital of £25,000 in ordinary shares of £1 each—Elder Dempster and Imperial Airways each taking a 50 per cent interest.[2] It was agreed that the whole of this capital be issued but that the shares would only be partly paid up until such time as additional resources were required.[3] Major G. F. Torry, M.C. and Mr Picton Hughes Jones were then appointed directors to represent Elder Dempster in the new firm, and it was decided that the registered office should be at Colonial House, Liverpool.[4]

Practical steps were then taken to implement the recommendations of the Report, and it was decided that an air-link between West Africa and Khartoum (and hence London) could best be achieved in three stages. During the first stage passengers, mail and freight would be carried from Khartoum to Kano by air and onward transmission to Lagos would be by rail. Then, when suitable arrangements could be made, the second stage would be brought into operation and the planes

[1] E.D.L.P., *Air Report*, pp. 9–10.

[2] E.D.L.P., Minute Book No. 1, Minute 295, 24 September 1935.

[3] Note that at this time the U.A.C. reaffirmed its decision not to take an active interest in the establishment of air services in West Africa. (U.A.C. Executive Committee Minutes No. 2, p. 291, 12 March 1935).

[4] E.D.L.P., Minute Book No. 1, Minute 305, 29 October 1935.

would continue to Lagos via Kaduna, Minna and Oshogbo. The final stage would permit the service to be extended to the Gold Coast.

These plans placed Kano in a key position and meant, consequently, a great deal of extra work for Elder Dempster's representative. As previously noted, Mr A. C. Wyness had been appointed to this position in 1930, and in the following years had successfully built up the Company's agency business. Then came the decision to operate the new air route. This meant that he was to be responsible for the collection and distribution of the mail, besides having to ensure that satisfactory arrangements were made for the provision of ground services. The early R.A.F. flights had landed at the polo ground but this was unsuitable for commercial flights (partly because of the fear of yellow fever) and the Nigerian government had to be encouraged to construct a proper aerodrome to the north of the city. This naturally took time, but Wyness had the pleasure of seeing the Emir of Kano cut the first sod for the new airfield and later was able to take him—together with the Governor of Nigeria—on one of the first flights from the new facility.[1]

A proving flight under the command of Captain O. P. Jones left London on 26 January 1936. This reached the Sudan on 1 February and then flew via El Obeid, El Fasher, Geneina, Abecher, Ati, Fort Lamy and Maidugori to Kano—the 1,700 mile journey from Khartoum taking fifteen hours' flying time at a speed of approximately 115 m.p.h. The plane then returned to what was to be its base in Khartoum and began a regular weekly service to Kano on 15 February.[2] In October 1936 the second stage was introduced and flights continued on to Lagos, stopping at Kaduna, Minna and Oshogbo. The following year the final stage of the original plan was reached when the service was extended to Accra, the capital of the Gold Coast.[3]

The aircraft used to inaugurate and operate the West African service were *Daedalus* and *Delia*. These were De Havilland 86's—four-engined biplanes with accommodation for up to eight passengers and a

[1] Wyness interview, op. cit.
The author visited Kano in August 1969, and is indebted to Mr J. W. Evans of the Survey Office who kindly traced the original plan of this airfield. (Reference Kano Aerodrome Site 'D', Plan No. 85.)
[2] A much fuller account of the flying aspects of the service is to be found in *The Time Shrinkers* by D. M. V. Jones (London: David Rendel Ltd, 1971).
[3] Wyness interview, op.cit. Wyness left Kano in 1937 and helped to organise the new section between Lagos and Accra.

crew of three. They proved to be quite suitable for the route and, in fact, planes of this type continued the service until after the fall of France in 1940.[1] They were then replaced by Lockheed 14's which had a bigger payload and a longer range.[2]

Further internal developments within West Africa included the establishment of a weekly seaplane service between Bathurst and Freetown. In some respects this was to be the real start of Elders Colonial Airways activities, for until then Imperial Airways had provided most of the organisation as well as the technical know-how. In the case of the Coastal Seaplane Service, however, Elder's Colonial Airways acted as commercial managers for Elder Dempster Lines, while Imperial Airways were responsible for operational matters.

Elders Colonial Airways also began experimental flights between Lagos and Takoradi in 1939, but all of their flying activities came to an end in June, 1940, when these were taken over by the government for the duration of the war.

[1] Author's interview with W. L. Leinster, 6 May 1969. Wyness was succeeded at Kano by Wyatt Haywood. In turn, Haywood was followed by Leinster who served there from July 1937 to 1941.

[2] The route was then changed so that the service operated from Takoradi, through Lagos, Douala, Bangui, Libenge, Arua, Juba and Khartoum to Cairo. (See F. J. Pedler, op. cit.)

Chapter 12

The Second World War

The Effect of the War on British Shipping

With the outbreak of war in September 1939, British shipping became subject to progressive degrees of control.[1] This was essential in order to safeguard the nation's supplies of food and raw materials and, unlike the situation during the First World War, the imposition of control was a very rapid process. Very briefly, the Government immediately requisitioned those ships it required for specific purposes as soon as hostilities began.[2] Then in November 1939 it created the Ships Licensing Committee for Overseas Voyages. This body had the task of licensing ships for particular trades, but it only operated for a few weeks, because in December an order was made for the general requisitioning of all British ships. The Government then possessed complete authority over the allocation of shipping space but the particular conditions of each trade were not overlooked and varying degrees of freedom were given to shipping lines to organise their resources in accordance with the peculiar requirements of their own services.

Within the framework of overall control, therefore, the British shipping firms were instructed to act in concert with the other companies who normally operated on the same route. Thus, subject to the exigencies of war, shipping lines were encouraged to maintain their former services and because of the special knowledge and experience

[1] C. B. A. Behrens, *Merchant Shipping and the Demands of War* (London: H.M.S.O., 1955).
[2] The Admiralty assumed operational control of merchant shipping on 26 August 1939. (See S. W. Roskill, *A Merchant Fleet in War—Alfred Holt & Co. 1939/45* (London: Collins, 1962), pp. 19–23.)

which each firm had in the conduct of its own trade, this proved to be very much in the national interest.[1]

It was fortunate that such an efficient system was adopted at the beginning of hostilities, for the Second World War proved to be an even more testing period for the British mercantile marine than the First World War. During the years from 1939 to 1945 the Merchant Navy lost over 33,000 men.[2] This was more than double the number of seamen killed and missing in the Great War. Losses of British and Commonwealth vessels also increased and rose from less than eight[3] to nearly twelve million gross tons.[4]

In addition there were further losses during the war from so-called 'normal' marine hazards. These amounted to 633,000 gross tons whereas if the average for the thirties had merely been continued the total would only have been about 320,000 gross tons. Thus about half of these 'normal' losses must be blamed on the special conditions caused by the war, and when the war and marine casualties are added together they amount to 52 per cent of the 1939 U.K. fleet.[5] Approximately ten million gross tons of allied and neutral shipping were also lost and about the same amount of enemy tonnage. If these losses are added to those suffered by Britain and the Commonwealth it will be seen that total world sinkings amounted to thirty-two million gross tons, or about half of the pre-war fleet. On the other hand, about forty-three million gross tons were constructed during the war years, so that by 1946 the world fleet was over eleven million gross tons larger than in 1939.[6] This was chiefly because of the immense building programme undertaken by the Americans after they had entered the war in 1941. It should be appreciated, however, that the pattern of replacements, simple standardised vessels, meant that the composition, character and ownership of world tonnage changed substantially during the Second World War.[7]

[1] All vessels were operated for government account. The shipping companies were paid for the use of the ships—a complicated requisitioning scheme regulated the hire rates.

[2] R. H. Thornton, *British Shipping* (London: Cambridge University Press, 1959),p. 93.

[3] See above, Chapter 8, p. 205.

[4] M. G. Kendall, 'Losses of U.K. Merchant Ships in World War II,' *Economica*, N.S., Vol. XV (1948), p. 289.

[5] Ibid., p. 291.

[6] S. G. Sturmey, *British Shipping and World Competition* (University of London, Athlone Press, 1962), p. 138.

[7] See below, Chapter 13, p. 317

The West African Trade during the War

In the West African trade the immediate impact of war resulted in a change in the structure of the Conference. The German lines ceased to be active members and the Dutch were unable to maintain their former co-operation. On instructions from the Government, therefore, a West African Co-ordination Committee was formed by Elder Dempster, John Holt and the United Africa Company. This committee then acted on behalf of the Ministry of War Transport as the general regulating body for this particular trade, beginning its effective work in February 1940. In practice, this placed the detailed operation of the trade in Elder Dempster's hands—all outward cargo being booked through them or their agents. By degrees, homeward cargoes came under the authority of various United Kingdom ministries and the allocation of shipping space from West Africa was then mainly made by Elder Dempster personnel acting in their capacity as agents for the Ministry of War Transport.[1]

Thus Elder Dempster's organisation and staff in West Africa came in for a great deal of extra work during the Second World War. The change from peace-time conditions was relatively slow, however, and it was not until Italy's entry into the conflict, together with the fall of France, that the situation at sea became really serious. The Mediterranean was then closed, so practically all vessels had to travel round the Cape of Good Hope in order to reach East Africa, India, the Far East and Australasia. When Japan entered the fray some vessels were diverted and sailed via Panama but, even so, an enormous tonnage continued to use West African facilities as Freetown was a vital assembly and dispersal point for the convoy system.

West Africa was, furthermore, a key staging region for the Western Desert. Not only did vessels for this area call for fuel and repairs but also many aircraft were disembarked, reassembled and then flown overland to Egypt. Many passengers travelled by sea to Lagos and then continued their journey by air across Africa. This was by far the quickest and most convenient form of communication between Britain, the Middle East and India, and during the course of the war years it grew from practically nothing to very large proportions.[2] In addition, while

[1] A few non-Elder Dempster personnel also took part—at Dakar, for example, Hervey Black of the Donaldson Line was in charge of operations.

[2] A few V.I.P.s and persons with very high degrees of priority travelled by air all the way, e.g. Gibraltar, West Africa, Egypt.

these new demands were made on Elder Dempster's resources, it was essential for the war effort that normal West African exports such as oils, fats and timber be not only maintained but increased. The production of tin ore and bauxite was also encouraged on a large scale and added substantially to the cargoes to be moved to Britain.

Throughout the war Mr G. H. Avezathe was in charge of all Elder Dempster activities in Nigeria. He was also appointed the representative of the Ministry of War Transport so that the movement and loading of all vessels from the Congo to Dakar became his responsibility. These were very demanding tasks but they were completed with an expertise borne of long experience so that time could be spared to give special attention to the working of Lagos and Apapa. Working in co-operation with Mr Avezathe were Mr R. P. H. Davies, Elder Dempster's Gold Coast manager, and Mr Eric Wheeler, who was in charge of Sierra Leone and the Gambia for most of the war period.

In the case of Nigeria, the best account of Elder Dempster's activities is the one written by Mr Avezathe himself:

'The war increased the demands on the Company in Nigeria considerably. First came the need for ships' essential repairs to enable them to proceed safely and expeditiously on their voyages and much of this work was accomplished at Lagos where Elder Dempster Lines already had in being a repairs depot fitted however only for minor repairs to Main Liners and for construction and repairs of small craft. It soon became essential for this depot to increase its scope and attend to the many and varied requirements of ocean ships. It can safely be said that this was most successfully accomplished and many a Liner owes a big debt to this organisation for repairs that previously the Wilmot Point Works could not have attempted.

The working of Apapa Wharf and Lagos Customs Wharf Stevedoring was called upon to undertake a 24 hour day and vessels were enabled thereby to join convoys which they would otherwise have missed.

A Bonded store for Merchant ships was arranged and stores were made available for vessels who by length of their voyages had insufficient supplies.

The Crew Department was enlarged and African Seamen trained and engaged to help relieve the shortage of Merchant Seamen.

The Company took on Agency work and repairs of all troop transports, and also the management of a large coasting fleet for the movement of services stores and petrol for the R.A.F.

The Ministry of War Transport appointed the Nigerian Manager as their Representative and the control, programming and filling of all vessels from the Congo to Dakar became his responsibility. The cabling of all movements and loading programmes had necessarily to be communicated in high grade cypher, this necessarily resulted in all Shipping Companies' cables being passed through this one source.

The coal shortage resulted in a large increase in production and ocean movements of local coal to all territories, and the responsibility and programming of this large project was centred on the Ministry of War Transport's Representative.

The Accountancy section undertook the heavy responsibility of recording and paying the varied accounts of the Ministry's shallow to deep coasting scheme.

After the closing of the Mediterranean to merchant shipping, Lagos became one of the most important "travel junctions" in the Empire. Most people travelling between England and every part of the Middle East proceeded Sea/Air via Lagos and as the seaborne section between England and Lagos was made by vessels owned or managed by Elder Dempster Lines, it can be appreciated that our passenger department by efficiently handling all those passengers travelling under British or Allied Government auspices contributed usefully to the war effort.'[1]

Although Lagos was obviously of supreme importance, the Nigerian 'River Ports' also had a key role to play. The Elder Dempster agent at Port Harcourt assisted the export of substantial amounts of Udi coal to other parts of West Africa, while items such as tin, palm oil and seeds were also loaded there and at Burutu, Calabar,[2] Sapele and Warri.[3] These ports were able to work fairly normally during the war period, but the demand for produce and, in particular, for timber was so great that a special arrangement was made in order to increase their capacity. This was the 'Shallow to Deep Coasting Scheme' and it provided for the sea-going ships to be loaded with timber to the limit imposed by their draught in the shallow waters of the Niger delta. Coasters then brought out more easily managed commodities and these were then transshipped to the partially filled ocean vessels at Lagos. This was an expensive method of operation but commercial considerations were of little consequence at a time of wartime necessity.

Mr R. P. H. Davies was Elder Dempster's manager in the Gold Coast. At the outbreak of war the Company was using Accra, Cape Coast, Winneba and Takoradi but in 1941, following the sinking of *Sangara*,[4] all traffic was concentrated at the latter port. The importance of Takoradi had been recognised at an early date and a defensive boom

[1] E.D.L.P. Letter from G. H. Avezathe to W. L. Robinson, 18 February 1946.
[2] The 'Cross River' Ferry service was operated from Calabar. Mr J. C. Lucas was agent there from 1939 to 1941, and Mr C. N. Hodge followed him in that position.
[3] Mr T. Hughes was agent at Warri for part of the war.
[4] See below, p. 305.

had been built in 1939. The port itself was of recent construction[1] but it was not designed for the volume and diversity of cargo it had to handle during the war.

The pressure on Takoradi was, in fact, so great that round-the-clock working was only a partial solution. Extra labour had to be recruited, trained and housed and Mr Davies, assisted by the Takoradi agent, Mr E. C. C. Smith, was very active in ensuring the efficiency and well-being of the new staff. In spite of his efforts, however, many difficulties remained and could only be solved by almost continuous hard work when convoys were preparing to sail. Furthermore, the shortage of essential equipment meant that many improvisations were necessary. An example of what could be achieved with the right men and the right organisation concerns the handling of bauxite. This ore, vital for air-craft construction, was brought from the interior in ever-increasing quantities but with the aid of only six lighters, a small belt conveyor and two Scotch derricks, up to 2,500 tons per twenty-four hours were loaded.

The landing of aeroplanes also presented serious difficulties:

'. . . at the outset there was no crane capable of handling cased planes and that sometimes the carrying vessels themselves were not fitted with derricks suffici-ently powerful to lift the aircraft aboard them (loaded in U.K. with cranes) . . . One common expedient was to put a ship alongside capable of handling the heavy lifts, and take the lift from the other ship, passing it over the deck of the lifting ship to the R.A.F. vehicle waiting to receive it on the wharf . . .'[2]

In spite of the lack of facilities and the use of, at first, unsuitable labour, the enthusiasm generated by Mr Davies plus the skill of the ships' officers inspired African stevedores, such as Willie Toe, and European riggers, like Young and Barclay, so that few of the several thousand planes that were landed suffered any damage.[3] Other work undertaken by Elder Dempster at Takoradi included the bunkering of

[1] Takoradi was opened in 1928. See R. J. Harrison-Church, *West Africa* (London: Longmans, 1966), pp. 376–7.

[2] E.D.L.P. Letter from R. P. H. Davies to W. L. Robinson, 2 February 1946.

[3] William Toe worked directly under the ship's officers and was the foreman respon-sible for the landing of all these aircraft. According to his testimony not a single one was either damaged or lost while under his care. After the war he continued in the Company's employment at Takoradi for many years, becoming well known as an expert loader of logs. He is now engaged in a similar position for the Ghana Cargo Handling Company.

Source: Author's interviews with William Toe at Takoradi, 27 August 1969 and 24 September 1969.

both Admiralty and merchant vessels. An average of 2,000 tons per month was supplied—much of it at a day's notice—usually when the Royal Navy was unable to do this work for itself.

As a result of the closure of the port in 1941, the boats and crews at Accra were unable to continue their normal work. Arrangements were therefore made for them to be moved to Takoradi and they were mainly responsible for dealing with the enlarged quantities of cement that, in the absence of local production, were being imported for war purposes.

The obvious importance of Takoradi did not, strangely enough, lead to any enemy attacks, although vessels were torpedoed within short distances of the port. The greatest threat to its existence came when *City of Edinburgh* went on fire, for so much water had to be pumped into her that there was a serious danger that she would capsize and block the main channel. Fortunately it was possible to put the fire out and, after the vessel had been re-stowed, she was able to proceed on her way.[1]

Mr Eric Wheeler was Elder Dempster's Sierra Leone manager from 1940 to 1944 at a time when Freetown's strategic position as a main convoy assembly point—it may have been the largest in the world—meant that large numbers of vessels were frequently at anchor there. In these circumstances the work performed by Elder Dempster fell into two main parts. Firstly there was the normal task—enlarged by wartime demand—of loading and unloading the vessels engaged in the West African trade. Many of these required repairs and servicing while all needed fuel and stores in various quantities. Secondly the Company acted as agents for about forty lines which were using the port because of the war.[2] There were so many of these vessels, in fact, that Elder Dempster found it essential to have a man permanently engaged on boarding-duties to take orders for fuel, food, water and supplies.[3]

The demand for repairs to ocean-going vessels was so great that the Company's 'King Tom' Works at Freetown had to be considerably enlarged. These eventually employed eight British staff[4] plus three

[1] Interview with Mr J. C. Lucas, 31 March 1969.
[2] Interview with Mr Eric Wheeler, 21 April 1969.
[3] For much of the war this situation was held by Mr K. Postance.
[4] These included E. B. A. (Bert) Peate (Engineer in Charge), T. H. Cowley (2 1/C), Andrews (1/C Plating), Scott (1/C Electrician), Baines (1/C Machinery) and H. Diamond (1/C Foundry Work).

hundred Africans and about fifty Italian tradesmen who were prisoners of war. A seven-day week was worked—twenty-four hours per day when essential—but although output increased enormously it was frequently necessary to call on the assistance of the railway workshops at Clinetown. Furthermore, although a large stock of plates, tubing, spares and parts had been built up before the war had started, the tremendous demand for repairs quickly necessitated the local manufacture of many new items.[1] In addition to this extra war work the normal functions of the works had to be continued. Thus up to thirty lighters and tugs had to be regularly slipped and maintained, tanks had to be cleaned and, as at Wilmot Point, three or four new lighters had to be constructed each year.[2]

Elder Dempster's agent at Bathurst, Wyatt Haywood, came under the authority of the Sierra Leone manager for the duration of the war. The Gambia possessed only a small trade but its close proximity to French-held Senegal made it of great strategic value at certain times.

Elder Dempster During the War

In 1939 Elder Dempster's ocean-going fleet consisted of five passenger ships and thirty-six cargo vessels. These totalled 228,777 gross tons and the Company also owned four coasters which were used on the West African Coast. By the end of the war in 1945 over half of this tonnage had been lost.[3]

It should be appreciated, however, that essential West African services were frequently assisted by the transfer of vessels from less important—or temporarily suspended—routes.[4] Thus while up to a hundred ships might have been engaged in the trade at any one time, many were strangers to the run. All of this tonnage was organised by the West African Lines Co-ordination Committee and a number of these additional vessels were directly managed by Elder Dempster.

[1] Iron tug propellers of up to 6[1] diameter were cast for the first time.
[2] The Wilmot Point Works at Lagos operated under Messrs Hooper and Glendinning during the period of hostilities. Its activities, and difficulties, were identical with those of the King Tom Works.
Source: Interview with A. S. Glendinning, May 1969.
[3] See Appendix, p. 417, Table 23.
[4] Many requisitioned Dutch ships and enemy prizes were placed under Elder Dempster management and used to supplement the West African services.

They, too, suffered severe losses from enemy action or collision, seven ships totalling 33,610 gross tons being sunk.[1]

Elder Dempster suffered no losses of any description in 1939 but five vessels were lost during 1940. The following year, 1941, was the worst of the war, for ten Company ships and two managed vessels became casualties. The next year, 1942, was another bad one—eight Company ships and two more managed vessels being sunk. By 1943, however, the situation was much brighter—only three Company ships and two managed vessels being lost. Furthermore the purchase of three second-hand motor ships, *Thurland Castle*, *Greystoke Castle* and *Penrith Castle* significantly strengthened the fleet in that year. (These were later renamed *Fulani*, *Freetown* and *Fantee*). Two new buildings, *Tarkwa* and *Tamele*, also provided additional capacity in 1944. No Company tonnage was destroyed in either 1944 or 1945, but one managed vessel was torpedoed in the last year of the war.

More tragic even than the loss of the ships was the death of many fine men—478 of Elder Dempster's sea-going staff being killed.[2] The loyalty and bravery of the staff was recognized by the granting of seventeen awards which included ten O.B.E.'s, three B.E.M.s, two M.B.E.s, one Czech Cross and one Lloyd's War Medal. Fourteen more received commendations, while another was mentioned in despatches.[3]

During the Second World War Elder Dempster was also attacked at home. The Company had moved its head office from Colonial House to India Building (both in Water Street, Liverpool) on the 1 July 1939.[4] The new accommodation was greatly appreciated, particularly as the opportunity was taken to replace the high stools and desks that had remained from the Alfred Jones era! After less than two years, however, a second move had to be made.[5] This was as a consequence of an enemy air raid which, on 3 May 1941, caused the almost complete destruction of India Building, Elder Dempster's office being gutted by fire. There was naturally much dislocation and confusion, but this was

[1] See Appendix, p. 418, Table 24.
[2] F. Bateman Jones, 'Elder Dempster Lines', Pamphlet published by the Company (September 1945), p. 4.
[3] Ibid., p. 8.
[4] E.D.L.P. Directors Minute Book No. 1, Minutes 467 and 487.
[5] Note that the Master Porterage, Stevedoring, Victualling and Marine Departments were not affected as they were situated at Toxteth Dock, Liverpool.

greatly reduced by the plans which the Company had made to deal with just such an emergency.

Many important documents and books were transported by trolly each evening and were kept overnight in a special room on a lower floor—items of special value being placed in fireproof safes, together with photographic records. Some of these papers had charred covers but all were intact, so the Company's precautions had saved its administration and, incidentally, the Inland Revenue, from many future headaches.

Elder Dempster's main office was re-established at 3 Linnet Lane in Liverpool 17. This was a large house that had been previously acquired and prepared in case of need. Space there was extremely limited—the directors' office was in a hayloft over the stables—so a second house was bought in nearby Mannering Road. Even then accommodation proved to be insufficient and within a few weeks the accounts department moved to The Chase, Barton Road, Hoylake. By 1943, however, it was possible to move the crew department back into India Building, where it occupied the undamaged mezzanine floor, together with representatives of other departments. These arrangements then continued until 1946 when India Building again became the Company's administrative centre, but it was not until 24 November 1952 that repairs and decorations were finally completed.[1]

Fleet Losses and Incidents
It is only possible to give a brief outline of the loss of the twenty-four Elder Dempster vessels that were sunk as a result of enemy action during the Second World War.[2] Some, like *Bassa*, have little to relate. She sailed from Liverpool for the United States in September 1940, and she and her crew of fifty were never heard of again. Most of the Company's losses were not of this type, however, and in many cases the skill and courage of the sea-going staff were sufficient to reduce the effect of both torpedo and bomb. Thus *Bodnant*, *Daru*, *Edward Blyden* and *New Columbia* were sunk without a single casualty and a further seven vessels each had less than four killed. On the other hand there were a number of instances where bad weather, other adverse

[1] Author's interview with Mr T. Keenan, 4 June 1969.
[2] The names of the vessels lost during the Second World War are given in the Appendix, p. 417, Table 23.

conditions, or ill-luck handicapped rescue attempts and resulted in heavy losses.

The first vessel to be lost was the *Accra*, a passenger mail ship of 9,337 gross tons, that was under the command of Captain J. J. Smith. She left Liverpool on 23 July 1940, and three days later, when about two hundred miles to the West of Ireland, was torpedoed without warning. Although *Accra* sank an hour after being hit, all her boats were got away successfully and the survivors were quickly picked up by other ships in the convoy. As a result, only nineteen of a total of nearly five hundred passengers and crew on board lost their lives.

A few days later *Boma*, under Captain E. C. Anders, had the unwanted distinction of being the first Elder Dempster cargo vessel to be sunk. This was followed by the disappearance of *Bassa* in the North Atlantic and by the sinking of *Apapa*—a sister of the *Accra*. In the latter case it was a sudden air attack which caused the damage—a bomb dropping on number three hatch setting on fire the cargo of palm kernels. Owing to damage in the engine room it was not possible to control this outbreak, so passengers and crew were ordered to abandon ship. This was achieved with no sign of panic: 'Everybody behaved in an orderly manner and very steadily',[1] and in consequence only twenty-six out of two hundred and sixty-one were killed. A final blow for the Company in 1940 was the loss of *Bodnant*, fortunately without loss of life, after a collision in convoy with *City of Bedford*.

The first incident of 1941 was a particularly tragic one. This concerned the *Seaforth* (Captain W. Minns) which was missing after sending a wireless message that she was being attacked by a submarine some 370 miles to the north-west of Ireland. Her crew of forty-nine and her ten passengers were later presumed to be dead. The next Elder Dempster vessel to be lost was the *Swedru*. She was sailing from Freetown to Liverpool in a heavily escorted convoy when she was struck by two enemy bombs. These caused many casualties, the captain, chief engineer, chief officer and chief steward being killed instantly and the second officer receiving injuries from which he subsequently died. The third officer then took over command and, after seeing the extent of the damage and the rapidity with which fire was spreading, ordered the boats away. Thirty-two survivors were quickly picked up by H.M.S.

[1] E.D.L.P., Elder Dempster Lines Casualties, File 1, No. 1, Statement by Captain E. V. Davies.

Gladiolus and taken to Londonderry, but seventeen had died in the attack.

Dunkwa (Captain J. W. Andrew) was on a voyage from Glasgow to Freetown, travelling independently, when on 6 May she was torpedoed. *Dunkwa* sank in eight minutes and it proved to be difficult to fill and launch the boats in time. The submarine surfaced and assisted the survivors who then set sail for Freetown in their two lifeboats. After two days, when 110 of the 220 miles had been covered, the *Polydorus* came into sight and eventually landed the crew, less eight casualties, at Oban.

The following month saw the loss of *Alfred Jones* (Captain H. Harding). In October, 1940, this vessel had been severely damaged by enemy aircraft and eleven of her crew had been killed. She returned to service after repair, but on 1 June was torpedoed and sank with the loss of two men when about 140 miles west of Freetown. A few days later the passenger liner *Adda* was torpedoed when eighty miles west of Cape Sierra Leone. Although she was carrying 260 passengers and a crew of 159 there were only nine casualties. This was partly because of good weather but also because a radio message to Freetown enabled a rescue vessel to collect the survivors within a few hours. Twelve members of *Adda*'s crew subsequently left Sierra Leone for Liverpool on *Empire Ability*, a vessel being managed by Elder Dempster on behalf of the Ministry of War Transport. This was torpedoed on 26 June but, although two members of her complement were killed, her passengers escaped harm, returning safely to Freetown.

It might be thought that those members of *Adda*'s crew that were sunk twice in the same month had just cause for complaint, but their feelings of outrage were small compared with those felt by the officers and men of *Sangara*. This vessel was actually lying at anchor off Accra when she was torpedoed. There was only a single death but the dangers were obvious and from June 1941, all cargo was diverted to the more easily protected port at Takoradi. As *Sangara* sank in shallow water it was possible to raise her and, after the war, following temporary repairs at Lagos, she was towed to England, re-fitted and then re-entered the Company's service.[1]

---

[1] It was necessary to re-purchase *Sangara* from the salvors as these had bought the wreck from the government who, in turn, had settled Elder Dempster's claim on a total loss basis.

Elder Dempster was to suffer three more losses before 1941 came to an end and all occurred within a nine-day period in September. *Daru* (Captain W. Rowlands) was bombed and sank on the 15th even though she was sailing in a heavily guarded convoy. *Edward Blyden* (Captain W. Exley) and *Dixcove* (Captain R. Jones) were sailing in another convoy from Freetown to Liverpool and were torpedoed on the 22nd and 24th respectively. Only four of the eleven ships in this particular convoy reached their destination safely. The only satisfactory aspect of these terrible incidents was that the loss of life was low—the third engineer of *Dixcove* being the sole fatality.

The fleet suffered no further losses until May 1942, when *New Brunswick* (Captain C. M. Whaley) was torpedoed on a voyage from Glasgow to West Africa. The survivors were picked up almost immediately by H.M.S. *Woodruff* but three of the crew and a ship's gunner were found to be missing. The next to be sunk was *Mattawin* (Captain C. H. Sweeny) which was on a voyage from New York to Alexandria. On 2 June, when three days out, she was torpedoed and foundered in seven minutes. In spite of this, four boats were launched and every person on board—including two who had been blown over the side—embarked safely. Orders were then given for each boat to make its own way to Cape Cod some two hundred miles distant. The next day, two of the boats were picked up by the Norwegian vessel *Torvanger* and a third, which was fitted with an engine, reached port on 5 June. But the fourth boat under the command of G. H. Griffiths (third officer) had a more difficult passage. After winds and currents had separated it from the other boats it was missed by *Torvanger* and its crew suffered from heavy rain and a thick fog. Each night was bitterly cold but on 6 June the weather cleared and they were spotted by a flying-boat. The U.S.S. *General Greene* arrived the following morning. This quickly transported the occupants to Nantucket where it was learned that every member of the crew, plus twelve American soldiers, had been rescued without loss.

A letter was subsequently written to Elder Dempster by one of the American personnel that had survived the loss of *Mattawin*:

'I have just returned from one of your ships that was sunk and wish to take the liberty of praising the person in charge of the life-boat I was on, for his splendid leadership and the order he kept, also for keeping the morale up. I do not know his name but he was Third Mate of the s.s. *Mattawin* which was sunk June 1st or 2nd. We were the lifeboat that was picked up on the sixth day.'[1]

The next casualty to be suffered by the fleet came on 1 September when *Ilorin* was torpedoed. Although an old vessel, built in 1920, she was an important link in the West African coasting trade.[2] The real tragedy, however, was in the loss of thirty-two members of the crew—there being only five survivors. This was also the case when *Abosso* (Captain R. W. Tate) was sunk on 30 October. *Abosso* was the largest (11,330 gross tons) and newest (built 1935) of the Company's express mail and passenger ships but her loss was of little consequence when compared with the near annihilation of her crew and passengers—more than a third of all Elder Dempster's casualties during the Second World War being suffered in this one disaster.

Abosso left Capetown for Liverpool on 8 October 1942. She had a crew of 182 and carried 100 passengers. These included 16 civilians, 3 British sailors, 3 British naval ratings, 34 members of the Royal Netherlands Navy and 44 internees.[3] Three weeks after leaving port when the vessel had reached a position about 700 miles North of the Azores, (44°N 28°W) she was torpedoed without warning. This occurred at 18.15 hours, just after dark. The explosion stopped the engines and a thirty degree list to port developed almost immediately. Attempts to lower the boats were handicapped by heavy seas and by the failure of the ship's lights, while the heavy list added to the difficulties. Nevertheless, at least three and probably five lifeboats did get away successfully before a second torpedo completed the destruction of *Abosso*, which sank a few minutes later. The weather then deteriorated still further and gale force eight winds, non-stop rain and tremendously high seas made survival a desperate matter.

Quartermaster A. V. May in charge of boat No. 5 found it difficult to keep his craft's head to the wind. The crew members aboard were mainly stewards, 'not accustomed to handling oars'[4] and although they did their best it became necessary to put out a sea anchor. With the aid of an oil bag and constant bailing the boat was kept afloat through the

[1] E.D.L.P. Elder Dempster Lines Casualties, File 1, No. 23, Letter from C. C. Wilson, American Field Service, New York, to Elder Dempster Lines Limited, 24 June 1942.
[2] Formerly the *Smerdis,* she had been acquired by Elder Dempster in 1934.
[3] E.D.L.P. *Ship Incidents* File; *Abosso,* Passenger list.
[4] E.D.L.P. Elder Dempster Lines Casualties, File No. 1, No. 26, Evidence of Albert Victor May.

night. The following day it was possible to use a sail for a time but then the weather worsened and a second terrible night had to be endured. At dawn, the wind having moderated, the sail was raised again and at 10 a.m. a convoy was sighted. An hour later all were on board H.M.S. *Bideford*, but the joy of rescue was gradually saddened by the realisation that the thirty-one occupants of boat No. 5 were the sole survivors of *Abosso*—168 Elder Dempster men and 83 passengers had perished.

Hardships of a different kind followed the sinking of *Dagomba* (Captain J. T. Marshall) on 3 November. She was hit simultaneously by three torpedoes, so went down very quickly. In spite of this, two of the four lifeboats were successfully launched, and the crew, with some exceptions—including the captain and chief engineer—were able to embark in time. Those still on board were taken down by the undertow but all managed to regain the surface where they were picked up by the chief officer in No. 2 boat. The submarine, an Italian one, surfaced soon after and provided stores and a course, for Freetown, 450 miles to the East.[1]

The lifeboats set out for Freetown together but parted company during the ensuing night. No. 2 boat then sailed and rowed a distance of 300 miles in eleven days before being sighted by the Portuguese warship, *Bartholomew Dias*. The survivors were given every kindness on this vessel and were eventually landed at Luanda.

No. 4 boat was under the command of the third officer (D. G. Wickstead) as the second officer had been fatally injured when *Dagomba* went down. This also made its way towards the West African Coast under arduous conditions. On the eighth day a convoy was sighted and it was thought that all difficulties were at an end. Unfortunately the ships proved to be under the control of the German-dominated French Vichy Government with whom British relations were extremely strained. The survivors were taken on board a sloop, *Aviso Annamite* and were imprisoned in the capstan flat for a period of five days. They were then landed at Dakar and taken to an internment camp at Sebikotane. Food and amenities were extremely sparse and it was not until 12 December that arrangements could be made for the men to be repatriated.[2] Even then their troubles were not completely over for

[1] E.D.L.P. Elder Dempster Lines Casualties, File No. 1, No. 32, Evidence of Captain J. T. Marshall.
[2] The attitude of the Senegal authorities towards their British internees changed drama-

transportation was a serious problem and after a train and lorry journey the party ended by walking the last ten miles to the Gambian border.[1] By the time these members of *Dagomba*'s crew reached Bathurst, thirty-eight days had elapsed since their ship had been sunk. In spite of all these difficulties, however, forty-three out of a total of forty-nine survived their dangerous journeys to safety.

There were two further casualties in 1942, *New Toronto* (Captain C. J. Knowles) and *Henry Stanley* (Captain R. Jones) being sunk on 5 and 6 December. The former was torpedoed and sank in twenty minutes while off Cotonou. The crew were picked up almost immediately by an escort vessel but three were subsequently found to be missing. The loss of *Henry Stanley* was much more costly. She was on a voyage from Liverpool to Freetown and had reached a point some 580 miles West of Fayal when she was hit. The boats were launched successfully, all passengers and crew embarking in safety. A little while later the submarine appeared and Captain Jones was forced to go aboard. During the night a terrible gale developed and it must be assumed that it was at this time that the lifeboats were lost, for they were never seen again. Captain Jones, however, did survive but it was not until his liberation from a German prison camp in April 1945 that he could give the only eye-witness account of the loss of his ship.[2] The sinking of *Henry Stanley* had cost the lives of fifty-two Elder Dempster men and eleven passengers.

Elder Dempster were to lose three more Company-owned vessels during the Second World War, and all of these casualties occurred in 1943. *William Wilberforce* (Captain J. W. Andrew) was sunk on 9 January while travelling without escort on a voyage from Takoradi to Hampton Roads. Ten days out of harbour, when about 500 miles West of the Canary Islands, she was struck by two torpedoes. Three members of the crew were killed at this time, but the remainder of those on board were able to get away in two boats. These were both subsequently sighted by the Spanish vessel, *Monte Arnabal*, and the

---

tically following the landing of allied troops in North Africa on 8 November. The subsequent occupation of Vichy, France by the Germans and the scuttling of the French fleet at Toulon on 27 November 1942, completed this transformation.

[1] E.D.L.P. Elder Dempster Lines Casualties, File 1, No. 31, Evidence of D. G. Wickstead.

[2] E.D.L.P. Elder Dempster Lines Casualties, File, 1, No. 25.

survivors were landed at Tenerife. Another Spanish ship then transported the party to Gibraltar where it was split into several groups for onward transmission to the U.K.[1] One of these groups consisted of Captain Andrew, the chief officer, second officer, chief engineer, second engineer, chief steward and the two cadets. They were allocated to Elder Dempster's *Mary Slessor* which had just arrived after landing troops and cargo at Algiers.

Mary Slessor sailed from Gibraltar on 7 February at 5 p.m. She was the commodore-ship in a thirty-six vessel convoy and was leading the centre column. Just before midnight, while still in the Straits, *Mary Slessor* struck two mines almost simultaneously and went down with great rapidity. None of the boats was launched successfully, so those who survived had to cling to rafts and wreckage until they were picked up by escort vessels some three or four hours later. Amongst those rescued was the Captain, C. H. Sweeney, who had been master of the *Mattawin* when she was sunk in June 1942, but there was a high death-rate. *Mary Slessor* had carried a crew, with survivors, of seventy-four, and thirty-two of these lost their lives—the casualties including both the chief officer and second officer of *William Wilberforce*.[2]

The final loss suffered by the Company's fleet during the war occurred on 31 October 1943. At about 9.15 p.m. on that date *New Columbia* (Captain F. B. Kent) was torpedoed while travelling unescorted from Libreville to Lagos at a point approximately 155 miles S.S.E. of the latter port. The weather was kind, so all four boats were launched and filled without difficulty and a course was set for Lagos. Next morning they were sighted by a Sunderland flying-boat which then guided *Conakrian* to their rescue. All members of the crew were quickly taken on board and were landed at the Nigerian capital the following day.[3] There were no fatal casualties and only a few slight injuries, so there was much to be thankful for—particularly as Elder Dempster's vessels bore a charmed life for the remainder of hostilities.

Thus there were no casualties during 1944 and the only one in 1945 was *Point Pleasant Park*. This was owned by the Canadian government's Park Steamship Company and was managed by Elder Dempster. She was torpedoed on 23 February while on a voyage from

[1] E.D.L.P. Elder Dempster Lines Casualties, File 2, No. 1.
[2] E.D.L.P. Elder Dempster Lines Casualties, File 2, Numbers 2, 2a, 3, 4, and 5.
[3] E.D.L.P. Elder Dempster Lines Casualties, File 2, Numbers 17, 18, 19 and 20.

Canada to South Africa. Nine men were killed during the attack, but the remainder sailed their boats for nine days, covering a distance of 400 miles, before being picked up at a point near Luderitz Bay, in South-West Africa.

This brief account of the losses of the Elder Dempster fleet during the Second World War ought not to disguise the fact that even those vessels which survived were subjected to tremendous strains. The long hours, hard work, boredom and discomfort endured by the sea-going staff were continuous problems that lasted as long as the war itself. Thus, although *Aba* sailed in many campaigns and suffered many attacks, she was never seriously damaged and few lives were lost. Indeed some Elder Dempster vessels were not involved in any incidents but all were under a constant atmosphere of uncertainty. The element of danger was, of course, always present, but tended to be submerged in the arduous routine of the daily grind. The normal hazards of the sea remained and were accentuated by the possibility of enemy action—and by the need to conform to the stringent regulations imposed by wartime necessity.

Chapter 13

Post-War Reconstruction

Post-War Problems

The ending of the Second World War in 1945 saw Elder Dempster Lines with many pressing problems. In the first place, in spite of wartime purchases and construction, its fleet had been reduced to only half of its tonnage in 1939:

Elder Dempster Fleet 1939–1945 (including Coasters)

1939	=	228,777 gross tons
Wartime losses (from all causes)	=	144,465[1]
		84,312
Less: Sale *Egba* in 1943	=	4,989
		79,323
Plus: Wartime purchases	=	18,225
		97,548
Plus: Wartime construction	=	14,588
1945	=	112,136

Furthermore, the pattern of losses was such that the Company was left without a main-line passenger ship. Four of these had been sunk and although *Aba*, the pre-war reserve, had survived a dangerous career as a hospital vessel, she was very elderly and after much discussion it was decided not to refit her and she was sold.[2] Most of the

[1] See Appendix p. 23, Table 417, for details of these losses.

[2] *Aba*, built in 1918 for the Glen Line, was purchased in 1920. Formerly operated under

remaining tonnage was badly in need of renovation at a time when repair facilities throughout the world could not cope with the demand for their services and the age structure of the fleet (the average vessel was nearly eighteen years old at the end of 1943) meant that major maintenance problems were always present.[1]

A second serious post-war problem for Elder Dempster concerned its head office accommodation. As previously noted, the wartime blitz and fire had led to the dispersal of the various departments between a number of different sites.[2] This was obviously detrimental to efficient working, so the Company put a great deal of effort into its attempts to return to its former home in India Buildings. Although reconstruction was incomplete, the desired moves were achieved in 1946 but the effects of the dislocation were not finally removed until 1952.

The third and, potentially, most important of the Company's difficulties began in January 1944 for it was then that the management agreement with Alfred Holts came to an end. Holt's decision, no doubt prompted by a shortage of experienced administrators, did not mean an end of their interest in Elder Dempster. They continued to be the largest shareholder in Elder Dempster Lines Holdings Limited, and at least two of their nominees were always members of its board. In addition, they were always prepared to recommend directors to the operating firm and over the next decade several Holt men were to provide valuable expertise. In spite of these remaining links with Alfred Holts, however, the ending of the management agreement did make a number of senior appointments essential, for three of the five directors of Elder Dempster Lines Limited resigned at the end of 1943.

The board of Elder Dempster Lines had remained fairly static since its creation in 1932. Sir Richard Durning Holt acted as chairman from that date until his death in 1941 and the Hon. L. H. Cripps, also a member of the original board, then succeeded him in the chair. Both G. F. Torrey, appointed 1932, and L. D. Holt, appointed 1936, served until 1943, but Picton Hughes Jones—also a 'founder' director—re-

---

the name of *Glenapp*, as a cargo vessel, she was refitted to carry 360 passengers and was the world's first large passenger liner to be propelled by diesel engines. After being sold to the Bawtry Steamship Company in 1947 she was renamed *Matrona* and while being renovated turned turtle in Bidston Dock, Birkenhead. Although eventually righted she was then scrapped.

[1] E.D.L.P. 'Fleet values at 31 December 1943'.   [2] See Chapter 12, pp. 302–3.

signed in 1940. R. A. Smye, chief accountant, was then elected to replace Mr Jones, while J. R. Hobhouse (1941–2) and later R. H. Thornton (1942–3) replaced Sir Richard Durning Holt.[1]

At the beginning of 1944, therefore, Elder Dempster Lines lost Holt, Thornton and Torrey. They were replaced by Colonel (later Sir) A. C. Tod[2]—The Chairman of the 'Holding' Company—and by J. H. Joyce[3]—W. L. Robinson, the Line's chief superintendent engineer, joined the board a little later. Cripps remained as chairman for a further year and was succeeded for a single year by Smye. The resignations of these directors in 1945 and 1946, respectively, then led to the election of G. H. Avezathe[4] and C. T. J. Cripps, and to the appointment of J. H. Joyce to the chair. Joyce's long tenure in this position (1946–1963) and Tod's lengthy term as a non-executive director (1944–1962) permitted a valuable continuity to be maintained and they may be said to have largely instigated and guided the post-war development of the Company.

The settlement of the immediate post-war management and accommodation problems were, of course, only prerequisites, however essential, to the main task which faced the reorganised board of directors—nothing less than a complete reshaping of the Company's business. It was accepted that technical progress, plus the differences either formulated or accelerated by the war, implied a considerable degree of change, but the plan for the future had necessarily to be based on the past. Consequently the following figures were compiled from the Company's records (see p. 315).

The new development plan, based on the pre-war figures, contained two basic assumptions. Firstly that Elder Dempster together with the other surviving member of the conference—the Holland West Africa

[1] See Appendix p. 463, Table 59, for the list of directors of Elder Dempster Lines Limited, 1932–7[2].

[2] See Appendix p. 464, Table 60, for the list of directors of Elder Dempster Lines Holdings Limited, 1936–52 and Liner Holdings Company Limited, 1953–72.

[3] John Hall Joyce was born in 1906, educated at Repton School and thereafter, from 1926 to 1937, was engaged in a number of engineering activities both in the construction and in the oil refinery spheres. In 1937 he first became directly concerned in shipping affairs, when he joined James Spencer and Company, the well known Glasgow stevedores, with whom he remained as a partner until 1943 when he was asked by the then Holdings Company to join Elder Dempster Lines as a Director . . .

(*Sea*, Vol. V, No. III (Autumn 1963), pp. 12–13.)

[4] See above, Chapter 12, p. 297.

Summary of Elder Dempster's Pre-War Carrying
(1936–7–8 Averages)

West Africa to/from:	Freight tons	Freight tons
Liverpool	201,000 (53 ships)	182,000 (53 ships)
London, Continent	93,000 (18)	74,000 (18)
Extras	28,000 —	150,000 (31)
Total	322,000 (71)	406,000 (102)
U.S.A.	75,000 (14)	83,000 (18)
Canada	152,000 (23)	78,000 (10)
	549,000	567,000[1]

Line—and the two British 'merchant' lines, John Holt's and the United Africa Company, would commit themselves to providing facilities for the carriage of all West African cargoes and passengers on the United Kingdom and the North Continental routes. The second assumption was that the prosperity of the West African countries must have an overriding priority, and this necessarily implied that the traders should have the ability to ship without difficulty at a reasonable cost. These were neither altruistic nor unselfish policies, but were reflections of the view that the long-term viability of the shipping companies could only be assured if West Africa itself was also affluent.

Elder Dempster's leading position in the West African shipping trade could not assure that its plans for the future would be automatically accepted by the other interested parties. The fact that they were largely followed was due to a wide variety of reasons—most of which were peculiar to the immediate post-war situation. The Holland West Africa Line, for example, had suffered badly during the war and it required time and capital to rebuild its organisation and fleet. Consequently when J. H. Joyce visited Amsterdam shortly after the liberation of the Netherlands in 1944 he received a warm welcome. Agreement in respect of future policy was quickly achieved in these circumstances and working arrangements were settled so that the Dutch could begin to take an active part in the trade once more.

The case of the two British 'merchant' lines was rather different. As noted earlier, a West African Lines Co-ordination Committee had been formed by Elder Dempster, John Holt and the United Africa Company

---

[1] E.D.L.P. J. H. Joyce Mss., p. 1.

in the early days of the war.[1] Ministerial control lasted until 30 September 1947, though from 2 March 1946 the process of derequisitioning began to be put into effect under the auspices of the United Maritime Authority.[2] Then from 1 October 1947 transitional arrangements came into force and after 10 November 1948 British tonnage was freed from all restrictions and could engage in normal commercial activities. During the period of control, co-operation amongst the three British shipping companies had proved to be particularly successful and so when requisitioning came to an end there were obvious reasons for continuing these close ties. It was therefore decided:

'. . . not merely to continue the war-time Co-ordination Committee arrangements, but to operate the trade among these three Owners equitably on an historical basis as to volume, but as an overall service for all cargo offering irrespective of the fact that two of the Owners themselves were very large Shippers of cargo. This voluntary arrangement was really continuing the War-time practice, but extending it in such a way that it should form and did form, a basis for the future handling of the trade when there was complete freedom . . .'[3]

It should also be remembered that both John Holts and the United Africa Company were primarily concerned with their merchanting interests. Consequently they were less anxious about freight rate levels than either Elder Dempster or the Holland West Africa Line, as any reduction in profitability on the shipping side could theoretically be offset by an equivalent rise from their other activities.

The Merchants Freight Association was, of course, vitally interested in securing and maintaining freight levels that would assist its members to compete in world trade. It recognised, however, that a certain return was essential if the shipowners were to replace and extend their fleets at the rate which it was agreed was both necessary and desirable. As a result, discussions of an amicable nature fixed freight rates at levels

[1] See above, Chapter 12, p. 296.
[2] The United Maritime Authority was created in 1944 by agreement with the other governments of the allied powers in order to '. . . ensure that allied ships reverting from the common pool to their respective Governments' control should be available to fulfil the essential programmes of every country—as opposed to leaving any country with ships' capacity more than its essential needs in an advantageous position to start ordinary commercial activities ahead of other countries short of ship capacity for its essential needs'. E.D.L.P. Letter from J. H. Joyce to A. W. Richards (Messrs. Alsop Stevens and Company) 31 October 1955.
[3] E.D.L.P. J. H. Joyce to John Holt & Co. (Liverpool) Ltd, 28 January 1954.

which gave satisfaction to shipowner and merchant alike and which, in the long term, were equally beneficial to each party.[1]

Elder Dempster's reasonable attitude in respect of freight rates is seen to be all the more praiseworthy when it is considered against the post-war shipping situation. As previously noted[2] the excess of ship-building over losses during the period 1939 to 1946 had meant a net gain of $11\frac{1}{2}$ million tons to the world's merchant fleet. However, many of these ships were American-built standardised vessels with only a limited commercial value. Thus, although some were sold to foreign owners, and some continued to be operated by American interests, a large proportion were transferred to the United States Reserve Fleet and became inactive. The consequent shortage of shipping could not be relieved by new construction for in most countries building capacity had been badly damaged, so annual tonnage launched did not reach the 1938 level until 1949. Severe port congestion, particularly in Australia and Africa, further reduced the efficiency of existing vessels and so strengthened the demand for their services. The resulting boom in shipping might have ended in 1950 but it was, in fact, extended firstly by the Korean War and then, after a brief recession, by the block-age of the Suez Canal in 1956.[3] These factors, aided by an element of inflation, ensured a continuous upward trend in freight charges but— as will be seen later—the rise in West African rates was considerably less than the world average.[4]

Reconstruction of the Fleet

On 1 January 1944, when the management agreement with Alfred Holts came to an end, the Elder Dempster fleet consisted of only sixteen ocean-going vessels. These included the twenty-five-year-old *Aba* still in use as a hospital ship, nine motor vessels with an average age of twelve years and six steamships whose average age was nearly twenty-three years.[5] Two other ships, *Tarkwa* and *Tamele* were building and

[1] The pre-war agreement between the Conference and M.F.A. had been 'frozen' for the duration.

[2] See above, Chapter 12, p. 295.

[3] R. H. Thornton, *British Shipping* (London: Cambridge University Press, 1959), pp. 93–95.

[4] See below, p. 326 and Chapter 14, pp. 372–3.

[5] E.D.L.P. 'Fleet values at 31 December 1943'.

the salvaged *Sangara* had been purchased from the salvors and was lying in Lagos.

It was obvious to the new board of directors that even without further losses an extensive rebuilding programme would be necessary as soon as the war was over. To meet the cost of such a reconstruction the Company possessed certain funds which it had been acquiring for this purpose. These included £3,408,509 in the Fleet Replacement Account; £1,089,010 held by the government as a Reserve for Fleet Replacement and a general Reserve Account of £575,000 which could be utilised if it were considered absolutely essential.[1] Altogether, therefor, Elder Dempster had access to over five million pounds with which to replace its war losses and make provision towards the eventual renewal of what remained of its ageing fleet. Whether or not this suggests that Elder Dempster and other British shipping companies received adequate compensation for their casualties is not clear. Sturmey felt that hire rates during the war were fair but that shipowners could not make fortunes, and he concluded that,

> 'For replacements, the compensation was reasonable but rising prices in relation to depreciation reserves meant that in 1946 practically the whole of the wartime gains were needed to restore fleets to their pre-war strengths while subsequent increases in replacement costs could only be met by drawing on general reserves accumulated before 1939, by increasing capital, or directly from post-war profits. . . .'[2]

During 1944, therefore, Elder Dempster gave a great deal of thought to future policy and, having settled the general principles, turned to a consideration of their practical application. Both *Tarkwa* and *Tamele* entered into service in the year, but no other vessels were actually acquired or ordered as it was necessary to decide precisely what was required. The replacement of the passenger-carrying ships was a particularly thorny problem because of the anticipated competition from air transport:

> 'On the one hand, busy business executives, would doubtless wish to travel expeditiously, both out and home by air, but others, that is those who earn their daily bread in West Africa, might have varying wishes according to whether they were embarking on a new tour or coming home for that much needed and

[1] Elder Dempster Lines Ltd, Balance Sheet 31 December 1943.

[2] S. C. Sturmey, *British Shipping and World Competition* (University of London: Athlone Press, 1962), p. 151. For a comprehensive discussion of this topic see pp. 144–150 of his work.

longed for leave. Whereas many would be content to use air for the outward voyage they would not look with equanimity upon a swift transition from tropical heat to the unkinder English climate, particularly in the midst of winter. Furthermore, as most Coasters know full well, the homeward voyage does so much to bring them round to a better state of health than that in which they usually leave the Coast for home after a strenuous tour in the humid energy-absorbing climate of West Africa.'[1]

In view of the uncertainty which obscured the future of passenger traffic a sensible middle course was adopted and in February 1945 *Accra* and *Apapa* were ordered so as to provide a three-weekly service from Liverpool to Lagos. These vessels were delivered in September 1947 and March 1948 respectively at a cost of just over £900,000 each. Then as the post-war pattern of the passenger trade became clearer, a third ship—*Aureol*—was ordered in March 1949. She was delivered in October 1951, but although only a little larger, (14,083 gross tons compared with 11,600 gross tons of the earlier passenger liners) she cost about twice as much. A fortnightly sailing was then introduced and this remained an established feature of the trade until 1967.

Six diesel-engined cargo vessels were also ordered in 1945. These were a slightly larger and modernised version of the pre-war 'S' class (4,800 gross tons instead of 4,100 gross tons). As a result *Sherbro*, *Shonga* and *Salaga* were delivered in 1947 and *Sekondi*, *Sulima* and *Swedru* were commissioned in 1948. Each of these vessels cost approximately £450,000.

The immediate post-war building programme was further supplemented by the purchase of second-hand tonnage and three steamships of 7,200 gross tons were acquired from the United States Maritime Commission. These had been constructed in 1943 as *Samos*, *Samota* and *Samyale* but Elder Dempster renamed them *Zini*, *Zungeru* and *Zungon*. In addition to these 'Liberty' ships, five Canadian 'Park' vessels of about the same size were bought to operate in the Canada/South Africa trade. These were named *Cabano*, *Cargill*, *Cambray*, *Chandler* and *Cottrell*.[2] A further addition to Elder Dempster's ocean-going fleet came in 1946 when the *Sangara*, torpedoed in 1941, was recommissioned and re-entered the Company's West African service.[3]

[1] F. Bateman Jones, pp. 5–6.
[2] Built in Canada in 1943/4 they were formerly named *Strathcona Park*, *Wascana Park*, *Bridgeland Park*, *Crystal Park* and *Goldstream Park*—all were steamships.
[3] See above, Chapter 12, p. 305.

It was also necessary for Elder Dempster to purchase a number of small vessels to assist in the operation of the West African creek and coastal trades. Two coasters, *Warri* and *Sapele* were therefore bought new from the British Government under the 'Tonnage Disposal Scheme' in 1946. Another similar vessel, also of 974 gross tons, the *Forcados*, was acquired from its first buyer in 1948.[1] A specialised post-war coastal activity was concerned with the Port Harcourt/Takoradi coal trade. The Ministry of War Transport pressed Elder Dempster to provide a collier service, so *Oxford* and *Knowlton*, two old 'lakers' of about 2,000 gross tons, were purchased specially for this work in 1946. The final stage of the immediate post-war coastal programme was completed in 1948 when *Calabar*, a 2,000 gross ton passenger vessel which operated between West and South Africa, was completely overhauled and re-conditioned.[2]

The net result of Elder Dempster's post-war construction and purchasing policies was as follows: *Aba* sold 1947 and *Fantee*[3] lost 1949 must be deducted from the 112,136 gross tons which the Company owned in 1945. In fact the latter vessel was replaced by the war-built *Prah*, formerly the *Avis Bay*, in 1949 so that by the end of that year the fleet consisted of 222,471 gross tons.[4] There were, furthermore, another 35,844 gross tons under construction for Elder Dempster at that time. Thus in a comparatively short space of time the fleet had been almost restored to its pre-war size of 228,777 gross tons, but it should be remembered that five ships—amounting to nearly 36,000 gross tons—were permanently engaged on the Canada/Cape service.

Changes in the Trade
In physical terms, the growth of the West African trade after the war can be simply stated. If the average import and export tonnages for the period form 1936 to 1939 are expressed as 100, the comparative figures for 1946 to 1950 show that imports had increased to 147 and exports

[1] These vessels had been completed in 1945 and had been registered as *Empire Pampas*, *Empire Pavilion* and *Empire Pattern*.
[2] *Calabar* was built for Elder Dempster in 1935 and was used as an on-carrier for the mail service. When the mail vessels were lost she was switched to a provisional West/South African service.
[3] *Fantee* was wrecked on the Seven Stones Rocks in the Scillies on 6 October 1949. There was no loss of life or injury.
[4] See Appendix, p. 419, Table 25.

James Howie, an Elder Dempster Agent, with his staff, *c.* 1895.

PLATE 19

James Howie during a cricket match, *c.* 1895.

James Howie (right front) and friends, *c.* 1895.

PLATE 20

An Elder Dempster Agent at work, *c.* 1895.

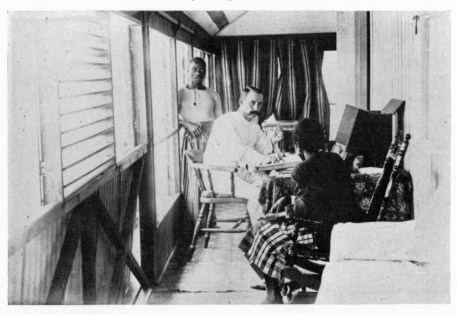

had risen to 140.[1] A more detailed examination of the post-war figures shows that between 1946 and 1950 imports rose by 74 per cent and exports increased by 27 per cent.[2]

There were many reasons why exports did not rise as rapidly as imports. One of these was the imbalance in the trade at that time which made southbound space easier to obtain than northbound. On the latter route it was necessary to use chartered vessels on occasions—sometimes at heavy loss to the shipping companies—in order to ensure that produce was not left behind, but even so the pressure on capacity was generally severe. The fact that the export of palm oil and palm kernels remained relatively static can be partly explained by the post-war shortages in the supply of all kinds of merchandise and foodstuffs from Britain and the resulting lack of incentive to the producers. This had a material effect on the composition of the export trade, for while these items remained at a stable level[3] other products increased at a much more satisfactory rate. Thus cocoa and cotton rose by 35 per cent, hides by 100 per cent and timber by 800 per cent.[4] In other words, the particular conditions of the immediate post-war years not only altered the supply and demand for specific products but also changed their position in the trade as a whole.

The changing composition of the West African trade and the extent to which its imports and exports had developed between 1939 and 1949 have now been indicated, but they require further clarification before their true significance can be finally assessed. For example, conditions of trade and the relationships between shipowners and merchants had been subjected to varying degrees of control during the war and these controls, suitably modified to serve post-war conditions, were retained in a variety of forms. These, in turn, led to changes in the links between the shipping lines and the merchants, and eventually to alterations in the structure of the West African Lines Conference itself. In addition, these main developments were influenced by a variety of subsidiary pressures such as the demand for cargo space and the impact of increasing competition from external shipping lines. Thus, although the

[1] See Appendix, p. 399, Table 5.   [2] See Appendix, p. 400, Table 6.

[3] In many areas there was little scope for further expansion of palm oil, palm kernel or ground nut production P. T. Bauer, *West African Trade* (London: Cambridge University Press, 1954), p. 196.

[4] The expansion of timber exports was helped by the fact that it could be carried as deck cargo. See also Appendix, p. 400, Table 7.

British companies had regained their pre-war tonnage, they found it difficult to meet all demands for capacity—hence the need to charter—and were faced with a completely new set of conditions in which to carry on their services. To this extent it can be affirmed that the war and its aftermath had resulted in an irrevocable break in the traditional and historical ties which bound Britain with West Africa.

The first and most important element in change arose from the continuation of the functions of the war-time West African Produce Control Board. This authority[1] exercised a virtual monopoly over the export of West Africa's principal products in an attempt to ensure regularity of supply to the United Kingdom and other markets. This had the double effect of maintaining supplies of vital primary products and of underwriting the economic position of the producer through the guaranteed purchase of his crop. Minimum prices were fixed for each commodity and the former merchants were remunerated by '. . . commissions calculated to cover expenses and an agreed margin of profit'.[2] In practice, the statutory monopoly exercised by the West African Produce Control Board led to the establishment of a direct relationship with the West African Lines Co-ordination Committee. Thus as far as the shipping companies were concerned their contact for the supply of West African produce was now a single agency instead of, as previously a large number of separate merchant houses.

When the war ended, the functions of the West African Produce Control Board were gradually vested in a series of separate marketing boards which were created to deal with individual products on a regional basis.[3] An example of the functions of these new authorities concerns the Gold Coast Cocoa Marketing Board:

[1] It was thought that the outbreak of war would result in a socially and politically disastrous fall in cocoa prices so Britain arranged to buy the whole crop at prices to be fixed each year. This was first organised by the Cocoa Control of the Ministry of Food but in 1940 the Cocoa Control Board was set up under the authority of the Colonial Office. In 1942 the title of this body was altered to the West African Produce Control Board and it then became responsible for the purchase and export of all vegetable oils and oil seeds from the British territories as well as continuing its control over cocoa.

[2] P. T. Bauer, op. cit., p. 200.

[3] Nigeria Cocoa Marketing Board, established in 1947; Gold Coast Cocoa Marketing Board, established in 1947; Nigeria Groundnut Marketing Board, established in 1949; Nigeria Oil Palm Produce Marketing Board, established in 1949; Nigeria Cotton Marketing Board, established in 1949; Gold Coast Agricultural Products Marketing Board, established in 1949; Sierra Leone Agricultural Marketing Board, established in 1949; Gambia Oil Seeds Marketing Board, established in 1949.

'. . . It shall be the duty of the Board to secure the most favourable arrangements for the purchase, grading, export and selling of Gold Coast cocoa, and to assist in the development by all possible means of the cocoa industry of the Gold Coast for the benefit and prosperity of the producers.'[1]

This somewhat high-sounding phraseology covered a series of operations which, in turn, altered some of the traditional functions of the export merchant. The most important of these changes concerned the relationship between the merchant and the shipowner in the determination of freight rates. In the import trade there was little alteration in the existing practice and merchants continued to ship their own goods in the usual way. Their business remained largely a retail one—hence their need to maintain a multitude of selling-posts scattered over the entire area. In pre-war days most import merchants were also export merchants but under the new system they no longer bought much produce on their own account.[2] Instead, they chiefly acted as buying agents for the various boards. Thus the old pattern of trade under which the merchant bought produce and sold trade goods and largely financed the transmission of these cargoes was now replaced by a centralised system under government authority. As a result, the responsibility for the shipment of West African exports, apart from a few small items, rested with the marketing boards and these bodies negotiated directly with the conference and fixed freight rates for the whole of the year's production.[3] It was this particular change in the function of the export merchant which provided, as we shall see later, an important factor in inducing the United Africa Company and John Holts to join the West African Lines Conference.

In any examination of the terms governing the carriage of produce and merchandise in the immediate post-war period it is necessary to distinguish between the rate structure of the southbound and northbound services, (i.e. from Europe to West Africa and from West Africa to Europe). This was because of the traditional imbalance in the trade, the northbound cargoes of produce being larger than the southbound

[1] *Gold Coast Ordinance*, No. 16 of 1947, quoted by P. T. Bauer, op. cit., p. 276.

[2] 'In all four colonies the marketing boards control practically 100 per cent of agricultural exports produced by Africans, including quite minor and even insignificant production'. Ibid., p. 276.

[3] The year's production really refers to the season's crop but it should be remembered that the season varied for different products.

shipments of merchandise. In the immediate post-war period, however, this difference was less marked than in the thirties, owing to the large quantities of cement, building materials, plant and capital goods required for constructional purposes in West Africa.

On the southbound route freight rates were subject to three distinct influences. The first of these concerned the Merchants Freight Association which, by virtue of the fact that its members were responsible for the bulk of merchandise shipped to West Africa, was in a relatively strong position to negotiate terms with the conference. In practice, the shipping companies developed an arrangement with the Merchants Freight Association under which its members received the normal 10 per cent deferred rebate off the tariff rates which was available to any other 'loyal' shippers. Its members did not receive any preferential rates, but they were guaranteed that no alterations in freight rates would be made without prior consultation—a matter of prime consideration to them as import merchants. In addition, regular official meetings were held between the M.F.A. and the conference lines, and a close liaison developed between Mr Joyce (as conference chairman) and the chairman of the M.F.A.

A second influence on freight rates was exercised by the Crown Agents for the Colonies as they were responsible for supplying the needs of the four West African Colonial governments. These cargoes were not normally 'trade' goods, so could be given special rates outside the tariff without upsetting the merchants, although sometimes difficulties of classification did arise. The third determinant of southbound freight rates was induced by the growth in the number of civil engineering projects being undertaken in West Africa. These called for large quantities of heavy equipment and building materials and the rates for such items (also outside the normal tariff) were usually agreed between the conference and the particular contractor concerned.

On the northbound route there was a considerable difference in emphasis. The Merchants Freight Association was responsible for only a small proportion of the cargoes exported from West Africa, such commodities as they sent being mainly composed of hides, skins, piassava[1] and timber, all items which did not come under the scope of the marketing boards. Apart from timber shipments, which were important, the other items were relatively insignificant. Similarly, the

[1] 'Piassava' is a vegetable fibre used in the manufacture of brushes and brooms.

Crown Agents for the Colonies had almost no interest at all in north-bound cargoes, the bulk of which—including practically all exports of agricultural produce—came under the direction of the West African Produce Control Board and later under that of the Marketing Boards created to deal with individual products on a national basis. Rates for these items were fixed on a seasonal basis and were determined by direct negotiation between a conference sub-committee and Sir Eric Tansley[1] on behalf of the Marketing Boards.

Sir Eric Tansley was convinced of the value of arranging bulk shipments with the conference. He estimated that the West African Produce Control Board paid less than 75 per cent of freight rates charged on other routes for similar cargoes after allowing for mileage. This, he suggested, was because the conference lines received practically all of the Board's produce and could plan in advance what ship-tonnage to put on the berth to cover northbound requirements. They were therefore in a position to quote very low figures. Freight rates were normally agreed annually, although meetings took place more regularly than this and on occasion the Board was agreeable to the making of some allowance in the rates towards the high cost of chartering additional vessels when this was essential. Sir Eric was satisfied that freight rates rose only slowly in the period between 1945 and 1950 even though this was at a time of rapidly rising produce prices, and increases in shipping costs could have easily been absorbed or passed on to the consumer.[2]

The only important exceptions to these arrangements for the north-bound route were timber and minerals. Timber had been controlled during and immediately after the war by the Ministry of Supply. On decontrol it was imported into Britain by timber-merchants who in most cases were not themselves West African traders. Acting through their trade organisation, these importers made special arrangements with the conference lines for the carriage of their timber, and these terms required the provision of a three-month notice of changes in freight rates. In the case of tin, a relatively small item, freight rates were

[1] Sir Eric Tansley had been chairman of the London Cocoa Terminal Market Association in 1932 and of the Cocoa Association of London in 1936-7. From 1940 to 1947 he was Marketing Director of the West African Produce Control Board, and from then until 1961 he was Managing Director of the Ghana Cocoa Marketing Co. and Adviser to the Nigerian Produce Marketing Co. (See *Who's Who*, 1970, p. 3044.)

[2] Author's interview with Sir Eric C. Tansley, 7 June 1967.

agreed by the conference with the Chamber of Mines after discussion with the mining companies concerned.[1] Other minerals, including bauxite, iron and manganese were largely handled by tramp ships and their freight rates were not affected by conference agreements, although an annual agreement was usually made for the carriage of manganese to the U.S.A.

Two further points need to be mentioned. At the beginning of the war, all freight-rate agreements were suspended by mutual consent, with the proviso that they would be reactivated on the termination of hostilities. Freight rates in fact were increased substantially during the war but this did not benefit the shipping companies significantly as their fleets were under government requisition and they only received the agreed hire charge. With the ending of requisitioning, however, the shipping companies once again retained all the receipts obtained from the carriage of goods and passengers, and on the southbound route the war-time level of charges then proved to be sufficiently remunerative for them to be maintained without increase until January 1951.[2] On the northbound route, where the pressure on shipping space was more acute, some adjustments were made to freight rates during this period but the evidence of Sir Eric Tansley would suggest that the increase tended to be small and well justified.[3]

The second consideration which needs to be mentioned is of more importance to the structure of the West African trade after 1950 than in the immediate post-war period. Nevertheless, it is relevant to note that changes were taking place in the trans-shipment trade as early as 1945, although they were almost unnoticed at the time. Hitherto, British West Africa's shipping connections with the outside world had been largely confined to Britain, Germany, North America and Japan. Consequently, large trans-shipment trades had grown up at Liverpool and Hamburg, and these had been carefully maintained by the conference lines, who quoted very low freight rates for through carriage. In 1945, however, the Scandinavian West Africa Line began a direct service to West African ports and this reduced the trans-shipment trade

[1] Author's interview with Mr J. Griffiths, Secretary of the Chamber of Mines, Jos, Nigeria on 16 September 1969.

[2] S. F. Klinghofer, 'A report on a preliminary survey of factors contributing to level of freight rates in the seaborne trade of Africa'. United Nations Economic Commission for Africa. 1965, Table 25.

[3] For details of subsequent changes see Appendix p. 479, Table 81.

in stockfish.[1] This was a relatively small item of cargo, but the implications of this change were to have widespread repercussions on the trade of West Africa as a whole in later years. It marked an important step towards active competition from shipping lines which were outside the previous pattern of services.

The Extension of the Conference

The reference, above, to the inauguration of a direct service by the Scandinavian West Africa Line is a significant indication of the changes which had taken place since 1930. In the thirties the United Africa Company had frequently chartered Norwegian and Swedish ships. These were normally engaged in the South African trade, but during the depression were quite content to sail to West African ports if cargo was available. To this extent, therefore, a link had been established before the war between Scandinavia and West Africa. In the post-war period the acute shortage of shipping space provided conditions suitable for the establishment of a direct service, and in the circumstances this was effected without active or effective opposition from the West African Lines Conference. Thus the Scandinavian West Africa Line,[2] formed in 1945, had 34,000 gross tons in service four years later and this, together with the 35,000 gross tons introduced by the Hoegh Line[3] in 1949, helped to fill the gap created by the exclusion of the Woermann group and the growth of trade.

The Holland West Africa Line, with the agreement of the conference, also took advantage of the boom and increased its fleet from the 18,000 gross tons employed before the war to 50,000 gross tons by 1949. By the same date Elder Dempster had recovered from the effects of its wartime losses and its fleet had been restored to approximately its 1939 tonnage. Similarly, both the United Africa Company[4] and John

[1] Until then it was customary for stockfish to be shipped from Norway to Newcastle by the Bergen Line. It was then sent to Liverpool by rail and taken to West Africa by Elder Dempster who quoted low through rates for this item.

[2] The Scandinavian West Africa Line was established by the Transatlantic Rederi A.B. of Gothenburg, Sweden; the Bergenske Dampskibsselskab of Bergen and Messrs Fearnley and Eger of Oslo, Norway. Wilh. Wilhelmsen of Oslo also intended to join but were dissuaded by Elders and the U.A.C.

[3] This was the Leif Hoegh Company of Oslo.

[4] The United Africa Company lost 9 of the 16 ships it owned in 1939 and, in addition, 2 were captured at Dakar by the Vichy French. These were treated as a total loss at the

Holt[1] had rebuilt their fleets to a size that was almost identical with those owned at the outbreak of hostilities, 82,000 and 19,000 gross tons respectively. These changes and similarities, as compared with 1939, were then reflected both by the conference share of the trade and by the proportions carried by each individual company.[2]

In 1939 the fleets operated by the conference lines amounted to 317,000 gross tons. This represented some 75 per cent of the total tonnage on the route; Elder Dempster owning 72 per cent, Woermann 22 per cent, and Holland West Africa Line 6 per cent of the conference share. By 1949 the conference fleets had declined to 276,000 gross tons and this represented a fall to only 62 per cent of the total. Elder Dempster's share of this was 82 per cent, while the Holland West Africa Line possessed the remaining 18 per cent of the conference proportion.[3] It should be noted, however, that by 1949 the total owned and employed on West African routes had risen by 27,000 gross tons (compared with 1939) and that while the tonnage controlled by the British Lines had fallen slightly, the two new entrants—the Scandinavian West Africa Line and the Hoegh Line—now operated 16 per cent of the company-owned fleets.[4]

If the immediate pre-war years are compared with the immediate post-war period it will be seen that an increase of nearly 50 per cent in the volume of trade was matched by a rise of less than 7 per cent in the gross tonnage of the shipping lines carrying this trade. That a larger volume of cargo was lifted by practically the same tonnage may be

time but were subsequently bought back from the M.O.T. under the Government disposal scheme.

[1] John Holt and Company (Liverpool) Limited, lost three of their five pre-war ships and one war-time replacement. (See P. N. Davies, *A Short History of the ships of John Holt & Co. (Liverpool) Limited, and the Guinea Gulf Line Limited*, p. 10. Published privately by John Holt, Liverpool, 1965).

[2] It should be made clear, however, that the U.A.C. and John Holt shares were based on the previous ratio of carrying. The shares were by cargo tons—not ships—and each firm could use owned or chartered vessels at its discretion and convenience.

[3] Based on C. Leubuscher, *The West African Shipping Trade 1909–1959* (Leyden: A. W. Sythoff, 1963), p. 99, Table 1, but note that the tonnages (hence the percentages) differ somewhat as the dates are not identical.

[4] Note that this does not mean that they enjoyed 16 per cent of the total trade. Differences in ships, speed of turnround and voyage patterns, plus the extensive chartering of the Conference Lines, ensured that the latter kept a much bigger share than the fleet tonnages would indicate.

explained in a number of ways. The shortage of shipping meant that
existing vessels enjoyed higher load factors than those customary before
the war, and the better-designed vessels of the post-war period had a
greater deadweight capacity for a given gross tonnage than those constructed in the nineteen-twenties and thirties.

It would, however, be wrong to infer that there was any substantial
increase in efficiency in the post-war operation of the West African
carrying trade. While it is true that the shipping companies were successful in handling a large rise in the volume of trade, this was accomplished against a background of severe port congestion on the Coast.[1] As
a result, lengthy delays precluded any improvement in turnround and
lessened the number of voyages which could be achieved each year.[2]
Most of the additional cargo was, in fact, carried by an unspecified
amount of tonnage which was chartered for the purpose by the conference lines. This was part of a deliberate policy by all the British firms,
though the U.A.C. were usually the largest charterers. It represented
an attempt to prevent other lines from gaining a foothold in West
Africa and, until 1950, it frequently involved a financial loss to the Companies. After that date, however, a chartering surcharge was agreed
with the major shippers so as to spread the loss on chartered voyages
over the whole trade.[3]

The success, or otherwise, of this policy may be judged by the fact
that even under such favourable conditions as existed after the war, only
the two Scandinavian lines were able to secure a permanent share in
the West African shipping trade. Any resentment which the conference
lines felt towards these 'interlopers' was diminished by the continuing
growth of cargoes in both directions. Nevertheless, the rapid increase
in new tonnage in 1949 carried with it a potential threat which could
not be ignored—either by the conference or the British 'merchant'
lines. As far as the conference was concerned, the existing system pro-

[1] G.G.L.Mss. 'Length of Outward Voyages to West Africa'. 30 August 1949. Con/2A
(History). See also 'The extent and causes of port delays', *Statistical and Economic Review*,
No. 19 (March 1957), pp. 14–21.
[2] Elder Dempster Lines Holdings Limited, Chairman's Statement at the 14th A.G.M.
April 1950 '. . . the time for a round voyage of a cargo liner to the regular ports now
averages 20 per cent longer than in 1939 . . .'
[3] Elder Dempster Lines Holdings Limited, Chairman's Statements at 15th and 16th
A.G.M.'s, April 1951 and April 1952. Also interview with J. H. Joyce Esq., 3 March
1967.

vided a high degree of flexibility and a reasonable level of profitability. This was particularly true on the northbound route, where the normal practice was for the Marketing Boards to arrange with the conference for the carriage of their entire crops of produce, and for the conference to use their own ships and those of John Holt and the United Africa Company to carry these cargoes. It was obviously of advantage for the conference to be able to call upon the tonnage owned by the West African merchants. On the reverse side of the coin it was equally advantageous to Holt's and the United Africa Company to be able to employ their ships in this way, bearing in mind that there was little northbound cargo from British West African territories other than that controlled by the Marketing Boards. In short, Although there was no formal agreement, both John Holt and the United Africa Company had virtually become members of the conference in all but name.[1]

The intrusion of the Scandinavian lines into the West African trade and the prospect of further rapid expansion of their tonnage, together with the anticipated re-entry of the Woermann Line, (which, in fact, took place in 1952), forced Elder Dempster to reconsider the structure of conference relationships. The co-operation between the British lines which had been built up during and immediately after the war had fostered mutual trust and identity of interest between the participating companies. Faced with the threat of more intense foreign competition, the obvious course was to seek a strengthening of the bonds which held the conference lines and the shipping departments of the two West African merchants together.

Considerable discussion with the Merchants Freight Association then followed and ultimately a formula was agreed which ensured that the United Africa Company and John Holt would not profit from their shipping activities to any greater extent than they would have done in any case by merely continuing to carry their own historic share of the trade.[2] After this arrangement was finalised, John Holt and the United

[1] There were a number of specific agreements. Up to the time of derequisitioning, the wartime measures designed to ensure the economic workings of the available ships were continued. During this period agreement was reached by the interested parties so that future developments were to be based on the pre-war ratios of cargoes.

[2] E.D.L.P. J. H. Joyce Mss. The arrangements were made with the goodwill and approval of the Merchants Freight Association who appreciated that all the ships were needed to provide a comprehensive service with equal terms and opportunities for all shippers.

Africa Company were admitted as full members of the West African Lines Conference and the Merchants Freight Association as from 1 January 1950.

It was considered desirable to make it clear that the shipping and merchanting functions of the United Africa Company and John Holt were completely separate. In order to achieve this, it was decided to transform the shipping departments of the two firms into independent shipping companies and thus the Palm Line Limited and the John Holt Line Limited were created in 1949 and 1950 respectively.

The new conference lines automatically gained the status of common carriers, but this only gave formal recognition of the position they had occupied since they were requisitioned in 1939.[1] By this action the conference gained added strength and importance as it then controlled 84 per cent of all tonnage employed on the U.K. and Continental routes to the Coast.[2]

Thus over a period of forty years, the wheel had turned full circle. On the death of Sir Alfred Jones at the end of 1909, the West African Shipping Conference—a legacy of his life's work—had been responsible for almost all the tonnage serving British West Africa; in 1950, after forty years, which included two world wars, economic depression, financial disaster and internal dissension, the conference was ostensibly in the same pre-eminent position in which it had been left by Jones. Furthermore, Elder Dempster remained the largest operator in the trade and its leadership in 1950 was comparable, on the surface at least, with the paramount position it had held in 1910.

Company Structure and Development

At the end of the war the Ocean Steam Ship Company[3] remained the largest shareholder in Elder Dempster Lines (Holdings) Limited which, in turn, continued to own all the ordinary share capital of Elder Dempster Lines Limited.

Elder Dempster Lines Limited retained its ownership of the West African Lighterage and Transport Company, and of its dormant German

[1] P. N. Davies. *A Short History of the Ships of John Holt and Company (Liverpool) Limited*, op. cit.. p. 10. Also *Statistical and Economic Review*, March 1957. op. cit., p. 2.

[2] Based on C. Leubuscher, op. cit., p. 99, Table 1, but note that the tonnages (hence the Percentages) differ somewhat as the dates are not identical.

[3] The Ocean Steam Ship Company changed its name to Ocean Transport and Trading Limited on 15 January, 1973.

interests—Elder Dempster Lines G.m.b.H.[1] It also continued to own a share in Elders Colonial Airways and had been increasing its interests in both Canada and South Africa. Thus a new concern, Canadian and African Stevedores Limited, had been formed in 1943 to carry out the stevedoring work on the Canadian government-owned 'Park' ships which Elder Dempster's Montreal office was operating for the Dominion's account in the Canada/South Africa trade. In 1945 this was followed by the establishment of Elder Dempster Lines (Canada) Limited, primarily to purchase and operate five 'Park' ships on the Canada/Cape service.[2] These were offered to the Company on special terms and the Bank of England made the necessary dollars available quite readily, on the grounds that substantial dollar earnings could be anticipated.

In fact, Elder Dempster Lines (Canada) Limited had only a short active life. It provided a service from Montreal and St John to South and East African ports—mostly returning via West Africa. Early results were very encouraging but a shortage of foreign exchange in South Africa led to difficulties after 1948. These were intensified by the strike of Canadian seamen during the following year and by a continued reduction of the cargoes offered. Accordingly, in 1950, the ships were transferred to the United Kingdom registry and operated thereafter on a demise charter. The Montreal organisation was then closed down and the Company's operations and trading rights were placed in the care of local agents.[3]

The financial results of the Canadian venture were quite satisfactory —its accumulated profit since its inception amounted to C.$1,599,706 after payment of Canadian tax—so it was unfortunate that factors outside Elder Dempster's control prevented the enterprise from becoming a permanent one.[4] It was subsequently decided to liquidate Elder Dempster Lines (Canada) Limited and to perpetuate the name of the

[1] Elder Dempster and Company had first established a Branch Office in Hamburg in 1887. See Company Register I, Register No. 24,372, p. 162. (A copy of this is held as part of E.D.L.P.)

[2] Services on this route had formerly been operated for many years. See above, Chapter 5, pp. 128-9, and Chapter 11, p. 279.

[3] Elder Dempster continued to call at Halifax and other Canadian ports as part of its West Africa–North America service. A further link was inaugurated early in 1971 when a new route was developed (in conjunction with *Chargeurs Reunis*) through the St Lawrence Seaway to the Great Lakes. Details of this are given in *Sea*, Vol. VIII, No. IV (July 1972), pp. 6-8.

[4] Elder Dempster Lines (Holdings) Limited, Chairman's statement, 21 May 1951.

company in Canada by changing the name of Canadian and African Stevedores Limited to Elder Dempster Lines (Canada) 1962 Limited.[1]

A second new firm, Elders of South Africa (Proprietary) Ltd was also formed in 1943. It was intended that Major L. H. Cripps would take charge of this when he retired from the board of the parent company but, although the concern was moderately successful in its stevedoring activities and its investment in a wholesale grocer was prospering, it was determined to terminate the undertaking in its existing form. Accordingly the stevedoring side was transferred to Mitchell Cotts—Elder Dempster's agents—and the interest in Messrs Figg Brothers and Sacks was handed over to the West African Lighterage and Transport Company in 1945.

Elder Dempster's interest in the development of air transport in the thirties has already been noted[2] and during the war the technical improvements which took place gave rise to hopes that the Company might be able to operate a service between the United Kingdom and Lagos.[3] The feasibility of such a project was demonstrated by a proving flight made in 1945[4] when W. L. Robinson and F. Bateman Jones travelled directly to the Coast by air, but the British Government's decision to nationalise trunk-route flying precluded any further action from being taken at that time. There then seemed to be no possibility of joint action by the Company and the nationalised airlines, so in 1948 Elder Dempster purchased the British Overseas Airways Corporation's share of the jointly owned but inoperative Elders Colonial Airways, the price being based solely on net asset values.[5]

In 1948 the Company also bought the share capital of Elder Dempster (Cardiff) Limited. This firm had been owned by outside interests since 1935 and it was re-acquired in order to recover its name rather than its business. It then lay dormant until 1954 when its title was changed to Elder Dempster (Agencies) Limited and its functions were completely revised.[6]

In spite of the rapid growth of the Elder Dempster fleet after the war, the development of West African trade was so swift that regular recourse to chartered tonnage was frequently necessary. Many different

---

[1] Elder Dempster Lines Limited, Directors report, 9 April 1962.
[2] See above, Chapter 11, pp. 289–93.   [3] *Fairplay*, 12 March 1914, p. 320.
[4] F. Bateman Jones, op. cit., p. 7.   [5] E.D.L.P. J. H. Joyce Mss., p. 5.
[6] See below, Chapter 14, p. 340.

vessels were utilised for this purpose but amongst the most suitable were the 'K' class ships owned by the British and Burmese Steam Navigation Company Limited. The decline in Anglo-Burmese trade had encouraged the line to build the 'K' class specifically for charter, and for long periods they were employed by Elder Dempster almost continuously. A happy and profitable relationship thus developed between the two companies, so in 1951 Elder Dempster took the logical step of opening negotiations to buy the whole of the British and Burmese ordinary stock. These were quickly concluded on its behalf by Elder Dempster Lines (Holdings) Limited,[1] in spite of rumours of a proposed take-over by another shipping group.

At the time of its purchase the British and Burmese—better known as the 'Paddy Henderson Line'—owned two passenger ships and two fast cargo ships which were employed in its traditional trade. It also possessed six post-war 'K' class vessels—all of which were on charter to Elder Dempster when their sale was being arranged—and it had a further five vessels of this type on order.[2] The payment for the British and Burmese amounted to over six million pounds, and the ease with which this large sum was found is a complete vindication of Elder Dempster's post-war financial policies. The transaction was financed largely from Group resources—arranged by a capital distribution of £3,000,000 by Elder Dempster Lines Limited to its parent company together with a loan of £2,250,000. The Holdings Company financed the balance of the purchase price by issuing a further 687,149 £1 ordinary shares at a premium of 10s per share.[3]

Following Elder Dempster's acquisition of the British and Burmese, its management continued in the hands of Messrs P. Henderson and Company of Glasgow.[4] In practice, this meant that they looked after the Burma trade and the ships employed in it, but the operation of the 'K' class ships in the West African trade was made the responsibility of Elder Dempster Lines Limited.[5]

[1] Elder Dempster's parent company subsequently changed its name to Liner Holdings Company Limited, in order to distinguish its wider interests in the shipping world.

[2] This was particularly valuable as tonnage continued to be in short supply.

[3] Elder Dempster Lines (Holdings) Limited, Directors' report, 13 April 1953.

[4] D. Laird, *Paddy Henderson. The Story of P. Henderson and Company* (London: George Outram, 1961). This gives an outline of the company's history from 1834 to 1961. Chapter 16 (pp. 217–221) gives a brief account of the sale to Elder Dempster Lines (Holdings) Limited.

[5] Elder Dempster Lines (Holdings) Limited, Chairman's Statements, 19 May 1952.

Thus by the early fifties the short-run problems of post-war reconstruction had been largely resolved. It now remains for us to examine the long-term effects of the Second World War and to see how these, and other underlying influences, were to mould the future of the Company and its relationships with West Africa.

Chapter 14

Recent Developments

The Post-War Era

The disruption engendered by the Second World War was followed by
a period of reconstruction which may be said to have been completed
by about 1950. This is not to suggest that the 1939 situation had been
restored, for many permanent changes had taken place, but rather that
most of the short-term effects of the war had by then been either reme-
died or greatly modified.

It is the longer-term changes which must now be considered and
these were essentially of a much more fundamental nature than any
previously examined. The basic causation was the move towards
political and then economic independence by the West African colonies
of the European powers, but this prime factor was closely allied to the
greatly accelerated speed of technological progress. Neither of these
movements had been instigated by the war, but both had received a
tremendous boost during the period of hostilities, and together they
were to be responsible for the rapid evolution which occurred in the
fifties and sixties.

In the British West African possessions the administration had been
consciously preparing its subjects for independence, but this had been
envisaged as taking place in the far-distant future. Consequently the
demands for fuller representation were at first received with little sympathy, but such was the 'wind of change' that full autonomy was granted
to Ghana in 1956; to Nigeria in 1960; and to Sierra Leone and the
Gambia in 1961 and 1965 respectively. As other European powers were
simultaneously engaged in altering their relationships with their own
colonies, West Africa was quickly transformed to a region where most
states enjoyed freedom from much external direction.

The very force of these developments and of the economic changes which followed intensified many problems within West Africa and could have provided a potentially serious threat to the future of Elder Dempster's traditional trade. In fact, the new circumstances were accepted as a fresh challenge by the Company and, in spite of numerous setbacks, it was able to retain a substantial share of the West African shipping business throughout the sixties. This was a great tribute to Elder Dempster's adaptability and efficiency and thus, to a large extent, to its board of directors.[1]

At the beginning of the nineteen-fifties, Elder Dempster's directors were J. H. Joyce (chairman), A. C. Tod, C. T. J. Cripps, G. H. Avezathe and W. L. Robinson. The latter resigned in 1951 and was replaced by M. B. Glasier. Two additional directors, A. E. Muirhead and A. M. Bennett, were appointed in 1952 but Mr Avezathe retired during the following year. Mr Cripps also left the board a little later and his place was taken by P. G. H. Arundell. No further changes occurred until 1962 when F. L. Lane was appointed a director, becoming chairman in succession to Mr Joyce twelve months later. In addition to losing their chairman, Mr Arundell and Sir Alan Tod[2] also resigned in 1963— the latter's seat being occupied by Brigadier P. J. D. Toosey, the new chairman of the 'Holding' Company. G. J. Ellerton and Sir John N. Nicholson[3] became directors in 1967 and J. D. Robertson was appointed in 1969. Mr Bennett and Mr Muirhead, however, retired in 1968, so that at the end of the decade the board consisted of F. L. Lane[4] (chairman), M. B. Glasier, G. J. Ellerton, J. D. Robertson, P. J. D. Toosey and Sir John N. Nicholson.

Since then, Mr Lane, Mr Glasier,[5] Brigadier Toosey and Sir John N. Nicholson have all retired. Mr Lane was succeeded as chairman by G. J. Ellerton[6] at the end of May 1972—the other members of the board at that date being J. D. Robertson, P. F. Earlam (appointed in 1971) and P. H. D. Toosey (appointed in 1971).

[1] Details of the Directors of Elder Dempster Lines Ltd, are given in the Appendix, Table 59, p. 463.
[2] *Sea*, Vol. VII, No. V (January 1971), p. 25.
[3] Sir John N. Nicholson was a director, ex officio, as chairman of the Ocean Steam Ship Company.
[4] *Sea*, Vol. VIII, No. IV (July 1972), p. 24.
[5] *Sea*, Vol. VIII, No. II (July 1971), p. 24.
[6] *Sea*, Vol. VIII, No. IV (July 1972), p. 21.

It was to be anticipated that the newly independent states of West Africa would wish to secure a greater degree of control over their external communications than had previously been the case. Thus in 1958 the West African Airways Corporation—an enterprise owned jointly by Nigeria, Ghana, Sierra Leone and Gambia—was dissolved. Then at the invitation of the Nigerian Federal Government, Elder Dempster and the British Overseas Airways Corporation participated with the government in forming W.A.A.C. (Nigeria) Limited.[1] This was a new company which took over the Nigerian internal and long-distance air services and established them on a profitable basis. The local government then desired that it should be a 100 per cent Nigerian affair, so in 1961 it was reorganised and both Elder Dempster and the B.O.A.C. sold their interests to the Nigerian Government.[2]

A more momentous development, however, concerned the provision of their own shipping services by both Ghana and Nigeria. In 1957 the Nigerian government had discussed the setting up of a joint company with its neighbouring states, but Ghana wished to establish its own line, and Sierra Leone and the Gambia did not feel able to make a large investment at that time, so the project was abandoned.[3] The Ghanaian government then finalised its plans and the Black Star Line began a service to Europe in the summer of 1957. Elder Dempster had been quite prepared to assist in this venture but, in the event, it was Israel's Zim Line which took a 40 per cent share and undertook to put the new concern on its feet. The West African Lines Conference admitted the Black Star Line immediately, but at first it was limited to a maximum of five ships. This number was considerably increased after 1959, though this was partly because the Company joined the American West African Freight Conference and began a service to North America.[4] Eight new cargo vessels were then ordered,[5] but as the Zim Line was not prepared to provide the additional capital necessitated by this expansion, it sold its shares to the Ghana Government.[6] It was arranged, however, that

[1] Chairman's statement at A.G.M. of Liner Holdings Co. Ltd, 19 May 1959.
[2] Chairman's statement at A.G.M. of Liner Holdings Co. Ltd, 15 May 1961.
[3] *Debates of the House of Representatives*: Nigerian Minister of Transport, 10 September 1957.
[4] *West Africa* (1959), p. 698.
[5] *West Africa* (1960), p. 1207.
[6] It appears likely that the Ghana Government welcomed this development as it wished to be the sole owner of the line.

Zim would continue to supply managerial and technical help for a further period.

Faced with the Ghanaian example and influenced by growing pressure within parliament, the Nigerian government also decided to establish its own shipping lines. Negotiations began with a number of companies who offered their assistance but, in February 1959, it became known that Elder Dempster and the Palm Line were to take an active part. It was then agreed that the Nigerian National Shipping Line be set up with an authorised capital of £2,000,000—the Government's shareholding being 51 per cent while Elder Dempster and Palm acquired 33 per cent and 16 per cent respectively. The two British lines arranged to manage the new company and it was agreed that they would help to train Nigerians in all aspects of navigation, engineering and management.[1] They also gave their support to ensuring that it was able to join the conference without difficulty. The new line was limited to six vessels in 1959, eight in 1960 and ten in 1961, and it was stipulated that at least 50 per cent of these must be company-owned and not chartered tonnage. The joint association between Elder Dempster, Palm and the Nigerian government came to an end in 1961, when a satisfactory transfer of shares and a friendly hand-over of the management were both achieved.[2] This did not, of course, mean an end to the co-operation between the firms for, as in the case of the Black Star Line, all continued to be loyal members of the West African Lines Conference.

Elder Dempster also foresaw that the forthcoming independence of their trading area would lead to major changes in the structure and organisation of its shore-based activities. Accordingly, in 1954, several years before the first West African nation secured its political freedom, the Company made a major policy decision which had the effect of confining Elder Dempster Lines operations to purely ocean carriage.[3] This entailed divesting the Company of all its shore-based activities and assets in West Africa and was effected by the formation of a new company styled West African Properties Limited, which acquired the ownership of all properties, offices, residences, wharves, warehouses and work-

[1] *Debates of the House of Representatives*: Nigerian Minister of Transport, 19 February 1959.
[2] Chairman's Statement, Liner Holdings Company Limited, A.G.M., 14 May 1962.
[3] It also meant that the Lines were not directly committed to the employment of large numbers of employees in West Africa.

shops situated in what were then the four British colonies of Gambia, Gold Coast, Nigeria and Sierra Leone.

Elder Dempster (Cardiff) Limited, then dormant, changed its name to Elder Dempster (Agencies) Limited, and began to function as Elder Dempster Lines' agent at all ports where representation had previously been by branch offices. Elders Colonial Airways Limited changed its name to Elders Engineering and Airways Company Limited, and assumed the operation of the marine repair establishment which Elder Dempster Lines had formerly operated under the title Wilmot Point Repairs Department. The old-established West African Lighterage and Transport Company Limited transferred its fixed assets to the new property company but relinquished its ship agency responsibilities in certain ports, mainly in the then Gold Coast, to Elder Dempster (Agencies) Limited.

At a time of rapid political change, the advantages of separating the 'Lines' Company from any direct establishment on the coast are obvious and these have undoubtedly played an important role in maintaining the customary good-will between the Company and the West African states. This has been of the utmost significance during a period when Elder Dempster's political relationship with the administration was inevitably changing. Formerly the Company's Nigerian manager was traditionally a member of the Nigerian Legislative Council, while a number of other employees held similar situations in other parts of the coast. This position was not basically altered by the establishment of the House of Representatives in 1952, but after independence the practice of appointing expatriate nominees came rapidly to an end.

The formation of a number of firms specifically associated with West Africa also facilitated the process of Africanisation. From the early days of Alfred Jones, who had a great respect for African abilities, it had been Company policy to train and employ a high proportion of the local inhabitants whenever possible. At first these were used solely as labourers, but the more able gradually undertook more responsible work as clerks, checkers, warehousemen and semi-skilled engineers. By 1939, this process had gone quite a long way, but most of the senior posts were still filled by Europeans. The wartime shortage of experienced staff gave many Africans an opportunity to demonstrate their true abilities and by the end of hostilities a few were occupying quite demanding positions. This tendency continued during the early post-war years and was accelerated in the fifties by the advent of better qualified and educated candidates for employment. By the time that independence was achieved a number of Africans had reached managerial status and recent progress in this direction has been so complete that, by 1973, Elder Dempster only employed twenty expatriates in the whole of West Africa, compared with 50 in 1965, 110 in 1960, and some 150 in the mid-fifties.[1]

Another change which had its roots in the first half of the twentieth century, but which was to assume a greater momentum after the Second World War, was concerned with the establishment and extension of new ports. It will be appreciated that the lack of natural deep-water harbours, apart from those at Bathurst and Freetown, had necessitated the use of 'surf ports' at many points on the Coast. At such places the steamship had to anchor off shore while her cargo was unloaded into open boats which were paddled to the beach, bulky lifts such as motor cars being conveyed on two boats lashed together. In 1910 most of the 'boating' companies which undertook this work were either owned or controlled by the conference lines, but in the twenties and thirties the United Africa Company developed its own facilities for the handling of cargo. These then provided an alternative to the services provided by the regular shipping companies, but co-operation between Elder Dempster and the U.A.C. during the war and the latter's association in the West African Lines Conference after 1950 meant that their subsidiary activities tended to be complementary rather than competitive. It should be made quite clear, however, that at no stage in the post-war era was the ownership of landing facilities used as a weapon to fight new entrants to the trade:

'. . . It is agreed that we cannot withhold Lighterage services from unfriendly competitors, as this is regarded as a form of public service. We shall, however, refuse to act as Agents for unfriendly competitors and it is very unlikely that we could undertake to give unfriendly competitors repair facilities for their main line or local craft . . .'[2]

Elder Dempster, in fact, went so far as to ensure that no priority was even given to their own vessels,[3] but the changing circumstances after

[1] E.D.L.P., Information supplied by H. Watson, Coast Administration Department. It should be appreciated that the changing functions of the Company within West Africa meant that a number of jobs had ended or been severely reduced in importance.

[2] E.D.L.P., Letter from J. H. Joyce to Zone Managers on the Coast, 11 September 1946.

[3] E.D.L.P., J. H. Joyce, Mss.

the war quickly lessened the value of these arrangements. As early as 1928 a new port had been completed at Takoradi on the Gold Coast and the success of this venture eventually prompted a similar development at Tema, which was intended to replace the surf port at Accra. Construction at Tema began in 1951 and it was opened for restricted commercial operations ten years later.[1] The effect of this, plus the extensions to Takoradi which were completed in 1955, was the concentration of all Ghanaian traffic at their two deepwater ports—a tremendous achievement when it is realised that in 1961 Accra had handled 1,187,000 tons of cargo.[2]

In Nigeria, port development has followed a similar pattern. The Lagos-Apapa harbour,[3] first opened to sea-going vessels in 1913, was improved during the twenties, but substantial extensions were not started until 1952. Since then the port has been further enlarged and now, 1972, has a total of seventeen berths including one (without cranes) for container traffic. At Port Harcourt, established during the First World War as an outlet for Udi coal and improved during the twenties, large-scale extentions were completed in 1960. As a result of these developments and of more recent modernisation programmes, Lagos and Port Harcourt now have annual capacities of four million tons and one and a half million tons respectively and are responsible for a large proportion of the country's trade. The Nigerian Ports Authority, established in 1954, controls these activities and also looks after a number of small ports including Sapele, Calabar and Koko.[4] Recently the N.P.A. acquired Warri (formerly owned by John Holt and Company) and Burutu (previously owned by the United Africa Company) but Bonny remains outside its sphere, being organised for the export of crude petroleum by Shell and B.P. Limited. Access to the Delta Ports is now normally via Escravos bar, and the N.P.A. is responsible for the dredging and similar work which is necessary to ensure an adequate depth of water.

[1] David Hilling, 'Tema: the Geography of a New Port', *Geography*, Vol. LI, part 2 (April 1966), pp. 111–125.

[2] David Hilling, 'The Evolution of the Major Ports of West Africa', *The Geographic Journal*, Vol. CXXXV, Part 3, (September 1969).

[3] Lagos and Apapa were originally regarded as separate ports, but are now looked on as parts of the same complex.

[4] The N.P.A. is responsible for most aspects but private enterprise undertakes the cargo handling.

Sierra Leone is fortunate in possessing a fine natural harbour at Free-town, but until 1954 this only had facilities for lighters. In that year the Queen Elizabeth II Quay was opened and a substantial extension to this was completed during 1970. Practically all of the country's general cargo passes through Freetown, but Pepel exports a large quantity of iron ore and Sherbro is used for the shipment of piassava and palm kernels. Bathurst, Gambia's sole port, also possesses deep-water and other natural advantages but, like Freetown, was a lighter port until the post-war period. Government Wharf was completed in 1952 and has since provided fairly satisfactory, if limited, facilities for cargo vessels while the Admiralty Wharf now caters mainly for petroleum products.[1]

The main developments in other West African states since the Second World War include an increase in general cargo capacity as well as the provision of special equipment—ports in some cases—to deal with the bulk handling of certain items. At Port Étienne, in Mauritania, recent construction has provided facilities for the bulk loading of iron ore and the landing of petroleum, while Dakar, in Senegal, has continued to grow in a most sophisticated manner, largely because of its function as an important bunkering depot. Conakry, in Guinea, has expanded rapidly since before the war and now has berths for nine ocean-going vessels which are used to handle mineral ores as well as general cargoes. In Liberia new ports were built at Monrovia in 1948 and at Buchanan in 1963. Both cater for the export of iron ore, but Monrovia also deals with most of Liberia's other imports and exports. On the Ivory Coast, Abid-jan began to develop in 1950, when it was first connected to the sea by the Vridi Canal. It is now one of the largest and most modern ports in West Africa and specialises particularly in the export of timber, besides catering for all types of import. Abidjan has now completely eliminated Port Bouet and Grand Bassam which formerly handled cargoes for this region and the construction of a new harbour at San Pedro will soon replace the poor arrangements at Sassandra.[2]

A new port to deal with general cargo was opened at Lomé in 1968, and Togo has also recently constructed a special facility to load phos-

---

[1] The World Bank has now (1972) agreed to finance proposals for the rebuilding of the Admiralty Wharf. This will then cater for most imports and this will leave the Government Wharf to handle the export of ground-nut oil and cake.

[2] *Sea*, Vol. VII, No. 5 (January 1971), p. 24.

phates at Kpéme. Dahomey has followed a policy similar to that of Togo and a deep-water harbour was completed at Cotonou in 1965, thus obviating the need for lighterage. In the Cameroon, Douala now has twelve berths for ocean-going ships and special installations for handling bananas, petroleum and bauxite. Tiko has a single berth which is used almost exclusively for the loading of bananas, but Bota-Victoria remains virtually unchanged since 1914, with facilities only for lighters. Ports to the south of Cameroon may or may not be regarded as part of the West African shipping range but, irrespective of this, it is clear that Libreville, Port Gentil, Pointe Noire, Boma, Matadi, Luanda and Lobito are generally handling substantially enlarged quantities of imports and exports and, in most cases, their facilities have been markedly improved since 1945.[1]

The post-war development of ports has thus been substantial,[2] but it has been overshadowed by the dramatic increase in West African trade from seven to over seventy-five million tons since 1946. This figure tends to overstate the case, as a large proportion of the addition consists of bulk cargoes, including oil, which are easily handled by special installations and ships. Nevertheless, the expansion of general cargo has outstripped capacity in many ports—only a few are under-utilised—and delays to vessels have, at times, proved to be very extensive and expensive.[3]

A natural corollary to the growth of commerce and the expansion of West African ports has been the development of facilities in the United Kingdom. Elder Dempster's main terminal was traditionally at Liverpool, but after the war the London trade experienced a tremendous increase.[4] As a result it was decided—in association with Palm Line and the Guinea Gulf Line—to form a stevedoring firm to operate at Tilbury Dock, and West African Terminals Limited was incorporated

[1] Author's visit to West and South Coast ports in 1969.

[2] For a more detailed examination of this topic, see D. Hilling, op. cit., H. P. White, 'The Ports of West Africa', *Tijdschrift voor Economische en Sociale Geographie*, Vol. L (1959), pp. 1–8; R. G. Albion, *Seaports South of the Sahara* (New York: Appleton-Century, 1959); and B. S. Hoyle & D. Hilling, (Eds.), *Seaports and Development in Tropical Africa* (London: MacMillan, 1970).

[3] Guinea Gulf Line Mss. Length of Outward Voyages to West Africa (30 August 1949, Con/2A History). See also 'The Extent and Causes of Port Delays', *Statistical and Economic Review*, No. XIX (March 1957), pp. 14–21. For more recent information (1962–1965) see 'The West African Shipping Range by Dag Tressel' (New York: United Nations 67-11-D. 24, 1967).

[4] 'London and the West African Trade', *Sea*, Vol. III, No. II (Spring 1958), pp. 1–5.

in November 1955. It operated from temporary accommodation for two years while a purpose-built office was constructed, but it then possessed an ideal building for its work.[1] The Company was wound up in 1966, however, for its functions were taken over by Metropolitan Terminals Limited—a concern in which Elder Dempster, Palm Line, the Furness Withy Group and the British Commonwealth Group each took a 25 per cent interest.[2]

The success of the London arrangements were such that it was decided to create a similar organisation in Liverpool. Accordingly in July 1961 the Liverpool stevedoring and master porterage work of Elder Dempster, Palm and Guinea Gulf was consolidated in Liverpool-West African Terminals Limited: this then performed all the stevedoring, wharfingering and master porterage for the three lines and for the other lines in the West African trade for which they were loading-brokers.[3] In July 1966 the Company was joined by the stevedoring department of the Booker Group and it was then renamed Liverpool Maritime Terminals Limited.[4]

The attempts to improve efficiency in West Africa and European ports have been assisted by recent developments in containerisation and palletisation. Elder Dempster and Palm Line, in fact, undertook a lengthy research programme before deciding that there appeared to be a case for experimenting with containers in the West African trade.[5] They then consulted the Nigerian National Shipping Line and the three lines established the African Container Express Limited. Operations began in 1965—the containers used being made of fibreglass to help insulation and measuring 8 by 8 by 10 feet—and the service has gradually been increased. At first, progress was relatively slow, for while containers are very suitable for certain items on the southbound route

[1] 'New Office Building for West African Terminals', Sea, Vol. III, No. IV (Spring 1959), p. 8.

[2] Although each company had a 25 per cent nominal shareholding, the West African trade is by far the largest contributor to throughput.

[3] 'Liverpool West African Terminals Limited', Sea, Vol. IV, No. IV (Winter 1961-2), p. 11.

[4] 'Appointments', Sea, Vol. VII, No. 1 (Summer 1968), p. 22. For a variety of reasons it was decided to end Ocean's stevedoring activities at London and Liverpool and these businesses were sold during 1973 to the Port of London Authority and the Mersey Docks and Harbour Company.

[5] 'This Containerisation Business', Palm Bulletin, Vol. V, No. II (Summer 1965), pp. 4-5.

there were a number of complications on the return journey. Tropical produce is not the ideal cargo for this type of carriage and it is obviously undesirable to carry empty containers. Nevertheless, the demand has continued to expand steadily and the provision of specialised vessels loaded exclusively with containers would appear to be the logical outcome in due course.

Parallel and complementary to this development has been the introduction of palletisation. Originally most of the pallets were of the returnable type and the shipping companies, together with the Nigerian Ports Authority and the Ghana Cargo Handling Company, formed a 'pallet pool'. Recent trends have been towards the use of disposable pallets and it is likely that they will eventually replace 'returnables' for most items.[1] Many southbound cargoes are palletised by the Company at Liverpool or Tilbury but, in some cases, they are now loaded by the manufacturer and remain as a unit until they reach the importer's own warehouse. Fork-lift trucks, both ashore and on ship, move the loaded pallets and save expensive man-handling as well as time. Thus palletisation has proved to be successful and has made it possible to reduce voyage times on the scheduled services.

The new system, by doubling or even trebling loading and discharging speeds, has reduced overtime payments and less cargo has been shut out. It also has the advantage over containers in that the backloading of 'returnables' occupies little space and the saving in time when unloading more than pays this freight charge. With 'disposables', of course, there is no return freight rate to consider. Future progress in raising the size of unit loads is conditional upon many extraneous factors, but even at the present stage of development has significantly benefited all concerned.[2] This is especially true for the shipper, as reduced rates are charged for palletised cargoes,[3] while items sent in containers have a greater freedom from either damage or pilferage.[4]

A final development which has approached maturity in the post-war era has been in the field of communications. In the nineteenth century, the sole means of keeping in touch with masters and agents on the coast

[1] The use of returnables has now ceased (May 1973).

[2] 'Containers and Palletisation', *Sea*, Vol. VI, No. II (Autumn 1965), pp. 9–11.

[3] 'Palletised Cargo Rates Slashed', *Nigerline* (Magazine of the Nigerian National Shipping Line), Vol. I, No. X (June 1967), pp. 9–11.

[4] 'Economics of Containerisation', *Nigerline*, Vol. II, No. I (September 1967), pp. 6 & 8.

was by letters carried by the Company's own vessels. Thus the senior men on the spot bore a heavy responsibility when decisions were required for, in most instances, it would have taken many weeks to have obtained a reply from head office. These circumstances changed dramatically when West Africa was connected to England by cable. This reached Bathurst and Freetown in 1886 and, three years later, it had been extended to include Accra, Lagos, Brass and Bonny.[1] Marconi's invention of wireless telegraphy further strengthened the contact between the Coast and Liverpool and, after 1929, both services were operated jointly by Cable and Wireless Limited.[2] The value of wireless as a means of communication between ship and ship, and ship and shore, was early appreciated by Elder Dempster—its *Lake Champlain* being the first British vessel to be fitted with Marconi's installation.

With the development of improved facilities came the gradual emergence of a communications centre on the coast. This was first sited at Accra and for most of the thirties all northbound cargoes were arranged by the Gold Coast manager. By 1938, however, it was found to be more convenient to use Lagos for this purpose, and its position was strengthened in 1939 by the appointment of the Company's Nigerian manager as the Ministry of War Transport's representative with responsibility for the movement and loading of all vessels from the Congo to Dakar.[3] Communications were consequently concentrated on Lagos for the duration of hostilities and, since then, Elder Dempster have continued to use this port for co-ordinating their activities on the Coast. Lagos is, therefore, the present location of its Ocean Traffic Controller who directs the routing of the Company's vessels when they are in West African waters—a task greatly simplified by recent developments in radio telephones, which can provide a vital link between ship and shore.

In the later thirties, Elders Colonial Airways helped to stimulate and operate a regular air service to West Africa and thus provided an additional link with Europe.[4] This assumed a much greater importance after the war, when direct routes were established and flying time was significantly reduced. Airmail, together with the introduction of the long-distance telephone and the continuing use of cable and wireless facilities, then provided an adequate—if not completely satisfactory—service

[1] 'Message Communication Part I', *Standard Bank Review* (October 1969), p. 5.
[2] 'Message Communication Part II', *Standard Bank Review* (November 1969), p. 8.
[3] See above, Chapter 12, p. 297.   [4] See above, Chapter 11, pp. 289–93.

during the forties and fifties. Any deficiencies in the system were, however, largely ended in December 1959, when the first direct teleprinter
link between Liverpool and West Africa was installed at Elder Dempster's Lagos agency and at its head office in India Building.[1] This direct
link still continues but is now complemented by the use of the international telex network which covers all the Company's main offices and
agencies.

Changes in Conference Membership and Structure
In 1939 the West African Lines Conference (WALCON) had consisted
of Elder Dempster, the Woermann Linie of Hamburg, and the Holland
West-Africa Lijn. The Second World War prevented the previous pattern of sailings from continuing and when the conference agreement
came to an end in 1941 it could not be renewed. At a meeting held on
7 July 1944, the Holland West-Africa Lijn accepted the view of their
solicitors that WALCON had, in fact, expired on 14 March 1941.[2] It
was decided, therefore, to recreate the former structure and the Hon.
L. H. Cripps, chairman of Elder Dempster, was appointed to the chair.[3]
When peace returned in 1945 Elder Dempster continued to provide
most of the tonnage for the trade, but the Holland West-Africa Lijn
rapidly rebuilt its fleet and, by 1949, this was three times larger than it
had been before the war. The Woermann-Linie was in a moribund
state and without ships when hostilities came to an end, and was not
invited to rejoin the conference until much later.

The gap left by the absence of the Woermann Linie was partly filled
by the expansion of the Holland West-Africa Lijn and by services begun
by the Scandinavian West Africa Line and the Hoegh Line in 1945 and
1949 respectively. These latter companies were, of course, operating
outside the conference framework at this time and, in the peculiar
circumstances of the early post-war years, there was little that WAL-
CON could do to restrict their activities. The close association of the
two British merchant lines with the conference after the war was recognised, however, and both the John Holt Line and the Palm Line were
admitted to full membership in January 1950.[4]

[1] *Sea*, Vol. IV, No. II (Summer 1960), p. 17.
[2] WALCON, meeting held 7 July 1944, Minute No. 1.
[3] WALCON, meeting held 7 July 1944, Minute No. 2.
[4] The John Holt Line and the Palm Line were formed from what had been the shipping.

During the fifties, a number of factors led to a further substantial expansion of WALCON. The development of German trade led to the Woermann Linie being readmitted in 1952—partly as a means of combating Scandinavian intervention, but also because of the growing competition from the Union Africa Linie and the Hanseatischer Afrika-Dienst, two German firms operating in the Antwerp-Hamburg range.[1] Well-remembered personal relationships facilitated this arrangement—Elder Dempster's attitude being that if it were essential to admit a German line it might as well welcome an old friend with which it knew it could work amicably.[2] Competition then developed between WALCON, the two German 'outsiders', and the two Scandinavian shipping companies. Thus the rates for stockfish, cement and beer were greatly reduced, while on the northbound route to the Continent and the United Kingdom payers of freight were given a 10 per cent loyalty rebate.[3] There was, however, some co-operation between the conference lines and the Scandinavian firms, for in the early fifties both Scandinavian West Africa Line and Hoegh had copies of WALCON tariff and received amendments to this, unofficially, from individual conference members. This arrangement was terminated in 1954 in view of the increased activities of the two lines, and further competition developed. Wiser councils then prevailed and the Scandinavian West Africa Line joined the Conference in September 1955. It was not possible to reach an agreement with the Hoegh Line until August 1957, but then it too became a member of WALCON. A few months later the newly formed Black Star Line of Ghana also joined the conference and this was followed by the admittance of the Nigerian National Shipping Line when it was established in May 1959.

---

departments of John Holt and the United Africa Company. See above, Chapter 13, pp. 330–1.

[1] The vessels of the Union Africa Linie were absorbed into the Woermann fleet in the mid-fifties and in 1964 Woermann signed an agreement with Hanseatischer Afrika Dienst whereby it took over the management of that company for a ten-year initial period under the name, flag and funnel mark of Woermann-Linie.

[2] Author's interview with J. H. Joyce.

[3] There were two rebates for timber at this time, 10 per cent to the shipper and 10 per cent to the payer of freight. The shippers have always received their loyalty rebate on a deferred basis, irrespective of the destination of their shipments. The rebate to loyal payers of freight on the Continent has also always been on a deferred basis—it was only the payers of freight in the U.K. who were given the option of an immediate rebate in the absence of competition on this route.

The fact that new entrants to the trade found it convenient to join WALCON must not be taken to imply that each was completely satisfied with the terms on which it was accepted. Woermann's allocation of sailings was far less than before the war and, although this was gradually increased, it never reached the percentage share it enjoyed up to 1939. The two 'national' lines also received a smaller share of the business than they would have wished, when they first began their operations.[1] So far as these companies are concerned, however, these initial irritations have largely disappeared with the passing of time. In the case of the two Scandinavian lines it was found to be extremely difficult to fix their shares of the trade on a permanent basis and both disliked the understanding which prevented them from carrying West African Marketing Board produce to other than Scandinavian ports. WALCON's attempts to meet the criticisms from these lines were only partly successful—the Scandinavian West Africa Line remained within the conference, but Hoegh resigned in August 1963.[2]

Thereafter the Hoegh Line operated outside WALCON and attempted to break into the United Kingdom-West African routes. The resulting freight-war caused some degree of confusion and this was only finally resolved when the conference structure was completely reorganised on 1 January 1968. From that date WALCON was divided into two new conferences—the U.K. and Eire services to and from West Africa being undertaken by the United Kingdom-West Africa Lines Joint Service (UKWAL) and the Continental and Scandinavian services to and from West Africa being carried out by the Continent West Africa Conference (COWAC).[3]

Before 1939 West Africa's trade links with the outside world were mainly limited to Britain and Europe.[4] In consequence, extensive

[1] The Black Star Line, which joined WALCON for a four year period in 1957 had its agreement revised in 1959 and increased its share of the trade substantially. When the Nigerian National Shipping Line was admitted to WALCON, it did not own any ships, merely using chartered vessels. It has since acquired a progressively larger share of the trade, but as in the case of Black Star and all other Conference members, must operate a high proportion of Company-owned tonnage.

[2] Hoegh was particularly dissatisfied with their tonnage allocation from Hamburg. They negotiated improved terms in October 1959, two years after joining WALCON, but could not make sufficient progress when negotiations were undertaken for the Conference Agreement which was to become effective from 1 January 1962.

[3] See Appendix, p. 480, Table 82.

[4] Elder Dempster also provided a direct service from India to West Africa and operated ships between the Coast and North America.

trans-shipment facilities, based on through rates, were developed at Liverpool, Hamburg, Rotterdam and New York. The O.S.K. line[1] operated an occasional service between Japan and the coast from 1934 to 1937, but apart from this it was not until after the Second World War that direct services were established on any scale. One aspect of this development was the creation of links with Scandinavia, while the further extension of regular sailings to North America was another. In the fifties direct services between West Africa and India were started, in opposition to Elder Dempster sailings, by the Indian Scindia Line, and three Japanese companies began the operation of routes from the Far East.[2] Other links formed at this time were to Capetown for onward transmission to Australia and New Zealand, and directly to South America.[3] The shipping lines which operated these services gradually organised themselves into conferences in order to regulate their particular routes to West Africa,[4] and by 1964 practically all important services, except those to Australasia, were covered by conference agreements.[5] These conferences then developed a policy of co-operation with WALCON and this has persisted to the present day.

Elder Dempster, while retaining its position in WALCON, remained members of two of the more important conferences which govern the direct trades—the Italian West African Conference and the American West African Freight Conference. The Company also reached an agreement with the South France and North Africa/West Africa Conference (OTRAMA) in respect of calls at Casablanca en route from Italy to the coast and for calls at Marseilles northbound from West Africa to Italy, but it did not join either the Far East-West Africa Conference or the Lignes de Navigation Resservant la Coa. The recent splitting of WALCON into the UKWAL Joint Service and COWAC has not materially altered this position.

The Development of Trade
The trade of West Africa showed a remarkable increase in the early

[1] The Osaka Shozen Kaisha Line of Tokio.
[2] These were the O.S.K., the Mitsui and the Kawasaki Kisen Kaisha Lines (the latter is known as the 'K' line).
[3] There were a few direct sailings to Australia, almost entirely for cocoa.
[4] In the main these conferences had been formed in the inter-war period but had then lain dormant until the fifties.
[5] See Appendix, p. 481, Table 83.

post-war years[1] and this tendency continued during the fifties. Imports into the former British colonies more than doubled in this period—partly because of the large number of capital projects which were being undertaken—while the rise in exports was nearer 25 per cent. Trade has continued to develop in the sixties but, as the following table indicates, the rate of expansion has declined considerably:

External Trade of the former British Colonies in West Africa.[2]
(U.S. $ million)

Year	Imports					Exports				
	Gambia	Ghana	Nigeria	S.Leone	Total	Gambia	Ghana	Nigeria	S.Leone	Total
1937	4	62	72	9	147	4	61	95	13	173
1938	2	38	42	7	89	2	32	47	11	92
1948	9	127	169	20	325	9	202	252	22	485
1952	10	187	317	29	443	11	214	363	30	618
1953	6	207	303	31	547	8	224	348	33	613
1954	7	199	319	36	561	9	293	419	32	753
1955	10	246	381	48	685	7	243	370	29	749
1956	10	249	428	65	752	7	222	377	37	643
1957	13	271	427	79	790	12	229	357	52	650
1958	11	237	466	67	781	12	263	380	55	710
1959	9	317	500	66	892	8	286	458	55	807
1960	9	363	605	74	1,051	8	294	475	83	860
1961	13	394	623	91	1,121	9	292	486	82	869
1962	13	333	569	85	1,000	10	291	472	58	831
1963	12	365	581	84	1,042	9	273	531	81	894
1964	12	341	711	99	1,163	9	293	601	95	998
1965	16	445	770	108	1,339	14	291	751	89	1,145
1966	*16	352	718	100	1,186	*14	244	795	83	1,136
1967	*16	307	626	90	1,039	*14	278	677	70	1,039

(* estimated figures)

These statistics give a general impression of the changes in the magnitude of West African trade and show the progress achieved by each nation. The four states have many similarities, but a detailed examination also indicates many differences.[3] Areas in West Africa that were not formerly controlled by Britain have also developed rapidly in the post-war era, so that the whole region now plays a much more significant role in world trade. This is made very clear by a comparison of the situation in 1913 with that in 1963:

[1] See above, Chapter 13, pp. 320-1.

[2] Based on information in the United Nations Statistical Year Books for 1957, 1962 and 1968. (Copyright: United Nations, 1957, 1962 and 1968. Reproduced by permission.) Note that the amounts are in millions of U.S. dollars and that no allowance has been made for changes in the value of this currency over the period.

[3] See Appendix, p. 401, Table 8.

An Elder Dempster Agent's sitting room, *c.* 1895.

PLATE 21

An Elder Dempster Agent's dining room, *c.* 1895.

PLATE 22   One of the two aircraft used by Elders Colonial Airways from 1936 to 1940 on the Khartoum–West Coast route.

West Africa's changing position in the world dry cargo trade[1]
(million metric tons)

Year	Total world dry cargo trade	West African exports	West African exports as a % of world trade	West African imports	West African imports as % of world trade
1913	289	1.34	0.46	2.76	0.96
1963	620	11.06	1.78	8.16	1.32

In addition to West Africa's increasing share of world commerce there has also been a substantial change in the direction of its trade. Even so, the United Kingdom, together with northern and western Europe, continue to provide a high proportion of the region's imports and accept nearly two-thirds of its exports.[2]

Changes in the Elder Dempster Fleet
Elder Dempster's replacement of wartime losses was virtually complete by the end of 1949, for in terms of tonnage the pre-war situation had been largely restored.[3] A number of these vessels, however, were either elderly and past their prime or were of a wartime design that was uneconomic for commercial service. If the standards of the service were to be maintained and ultimately improved, and if provision was to be made for the further growth of trade, a major building programme was obviously a necessity. By 1948 Elder Dempster had already gained sufficient experience to plan ships that were specifically designed to meet the changed conditions of the post-war era. Two 'E' class vessels, primarily intended for the Canada-Cape or United States-West African trades were then laid down and were commissioned as *Eboe* and *Ebani* in 1952. Two new coasters, *Baro* and *Benin*, and a passenger ferry, *Eket*, were also ordered at this time and all three came into service during 1950. Construction of the earlier ships of the 'O' class began in the early fifties. These were a little larger than the post-war 'S' vessels, as the pattern of trade had shown that bigger units were likely to be more profitable than the previously accepted standard. *Obuasi* and *Onitsha* were completed in 1952, the latter being equipped with a 150-ton derrick to enable her to continue the work of the ageing *Mary Kingsley*. At the date of construction this derrick was the heaviest to be fitted to any

[1] United Nations Conference on Trade and Development, *The West African Shipping Range*, by Dag Tresselt, United Nations, New York, 1967, Table 2, p. 10.
[2] See below, p. 363.   [3] See above, Chapter 13, pp. 317–20.

British vessel. A third member of the 'O' class was *Owerri* and she entered the Company's service in 1955.

The regular use of large warbuilt vessels in the West African trade suggested that a further rise in size would be profitable for a proportion of the fleet. Accordingly *Perang* was ordered in June 1951 and *Patani* in April 1953. They were each of 6,200 gross tons compared with 4,800 gross tons of the post-war 'S' class, and were delivered in 1954. These vessels were notable in that they pioneered a simplified circuit for direct current fluorescent lighting which has since become standard practice. Furthermore, while the main engine of *Patani* was on the test bed, water cooling was replaced by oil cooling in one cylinder lower piston, as this had been an important source of the corrosion hazards in Doxford engines. The experiment proved to be successful and has since been widely adopted in subsequent buildings.

Two additional 'O' class vessels were laid down in 1954 and these were subsequently commissioned two years later as *Oti* and *Ondo*. *Oti* was the first ship to be fitted with an inert gas fire-extinguishing system in her hold—a method of fire control that had been developed jointly by Pyrene and Elder Dempster, while *Ondo* was equipped with the first 'wrong order' alarm for electric telegraphs. A third 'E' ship, *Egori*, was also built and entered the United States-West Africa route in 1957. She was fitted with the first supercharged Doxford engine to be constructed as such, and possessed oil-cooled lower pistons and a diaphragm between the crankcase and cylinder.[1]

Until 1955 all the new units (except passenger vessels and the 'E' class intended for the Canadian and American services) were in the 11 to 12½ knot range. On the pure economics of carrying a ton of cargo in the U.K. or Continental-West African trade, this range of speeds was probably the cheapest, but the competition of other lines forced the Company to reconsider its traditional policy. *Aureol* had been built with her engines arranged to burn heavy oil instead of diesel fuel and this had proved to be a viable experiment. To some extent, therefore, the use of a cheaper propellent meant that the increased cost of extra speed could be offset, so, in 1955, it was decided to design rather faster ships for the

[1] Author's interview with Mr A. M. Bennett, March 1968, Director of Elder Dempster Lines with special responsibility for marine engineering. It was generally recognised in the shipping trade that the vessels constructed for Elder Dempster Lines were always technically well advanced. (Author's interview with Mr M. B. Glasier, Director of the Ocean Steam Ship Company and Elder Dempster Lines, January 1972.)

main U.K. and Continental-West African routes. Three 'D' class vessels, *Daru*, *Degema* and *Dixcove*, of similar size to the 'P' types, but with a service speed of fourteen knots, were ordered in November 1955. *Dunkwa* was laid down in 1957 and *Deido* and *Dumurra* completed the series in 1961.

The success of the 'D' class then led to a decision to build a number of even faster vessels. These were the 'F' group, capable of sixteen knots, and comprised *Fourah Bay* (1961), *Falaba* (1962), *Forcados* (1963) and *Fian, Freetown* and *Fulani* (1964). All of these were approximately 7,700 gross tons and this combination of size and speed appears to be ideal for the present state of the trade.

In addition to the construction of new vessels, Elder Dempster also acquired a certain amount of second-hand tonnage during the fifties. Two coasters, *Bida* and *Benue*, were purchased in 1951 to assist in the Nigerian coal trade, but they were disposed of in 1952 when the volume of this business rapidly declined. Two further ships were purchased in 1957.[1] These were renamed *Winneba* and *Calabar* and were bought with the object of establishing a monthly passenger service between London and the West Coast of Africa. Each was of approximately 8,300 gross tons with accommodation for over a hundred passengers and considerable space for refrigerated and general cargo. The service proved popular for a few years, but the decline in passenger traffic caused by the increasing competition of air transport led to the sale of the ships in 1962.[2]

Of much greater significance than these purchases of specialised vessels was the acquisition of the British and Burmese Steam Navigation Company Limited in 1952.[3] The tonnage which was then taken over was made up of four cargo liners totalling 25,700 gross tons and seven cargo vessels totalling 38,100 gross tons.[4] After this date the British and Burmese continued to operate in the Burma trade with a small number of vessels which were managed by Messrs P. Henderson and Company of Glasgow.[5] The 'K' class vessels, however, which had formerly been largely chartered to Elder Dempster, contined to sail almost exclusively

[1] They were formerly *Umgeni* and *Umtali*, built in 1938 and 1936 respectively.

[2] This was anticipated by the Company but it had been decided that it had to meet the demand if it were keep faith with the public.

[3] See above, Chapter 13, p. 334.   [4] See Appendix, p. 420, Table 26.

[5] Elder Dempster Lines Holdings Limited, Accounts for the year ending 31 December 1952.

in the West African trade, and were still managed by Hendersons.[1] A number of other new vessels joined the British and Burmese fleet during the next decade and, by 1961, it totalled 128,405 gross tons, practically all of which was always employed on West African routes.[2]

As new tonnage was delivered to Elder Dempster and as the British and Burmese 'K' class was extended, older vessels were scrapped or sold for service in less demanding trades.[3] Only two vessels were lost during this period. In 1956, *Warri*, a coaster of 974 gross tons, built in 1945, was stranded and became a total loss. There was no loss of life or personal injury in this case, but fate was not so kind when *Ondo* went aground at the mouth of the River Elbe in December 1960. This vessel of 5,435 gross tons, completed in 1956, was lost without any of her crew being hurt, but three members of the German Pilot Service were drowned when their launch capsized while attempting to come alongside.

In 1963 there was a number of amalgamations between the floating and technical staffs of Elder Dempster and the British and Burmese. These were instigated by the continuing decline in the trade with Burma, and the fierce competition in the West African services which made it essential to maximise the efficiency of the two companies. A complete reconstruction followed in 1964. The British and Burmese Steam Navigation Company Limited became non-operative and its activities were undertaken by the Henderson Line Limited—a new, wholly-owned subsidiary of Liner Holdings Company Limited. Three vessels were transferred from the British and Burmese to the Henderson Line, *Bhano*, *Kaduna* and *Pegu*, and Elder Dempster contributed *Prahsu* which was renamed *Kalaw* to give the new company a fleet of four ships. Later that year the British and Burmese purchased the six-year-old, 15,000 ton deadweight bulk carrier, *Gjendefjell*. This was renamed *Sunjarv* and placed on a six-year time charter.

The ten other vessels owned by the British and Burmese were transferred to Elder Dempster. These were *Dalla*, *Donga*, *Dumbaia*, *Kabala*, *Kadeik*, *Kandaw*, *Kentung*, *Kohima*, *Koyan* and *Kumba*. Then in 1965 *Kaduna* and *Kalaw* moved from Henderson to Elder Dempster, while *Daru* (renamed *Yoma*) moved from Elder Dempster to Henderson.

[1] R. Borland and A. McCrae of P. Henderson remained on the board of the British and Burmese S.N. Co. Ltd. J. H. Joyce, M. B. Glazier and A. E. Muirhead joined this board on behalf of Elder Dempster, Mr Joyce becoming chairman.
[2] See Appendix, p. 420, Table 27.   [3] See Appendix p. 421, Table 28.

Kohima, together with a number of other 'K' class ships, was sold in 1966, but *Kalaw* (formerly *Prahsu*) was renamed *Kohima* to preserve the name.

Further fleet movements followed the purchase of the Guinea Gulf Line on 1 March 1965. This firm, the shipping department of John Holts until 1950,[1] had found it to be uneconomic to operate only four ships in the difficult days of the early sixties. In consequence, it had been decided to rely on conference services and, after an abortive sale to the Nigerian National Shipping Line, successful negotiations were concluded with Liner Holdings Company Limited.[2] The effect of the transaction was to give Guinea Gulf's share in the Conference to Elder Dempster, which was very desirable, but it also meant that it acquired four vessels which it did not wish to operate. These were *Mary Holt, Elizabeth Holt, Florence Holt* and *Rose of Lancaster,*[3] all being oil-fired, steam-turbine ships that could not be easily integrated into Elder Dempster's fleet of motor vessels. Thus, although they were generally considered to be very reliable and comfortable ships, they did not go into service for Elder Dempster, but were sold as soon as possible to other owners. Six of the Company's 'S' class were then transferred to the Guinea Gulf Line and renamed as follows: *Shonga* became *Mallam, Salaga* became *Mamfe, Sekondi* became *Mampong, Sulima* became *Mano, Swedru* became *Maradi* and *Sherbro* became *Matru.*

In the years which followed, a number of the older vessels were either scrapped or sold in order to maintain the fleet at a high level of efficiency and also to keep it in line with the requirements of the Company's share in the West African trade.[4] The sale of these vessels then led to a further rationalisation of the Elder Dempster, Henderson, and Guinea Gulf Line fleets. The continuing decline in the Burma trade had made it uneconomic to maintain even a small number of ships on that route. As a result, *Bhamo, Pegu* and *Yoma* were transferred to the Guinea Gulf Line—the latter vessel reverting to her former name of *Daru.* This left Hendersons without any general cargo vessels, so an agreement was made with Bibbys for the operation of a joint service to carry what re-

[1] See above, Chapter 13, pp. 330–1.

[2] P. N. Davies, *A Short History of the Ships of John Holt and Company (Liverpool) Limited and the Guinea Gulf Line Limited* (Published privately by the Company, Liverpool, 1965).

[3] This ship was owned by the Red Rose Navigation Company (a subsidiary of Holt's) and on charter to Guinea Gulf.

[4] See Appendix, p. 422, Table 29.

mained of their trade to and from Burma. Since 1968 Henderson's share
of this limited business has been conducted by tonnage chartered from
Elder Dempster.[1] The line is managed by Roxburgh Henderson and
Company Limited of Glasgow (successors to Messrs P. Henderson and
Company, Ship Managers Limited) and it was responsible for the bulk
carrier *Sunjarv* which operated on a long-term charter until it was sold
in July 1970.

The Guinea Gulf fleet consisted of six 'S' class vessels until 1967, but
these were then sold. They were replaced by the three ships transferred
from the Henderson Line, plus *Freetown* and *Kumba* supplied by Elder
Dempster. The latter reverted to Elder Dempster during 1968, and
since then *Bhamo*, *Pegu*, *Daru* and *Freetown* have been the only units
operating under the Guinea Gulf flag and colours.

Elder Dempster's traditional passenger service from Liverpool to
West Africa has suffered greatly from the competition of air transport.[2]
As late as 1939 the Company employed four liners, with a fifth in reserve,
on this route, with alternative voyages terminating in Calabar or Port
Harcourt.[3] The post-war pattern of fortnightly sailing from the Mersey
to Lagos began when *Aureol* came into service in 1951, but by the middle
of the sixties load factors for the three ships had dropped to an unprofitable level.[4] In the absence of adequate trade it was decided, therefore,
not to spend the very large amounts which would have been necessary
to keep *Accra* and *Apapa* at the desired level of efficiency and they were
sold in 1967 and 1968 respectively.[5] This then left *Aureol* to provide a
six-weekly service from Liverpool to the coast and this continued until
March 1972, when her sailings were transferred to Southampton. The
prime cause of this change was the closure of Prince's Landing-stage

[1] This arrangement continued until 1970 when it was decided to end the Henderson
sailings for the time being. The Company's conference rights have been maintained, and
it will re-enter the trade if circumstances permit. Author's interview with Mr A. McCrae,
24 April 1970.
[2] The total number of passengers carried out and home on all services amounted to
8,102 in 1948; 15,376 in 1952; 28,107 in 1960; 11,302 in 1966 and 5,331 in 1971. E.D.L.P.
Summary Passengers carried. Kindly supplied by Elder Dempster Lines Passenger Department.
[3] E.D.L.P. West African Mail Service Sailing Schedule, No. 11 (April 1938 to March
1939).
[4] Apart from the competition of air transport, the reduction in the number of expatriate
government servants was the most important factor in this decline.
[5] Note also the reduction in the London–West Africa passenger service, See above, p.
355.

and the absence of alternative facilities at Liverpool, but the move to Southampton has provided an opportunity to instigate further alterations to the service. Thus *Aureol* now carries no northbound cargo and the quicker turnround in Lagos, together with the slightly shorter route, permits a voyage pattern of thirty-five instead of forty-two days.

There has been much speculation as to the future of sea-passenger traffic between the United Kingdom and West Africa, but at the time of writing it would appear that it is sufficient to justify the retention of one vessel. Since the sale of her consorts, *Aureol* has been almost fully booked and her new schedule will enable her to complete ten as against eight or nine voyages per year. She is, of course, over twenty years old and cannot continue indefinitely, but it would seem that she will repay any decision to retain her for a further period, providing that existing load factors can be maintained.

The Elder Dempster fleet reached its post-war peak of 293,853 gross tons in 1965.[1] Since then it has declined to the 1972 total of 205,989 gross tons, and both the Burma trade and the sea-passenger traffic to West Africa have greatly contracted. Some compensation for these losses could, however, be obtained from Elder Dempster's successful entry into a completely new field. This enterprise was organised by the wholly owned subsidiary, Seaway Car Transporters Limited, which was incorporated in 1965. Its original object was to provide a service from Felixstowe to carry vehicles of British manufacture to the Scandinavian ports of Copenhagen, Malmo, Drammen and Gothenburg, and it was hoped that on some return-voyages Swedish-built cars and trucks could be brought back. Actual operations began in 1967 with the specially designed *Carway*[2] which, although of only 1,597 gross tons, can carry as many as 400 export cars.[3] The success of this vehicle ferry under the commercial management of the Mountwood Shipping Company led to the purchase of a second vessel in 1969. This was renamed *Clearway*,[4] and with her acquisition it was possible to offer a twice-weekly service. The experience gained in operating these ships between Britian and Scandinavia then led to a decision to double the Company's tonnage

[1] Details of the growth of the Elder Dempster fleet from 1940 to 1964 are given below, p. 368.

[2] Author's interview with J. D. Wilson, Esq., Chairman and Managing Director of the Mountwood Shipping Company, 25 November 1969.

[3] *Sea*, Vol. VII, No. I (Summer 1968), pp. 8–9.

[4] She was formerly known as *Sealord Challenger*.

on this route and *Speedway*, similar to but of larger capacity than *Carway*, was launched in February 1970. The advantages of a vessel that is purpose-built for a particular trade are obvious, but there are certain snags:

'By the mere fact of specialisation, she is somewhat inflexible as to alternative use, and carries therefore an inbuilt commercial risk. She has been built without the backing of any firm contract with any part of the motor industry—but we think we can meet their needs sufficiently competently to satisfy their requirements and attract their support.'[1]

In April 1970, the second-hand *Mandeville* (similar to *Clearway*) was purchased and renamed *Skyway*. Two months later *Speedway* entered the service to make a total of four company-owned vessels, and in the following October m.v. *Saaletal* was acquired on time-charter to become a fifth member of the fleet.[2] This increase in tonnage permitted the Company to extend its services so that four ships operated between the east coast of the United Kingdom and Scandinavia, while the other vessel normally sailed between the Continent and either the United Kingdom or Denmark.[3]

The operation of the *Seaway* fleet on the short sea-routes has been followed by an extension of its activities to the West African trade. In June, 1971, *Clearway* was chartered to UKWAL Joint Services and began a service from Poole in Dorset to Nigeria.[4] Since then Clearway has operated a 28-day voyage cycle, spending less than twelve hours at a guaranteed berth at Apapa Quay and taking only a day to turn round in the United Kingdom. The introduction of this service has proved a great benefit in satisfying the ever-increasing demand for cars and commercial vehicles in West Africa—the trade amounted to 16,000 units in 1970—but unfortunately there is little or no cargo that, at present, can be conveniently carried on the northbound route.[5] The Scandinavian services of Seaway Ferries Limited[6] were rationalised in 1972 following

[1] Statement by F. L. Lane, Esq., Chairman of Elder Dempster Lines, Limited, at the launch of *Speedway* on 18 February 1970.

[2] Note that *Speedway* and *Clearway* exchanged names during September 1970.

[3] *Carway* and (new) *Clearway* are essentially car-carriers; the other vessels carry cars but are essentially Roll-on/Roll-off trailer ships.

[4] *Sea*, Vol. VIII, No. II (July 1971), p. 18.

[5] Ukwal Joint Service, News Release. Statement by P. F. Earlam, Director of Elder Dempster Lines, at a Press Conference held on 16 June 1971.

[6] The Mountwood Shipping Company was acquired by the Ocean Group in 1971 and Seaway Car Transporters Ltd became Seaway Ferries Ltd in January 1972. It was felt.

losses experienced during 1971.[1] The losses continued, however, and as a result it was decided to end the Scandinavian services in January, 1973.[2] At its peak the Seaway Fleet amounted to 5,136 gross tons. At 1 May 1972, the Elder Dempster fleet comprised 205,989 gross tons and, if the Guinea Gulf tonnage (25,686) and Seaway ships are taken into account, this means that the Company operated a total of 236,811 gross tons.[3] The average age of this combined fleet was approximately thirteen years.

Post-War Change and Diversification
Elder Dempster's traditional business had been to carry cargo and passengers between West Africa and either the United Kingdom or the continent of Europe. Until 1914 the trade had been shared with a single competitor—the Woermann Linie of Hamburg—but in the inter-war period the Holland West-African Lijn and the shipping departments of the United Africa Company and John Holt had also secured a footing. In spite of this increased rivalry, Elder Dempster retained a predominant position in the trade and this was reinforced by the absence of the Woermann Linie during the Second World War. Events since 1945, however, have greatly reduced the Company's share of WAL-CON's sailings.

Elder Dempster is now but one, albeit the strongest, of a large number of lines that are engaged on their customary routes—see table overleaf. Furthermore, a significant quantity of West African imports and exports are now carried directly to and from the country concerned instead of being trans-shipped at Liverpool or Hamburg—details are provided on page 362. Elder Dempster attempted to deal with this changing situation as it evolved. It reorganised its external services such as the Canada/Cape and West Africa/North America as well as providing a number of new or extended coastal routes. Some of these activities involved the establishment of new companies like Elder

---

that this change of name was more in keeping with the Company's present business activities. See: *Seaway Ferries News*, No. I (May 1972).

[1] Seaway Ferries Limited, Press Release, 28 July 1972.
[2] See Ocean Transport and Trading Limited, Annual Report and Accounts for 1972, Chairman's Review, p. 6.
[3] See Appendix, Table 30, p. 423. Note that this total does not include the two ships *Eket* and *Oron* operated by the West African Lighterage & Transport Company Ltd.

Number of Vessels operated and Monthly Sailings provided by
WALCON in 1964[1]

Line	No. of vessels operated	Sailings per month
Elder Dempster Lines, Limited	43	14/15
Holland West Afrika Lijn, N.V.	12	5
Palm Line Limited	22	6
Guinea Gulf Line Limited	3	2
Woermann-Linie	27	12
Scandinavia West Africa Line	13	3
Black Star Line Limited	10	3
Nigerian National Shipping Line Ltd	15	4
Total:	145	49/50

Direction of West African Maritime Trade in 1963.[2]
(*Excluding Spanish and Portuguese Territories*)

	Northern & Western Europe & United Kingdom	Mediterranean	U.S.A. & Canada	Far East	Coastal	Other	Total
Imports	38.6	28.2	13.6	2.0	4.8	3.5	100.0
Exports	62.5	8.1	11.0	0.3	6.5	10.0	100.0
Total	49.3	19.2	12.5	1.2	5.5	6.5	100.0

Dempster Lines (Canada) Limited and Elders of South Africa (Proprietary) Limited, and some were arranged with the co-operation and assistance of other conference members. The Company was also quick to join new conferences as they were formed to cater for direct services to West Africa, and it attempted—without success—to obtain a share in the growing air transport business which it had helped to pioneer in 1936.

The acquisition of the British and Burmese Steam Navigation Company in 1952 was primarily designed to secure the 'K' class vessels which

[1] S. F. Klinghofer, 'A Report on a Preliminary Survey of Factors contributing to level of freight rates in the Seaborne Trade of Africa' (New York: U.N. Economic Commission for Africa, 1965), Table No. 2 (supplied by WALCON Secretariat).
[2] Ibid., Table No. 4 (also quoted by Dag Tresselt, op. cit., Table No. 1, p. 10).

were so well suited to West African conditions, but it also enabled Elder Dempster to diversify on to the Burma route. This was recognised to be a declining trade, but for over ten years it gave semi-profitable employment to a small number of vessels—calls at Egyptian ports, the Sudan, and Aden supplementing the limited cargo available on the eastward leg of the voyage. Throughout this period it was always possible, if unlikely, that business would improve, but it continued to decline[1] and the Company was eventually forced to rationalise its service by making a suitable arrangement with the Bibby Line. Another shipping firm was acquired in 1965. In this case the object was to reinforce Elder Dempster's position in its traditional trade; for the purchase of the Guinea Gulf Line secured its share of WALCON. The four vessels obtained at this time were not considered suitable to be integrated into the Company's fleet and were sold to other owners as quickly as possible.

Changing conditions, both in the achievement of political independence and in the growth of internal communications, have considerably altered Elder Dempster's activities within West Africa since the war. The extension of rail and river services and, in particular, the tremendous expansion of road transport has enabled trade to be concentrated at fewer and fewer ports. This has inevitably meant that the Company's agencies on the Coast have tended to become larger while their number has been simultaneously declining. One result of this development has been the reorganisation of the Company's structure within West Africa: since 1954 the West African Lighterage and Transport Company, Elders Engineering and Airways Company, West African Properties, and Elder Dempster (Agencies) Limited have all undertaken specific duties which have been completely divorced from the activities of Elder Dempster Lines, which now exists solely to provide external shipping services. A second aspect of these changes has been the growing co-operation between Elder Dempster and the Palm Line, which has been especially important in the arrangement of port facilities. A joint agency was first established by the two firms in Hamburg in 1963[2] and later similar institutions were created in Sierra Leone (1965) and in

---

[1] The closing of the Suez Canal in 1967 was the final straw as it made it uneconomic to call at Port Sudan and Aden.

[2] Elderpalm Schiffahrts–Agentur G.m.b.h. took over the work formerly undertaken by Elder Dempster Lines G.m.b.h.—the latter firm has since lain dormant.

Ghana (1969). Liner Agencies (Ghana) Limited are housed in fine premises originally purpose-built by Elder Dempster at Takoradi; the Accra offices are situated in the recently constructed Standard Bank Building, while at Tema accommodation has been successfully adapted from a warehouse near the harbour.

A new building for Elder Dempster Agencies at Apapa was completed in September 1956,[1] and another to house the Lagos administrative centre was opened in October 1963.[2] The latter office is sited on the Marina in the middle of the commercial area and occupies a most advantageous position. Close by is Elder Dempster's own wharf, which provides a convenient point to board the Company's launches.[3] In Freetown, Sierra Leone Shipping Agencies Limited have their offices in a fine new building which stands within a few yards of the Queen Elizabeth II Quay. It stands on land which was originally purchased by Elder Dempster and Company in the early twenties but which was sold in 1935 after the government had refused to consider moving the port to that site. This decision was rescinded in 1952, so Elder Dempster were forced to re-acquire a small part of their former holding at a greatly enhanced price.[4]

The net effect of these changes is that Elder Dempster Lines now has little direct business within West Africa and even its subsidiary companies play a much smaller role than in pre-war days. The extensive workshop facilities at King Tom and Wilmot Point are no longer operated by the Company, and its subsidiaries' only remaining activities are concentrated at Calabar where *Eket* and *Oron* continue to provide valuable ferry services.[5]

A more recent venture has been the formation of the Volta Lake Transport Company Limited in association with Scanship (Ghana) Limited and the Volta River Authority. This will have the task of providing a water-transport service for passengers and cargo on the lake created on the Volta by the dam at Akosombo. The flooded area is approximately 3,300 square miles and extends to Yapei, about 250 miles

---

[1] *Sea*, Vol. II, No. III (Autumn 1956), pp. 13–16.
[2] *Sea*, Vol. V, No. III, (Summer 1954), rear page.
[3] *Sea*, Vol. VII, No. I (Summer 1968), p. 26.
[4] Author's interview with the late Mr Ade Lewis-Coker in Freetown, 12 July 1969. See also *Sea*, Vol. XII, No. II (Spring 1956), pp. 1–5 and Vol. VII, No. V (January 1971) p. 25.
[5] '500,000 a year', *Sea*, Vol. VIII, No. IV (July 1972), pp. 10–11.

to the north of the dam, so there is great scope for this particular enterprise. The Volta Lake Transport Company was registered in Ghana during 1969 and limited operations began at that time.[1]

The rationalisation of company structure and close working with the Palm Line overseas have had parallel lines of development in other spheres. Thus, Liverpool Maritime Terminals Limited and Metropolitan Terminals Limited are partly owned by the two companies. They co-operated in helping in the establishment of the Nigerian National Shipping Line, and the three lines later joined together to form African Container Express Limited. The two lines, Elder Dempster and Palm, also act together in many other ways because of their common membership of the various conferences. Thus Elder Dempster, Palm, Guinea Gulf, Black Star, Nigerian National and Hoegh Lines now operate joint services between the United Kingdom and Eire to West Africa; Elder Dempster, Palm, Guinea Gulf and Hoegh provide a Continent joint service,[2] and Elder Dempster and Chargeus Réunis maintain a co-ordinated service from the Coast to North America.[3] Co-operation within the conference structure has also resulted in special arrangements being made to encourage the use of through pallets. Shippers benefit by paying a reduced rate to the shipowner and, as a number of port authorities charge less for palletised cargo, considerable savings are possible. The shipping lines and ports gain, of course, from the more rapid speed of turnround.[4]

The present position of Elder Dempster Lines Limited, as a wholly-owned subsidiary of Liner Holdings Company Limited, has not changed since the latter firm was established as Elder Dempster Lines (Holdings) Limited in 1936. There has, however, been a significant alteration in the shareholding of Liner Holdings, for on 1 January 1965 the Ocean Steam Ship Company Limited—now Ocean Transport and Trading Limited —became the sole owner of its entire share capital.[5] As a result the Ocean board of directors—not the board of Liner Holdings—became the

---

[1] *Sea*, Vol. VII, No. III (January 1970), pp. 14–18.

[2] Elder Dempster Lines, News Release, 13 February 1970. 'Joint Continental Service to West Africa'.

[3] It is expected that the Compagnie Maritime Belge will participate in this service in the near future.

[4] UKWAL publication, 'Palletised cargoes to West Africa, and the Unit Load.'

[5] Liner Holdings Company Limited, Directors' Report for the year ending 31 December 1965.

ultimate authority for the policies adopted by Elder Dempster Lines. It also marked the introduction of a period of ever-closer co-operation between what had become Ocean's two main operating companies—Elder Dempster Lines and the Blue Funnel Line—and this was to be the beginning of a comprehensive policy of integration.[1]

Since the ending of the Second World War, Elder Dempster's traditional policy of reliance upon a single geographic area has been increasingly questioned. Until then this had always been regarded as a source of strength, but the many changes which have taken place in the post-war era have led some directors to consider it a potential source of weakness. Accordingly, while every effort has been made to maintain Elder Dempster's position in all aspects of the West African trade, the Company has also been quite prepared to examine other possibilities. As previously noted, the acquisition of the British and Burmese Steam Navigation Company gave an entry to Burmese routes.[2] If this trade had developed it would have given a useful geographic 'spread', but in the event it continued to decline, from factors which were quite beyond the Company's control. The purchase of a number of other lines was also considered, but no definite offers were made. Investigations showed that these prospects were not commercially viable; were a poor 'fit' with the Company's current services; or would put too great a strain on already stretched managerial and administrative capacity. It was decided, therefore, not to attempt to acquire any more existing companies,[3] but to seek to diversify into other activities—in particular, into the bulk trades and into the European car ferry and trailer business. The latter object appeared to be achieved with the formation of Seaway Car Transporters, but discussions with a major oil company in respect of the carriage of oil were inconclusive. An examination of various ore routes was then undertaken and some of these showed considerable promise. However, the link with Ocean in 1965 ended the necessity for diversification outside the Group, as it already operated world-wide services in many fields. Since then the search for new ventures has been organised centrally and this has provided wider opportunities for suitable investment.

[1] The present (1972) structure of the Group is given in the Appendix, p. 467, Table 63.
[2] See above, pp. 355–6.
[3] The acquisition of the Guinea Gulf Line in 1965 was regarded as a special case. See above, p. 357.

Profitability and Success of Elder Dempster Lines

The economic efficiency of a company can best be judged by its financial returns, although these cannot be judged in isolation from other relevant factors. As a yardstick these financial returns may be varied in the short run by internal or external influences, but in the long term they provide the only satisfactory guide to the extent to which a firm has been able to take advantage of the opportunities available in a particular trade or business. Elder Dempster Lines' results are, therefore, a reflection both of the quality of the opportunities available in the West African trade and an indication of the excellence of its management, organisation and personnel.

It is possible to calculate profitability in a wide variety of ways, but a method based on the annual return per gross registered ton would seem to possess the fewest disadvantages.[1] In the table on page 368 this has been refined so that the size of the fleet is the mean for each year, and both administrative costs and depreciation have been deducted.[2]

According to one authority who examined 'Profits from sailings per gross ton owned tonnage of British liner/cargo firms' for the period 1948 to 1964, Elder Dempster's earnings from voyages in the West African trade were considerably more than the average for the lines listed in *Fairplay*'s selection of liner/cargo firms.[3] The tables below would seem to confirm this view, in that since its inception in 1932, Elder Dempster Lines has been remarkably successful in obtaining a reasonable return from its vessels.[4] They also indicate, as might be expected, that the level of profitability has fluctuated with the state of trade. Thus the depressed thirties gave only a moderate yield and,

---

[1] This method overcomes a number of the difficulties which make inter-company comparison so uncertain for capital structure, taxation, interest charges and dividend policy can be ignored.

[2] Any comparison of these particular figures with the returns obtained by other firms must take account of marginal differences in administrative costs and in rates of depreciation.

[3] D. Tresselt, op. cit., Graph IV-2, p. 40.

[4] These financial results could only have been achieved if the excellence of the commercial organisation was paralleled by the efficiency of ship operations. In fact, a very high level of competence and dedication was demanded from the Captains of Elder Dempster vessels and this established a pattern that permeated all activities. A typical example of the care and thought given to ship operations is provided by the 'Notices to Masters' issued by the Company which covered all aspects of the Captain's duties. Author's interview with Mr M. B. Glasier, January 1972.

Profit of Elder Dempster Lines' Vessels per G.R.T., 1940–1964[1]

Year	Average G.R.T. of main line Ships	Net voyage profit after administrative costs & depreciation £	Average profit per G.R.T.
1940	194,232	600,250	3.01
1941	154,034	555,724	3.61
1942	111,572	235,085	2.11
1943	91,460	227,651	2.49
1944	98,251	199,850	2.03
1945	105,544	310,269	2.94
1946	105,544	1,369,911	12.98
1947	127,566	1,971,218	15.45
1948	162,607	2,296,362	14.12
1949	172,441	2,461,750	14.28
1950	172,925	1,657,398	9.58
1951	180,934	1,982,201	10.96
1952	201,247	2,732,397	13.58
1953	213,202	3,774,052	17.70
1954	210,088	2,761,533	13.15
1955	206,962	2,700,056	13.05
1956	208,403	3,033,306	14.55
1957	226,358	2,583,871	11.42
1958	219,488	2,145,368	9.77
1959	221,591	1,751,226	7.90
1960	230,783	1,615,645	7.00
1961	222,218	1,404,338	6.32
1962	229,782	735,660	3.20
1963	227,085	737,386	3.25
1964	263,225	776,473	2.95

while the fleet was requisitioned during the war, returns were unspectacular, if steady. The post-war shipping shortage, allied to the expansion of the West African trade, made the late forties and fifties a highly profitable era for the Company. The subsequent intensification of competition and a slowing in the pace of expansion then led to poorer, if satisfactory, results in the sixties—these being exacerbated in 1966 and 1967 by the effects of the disastrous seamen's strike and the fight with

[1] Compiled from figures kindly made available by Mr T. Kennan, Chief Accountant of Elder Dempster Lines Limited in January 1970. Similar details for the period 1933 to 1939 are given in Chapter 11, p. 278.

Note that all figures are subject to any limitations which may have been imposed under the Shipping Companies Exemption Order of 1948.

the Hoegh Line. Since then there has been some improvement, but this was considerably hampered by the dislocation engendered by the Nigerian Civil War and its aftermath.

During the period from 1932 to 1965, the Company has also received an income from its investments and, at times, this has provided a very substantial proportion of total earnings. Indeed, in 1965, investments supplied over 50 per cent of the balance for the year, while in both 1943 and 1944 receipts from this source were only a little less than net voyage profits. In general, however, reserves have been accumulated to build a hedge against various possible contingencies and, although interest and dividends have been welcomed, they have essentially been of secondary importance. On the occasions when very large sums have been invested in securities rather than ships, the potential earning of the fleet has been correspondingly reduced, but it will be appreciated that the achievement of smaller voyage-profits in these circumstances does not affect the net returns per gross ton, which remains a valid yardstick of efficiency.

Another test of Elder Dempster's efficiency is the extent to which it has been able, over the years, to maintain its position in the West African trade. There are a number of ways in which this can be calculated, but the most satisfactory indication of change is given by the shares allocated by successive conference agreements. These are particularly valuable in that they formalise and, perhaps, rationalise the often conflicting claims and abilities of each company at given points in time:

The details given below refer only to Elder Dempster's share of WALCON which does not, of course, cover the entire trade with the Coast and which, at times, has not included all cargoes from the British territories. Thus in the years up to 1939 the northbound and southbound shipments to or from the United Kingdom and Eire took no account of the freight controlled by either the United Africa Company or John Holt. Arrangements were then made between the three British companies, and these persisted after the war, but until 1950 the Merchant Lines were not officially recognised by conference agreements. The fall shown in Elder Dempster's proportion of this trade is, therefore, only a statistical quibble for, after 1950, it includes these two lines without indicating that they brought their own cargoes with them, i.e. Elder Dempster's smaller share was of a larger trade. Since that date

there has been a gradual decline in outward shares owing to the inclusion of other lines, but the homeward route has not been significantly
affected.

Elder Dempster's Shares in WALCON 1924–1967[1]

Year	U.K. & Eire to West Africa %	West Africa to U.K. & Eire %
1924	100.0	100.0
1929	100.0	100.0
1939	100.0	100.0
1944	100.0	100.0
1950	64.0[2]	43.2
1953	71.5[3]	49.5
1955	63.0	49.5
1957	63.0	49.5
1958	63.0	49.5
1959	63.0	49.5
1962	55.19	46.6
1963	54.53	45.8
1964	53.88	45.0
1965	53.23	44.2
1966	53.23	49.2
1967	47.84	49.2

Elder Dempster's share of the Continental–West African service has
also declined both outward and homeward but there are no adequate
statistics. There were no restrictions on carriage in the earlier period
although many informal conventions were observed. After 1955 the
lines engaged in the United Kingdom and Eire–West Africa service did
make an agreement restricting their share of return cargoes to the Continent, but it must be emphasised that their collective share was much
less than 50 per cent of the total, as it did not include shipments made by
other conference members. The Black Star Line and the Nigerian
National Shipping Line joined in this arrangement when they began
their sailings in 1958 and 1959 respectively, but the former withdrew
from the scheme in 1966.

The decline in Elder Dempster's share of WALCON cargoes has

[1] Based on statistics kindly supplied by Mr J. McCormick, former Secretary of WAL-
CON and currently (1972) Secretary of UKWAL. Note that these shares refer only to
Conference cargoes and not to the whole trade.
[2] This proportion was at 709,653 tons.　　[3] This proportion was at 1,250,000 tons.

the natural corollary that other lines have entered the trade, or have increased their share of it since the early days of the post-war era. The
situation in 1964 was as follows:

Shares in WALCON for 1964

	%		%
Elder Dempster	30.0	Woermann Line	18.6
Palm Line	15.1	Scandinavian W.A.L.	9.0
Guinea Gulf	2.0	Black Star Line	6.8
Holland W.A.L.	8.2	Nigerian N.L.	10.3

The details given above show that Elder Dempster's share had
fallen to approximately 30 per cent by 1964. This estimate is based on
the number of vessels operated in the trade,[1] but the use of chartered
vessels and the possibility that some proportion of company-owned
tonnage might sometimes be operated on other services means that it is
an unreliable guide.[2] Yet even if we accept the inadequacies of these
statistics—which tend to understate the Company's position, as its
vessels were somewhat larger than the average for the route—it is still
quite clear that its percentage of the trade had declined substantially
since 1948/9. At that time Elder Dempster's proportion based on similar
criteria, had been 57 per cent of the fleets serving WALCON territories,[3] but it would be unfair to regard the loss as a disaster—it was
inevitable and in some ways may be regarded as actually desirable from
the Company's point of view.

The growth of the Palm Line, for example, has reduced Elder
Dempster's nominal share of the trade, but it has also had many beneficial effects—the present friendly co-operation between the two lines is
far preferable to the bitterness of the twenties. The formation of the two
National Lines may also be considered in this light. Their emergence
must be accepted as a natural development which could hardly have
been resisted and the stability of the trade has benefited from their in-
corporation within the conference structure. The entry of a Dutch
company after the First World War and of two Scandinavian lines after

[1] See above, this Chapter, p. 362.
[2] Apart from the general criticisms of this type of evidence the Hoegh Line were not
members of WALCON at that particular time, although they continued to operate on the
West African routes as previously.
[3] C. Leubuscher, *The West African Shipping Trade, 1909-1959* (Leyden: A. W. Sythoff
1963), p. 99, Table 1. (Also, see above Chapter 13, pp. 327-8.)

the Second World War were made possible by the special conditions ruling at those times and not by any particular omissions on the part of Elder Dempster. This is not to suggest that the Company has made no mistakes in protecting what were its legitimate interests—rather that on balance it has been moderately successful in adapting its position and policies to changing circumstances. It was unlikely that the duopoly of the Alfred Jones era or the oligopoly of the inter-war period could be maintained indefinitely, and it is to the Company's credit that this was recognised so that fundamental changes could be made with relative ease. It should also be noted, however, that the assimilation of each new line has been at the expense of the entire trade, for all have felt obliged to follow Elder Dempster's policy,[1] and that the process of change has been greatly assisted by the continuing growth of cargoes, so that the smaller percentage has not always been reflected by the carriage of smaller annual tonnages. Thus Elder Dempster carried an average of 549,000 freight tons outward, and 567,000 freight tons inward during the years 1936 to 1938,[2] but this was exceeded by 11 per cent in 1951, 35 per cent in 1960 and 37 per cent in 1969.[3]

Although Elder Dempster Lines can justly claim to have consistently maintained a reasonable level of profitability, it might be argued that this has been as a consequence of excessive rates of freight rather than from any particular expertise or competence. This suggestion was, in fact, made before the United Nations Economic Commission for Africa in 1964 when delegates called for:

'stable and guaranteed agreement on the standardisation of freight rates at levels equitably fixed in comparison with similar rates prevailing in other parts of the world'.[4]

A 'Report on a Preliminary Survey of Factors contributing to levels of freight rates in the seaborne trade of Africa' was accordingly prepared for the E.C.A. by Mr S. F. Klinghofer and it was published in July 1965.[5]

---

[1] The division of WALCON into UKWAL and COWAC in January 1968 has further reduced Elder Dempster's shares of both the British and Continental routes. The reductions are quite small, however, and do not invalidate the points made above.

[2] See above, Chapter 13, p. 315.   [3] See Appendix, p. 466, Table 62.

[4] Resolution 101 (VI) adopted by the Economic Commission for Africa at its 112th Plenary Meeting on 29 February 1964.

[5] Reference 65/2281 (E/CN. 14/Trans/27), : July 1965.

The Report was critical of many aspects and details of the West African shipping trade, but commenting on the motion it stated:

'Should the above intentions be realised, the sub-regions freight rates would be revised upwards and trade would in most instances become adversely affected.'[1]

And its conclusion was that:

'From the findings of the Mission it would appear that as far as the West-African sub-region is concerned, some of the assertions contained in Resolution 101 (VI) are at variance with the actual state of affairs, i.e. the sub-region actually enjoys very reasonable maritime freight rates in its international trade for the bulk of goods exchanged.'[2]

It could also be argued that as much of West Africa's external communications is organised by shipping conferences in which Elder Dempster takes a leading part, any success in retaining its pre-eminent position is the result of some form of restrictive practice. This, however, is to miss the point that every conference concerned with West Africa is sufficiently flexible to accommodate new companies in accordance with the needs of trade, i.e. note the immediate membership obtained by the Black Star Line and the Nigerian National Shipping Line. Furthermore, although freight rates are agreed there is still considerable competition within the conference structure as companies endeavour to win new customers by the excellence of their service or their special care of particular sorts of cargoes. Finally it must be borne in mind that the West African trade does not operate in isolation from other world trades, and that any attempt to raise freight rates must be justified or it would inevitably bring in tonnage from other regions.

A last point to consider when attempting to assess Elder Dempster's economic efficiency is the rate of return it obtains on the capital employed in its business. The table on page 374 shows how the employed capital has risen from under £3 million in 1933 to over £43 million in 1965, and these figures are then used to form the basis of the table on page 375.

The net profits indicated above show a distinct correlation with the average net profits per gross ton discussed earlier.[3] Both reflect the same trends in the level of international trade, although there are a number of differences in the form of leads and lags. The tables also demonstrate quite forcibly the conservative financial policy carried out

[1] S. F. Klinghofer, op. cit., p. 7, para. 25.   [2] Ibid., p. 94, para. 390.
[3] See above, Chapter 11, p. 278, and this chapter, p. 368.

Liner Holdings Group of Companies[1]
Capital Employed

Year end 31–12	Authorised capital	Issued capital	Reserves & retained profit	Total
1933	2,500,000	2,500,000	386,579	2,886,579
1934	2,500,000	2,500,000	254,704	2,754,704
1935	2,500,000	2,500,000	364,528	2,864,528
1936	2,500,000	2,500,000	460,359	2,960,359
1937	3,000,000	2,214,111	1,794,950	4,009,061
1938	3,000,000	2,555,798	1,559,260	4,115,058
1939	3,000,000	2,748,596	1,277,455	4,026,051
1940	3,000,000	2,748,596	2,374,282	5,122,878
1941	3,000,000	2,748,596	3,626,090	6,374,686
1942	3,000,000	2,748,596	4,409,321	7,157,917
1943	3,000,000	2,748,596	4,616,915	7,365,511
1944	3,000,000	2,748,596	4,438,856	7,187,452
1945	3,000,000	2,748,596	4,457,056	7,205,652
1946	3,000,000	2,748,596	4,258,322	8,006,918
1947	3,000,000	2,748,596	6,417,751	9,166,347
1948	3,000,000	2,748,596	8,185,857	10,934,453
1949	3,000,000	2,748,596	9,724,350	12,472,946
1950	3,000,000	2,748,596	10,749,184	13,497,780
1951	3,000,000	2,748,596	11,821,907	14,570,503
1952	4,000,000	3,435,745	13,113,940	16,549,685
1953	7,000,000	6,871,490	12,083,998	18,955,488
1954	7,000,000	6,871,490	14,115,901	20,987,391
1955	7,000,000	6,871,490	16,275,048	23,146,538
1956	7,000,000	6,871,490	19,018,503	25,889,993
1957	7,000,000	6,871,490	22,178,128	29,049,618
1958	7,000,000	6,871,490	24,787,693	31,659,183
1959	7,000,000	6,871,490	28,097,193	34,968,683
1960	7,000,000	6,871,490	31,058,300	37,929,790
1961	7,000,000	6,871,490	33,402,825	40,274,315
1962	7,000,000	6,871,490	34,829,036	41,700,526
1963	7,000,000	6,871,490	34,956,152	41,827,642
1964	7,000,000	6,871,490	35,474,682	42,346,172
1965	7,000,000	6,871,490	36,391,232	43,262,722

[1] The 'Liner Holdings Group' for this purpose includes Elder Dempster Lines and West African Lighterage and Transport until 1936; Elder Dempster Lines Holdings, Elder Dempster Lines and West African Lighterage and Transport from 1936 to 1945; plus Elder Dempster (Canada) Ltd from 1946 to 1952. After that date the employed capital is based on Elder Dempster Lines Holdings Consolidated Accounts (for 1952) and thereafter on Liner Holdings Consolidated Accounts.

RECENT DEVELOPMENTS

| | | Liner Holdings Group of Companies[1] Return on Capital | | | Net profit as % of capital employed | |
Year	Capital employed 1st Jan.	Net Profit	Plough-back	Dividend[2]	Plough-back	Dividend
1933		85,308	55,308			
1934	2,886,579	109,050	50,925	58,125	1.76	2.01
1935	2,754,704	203,461	106,586	96,875	3.87	3.52
1936	2,864,528	199,288	84,913	114,375	3.00	3.99
1937	2,960,359	412,954	294,741	118,213	10.00	3.99
1938	4,009,061	289,006	112,061	176,945	2.80	4.41
1939	4,115,058	234,452	60,186	174,266	1.51	4.33
1940	4,026,051	251,916	108,670	143,246	2.70	3.56
1941	5,122,878	255,861	122,628	133,233	2.39	3.60
1942	6,374,686	186,249	59,308	126,941	.93	1.99
1943	7,157,917	175,881	52,915	123,686	.74	1.73
1944	7,365,511	211,388	87,702	123,686	1.19	1.68
1945	7,187,452	241,889	118,202	123,687	1.64	1.73
1946	7,205,652	703,766	514,800	188,966	7.14	2.62
1947	8,006,918	1,537,355	1,348,389	188,966	16.84	2.36
1948	9,166,347	1,674,818	1,485,852	188,966	16.21	2.06
1949	10,934,453	1,479,900	1,281,934	188,966	11.72	1.73
1950	12,472,946	1,137,459	910,700	226,759	7.30	1.82
1951	13,497,780	1,352,961	1,136,509	216,452	8.42	1.60
1952	14,570,503	2,007,007	1,736,442	270,565	11.92	1.86
1953	16,549,685	2,110,415	1,770,276	340,139	10.70	2.06
1954	18,955,488	1,904,719	1,564,580	340,139	8.25	1.79
1955	20,987,391	2,177,281	1,742,659	434,622	8.30	2.07
1956	23,146,538	2,452,660	1,939,016	513,644	8.38	2.22
1957	25,889,993	2,569,029	2,055,385	513,644	7.94	1.98
1958	29,049,618	2,051,139	1,537,495	513,644	5.29	1.77
1959	31,659,183	1,995,991	1,448,849	547,142	4.58	1.73
1960	34,968,683	2,472,500	1,925,358	547,142	5.51	1.56
1961	37,929,790	2,517,165	1,970,023	547,142	5.19	1.44
1962	40,274,315	1,638,889	1,091,745	547,142	2.71	1.36
1963	41,700,526	1,238,658	691,516	547,142	1.66	1.31
1964	41,827,642	1,305,591	772,192	533,399	1.85	1.28
1965	42,346,172	1,231,005	988,785	242,220	2.34	.57

[1] Compiled on the same basis as the previous table.
[2] Dividend before 1965 is net.

by the board of directors. Dividends only averaged about 27 per cent of net profit between 1934 and 1965, so the balance of 73 per cent was available to be ploughed back. To a large extent this policy enabled the expansion of Elder Dempster Lines to be undertaken without recourse to the market but, of course, it meant a reduction in the amount available for distribution to the shareholders. Consequently the amount they received in dividends would appear to be little more than the yield they would have obtained if they had invested in Consols.[1] On the other hand it should be appreciated that the profits retained by the company enhance what is, after all, the shareholders' property and provide a broader base for future, potentially larger, dividends. In the meantime the shareholder may be compensated, to some extent, for the loss of income by the advance in the value of his shares.

In any case it is not possible to compare accurately an investment in British Government Securities with one in a private concern, because of the risk element which is a necessary part of a commercial venture. For this reason it is better to contrast Elder Dempster's results with those of similar firms; the inclusion of the running yield on Consols in the table below may, however, be thought valuable as it gives a rough yardstick of the risk free returns available at the time:

The figures above indicate that during the sixties the shipping industry has been relatively unprofitable when compared with the average

Comparison of Returns on Employed Capital[2]
(Profits are gross, before taxation and interest charges,
but after depreciation)

Year	Times 300 Companies	Shipping Co's including Ocean	Ocean	Elder Dempster Lines	2½% Consols
1963	11.5	1.5	6.4	5.0	5.58
1964	13.5	2.7	7.6	4.5	6.03
1965	13.0	3.0	6.5	4.6	6.42

[1] It is not easy to be definite on this type of comparison. The correct procedure is to compute the rate of return obtained on an investment in a given year, the return being derived from annual or semi-annual dividends plus what is realised from the eventual sale of the investment. This rate of return may then be compared with an investment, starting and ending in the same years in Consols or Equity Shares in general. Strictly speaking, however, the figure for Consols is a yield against the market price. The figures for the return on employed capital do not take account of differences between the book value of the shares (plus retained profits) and their market price.

[2] Based on The Times 300 and the Ocean Steam Ship Company Limited's Annual Report and Accounts for 1969. The Elder Dempster statistics, both here and in the two preceding tables, were provided by the Company's Accounts Department.

performance of three hundred of the largest industrial firms in the United Kingdom. Ocean and Elder Dempster, however, have been much more successful than the average shipping company, so should be well placed to take advantage of any increase in world trade or improvement in freight rates if and when they occur. Nevertheless, the table makes it clear that shipping is not an industry where profits are easily made, so it is against this background that a final assessment of Elder Dempster Lines financial results should be reached.

In the period between 1934 and 1965 the Company's average net profit per year represented a return of 7.98 per cent on the capital employed.[1] This was after the customary depreciation of 5 per cent per annum on the fleet[2] and the fullest possible provision for the maintenance and replacement of all the Company's assets. By the standards of domestic industry this may not be a high figure but in the world of shipping it indicates a very solid achievement. The very high level of plough-back demonstrates, far more eloquently than words, the long-term view which Elder Dempster took of its association with West Africa. Equally, the smallness of its dividends—an annual average of only 2.21 per cent of the employed capital—shows that claims of possible exploitation on behalf of the shareholders are far from the truth. At the same time it may be considered that Company policy has not always been as flexible as might have been desired. The decline in Elder Dempster's share of the West African trade may be excused on the grounds that it is a smaller percentage of a larger business, while the legitimate aspirations of African nations to operate their own vessels had obviously to be taken into account. Nevertheless, it is clear that the Company has neglected many of the opportunities that have been available in the growing oil, ore and timber trades. The concentration

[1] Note the range of returns shown on p. 375 indicates periods of very high and very low profits so the average return given here may not provide a satisfactory picture of the Company's performance.

[2] It will be seen that Ocean's return on employed capital is slightly higher than Elder Dempster's. This is partly explained by the fact that the former depreciates its ships over a longer period, i.e. 24 years instead of 20 years. The two companies have also had a different approach to marine insurance which may have influenced these figures. Elder Dempster's traditional policy has been to lay off most of its insurance on to the market whereas Ocean usually carried all of the risk itself. In recent years both have modified these policies so that Elder Dempster has carried an increasing proportion of any loss and Ocean has resorted to the market to obtain cover for the extremely expensive specialised vessels it is currently operating.

on traditional routes, cargoes and methods resulted in a high level of efficiency, and satisfactory financial returns were obtained throughout the fifties. This very success may then have induced an over-cautious approach to new ideas and change and the consequent failure to diversify early enough, on a sufficiently large scale, suggests that avoidable mistakes were occasionally made.

Chapter 15

The Future

Difficulties Ahead in the Seventies

The long history of Elder Dempster and its predecessors since 1852 has shown its remarkable capacity for survival during periods of great difficulty. The years following the Second World War—like those round the beginning of the century—were extremely profitable for the Company, but by the early sixties many problems were again causing much concern. Various forms of remedial action were then adopted and gave some measure of relief, but there is little doubt that the seventies will provide a serious challenge to further progress and viability. The pattern which these strains will take is already largely apparent, for there is the likelihood of further changes in both the organisation of trade and in the West African countries themselves.

Some cargoes are now subject to regulation by the exporting state, but this has not lessened Elder Dempster's traditional preoccupation with the need to maintain friendly relations with the merchant body. The establishment of the West African Merchants Freight Association in 1930 ensured that its members received adequate notice of any changes in freight rates, and that they paid no more for their carriage than other shippers. In return each merchant undertook to remain loyal to WALCON.[1] The Association provided a useful forum for discussion, but it is doubtful if it was able to exert very much influence on events in the thirties, as it did not include either the United Africa Company or John Holt. These two firms did join in 1950, at the same time as their shipping departments were reorganised as the Palm Line

[1] WAMFA & WALCON agreements dated 14 March 1931 and 23 December 1935. (See also above, Chapter 10, pp. 250-1.)

and the John Holt Shipping Line, and became members of WALCON.[1] The dual interests of the U.A.C. and Holts make it unlikely that their presence was a source of strength to the Association, and they may have been the main cause of its dissolution in 1959.

A new body to replace the Merchants Freight Association was formed in 1959. This was the West African Shippers Association, and as it included manufacturing interests it seems to have been more appropriate than the former group to the changing circumstances of the trade. The new Association aimed at attracting all companies who were concerned, '. . . with the movement and handling of cargo and passengers to or from West Africa by sea or air . . .' and it quickly built up to a membership of ninety. Early enthusiasm was, however, not maintained—partly owing to an internal dispute over the proposed introduction by the lines of an immediate rebate system—and this caused support to dwindle to only forty firms. The division of WALCON at the beginning of 1968 then revitalised WASA for it was recognised by UKWAL almost at once, and by COWAC a little later. By January 1970, when five important firms rejoined, the Association may be said to have achieved its aim and was representing a substantial proportion of the British shippers to West Africa.[2] A number of formal and informal meetings are now held between WASA and the conference lines each year, and all parties seem to be reasonably satisfied with the present arrangements for consultation and discussion.[3]

Of equal importance are the Company's relationships with the West African marketing boards, for these are responsible for the sale and export of a very large part of the region's produce and so are the source of considerable northbound cargoes.[4] The special relationship[5] established in the early post-war years when Elder Dempster controlled a large proportion of available tonnage has now been replaced by new commercial arrangements. The watershed in this respect came in the

[1] WAMFA & WALCON agreements dated 6 August 1952. (See also above, Chapter 13, pp. 330-1.)

[2] Note the existence of the 'Holland Branch' of WASA and of the current attempts to enlarge this to form a European Association which will include France and Germany.

[3] Author's interviews with Mr J. D. Robertson, Director of Elder Dempster Lines and Mr D. J. T. Owen, Secretary of WASA May 1970.

[4] The ending of crushing in the U.K. has lessened the importance of these cargoes to the shipping companies as the volume is less. This does not apply to the Continental routes where the trade remains largely unaltered.

[5] See above, Chapter 13, pp. 324-5.

1964–5 season when a dispute arose over the freight rate for oilseeds.[1] The Nigerian Produce Marketing Board then announced a public tender for the carriage of the entire crop and was able to obtain a rate of U.S. $11.30 per long ton, i.e. U.S. $0.79 less than the previous conference figure.[2]

Nevertheless, the tender cannot be regarded as a success. Bids only covered 50 per cent of the anticipated tonnage and eventually WALCON carried most of the balance. Of more importance, however, were the contract terms on which the produce was moved. Whereas the Conference normally carried any quantity from and to any port in its range, these tenders were based on full cargoes between a strictly limited number of loading and discharging harbours.[3] The inconvenience of these arrangements is obvious and more than offsets any slight reduction in the rate of freight. Consequently, when a second attempt at tendering proved to be no more successful than the first, the Board did not repeat its experiment. Since that time the Nigerian Produce Marketing Board has given most of its exports to the Nigerian National Shipping Line. This Company does not have the capacity to lift this quantity of cargo, so divides it amongst the other lines engaged in the trade. Elder Dempster's allocation is accordingly now based on its ability to provide a service which is at least as good as its competitors, and there can be no complaint if it fails to hold its share of northbound cargoes as a result of inefficiency or a lack of suitable tonnage. On the other hand, it must be hoped that the assignment of produce continues to be made on a commercial basis and that decisions are not unduly influenced by pressures from governments or state agencies.

The seventies will see a very natural desire on the part of the West African nations to see an ever-increasing volume of their trade carried in vessels owned and operated by themselves. From a political viewpoint it may be considered essential that the share of the national lines should continue to grow, but this is open to question on purely economic grounds. The importance of making the best possible use of scarce resources at least makes arguable the wisdom of diverting large

[1] An account of this from the Nigerian Produce Marketing Company's viewpoint was given in a Press Announcement published in the *Nigerian Daily Express,* 8 February 1964.

[2] S. F. Klinghofer, 'A Report on a Preliminary Survey of Factors, contributing to level of freight rates in the Seaborne Trade of Africa' (New York: U.N. Economic Commission for Africa, 1965), p. 12, para. 43.

[3] Ibid.

amounts of capital to the expansion of shipping services when these are already being efficiently provided. This is especially true in the case of an under-developed country where many additional worthwhile investments that are vital to the nation's economic growth can easily be discerned. This is, clearly, the present situation in West Africa, where the development of roads, railways and port facilities still lag behind the growth of trade.

It will be appreciated that a national fleet has a definite value, both as a measurement of real costs and as a means of influencing the key decisions of a conference. Beyond a certain size of fleet, however, these factors tend to lose some of their force and there is no evidence to suggest that either the Black Star Line or the Nigerian National Shipping Line needs to be increased on these grounds. It may, nevertheless, be felt necessary in some circumstances to gain a larger share of a carrying trade as a means of protecting an economy from either existing or potential abuse. In the West African case, Klinghofer has shown that current arrangements and levels of freight rates were quite satisfactory to the shippers[1] and additional protection is, of course, always available because of the organisation of a high proportion of northbound produce by the state controlled marketing boards.

The Black Star Line now (1972) owns sixteen ships totalling 81,974 gross tons and the Nigerian National Shipping Line has twelve vessels amounting to 81,943 gross tons. It has been possible to accept and assimilate these large fleets in the relatively short period since 1958 because there has been a simultaneous and corresponding growth in trade and because time-expired vessels in other conference lines fleets have not been replaced. The pace of trade expansion has now slowed,[2] so any further increases in overall tonnage should be related to the total demand for shipping capacity, or freight rates will be forced down to unremunerative levels. If this has the effect of penalising the least efficient companies and vessels through the normal competitive process, none can complain, but if the market is distorted by commercially non-economic factors, it is likely that in the long term the real cost of West Africa's shipping services will be higher, not lower, than at present.

Arguments of this nature apply equally to competition from Eastern European countries. This began in 1958 when the Polish Ocean Lines

[1] See above, Chapter 14, pp. 372–3.
[2] The trade of Nigeria resumed its upward trend during 1972.

established a West African service.[1] In 1961 this was followed by the Rostock-based Deutsche Seereederei and almost at once these two lines started joint operations under the name of Uni-Africa. The name has now been changed to United West African Services and includes the Estonian Shipping Company. Their main route is from Poland and East Germany to Guinea, Ghana and Nigeria, but this is supplemented by calls at Continental ports according to demand. Originally their main southbound cargo was cement, but a steadily increasing proportion of general goods is now carried. On the northbound route timber, cocoa and ground-nuts, together with ores and concentrates, were their main cargoes but they now carry a much wider range of commodities both to the North Continent and to the Baltic ports.

In the past decade a developing if still somewhat distant relationship has gradually evolved between the East European lines and the other firms operating to the Coast although UWAS freight charges have been deliberately kept somewhat below the conference rates. But what of the future? The principal motivations of UWAS are the desire to earn hard currency; the political importance of maintaining close links with the under-developed countries of Africa; and the need to employ the large number of ships being constructed in Eastern Europe. In these circumstances it is clear that commercial considerations could take second place to non-economic factors at any time. In this event the long-run stability of the present system might be sacrificed in order to benefit from some transitory short-term reduction in rates. This would, of course, affect the National lines equally with the other members of the Conference and the ensuing reaction would lead to endless recriminations and disruption. On the other hand it is quite possible that the existing contacts between the two sides may lead to some form of closer co-operation and this would be mutually beneficial in helping to solve the problems which are currently affecting liner shipping throughout the world.

Possible Solutions
Elder Dempster took a leading part in the re-establishment of the shipping conference in 1924[2] and have continued to give it their complete

[1] D. Tresselt, 'The West African Shipping Range' (Geneva: U.N. Conference on Trade and Development, 1967), pp. 45–51, paras. 312–329.

[2] See above, Chapter 9, pp. 217–21.

support. The original motivation was to regulate the trade at a time when too many ships were chasing too little cargo, but in the post-war era, up to the early sixties, the reverse was true and WALCON was under extreme pressure to meet all its obligations. Since then, however, supply and demand have been more evenly balanced, but there have, inevitably, been periods of glut and scarcity of both tonnage and cargoes. In each of these situations the conference has had an important role to play. At times of excess capacity, rates have not been forced down to unremunerative levels which could not be maintained and vessels have been chartered, sometimes at a loss, when shipping has been in short supply, in order to ensure that all cargoes have been cleared without undue delay.

Thus it may be argued that the conference system is of benefit to all who are genuinely interested in the long-term well-being of the trade. The advantages to an individual shipping company are obvious: rates fluctuate less and tend to be marginally higher at times than they would be with wholly unregulated competition. The shippers also dislike constant changes in rates and would welcome the stability and regularity of service guaranteed by the conference, even if it meant that freight charges were fractionally more. In fact, the pooling of shipping capacity and the consolidation of cargoes encouraged by a shipping conference should provide a number of positive savings which could mean that the real cost of carriage is considerably reduced. It is possible, therefore, for the shipowner to set slightly lower rates for his service than would otherwise have been the case, and still get a better return on his capital. It may well be that the optimal size of fleet required for the West African trade is relatively small and that most economies of scale are achieved at an early stage, but the maintenance of high load factors—the really crucial point—necessitates at least some degree of regulation. The gradual development of an optimal liner circuit with joint services, joint loading brokers and, to some extent, joint agencies must imply that the technical organisation is geared towards providing a high level of efficiency. Klinghofer suggests that this is reflected in the moderate freight rates that are charged in comparison with other routes. But the present system is by no means perfect and if Elder Dempster are to retain a substantial share of their traditional trade they must try to ensure that co-operation within the conference is further increased and the economic advantages stemming therefrom are fully utilised.

PLATE 23   The route taken by aircraft flying from Europe to Nigeria
before World War II.

The beginning of work at Kano airfield in 1935.

PLATE 24

The arrival of the first mail at Kano airfield, February, 1936.
The E.D. Agent, A. C. Wyness, is in the centre.

THE FUTURE

The character of WALCON and its successors, UKWAL and COWAC, has changed considerably since the inter-war period. Instead of being primarily concerned with relationships with individual firms of merchants it now acts as the main negotiating body for the member-lines with the produce marketing boards and the associations of various trades and shippers. In turn, since the end of the Second World War there has been a significant alteration in the method of operation. The deferred rebate system was re-introduced for southbound shipments in 1947—5 per cent of the freight rate being returned after a six months' period, plus a further six months' wait, to shippers who remained loyal to the conference. In 1958 this rebate was increased to $7\frac{1}{2}$ per cent and continues at the same level at the present time. The significant change, however, came in 1968 when an alternative to the deferred rebate was offered to all southbound shippers. This was the immediate rebate contract which gave a $7\frac{1}{2}$ per cent discount when freight was paid if the shipper contracted to send all his future cargo to the coast via conference vessels. The contract which had to be signed was for an indefinite period, but it could be terminated by the giving of six months' notice. For various reasons, many of the merchants preferred to continue using the deferred rebate system, but recently there has been a gradual wing to contractual agreements, and these now cover about three-quarters of the southbound trade, if we exclude the special arrangements which are usually made when large projects are under construction.[1]

The situation on the northbound route was rather different because of the presence of the produce marketing boards. As previously noted,[2] these were responsible for a large proportion of West African exports, and as they negotiated their rates directly with the conference there was less need for a rebate system in the trade generally. Nevertheless, one was announced for timber in 1952, but this was quickly cancelled and only came into force after further discussions in 1958. The northbound deferred rebate system was subsequently extended to cover most types of produce in 1960, but it is unlikely that this has made any difference to the net rates paid by the statutory authorities.[3] Special contract rates

[1] COWAC shippers have been slower to use immediate rebate contracts, but the new system is gradually gaining ground in the Continental trades.

[2] See above, Chapter 13, pp. 322–3.

[3] Cocoa, Coffee, Cotton, Ginger, Oilseeds, Groundnut Oil, Palm Oil and Palm Kernel Oil were subject to a $7\frac{1}{2}$ per cent rebate in 1960: this was raised to 10 per cent in

are also available to a limited number of firms—mainly 'crushers'—but the immediate rebate contract system is not used in the northbound trade.

A final factor which must be taken into account when considering Elder Dempster's place in the West African trade of the future is concerned with the physical aspect of carrying cargo. During the past ten years there have been two distinct tendencies in world shipping. On the deep-sea routes many economies of scale have been secured by the building of larger and larger units. Unfortunately, the limitations of West African ports and, to some extent, the character of the general trade has prevented and will continue to prevent the use of very big ships on the coast. There has also been a fresh approach to the whole concept of seaborne carriage, which has concentrated its attention on the weakness of the present system—the length of the unproductive time spent in port.

Thus containerisation and palletisation have been introduced on many services in order to increase the rate of loading and discharging— there are other benefits—because of an appreciation that time equals money. Any increase in the unit size of cargo is helpful in this respect, but the expense involved can only be justified either if the cargo is suitable, physically and financially, or if the cost of handling in the traditional break-bulk form is escalating rapidly. It is the latter consideration which is paramount today, but the full benefit of containerisation can only be obtained when there are opportunities for substantial savings at both ends of the sea-link. In the United Kingdom these could be achieved by a reduction in the transport and handling costs charged for moving cargo from inland areas, but there is not so much scope for economies of this type in West Africa at the present time since the ultimate destination of most goods lies close to the port of entry. This pattern, however, is likely to change in the future, so containerisation will become more attractive from that point of view. On the other hand, the continuing growth of southbound cargoes has led to a change in the inbalance of the liner trade. Southbound tonnages, which lend themselves to containerisation, are now greater than northbound tonnages which, generally speaking, do not. In these circumstances it is inevitable that a high, perhaps increasing, proportion of empty containers will have to be returned to Europe—a prospect

1962. Rubber was granted a $12\frac{1}{2}$ per cent and Timber, a 10 per cent plus 10 per cent rebate at this time.

which cannot be expected to enhance the economic efficiency of the system.

In these circumstances it is not surprising that containerisation is only now beginning to make progress and today forms only a small—though increasing—part of the total trade. It could be fairly argued, however, that this, in part, is a reflection of the limitations imposed on the present system operated by African Container Express Limited by the use of ordinary cargo liners—not the purpose-built vessels which would be essential for a fully integrated service. The capital requirement is greatly reduced but so is the efficiency, so it would be fair to comment that the sophisticated container concept has not yet been adequately tested for the West African trade. On the other hand, the vessels presently in the trade are susceptible to palletisation, which has already proved itself to be of value, and the proportion of cargo dealt with by this method continues to grow each year. The pallets are relatively cheap to make and can either be disposable or can be continually returned as they take up little space.[1] Consequently palletisation has been introduced at a relatively small cost, and the saving in time when loading and discharging has resulted in economies for both the shipper and the shipowner.[2]

It seems probable, therefore, that the future will see a further development of palletisation schemes, but there is a limit to their application, and other alternatives must also be carefully investigated. One distinct possibility is that, in spite of the problems outlined above, constant consideration will be given to the introduction of a comprehensive container system as and when it is felt to be justified by the evolution of the trade. In view of the relative smallness of the cargoes passing through most West African ports it seems inevitable that any such system would have to be based on Nigeria which provides 70 per cent of the total trade. In this event the most likely development would be the extension of the existing facilities at Apapa, perhaps by the construction of a suitably equipped container berth.

Another possible solution would be for each ship to be self-contained so that it could load and unload its containers with its own gear. Yet another possibility which warrants consideration is the adoption of a

[1] The use of returnable pallets has now come to an end in the West African trade.
[2] See above, Chapter 14, p. 346.

'lighter aboard ship' (LASH) system. This could provide a satisfactory answer to many of the current difficulties in West African ports, but the system is very expensive and is yet to be proved. A third course of action is for some type of 'roll-on roll-off' technique to be adapted to West African conditions, but although one version of this system is currently working well for motor vehicles[1] it appears to be unlikely that it can be extended to satisfy all requirements at a viable cost.

Nevertheless, it remains true that the growth of port facilities in West Africa has barely kept pace with the development of trade. It is essential, therefore, that Elder Dempster continue to watch the technical innovations discussed above in order to be able to make and implement a quick decision when the time is ripe. It is also important that the Company keeps itself well informed on the progress being made in new technical matters and in such projects as the possible development of an overland route to West Africa. Elder Dempster's current policy appears to be the correct one in that it is keeping open the whole range of the options available to it. The importance of this will, perhaps, be better appreciated after an examination of the forecasts made for the future increase of the trade of West Africa.

Forecasts of Future Growth in West African Trade

Klinghofer, writing in 1964, anticipated that ore exports would have increased 250 per cent by 1974 and that the 'over-all shipping tonnage of the (West African) sub-region might thus be expected to more than double within ten years.'[2] Tresselt's projection, compiled two years later, gives a sound analysis of future expansion.[3] His estimate of 'Exports of Liner and Tramp Cargoes from West African to Northern Europe in 1965 and Forecast for 1980' shows that the 6,300,000 metric tons of 1965 will have risen to 12,910,000 metric tons by 1980 i.e. an annual average growth of 5 per cent.[4] Complementary to this table is

[1] See above, Chapter 14, p. 360.

[2] S. F. Klinghofer, op. cit., paras. 188 and 290.

[3] This does not imply that all his conclusions should be uncritically accepted. Some authorities feel that both Klinghofer and Tresselt over estimate the growth of the liner and bulk trades.

[4] D. Tresselt, op. cit., Table 4, p. 13. Original source of this information is O. E. C. D. Commodity Trade Imports, Series C, January-December 1965. It covers the E.E.C. countries (excluding Italy) and E.F.T.A. countries (excluding Portugal) plus Ireland. The total annual average growth does not include items for which no 1980 estimate is given.

his 'Exports of Typical Bulk Cargoes from West Africa to Northern Europe in 1965 and Forecast for 1980' and this suggests that the 32,626,000 metric tons of 1965 will have grown to 263,286,000 metric tons by 1980, i.e. an annual average increase of 15.2 per cent.[1]

Tresselt's estimates show that the composition of West African exports will change substantially in some respects during the next decade. In 1965 timber was the largest single item in the liner trades and as it will grow at a rapid rate it will easily retain this position. Oilseeds, nuts and kernels, although increasing at a relatively slow pace, may maintain their second place and cocoa, although only progressing at a modest pace, will continue to be third in importance. A major growth-point will be in aluminium, for Tresselt anticipates that exports of this metal will increase by 21.5 per cent per year and by 1980 he believes that it will have risen from the fourteenth to the fourth position by weight. The export of unwrought copper and zinc will also expand at a substantial rate, while bananas and coffee will continue to make steady progress.

In the bulk trades, a number of major changes will also occur. The most important item by weight in 1965 was iron ore. This will grow at a rapid pace, but nevertheless petroleum will occupy first place before 1980. The export of manganese, alumina, bauxite, zinc and lead ores will continue to rise throughout this period, but tin will increase only slowly, and natural phosphates, though likely to show some expansion, will not maintain their current position in third place.

A more recent analysis of the future growth of Nigerian trade is given in the NEDECO Report.[2] This uses a number of consultants' reports,[3] some of which may not have been officially accepted by the Nigerian Government, in order to estimate probable tonnages for imports and exports in 1980 and 1990. Agricultural exports are expected to rise from the 1,852,000 tons of 1965 to 2,471,000 tons in 1980 and to 3,640,000 tons in 1990.[4] Non-agricultural exports (excluding mineral oil) are similarly expected to increase from the 472,000 tons of 1965 to

[1] Ibid., Table 6, p. 17. Original source of this information is O.E.C.D. Commodity Trade Imports, Series C. January-December 1965. It covers the E.E.C. countries (excluding Italy) and E.F.T.A. countries (excluding Portugal) plus Ireland. The total annual average growth does not include natural phosphates.

[2] Netherlands Engineering Consultants, *Development of the Ports of Nigeria*, 1970–1990, 3 Vols. (The Hague, 1970).

[3] Ibid., Vol. II, II/14–15.   [4] Ibid., Vol. II, Table II. 18.

708,000 tons in 1980 and to 979,000 tons in 1990.[1] Totalled together and using 1965 as a base year these figures indicate a growth of 2.5 per cent per annum up to 1980 and 6.2 per cent from 1980 to 1990. The analysis of imports is complicated by such items as the proposed iron and steel complex and by the extent to which Nigeria will become self-sufficient in petroleum products with the development of local refining capacity based on Nigerian crude oil. After making suitable allowances for these factors, the NEDECO Report comes to the conclusion that non-oil imports, which grow at a rate of 3.5 per cent from 1956 to 1965, will expand at 3.8 per cent from 1965 to 1980 and at 4.8 per cent from 1980 to 1990.[2]

Apart from changes in the composition of the liner and bulk trades,[3] it is also necessary to consider any variations in their direction. Until after the Second World War traditional services persisted and the vast majority of West African imports and exports originated or terminated in the United Kingdom or on the continent of Europe. In 1963 trade was still following these previous lines, but new trends were developing and the pattern was becoming more and more diffused.[4] Klinghofer thinks that this process will continue and that Eastern Europe, North America and perhaps Japan will increase their share of the market.[5] In spite of this, however, he feels that the United Kingdom and Europe will remain West Africa's largest trading partner. Tresselt agrees with these views, but stresses the point—also made by Klinghofer—that within the general framework there will be a move away from British, Irish and French Atlantic ports to other Continental harbours.[6] Britain's entry into the European Economic Community in 1973 may well reinforce this movement.

Conclusions

What then are the prospects for Elder Dempster in the future? According to Tresselt there is an average annual growth of 5 per cent to be

---

[1] Ibid., Vol. II, Table II. 19.   [2] Ibid., Vol. II, Table II. 22.

[3] The forecasts given above provide the best data currently available in respect of the future of West African trade. Consequently they are an essential part of any serious attempt at forward planning but their limitations are such that they should not be regarded as precise indicators. Nevertheless certain clearly discernible trends are apparent and it is these, rather than the actual statistics, that should be noted.

[4] See above, Chapter 14, p. 362.   [5] S. F. Klinghofer, op. cit., para. 291.

[6] D. Tresselt, op. cit., para. 172.

expected in West African liner-trade products.[1] It should, therefore, be
a simple matter for the Company to maintain the actual tonnages it is
carrying at the moment. But is this enough? The African carriers
certainly anticipate that their share of the trade will increase with the
passage of time. This is a legitimate ambition but it is not necessarily
incompatible with Elder Dempster's own desire to continue to maintain a substantial position on its traditional routes. With a rising level of
activity it should be quite possible for the Company to increase the size
of its shipments even though its percentage share of the liner trade
gradually declines.

The projections for the future show that there are significant differences in each commodity's rate of growth. Hence it is desirable for
particular attention to be given to items such as aluminium, zinc and
timber which are expanding at above the average rate. This added pre-
caution must be taken if Elder Dempster is to be able to deal with the
intensification of normal competition, the aspirations of the national
lines, and the possible further development of Eastern European and
Japanese interests.

Apart from the Company's defence of its share of liner cargoes there
is also the question of its entry into the West African bulk trades. As
noted above, it is anticipated that these will increase at an average
annual rate of over 15 per cent,[2] i.e. three times as quickly as in the
liner trades. In the past, developments of this type have been largely
ignored by Elder Dempster—perhaps for reasons which appeared to be
adequate at the time—but this ought not to mean that similar opportunities need to be missed in the future. The enormous growth of the
Nigerian petroleum industry is a case in point. Following the war-time
setback, production has increased rapidly. Thus only 500,000 barrels per
day were produced in January 1970, but by January 1973 output had
reached 1.9 million barrels a day. It is not anticipated that this rate of
progress can be maintained in the future but the massive investment
plans of the international oil companies (Shell/B.P. alone spent
£ N65 million in 1971) and of the Nigerian National Oil Corporation,
are certain to ensure a continued expansion of the industry and of its
ancillary services.[3]

Another example of tremendous growth is that of iron ore, for it is

[1] See above, this Chapter, p. 388.   [2] See above, this Chapter, p. 389.
[3] Standard Bank, *Annual Economic Review, Nigeria* (June 1972), pp. 9–10.

calculated that exports will rise from the eighteen million metric tons of 1965 to eighty-nine million metric tons in 1980. The production of alumina and bauxite, and of zinc, lead and manganese ores will also increase at what would previously have been considered to be incredible rates. Taken collectively, these developments provide a challenge to Elder Dempster which warrants, at the very least, an exhaustive and continuous investigation. An examination of the bulk trade in timber might prove to be particularly fruitful.

The prospects for passenger traffic are not so encouraging. Competition from air transport has so reduced demand since 1945 that a single vessel can now cope with the entire business at most times of the year.[1] This situation is not unique to West African services, for practically all international routes have suffered from the same problem. Even in the passenger field, however, the future is not entirely gloomy. Recent experience has raised hopes that the passenger liner may yet have a viable part to play in transportation and there is some evidence to indicate that the number of people wishing to travel one way by sea may be gradually increasing. If this general trend continues and applies equally to West Africa it should ensure the retention of *Aureol* for a further number of years.

The name of Elder Dempster is synonymous with West Africa to most people, but in recent years the Company has acquired interests in other parts of the world and the future of these must also be considered. The purchase of the British and Burmese Steam Navigation Company in 1952 has not, unfortunately, provided a permanent new trade for the Company to develop. Sailings on this route have now ended and although Elder Dempster has reserved its conference rights there seems little chance that it will again operate a profitable service to Burma.[2] On the other hand, the recent extension of the West African–North American service to the Great Lakes appears to offer every promise of success[3] and is a clear indication of the Company's intention of pursuing profitable opportunities as and when they occur.

From the foregoing it would appear that, on balance, Elder Dempster can face the seventies with some degree of confidence. Many of its current problems can be overcome by an application of imagination

[1] See above, Chapter 14, pp. 358–9.
[2] See above, Chapter 14, pp. 362–3.
[3] See above, Chapter 13, p. 332.

tempered with common sense, while there are several particularly bright prospects which may come to maturity in the near future. On the other hand, some factors lie outside the control of the Company, and the extent to which these can be accepted or modified will be a severe test of the quality and flexibility of its management and staff. These strains are, of course, an acceptable part of any competitive commercial operation but it is to be hoped that market forces will remain as the ultimate criteria of the services provided. Discrimination by flag or interference from other, non-economic, sources must be avoided if the trade as a whole—not only Elder Dempster—is to avoid significant increases in the cost of carriage.

Elder Dempster's future prospects, however, cannot be divorced from those of Ocean Transport and Trading Limited of which it has formed a part since 1965.[1] Ocean's policy of development and diversification has considerably widened its interests during the past decade and with the recent acquisition of Wm. Cory and Son[2] its employed capital has grown to approximately £220 million. One consequence of this expansion has been the complete reorganisation of the Company from a geographical to a functional basis,[3] but even this upheaval is unlikely to be the end of the transformation, for Ocean has a sizeable commercial and technical team continually engaged in studying numerous plans for the further extension of its resources and enterprise. These include some of the commercial developments already suggested for Elder Dempster, and there is no doubt that all will receive expert and sympathetic consideration.

Elder Dempster's position today, then, is that it is financially viable in its own right and is highly competitive in its traditional trade with West Africa. In addition, Elder Dempster has been immeasurably strengthened by its association with Ocean Transport and Trading Limited and this should prove to be a decisive influence on its progress in the years that lie ahead.

[1] See above, Chapter 14, p. 365.
[2] *Ocean Mail*, No. XV (May 1972).
[3] *Ocean Mail*, No. XVI (June 1972) and *Ocean Mail Supplement* (September 1972).

List of Appendices

APPENDICES

395

Table 1 EXPORTS FROM BRITISH WEST AFRICA TO THE UNITED KINGDOM, 1854–1913

Commodity	1854 %	1884 %	1900 %	1913 %
Palm Oil	40.2	53.9	40.7	39.5
Nuts for Oil	3.0	25.9	12.5	15.4
Cocoa	—	—	—	9.9
Tin Ore	—	—	—	8.3
Timber	36.4	—	14.4	8.2
Rubber	—	12.8	27.4	4.7
Other raw materials	—	—	—	4.3
Cotton	—	1.3	—	3.3
Manufactured articles	—	—	—	1.4
Grain, Corn and Maize	—	—	—	1.0
Gold	—	—	—	.5
Ivory	.6	1.1	1.2	.3
Gum	2.5	1.9	.5	.1
Ginger	3.1	1.1	.9	.1
Wax	7.9	.2	.1	.05
All other items	6.3	1.8	1.8	2.95
	100.0	100.0	100.0	100.0

Total Values: £252,814   £1,099,256   £2,137,023   £5,173,553[1]

[1] Details of the trade of British West Africa with Britain are given in the 'Annual Statements of the Trade of the United Kingdom with Foreign Countries and British Possessions', published by Her Majesty's Stationery Office. A comprehensive list of the value and weight of the principal commodities is given, but due to changes in political boundaries it would be unwise to compare the individual totals of the separate colonies with earlier or later years. A further complication is caused by the fact that many of the commodities arriving in Britain were without a specific port of origin, and were shown as 'not particularly designated', and were thus not included in the totals of imports from British possessions. The best available guide to the intricacies of West African trade statistics is that provided in the Statistical Appendices, 1800 to 1914, provided in C. W. Newbury, *British Policy towards West Africa, Select Documents 1875–1914* (London: Oxford University Press, 1971).

Table 2 EXPORTS OF CERTAIN COMMODITIES FROM NIGERIA
AND THE GOLD COAST 1899–1951

Nigeria

'000 tons	1899–1901	1919–21	1929–31	1935–37	1951
Palm Oil	14	80	129	150	150
Palm Kernels	52	192	255	346	347
Groundnuts	—	45	151	242	141
Cocoa	—	20	53	91	122
Cotton	—	4	6	11	15
Hides and Skins	—	4	6	7	14
Timber	27	29	34	44	394
	93	374	634	891	1,183

Gold Coast

Cocoa (000 tons)	1	145	218	272	230
Timber (£000's)	70	123	104	112	4,977

Source: P. T. Bauer, *West African Trade* (London: Cambridge University Press, 1954),
Adapted from Table II, p. 195.

Table 3 INDEX NUMBER OF AVERAGE VALUES

Year	Imports	Exports
1924	100	100
1925	100.1	97.3
1926	91.6	91.7
1927	87.6	86.5
1928	88.6	86.3
1929	86.2	84.1
1930	75.7	80.3

Source: Statistical abstract for the U.K. Cmd. 5553 (1937).

Table 4 TRADE FIGURES OF THE BRITISH WEST AFRICAN
COLONIES

	Imports of Merchandise		Exports of Domestic Produce	
	Monetary Terms	Real Terms	Monetary Terms	Real Terms
1928	100	100	100	100
1929	84	86.3	96	98.5
1930	77	90.1	78	83.8
1931	41	59.3	50	60.1
1932	47	73.5	52	67.1
1933	42	68.9	48	62.9

Source: Based on Table 96 (Total Imports of Merchandise) and Table 100, (Total Exports of Domestic Product) 'Statistical Abstract for the British Empire' (1935), Cmd. 4819.

Table 5 WEST AFRICAN IMPORTS AND EXPORTS

	1936–9 tons	1946–50 tons
Imports		
Nigeria	518,000	785,000
Ghana	469,000	665,000
Gambia	20,000	29,000
Total	1,007,000	1,479,000
Exports		
Nigeria	1,111,000	1,314,000
Ghana	735,000	1,281,000
Gambia	54,000	56,000
Total	1,900,000	2,651,000

Source: *Statistical and Economic Review*, No. XIV (March 1957), p. 18. (Note: This is produced and published by the United Africa Company.) The Sierra Leone, and Non-British Colonies, also increased in a similar way.

Table 6 WEST AFRICAN IMPORTS AND EXPORTS

	1946 tons	1948 tons	1950 tons
Imports			
Nigeria	549,000	756,000	1,069,000
Ghana	414,000	645,000	881,000
Sierra Leone	247,000	136,000	139,000
Gambia	14,000	29,000	42,000
Total	1,224,000	1,566,000	2,131,000
Exports			
Nigeria	1,203,000	1,265,000	1,450,000
Ghana	1,301,000	1,259,000	1,373,000
Sierra Leone	719,000	1,025,000	1,248,000
Gambia	38,000	69,000	59,000
Total	3,261,000	3,618,000	4,130,000

Source: *Statistical and Economic Review*, No. XIX (March 1957), p. 18.

Table 7 EXPORTS OF CERTAIN COMMODITIES FROM NIGERIA AND THE GOLD COAST

	1935–7 tons	1951 tons
Nigeria		
Palm Oil	150,000	150,000
Palm Kernels	346,000	347,000
Ground Nuts	242,000	141,000*
Cocoa	91,000	122,000
Cotton	11,000	15,000
Hides and Skins	7,000	14,000
Timber	44,000	394,000
(*not representative because the crop failed in 1950)		
Gold Coast		
Cocoa	272,000	230,000
Timber	£ 112,000	£4,977,000

Source: P. T. Bauer, *West African Trade* (London: Cambridge University Press, 1957), p. 195.

Table 8 EXTERNAL TRADE OF NIGERIA, GHANA, SIERRA LEONE AND THE GAMBIA IN THE POST-WAR ERA

Nigerian Imports (£ million)

	1949	1950–5	1956	1957	1958	1959	1960	1961
Cotton Piece Goods	17.9	18.0	14.4	14.5	16.3	14.9	22.4	26.4
Rayon Piece Goods	2.4	7.9	14.9	11.4	10.8	7.9	8.6	7.4
Clothing	0.9	1.1	3.2	2.8	3.8	4.4	5.7	5.8
Footwear	0.6	1.1	2.7	2.4	2.7	2.6	3.7	3.3
Fish	0.4	2.5	6.8	8.5	7.5	8.7	8.8	8.3
Wheat Flour	0.4	1.0	2.0	2.3	2.1	2.6	3.2	3.2
Sugar	0.4	1.0	3.1	2.6	3.4	3.2	3.8	3.2
Beer	0.8	1.7	3.2	3.2	3.3	3.6	3.9	3.9
Electrical and	3.1	6.4	5.0	5.2	5.9	7.8	9.7	8.2
Machinery			9.0	9.3	11.7	15.7	15.4	18.0
Commercial Vehicles	1.6	2.8	7.5	5.2	6.8	5.8	6.3	7.8
Cars	0.9	1.6	3.7	4.1	4.4	5.3	8.2	8.1
Petroleum Oils	2.1	4.7	6.7	7.7	8.2	9.6	10.5	11.7
Iron and Steel	2.4	4.1	7.6	9.2	8.9	10.3	9.1	10.2
Cement	1.0	2.2	4.3	4.6	4.1	4.4	5.4	3.7

Nigerian Exports (£ million)

	1949	1950–5	1956	1957	1958	1959	1960	1961
Palm Kernels	16.9	20.4	20.4	18.0	20.5	26.0	26.1	19.2
Palm Oil	11.9	13.8	14.9	13.8	12.7	13.8	14.0	13.2
Cocoa	14.7	26.0	24.0	26.0	26.8	38.3	36.8	33.7
Ground-nuts (raw)	18.9	17.9	27.8	20.1	26.9	27.5	22.9	31.2
Ground-nut Oil	—	1.2	4.1	4.6	3.7	4.6	5.3	4.9
Rubber	0.6	4.4	6.4	7.0	7.6	11.6	14.2	11.0
Cotton	1.4	5.0	7.1	6.3	7.8	7.3	6.2	11.1
Bananas	1.9	2.3	2.4	2.8	3.3	2.6	2.6	3.8
Benniseed	1.0	0.8	1.4	1.4	0.9	1.2	1.8	1.5
Hides and Skins	3.9	5.2	3.0	3.1	3.3	4.2	4.3	4.0
Log and Timber	1.4	4.2	4.8	4.9	6.2	7.1	8.1	7.9
Tin Ore and Concentrates	5.5	7.4	7.2	7.6	3.9	4.2	6.0	6.6
Columbite	0.2	1.5	1.8	0.8	0.5	1.1	2.1	1.2
Coal	0.1	—	0.3	0.5	0.5	0.4	0.1	0.2
Petroleum	—	—	—	—	0.5	2.7	4.4	11.5

Source: 'Commonwealth Development and Its Financing', No. 5, *Nigeria* (London: H.M.S.O., 1963).

Nigerian Imports (£ million)

	1962	1963	1964	1965	1966
Food	23.4	21.9	20.6	23.0	25.7
Beverages and Tobacco	4.7	2.9	2.9	2.0	2.2
Crude Materials	2.4	3.1	3.6	6.5	7.2
Mineral Fuels	14.0	15.5	19.5	17.3	13.8
Animal and Vegetable Oils	0.8	0.8	0.1	0.1	0.1

Nigerian Imports (£ million)

	1962	1963	1964	1965	1966
Chemicals	12.3	14.4	17.0	20.1	20.7
Manufactured Goods	73.0	74.1	89.6	90.0	79.3
Machinery	48.2	50.5	74.9	92.4	95.4
Miscellaneous manufactured articles	21.6	21.3	22.4	20.5	18.8
Miscellaneous transactions	2.8	3.4	2.9	3.0	0.8

Nigerian Exports (£ million)

Food	37.4	37.0	47.1	49.7	37.5
Beverages and Tobacco	0.1	0.1	0.1	0.1	0.1
Crude Materials	82.2	96.7	105.7	115.1	100.3
Mineral Fuels	11.7	17.5	32.2	68.1	93.1
Animal and Vegetable Oils	15.1	16.1	19.4	24.2	24.4
Chemicals	0.2	0.1	0.1	0.1	0.1
Manufactured Goods	8.8	10.6	2.2	2.8	18.9
Miscellaneous transactions	3.1	3.7	3.4	3.0	3.9
Re-exports	4.6	4.1	4.1	5.0	5.3

Source: *Nigeria Trade Journal*, for the relevant years, published by the Federal Ministry of Information, Lagos.

Imports into Ghana (£ G'ooo)

	1961	1962	1963	1964
Food and live animals	26,236	23,140	18,452	20,042
Beverages and tobacco	3,511	1,326	1,194	707
Crude materials—not fuels	875	788	930	997
Minerals, fuels and lubricants	6,533	7,321	7,634	7,074
Animal and vegetable oils and fats	454	323	838	1,449
Chemicals	10,121	9,677	9,577	7,487
Manufacture goods	44,462	40,542	42,137	39,664
Machinery and transport equipment	33,083	25,893	37,072	35,631
Misc. manufactured articles	13,438	8,826	10,674	7,523
Misc. commodities and transactions	2,068	1,246	1,802	917
Transactions in gold and monetary items	2,049	18	105	100

Exports from Ghana (£ G'ooo)

Food and live animals	72,534	73,005	73,205	74,247
Beverages and tobacco	91	25	1	2
Crude materials—not fuels	29,519	26,399	21,167	26,438
Minerals, fuels and lubricants	14	10	76	1,044
Animal and vegetable oils and fats	24	165	86	5
Chemicals	63	95	156	248
Manufactured goods	954	1,549	1,269	1,157
Machinery and transport equipment	456	973	747	486
Misc. commodities and transactions	377	1,220	736	593
Misc. manufactured articles	355	341	108	112
Transactions in gold and monetary items	10,750	11,125	11,288	10,308
Re-exports	1,961	3,359	2,004	1,434

Source: *West African Directory*, 5th edition (1966–7), p. 108.

APPENDICES

Imports into Sierra Leone c.i.f. value

	1962 £	1963 £	1965 Le.
Food, beverages and tobacco	6,819,340	4,805,782	6,348,551
Mineral fuels	3,556,838	2,700,408	3,383,954
Chemicals	1,379,793	1,115,431	2,073,217
Manufactured articles	8,670,364	5,621,180	9,990,577
Machinery and transport equipment	5,791,652	3,984,568	10,944,294
Misc. manufactured articles	3,222,112	2,208,771	3,418,918

Exports from Sierra Leone f.o.b. value

	1962	1963	1965
Food, beverages and tobacco	1,315,563	1,113,618	2,013,413
Crude materials	7,983,022	5,970,683	9,501,448
Animal and vegetable oils and fats	21,176	4,901	—
Manufactured articles	1,708,997	13,219,597	18,474,632

Source: *West African Directory*, 6th Edition (1967-8), pp. 432-3.

Imports into the Gambia

	1961 £	1962 £	1963 £	1964 £
Manufactured goods	1,769,354	1,370,443	1,198,451	1,279,230
Machinery and transport equipment	545,038	715,947	624,870	548,441
Misc. manufactured articles	139,079	125,602	150,502	101,189
Transactions in gold and monetary items	21	—	—	—
Customs Protectorate	89,622	84,961	68,264	78,969

Exports from the Gambia

	1962 £	1963 £	1964 £
Ground-nuts decorticated	3,320,621	2,189,067	1,696,833
Beeswax	440	—	—
Hide, raw	4,780	4,471	4,561
Skins, raw	771	33	—
Palm kernels	89,306	95,900	71,696
Others	62,015	694,882	1,397,478
Re-exports	90,739	112,286	125,081

Source: *West African Directory*, 5th Edition (1966-7), pp. 69-70.

Table 9 VESSELS USED BY MACGREGOR LAIRD'S EXPEDITION IN
1832

The three vessels were registered at Liverpool on 5 July 1832. The shareholders were Joseph Hornby, Alexander Smith Junior, William Dixon and Thomas Forsyth—all being described as 'merchants of Liverpool'. They were also the four trustees appointed by trust deed of 19 March 1832, and together with other members have associated themselves as a joint stock company by the aforesaid deed in the name of the African Inland Commercial Company.

Columbine—a sailing ship of 176 tons built at Douglas in 1826. Captain Robert Miller. Sold by the trustees on 23 July 1834.

Quorra—a paddle steamer of 83 tons built at Birkenhead in 1832 by Seddon and Langley. Captain S. L. Harris. Broken up at Fernando Po in 1841.

Alburkah—a paddle steamer of 35 tons built at Liverpool by Macgregor Laird and Company in 1832. Captain Joseph Hill. Broken up at Fernando Po in 1838.

Source: Liverpool Shipping Registers. Entry 92 and 93, 5 July 1832.

Table 10 PROPOSED CHARTER OF *BEESWING*

Charges		Receipts		
3 months hire at £560 (including feeding, wages and insurance)	£1,680	Freight out: 1,600 tons at 22/6d	=	£1,800
400 ton coal at 16/–	320	Freight home: 900 tons at 27/6d	=	£1,237
50 ton Madeira at 30/–	75	Intercolonial earnings	=	£250
Liverpool charges including stowing cargo	100			
Commission and other charges	50			
Expenses entering and discharging Havre	150			
Expenses on return to Liverpool —discharging commission	100			
Expenses at Sierra Leone	30			
Labour of Kroomen	100			
Contingencies	100			
	£2,705			£3,287

Source: John Holt Papers, 4/1. Letter from George Miller to John Holt, 12 March 1884.

Table 11 EXPANSION OF THE ELDER DEMPSTER FLEET, 1896–1909 (net tons)

	African Steam Ship Co. Net tons ships	British & African	Elder Dempster & Co.	Compagnie Maritime Belge	Elder Dempster Shipping Ltd	Totals
1896	50,315 (29)	29,304 (23)	2,045 (3)	7,716 (3)	—	89,380
1897	46,695 (32)	27,458 (22)	20,580 (9)	4,881 (2)	—	99,614
1898	56,856 (33)	31,488 (24)	35,404 (15)	6,008 (2)	—	129,756
1899	44,868 (28)	33,349 (24)	13,101 (7)	10,833 (4)	50,234 (17)	152,385
1900	38,768 (26)	33,934 (25)	26,224 (10)	15,645 (6)	54,379 (15)	168,950
1901	42,775 (29)	63,308 (34)	33,401 (21)	8,004 (3)	50,744 (15)	198,232
1902	42,818 (28)	65,814 (34)	29,052 (16)	8,004 (3)	48,798 (16)	194,486
1903	45,595 (29)	65,127 (37)	9,089 (6)	7,833 (3)	35,450 (16)	162,994
1904	39,084 (25)	57,058 (36)	13,883 (7)	10,730 (4)	37,884 (18)	158,639
1905	38,906 (25)	59,714 (38)	10,321 (8)	8,107 (3)	45,585 (21)	162,633
1906	39,125 (23)	56,506 (37)	15,872 (9)	10,684 (4)	42,656 (21)	164,843
1907	44,136 (24)	60,329 (39)	25,059 (15)	8,175 (3)	46,998 (23)	184,697
1908	44,586 (25)	57,799 (36)	22,207 (13)	8,175 (3)	49,231 (25)	181,998
1909	42,549 (22)	58,643 (36)	19,038 (11)	9,451 (3)	48,005 (15)	177,686

Source: Lloyds Registers of Shipping for the relevant years.

Table 12 ELDER DEMPSTER NON-WEST AFRICAN FLEETS, 1896–1909

(Net tons)

	Imperial Direct Line	Beaver Line	Ocean Transport
1896	—	—	11,263 (4)
1897	—	—	11,263 (4)
1898	—	—	11,263 (4)
1899	—	8,197 (3)	3,398 (2)
1900	—	20,303 (6)	1,433 (1)
1901	—	15,548 (5)	1,433 (1)
1902	13,441 (6)	—	—
1903	8,092 (5)	—	—
1904	8,092 (5)	—	—
1905	11,933 (6)	—	—
1906	13,625 (6)	—	—
1907	13,625 (6)	—	—
1908	13,625 (6)	—	—
1909	13,625 (6)	—	—

Source: Lloyds Registers of Shipping for the relevant years.

Table 13 COMPARISON OF ELDER DEMPSTER AND WOERMANN
FLEETS
(Net tons)

	Elder Dempster	Woermann
1896	89,380	15,709
1897	99,614	18,831
1898	129,756	21,430
1899	152,385	24,569
1900	168,950	22,737
1901	198,232	34,363
1902	194,486	43,291
1903	162,994	49,139
1904	158,639	46,914
1905	162,633	62,850
1906	164,843	71,966
1907	184,697	62,781
1908	181,998	56,736
1909	177,686	53,976

Source: Lloyds Registers of Shipping, for the relevant years.

Table 14 SALE OF THE BEAVER LINE IN 1903

Elder Dempster and Company sold their Canadian interests to the Canadian Pacific
Line for the sum of £1,417,500. This included provision for 'goodwill' and the following vessels, but note that part of the fleet, formerly used on the Canadian service,
was retained by Elder Dempster and used for other purposes:

Vessels Transferred to Canadian Pacific		
Name	Built	Gross Tons
Montreal	1900	6,870
Montezuma	1899	7,345
Milwaukee	1897	7,323
Montcalm	1897	5,505
Monteagle	1899	5,498
Montfort	1899	5,519
Mount Royal	1898	7,064
Mount Temple	1901	7,656
Monterey	1898	5,455
Montrose	1897	7,094
Lake Champlain	1900	7,392
Lake Erie	1900	7,550
Lake Manitoba	1901	8,852
Lake Michigan	1902	7,000

Source: F. C. Bowen, *History of the Canadian Pacific Lines*. (London, Marston, 1928),
pp. 84–5.

Table 15 SHIPPING EMPLOYED BETWEEN U.K. AND WEST AFRICA, 1914–1919

Date	British	German	Total
July 1914	274,000	133,000	407,000 tons
Sept. 1914	270,000	—	270,000 tons
1915	200,000 (E)	60,000 (E)	260,000 tons
May 1917	134,000 (E)	50,000 (E)	184,000 tons
Minimum			
between			
May 1917 and	112,000 (E)	40,000 (E)	152,000 tons
Nov. 1918			
Nov. 1918	129,000 (E)	40,000 (E)	169,000 tons
Feb. 1919	166,000 (E)	40,000 (E)	206,000 tons

Note: In the July 1914, figures the German—West African trade is included so these are not directly comparable with those of other dates. The figures for German vessels refer to captured ships after September 1914, and these were all operated by Elder Dempster on Government account. Certain details in the breakdown between British and German steamers are estimates (indicated by 'E'), but the totals are reasonably firm. This is not to say that they necessarily agree with those quoted by other authorities, for it is extremely difficult to determine how many Elder Dempster and Woerman lines were temporarily engaged on other routes. The table was compiled by the author from the following sources:

C. Ernest Fayle, *The War and the Shipping Industry* (London: Oxford University Press, 1927), Table 17, p. 430, *Fairplay*, 15 June, 1916, p. 940. *Annual General Meeting of Elder Dempster and Company, Limited,* and 'Report of the Committee on Edible and Oil Producing Nuts and Seeds (H.M.S.O., 1916), CD.8248, Q.6027, Evidence of Sir Owen Philipps.

Table 16 ELDER DEMPSTER SHIP LOSSES, 1914–1918

Year	Lost by Natural Causes	Gross Tons	Sunk by Enemy Action	Gross Tons	Total
1914	*Degama*	3,507	*Nyanga*	3,066	
	Muraji	3,238			
		6,745		3,066	9,811
1915	*Delta*	585	*Ilaro*	2,799	
	Abeokuta	1,817	*Falaba*	4,806	
	Dakar	4,081	*Bonny*	2,702	
			Eithiope	3,794	
		6,483		14,101	20,584

Year	Lost by Natural Causes	Gross Tons	Sunk by Enemy Action	Gross Tons	Total
1916	*Madeira*	1,773	*Nil*	—	
	Bornu	3,238			
	Niger	980			
		5,991			5,991
1917	*Mendi*	4,230	*Memnon*	3,176	
	Gando	3,809	*Asaba*	972	
	Nigeria	3,755	*Andoni*	3,188	
			Yola	3,504	
			Adansi	2,644	
			Tarquah	3,859	
			Sapele	3,152	
			Addah	3,149	
			Karina	4,222	
			Agberi	3,463	
			Aburi	3,730	
			Tamele	3,924	
			Akassa	3,918	
			Abosso	7,782	
			Apapa	7,832	
			Elele	4,831	
			Eloby	4,820	
			Obuasi	4,416	
			Gold Coast	4,255	
			Benito	4,712	
			Ikbal	5,434	
		11,794		86,983	98,777
1918	*Burutu*	3,863	*Boma*	2,510	
	Konakry	4,397	*Badageri*	2,952	
			Hartley	1,150	
		8,260		6,612	14,872
		39,273		110,762	150,035

Source: Compiled by the author from Elder Dempster's fleet list.

Table 17 SHIPS PURCHASED BY ELDER DEMPSTER: 1919–21

Year	Name	Gross Tons	Year	Name	Gross Tons
1919	Bassa	5,267	1920	Ekari	6,711
	Badagry	5,161		Burutu	5,275
	Bereby	5,248		Boma	5,408
	Bonny	5,173		New Brighton	6,538
	Boutry	5,182		New Brooklyn	6,546
	Bakana	5,384		New Columbia	6,574
	Barracoo	5,234		Jebba	5,875
	Bata	5,260		Jekri	5,875
	Bodnant	5,258		Aba	7,373
	Bathurst	5,437		Fantee	5,663
	Biafra	5,405			———
	Matadi	3,097			61,838
	Mateba	2,955			———
	New Brunswick	6,529	1921	Bompatra	5,570
	New Georgia	6,566		Calgary	7,206
	New Mexico	6,566			———
	New Texas	6,568			12,776
	New Toronto	6,568			———
		———		Grand Total:	171,472
		96,858			———

Source: Compiled by the author from the Elder Dempster fleet list.

Table 18 NUMBERS OF NON ELDER DEMPSTER SHIPS REPORTED IN WEST AFRICA 1920–30

July	Swedish West Africa Line	Holland West Africa Line	German African Line	Bull Line (USA)	Trans-Atlantic West African Line	A. Krohn Service (Danish)	Société Navale de L'Ouest (Fr)	Chargeurs Réunis (Fr)	C. Fabre (Fraissinet Line) (Fr)	Venture Weir (Fr)	Italian West Africa Line	Roma Societa di Navigazione	Congo Line Navigasione Liberia
1920	3	5	—	—	—	—	—	—	—	—	—	—	—
1921	*	9	—	13	—	4	5	—	—	—	—	1	—
1922	—	11	—	5	—	5	10	2	—	—	2	2	—
1923	—	10	26	6	—	—*	—	3	3	7	2	—	—
1924	—	11	28	8	—	—	7	3	8	6	3	—	—
1925	—	11	28	8	—	—	6	7	10	9	3	—	—
1926	—	12	31	8	—	—	7	5	13	—	5	—	—
1927[1]	—	13	32	10	—	—	4	15	11	5	3	—	—
1928	—	15	34	11	—	—	8	15	9	4	5	—	4
1929	—	11	35	11	4	—	5	16	12	4	—*	—	4
1930	—	8	30	11	—*	—	6	13	10	3	—	—	—*

[1] June.   * End of service

Source: Based on details given each week in the magazine *West Africa*. It is not suggested that these are completely accurate, but as any faults are likely to be constant they form a useful guide in comparing one year with another.

411

Table 19 BRITISH VESSELS ENTERED AND CLEARED THE BRITISH
WEST AFRICAN COLONIES: 1919–29

		%
1919	—	90.5
1920	—	80.1
1921	—	71.1
1922	—	67.4
1923	—	63.4
1924	—	63.0
1925	—	64.6
1926	—	60.5
1927	—	60.75
1928	—	56.2
1929	—	56.9

Source: Compiled from details given in the 'Statistical abstract for British Overseas Dominions and Protectorates'. Cmd. 2738 (1926), and 'Statistical abstract for the British Empire'. Cmd. 4393 (1933).

Table 20 VESSELS ACQUIRED BY ELDER DEMPSTER LINES
LIMITED ON ITS FORMATION IN 1932

Operating Company No. 2 (West African Lines)—To this Company will be transferred the vessels which are set out in the first column of the following Schedule by the Companies whose names appear in the second column of such Schedule freed from the mortgages and charges specified in the third column of such Schedule, and all other mortgages and charges (if any) thereon, viz.:

Name of Vessel	Owned by	Particulars of Mortgages and Charges
S.S. *Milverton*	Elder Dempster & Co., Limited	A specific charge to Trustees for 5 per cent Debenture Stock. A specific charge to Trustees for 5 per cent 'A' Debenture Stock.
M.V. *Deido*	African Steam Ship Company	A specific charge to Trustees for the 6 per cent Debenture Stock
M.V. *Mattawin*	,,	,,
S.S. *Cochrane*	,,	,,
M.V. *Adda*	,,	,,
S.S. *New Columbia*	,,	,,
S.S. *Fantee*	,,	,,
S.S. *New Brighton*	,,	,,
S.S. *Barracoo*	,,	,,
S.S. *Bata*	,,	,,
S.S. *Bereby*	,,	,,
S.S. *Bodnant*	,,	,,
S.S. *Biafra*	,,	,,
S.S. *Boutry*	,,	,,
S.S. *Bassa*	,,	,,
S.S. *Jebba*	,,	,,
S.S. *Egori*	,,	,,
S.S. *Egba*	,,	,,
S.S. *Eboe*	,,	,,
S.S. *Sir George*	,,	,,
S.S. *Uromi*	,,	,,
S.S. *Abinsi*	,,	,,
S.S. *Ibadan*	,,	,,
S.S. *New Mexico*	Elder Line Limited	None
S.S. *New Brunswick*	,,	,,
S.S. *Bathurst*	,,	,,
S.S. *Attendant*	,,	,,

Name of Vessel	Owned by	Particulars of Mortgages and Charges
M.V. *Dagomba*	The British and African Steam Navigation Company Limited	A specific mortgage to the Royal Exchange Assurance
M.V. *Daru*	"	"
M.V. *Dixcove*	"	"
M.V. *Dunkwa*	"	"
M.V. *Apapa*	"	A specific mortgage to the Midland Bank Limited and the Bank of Ireland
M.V. *Accra*	"	"
M.V. *Aba*	"	"
S.S. *Bompata*	"	"
S.S. Calgary	"	"
S.S. *New Brooklyn*	"	none
S.S. *Boma*	"	"
S.S. *New Toronto*	"	"
S.S. *New Texas*	"	"
S.S. *New Georgia*	"	"
S.S. *Burutu*	"	"
S.S. *Jekri*	"	"
S.S. *Gambia*	"	"
S.S. *Gaboon*	"	"
M.V. *Ila*	"	"
S.S. *Appam*	"	A specific mortgage to the Midland Bank Limited and the Bank of Ireland
S.S. *Ebani*	"	none
S.S. *Otta*	"	"
S.S. *Onitsha*	"	"
S.S. *Lokoja*	"	"
S.S. *Ilorin*	"	"
S.S. *Calumet*	Imperial Direct Line Limited	none
S.S. *Badagry*	"	"
S.S. *Benguela*	"	"

Source: Elder Dempster Lines, Ltd. File 267738 (live at Companies House). Formation Documents, 15 August 1932.

Table 21 DISPOSAL OF ELDER DEMPSTER SURPLUS SHIPS, 1933–4

Name	Gross Tons	Built	Price obtained
Abinsi	6,365	1908	£ 6,100
Badagry	5,161	1919 ⎤	
Bata	5,328	1919 ⎬	£22,500
Boutry	5,182	1919 ⎦	
Bathurst	5,438	1919	£ 6,200
Benguela	5,520	1910	—
Gambia	3,296	1915	£ 8,250
Jebba	5,875	1917	—
Jekri	5,875	1917	—
New Brighton	6,538	1920	£ 3,500
New Georgia	6,566	1919	—
New Mexico	6,566	1919	£ 6,850
Fantee	5,663	1920	—
Bompata	5,570	1921	£ 8,000
Burutu	5,275	1918	—

The above ships were redundant and never commissioned by the new Company. In addition, a number of vessels which had been in service for Elder Dempster Lines were also sold during this period.

Source: Elder Dempster Lines Papers, Accounts Department, Black Books.

THE TRADE MAKERS

Table 22 SHIPPING ENTERED IN THE PORTS OF BRITISH WEST
AFRICA (NIGERIA, GOLD COAST, SIERRA LEONE AND THE
GAMBIA)

Year	Total Shipping Entered	British Shipping Entered	British Shipping Entered	British Proportion of Annual Enterings
1930	100	100	100	56.9
1931	85.8	76.8	97.9	50.9
1932	71.4	68.1	75.7	54.3
1933	76.0	69.4	84.7	52.0
1934	89.1	83.0	97.1	53.1
1935	100.1	95.4	106.3	54.3
1936	102.6	104.8	99.7	58.1
1937	111.3	118.8	110.7	57.2
1938	103.6	103.9	103.2	57.1
1939	60.0	61.4	58.0	58.3

Based on the 'Statistical Abstract for the British Empire' (1935). Cmd. 4819, pp. 81–93
and the 'Statistical Abstract for the British Commonwealth' (1950). Cmd. 8051, pp. 264–6.

Forerunner, the first ship of the African Steam Ship Company, 1852–1854.

Hope, 1853–1860.

Roquelle, the first ship of the British and African Steam Navigation Company, 1869–1882.

PLATE 25

PLATE 26

Yoruba under sail, 1871–1873.

Lake Megantic built 1884 was acquired as *Arawa* in 1899. She was re-named *Port Henderson* in 1905 and sailed under that name until sold in 1912.

Batanga operated by the British and African Steam Navigation Company from 1893 to 1922.

Table 23 ELDER DEMPSTER SHIPS LOST DURING THE SECOND
WORLD WAR

Year	Lost by 'Normal' Maritime Hazards	Gross Tons	Sunk by Enemy Action	Gross Tons	Total
1940			*Accra*	9,336	
			Boma	5,408	
			Bassa	5,267	
			Apapa	9,332	
			Bodnant	5,342	
				34,685	34,685
1941	*Bereby*	5,248	*Seaforth*	5,459	
			Swedru	5,378	
			Dunkwa	4,752	
			Alfred Jones	5,012	
			Adda	7,816	
			Sangara	5,445	
			Daru	3,854	
			Edward Blyden	5,002	
			Dixcove	3,789	
		5,248		46,507	51,755
1942	*Kwaibo*	396	*New Brunswick*	6,528	
			Mattawin	6,918	
			Ilorin	814	
			Abosso	11,330	
			Dagomba	3,845	
			New Toronto	6,567	
			Henry Stanley	5,025	
		396		41,027	41,423
1943			*William Wilberforce*	5,003	
			Mary Slessor	5,026	
			New Columbia	6,573	
				16,602	16,602
		5,644		138,821	144,465

Source: Elder Dempster Lines Papers, Compiled by the author from the 'Ship Incidents' file.

Table 24 VESSELS MANAGED BY ELDER DEMPSTER AND LOST
DURING THE SECOND WORLD WAR

Date of Loss		Name of Vessel	Gross Tonnage	How Lost
26 June	1941	S.S. *Empire Ability* (ex Uhenfels)	7,602	Torpedoed
24 July	1941	S.S. *Macon*	5,134	Torpedoed
6 November	1942	M.V. *Hai Hing*	2,561	Torpedoed
10 November	1942	S.S. *Qued Grou*	792	Torpedoed
26 March	1943	S.S. *Lafonia*	1,961	Collision in Convoy
8 July	1943	S.S. *De La Salle*	8,400	Torpedoed
23 February	1945	S.S. *Point Pleasant Park*	7,160	Torpedoed

Source: Elder Dempster Lines Papers, Compiled by the author from the 'Ship Incidents' file.

Table 25 ELDER DEMPSTER FLEET, 31 DECEMBER 1949

Passenger Vessels	gross tons	Cargo & Cargo Passenger Vessels	gross tons
M.V. *Accra*	11,600	M.V. *David Livingstone*	4,091
M.V. *Apapa*	11,607	M.V. *Deido*	3,894
M.V. *Calabar*	1,964	M.V. *Freetown*	5,853
		M.V. *Fulani*	6,539
Inter-Coastal Vessels		M.V. *Macgregor Laird*	4,081
M.V. *Auchmacoy*	255	M.V. *Mary Kingsley*	4,083
S.S. *Forcados*	974	S.S. *New Brooklyn*	6,546
S.S. *Knowlton*	2,068	S.S. *New Texas*	6,568
M.V. *Oron* (Ferry)	277	S.S. *Prah*	7,339
S.S. *Oxford*	1,893	M.V. *Salaga*	4,810
S.S. *Sapele*	974	M.V. *Sangara*	4,189
S.S. *Warri*	974	M.V. *Sansu*	4,174
		M.V. *Sekondi*	4,811
Cargo & Cargo Passenger Vessels		M.V. *Sherbro*	4,811
S.S. *Biafra*	5,405	M.V. *Shonga*	4,810
S.S. *Cabano*	7,157	M.V. *Sobo*	4,124
S.S. *Calgary*	7,275	M.V. *Sulima*	4,819
S.S. *Calumet*	7,405	M.V. *Swedru*	4,809
S.S. *Cambray*	7,165	M.V. *Tamele*	7,172
S.S. *Cargill*	7,152	M.V. *Tarkwa*	7,416
S.S. *Chandler*	7,161	S.S. *Zini*	7,256
S.S. *Cochrane*	7,276	S.S. *Zungeru*	7,273
S.S. *Cottrell*	7,163	S.S. *Zungon*	7,267

Source: Based on fleet list given in Elder Dempster Lines Holdings Limited, Directors' Report and Statement of Accounts for the twelve months ending 31 December 1949.

Table 26 BRITISH AND BURMESE FLEET IN 1952

Liners		Cargo Vessels	
Martaban	5,740 gross tons	Kadeik	7,489 gross tons
Prome	7,043 ,, ,,	Kaladan	4,916 ,, ,,
Salween	7,063 ,, ,,	Kanbe	4,878 ,, ,,
Yoma	5,909 ,, ,,	Kalewa	4,876 ,, ,,
		Katha	4,878 ,, ,,
		Kindat	5,530 ,, ,,
		Koyan	5,537 ,, ,,

Source: Compiled by the author from the annual accounts of Liner Holdings Company Limited.

Table 27 ADDITIONS TO THE BRITISH AND BURMESE FLEET 1953-61

1953	Kohima	5,957 gross tons
1954	Kentung	5,558 ,, ,,
1955	Kandaw	5,599 ,, ,,
1955	Kaduna	5,599 ,, ,,
1957	Bhamo	5,932 ,, ,,
1958	Kumba	5,439 ,, ,,
1958	Kabala	5,445 ,, ,,
1960	Donga	6,565 ,, ,,
1960	Dumbaia	6,558 ,, ,,
1961	Dalla	6,564 ,, ,,
1961	Pegu	5,764 ,, ,,

Source: Compiled by the author from the annual accounts of Liner Holdings Company Limited.

Table 28 DISPOSAL OF SURPLUS ELDER DEMPSTER SHIPS,
1950 TO 1963

Year	Name of Ship	Gross Tonnage	Built	Acquired
1950	S.S. *Oxford*	1,893	1923	1946
	S.S. *Knowlton*	2,068	1922	1946
1951	S.S. *Biafra*	5,405	1919	1919
1952	S.S. *Bida*	1,791	1942	1951
	S.S. *Benue*	1,814	1943	1951
	M.V. *Macgregor Laird*	4,081	1930	1930
1953	M.V. *David Livingstone*	4,091	1930	1930
	M.V. *Calabar*	1,964	1935	1935
1954	M.V. *Mary Kingsley*	4,083	1930	1930
	S.S. *New Brooklyn*	6,546	1920	1920
	S.S. *New Texas*	6,568	1919	1919
1955	S.S. *Calumet*	7,405	1923	1923
1957	S.S. *Calgary*	7,275	1921	1921
	S.S. *Cochrane*	7,276	1923	1923
1958	M.V. *Deido*	3,894	1928	1928
	M.V. *Freetown*	5,853	1928	1943
	M.V. *Fulani*	6,539	1929	1943
	S.S. *Zungeru*	7,273	1943	1947
	S.S. *Zungon*	7,267	1943	1947
	S.S. *Prah*	7,339	1945	1949
1959	S.S. *Cabano*	7,157	1943	1946
	S.S. *Chandler*	7,161	1944	1946
	S.S. *Zini*	7,256	1945	1947
1960	S.S. *Benin*	2,483	1950	1950
	M.V. Sangara	4,189	1939	1939
	M.V. *Sansu*	4,174	1939	1939
	S.S. *Cambray*	7,165	1944	1946
	S.S. *Cargill*	7,152	1943	1946
	S.S. *Cottrell*	7,163	1944	1946
1961	S.S. *Baro*	1,517	1950	1950
1962	S.S. *Forcados*	974	1945	1948
	S.S. *Sapele*	974	1945	1946
	S.S. *Calabar*	8,305	1936	1956
	S.S. *Winneba*	8,355	1938	1956
	S.S. *Prome*	7,043	1937	1952
	S.T. *Salween*	7,063	1938	1952
1962	M.V. *Katha*	4,878	1947	1952
	M.V. *Kanbe*	4,878	1948	1952
1963	M.V. *Sobo*	4,173	1937	1937

Year	Name of Ship	Gross Tonnage	Built	Acquired
	M.V. *Kaladan*	4,916	1950	1952
	M.V. *Kalewa*	4,876	1947	1952
	M.V. *Kindat*	5,530	1950	1952
	S.T. *Martaban*	5,740	1950	1952
	S.T. *Yoma*	5,809	1948	1952

Source: Compiled by the author from the annual accounts of Liner Holdings Company Limited.

Table 29 DISPOSAL OF SURPLUS ELDER DEMPSTER SHIPS, 1964 TO 1972

Year	Name of Ship	Gross Tonnage	Built	Acquired
1966	M.V. *Koyan*	5,537	1952	1952
	M.V. *Kohima*	5,597	1953	1953
	M.V. *Kentung*	5,558	1954	1954
	M.V. *Kadeik*	7,489	1952	1952
	M.V. *Itu*	129	1954	1954
1967	M.V. *Tamele*	7,173	1944	1944
	M.V. *Tarkwa*	7,414	1944	1944
	M.V. *Kandaw*	5,599	1955	1955
	M.V. *Accra*	11,644	1947	1947
	M.V. *Mallam*	4,810	1947	1947
	M.V. *Mampong*	4,811	1948	1948
	M.V. *Mano*	4,810	1948	1948
	M.V. *Maradi*	4,809	1948	1948
	M.V. *Matru*	4,811	1947	1947
1968	M.V. *Mamfe*	4,810	1947	1947
	M.V. *Apapa*	11,651	1948	1948
1970	M.V. *Sunjarv*	15,000 d/w	1958	1964
1972	M.V. *Onitsha*	7,267	1952	1952
	M.V. *Perang*	6,177	1954	1954
	M.V. *Owerri*	5,798	1955	1955
	M.V. *Oti*	5,485	1956	1956

Source: Compiled by the author from the annual accounts of Liner Holdings Company Limited.

Table 30 ELDER DEMPSTER LINES FLEET, I MAY 1972

Name of Ship	Gross Tonnage	Built	Acquired	Type
M.V. *Aureol*	14,083	1951	1951	Passenger
M.V. *Carway*[a]	1,597	1967	1967	Car Ferry
M.V. *Clearway*[a]	1,160	1970	1970	Car Ferry
M.V. *Dalla*	8,831	1961	1961	Cargo
M.V. *Degema*	8,153	1959	1959	Cargo
M.V. *Deido*	8,254	1961	1961	Cargo
M.V. *Dixcove*	8,138	1959	1959	Cargo
M.V. *Donga*	8,868	1960	1960	Cargo
M.V. *Dumbaia*	8,876	1960	1960	Cargo
M.V. *Dumurra*	8,238	1961	1961	Cargo
M.V. *Dunkwa*	8,254	1960	1960	Cargo
M.V. *Ebani*	9,376	1952	1952	Cargo/Passenger
M.V. *Eboe*	9,380	1952	1952	Cargo/Passenger
M.V. *Egori*	8,331	1957	1957	Cargo
M.V. *Eket*[b]	394	1950	1950	Ferry
M.V. *Falaba*	7,703	1962	1962	Cargo
M.V. *Fian*	7,689	1964	1964	Cargo
M.V. *Forcados*	7,689	1963	1963	Cargo
M.V. *Fourah Bay*	7,704	1961	1961	Cargo
M.V. *Fulani*	7,689	1964	1964	Cargo
M.V. *Kabala*	5,445	1958	1958	Cargo
M.V. *Kaduna*	5,599	1956	1956	Cargo
M.V. *Kohima*	5,445	1959	1959	Cargo
M.V. *Kumba*	5,439	1958	1958	Cargo
M.V. *Obuasi*	5,895	1952	1952	Cargo
M.V. *Onitsha*	7,267	1952	1952	Cargo
M.V. *Oron*[b]	277	1938	1938	Ferry
M.V. *Oti*	5,485	1956	1956	Cargo
M.V. *Owerri*	5,798	1955	1955	Cargo
M.V. *Patani*	6,183	1954	1954	Cargo
M.V. *Perang*	6,177	1954	1954	Cargo
M.V. *Speedway*[a]	1,204	1968	1970	Roll-on/Roll-off Trailer ship.
M.V. *Skyway*[a]	1,175	1968	1970	Roll-on/Roll-off Trailer ship.

[a] Owned by Seaway Ferries Ltd.
[b] Owned by West African Lighterage & Transport Co. Ltd

Guinea Gulf Line Fleet, 1 May 1972

Name of Ship	Gross Tonnage	Built	Acquired	Type
M.V. *Bhamo*	5,932	1957	1957	Cargo
M.V. *Daru*	6,301	1958	1958	Cargo
M.V. *Freetown*	7,689	1964	1964	Cargo
M.V. *Pegu*	5,764	1961	1961	Cargo^c

^c Note that in the fleet list published on p. 23 of the Ocean Steam Ship Company Limited's Annual Report and Accounts for 1971 three additional ships are included under the Elder Dempster section. These are *Akosombo* (formerly *Ascanius*), *Calchas* and *Mano* (formerly *Menelaus*) which have been transferred either on a temporary or permanent basis from the Blue Funnel Line. In view of the uncertainty that surrounds the future of these vessels they have not been included here or in the combined fleet referred to on p. 361. In fact *Calchas* has now (August 1972) been transformed back to the Blue Funnel fleet. Note also that in the period from May to August 1972 the following Elder Dempster vessels have been sold: *Onitsha*, *Oti*, *Perang* and *Owerri*, and that *Dixcove*, of Elder Dempster, and *Freetown* and *Pegu* of Guinea Gulf are currently operating on Far Eastern routes on a temporary basis.

Table 31   MESSRS FLETCHER, PARR AND COMPANY

Mr Walter Samuel Partridge was born in 1834.
'He launched into business in 1851 as a clerk in the office of Messrs. H. and H. Willis and Co., ship and insurance brokers, of 3, Crosby Square, London. In 1859, however, he left that employ, and became connected with the firm of Messrs. W. and H. Laird, coal merchants, of Liverpool. On Mr. W. Laird retiring in 1863, Mr. W. S. Partridge was taken into partnership, the direct object of the enlargement of the firm being the establishment of a branch house in London. This was effected under the style of Messrs. Fletcher, Parr and Co. In due course Messrs. Fletcher and Parr passed out of the firm, with the result that in 1875 our "Headlight" was the only remaining representative of the original London combination, and he therefore altered the style to the present—i.e. Messrs. W. S. Partridge and Co.'

The original partnership arrangements for the London business were that Fletcher & Parr, I. P. Higginson and Partridge each received one third of any profits. This was subject to revision if the profits were below £400 in any year, and was subsequently altered so that Fletcher and Parr, and Higginson, received half of the profits and Partridge received the balance.

Source: *Our Shipping Headlights*, published by (The Syren and Shipping Limited, 1908), p. 158.
See also African Steam Ship Company Papers, Fletcher and Parr's Private Journal, No. 1.

Table 32

The constituent firms forming the African Association, Limited, in 1889 were:

i.	Thomas Harrison and Company	(of Liverpool)
ii.	British & Continental African Company	(of Liverpool)
iii.	Couper, Johnstone and Company	(of Glasgow)
iv.	Hatton and Cookson	(of Liverpool)
v.	Holt and Cotterell	(of Liverpool)
vi.	Richard and William King	(of Bristol)
vii.	Stuart and Douglas Limited	(of Liverpool)
viii.	Taylor, Laughland and Company	(of Glasgow)
ix.	George Watts and Company	(of Liverpool)

Source: *The History of the United Africa Company to 1938*, circulated privately by the Company (London, 1938), p. 73.

Table 33 CAPITAL STRUCTURE
BRITISH & AFRICAN STEAM NAVIGATION COMPANY

1868	Nominal Capital: 400 shares of £500 each =	£200,000
	Issued Capital:	
	192 'A' Shares (£275 called up) ⎫ = 322 shares 130 'B' Shares (£120 called up) ⎭	£ 68,400
6.4.1872	Change from 400 Shares @ £500 to 320 Shares @ £625. Nominal Capital remained at	£200,000
28.3.1881	Change from 320 Shares @ £625 to 2,500 Shares @ £100 (£90 called up) 156 Shares not issued. Nominal Capital =	£250,000
23.4.1883	Became *Limited* Company. 15,000 Shares @ £50. 11,720 taken up. (£42 called up) Nominal Capital =	£750,000
19.3.1884	1,280 new shares issued (£25 called up) = 13,000 shares.	£524,240
18.3.1885	New shares made equal to old by calling up £17 on them. Now 13,000 shares @ £42 called up =	£546,000
15.6.1886	Nominal Capital reduced from £750,000 (15,000 @ £50) to £600,000. (15,000 @ £40).	
16.2.1887	£5 per share returned leaving 13,000 issued @ £35.	
16.3.1887	Nominal Capital 15,000 @ £40 =	£600,000
	Issued Capital: 13,000 @ £40 =	520,000
	Issued Capital	
	(reduced): 13,000 @ £35 =	455,000
18.1.1888	£5 per share returned leaving 13,000 issued @ £30. Reduced Issued Capital: 13,000 @ £30 =	£390,000
26.3.1890	Liability of £10 per share cancelled and each share divided into 3 new shares now 45,000 @ £10. (39,000 issued and fully paid) =	£390,000
1.3.1899	Articles of Association changed	
28.9.1900	Company voluntarily wound up. Liquidators were A. Elder, J. B. Mirrlees, John Wilson, Tom Davidson, J. Dempster, D. Murray.	

Source: File E.67206, dissolved at the Companies Registration Office, Edinburgh.

Table 34 SUMMARY OF CAPITAL AND SHARES OF THE BRITISH
AND AFRICAN STEAM NAVIGATION COMPANY, MADE UP TO THE
FOURTH DAY OF MARCH, 1870

Nominal Capital £200,000 divided into 400 shares of £500 each.
Number of Shares taken up to the Fourth day of March, 1870—322, whereof 192
are 'A' shares 130 are 'B' shares.
There has been called up on each 'A' share £275 and on each 'B' share £120.
Total amount of calls received —£68,400
Total amount of calls unpaid   — —
Total amount of shares forfeited— —

4 March 1870
List of persons holding shares.

BRITISH AND AFRICAN STEAM NAVIGATION COMPANY
SHARE DISTRIBUTION ON 4TH MARCH 1870

'A' SHARES

Brush	Peter	Leith	Merchant	54
Randolph	Charles	Glasgow	Engineer	27
Cunliff	Richard S.	21, Carlton Place, Glasgow	Engineer	9
Laury	Robert Frew	Liverpool	Master Mar.	9
Cunliff	James L.	Fairfield	Engineer	6
Jamieson	John L. K.	22, Carlton Place, Glasgow	Engineer	3
Cook	Robert	Woodbine Cottage, Pollokshields	Engineer	3
Muir	Thomas	Tradeston Mill, Glasgow	Merchant	3
Dunlop	David John	298, Bath Crescent, Glasgow	Engineer	3
Lorimer	John	19, St Enoch Square, Glasgow	Merchant	3
Moyes	William	19, St Enoch Square, Glasgow	Merchant	3
Mirrlees	James Buchanan	Scotland Street, Glasgow	Engineer	12
Walker	Alexander	158, Leadenhall Street, London	Merchant	6
Davison	Thomas	248, Bath Crescent, Glasgow	Engineer	3
Harrison	Michael	3, Mountjoy Square, Dublin	Judge	3
Elder	Alexander	2, Brunswick St, Liverpool	Merchant	3
Marmon	James	45, Regent Road, Liverpool	Contractor	3
Garthside	James	69, Rodney Street, Liverpool	Surgeon	3
Jack	John	Victoria Works, Liverpool	Engineer	2
Jones	James Fisher	38, Chapel Street, Liverpool	Sailmaker	3
Todd	Michael	Barry	Merchant	6
McOnie	Andrew	Scotland St, Glasgow	Mfg. Chemist	1
Wilson	John	18, Oswald Street, Glasgow	Merchant	3
Spiers	Robert	18, Oswald Street, Glasgow	Merchant	5
Wilson	S. R.	Liverpool	Merchant	25

BRITISH AND AFRICAN STEAM NAVIGATION COMPANY
SHARE DISTRIBUTION ON 4TH MARCH 1870

'B' SHARES

Dunlop	David John	298, Bath Crescent, Glasgow	Engineer	6
Neish	Theodore L.	12 Centre St, Glasgow	Engineer	6
Folland	N. S.	90, Irlam Lane, Bootle	Master Mar.	3
Woolcott	Henry J.	Beresford Road, Claughton	Gentleman	6
Rodger	John	Inveraray	Chemist	3
Muir	Thomas	Tradeston Mill, Glasgow	Merchant	4
Davison	Thomas	248, Bath St, Glasgow	Engineer	4
Coats	Thomas	Ferguslie, Paisley	Thread Mfg.	4
Griffiths	John	12, Glover Street, Birkenhead	Master Mar.	1
Ford	James	26, Regent Terrace, Edinburgh	Merchant	13
Cook	Robert	Woodbine Cottage, Pollokshields	Engineer	8
Ross	Robert	176, St Vincent St, Glasgow	Writer	6
Harrison	Michael	3, Mountjoy Square, Dublin	Judge	2
Salisbury	Edward	248, Bath St, Glasgow	Gentleman	2
Nicholl	William	Liverpool	Shipowner	2
Robinson	Henry Oliver	194, West George St, Glasgow	Civil Engineer	2
MacLellan	Walter	129, Irongate, Glasgow	Iron Merchant	6
Comrie	Mrs Ann	Bute Hotel, Rothsay	Hotel Keeper	3
Mirrlees	James Buchanan	Scotland St, Glasgow	Engineer	5
Cunliff	Richard S.	21, Carlton Place, Glasgow	Engineer	3
Jones	James Fisher	38, Chapel Street, Liverpool	Sailmaker	3
Moyes	William	19, St Enoch Square, Glasgow	Merchant	2
Lorimer	John	19, St Enoch Square, Glasgow	Merchant	5
Marmon	James	45, Regent Road, Liverpool	Contractor	8
Jamieson	John L. K.	22, Carlton Place, Glasgow	Engineer	6
McOnie	William	Scotland Street, Glasgow	Engineer	3
Elder	Alexander	2, Brunswick Street, Liverpool	Merchant	2

Total: 'A' Shares 204
'B' Shares 117
———
(4th March 1870) 322

Source: File E.67206, dissolved at the Companies Registration Office, Edinburgh.

Table 35 BRITISH & AFRICAN STEAM NAVIGATION COMPANY (UNLIMITED: 1869–1883)

SHARES DISTRIBUTION

NAME	1870	1871	1872	1873	1874	1875	1876	1877	1878	1879	1880	1881	1882	1883
A. Elder	6	6	6	10	10	11	19	19	19	19	10	25	200	200
*J. Dempster & Seligmarm	1	1	1	5	5	6	9	9	9	9	9	12	96	96
	6													
A. L. Jones	—	—	—	—	—	—	—	—	—	—	—	1	8	8
W. J. Davey	—	—	—	—	—	—	—	—	—	—	—	1	8	8
W. McOnie	8	8	8	7	7	7	8	8	8	8	15	15	120	120
A. McOnie	7	7	7	7	7	7	7	7	7	7	7	7	56	56
McOnie (Jnr)	—	—	—	1	1	1	1	1	1	1	1	1	8	8
J. B. Mirrlees	25	25	25	25	25	25	25	25	25	25	25	25	200	200
T. Coats	30	30	35	35	35	35	35	35	35	35	35	35	265	265
J. Holt	—	—	—	—	—	—	—	—	—	Ex.	Ex.	—	—	—
C. Randolph	—	27	27	27	27	27	27	27	27	27	27	—	—	—
P. Brush	—	22	8	—	—	—	—	—	—	—	Ex.	Ex.	Ex.	Ex.
J. L. Cunliff	—	17	17	17	17	20	20	20	20	20	20	20	160	160
Total Number of Shares:	322	322	322	320	320	320	320	320	320	320	320	320	2,344	2,344
Number of Shareholders:	46	49	50	52	50	50	50	50	50	50	50	53	53	53

* Note that Dempster & Seligmarm held 6 joint shares.

BRITISH & AFRICAN STEAM NAVIGATION COMPANY (LIMITED: 1883–1900)

SHARES DISTRIBUTION

Shareholder		1883 (April)	1883	1884	1885	1886	1887	1888	1889	1890	1891	1892	1893
Alexander Elder, Merchant, 48 Castle Street, Liverpool.	New:	—	—	—	—	—	—	—	—	—	—	—	—
	Old:	1,000	1,000	800	732	732	732	732	732	732	2,196	2,196	2,296
Mrs A. Elder	New:	—	—	—	—	—	—	—	—	—	—	—	120
	Old:	—	—	—	—	—	—	—	—	—	—	—	—
John Dempster, Merchant, 48 Castle Street, Liverpool.	New:	—	—	—	—	—	—	—	—	—	—	—	—
	Old:	480	470	470	545	545	668	668	676	653	1,959	2,025	2,871
William Dempster	New:	—	—	—	—	—	—	—	—	—	—	—	20
	Old:	—	—	—	—	—	—	—	—	—	—	—	—
A. L. Jones, Steamship Agent, 66 Cressington Park, Aigburth.	New:	—	40	100	150	150	30	30	332	332	996	1,155	459
	Old:	40	40	40	—	—	—	—	—	—	—	—	—
W. J. Davey, Steamship Agent, 24, Brompton Avenue, Liverpool.	New:	40	20	50	—	—	—	—	—	23	69	69	69
	Old:	40	40	40	—	—	—	—	—	—	—	—	—
John Holt, Merchant and Family.	New:	—	—	—	—	—	—	—	—	—	—	—	—
	Old:	—	—	—	40	40	40	40	200	357	801	801	801
AFRICAN ASSOCIATION.	New:	—	—	—	—	—	—	—	—	—	—	—	—
	Old:	—	—	—	—	—	—	—	—	—	—	—	—
William McOnie, Engineer, of Glasgow, and Family.	New:	—	—	—	—	—	—	—	—	—	—	—	—
	Old:	920	920	920	970	970	970	970	707	660	1,980	1,980	1,980
James B. Mirrlees, Engineer, of Glasgow.	New:	—	—	1,000	—	—	—	—	—	—	—	—	—
	Old:	1,000	1,000	1,000	1,000	1,000	1,000	1,000	800	800	2,400	2,000	1,500
Thomas Coats, Mfr, of Ferguslie, Paisley, and Family.	New:	—	75	75	—	—	—	—	—	—	—	—	—
	Old:	1,325	1,130	1,280	1,380	1,380	1,380	1,380	1,380	1,380	4,140	4,140	4,140
TOTAL NUMBER OF SHARES:		11,720	11,720	11,720	13,000	13,000	13,000	13,000	13,000	13,000	39,000	39,000	39,000
NUMBER OF SHAREHOLDERS:		—	—	87	87	88	88	88	88	88	90	90	91

BRITISH & AFRICAN STEAM NAVIGATION COMPANY. (LIMITED 1883–1900)
SHARES DISTRIBUTION

Name	1894	1895	1896	1897	1898	1899	1900
A. Elder	2,596	2,596	2,051	2,061	2,185	2,185	2,559
Mrs A. Elder	129	129	129	129	129	129	150
J. Dempster	2,871	2,871	1,755	1,565	1,595	1,665	1,831
W. Dempster	20	20	20	120	40	40	46
A. L. Jones	189	39	55	155	205	205	179
W. J. Davey	69	69	69	69	69	69	79
J. Holt and Family	776	711	2,761	621	415	643	920
African Association	—	—	—	—	40	2,160	2,492
W. McOnie and Family	1,380	1,380	60	60	60	60	69
J. B. Mirrlees	1,500	1,500	1,500	1,500	1,500	1,500	1,740
T. Coats and Family	4,140	4,140	4,140	4,140	4,140	4,140	4,534
Total number of shares:	39,000	39,000	39,000	39,000	39,000	39,000	45,000
No. of Shareholders:	92	98	111	121	125	127	138

BRITISH & AFRICAN STEAM NAVIGATION COMPANY (1900) LIMITED

	1901	1902	1903	1904	1905	1906	1907	1908	1909	1910
Jones & Davey	62,442	54,440	52,140	47,140	47,140	47,140	42,140	42,140	39,190	11,000
A. L. Jones	280	281	281	281	281	281	281	281	281	281
W. J. Davey	280	281	281	281	281	281	281	281	281	—
J. Dempster	10	10	10	10	10	10	10	10	5	5
Warr	1	1	1	1	1	1	1	1	1	1
Dun	1	1	1	1	1	1	1	1	1	—
Dixon	250	250	—	—	—	—	—	—	—	500
Pirrie	10	10	10	10	10	10	10	10	10	10
Bateson	1	1	1	1	1	1	1	1	1	1
Crawford	1	1	1	1	1	1	1	1	1	1
Harland & Wolf	—	8,000	8,000	8,000	8,000	8,000	8,000	8,000	8,000	8,000
Lady Dixon	—	—	250	250	250	250	250	250	250	250
Webb & Vaisey	—	—	2,000	2,000	2,000	2,000	7,000	7,000	7,000	7,000
B. Pinnock (J's Niece)	—	—	100	100	100	100	100	100	100	100
M. I. Pinnock (J's Sister)	—	—	100	100	100	100	100	100	100	100
Mrs Williams (J's Niece)	—	—	100	100	100	100	100	100	100	100
E. D. Shipping Limited	—	—	—	5,000	5,000	5,000	5,000	5,000	5,000	5,000
O. H. Williams & Ross	—	—	—	—	—	—	—	—	2,700	2,450

J. Craig	—	—	—	—	—	—	—	—	250	250
W. Dempster	—	—	—	—	—	—	—	—	5	5
Porter	—	—	—	—	—	—	—	—	—	1
Stewart & Hughes (Bankers)	—	—	—	—	—	—	—	—	—10,000
O. Phillips	—	—	—	—	—	—	—	—	—	250
Elder, Dempster & Co.	—	—	—	—	—	—	—	—	—15,195
Total number of Shares:	63,276	63,276	63,276	63,276	63,276	63,276	63,276	63,276	63,276	65,000

Notes on the Movements of the Above Shares

1902:   2 Shares ex Jones & Davey Joint holding to their separate holdings.

8,000 Shares ex Jones & Davey Joint holding to Harland & Wolf.

250 Shares ex Sir Dixon to Lady Dixon.

1903:   100 Shares ex Jones & Davey Joint holding to Miss B. Pinnock.

100 Shares ex Jones & Davey Joint holding to Mrs M. I. Pinnock.

100 Shares ex Jones & Davey Joint holding to Mrs O. H. Williams.

2,000 Shares ex Jones & Davey Joint holding to Webb & Vaisey.

1904:   5,000 Shares ex Jones & Davey Joint holding to E. D. Shipping Limited.

1907:   5,000 Shares ex Jones & Davey Joint holding to Webb & Vaisey.

1909:   2,700 Shares ex Jones & Davey Joint holding to G. H. Williams.

250 Shares ex Jones & Davey Joint holding to J. Craig.

5 Shares ex J. Dempster to W. Dempster.

1910:   281 Shares ex Davey to Elder Dempster and Company.

1 Share ex Dun to Porter.

10,000 Shares ex Davey & Jones Joint holding to Stewart & Hughes.

5,000 Shares ex Davey & Jones Joint holding to Dixon.

13,190 Shares ex Davey & Jones Joint holding to Bates.

13,190 Shares ex Davey & Jones Joint holding to Elder Dempster & Co. (via Bates)

250 Shares ex O. H. Williams to Phillips.

1,724 new shares issued, and taken up by Elder Dempster & Co.

Source: File E.67206, dissolved at the Companies Registration Office, Edinburgh.

APPENDICES

Table 36 SIERRA LEONE COALING COMPANY
Known as 'THE OLD COMPANY'
Bank Buildings, Water Street, Freetown.

Retail–Wholesale Warehouse

Always a plentiful supply of Tinned meats, White lump and light brown sugar; 1 cwt. and 2 cwt. barrels, flour, Biscuits, Potatoes and Rice, Ham and Bacon, Beef and Pork in Barrels of 200 lbs. each, Butter and Lard in tins of various sizes.

Paints, assorted oils, Glass, Ropes and Disinfecting fluid. The mineral Sperm is an invaluable non-explosive oil for lamps; highly recommended to Clergymen, Lawyers and Students.

A full assortment of Sundry Provisions always kept in stock.

The *Sierra Leone Coaling Company* do all kinds of Ship's business including entering and clearing at the Customs at a moderate charge. They have a large stock of Wines, Beer and Spirits, Puncheon and Demijohn Rum in Bond as well as duty paid. Also very Old Jamaica Rum in Bottles.

Merchants and Traders in Cotton and other goods are especially invited to call and inspect the large assortment of Cotton Goods in Stock. Also Gents and Ladies Boots and Shoes, Silk Handkerchiefs, Tweeds, Cloths, etc.

They have also a stock of fashionable Pique Fronts, Berlin Shirts, Flexible Zepheyrs, Super Rim, Terai hats, Masher Helmets, Walking Sticks and other Gents' and Ladies wearing apparel and Fancy goods.

For Cheapness Variety and Durability of Articles 'The Old Company' Cannot be Beaten.

Source: Advertisement in the *Sierra Leone Weekly News*, 17 October 1891.

Table 37 THE WEST AFRICAN BANK LIMITED

Directors: Edward Gratto, Esq., J.P. *Auth. Capital:* £250,000
Edward Draftmere, Esq. First series of: £50,000
C. Marcus Westfield, Esq.
James Fraser, Esq.

Bankers: London—The London & County Banking Company, 21 Lombard Street.
Liverpool—Messrs Edward W. Yates & Company, 37 Castle Street.

Solicitors Messrs Peacock & Goddard, 3 South Square, Gray's Inn, W.C.

Auditors: Messrs James Fraser & Sons, Chartered Accounts, 2 Tokenhouse Buildings, London, E.C.

Head Office: (pro tem) 2 Tokenhouse Buildings, London, E.C.

Branches: Freetown, Sierra Leone.

The West African Bank Limited
Terms

1. *Current Accounts:* On the same plan as that usually adopted by London bankers. A commission of half a per cent will be charged on the Dr. side of the Account.
2. *Deposits at 14 Days Notice and Fixed Deposits* will be received at interest to be agreed upon which will vary according to the length of time the deposit is made for.
3. *Advances on African Gold* will be made at the rate of 40s per ounce and the surplus credited after assey and report. A commission will be charged on the proceeds of one per cent to customers having current accounts and two per cent to others.
4. *Bills for Collection* in Europe or at the Branches and Agencies will be charged a commission of 2½ per cent if in Europe and 5 per cent if in West Africa.
Parties not keeping current accounts will be charged an extra one per cent. To those keeping current accounts an advance varying from half to three fifths will be made if accompanied by invoice of goods and Bills of Lading against which they are drawn.
5. *Purchase of Bills of Exchange* On Europe will be made at a rate of exchange based on the current rates of interest. To parties not having a current account an additional commission of 1 per cent will be charged and no bills will be purchased off them unless drawn against 3/5ths of the market value of produce shipped and accompanied by Bills of Lading. When the Bank has to sell the produce against which Bills are drawn in order to encash their amount an additional commission of 2½ per cent will be charged beyond the London brokerage.
6. *Drafts on London, Paris, Hamburg and New York* will be issued in sterling only, at a premium to be fixed at the time.
7. *Approved Trade Bills* having not more than three months to run will be discounted.

p.p. West African Bank Ltd
John Evans

Source: *Sierra Leone Weekly News*, 12 September 1891.

APPENDICES

Table 38 BANK OF BRITISH WEST AFRICA LIMITED

Formed: 30.3.1894

Capital: 10,000 shares at £10 each = £100,000 (Nominal)

Agreement: 26.7.1894 shows that the company owed Jones (£6,932), Davey (£1,732) and Sinclair (£1,732). They then received the following shares, each with £4 per share paid up:

          Jones—1,733   Davey—433   Sinclair—433.

Directors: Henry Coke
          Alfred Lewis Jones
          George W. Neville
          Owen Harrison Williams

8.10.1900:   Capital increased to £250,000 by the issue of 15,000 shares at £10 each.

28.10.1907:   Capital increased to £1,000,000 by the issue of 75,000 shares at £10 each.

1957:   Name changed to Bank of West Africa Limited.

31.8.1966:   Name changed to Standard Bank of West Africa, Limited.

Source: File 40828, live at Companies House, London.

Table 39 BANK OF BRITISH WEST AFRICA LTD

Distribution of Shares

Name	Occupation	1894	1895	1896	1897*	1898	1899	1900	1901	1902	1907
E. Laurence	Merchant	50	50	50	50	50	50	50	50	50	50
D. H. Williams	Cotton Broker	100	100	100	100	100	100	100	100	100	100
W. Ross	Clerk	1	1	1	11	1	11	10	10	10	—
F. Bond	Gentleman	50	50	50	100	50	100	100	100	100	—
H. Coke	Merchant	50	50	50	100	50	100	200	200	200	200
J. Pinnock	Merchant	100	100	100	100	100	100	100	100	100	—
J. Roxburgh	Cotton Broker	50	50	50	80	50	100	100	100	100	130
A. L. Jones	Ship Owner	1,733	1,628	1,628	1,648	1,648	1,648	1,723	1,820	2,161	4,739
W. J. Davey	Ship Owner	433	433	433	433	433	433	433	433	433	520
A. Sinclair	Ship Owner	433	433	433	433	433	433	433	433	433	—
G. W. Neville	Manager	—	100	100	100	100	100	100	150	150	100
†Edward Jones	Manager	—	2	2	2	2	2	2	2	2	2
John Manning	Secretary	—	2	—	—	—	—	—	—	—	—
Leslie Murg	—	—	1	—	—	—	—	—	—	—	—
†Mary Jones	—	—	3	3	3	3	3	3	3	3	3
		3,000	3,000	3,000	5,535	5,788	6,945	8,700	10,475	11,680	15,000

* No new shareholders are shown starting in 1897.
† Hertford Drive, Liscard, later 10, Walton Park, Walton.

Source: File 40828, live at Companies House, London.

Table 40 ELDERS NAVIGATION COLLIERIES LIMITED

Founded: 5.3.1900
Directors: A. L. Jones
W. J. Davey
Raylton Dixon
David Highgate
David Jones
William Dempster
Laurence Jones
Capital: 5,000 @ £10 each = £ 50,000
5% Debentures = 75,000
———
£125,000
———

Jones received £124,930 by allotment of 4,993 shares, value £49,930 and the debentures making a total of £124,930
19.12.10: Name changed to Elders Collieries Ltd
20.4.15: Name changed to Celtic Collieries Ltd
1930: Wound up
Colliery situated at Garth, Maesteg, Glamorgan

Source: File 65244, dissolved at Companies House, London.

Table 41 ELDERS NAVIGATION COLLIERIES LIMITED

Name	1901	1902	1903	1904	1905	1906	1907	1908	1909	1910
*A. L. Jones	4,993	3,993	4,893	4,893	4,893	4,893	4,893	4,793	4,793	—
*W. J. Davey	1	1,001	101	101	101	101	101	101	101	—
R. Dixon	1†	1	1	1	1	1	1	1	1	1
D. Highgate	1	1	1	1	1	1	1	1	1	1
D. Jones	1	1	1	1	1	1	1	1	1	1
W. Dempster	1	1	1	1	1	1	1	1	1	1
L. Jones	1	1	1	1	1	1	1	1	1	1
J. Craig	1	1	1	1	1	1	1	1	1	101
	5,000	5,000	5,000	5,000	5,000	5,000	5,000	5,000	5,000	—
O. H. Williams	—	—	—	—	—	—	—	—	—	100 (Ex A.L.J.)
Elder Dempster & Co.	—	—	—	—	—	—	—	—	—	4,794 (Ex A.L.J. W.J.D.)
										5,000

* Directors.   † Lady Dixon.

Source: File 65244, dissolved at Companies House, London.

Table 42 ELDERS AND FYFFES LTD

Formed: 9.5.1901

Directors:

A. L. Jones	Ship Owner	H. Wolfson	Fruit Mcht.
A. H. Stockley	Fruit Mcht.	J. M. Leacock	Fruit Mcht.
A. R. Ackerley	Fruit Mcht.	E. C. Barker	Fruit Mcht.
R. Ackerley	Fruit Mcht.		

Registered Office: 9/12 Bow Street, London.

Capital: £150,000 in 150,000 shares of £1 nominal, divided into 'A', 'B' and 'C' shares. £160,000 in Debenture Stock issued 10.6.1901.

Trustees: Owen Harrison Williams, Alfred Lloyd Barrell.

The Company took over the business in certain spheres of Messrs Elder Dempster & Co. & of Messrs Fyffe, Hudson & Co. Ltd. Alfred Jones was to be Chairman as long as he remained a Director but neither he nor W. J. Davey were to be paid for services as Chairman or Director.

Satisfaction of Debentures

£20,475 repaid on 30.6.02
10,000 repaid on 16.9.02
10,000 repaid on 1.7.03
10,000 repaid on 30.6.04
10,000 repaid on 30.6.05
10,000 repaid on 30.6.06
10,000 repaid on 30.6.07
10,000 repaid on 30.6.08

Increase of Capital

10.2.03 + 122,460 = 272,460 total
16.2.04 + 77,540 = 350,000
23.12.04 + 100,000 = 450,000
30.8.13 + 550,000 = 1,000,000

Mortgages on Ships

12.5.04. Mortgage of £50,000 to Barclay & Co. Satisfied on 11.2.05
13.2.05. Mortgage of 75,000 to Barclay & Co. Satisfied on 30.9.05
2.10.05. Mortgage of 75,000 to Barclay & Co. Satisfied on 23.8.06
(Also borrowing on the S.S. *Miami*, S.S. *Matina*, S.S. *Manichee*)

ELDERS AND FYFFES LIMITED SHARE DISTRIBUTION

Year	1901	1902	1903	1903	1905	1905	1908	1908	1909	1909
A. L. Jones	70,500	70,505	55,449	—	83,254	1	55,503	27,752	20,000	27,752
W. J. Davey	23,493	23,495	13,479	—	20,237	1	13	6,752	13	6,746
A. H. Stockley	2,000	2,000	5,998	4,000	9,006	6,006	10,008	5,004	10,008	5,004
A. H. Ackerley	2,000	2,000	2,998	1,000	4,501	1,502	4,004	2,001	4,002	2,001
R. Ackerley	2,000	2,000	1,998	—	2,999	1	2,000	1,000	2,000	1,000
'A' Shares	99,993	100,000	100,000							
H. Wolfson	2,000	2,667	—	21,644	1	32,497	21,665	10,833	21,665	10,833
J. W. Leacock	22,000	2,667	—	21,644	1	32,496	21,665	10,832	21,665	10,832
E. C. Barker	2,000	2,606	—	21,643	1	32,496	21,665	10,832	21,665	10,832
Wolfson, Leacock, Barker	42,180	42,180	—	—	—	—	—	—	—	—
L. Wolfson	1,820	—	—	—	—	—	—	—	—	—
'B' Shares	50,000	50,000								

Subscribers:

4	A. Preston	
1	J. Jones	
1	B. Parmer	
1	M. Keith	
7	C. Hubbard	
	F. Hart	

	1903	1903	1905	1905	1908	1908	1909	1909
A. L. Jones	16,900	12,100	31,509	31,100	67,229	37,500	67,229	37,500
W. J. Davey	12,520	11,700	22,520	19,700	—	—	—	—
A. H. Stockley	11,350	10,300	21,350	14,300	25,150	10,500	25,150	10,500
A. R. Atcherley	9,500	9,116	20,600	19,784	18,616	—	18,666	—
SUBSCRIBERS: C. Hubbard	8,600	8,000	9,500	9,116	18,000	18,000	22,384	18,000
F. Hart	6,521	6,000	14,521	11,000	16,521	9,000	16,521	9,000
	145,313	127,147	240,000	210,000				
	272,460		450,000					

	1908	1908	1909	1909
R. Clark	100	—	100	—
Williams & Ross	13,479	—	13,479	—
Robertson & Hughes (Bankers)	—	—	35,503	—
	300,000	150,000	300,000	150,000
	450,000		450,000	

440

ELDERS & FYFFES LTD

Name	1910 Fully Paid	1910 Partly Paid
'A' Shares		
A. L. Jones	—	—
W. J. Davey	—	—
A. H. Stockley	10,008	4,904
A. R. Ackerley	4,002	2,001
R. Ackerley	2,000	1,000
'B' Shares		
H. Wolfson	21,665	10,833
J. W. Leacock	21,665	10,832
E. C. Barker	21,665	10,832
Wolfson, Leacock & Barker	—	—
L. Wolfson	—	—
A. Preston	67,229	37,500
J. Jones	—	—
B. Palmon	25,150	10,500
M. Keith	18,616	—
C. Hubbard	22,384	18,000
F. Hart	16,521	9,000
R. Clark	100	—
Robertson & Hughes (Bankers)	—	—
R. Miller	—	100
Sir P. Bates	—	—
Elder Dempster & Co. Ltd	68,995	34,498
	300,000	150,000
	450,000	

NOTES:

18.12.1907: Agreement made with the United Fruit Co. of New Jersey re bananas.

4.10.1913: New shares issue of £550,000 in £1 shares taken up by the United Fruit Company.

Dec. 1913: This return shows that Elder Dempster's had sold their 68,995 fully paid & 34,498 partly paid shares to A. Preston.

Source: File 70123, live at Companies House, London.

Table 43 IMPERIAL DIRECT WEST INDIA MAIL SERVICE CO. LTD

Formed: 9.12.1901

Capital: 50,000 shares @ 10 = £500,000

Agreement: 31.12.1901. Between A. L. Jones and W. J. Davey, and the new company. This provided for the sale to the company of the U/M ships valued at £475,000 plus £25,000 for goodwill:

Port Royal	*Port Antonio*	*Port Maria*
Port Morat	*Montrose*	*Garth Castle*
Delta		

In return Jones received £250,000 in cash and 25,000 shares @ £10 each—a total of £500,000

Mortgages: 14.1.02. 1st Mortgage of £250,000 4½% debentures. (Trustees: Sir Edward Laurence, Charles McArthur, J. S. Harwood-Rowe)

16.3.04. Addition of *Port Kingston*

1937—Wound up

IMPERIAL DIRECT WEST INDIA MAIL SERVICE CO. LTD. SHARE DISTRIBUTION

	1901	1902	1903	1904	1905	1906	1907	1908	1909	1910	1911
A. L. Jones*	18,672	18,672	18,672	8,672	8,672	8,672	8,672	8,672	8,472	—	—
W. J. Davey*	6,224	6,224	6,224	6,224	1,224	1,224	1,224	1,224	1,224	—	—
H. R. Dixon*	100	100	100	100	100	100	100	100	100	100	100
Sir W. H. Wills	1	1	1	1	1	1†	1	1	1	1	1
A. Elder	1	1	1	1	1	1	1	1	1	1	1
P. Napier Miles	1	1	1	1	1	1	1	1	1	1	1
John Dempster	1	1	1	1	1	1	1	1	1	1	1
British & African Steam Nav. Co.	—	—	—	10,000	10,000	10,000	10,000	10,000	10,000	10,000	—
E. D. Shipping Ltd	—	—	—	—	5,000	5,000	5,000	5,000	5,000	5,000	—
John Craig	—	—	—	—	—	—	—	—	100	100	100
H. W. Davey	—	—	—	—	—	—	—	—	100	—	—
O. H. Williams	—	—	—	—	—	—	—	—	—	100	100
Elder Dempster & Co. Ltd	—	—	—	—	—	—	—	—	—	9,696	24,596
(Others)	—	—	—	—	—	—	—	—	—	—	100
TOTALS:	25,000	25,000	25,000	25,000	25,000	25,000	25,000	25,000	25,000	25,000	25,000

* Directors.   † Became Lord Winterstoke.

Source: File 72110, dissolved at Companies House, London.

443

Table 44 ELDER AND FYFFES (SHIPPING) LIMITED

Formed:	18.4.1902
Capital:	100,000 £1 shares = £100,000 nominal
Agreements:	1. Elders and Fyffes Ltd. agree to hire three steamers from the new firm

2. Elders and Fyffes agree to give the new firm the option of providing any new steamers they may require, but have certain rights if new shares are issued

3. W. A. Angone & Co. are appointed Managers. W. A. St Aubyn Angone, who is a promoter, and one of the first Directors of the Company shall be entitled to enter into an agreement with Elders and Fyffes in the terms of the draft already prepared whereby he is appointed sole Maritime Insurance Broker to Elders and Fyffes upon the terms therein mentioned

Directors:	W. A. St. Aubyn Angone	Insurance Broker
	John William Didsdale	Underwriter
	Arthur Henry Stockley	Fruit Merchant
	Edward Cecil Barker	Fruit Merchant
11.11.1902:	3 ships mortgaged for £12,500	
28.5.1907:	Company wound up	

ELDERS AND FYFFES (SHIPPING) LTD DISTRIBUTION OF SHARES

Name	Address	1902	1906	
		'A' Shares	'A' Shares	
W. A. A. Angove	9 Gracechurch Street	13,300	34,900	held by Elder & Fyffes
H. W. Richards	9 Gracechurch Street	4,000	100	held by all others
A. T. Richards	9 Gracechurch Street	2,000		
B. H. Hodgson	9 Gracechurch Street	4,000	35,000	
A. W. Symes	Borneo, Pangbourne	1,000		
J. W. Ridsdale	9 Gracechurch Street	500		
T. L. Maycock	9 Gracechurch Street	200		
		25,000		
		'B' Shares	'B' Shares	
Elder & Fyffes		12,000	46,900	held by Elder & Fyffes
		37,000	100	held by all others
			47,000	
		'C' Shares	'C' Shares	
H. Wolfson	9 Bow Street	5,000		
J. W. Leacock	9 Bow Street	5,000		
E. C. Barker	9 Bow Street	5,000		
Mrs E. Hinshaw	Brickhampton Hall, Parshaw	1,000	17,798	held by Elder & Fyffes
H. Donald	331 Holloway Road, N.	1,000	202	held by all others
A. H. Stockley	9 Bow Street	1,000	18,000	
		55,000		

Elders & Fyffes Ltd held 99,598 out of 100,000 shares
Taken over in 1907

'A', 'B' and 'C' are all ordinary shares and have similar rights for dividend & capital.

Source: File 73475, dissolved at Public Record Office, London.

Table 45 ELDER DEMPSTER SHIPPING LIMITED

Formed: 3.5.1899

Capital: 100,000 shares @ £10. = £1,000,000

Agreement: 5.5.1899. This provided for the purchase of the u/m ships for £1,100,000. i.e., £600,000. in cash and 50,000 shares @ £10. = £500,000.

Montcalm	Montclair	Monteagle
Montenegro	Monterey	Montfort
Montpelier	Mount Royal	Monarch
Andori	Ashanti	Banana
Degama	Lokoja	Milwakee
Yola	Yoruba	

Schedule:

Owners or Nominees	Amount in Shares and Cash	Numbers of Each Share
@ A. L. Jones & Davey	48,990 and £489,900	
A. L. Jones	250	2,500
W. J. Davey	250	2,500
A. Sinclair	250	2,500
R. Dixon	250	2,500
A. Elder	3	30
J. Dempster	3	30
J. Craig	2	20
D. Jones	1	10
H. D. Bateson	1	10
	50,000	500,000
E.D. & Co.		600,000
		£1,100,000

ELDER DEMPSTER SHIPPING LIMITED

Mortgages

18.5.1899   Trust Deed;   £600,000 Debenture Stock @ 4½ per cent

             Trustees;   Sir Edward Lawrence, Charles MacArthur, John Sutherland Harwood-Banner.

2.10.1901   S.S. *Bida,* S.S. *Hausa.*

27.12.1902   S.S. *Llandulas,* S.S. *Nyanga,* S.S. *Abeakuta.*

12.5.1903   S.S. *Melville.*

4.1.1904   S.S. *Etalia,* S.S. *Memman,* S.S. *Lycia.*

3.3.1904   S.S. *Canada Cape.*

3.5.1904   S.S. *Porto Novo.*

30.5.1904	S.S. *Muraji.*
20.7.1904	S.S. *Zunzeru.*
18.3.1905	S.S. *Benue.*
28.12.1905	S.S. *Dahomey,* S.S. *Angola.*
20.2.1906	S.S. *Port Morat.*
26.6.1906	S.S. *Coaling.*
12.7.1906	S.S. *Patani.*
3.10.1906	S.S. *Falaba.*
28.3.1907	S.S. *Ashogbo.*
14.9.1907	S.S. *Sobo.*
30.12.1907	S.S. *Forcados,* S.S. *Lagos.*
20.2.1909	S.S. *Jamaica.*
24.6.1909	S.S. *Badagri,* S.S. *Monrovia.*
21.5.1910	Name changed to Elder Line Limited.

In 1914 the African Steam Ship Company held 48,740 of the 50,000 shares.

In 1919 the African Steam Ship Company held 49,246 of the 50,000 shares.

In 1922 the new share issue of 50,000 was all retained by the African Steam Ship Company.

In 1929 the African Steam Ship Co. held 98,996 of the 100,000 shares.

11.6.1936.　　The Company was wound up.

Source: File 61912, dissolved at Public Record Office, London.

Table 46 ELDER DEMPSTER SHIPPING LTD
Share Distribution

Name	1899	1900	1901	1902	1903	1904	1905	1906	1907	1908	1909
Jones & Davey	48,990	48,990	48,990	48,990	48,990	15,990	15,990	15,990	15,990	15,990	16,240
A. L. Jones	250	250	250	250	250	250	250	250	250	250	250
W. J. Davey	250	250	250	250	250	250	250	250	250	250	250
A. Sinclair	250	250	250	250	250	—	—	—	—	—	—
R. Dixon	250	250	250	250	250	250	250	250	250	260	250
A. Elder	3	3	3	3	3	3	3	3	3	3	3
J. Dempster	3	3	3	3	3	3	3	3	3	3	2
J. Craig	2	2	2	2	2	2	2	2	2	2	2
D. Jones	1	1	1	1	1	1	1	1	1	1	1
Bateson	1	1	1	1	1	1	1	1	1	1	1
Jones, Davey & Sinclair	—	—	—	—	—	5,000	5,000	5,000	5,000	5,000	—
Harland & Wolff	—	—	—	—	—	7,000	7,000	7,000	7,000	7,000	7,000
O. H. Williams	—	—	—	—	—	250	250	250	250	250	250
Sir C. Furness	—	—	—	—	—	10,000	10,000	10,000	10,000	10,000	10,000
Webb & Vaisey	—	—	—	—	—	2,000	2,000	2,000	2,000	2,000	2,000
British & African S.N. Co.	—	—	—	—	—	9,000	9,000	9,000	9,000	9,000	9,000
Irvings Shipping	—	—	—	—	—	—	—	—	—	—	2,000
O. H. Williams & Ross	—	—	—	—	—	—	—	—	—	—	2,500
H. W. Davey	—	—	—	—	—	—	—	—	—	—	250
W. Dempster	—	—	—	—	—	—	—	—	—	—	1
Totals:	50,000										50,000

NOTE: 1914—48,748 shares held by the African Steam Ship Co.
1919—49,246 shares held by the African Steam Ship Co.
1920—50,000 shares (new issue) also held by the African Steam Ship Co.
1929—98,996 shares held by the African Steam Ship Co.
Company wound up—11/6/1936

Source: File 61912, dissolved at the Public Record Office, London.

ebba (ex *Albertville*) owned by the African Steam Ship Company from 1898 until she was lost at Hope Cove, Devon, in March 1907.

Nyanga built 1900 was sunk by a German surface raider in August 1914.

Fulani built 1907, wrecked in June 1914 on Carpenters Rock, Sierra Leone.

PLATE 27

Oshogbo built 1906, wrecked near Lagos, in July 1928.

Appam (1913–1936) was captured by the Germans during the First World War.

Aba (ex *Glenapp*) was the first large passenger vessel to be fitted with diesel engines (1918–1946).

PLATE 28

Mattawin (ex *Ediba*) built in 1923 was torpedoed in Long Island Sound in June 1942.

David Livingstone, one of the eight ships of the 'Explorer' class built during 1929 and 1930.

Abosso, the largest of the inter-war mail ships, was lost with great loss of life in October, 1942.

PLATE 29

Calabar built 1935 provided a service between West Africa and South Africa.

Oron, built 1938, alongside the new jetty at Calabar.

Prah (ex *Avisbay*) was acquired in 1950.

PLATE 30

Table 47 WILL OF SIR ALFRED LEWIS JONES

As Sir Alfred Jones had never married his next of kin were his sister, Mrs Mary Isabel Pinnock and his two nieces—Mrs Florence Mary Williams and Miss Blanche Elizabeth Pinnock—and these were the main beneficiaries. To his sister he left £1,500 plus an annuity of £2,500 per annum. She also received all the household goods at Oaklands, Aigburth, where she had kept house for Jones, and the use of this residence during her lifetime. Mrs Williams received £20,000 upon trust for life, and Miss Pinnock was left £30,000 on the same basis. There were also several bequests to friends, and provision was made for servants and clerks. The residue of the estate was then to be formed into a trust fund to help worthy causes—mainly those with a West African bias. The total value of the estate was originally estimated at £674,259 but was later re-sworn to £583,461. As will be imagined it was largely tied up in various companies and as many of the assets were mortgaged it was a complicated matter to settle.

The estate was not finalised until 1928. By then it was stated that over £325,000 had been distributed to charitable and other institutions. Included in the scheme were provisions for research work in tropical diseases, for technical education for the local people of West Africa, and for the relief of poor relatives and old employees. The administration of the will involved the investigation of over 11,000 claims to legacies by clerks who had been in Sir Alfred's employ (although only 800 were admitted) costing £70,000.

For full details of will see: A. H. Milne, *Sir Alfred Lewis Jones, K.C.M.G.* (Liverpool, Henry Young, p. 14). See also *West Africa*, 12 May 1928, p. 580.

Table 48 ELDER DEMPSTER AND COMPANY LIMITED

Formed:	31.3.1910		
Directors:	Lord Pirrie, Sir Owen Phillips		
Capital:	500,000 of £1 Cumulative Preference shares	=	500,000
	400,000 of £1 Ordinary Shares	=	400,000
	10,000 of £1 Management Shares	=	10,000

910,000

5 per cent of Debenture Stock   1,000,000

£1,910,000

Liverpool Managing Directors: John Craig
Owen Harrison Williams
David Jones
James Henry Sharrock (Accountant)
Edwin Bicker-Caarten (Secretary)

Allocation of Shares to Estate of Sir A. L. Jones
'Sale to the company of the business and goodwill of Elder Dempster and Company, The Grand Canary Coaling Company, The Teneriff Coaling Company and the Sierra Leone Coaling Company, and of the profits and assets mentioned in an agreement dated 2.4.1910.'

Total payments under this agreement were—

Cash	£200,000	
Debenture Stock	200,000	(Part of £1 million)
Preference shares	100,000	

£500,000

Agreement dated 2.4.1910 between Owen Harrison Williams, and Lord Pirrie and Sir Owen Phillips.

The First Schedule

Short Description of Property	*Particulars of Mortgages Thereon*
1. All that piece of land situate on the north side of Water Street east side of Tower Gardens and south side of Old Churchyard in the City of Liverpool containing in the whole 1,794 square yards more particularly described in the plan drawn on an indenture dated the 15th day of May 1905 and made between Sir Alfred Lewis Jones (then Alfred Lewis Jones) of the one part and Wm. John Davey of the	Mortgaged to the Royal Insurance Company Limited for £110,000 and interest at $3\frac{7}{8}$ per cent. per annum.

Short Description of Property

other part and thereon edged with red Together with the buildings erected thereon and called or known as 'Colonial House'.

2. All that piece of land fronting to Caryl Street Hill Street Warwick Street and Grafton Street in Toxteth Park in the said City of Liverpool containing in the whole 16,082 square yards or thereabouts more particularly described in the plan on an indenture dated the   day of   1905 and made between Annie Powell of the one part and the said Sir Alfred Lewis Jones and Wm. John Davey of the other part and thereon surrounded by blue red yellow and green lines on the said plan with the marble works cottages and stores thereon.

Mortgaged to Messrs. T. and J. A. Bartlett for £32,000 and interest at the rate of 4 per cent. per annum.

3. All those pieces of land situate on the south side of Hill Street aforesaid and more particularly delineated in the plan drawn upon an indenture dated the 2nd day of October 1906 and made between William Henrich Johnson of the one part and Henry Sanderson Paterson and George Bennett Paterson of the other part and therein coloured red and yellow with the smith's and wheelwright's shops and two cottages Nos. 24 and 26 Hill Street erected thereon.

4. All that piece of land on the east side of Back Grafton Street in the said City of Liverpool more particularly described in an indenture dated the 8th day of November 1906 and made between John Bennett Price and William Knowles of the one part and Henry Sanderson Paterson and George Bennett Paterson of the other part together with the two messuages and dwelling houses erected thereon.

5. The messuages or dwelling-houses and stables situate in Toxteth Park in the said City of Liverpool and conveyed to Messrs. Elder Dempster & Co. by five several indentures dated the 11th January 1882 and 7th February 1888 the 15th February 1888 and 6th March 1888 and the 13th March 1888.

The deeds are deposited with Parr's Bank Ltd. to secure an overdraft of the Grand Canary Coaling Co.

6. All that piece of land situate in Toxteth Park aforesaid bounded by Sefton Street on the west Stanhope Street on the north Crow Street on the east and Perry Street on the south. Together

1. Mortgaged to Miss Elizabeth Stringer for £12,500 (of which £10,000 remains owing)

Short Description of Property

Particulars of Mortgages Thereon

with the eight warehouses erected thereon which piece of land is delineated on a plan annexed to an indenture dated the 10th day of May 1899 and made between Samuel Withers and Henry Hartley Withers of the one part and the said Sir Alfred Lewis Jones (then Alfred Lewis Jones) Wm. John Davey and Alexander Sinclair of the other part.

and interest at 3½ per cent. per annum.
2. Mortgaged to Parr's Bank Limited to secure the overdraft of Elder Dempster and Co.

7. All those messuages and buildings situate in the parish of St. Nicholas in the City of Bristol and being No. 25 the Welsh Back and Nos. 29, 31, 33 and 35 Queen Charlotte Street delineated on the plan drawn on an indenture dated the 11th day of November 1898 and made between Herbert Alfred Burleigh of the one part and the said Sir Alfred Lewis Jones (Then Alfred Lewis Jones) Wm. John Davey and Alexander Sinclair of the other part.

Deposited with the Capital and Counties Bank Limited Bristol to secure an overdraft up to £6,500.
Nos. 31 & 33 Queen Charlotte St. aforesaid are subject to a fee farm rent of £12 per annum.

The Second Schedule—Foreign Properties in the Grand Canary

(A)   The property of *Elder Dempster and Company*

  1. Hotel Metropole and Annexe and Brown's House.
  2. Finca Alfredo Building Estate of about 33 acres on which are situate the Villa Alfredo and the Villa Flores.
  3. Finca Alcaravaneras Building Estate of about 53 acres on which are situate the Villas Alcaravaneras the Norwegian House Belle Vue House Swiss Cottage and Vista Alegro House.
  4. Escalaritas Estate.
  5. Zarita's Tank.
  6. Escorial Warehouse.
  7. Jetty and Mole at Santa Catalina.
  8. Stables at Santa Catalina.
  9. Land in Santa Catalina (5,762 square metres) with carpenter's shop and boat-house.
  10. Office on Santa Catalina Mole.
  11. Land in Calle Viera y Clavijo Las Palmas with timber store.
  12. Tras Palacio Warehouse.
  13. Warehouse at Las Palmas known as Elder and Fyffe's Warehouse.
  14. Office at Las Palmas.
  15. Hotel Victoria Monte.

(B)   The property of *Grand Canary Coaling Company*

    1. Offices.
    2. Coal Depot.
    3. Officers and Stores.
    4. Plot of land (1,500 square metres).
    5. Plot of land (5,856 square metres).
    6. Ship-building yard.
    7. Government concessions for slipway, dated 15 July 1896 and 25 October 1905.
    8. Petroleum stores and yard.
    9. Plot of land adjoining castle.
    10. Plot of land (containing 3,000 square metres).
    11. Office on Santa Catalina Mole.

In Tenerife

(A)   The property of *Elder Dempster and Company*

    1. Pino do Oro Hotel Santa Cruz Tenerife.
    2. Land and Offices in Calle Castello Santa Cruz aforesaid.

(B)   The property of the *Tenerife Coaling Company*

    1. Coal stores, Santa Cruz.
    2. Slipway, Santa Cruz.
    3. Petroleum store, Lana de los Molinos.
    4. Water tanks, Calle San Martin and at La Masita, Santa Cruz.

    NOTE: All the lighters steam tugs and other craft of the Grand Canary Coaling Company and the Tenerife Coaling Company are vested in the Compannia de Embarcaciones Canarias.

In Jamaica

The Property of *Elder Dempster and Company*

1.   Astwood's Wharf. Consisting of a piece of freehold land and storehouse situate in Port Royal Street and Princes Street in the city and parish of Kingston.

2.   Fink's Wharf. Consisting of a piece of freehold land and storehouses situate in Princes Street aforesaid.

3.   A freehold piece of land situate at the south-west corner of Port Royal Street and Luke Lane in the said city of Kingston containing by admeasurement from north to south 586 feet and from east to west 30 feet and 6 inches be the same more or less.

4.   Kingston Jamaica Steam Laundry. Consisting of a piece of land forming part of 40 Harbour Street Kingston held on a lease expiring 22 October 1910 at a rack rent of £48.

453

In West Africa

(A)   The property of *Elder Dempster and Company*

1.   Land at Banana Creek in the Congo State containing 5 hectares 41.85 centares registered on the district plan under the No. 7A.

2.   A piece of freehold land situate at Saltpond Gold Coast Colony delineated and edged round with pink on the map drawn on an indenture dated the 7th October 1909 and made between Gottlob Siegfried Rottman of the one part and Elder Dempster and Company of the other part.

3.   Land at Ilaro consisting of a freehold piece of land situate on the west bank of the River Yewa lying between the territories of Olseodau and Glegi.

4.   Land at Calabar Southern Nigeria consisting of—
    (a) A piece of land situate on the Calabar River held under a lease dated the 29th September 1905 for a term of fifty years from the 4th April 1905 at the yearly rent of £25.
    (b) A piece of land situate in Moor Road in the town of Calabar held under a lease dated the 21st February 1907 for so long as the land shall be used for the purposes of the business of the firm at the yearly rent of £15 : and
    (c) A piece of land situate at Marina Calabar on the left bank of the Calabar River containing an area of about 2,030 square yards held under a lease dated the 17th December 1909 for a term of fifty years from the date of the lease at a yearly rent of £50 for the first 30 years and subsequently as may be fixed by the Government of Southern Nigeria.

(B)   The property of the *Sierra Leone Coaling Company*

1.   Lemberg's Farm King Tom Point Sierra Leone consisting of a piece of freehold land and buildings delineated on the plan attached to an indenture dated the 28th May 1906 and made between Philip Lemberg of the one part and Sir Alfred Lewis Jones of the other part.

2.   Two town lots of freehold land situate at the corner of Oxford Street and Rawdon Street in Freetown in the Colony of Sierra Leone numbered 242 and 243 in the Public Register and plan of town lots of land for Freetown.

Source: File 108502, dissolved at Companies House, London.

Table 49 SHARES RECEIVED BY ELDER DEMPSTER & CO. LTD
ON ITS FORMATION

African Steam Ship Company	26,328 shares of £20 each fully paid
African Oil Mills Company Limited	3,751 shares of £10 each fully paid
	3,747 shares of £10 each £5 paid
African Association Limited	3,598 ordinary shares of £8 each fully paid
	49 Founders' shares of £8 each fully paid
Accra Boating Company Limited	6,000 shares of £1 each fully paid
	200 shares of £1 each 7s. 6d paid
British and African Steam Navigation Company Limited	62,140 shares of £10 each fully paid
Bank of British West Africa Limited	7,745 shares of £10 each £4 paid
	4,888 shares of £10 each £2 paid
Bristol Lighterage Company Limited	885 shares of £10 each fully paid
British West Africa Timber Company Limited	1,000 shares of £1 each fully paid
Cape Coast Castle Boating Company Limited	2,000 shares of £1 each fully paid
	200 shares of £1 each 7s 6d paid
Cunard Steamship Company Limited	6,071 shares of £20 each fully paid
	3,978 shares of £20 each £10 paid
Elder Dempster Shipping Limited	49,240 shares of £10 each fully paid
Elders and Fyffes Limited	68,995 shares of £1 each fully paid
	34,498 shares of £1 each 5s paid
	£15,437 debenture stock
Imperial Direct West India Mail Service Company Limited	24,896 shares of £10 each fully paid
	£7,500 debenture stock
Jamaica Hotels Limited	9,995 shares of £1 each fully paid
Mersey Engine and Producer Company Limited	3,000 shares of £1 each 3s 4d paid
Nigerian Dry Dock and Engineering Company Limited	150 shares of £1 each fully paid
Sekondi Lighterage and Hotel Company Limited	24,495 shares of £1 each fully paid
Swan Hunter and Wigham-Richardson Limited	20,383 ordinary shares of £1 each fully paid
	4,010 preference shares of £1 each fully paid
	£10,000 debenture stock
Union Cold Storage Company Limited Montreal	360 shares of $100 each fully paid
Wilson and Coventry Limited	950 preference shares of £1 each fully paid

G. B. Ollivant and Company Limited — 338 7 per cent preference shares of
£1 each fully paid

H. Hope and Company Limited — £12 10s first preference stock

Mexican 3 per cent Silver Bonds — $20,000

Elders Navigation Collieries Limited — 4,993 shares of £10 each fully paid

Source: File 108502, dissolved at Companies House, London. Formation Documents of
Elder Dempster & Co., Limited, Third Schedule.

Table 50 ELDER DEMPSTER'S WEST AFRICAN SERVICES

From Liverpool

a) A weekly mail and passenger express service to Sierra Leone and the principal Gold Coast ports, and with mails, passengers, and cargo to Forcados and Calabar.

b) A fortnightly passenger and cargo service to Sierra Leone, the principal Gold Coast ports, Forcados, Akassa, Brass, Warri and Sapele.

c) A fortnightly passenger and cargo service to Sierra Leone, Gold Coast, Calabar, Bonny, Okrika, Port Harcourt, and Opobo.

d) A fortnightly passenger and cargo service to Dakar, Bathurst, Sierra Leone, Liberian Coast, French Ivory Coast and the smaller ports of the Gold Coast and Dahomey.

e) A monthly cargo service to Conakry, Sierra Leone, smaller Liberian ports, French Ivory Coast, and Gold Coast ports to Cape Coast Castle.

f) A monthly passenger and cargo service to Sierra Leone, Accra, and ports south of Calabar down to the Congo.

From London

g) A three-weekly service to Sierra Leone and Gold Coast and Nigerian ports to Calabar.

From the Continent

h) A service every 15 days from Hamburg and Rotterdam to Lagos and other Nigerian ports to Calabar.

i) A service every 15 days from Hamburg and Rotterdam to Sierra Leone, Gold Coast, Forcados, Warri and Sapele.

j) A monthly service from Hamburg and Rotterdam to Bathurst, Conakry, Sierra Leone, French Ivory Coast, and the principal river ports in Nigeria.

From New York

k) A bi-monthly service from New York to all ports terminating at Calabar one month and South West African ports the next month.

In addition about thirty steamers each year were loaded with coal outward and were available to deal with timber and palm kernels on the homeward journey as required.

Source: 'Edible & Oil Producing Nuts & Seeds Committee' (London: H.M.S.O., 1916), CD.8248. Evidence of Sir Owen Philipps. Appendix 1, p. 209.

Table 51 ELDER DEMPSTER & CO. LTD, TABLE OF RESULTS 1911–1925

Year	Profits	Capital and Debentures Issued	Reserve Account		Dividend on Ordinary Shares %	Amount carried forward
			Addition	Total		
1911	236,749	1,730,000	50,000	676,580	10	
1912	288,199	3,635,000	100,000	726,580	10	41,516
1913	307,605	3,885,000	75,000	800,000	8	44,089
1914	326,121	4,135,000	50,000	850,000	8	52,808
1915	349,444	4,135,000	50,000	900,000	9	73,878
1916	358,175	4,135,000	50,000	950,000	10	74,679
1917	366,901	4,385,000	50,000	1,000,000	10	83,630
1918	408,529	5,135,000	50,000	1,050,000	10	119,785
1919	523,031	6,135,000	100,000	1,150,000	10	162,592
1920	671,490	8,135,000	100,000	1,250,000	10	212,351
1921	564,602	9,235,000	75,000	1,325,000	8	154,368
1922	536,107	9,235,000	50,000	1,375,000	7	113,660
1923	528,095	10,235,000	—	1,375,000	6	101,796
1924	574,301	10,235,000	—	1,375,000	5	110,085
1925	579,315	10,235,000	−625,000	750,000	5	121,713

Source: *Fairplay*, 7 June 1923, p. 593, and 10 June 1926, p. 615.

Table 52 FINANCIAL POSITION OF ELDER DEMPSTER AND COMPANY LIMITED

		1913	1924
CAPITAL:	Ordinary	£1,200,000	£1,810,000
	Preference	675,000	6,425,000
	Management	10,000	NIL
	Debentures	2,000,000	2,000,000
Reserves		725,000	1,375,000
Sundry creditors and outstandings		895,430	2,064,379
Bills payable: Shipbuilders		427,032	713,750
General		59,388	23,203
Freehold and leasehold property		344,875	750,719
Ships and shipping, industrial and general investments		4,879,599	12,422,426
Payment on account of steamers building		190,000	NIL
Sundry debtors and outstandings		599,843	1,263,654
Cash		166,621	299,826
Profit		307,379	573,941
Transferred to reserve		75,000	NIL
Dividend		8%	5%

Source: *Fairplay*, 11 June 1925, p. 624.

Table 53 FINANCIAL POSITION OF ELDER DEMPSTER & CO. LTD
1925–1929

	1925	1926	1927	1928	1929
Capital:	£	£	£	£	£
Ordinary	1,810,000	1,810,000	1,810,000	1,810,000	1,810,000
5½% Pref.	425,000	425,000	425,000	425,000	425,000
6% Pref.	3,500,000	3,500,000	3,750,000	3,750,000	3,750,000
6½% Pref.	2,500,000	2,500,000	2,500,000	2,500,000	2,500,000
Reserve	750,000	700,000	500,000	475,000	475,000
Debentures	2,000,000	2,000,000	2,000,000	2,000,000	2,000,000
Sundry Creditors and Bills Payable	2,676,440	2,669,161	2,570,763	2,261,685	2,122,339
Freehold and Leasehold Property	733,266	719,956	705,498	699,652	719,078
Fleet and Shipping Investments	11,942,175	11,883,236	11,931,629*	11,805,573	—
Fleet	—	—	—	—	124,802
Investments	—	—	—	—	11,744,245
Sundry Debtors, Bills Receivable, Cash	1,344,833	1,365,198	1,309,189	1,127,548	869,542
Profits and Dividends	578,987	509,278	525,031	546,791	306,201
Transferred from Reserve	—	50,000	50,000	25,000	—
Dividends (%):					
Ordinary	5	4	4	4	0
5½% Pref.	5½	5½	5½	5½	5½
6% Pref.	6	6	6	6	3
6½% Pref.	6½	6½	6½	6½	3¼

* £625,000 was transferred from reserve account in 1925, reducing the fund from £1,375,000 to £750,000 and £150,000 in 1927 to meet depreciation in value of investments.

Source: *Fairplay*, 26 June 1930, p. 778.

Table 54 SHIPPING COMPANIES CONTROLLED BY LORD KYLSANT

	No. of ships	Gross tons	D/W tons	Average age
African Steam Ship	39	183,136	271,350	12
Argentine Navigation	47	46,398	59,210	23
Belfast Steamship	6	8,109	5,538	18½
British & African	25	114,787	165,000	13
British & Irish	11	16,022	15,303	11
Bullard King	8	32,198	48,233	19
Burns & Laird	19	20,114	14,591	25½
City of Cork	7	7,829	5,853	21
Coast Lines	37	28,987	38,555	14
Dundalk & Newry	4	1,811	1,950	39
Elder Dempster	1	7,275	9,500	2
Glen Line	11	90,682	124,285	6½
Imperial Direct	6	30,554	46,000	12
Lamport & Holt	47	311,513	418,049	12
MacAndrews	19	31,392	52,240	9
David MacIver	7	26,417	43,352	12½
Moss Steamship	13	36,464	61,158	9½
Michael Murphy	5	3,810	4,850	10½
H. & W. Nelson	12	79,111	82,480	18
Pacific Steam	26	163,577	220,150	11
R.M.S.P.	51	429,379	448,539	12
Union Castle	38	347,350	359,986	15
White Star Line (including proportion of Shaw, Savill & Albion's ships)	36	444,649	357,580	18
Totals	475	2,461,564	2,853,752	15

Source: *Fairplay*'s 'Annual Summary of British Shipping Finance', 1927, p. 361.

Table 55 ELDER DEMPSTER INVESTMENTS IN ASSOCIATED
SHIPPING LINES

African Steam Ship	£1,680,720	(85 % of The Ordinary Stock)
British & African	1,489,720	(99 % of The Ordinary Stock)
Coast Line	230,000	(11½ % of The Ordinary Stock)
Glen Line	489,019	(23 % of The Ordinary Stock)
Lamport & Holt	1,694,997	(35 % of The Ordinary Stock)
James Moss	348,900	(35 % of The Ordinary Stock)
Royal Mail	135,000	(16 % of The Ordinary Stock)
Union Castle	1,364,990	(50 % of The Ordinary Stock)
Total of Ordinary	£7,433,346	
British & African	400,000	(Preference)
African Steam Ship	296,085	(Preference)
Coast Line	20,000	(Preference)
Grand Total	£8,149,431	

Source: *Fairplay*, 11 June 1925, p. 623. Elder Dempster annual accounts.

Table 56 LOSSES OF ELDER DEMPSTER & CO. LTD

Investment in major subsidiary companies	Investment	Written off	Balance
(African Steam Ship Co. and British & African S.N. Co.)	£3,032,560	£3,000,000	£32,560
Investments in associated companies			
(Royal Mail Group Companies)	7,824,591	5,267,409	2,557,182
M.V. Milverton	110,000	82,302	28,698

In addition, 'other investments' standing at £1,261,815 had been written down to £724,271 by the transfer of £537,544 from reserve and profit on investments.

Source: *Fairplay*, 14 December 1933, Elder Dempster & Company's Earnings.

Table 57 PRINCIPAL ORDINARY SHAREHOLDERS IN ELDER DEMPSTER LINES LIMITED (REGISTERED: 15 AUGUST 1932)

NAME	1932	1933	1934	1935	1936	1967
The Duke of Abercorn & Another, 68, Mount Street, London W.	27,332	27,332	27,332	—	—	—
British & African S.N. Co. Ltd, Colonial House, Water Street, L'pool	201,713	201 713	201,713	201,713	—	—
Elder Line Ltd, Colonial House, Water Street, L'pool	110,241	110,241	110,241	110,241	—	—
Imperial Direct Line Ltd, Colonial House, Water Street, L'pool	104,774	104,774	104,774	104,774	—	—
W. James & Another, 11, Vernon Court, Hendon Way, London N.	901,968	901,968	901,968	901,968	—	—
London Maritime Investment Co. Ltd, 5, St Helens Place, London E.C.	807,762	807,762	807,762	807,762	—	—
Solicitor for the Affairs of H.M. Treasury, Storey's Gate, London S.W.	—	346,210	346,210	346,210	—	—
E.D. Realisation Co. Ltd, Royal Mail House, Leadenhall St, E.C.	—	—	—	27,332	—	—
Royal Exchange Assurance, Royal Exchange, London E.C.	346,210	—	—	—	—	—
Elder Dempster Lines Holdings Ltd, 19 Leadenhall Street, London E.C.	—	—	—	—	2,499,993	2,499,991
Misc.	—	—	—	—	7	9
Total Ordinary Shares:	2,500,000	2,500,000	2,500,000	2,500,000	2,500,000	2,500,000

Sources: *Fairplay's* 'Annual Summary of British Shipping Finance', the 'Syren' Financial Year Rook and the Stock Exchange 'Official Year Book, for the relevant years.

461

Table 58 PRINCIPAL ORDINARY SHAREHOLDERS IN ELDER DEMPSTER LINES HOLDINGS LIMITED (REGISTERED 2 JUNE 1936)

	1937	1938	1939	1940	1941	1942	1945
Alliance Ass. Co. Ltd, 'A' a/c Bartholomew Lane, E.C.	10,000	10,000	10,000	10,000	10,000	10,000	10,000
Alliance Ass. Co. Ltd, 'B' a/c Bartholomew Lane, E.C.	10,000	10,000	10,000	10,000	10,000	10,000	10,000
Alliance Invest. Co. Ltd, 8 Basinghall St E.C.	11,197	11,197	11,197	11,197	11,197	11,197	11,197
Barclays Nominees (Lombard St) Ltd, 54 Lombard St, E.C.	10,851	10,851	10,851	10,851	10,851	—	—
Barings Nominees Ltd, 8 Bishopsgate, E.C.	33,790	33,790	33,790	33,790	33,790	31,590	31,590
Bishopsgate Nominees Ltd, 15 Bishopsgate, E.C.	15,600	15,600	15,600	15,600	15,350	12,600	12,600
British Invest. Trust Ltd, 46 Castle St, Edinburgh	10,000	10,000	10,000	10,000	10,000	10,000	10,000
Consolidated Nominees Ltd, 52 Threadneedle St, E.C.	16,698	16,698	16,698	16,698	15,593	17,402	17,402
Cushion Trust Ltd, 11 Old Broad St, E.C.	221,885	221,885	221,885	221,885	221,885	15,525	15,525
Legal & General Ass. Soc. Ltd, 10 Fleet St, E.C.	10,000	10,000	10,000	10,000	10,000	10,000	10,000
Liverpool & London & Globe Ins. Co. Ltd, L'pool	17,500	17,500	17,500	17,500	17,500	10,900	10,900
London Nominees Union Bank of Scotland, 62 Cornhill, E.C.	19,900	19,900	19,900	19,900	19,900	18,150	18,150
London Office Royal Bank of Scotland Nominees Ltd	13,200	13,200	13,200	13,200	15,200	25,200	25,200
Midland Bank (Princes St) Nominees Ltd, 5 Princess St, E.C.	22,000	22,000	22,000	22,000	21,500	—	—
North of Scotland Bank, London Nominees, E.C.	16,411	16,411	16,411	16,411	16,411	17,911	17,911
Ocean Steamship Co. Ltd, 3 Linnet Lane, L'pool	674,750	674,750	674,750	674,750	674,750	674,750	674,750
Provident Mutual Life Ass., Alresford Pl., Old Alresford, Hants.	20,000	20,000	20,000	20,000	20,000	20,000	20,000
Prudential Ass. Co. Ltd, 142 Holborn Bars, E.C.	91,000	91,000	91,000	91,000	91,000	91,000	91,000
Rea Towing Co. Ltd, 20 Water St, Liverpool	22,614	22,614	22,614	22,614	22,614	22,614	22,614
Royal Exchange Ass., 'A' a/c Royal Exchange, E.C.	12,089	12,089	12,089	12,089	12,089	12,089	12,089
Royal Insc. Co. Ltd, North John St, Liverpool	32,500	32,500	32,500	32,500	32,500	11,500	11,500
U. K. Temp. & Gen. Prov. Institution, 196 Strand, W.C.	20,000	20,000	20,000	20,000	20,000	20,000	20,000
West Nominees Ltd, 41 Lothbury, E.C.	55,100	55,100	55,100	55,100	52,100	50,100	50,100
Total Ordinary Shares (£1)	2,214,111	2,555,798	2,748,596	2,748,596	2,748,596	2,748,596	2,748,596

Notes: Name changed to Liner Holdings Co. Ltd in 1953. The Ocean Steam Ship Co. Ltd became the sole ordinary shareholder in 1965.

Capital Structure	to 1951	to 1952	to 1967
Authorised:	£3,000,000	4,000,000	7,000,000
Issued:	£2,748,596	3,435,745	6,871,490

Sources: Fairplay's 'Annual Summary of British Shipping Finance' and the Stock Exchange 'Official Year Book' for the relevant years.

Table 59 DIRECTORS OF ELDER DEMPSTER LINES LIMITED

Chairman

1932–41	Sir Richard Durning Holt, Bart.	1932–41
1941–4	Hon. Leonard Harrison Cripps, C.B.E. (Major)	1932–45
	Major Gerald Franklin Torrey, M.C.	1932–43
	Mr Picton Hughes Jones	1932–40
	Mr Lawrence Durning Holt	1936–43
1944–6	Mr Richard Arthur Smye	1940–6
	Sir John Richard Hobhouse, M.C.	1941–2
	Sir Alan Cecil Tod, C.B.E.	1944–62
1946–63	Mr John Hall Joyce	1944–63
	Mr William Leslie Robinson	1944–51
	Mr Roland Hobhouse Thornton, M.C.	1942–3
	Mr Gerard Henry Avezathe	1946–53
	Mr Charles Thomas Joyce Cripps	1947–55
	Mr Malcolm Bruce Glasier, C.B.E.	1951–71
	Mr Allan Montgomerie Bennett	1952–68
	Mr Albert Edward Muirhead	1952–68
	Mr Philip Grenville Harris Arundell	1955–63
1963–72	Mr Frank Laurence Lane, C.B.E.	1962–72
	Brig. P. J. D. Toosey, C.B.E., D.S.O.	1963–70
1972–	Mr Geoffrey James Ellerton, C.M.B., M.B.E.	1967–
	Sir John Nicholson, Bart., K.B.E., C.I.E.	1967–71
	Mr John Duncan Robertson	1969–
	Mr Peter Francis Earlam	1971–
	Mr Patrick Henry Denton Toosey	1971–

as on 1 August 1972

Source: Directors Reports and Accounts of Elder Dempster Lines Limited.

Table 60 DIRECTORS OF ELDER DEMPSTER LINES HOLDINGS
LIMITED (1936–1952)
DIRECTORS OF LINER HOLDINGS COMPANY LIMITED (1953–1972)

Chairman

1936–62	Sir Alan Cecil Tod, C.B.E.	1936–70
	Sir Richard Durning Holt, Bart.	1936–41
	Mr Francis Cecil Howard	1936–43
	Hon. Leonard Harrison Cripps, C.B.E. (Major)	1936–45
	Mr Picton Hughes Jones	1936–43
	Mr Roland Hobhouse Thornton, M.C.	1944–53
	Colonel (Sir) James Geoffrey Brydon Beazley, M.C.	1944–55
	Mr Richard Arthur Smye	1945–8
	Mr John Hall Joyce	1948–68
	Mr Lawrence Durning Holt	1941–53
	Sir John Richard Hobhouse	1953–7
1963–70	Brig. P. J. D. Toosey, C.B.E., D.S.O.	1953–
	Sir John Nicholson, Bart., K.B.E., C.I.E.	1955–71
	Sir Reginald Stewart Mactier, C.B.E.	1957–67
1970–72	Mr Frank Laurence Lane, C.B.E.	1963–72
	Mr John Greenwood	1970–
1972–	Mr Geoffrey James Ellerton, C.M.B.	1971–
	Mr Charles Denis Lenox-Conyngham	1972–

as on 1 August 1972

Source: Directors Reports and Accounts of Elder Dempster Lines Holdings Limited, and Liner Holdings Company Limited.

Table 61 ELDER DEMPSTER AND THE CANARY ISLANDS

Elder Dempster's connection with the Canary Islands began in 1884 when the Grand Canary Coaling Company established a coaling station at Puerto de la Luz. Alfred Jones subsequently encouraged the growing of bananas in the Islands and arranged for them to be transported and marketed in England. At this time much land and property was acquired and the Inter-insular Steamship Company was formed to provide communications between the main ports. (See above, pp. 126–7).

After the death of Jones his estate passed to Philipps and Pirrie (See above, pp. 450–3) and in 1911 they sold a number of properties—including the Hotels Metropole and Victoria Monte—plus land on the Canteras beach, together with the site for the present Santa Catalina Hotel. The Inter-insular Steamship Company was sold during the following year. Apart from a dispute with the Canary Islands 'Coal Pool' (See above, pp.182–3), normal activities then continued until the end of the twenties—operations being channelled through Elder Dempster (Grand Canary) Limited, and Elder Dempster (Tenerife) Limited, which had been incorporated in 1912.

In the dark days of 1930 it was decided to dispose of such other assets as could be readily sold, but owing to the prevailing economic conditions very poor prices were obtained. (See above, pp. 258 et seq.) Then in 1934 the remaining assets and business in Las Palmas were purchased by the Company's local manager, Mr V. E. Pavillard, while a Mr Bellamy bought the Tenerife side of the business, and both retained the original titles of the companies they had acquired. Thus Elder Dempster (Grand Canary) Limited and Elder Dempster (Tenerife) Limited continued their existence under their new owners although, of course, they were not connected to the 'Lines' Company in any financial way.

In 1941 Elder Dempster (Canary Isles) Limited, was formed by Mr Pavillard and this then took over the assets and business of both Elder Dempster (Grand Canary) Limited and Elder Dempster (Tenerife) Limited. Until 1953 this new firm continued to act as agents for Elder Dempster Lines, but in that year the agency was transferred to Messrs Maritima Midway S.A., Paradoxically, Elder Dempster (Canary Isles) Limited retained their 'Blue Funnel' agency, and with the closure of the Suez Canal have found that this aspect of their work has assumed a new significance.

Elder Dempster Lines have several times approached their namesakes in the Canary Islands with a view to 'buying back their name'. Each time, however, they have been refused on the grounds that the long association of the 'Elder Dempster' name, and the continuing goodwill shown towards Alfred Jones's successors—he still has a main road named after him in Las Palmas—were above price.

In January, 1972, the agency of Elder Dempster Lines Limited, was transferred back to Elder Dempster (Canary Isles) Limited and thus the old association has been re-established.

Sources: See the formation documents of Elder Dempster (Grand Canary) Limited, Dempster (Tenerife) Limited, and Elder Dempster (Canary Isles) Limited, at Companies Registration Office, Companies House, City Road, London. These also give details of their capital structure and share-holdings.

The author would like to record his gratitude for the kind assistance given to him and his wife by Mr E. V. Pavillard during their visits to Las Palmas in September 1967, and in October 1969.

Table 62 ELDER DEMPSTER LINES—FREIGHT TONNAGES CARRIED TO AND FROM WEST AFRICA

		Outward	Inward
1951	U.K. and Continent	598,000 tons	467,000 tons
	U.S.A./Canada	63,000	118,000
		661,000	585,000
1960	U.K. and Continent	776,000	615,000
	U.S.A./Canada	59,000	61,000
		835,000	676,000
1969	U.K. and Continent	756,000	649,000
	U.S.A./Canada	55,000	70,000
		811,000	719,000

Source: From information kindly supplied by Mr J. C. Barlow of Elder Dempster Lines' Port and Voyage Services (Freight Statistics) Department.

Table 63 LINER HOLDINGS COMPANY LIMITED

(A wholly-owned subsidiary of Ocean Transport and Trading Limited)

Principal Subsidiary Companies:	Incorporated In:	Share Capital Held (%)
British and Burmese S.N.Co. Ltd	G.B.	100
Guinea Gulf Line Ltd	G.B.	100
Henderson Line Ltd	G.B.	100
Seaway Ferries Ltd	G.B.	100
West African Lighterage & Transport Co. Ltd	G.B.	100
West African Lighterage & Transport Co. (Nigeria) Ltd	Nigeria	100
West African Properties Limited	G.B.	100
West African Properties (Nigeria) Ltd	Nigeria	100
Marina Buildings Limited	Nigeria	100
Elder Dempster Agencies Ltd	G.B.	100
Elder Dempster Agencies (Nigeria) Ltd	Nigeria	100
Ocean Group Investment Ltd. (formerly Elders Engineering & Airways Co. Ltd)	G.B.	100
Industrial & Marine Engineering Company of Nigeria Ltd	Nigeria	100
Elder Dempster Lines Ltd	G.B.	100
Elder Dempster Lines (Canada) 1962 Ltd	Canada	100*
Elder Dempster Lines G.m.b.H.	Germany	100*
Elderpalm Schiffahrts-Agentur G.m.b.H.	Germany	60*
Principal Associated Companies:		
African Container Express Ltd	G.B.	42½*
Compagnie Maritime Belge (Lloyd Royale) S.A.	Belgium	11*
Sierra Leone Shipping Agencies Ltd	Sierra Leone	50*
Liverpool Maritime Terminals Ltd	G.B.	48
Metropolitan Terminals Ltd	G.B.	25
Liner Agencies (Ghana) Ltd	Ghana	50
Volta Lake Transport Co. Ltd	Ghana	24½

(Companies marked * are subsidiary/associated firms of Elder Dempster Lines Ltd)

Source: Based on information kindly made available by Mr A. J. White, Secretary of Ocean Transport and Trading Ltd. Note that the Group also has investments in other companies, but details of these are not given when its interest is less than 10 per cent of the share capital. The most important of these is the Mercantile Marine Engineering & Graving Dock Company, S.A., of Antwerp in which 16970 shares (8.6 per cent) are owned.

Table 64 JOHN HOLT AND COMPANY (LIVERPOOL) LTD

	Tonnage Outward (South Bound)		
	Total (tons)	Holt Ships (tons %)	Other Ships (tons)
1909–10	26,926	16,032 (59$\frac{1}{2}$)	10,894
1910–11	33,347	18,723 (56)	14,624
1911–12	33,632	18,153 (54)	15,470
1912–13	40,865	20,983 (51)	19,882
1913–14	30,076	16,303 (54)	13,773
	Tonnage Homeward (North Ward)		
1909–10	33,207	12,650 (38)	21,557
1910–11	48,078	17,277 (36)	30,801
1911–12	65,990	16,377 (25)	49,615
1912–13	70,691	19,512 (28)	51,169

Source: Guinea Gulf Lines Mss., History File, Con/2A, Memorandum dated 2 March 1914.

Table 65 THE JOHN HOLT FLEET DEPRECIATION ACCOUNT

S.S. *Balmore*

Purchased second hand in 1907 for	£7,253
Plus cost of refitting	£1,290
	£8,543
Less depreciation at 5% = 13 years @ £427 =	£5,551
	£2,992
Sold in 1920 for	£2,206
∴ Loss on depreciation a/c =	£786

S.S. *Jonathan Holt*

Purchased new in 1910 for	£23,250
Less depreciation @ 5% = 7 years @ £1,162 =	£8,134
	£15,116
Torpedoed in 1917 on 23rd voyage and amount recovered from insurance	£41,162
∴ profit on depreciation a/c =	£26,046

S.S. *Thomas Holt*

Purchased new in 1910 for	£23,250
Less depreciation @ 5% = 19 years @ £1,162 =	£22,078
	£1,172
Sold in January 1929 for	£14,250
∴ Profit on depreciation a/c =	£13,078

Source: Guinea Gulf Line Mss., History File, Con/2A.

Table 66 DEPRECIATION ACCOUNT OF JOHN HOLT VESSELS
BUILT IN 1926

Name of Ship	John Holt	Jonathan C. Holt	Robert L. Holt
New cost in 1926	£65,063	£65,063	£65,507
Depreciation @ 5%	39,000	39,000	49,125
Service	(12 years)	(12 years)	(15 years)
Book value when sold (or lost)	26,063	26,063	15,938
Amount realised when sold	34,960	38,182	x
Profit on depreciation a/c	8,897	12,119	x
(x = War loss in 1941)			

Source: Guinea Gulf Line Mss., History File, Con/29(1).

Table 67 COMPARISON OF JOHN HOLT FLEET IN 1930 AND 1939

		Built	Gross Tons
1930	Jonathan C. Holt (1)	1926	2,922
	Robert L. Holt (1)	1926	2,918
	John Holt (1)	1926	2,921
	Godfrey B. Holt (1)	1929	3,580
	Thomas Holt (2)	1929	3,599
			15,940
1939	Robert L. Holt (1)	1926	2,918
	Thomas Holt (2)	1929	3,599
	Godfrey B. Holt (1)	1929	3,580
	Jonathan Holt	1938	4,975
	John Holt (2)	1938	4,973
			20,045

Source: Guinea Gulf Line Mss., History File, Con/2A.

Table 68 PROFITS OF JOHN HOLT & CO. (LIVERPOOL) LTD.,
1935–1939

Year	Profits	Depreciation	Pensions	Profits (before all taxation)
1935	£83,599	£34,092	£3,465	£46,042
1936	£72,250	£31,632	£3,681	£36,937
1937	£258,153	£36,557	£10,378	£211,218
1938	£117,787	£33,841	£7,024	£76,922
1939	£108,952	£28,736	£14,968	£65,248

Profits including investment income, but after deducting all expenses (except depreciation, pension fund payments, but before all taxation).

Source: Harmood, Banner, Lewis & Mounsey (Chartered Accountants), Prospectus issued in 1950.

Table 69 SHIPS PURCHASED FOR THE BROMPORT STEAMSHIP
CO. LTD

Name of ship	Gross tons	Year built	Cost to Watsons	Cost to Levers
1. Colemere	2,119	1915	£36,765	£87,000
2. Delamere	1,524	1915	£27,708	£58,500
3. Flaxmere	1,524	1915	£27,719	£58,500
4. Linmere	1,578	1913	£26,258	£57,000
5. Oakmere	1,251	1910	£19,131	£48,000
6. Redesmere	2,122	1911	£25,644	£71,000
			£163,225	£380,000
7. Eskmere	2,292	1916	—	£68,368[a]
8. Rabymere	1,775	1916	—	£107,750[b]
				£556,118[c]

The table shows that Watsons obtained £380,000 for vessels which had cost them only £163,225 a year or so earlier. The true picture is even more favourable to them, for as a result of normal depreciation the steamers only stood in the company's books at £137,000.[d] Shortly after this Watsons went into liquidation[e] after selling its goodwill to Sir John Ellerman.[f]

[a] Lever's took up Watson's option on this vessel which was still under construction.
[b] Lever's bought this ship through Donaldson Brothers from J. C. Gould, Merchants Exchange, Cardiff.
[c] Compiled from the original documents in the author's possession.
[d] *Fairplay*, 20 April 1916, p. 628.
[e] *Fairplay*, 15 June 1916, p. 921.
[f] *Fairplay*, 25 May 1916, p. 810.

Table 70 FINANCIAL RECONSTRUCTION OF THE U.A.C.

This reconstruction was undertaken after its first two disastrous years when, on a capital of £15,731,600, a profit of only £24,000 was made in the year ending 30 April 1930 and a loss of £1,288,123 was made in the year ending 30 April 1931. It was decided to reduce the capital of the U.A.C. by £8,231,600—£6,967,620 of this being used to reduce the value of fixed assets and investments and £1,263,980 to cancel the debit balance from the first two years' trading. This left the U.A.C. with a capital of £7,500,000 held equally by the Niger Company and African and Eastern Trade Corporation. It was calculated that further liquid capital of £3,500,000 was essential for efficient working but the Corporation could only raise some £500,000. The balance of £3,000,000 was, therefore, provided by Unilever and as a consequence the Niger Company's share in the U.A.C. rose to 80 per cent while that of the African and Eastern fell to only 20 per cent.

Source: *History of the United Africa Company Ltd. to 1938*, circulated privately by the Company, London, 1938, pp. 126–129.

Table 71 PROFITS OF THE UNITED AFRICA COMPANY AFTER ITS RECONSTRUCTION IN 1931

Period	Profit	Dividend	General Reserve
5 months to Sept. 30 1932	141,359	1	—
12 months to Sept. 30 1933	428,386	2½	125,000
12 months to Sept. 30 1934	581,117	3¾	150,000
12 months to Sept. 30 1935	1,123,305	3	225,000
12 months to Sept. 30 1936	1,531,866	10	300,000
12 months to Sept. 30 1937	1,811,099	11	400,000

Source: *History of the United Africa Company Ltd. to 1938*, circulated privately by the Company, London, 1938, p. 131.

Table 72 VESSELS BUILT IN GERMANY FOR THE UNITED AFRICA COMPANY

		Gross Tons	Cost Price
1936	Congonian (2)	4,929	£88,135
	Ethiopian (2)	5,424	£77,015
	Guinean	5,205	£80,348
	Leonian	5,424	£77,411
	Liberian	5,205	£81,048
	Nigerian (2)	5,423	£77,740
1937	Gambian (2)	5,452	£117,948
	Takoradian	5,452	£118,002
		_____	
		42,514	

Source: United Africa Company Mss.

Table 73 VESSELS SOLD BY THE U.A.C. DURING 1935 AND 1936

		Gross Tons	Built	Selling Price
1935	Kumasian	3,400	1905	£5,400
	Lafian	3,832	1928	£34,000
	Nigerian	3,543	1925	£18,075
1936	Congonian	4,564	1929	£36,500
		_____		
		19,204		

Source: United Africa Company Mss.

Table 74 VESSELS BUILT IN THE U.K. FOR THE UNITED AFRICA COMPANY

		Gross Tons	Cost Price
1935	Ashantian (2)	4,917	£87,125
	Kumasian (2)	4,922	£86,915
1936	Matadian	4,275	£98,578
1937	Conakrian	4,876	£132,042
	Lafian (2)	4,874	£131,243
1938	Zarian (2)	4,871	£145,458
		_____	
		28,735	

Source: United Africa Company Mss.

Table 75 GROWTH OF THE U.A.C. FLEET (1934–39)

	No. of Ships	Total Gross Tons
U.A.C. fleet in 1934:	7	29,871
Less sold:	5	19,204
	2	10,667
Plus German constr'n:	8	42,514
	10	53,181
Plus British constr'n:	6	28,735
U.A.C. fleet in 1939:	16	81,916

Source: United Africa Company Mss.

Table 76 REBATE CIRCULAR IN WEST AFRICAN TRADE ISSUED BY MESSRS ELDER DEMPSTER & COMPANY

Liverpool, 1st October, 1905

Shippers (who are Principals) to and from ports of the above Coast, as far South as and including Tiger Bay, are hereby informed that on all shipments outwards and palm oil and palm kernels inwards made on and after the above date, and until further notice, and subject to the conditions and terms set out herein, each of the undernamed Companies and Lines of Steamers will allow a rebate of the = 10 per cent primage received by such Companies and Lines from such shippers on all shipments at tariff rates outwards and/or on palm oil and/or palm kernels inwards from or to Liverpool, Hamburg, Rotterdam, Havre, Antwerp and Bremen, or other ports or places in the United Kingdom or on the Continent.

The said primage to be computed every six months up to the 30th June and the 31st December in each year, and to be payable six months after such respective dates to those Principals only who until the date at which the primage shall become payable, shall have shipped exclusively by the steamers despatched by the undernamed Companies and Lines of Steamers respectively, from or to Liverpool, Hamburg, Rotterdam, Havre, Antwerp and Bremen, or other ports or places in the United Kingdom or on the Continent, to or from aforesaid ports of the above Coast, provided that such shippers have not, directly or indirectly, made or been interested in any shipments to or from such ports by vessels other than those despatched by the undernamed and also provided that the statement of claim for such primage shall be made in the annexed form within twelve months of the date of shipment to the Company or Line of Steamers which shall have carried the outward goods, or the palm oil and palm kernels, in respect of which the primage is claimed.

British & African Steam Navigation Co. (1900) Ltd
African Steam Ship Co.
Woermann-Line M.B.H.

West African Coast Steam Lines

Form for Statement of Primage Claimed in Respect of Shipments To be signed by the Merchant owning the Goods and/or Palm Oil and/or Palm Kernels.

190

Messrs
Gentlemen:

I/we beg to hand you the annexed list of my/our shipments by the steamers despatched by your Line during the six months ended upon which shipments I/we claim the rebate referred to in the Circular of the West African Coast Steam Lines dated — October, 1905, and such claim I/we make in accordance with, and on the terms and conditions of the said notice, which I/we have received, and with which I/we have complied in every particular.

The following are the particulars of the above-mentioned shipments, and they are in accord with the bills of lading and freight notes paid.

I/we remain,
GENTLEMEN,
Yours truly,

Signature to be that of the firm.
Name and Address in full.
Note: if B/L was taken out in any other name than your own, please state.

Table 77 CONFERENCE RATES OF FREIGHT FROM WEST AFRICA,
1905–12

Article	Sierra Leone	Axim, Seccondee and Accra	Lagos	Rivers
Palm Kernels	21s 6d	32s 6d	30s	21s 3d
Ground nuts (shelled)	45s	45s	45s	40s*
Shea nuts	21s 6d	32s 6d	30s	21s 3d
Palm oil	32s 6d	43s 6d	40s	27s 6d

*This was reduced to 30s in June 1909.

The usual primage of 10% was added to these rates, and a rebate of 10% was made in respect of shipments of palm kernels, shea nuts and palm oil.

RATES OF FREIGHT FROM WEST AFRICA, 1912 TO 1.7.1915

Article	Sierra Leone	Axim, Seccondee and Accra	Lagos	Rivers
Palm Kernels	24s	35s	32s 6d*	23s 6d
Ground nuts (shelled)	30s	35s	32s 6d*	32s 6d
Shea nuts	24s	35s	32s 6d*	23s 6d
Palm oil	35s	47s 6d	45s*	30s

*Reduced by 2s 6d in January 1914.

Primage and rebates of 10% were applied to shelled ground-nuts from 1 January 1914 onwards, in addition to the other items mentioned above, and a war time surcharge was introduced in August 1914.

Source: 'Report of the Committee on Edible and Oil Producing Nuts and Seeds' (London: H.M.S.O., 1916), CD.8248, pp. 209–10.

APPENDICES

Table 78 OUTWARD CONFERENCE RATES OF FREIGHT. PIECE
GOODS FROM U.K. TO LAGOS

Before the war	47s 6d + 10%
Feb. 1915	47s 6d
Feb. 1916	52s 6d + 10%
Feb. 1917	52s 6d + 10%
Feb. 1918	105s Net
Dec. 1918	80s Net
Feb. 1919	80s Net
Feb. 1921	80s Net or 1% value
Feb. 1923	67s 6d less 10 %

Source: C. Ernest Fayle, *The War and the Shipping Industry*, (London: Oxford University Press, 1927), Table 31, p. 441.

Table 79 PERCENTAGES OF INCREASE IN HOMEWARD RATES OF
FREIGHT SELECTED GOODS FROM LAGOS TO U.K.

Article	Rate on 1.8.14	17.8.14	5.9.14	1.10.14	7.12.14	1.7.15	1.10.15
		%	%	%	%	%	%
Palm kernels	30s	+ 25	+ 20	+ 15	+ 10	+ 28	+ 41
Palm kernel cake	30s	+ 25	+ 20	+ 15	+ 10	+ 28	+ 8
Ground nuts	30s	+ 25	+ 20	+ 15	+ 10	+ 28	+ 41
Shea nuts	30s	+ 25	+ 20	+ 15	+ 10	+ 28	+ 41
Palm Oil	42s 6d	+ 25	+ 20	+ 15	+ 10	+ 23	+ 25

Source: 'Report of the Committee on Edible and Oil Producing Nuts and Seeds' (London: H.M.S.O., 1916), CD.8248, Appendix II, pp. 210–11.

Table 80 HOMEWARD FREIGHT AVERAGES 1914–1919

Route	1914	1915	1916	1917	1918	1919
Calcutta to U.K. or continent	22s	67s 10¼d	174s 11¼d	325s	280s	175s
Northern range to U.K.	—	12s 6d	17s 9d	205s 3d	50s	8s 6d
River Plate (Lower ports) to U.K. or continent	16s 3¼d	66s 0¾d	141s 4¾d	162s 6d	—	cont. 195s / U.K. 62s 6d
Bilbao to Middlesbrough	4s 9¾d	13s 11¾d	20s 4¼d	40s	—	24s 9d
Bordeaux to Bristol Channel	—	15s 6d	17s 9d	20s 6d	17s 4d	20s

Source: C. Ernest Fayle, *The War and the Shipping Industry* (London: Oxford University Press, 1927), Table 29, p. 440.

Table 81 WEST AFRICAN LINES CONFERENCE. EXAMPLES OF
NORTHBOUND FREIGHT RATES FROM MAIN PORTS IN WEST
AFRICA (e.g. NIGERIA) TO BERTH PORTS IN U.K. AND ANTWERP/
HAMBURG RANGE
(RATES ARE SHOWN IN U.K. STERLING)

	Palm Oil in Bulk	Marketing Board Rates Cocoa	Oilseeds	Cotton	Tariff Rate Rubber
January 1952	99s Wt	110s Wt.	93s 6d Wt.	129s Wt.	157s Wt.
July 1952	106s Wt.	118s Wt.	100s 6d Wt.	138s 6d Wt.	—
October 1952	—	—	—	—	169s Wt.
June 1953	—	—	—	—	162s 6d Wt.
October 1953	95s Wt.	112s 6d Wt.	95s Wt.	130s Wt.	—
February 1954	—	—	—	—	142s 6d Wt.
February 1955	102s 6d Wt.	130s Wt.	102s 6d Wt.	145s Wt.	157s 6d Wt.
October 1955	110s Wt.	140s Wt.	110s Wt.	165s Wt.	173s 6d Wt.
April 1957	115s 6d Wt. —		115s 6d Wt.	173s 6d Wt.	182s Wt.
October 1957	—	147s Wt.	—	—	—
March 1958	110s 6d Wt.	140s Wt.	110s 6d Wt.	165s Wt.	—
October 1958	106s Wt.	135s Wt.	106s Wt.	160s Wt.	—
July 1960	110s 6d Wt. —		110s 6d Wt.	165s Wt.	191s Wt.
October 1960	—	140s Wt.	—	—	—
October 1961	118s 6d Wt.	150s Wt.	118s 6d Wt.	180s Wt.	210s Wt.
February 1962	—	—	100s 8d Wt. —		—
October 1962	—	135s Wt.	86s 4d Wt.	—	200s Wt.
August 1963	130s 6d Wt. —		—	198s Wt.	—
January 1964	—	—	104s Wt.	—	—
March 1964	—	120s Wt.	—	—	—
August 1964	95s Wt.	—	95s Wt.	180s Wt.	—
January 1965	—	115s Wt.	—	—	—
June 1965	—	—	—	—	210s Wt.
October 1965	97s 6d Wt. —		97s 6d Wt. —		—
March 1966	112s 6d Wt. —		—	—	—
December 1967 (to U.K. only)	131s 3d Wt.	140s Wt.	122s 6d Wt.	210s Wt.	236s Wt.

*United Kingdom/West Africa Lines Joint Service Rates are to U.K.,
Shown in Sterling*

| January 1968 | 131s 3d Wt. | 140s Wt. | 122s 6d Wt. | 210s Wt. | 236s Wt. |

Notes: 1. Rebates, where applicable, have been deducted.
2. Temporary surcharges imposed because of Korean and Suez Crises are not shown.

Source: Ukwal Secretariat, JMC/JF, 14 July 1969.

Table 82 WALCON CIRCULAR DATED 1 JANUARY 1968

The Member Lines of the West African Lines Conference (WALCON) have arranged that the activities of their Conference will be reorganised and that from 1st January 1968, two Conferences will operate to provide the services covering the trades and on the routes of the present WALCON.

The U.K. and Eire services to and from West Africa will be undertaken by the United Kingdom/West Africa Lines Joint Service whose Members will be:

Elder Dempster Lines Limited, Liverpool.

Palm Line Limited, London.

The Guinea Gulf Line Limited, Liverpool.

Black Star Line Limited, Accra.

The Nigerian National Shipping Line Limited, Lagos.

Leif Hoegh and Company, A/S, Oslo.

Continental and Scandinavian services to and from West Africa will be undertaken by the Continent West Africa Conference (COWAC) whose Members will be:

Woermann–Linie, Hamburg.

Holland West-Africa Lijn N.V. Amsterdam.

Elder Dempster Lines Limited, Liverpool.

Palm Line Limited, London.

The Nigerian National Shipping Line Limited, Lagos.

Black Star Line Limited, Accra.

The Guinea Gulf Line Limited, Liverpool.

The Scandinavian West Africa Line, Gothenburg.

Compagnie Maritime des Chargeurs Réunis, Paris.

Societe Navala Relmas-Vieljeux, Paris.

Societe Navale de l'Ouest, Paris.

Compagnie de Navigation Renis, Paris.

Leif Hoegh and Company, A/S, Oslo.

Source: WALCON Secretariat.

Sherbro built in 1947.

Aureol built 1951, passing the Pier Head, Liverpool.

Deido built in 1961.

PLATE 31

Kohima (1953–1966) was operated by the British and Burmese Steam Navigation Company before being acquired by Elder Dempster Lines.

Fian built 1964, is one of six 'F' Class vessels currently operated.

Carway, built 1967, was the first ship to go into service for Seaway Car Transporters.

PLATE 32

Table 83 INTERNATIONAL SHIPPING LINES SERVING WEST AFRICA IN 1964

(Excluding tankers, bulk carriers and other specialised trades or incidental services)

Trade Route	Conference Name	No. of Companies in this Conference	No. of Companies operating independently	Total No. of Companies
1. U.K., Continent and the Baltic to West Africa	West African Lines Conference	8	11	19
2. Italy to West Africa	Italian West African Conference	11	4	15
3. South France and North Africa to West Africa	O.T.R.A.M.A.	7	1	8
4. U.S. Atlantic Gulf Ports, Canadian, Atlantic and St Lawrence Seaway Ports to West Africa	American West African Freight Conference	18	0	18
5. Far East to West Africa	Far East/West Africa Conférence	6	1	7
6. French Atlantic Ports to West Africa	Conference des Lignes de Navigation Resservant la Coa	14	0	14
7. Australasia to West Africa	None	0	4	4

Source: Based on S. F. Klinghofer, 'A Report on a Preliminary Survey of Factors contributing to level of freight rates in the Seaborne trade of Africa', U.N. Economic Commission for Africa, 1965, Tables 1, 1a and 1b.

Table 84 THE NORTH ATLANTIC DIRECT SERVICES

Although Elder Dempster's principal interest was the operation of shipping services from British and European ports to West Africa, the Company was not averse to pursuing viable opportunities elsewhere as and when they became available. In accordance with this policy, vessels were occasionally chartered to other firms and frequently used on the North Atlantic. When Elder Dempster realised how profitable these ventures could be they built or purchased a number of ships specially designed for the trade. These included *Alexander Elder, Memphis, Plassey* and *Sobraon* (1890) *Assaye* (1891) *Mohawk* (1892) *Mobile* (1893) and *Etolia* and *Lycia* (1894).

In 1892 an agreement was made with the Atlantic Transport Line whereby some of the above-named ships sailed for the African Steam Ship Company (instead of being chartered) as part of a joint service. This arrangement appears to have come to an end in 1896 when *Mohawk* and *Mobile* were sold to the Atlantic Transport Line but Elder Dempster vessels continued to participate on other American routes, being particularly active in the seasonal cotton trade from Galveston and New Orleans. A number of especially large ships were built for this trade including *Milwaukee* of 7,323 gross tons (1897) and *Monmouth* (1898) and these formed the basis of the fleet transferred to Elder Dempster Shipping Limited, when it was established in 1899.[1]

Elder Dempster's interest in the U.K.—United States trade was paralleled by similar developments on Canadian routes.[2] At first only occasional voyages were made from this country to Quebec and Montreal, but in 1894 the Company took over the Bristol-Canada service formerly operated by the Dominion Line. Later, in 1899, the Beaver Line was acquired, and a regular schedule maintained from Liverpool to Avonmouth to Canada.[3] The Beaver Line was sold in 1903 and amongst the vessels transferred to the Canadian Pacific Railway Company at that time were a number previously owned by Elder Dempster Shipping Limited.[4] Other ships, formerly used by the Beaver Line, were retained by Elder Dempster and utilised on different routes.

During this period Elder Dempster had a further interest in the trade of the North Atlantic, for it managed the Ocean Transport Company Limited from 1894 to 1902. This firm was a wholly owned subsidiary of Harland and Wolff Limited and was consequently not integrated with Elder Dempster's other activities.

In 1901 Elder Dempster inaugurated a regular Canada to Cape (South Africa) service. This was later extended to include calls at West African ports on the Northbound route. A further development was the establishment of a West African to North American service which involved calls at both United States and Canadian ports.[5]

See also: *The Elder Dempster Companies and their Ships,* a typescript written by MR M. H. SMYE, the then Secretary of Elder Dempster Lines Limited in 1957. A copy is in the possession of the author of this present work.

[1] See above, Chapter 6, pp. 145–6.
[2] Full details of all Elder Dempster's Atlantic services in 1902 are given in Ocean Highways (an illustrated souvenir of Elder Dempster), London: Spottiswoode.
[3] See above, Chapter 5, pp. 128–9.
[4] See Appendix, Table 14, p. 407.
[5] See above, Chapter 5, 129 f/n2; Chapter 11, p. 279 f/n2 and Chapter 13, pp. 332–3.

Table 85 VESSELS OWNED BY ELDER DEMPSTER LINES, ITS PREDECESSORS AND SUBSIDIARY COMPANIES

Ref. No.	Ship's Name	Gross tons	Knots	Builder	Built	Pur- chased	Owning Companies	End of Service	
1	S.S. *Forerunner*	381	—	Laird	1852		African	Lost	1854
2	S.S. *Faith*	894	9½	Laird	1852		African	Sold	1855
3	S.S. *Hope*	894	9½	Laird	1853		African	Sold	1860
4	S.S. *Charity*	1,077	—	Laird	1853		African	Sold	1854
5	S.S. *Northern Light*	1,077	—	Laird	1853		African	Sold	1854
6	S.S. *Candace*	660	—	Laird	1853		African	Lost	1858
7	S.S. *Ethiope*	660	—	Laird	1854		African	Sold	1868
8	S.S. *Retriever*	329	9	Denny	1854		African	Sold	1867
9	S.S. *Athenian*	1,107	—	Smith	1854		African	Sold	1871
10	S.S. *Armenian*	1,107	—	Smith	1855		African	Lost	1865
11	S.S. *Gambia*	517	—	Port Glasgow	1855		African	Sold	1859
12	S.S. *Niger*	708	—	R. Napier	1856		African	Lost	1857
13	S.S. *Cleopatra*	1,280	—	Denny	1852	1859	African	Lost	1862
14	S.S. *Macgregor Laird*	969	—	R.-Elder	1862		African	Lost	1871
15	S.S. *Calabar*	1,122	—	R.-Elder	1864		African	Sold	1873
16	S.S. *Lagos*	1,199	—	R.-Elder	1865		African	Sold	1872
17	S.S. *Mandingo*	1,216	—	R.-Elder	1866		African	Sold	1872
18	S.S. *Biafra*	1,487	—	Laird	1868		African	Sold	1889
19	S.S. *Bonny*	1,277	—	R.-Elder	1869		B/A	Sold	1890
20	S.S. *Roquelle*	1,283	—	R.-Elder	1869		B/A	Sold	1882
21	S.S. *Congo*	1,283	—	J. Elder	1869		B/A	Sold	1882
22	S.S. *Benin*	1,530	—	J. Elder	1869		B/A	Lost	1881
23	S.S. *Liberia*	1,470	—	J. Elder	1870		B/A	Lost	1874
24	S.S. *Loanda*	1,474	—	J. Elder	1870		B/A	Sold	1889
25	S.S. *Volta*	1,477	—	J. Elder	1870		B/A	Sold	1891
26	S.S. *Rio Formoso*	163	—	Bowdler, C.	1870		B/A	Sold	1875
27	S.S. *Eboe*	653	—	T. Royden	1870		African	Sold	1875
28	S.S. *Soudan*	1,603	—	T. Royden	1870		African	Lost	1875
29	S.S. *Yoruba*	1,705	11	Laird	1871		African	Lost	1873
30	S.S. *Africa*	1,717	11	Laird	1871		African	Sold	1899
31	S.S. *Senegal*	1,625	—	Cunliffe	1872		B/A	Lost	1887
32	S.S. *Nigretia* (ex S.S. *Bentinck*)	1,810	—	Whitehaven	1872		African	Lost	1873
33	S.S. *Ambriz* (ex S.S. *Asiatic*)	2,121	—	T. Royden	1871	1873	African	Sold	1895
34	S.S. *Ethiopia*	1,761	—	T. Royden	1873		African	Lost	1882
35	S.S. *Elmina*	1,018	—	T. Royden	1873		African	Sold	1878
36	S.S. *Monrovia*	1,019	—	T. Royden	1873		African	Lost	1876
37	S.S. *Waydah*	418	—	London	1874		African	Sold	1893
38	S.S. *Forcados*	456	—	Cunliffe	1874		B/A	Lost	1904

Ref. No.	Ship's Name	Gross tons	Knots	Builder	Built	Pur- chased	Owning Companies	End of Service	
39	S.S. *Formoso*	461	—	Cunliffe	1876		B/A	Sold	1890
40	S.S. *Benguela*	1,860	—	J. Elder	1874		B/A	Lost	1905
41	S.S. *Cameroon*	1,862	—	J. Elder	1874		B/A	Lost	1904
42	S.S. *Corisco*	1,856	—	J. Elder	1876		B/A	Lost	1885
43	S.S. *Gaboon*	1,863	—	J. Elder	1878		B/A, African	Sold	1898
44	S.S. *Kinsembo*	1,868	—	Cunliffe	1876		B/A	Sold	1893
45	S.S. *Lualaba*	1,850	—	Cunliffe	1878		B/A	Sold	1895
46	S.S. *Opobo*	186	—	L'pool Forge	1877		African	Lost	1882
47	S.S. *Ramos*	233	—	Cunliffe	1878		B/A, African	Lost	1885
48	S.S. *Dodo*	531	—	Cunliffe	1879		B/A	Scuttled	1908
49	S.S. *Nubia*	1,958	—	Harland & W.	1879		African	Sold	1899
50	S.S. *Coanza*	1,518	—	J. Elder	1880		B/A	Lost	1893
51	S.S. *Malemba*	1,521	—	J. Elder	1880		B/A	Sold	1897
52	S.S. *Landana* (ex S.S. *Venetian*)	1,568	—	Harland & W.	1859	1880	African	Sold	1891
53	S.S. *Mayumba* (ex S.S. *Sicilian*)	1,492	—	Harland & W.	1859	1880	African	Sold	1882
54	S.S. *Akassa*	1,389	—	Harland & W.	1881		African	Sold	1903
55	S.S. *Winnebah*	1,391	—	Harland & W.	1881		African	Sold	1899
56	S.S. *Mandingo*	1,700	—	Harland & W.	1882		African	Sold	1905
57	S.S. *Congo*	1,687	—	Cunliffe	1882		B/A, African	Sold	1907
58	S.S. *Sherbro*	1,650	—	J. Elder	1882		B/A	Sold	1909
59	S.S. *Calabar*	1,701	—	J. Elder	1883		B/A	Lost	1898
60	S.S. *Lagos*	1,731	—	Dunlop	1883		B/A	Lost	1902
61	S.S. *Madeira*	1,773	—	Barclay	1884		B/A	Lost	1914
62	S.S. *Teneriffe*	1,800	—	Harland & W.	1885		B/A	Sold	1919
63	S.S. *Elmina*	1,764	—	Harland & W.	1885		African	Sold	1907
64	S.S. *Niger*	2,006	—	Harland & W.	1883		African	Sold	1903
65	S.S. *Opobo*	2,078	—	Barclay	1884		B/A	Lost	1890
66	S.S. *Roquelle*	2,013	—	Barclay	1884		B/A	Sold	1908
67	S.S. *Benin*	2,223	—	Harland & W.	1884		African	Sold	1905
68	S.S. *Benito*	712	—	Dunlop	1884		B/A	Lost	1894
69	S.S. *Clare*	2,034	—	T. Clark	1883	1887	E.D.	Sold	1890
70	S.S. *Nigretia*	2,477	—	R. Dixon	1888		E.D.	Sold	1893
71	S.S. *Teutonia*	2,376	—	Schlesinger	1881	1888	E.D.	Sold	1890
72	S.S. *Leon-y-Castillo*	529	—	Dunlop	1888		E.D., African	Lost	1910
73	S.S. *Viera-y-Clavijo*	529	—	Dunlop	1888		E.D., African	Sold	1912
74	S.S. *Perez Lavdos*	529	—	Dunlop	1888		E.D., African	Sold	1904
75	S.S. *Palmas*	2,428	10	Harland & W.	1888		E.D., African	Lost	1903
76	S.S. *Boma*	2,510	10	Naval C & A	1889		B/A	Lost	1918
77	S.S. *Matadi*	2,623	10	Naval C & A	1889		B/A	Lost	1896
78	S.S. *Soudan*	2,625	10	Naval C & A	1889		E.D., African	Lost	1891
79	S.S. *Coomassie*	2,625	10	Naval C & A	1890		E.D., African	Sold	1911

Ref. No.	Ship's Name	Gross tons	Knots	Builder	Built	Pur-chased	Owning Companies	End of Service
80	S.S. *Angola*	2,870	10	R. Dixon	1891		E.D., African, E.L.	Lost 1906
81	S.S. *Dahomey*	2,854	10	R. Dixon	1891		E.D., African, E.L.	Lost 1908
82	S.S. *Oil Rivers*	2,777	10	R. Dixon	1891		E.D., B/A	Sold 1907
83	S.S. *Eithiope*	2,893	—	R. Dixon	1889	1891	E.D.	Sold 1891
84	S.S. *Eboe* (ex S.S. *Simoon*)	2,070	—	C. Mitchell	1880	1889	African	Sold 1897
85	S.S. *Gambia* (ex S.S. *Sheikh*)	1,937	—	C. Mitchell	1880	1889	African	Sold 1897
86	S.S. *Yoruba* (ex S.S. *Sirocco*)	2,069	—	Wallsend	1880	1889	African	Sold 1897
87	S.S. *Biafra* (ex S.S. *Algarve*)	839	—	J. Priestman	1885	1890	E.D., African, E.L.	Sold 1896
88	S.S. *Loango* (ex S.S. *Knight of St George*)	2,935	—	T. Royden	1883	1890	E.D., African, E.L.	Sold 1905
89	S.S. *Earn*	181	—	Blackwood	1884	1890	E.D.	Sold 1911
90	S.S. *Isla*	109	—	Blackwood	1885	1890	E.D.	Sold 1911
91	S.S. *Alexander Elder* (renamed *Merrimac* in 1892)	4,173	—	Harland & W.	1890		E.D., African	Lost 1899
92	S.S. *Assaye*	5,129	—	Harland & W.	1891		African	Lost 1897
93	S.S. *Mayumba*	2,516	—	R. Dixon	1890		E.D., African	Sold 1915
94	S.S. *Monrovia*	2,402	—	R. Dixon	1890		E.D., African, E.L.	Lost 1914
95	S.S. *Ethiopia*	2,523	—	R. Dixon	1891		E.D., African	Converted into lighter 1909
96	S.S. *Memphis*	3,190	10½	Harland & W.	1890		E.D., African	Lost 1896
97	S.S. *Plassey* (renamed *Memnon* in 1892)	3,176	10½	Harland & W.	1890		African, E.L.	Lost 1917
98	S.S. *Sobraon* (renamed *Mexico* in 1893)	3,185	10½	Harland & W.	1890		African	Lost 1895
99	S.S. *Etolia*	3,270	10½	Harland & W.	1887	1894	African, E.L.	Lost 1906
100	S.S. *Lycia*	3,282	10½	Harland & W.	1888	1894	African, E.L.	Sold 1904
101	S.S. *Kwarra*	812	—	Naval C & A	1891		African	Lost 1908
102	S.S. *Bonny*	2,702	10½	Naval C & A	1891		B/A	Lost 1915
103	S.S. *Volta*	2,702	—	Naval C & A	1891		B/A	Sold 1908
104	S.S. *Loanda*	2,702	10½	Naval C & A	1891		B/A	Lost 1908
105	S.S. *Accra*	2,808	—	Naval C & A	1893		B/A	Sold 1920
106	S.S. *Batanga*	2,808	—	Naval C & A	1893		B/A	Broken up 1922
107	S.S. *Bathurst*	2,808	—	Naval C & A	1893		B/A	Lost 1917
108	S.S. *Axim*	2,793	—	Naval C & A	1894		B/A	Lost 1910
109	S.S. *Bakana*	2,793	11	Naval C & A	1894		B/A	Lost 1913
110	S.S. *Mohawk*	5,658	—	Harland & W.	1892		African	Sold 1896
111	S.S. *Mobile*	5,780	—	Harland & W.	1893		African	Sold 1896
112	S.S. *Europa*	2,232	—	M. Pearse	1881	1894	O.T.	Sold 1902

Ref. No.	Ship's Name	Gross tons	Knots	Builder	Built	Pur- chased	Owning Companies	End of Service
113	S.S. *Mariposa*	5,305	12	Mitchell	1891	1894	O.T.	Lost 1895
114	S.S. *Montezuma*	5,504	11	Harland & W.	1891	1894	O.T.	Sold 1898
115	S.S. *Niagara*	3,033	—	M. Pearse	1883	1894	O.T.	Lost 1899
116	S.S. *Marino*	3,819	—	Harland & W.	1895	1896	O.T.	Sold 1898
117	S.S. *Lagoon*	704	10½	Barclay	1895		B/A	Beached 1922
118	S.S. *Ilaro*	2,799	9	R. Dixon	1895		African	Beached 1915
119	S.S. *Banana*	2,817	9	J. Blumer	1897		E.D., E.L.	Sold 1919
120	S.S. *Biafra* (ex. *Leopoldville*)	3,363	—	R. Dixon	1895	1896	African	Sold 1910
121	S.S. *Queensmore*	3,878	11½	Gourley	1890	1896	E.D.	Sold 1898
122	S.S. *Ekuro*	485	9	Swan Hunter	1896		B/A	Scuttled 1914
123	S.S. *Ibadan*	793	—	Dunlop	1896		African	Sold 1901
124	S.S. *Ilorin*	946	9½	Dunlop	1896		African	Lost 1909
125	S.S. *Ashba*	972	9½	Caledon	1900		African	Lost 1917
126	S.S. *Iddo*	965	9½	Londonderry	1901		African	Dismantled 1923
127	S.S. *Bassa*	940	9½	Dunlop	1905		B/A	Sold 1917
128	S.S. *Oshogbo*	949	9½	Dunlop	1906		E.D., E.L.	Lost 1928
129	S.S. *Laguna* (ex. *Konigin Wilhelmina*)	1,596	—	Nederland	1892	1897	African	Sold 1898
130	S.S. *Ebani*	1,738	10	W. Gray	1896	1897	African	Sold 1898
131	S.S. *Yoruba* (ex. *Straits of Sunda*)	2,991	10	Barclay	1895	1897	E.D., E.L.	Lost 1911
132	S.S. *Montpelier*	3,483	10	McMillan	1897		E.D., E.L.	Lost 1900
133	S.S. *Landana*	2,834	9	R. Dixon	1897	1898	E.D.	Lost 1898
134	S.S. *Ashanti*	3,389	10	Swan Hunter	1897		E.D., E.L.	Lost 1919
135	S.S. *Lokoja*	3,458	10	Swan Hunter	1898		E.D., E.L.	Sold 1899
136	S.S. *Milwaukee*	7,323	12	Swan Hunter	1897		E.D., E.L.	Sold 1903
137	S.S. *Mount Royal*	7,045	12	Swan Hunter	1898		E.D., E.L.	Sold 1903
138	S.S. *Monarch*	7,296	12	Swan Hunter	1897	1899	E.D., E.L.	Sold 1926
139	S.S. *Montcalm*	5,478	12¼	Palmers	1897		E.D., E.L.	Sold 1903
140	S.S. *Montrose*	5,431	12¼	R. Dixon	1897		E.D.	Sold 1903
141	S.S. *Monterey*	5,443	12¼	Palmers	1898		E.D., E.L.	Sold 1903
142	S.S. *Monteagle*	5,468	12¼	Palmers	1899		E.D., E.L.	Sold 1903
143	S.S. *Montford*	5,481	12¼	Palmers	1899		E.D., E.L.	Sold 1903
144	S.S. *Andoni*	3,188	9½	Hamilton	1898	1899	E.D., E.L.	Lost 1917
145	S.S. *Gambia*	2,877	9	R. Dixon	1898		E.D.	Sold 1898
146	S.S. *Monmouth*	8,001	12	Harland & W.	1898		E.D.	Sold 1898
147	S.S. *Montclair*	3,806	10	McMillan	1898		E.D.	Sold 1901
148	S.S. *Melrose* (ex. *Strathnairn*)	4,038	10	W. Gray	1894	1898	E.D.	Sold 1899
149	S.S. *Montauk* (ex *Strathfillan*)	4,040	10	W. Gray	1894	1899	E.D., B/A	Lost 1911

Ref. No.	Ship's Name	Gross tons	Knots	Builder	Built	Pur- chased	Owning Companies	End of Service	
150	S.S. *Monmouth* (ex. *Fitzpatrick*)	4,071	10	Tyne Iron	1896	1898	E.D.	Sold	1899
151	S.S. *Parkmore*	3,318	12	C. J. Bigger	1890	1898	E.D.	Sold	1898
152	S.S. *Yola*	3,504	10	Sunderland	1898		E.D., E.L.	Lost	1917
153	S.S. *Olenda*	3,171	12¼	Barclay	1898		B/A	Sold	1913
154	S.S. *Oron*	3,171	12½	Barclay	1898		B/A	Sold	1919
155	S.S. *Bornu*	3,238	12½	Vickers	1899		B/A	Lost	1916
156	S.S. *Sokoto*	3,080	12½	Vickers	1899		B/A	Sold	1914
157	S.S. *Jebba* (ex. *Albertville*)	3,812	13	R. Dixon	1896	1898	African	Lost	1907
158	S.S. *Sekondi* (ex. *Leopoldville*)	3,765	13	R. Dixon	1897	1901	African	Sold	1910
159	S.S. *Nigeria*	3,755	13	R. Dixon	1901		African	Sold	1917
160	S.S. *Akabo*	3,806	13	R. Dixon	1902		B/A	Sold	1926
161	S.S. *Aro* (ex. *Albertville*)	3,805	13	R. Dixon	1898	1904	African	Sold	1914
162	S.S. *Degama*	3,507	8¾	F. Withy	1899		E.D., E.L.	Lost	1914
163	S.S. *Sangara*	3,530	—	F. Withy	1899		E.D.	Sold	1899
164	S.S. *Eko* (ex. *Frej*)	337	—	Stettiner	1890	1899	African	Sold	1905
165	S.S. *Sobo*	3,652	12½	Barclay	1899		African, E.L.	Sold	1915
166	S.S. *Fantee*	3,649	12½	Barclay	1899		African	Sold	1913
167	S.S. *Lake Huron*	4,040	13½	London	1881	1899	E.D.	Sold	1901
168	S.S. *Lake Megantic* (ex. *Arawa*, renamed *Port Henderson* in 1905)	5,115	13½	Denny	1884	1899	E.D., B/A, I.D.	Sold	1912
169	S.S. *Lake Ontario*	4,502	13½	J. Laing	1887	1899	E.D.	Sold	1905
170	S.S. *Lake Superior*	4,562	13½	J. & G. Thomson	1884	1899	E.D.	Lost	1902
171	S.S. *Montenegro*	4,408	10	Henderson	1898	1899	E.L.	Sold	1922
172	S.S. *Whydah* (ex. *Johann*)	1,381	—	Flensburger	1884	1899	African	Sold	1902
173	S.S. *Montezuma*	7,345	11½	A. Stephen	1899		E.D., B/A	Sold	1903
174	S.S. *Mount Temple*	7,656	11½	Armstrong, W.	1901		E.D.	Sold	1903
175	S.S. *Prah*	2,520	9½	W. Dobson	1899		E.D., B/A	Sold	1924
176	S.S. *Nyanga*	3,066	9½	W. Dobson	1900		E.D., E.L.	Lost	1914
177	S.S. *Sangara*	2,497	9½	Tyne Iron	1900		E.D., B/A	Sold	1919
178	S.S. *Warri*	2,493	9½	Tyne Iron	1901		E.D., B/A	Sold	1927
179	S.S. *Sansu*	2,495	9½	Tyne Iron	1901		E.D., B/A	Lost	1908
180	S.S. *Adansi*	2,644	9½	McMillan	1901		E.D., B/A	Lost	1917
181	S.S. *Ancobra* (renamed *Sokoto* in 1921)	2,646	9½	McMillan	1901		E.D., African	Sold	1924
182	S.S. *Boulama*	2,613	9½	Londonderry	1901		E.D., B/A	Sold	1923
183	S.S. *Lokoja*	2,604	9½	Clyde S & E	1901		E.D.	Lost	1902

Ref. No.	Ship's Name	Gross tons	Knots	Builder	Built	Pur- chased	Owning Companies	End of Service
184	S.S. *Egwanga*	2,600	9½	Clyde S & E	1902		E.D., B/A	Sold 1927
185	S.S. *Nembe* (ex. *Croxdale*)	2,842	9½	Tyne Iron	1902	1905	E.D., B/A	Burnt 1919
186	S.S. *Lusitania*	3,825	14	Laird	1871	1900	E.D.	Lost 1901
187	S.S. *Delta*	585	10	Swan Hunter	1900		B/A, E.D., I.D.	Scuttled 1915
188	S.S. *Lake Erie*	7,550	12½	Barclay	1900		E.D., B/A	Sold 1903
189	S.S. *Lake Champlain*	6,546	12½	Barclay	1900		E.D., B/A	Sold 1903
190	S.S. *Monmouth*	4,078	10½	R. Dixon	1900		E.D., B/A	Sold 1903
191	S.S. *Montreal*	6,870	13	Swan Hunter	1900		E.D., B/A	Sold 1903
192	S.S. *Abeokuta*	1,817	9	R. Duncan	1901		E.D., E.L.	Lost 1915
193	S.S. *Kano*	1,452	9½	Caledon	1901		E.D., B/A	Lost 1907
194	S.S. *Bida*	1,477	9½	J. Jones	1901		E.D., E.L.	Lost 1903
195	S.S. *Haussa*	1,477	9½	J. Jones	1901		E.L.	Lost 1903
196	S.S. *Egga*	1,445	9½	Londonderry	1901		African	Lost 1908
197	S.S. *Garth Castle*	3,704	—	J. Elder	1880	1901	E.D.	Sold 1901
198	S.S. *Lake Simcoe*	4,933	16	J. Elder	1884	1901	E.D.	Sold 1905
199	S.S. *Llandulas*	847	10	Selby S & E	1901		E.D., E.L.	Lost 1907
200	S.S. *Port Royal*	4,455	15	R. Dixon	1901		I.D.	Sold 1911
201	S.S. *Port Antonio*	4,458	15	R. Dixon	1901		I.D.	Sold 1911
202	S.S. *Port Maria*	2,910	16	Ramage & F	1901		I.D.	Sold 1910
203	S.S. *Port Morant*	2,831	16	A. Stephen	1901		I.D., E.L.	Sold 1909
204	S.S. *Wassau* (ex. *Trojan*)	3,652	—	J & G Thomson	1880	1901	E.D.	Sold 1902
205	S.S. *Lake Manitoba*	8,852	13	Swan Hunter	1901		E.D.	Sold 1903
206	S.S. *Lake Michigan*	7,000	13	Swan Hunter	1902		E.D.	Sold 1903
207	S.S. *Burutu*	3,863	—	A. Stephen	1902		E.D., B/A	Lost 1918
208	S.S. *Tarquah*	3,859	—	A. Stephen	1902		E.D., African	Lost 1917
209	S.S. *Melville*	4,391	10¾	R. Duncan	1902		E.D., E.L.	Sold 1926
210	S.S. *Porto Novo*	603	9	Dunlop	1903		B/A, E.L.	Scuttled 1921
211	S.S. *Port Kingston*	585	17	A. Stephen	1904		I.D.	Sold 1911
212	S.S. *Canada Cape*	4,283	10	Northumber- land	1904		E.L.	Sold 1912
213	S.S. *Kittiwake*	241	8	T. B. Seath	1899	1904	B/A	Lost 1908
214	S.S. *Puffin*	248	8	T. B. Seath	1899	1904	B/A	Hulked 1911
215	S.S. *Seagull*	241	8	T. B. Seath	1899	1904	E.D., E.L.	Sold 1906 Rebought 1912 Resold 1914

Ref. No.	Ship's Name	Gross tons	Knots	Builder	Built	Pur-chased	Owning Companies	End of Service	
216	S.S. *Zaria*	3,243	14	Clyde S & E	1904		B/A	Sold	1927
217	S.S. *Muraji*	3,238	14	Clyde S & E	1904		E.L.	Lost	1914
218	S.S. *Sapele*	3,152	12½	Palmers	1904		B/A	Lost	1917
219	S.S. *Addah*	3,149	12½	Palmers	1905		B/A	Lost	1917
220	S.S. *Chama*	3,152	12½	Palmers	1905		African	Sold	1930
221	S.S. *Benue*	3,111	12½	Swan Hunter	1905		E.L., African	Sold	1930
222	S.S. *Zungeru* (sailed as *Bruxellesville*, 1906–1909)	4,075	13	R. Dixon	1904		E.L., African	Sold	1910
223	S.S. *Landana* (ex. *Leopoldville*)	4,376	13	R. Dixon	1904	1908	African	Sold	1910
224	S.S. *Karina*	4,222	13	A. Stephen	1905		African	Lost	1917
225	S.S. *Mendi*	4,230	13	A. Stephen	1905		B/A	Lost	1917
226	S.S. *Patani*	3,465	13½	Workman C.	1905		E.D., E.L., African	Sold	1930
227	S.S. *Agberi*	3,463	13½	Workman C.	1905		E.D., E.L., African	Lost	1917
228	S.S. *Aburi*	3,730	13½	Harland & W.	1906		African	Lost	1917
229	S.S. *Fulani*	3,731	13½	Harland & W.	1907		E.D., African	Lost	1914
230	S.S. *Prahsu*	3,756	13½	Harland & W.	1907		E.D., African	Sold	1931
231	S.S. *Sierra Leone*	3,730	13½	Harland & W.	1907		African	Lost	1910
232	S.S. *Coaling* (renamed *Ethiope* in 1911)	3,794	9	Furness W.	1906		E.D., E.L.	Lost	1915
233	S.S. *Dakar* (ex. *Anversville*)	4,081	—	R. Dixon	1899	1906	African	Lost	1915
234	S.S. *Mandingo* (ex. *Philippeville*)	4,091	—	R. Dixon	1899	1906	African	Sold	1914
235	S.S. *Falaba*	4,806	—	A. Stephen	1906		E.D., E.L.	Lost	1915
236	S.S. *Bendu*	4,319	12	Swan Hunter	1906		E.D., E.L.	Sold	1929
237	S.S. *Benin*	4,313	12	Swan Hunter	1907		E.D., I.D.	Sold	1929
238	S.S. *Badagri*	2,952	9½	Tyne Iron	1907		E.D., E.L.	Lost	1918
239	S.S. *Abonema* (renamed *Sapele* in 1920)	2,952	9¾	Irvines S & D	1907		E.D., E.L.	Sold	1929
240	S.S. *Palma*	2,981	9½	Irvines S & D	1907		E.D., B/A	Sold	1930
241	S.S. *Lagos*	292	10¼	W. Harkness	1907		E.D., E.L.	Scuttled	1924
242	S.S. *Forcados*	397	10¼	W. Harkness	1907		E.D., E.L.	Scuttled	1925
243	S.S. *Salaga*	3,811	13¾	Workman C.	1907		E.D., I.D.	Sold	1930
244	S.S. *Gando*	3,809	13¾	Workman C.	1907		E.D., African	Lost	1917
245	S.S. *Niger*	980	9½	Dunlop	1907		E.D., African	Lost	1916
246	S.S. *Lokoja*	981	9½	Dunlop	1908		E.D., B/A	Scuttled	1934
247	S.S *Baro* (renamed *Ilorin* in 1919)	957	10	W. Harkness	1908		E.D., B/A	Scuttled	1933

Ref. No.	Ship's Name	Gross tons	Knots	Builder	Built	Purchased	Owning Companies	End of Service
248	S.S. *Bida* (renamed *Ibadan* in 1919)	963	10	W. Harkness	1908		E.D., African	Scuttled 1932
249	S.S. *Uromi*	962	10	W. Harkness	1909		E.D., African, E.D.L.	Scuttled 1936
250	S.S. *Jamaica*	1,138	—	W. Harkness	1908		E.L.	Sold 1912
251	S.S. *Konakry*	4,397	10½	R. Dixon	1908		B/A	Lost 1918
252	S.S. *Kaduna*	4,455	10½	R. Dixon	1910		E.D., I.D.	Sold 1923
253	S.S. *Kwarra*	4,441	10½	R. Dixon	1910		E.D., I.D.	Sold 1923
254	S.S. *Shonga*	3,044	10	Irvines S & D	1909		E.D., E.L., African	Lost 1928
255	S.S. *Winneba*	3,040	10	Irvines S & D	1909		E.D., B/A	Lost 1913
256	S.S. *Bassam* (renamed *Sulima* in 1921)	3,040	10	Irvines S & D	1909		E.D., B/A	Sold 1927
257	S.S. *Tamele*	3,924	10	Irvines S & D	1910		E.D., B/A	Lost 1917
258	S.S. *Akassa*	3,918	10	Irvines S & D	1910		E.L.	Lost 1917
259	S.S. *Onitsha*	3,921	10	Irvines S & D	1910		E.D., B/A	Sold 1932
260	S.S. *Benguela*	5,520	12½	Swan Hunter	1910		E.D., I.D.	Sold 1933
261	S.S. *Elmina* (ex. *Albertville*)	4,792	—	A. Stephen	1906	1910	African	Sold 1928
262	S.S. *Hartley*	1,150	—	Wood, Skinner	1903	1910	B/A	Lost 1918
263	S.S. *Sir George*	1,254	—	Dunlop	1909	1911	African, E.D.L.	Scuttled 1935
264	S.S. *Darro*	11,484	13½	Harland & W.	1912		I.D.	Sold 1915
265	S.S. *Drina*	11,483	13½	Harland & W.	1913		E.L.	Sold 1916
266	S.S. *Abosso*	7,782	13½	Harland & W.	1912		African	Lost 1917
267	S.S. *Appam* (sailed as *Mandingo*, 1917–1919)	7,781	13½	Harland & W.	1913		B/A, E.D.L.	Sold 1936
268	S.S. *Apapa*	7,832	13½	Harland & W.	1914		African	Lost 1917
269	S.S. *Ebani*	4,862	11½	Palmers	1912		B/A, E.D.L.	Sold 1938
270	S.S. *Eboe*	4,862	11½	Palmers	1912		African, E.D.L.	Sold 1938
271	S.S. *Elele*	4,831	11½	Irvines S & D	1913		B/A	Lost 1917
272	S.S. *Eloby*	4,820	11½	Irvines S & D	1913		B/A	Lost 1917
273	S.S. *Egba*	4,989	11½	Harland & W.	1914		African, E.D.L.	Sold 1943
274	S.S. *Egori*	4,995	11½	Harland & W.	1914		B/A, E.L., African, E.D.L.	Sold 1939
275	S.S. *Abinsi* (ex. *Leopoldville*)	6,365	13½	Harland & W.	1908	1914	E.D., E.L., African	Sold 1933
276	M.V. *Ife*	299	8	Hawthorn	1914		African	Scuttled 1930
277	M.V. *Ila*	299	8	Hawthorn	1914		B/A, E.D.L.	Scuttled 1935
278	S.S. *Obuasi* (ex. *Christopher*)	4,416	10¾	Tyne Iron	1910		B/A	Lost 1917
279	S.S. *Gaboon*	3,297	11¼	Tyne Iron	1915		B/A	Sold 1933

Ref. No.	Ship's Name	Gross tons	Knots	Builder	Built	Pur- chased	Owning Companies	End of Service
280	S.S. *Gambia*	3,296	11¼	Tyne Iron	1915		B/A	Sold 1933
281	S.S. *Gold Coast* (ex. *Hans Woermann*)	4,255	10	Dunlop	1900	1915	E.L.	Lost 1917
282	S.S. *Manxman*	4,827	—	Harland & W.	1888	1915	E.D.	Sold 1916
283	M.V. *Montezuma*	5,500	—	Harland & W.	1915		E.D.	Sold 1916
284	S.S. *Polladern* (ex *Emir*)	5,932	11½	Bremer V. V.	1911	1916	E.D.	Sold 1917
285	S.S. *Benito* (ex. *Falls of Nith*)	4,712	10½	Scotts	1907	1917	I.D.	Lost 1917
286	S.S. *Indore*	7,300	14	Workman C.	1898	1917	E.D.	Sold 1925
287	S.S. *Ikbal*	5,434	—	Harland & W.	1894	1917	E.D.	Lost 1917
288	S.S. *Roquelle*	4,364	10	Campbeltown	1918		I.D.	Sold 1927
289	S.S. *Bassa* (ex. *War Pointer*)	5,267	11½	Armstrong W.	1918	1919	African, E.D.L.	Lost 1940
290	S.S. *Burutu* (ex. *War Swan*)	5,275	11½	Sunderland	1918	1920	B/A	Sold 1934
291	S.S. *Badagry*	5,161	11½	Irvines S & D	1919		B/A, I.D.	Sold 1933
292	S.S. *Bereby* (ex. *War Raven*)	5,248	11½	Irvines S & D	1919		African, E.D.L.	Lost 1941
293	S.S. *Bonny* (ex. *War Stoat*)	5,173	11½	Irvines S & D	1919		B/A, E.L.	Lost 1928
294	S.S. *Boutry*	5,182	11½	Irvines S & D	1919		African	Sold 1933
295	S.S. *Bakana*	5,384	11½	Ropner	1919		B/A, E.L.	Sold 1929
296	S.S. *Barracoo*	5,234	11½	R. Thompson	1919		African	Sold 1933
297	S.S. *Bata*	5,260	11½	J. Brown	1919		African	Sold 1933
298	S.S. *Bodnant*	5,258	11½	J. Brown	1919		E.D., African, E.D.L.	Lost 1940
299	S.S. *Bathurst* (ex *War Alyssum*)	5,437	11½	Harland & W.	1919		B/A, E.L.	Sold 1933
300	S.S. *Biafra* (ex. *War Dahlia*)	5,405	11½	Harland & W.	1919		African, E.D.L.	Sold 1951
301	S.S. *Boma*	5,408	11½	Harland & W.	1920		B/A, E.D.L.	Lost 1940
302	S.S. *Bompata*	5,570	11½	Harland & W.	1921		B/A, E.D.L.	Sold 1934
303	S.S. *Matadi*	3,097	10¾	W. Dobson	1919		E.D.	Sold 1921
304	S.S. *Mateba*	2,955	10¾	R. Thompson	1919		E.D.	Sold 1921
305	S.S. *New Brunswick*	6,529	11½	Harland & W.	1919		E.D., E.L., E.D.L.	Lost 1942
306	S.S. *New Georgia*	6,566	11½	Harland & W.	1919		B/A	Sold 1933
307	S.S. *New Mexico*	6,566	11½	Harland & W.	1919		E.D., E.L., E.D.L.	Sold 1933
307	S.S. *New Texas*	6,568	11½	Harland & W.	1919		E.D., B/A, E.D.L.	Sold 1955
309	S.S. *New Toronto*	6,568	11½	Harland & W.	1919		E.D., B/A, E.D.L.	Lost 1942
310	S.S. *New Brighton*	6,538	11½	Harland & W.	1920		African	Sold 1933

Ref. No.	Ship's Name	Gross tons	Knots	Builder	Built	Pur-chased	Owning Companies	End of Service
311	S.S. *New Brooklyn* (ex. *War Romance*)	6,546	11½	Harland & W.	1920		B/A, E.D.L.	Sold 1954
312	S.S. *New Columbia* (ex. *War Pagent*)	6,574	11½	Harland & W.	1920		African, E.D.L.	Lost 1943
313	S.S. *Jebba* (ex. *War Lion*)	5,875	—	Kawasaki	1917	1920	African	Sold 1933
314	S.S. *Jekri* (ex. *War Pilot*)	5,875	—	Kawasaki	1917	1920	B/A	Sold 1933
315	M.V. *Aba* (ex. *Glenapp*)	7,373	14	Barclay	1918	1920	B/A, E.D.L.	Sold 1947
316	S.S. *Fantee*	5,663	—	Northumber-land	1920		E.D.	Sold 1933
317	M.V. *Milverton* (ex. *Glentara*)	6,754	11½	Harland & W.	1920	1929	E.D., E.D.L.	Sold 1934
318	T.S. *Ekari*	6,711	11½	J. Brown	1920		African	Sold 1926
319	M.V. *Ediba* (renamed *Mattawin* in 1929)	6,919	11½	Harland & W.	1923		African, E.D.L.	Lost 1942
320	T.S. *Calgary*	7,206	12	J. Brown	1921		B/A, E.D.L.	Sold 1957
321	T.S. *Calumet*	7,405	12	J. Brown	1923		I.D., E.D.L.	Sold 1955
322	T.S. *Cochrane*	7,203	12	J. Brown	1923		African, E.D.L.	Sold 1957
323	T.S. *Cariboo*	7,275	12	J. Brown	1924		E.D.	Lost 1928
324	M.V. *Adda*	7,816	14	Harland & W.	1922		African, E.D.L.	Lost 1941
325	M.V. *Accra*	9,337	15	Harland & W.	1926		B/A, E.D.L.	Lost 1940
326	M.V. *Apapa*	9,337	15	Harland & W.	1927		B/A, E.D.L.	Lost 1940
327	M.V. *Daru*	3,838	10	A. McMillan	1927		B/A, E.D.L.	Lost 1941
328	M.V. *Dixcove*	3,790	10	A. McMillan	1927		B/A, E.D.L.	Lost 1941
329	M.V. *Dunkwa*	3,789	10	A. McMillan	1927		B/A, E.D.L.	Lost 1941
330	M.V. *Dagomba*	3,845	10	A. McMillan	1928		B/A, E.D.L.	Lost 1942
331	M.V. *Deido*	3,878	10	Ardrossan	1928		African, E.D.L.	Sold 1958
332	M.V. *Kwaibo*	396	9½	J. Crichton	1928		N.T., E.D.L.	Lost 1941
333	M.V. *Henry Stanley*	4,028	12½	Ardrossan	1929		African, E.D.L.	Lost 1942
334	M.V. *Mary Kingsley*	4,017	12½	Ardrossan	1930		African, E.D.L.	Sold 1954
335	M.V. *Alfred Jones*	4,021	12½	Harland & W.	1930		B/A, E.D.L.	Lost 1941
336	M.V. *Edward Blyden*	4,021	12½	Harland & W.	1930		B/A, E.D.L.	Lost 1941
337	M.V. *David Livingstone*	4,022	12½	A. McMillan	1930		B/A, E.D.L.	Sold 1953
338	M.V. *Mary Slessor*	4,015	12½	A. McMillan	1930		B/A, E.D.L.	Lost 1943
339	M.V. *Macgregor Laird*	4,015	12½	Henderson	1930		African, E.D.L.	Sold 1953

Ref. No.	Ship's Name	Gross tons	Knots	Builder	Built	Pur-chased	Owning Companies	End of Service
340	M.V. *William Wilberforce*	4,013	12½	Henderson	1930		African, E.D.L.	Lost 1943
341	M.V. *Achimota*	10,000	16½	Harland & W.	1932		B/A	Sold 1932
342	S.S. *Ilorin* (ex. *Smerdis*)	815	9	London & Melrose	1920	1934	E.D.L.	Lost 1942
343	M.V. *Abosso*	11,330	15	Cammell Laird	1935		E.D.L.	Lost 1942
344	M.V. *Calabar*	1,932	12	Harland & W.	1935		E.D.L.	Sold 1953
345	M.V. *Swedru*	4,124	12½	Scotts	1936		E.D.L.	Lost 1941
346	M.V. *Sobo*	4,124	12½	Scotts	1937		E.D.L.	Sold 1963
347	M.V. *Sangara*	4,174	12½	Scotts	1939		E.D.L.	Sold 1960
348	M.V. *Sansu*	4,174	12½	Scotts	1939		E.D.L.	Sold 1960
349	M.V. *Seaforth*	4,199	12½	Caledon	1939		E.D.L.	Lost 1941
350	S.S. *Arete*	898	9¼	Mistley	1925	1937	E.D.L.	Broken up 1947
351	M.V. *Oron*	277		W. Denny	1938		W.A.L.T.	In service
352	M.V. *Auchmacoy*	255	8½	Hall Russell	1939	1941	E.D.L.	Scuttled 1950
353	M.V. *Fantee* (ex. *Penrith Castle* till 1946)	6,369	13½	Cammell Laird	1929	1943	E.D.L.	Lost 1949
354	M.V. *Fulani* (ex. *Thurland Castle* till 1946)	6,372	13½	Cammell Laird	1929	1943	E.D.L.	Sold 1958
355	M.V. *Freetown* (ex. *Greystoke Castle* till 1946)	5,853	13¾	Cammell Laird	1928	1943	E.D.L.	Sold 1958
356	M.V. *Tamele*	7,172	15	Cammell Laird	1944		E.D.L.	Sold 1967
357	M.V. *Tarkwa*	7,416	14	Caledon	1944		E.D.L.	Sold 1967
358	S.S. *Cabano* (ex. *Strathcona Park*)	7,157	11	Burrard	1943	1946	E.D.C., E.D.L.	Sold 1959
359	S.S. *Cargill* (ex. *Wascana Park*)	7,152	11	Burrard	1943	1946	E.D.C., E.D.L.	Sold 1960
360	S.S. *Cambray* (ex. *Bridgeland Park*)	7,165	11	North Vancouver	1944	1946	E.D.C., E.D.L.	Sold 1960
361	S.S. *Chandler* (ex. *Crystal Park*)	7,161	11	North Vancouver	1944	1946	E.D.C., E.D.L.	Sold 1959
362	S.S. *Cottrell* (ex. *Goldstream Park*)	7,163	11	North Vancouver	1944	1946	E.D.C., E.D.L.	Sold 1960
363	S.S. *Knowlton*	2,068	8	Fraser Bruce	1922	1946	E.D.L.	Sold 1950
364	S.S. *Oxford*	1,893	8	Swan Hunter	1923	1946	E.D.L.	Scuttled 1950
365	S.S. *Sapele* (ex. *Empire Pavilion*)	974	11½	Blyth D & S	1945	1946	E.D.L.	Sold 1962
366	S.S. *Warri* (ex. *Empire Pampas*)	974	11½	Smiths	1945	1946	E.D.L.	Lost 1956
367	S.S, *Forcados* (ex. *Empire Pattern*)	974	11½	Smith	1945	1948	E.D.L.	Lost 1962
368	S.S. *Zini* (ex. *Samos*)	7,255	11	Bethlehem	1943	1947	E.D.L.	Sold 1959
369	S.S. *Zungeru* (ex. *Samota*)	7,255	11	Bethlehem	1943	1947	E.D.L.	Sold 1958

Ref. No.	Ship's Name	Gross tons	Knots	Builder	Built	Pur-chased	Owning Companies	End of Service	
370	S.S. *Zungon* (ex. *Samyale*)	7,267	11	Bethlehem	1943	1947	E.D.L.	Sold	1958
371	M.V. *Salaga* (renamed *Mamfe* in 1965)	4,810	12½	Hawthorn	1947		E.D.L., G.G.	Sold	1968
372	M.V. *Sherbro* (renamed *Matru* in 1965)	4,811	12½	Furness W.	1947		E.D.L., G.G.	Sold	1967
373	M.V. *Sekondi* (renamed *Mampong* in 1965)	4,811	12½	Furness W.	1947		E.D.L., G.G.	Sold	1967
374	M.V. *Shonga* (renamed *Mallam* in 1965)	4,810	12½	Scotts	1947		E.D.L., G.G.	Sold	1967
375	M.V. *Sulima* (renamed *Mano* in 1965)	4,810	12½	Scotts	1948		E.D.L., G.G.	Sold	1967
376	M.V. *Swedru* (renamed *Maradi* in 1965)	4,809	12½	Scotts	1948		E.D.L., G.G.	Sold	1967
377	M.V. *Accra*	11,600	16	Vickers A.	1947		E.D.L.	Sold	1967
378	M.V. *Apapa*	11,607	16	Vickers A.	1948		E.D.L.	Sold	1968
379	S.S. *Baro*	1,517	11	Blyth D & S	1950		E.D.L.	Sold	1961
380	S.S. *Benin*	2,483	11	J. Lamont	1950		E.D.L.	Sold	1960
381	S.S. *Prah* (ex. *Avisbay*)	7,339	12	W. Gray	1945	1950	E.D.L.	Sold	1958
382	S.S. *Benue* (ex. *Benjamin Tay*)	1,814	13	Pacific Bridge	1943	1951	E.D.L.	Sold	1952
383	S.S. *Bida* (ex. *John W. Arey*)	1,791	13	Walter Butler	1942	1951	E.D.L.	Sold	1952
384	M.V. *Eket*	394		J. S. White	1950		W.A.L.T.	In service	
385	M.V. *Aureol*	14,803	16	A. Stephen	1951		E.D.L.	In Service	
386	M.V. *Eboe*	9,380		Scotts	1952		E.D.L.	In Service	
387	M.V. *Ebani*	9,376		Scotts	1952		E.D.L.	In service	
388	M.V. *Obuasi*	5,895		Harland & W.	1952		E.D.L.	In service	
389	M.V. *Onitsha*	7,267		Harland & W.	1952		E.D.L.	Sold	1972
390	S.T. *Martaban*	5,740		W. Denny	1950	1952	B.B.	Sold	1963
391	S.T. *Prome*	7,043		W. Denny	1937	1952	B.B.	Sold	1962
392	S.T. *Salween*	7,063		W. Denny	1938	1952	B.B.	Sold	1962
393	S.T. *Yoma*	5,909		W. Denny	1948	1952	B.B.	Sold	1963
394	M.V. *Kadeik*	7,489		Lithgows	1952	1952	B.B., E.D.L.	Sold	1966
395	M.V. *Kaladan*	4,916		Lithgows	1950	1952	B.B.	Sold	1963
396	M.V. *Kanbe*	4,878		Lithgows	1948	1952	B.B.	Sold	1962
397	M.V. *Kalewa*	4,876		Lithgows	1947	1952	B.B.	Sold	1963
398	M.V. *Katha*	4,878		Lithgows	1947	1952	B.B.	Sold	1962
399	M.V. *Kindat*	5,530		Lithgows	1950	1952	B.B.	Sold	1963
400	M.V. *Koyan*	5,537		Lithgows	1952	1952	B.B., E.D.L.	Sold	1966
401	M.V. *Kohima*	5,597		Lithgows	1953		B.B., E.D.L.	Sold	1966
402	M.V. *Kentung*	5,558		W. Denny	1954		B.B., E.D.L.	Sold	1966
403	M.V. *Patani*	6,183		Scotts	1954		E.D.L.	In service	
404	M.V. *Perang*	6,177		W. Gray	1954		E.D.L.	Sold	1972
405	M.V. *Itu*	129		Yarrow & Co.	1954		W.A.L.T.	Broken up	1966

Ref. No.	Ship's Name	Gross tons	Knots	Builder	Built	Pur-chased	Owning Companies	End of Service
406	M.V. *Owerri*	5,798		Harland & W.	1955		E.D.L.	Sold 1972
407	M.V. *Kandaw*	5,599		Lithgows	1955		B.B., E.D.L.	Sold 1967
408	M.V. *Kaduna*	5,599		Lithgows	1956		B.B., H., E.D.L.	In service
409	M.V. *Oti*	5,485		Harland & W.	1956		E.D.L.	Sold 1972
410	M.V. *Ondo*	5,435		Harland & W.	1956		E.D.L.	Lost 1960
411	M.V. *Egori*	8,331		Scotts	1957		E.D.L.	In service
412	M.V. *Winneba* (ex. *Umgeni*)	8,300		Swan Hunter	1938	1957	E.D.L.	Sold 1962
413	M.V. *Calabar* (ex. *Umtali*)	8,300		Swan Hunter	1936	1957	E.D.L.	Sold 1962
414	M.V. *Bhamo*	5,932		Lithgows	1957		B.B., H., G.G.	In service
415	M.V. *Daru*	6,301	14	Scotts	1958		E.D.L., H., G.G.	In service
416	M.V. *Kumba*	5,439		Lithgows	1958		E.D.L., G.G., E.D.L.	In service
417	M.V. *Kabala*	5,445		Lithgows	1958		B.B., E.D.L.	In service
418	M.V. *Degema*	8,153	14	W. Gray	1959		E.D.L.	In service
419	M.V. *Dixcove*	8,138	14	W. Gray	1959		E.D.L.	In service
420	M.V. *Prahsu* (renamed *Kalaw* in 1964 then *Kohima* in 1966)	5,445		Lithgows	1959		E.D.L., H., E.D.L.	In service
421	M.V. *Dunkwa*	8,254	14	Scotts	1960		E.D.L.	In service
422	M.V. *Donga*	8,868		Lithgows	1960		B.B., E.D.L.	In service
423	M.V. *Dumbaia*	8,876		Lithgows	1960		B.B., E.D.L.	In service
424	M.V. *Dalla*	8,831		Lithgows	1961		B.B., E.D.L.	In service
425	M.V. *Pegu*	5,764		Lithgows	1961		B.B., H., G.G.	In service
426	M.V. *Deido*	8,254	14	Scotts	1961		E.D.L.	In service
427	M.V. *Dumurra*	8,238	14	A. Stephen	1961		E.D.L.	In service
428	M.V. *Fourah Bay*	7,704	16	Scotts	1961		E.D.L.	In service
429	M.V. *Falaba*	7,703	16	Scotts	1962		E.D.L.	In service
430	M.V. *Forcados*	7,689	16	Lithgows	1963		E.D.L.	In service
431	M.V. *Fian*	7,689	16	Lithgows	1964		E.D.L.	In service
432	M.V. *Freetown*	7,689	16	Lithgows	1964		E.D.L., G.G.	In service
433	M.V. *Fulani*	7,689	16	Lithgows	1964		E.D.L.	In service
434	M.V. *Sunjarv* (ex. *Gjendefjell*)	15,000 d/w		J. L. Thompson	1958	1964	B.B., H.	Sold 1970
435	S.T. *Mary Holt*	5,577		W. Gray		1965	Acquired with the pur-	
436	S.T. *Elizabeth Holt*	5,580		Cammell Laird		1965	chase of the Guinea Gulf Line but did not go into	
437	S.T. *Florence Holt*	5,580		Cammell Laird		1965	service with E.D. Lines.	
438	S.T. *Rose of Lancaster*	5,197		W. Gray		1965		Sold 1965–6
439	M.V. *Carway*	1,597		Grangemouth	1967		S.F.	In service
440	M.V. *Clearway* (ex. *Speedway*)	1,160		Robb, D/Y Caledon	1970	1970	S.F.	In service

Ref. No.	Ship's Name	Gross tons	Knots	Builder	Built	Pur- chased	Owning Companies	End of Service
441	M.V. *Speedway* (ex. *Sealord Challenger,* ex. *Clearway*)	1,204		Werft Nobiskrug Rensburg	1968	1970	S.F.	In service
442	M.V. *Skyway* (ex. *Mandeville*)	1,175		Trosvik Verksted Brevik	1968	1970	S.F.	In service

Note: The table above is not strictly chronological as it attempts to take account of ship classes and series. In the case of vessels bought second-hand, the date of acquisition is normally used, not the date of construction. Abbreviations used for the 'Owning Companies' are as follows:

African African Steam Ship Company
B/A British & African S.N. Company
E.D. Elder Dempster and Company, and Elder Dempster and Company Limited
E.L. Elder Dempster Shipping Limited, and the Elder Line Limited
O.T. Ocean Transport Co. Limited
I.D. Imperial Direct West India Mail Service Company Limited
E.D.L. Elder Dempster Lines Limited
N.T. Nigerian Transport Company Limited
E.D.C. Elder Dempster Lines (Canada) Limited
G.G. The Guinea Gulf Line Limited
H. The Henderson Line Limited
B.B. The British & Burmese S.N. Company Limited
S.F. Seaway Car Transporters Limited, and Seaway Ferries Limited
W.A.L.T. West African Lighterage and Transport

Source: The table is based on the 'Elder Dempster Fleet List for 1852 to 1960', which was produced by the then Company Secretary, Mr M. H. Smye, in August 1960. Additional details have been obtained from the Annual Directors Reports and Accounts of the relevant companies. My thanks are also due to Mr C. E. Woodward, currently attached to Ocean's department of Naval Architecture, for his assistance with the latter part of the table.

Bibliography

a. *Manuscript Sources*

1. Private Collections

Elder Dempster Lines, Mss

Elder Dempster Lines Limited hold most of the remaining records of the African Steam Ship Company, the British and African Steam Navigation Company, Elder Dempster and Company and Elder Dempster and Company Limited. As a result of the changes in company structure which followed the Royal Mail crash, and because of the damage sustained during the wartime blitz on Liverpool, few items have survived, but many gaps have been filled from the archives of J. T. Fletcher and Company—formerly Messrs Fletcher and Parr. The papers of the present firm, Elder Dempster Lines Limited, are reasonably complete but, of course, only date back to its formation in 1932.

The John Holt Papers

These are an invaluable guide to the merchanting aspect of West African history and cover the period from about 1870 to the present day. They have been well catalogued by Dr J. E. Flint and are kept by John Holt & Co. (Liverpool) Limited at their offices in India Building, Water Street, Liverpool. The late Mr Cecil Holt, then a senior director of the firm, kindly permitted me to have ready access to these archives.

The Guinea Gulf Line MSS

The papers of the Shipping Department of John Holt and Company (Liverpool) Limited, the John Holt Line Limited, and the Guinea Gulf Line Limited, have been collected under the above heading and were kindly made available to me by Mr Douglas Mather, the former chairman of the firm.

Royal Niger Company Papers

These are now kept at the Rhodes House Library in Oxford having been presented by the Earl of Scarborough. The relevant files are:

    Mss. Afr. S.95.   Vol. 7 Transport
                        Vols 11, 12 & 13 Miscellaneous.

United Africa Company Papers

These papers are held at United Africa House, Blackfriars Road, London. The general index gives details of items kept on behalf of the U.A.C. and of its constituent firms including the Niger Company, Millers, the African and Eastern Trade Corporation, Swanzys and the Southern Whaling and Sealing Company. With the exception of the last these organisations are concerned almost exclusively with merchanting, mainly in West Africa. The index also lists many documents in respect of the Bromport Steamship Company and later shipping activities, but most of these have now been handed over to the Palm Line Limited.

Lever Brothers MSS
The *Minutes of the Directors' Conference* of Lever Brothers Limited, provide the best possible guide to the activities of the Lever organisations in West Africa. All aspects of merchanting and shipping policies are fully discussed and all key decisions noted. I am greatly obliged to Mr R. F. Taylor, Assistant Secretary of Unilever, for permission to examine these records which are kept at Unilever House, London.

Palm Line Papers
The Company possesses many of the surviving papers of the Bromport Line and of the shipping department of the United Africa Company. Technical and financial details of the Line's operations since 1950 are also available. A number of house history pamphlets, written at various dates, provides a simple guide to the development of the firm and its fleet.

Henry Tyrer MSS
Henry Tyrer and Company Limited of Liverpool operated chartered vessels to West Africa during the Alfred Jones era and subsequently acted as managing agents for the ships of the Bromport Line, the African and Eastern Trade Corporation, the Niger Company and the United Africa Company. This association only terminated in 1950 after the Palm Line had been established and the whole structure of Lever's shipping interests had been reorganised.

A number of important papers and documents concerning the above firm were made available to me by the late Mr. Frederick Cutts who gave me the benefit of his seventy years' experience in the West African trade.

The E.D. Morel Papers
This huge collection of the letters and documents of E. D. Morel is now kept at the British Library of Political and Economic Science, London School of Economics, Houghton Street, London. The relevant files are as follows:

Box F. 8/1   Letters from Sir Alfred Jones.
Box F. 8/2   Letters from John Holt.

The Mocatta Papers
Mrs Florence Norah Mocatta of Hoylake, Wirral, is the great niece of Sir Alfred Jones. She has in her possession the remaining private papers of Sir Alfred. These include only a small number of letters and telegrams, but also of value is the scrapbook of Florence Mary Pinnock, (Jones's niece), compiled whilst she was living at her uncle's house. Other items of interest include a short, handwritten biography of Jones by his sister, Mrs Isobel Mary Pinnock and a detailed 'Book of Obituary'.

2. Company Files

The following files of live companies are kept at Companies House, 55–71, City Road, London:

Reference No. 40828 Bank of British West Africa Limited
     70123 Elder and Fyffes Limited
     267738 Elder Dempster Lines Limited
     267738 Elder Dempster Lines (Holdings) Limited and Liner Holdings Company Limited
     51851 John Holt and Company (Liverpool) Limited
     734040 Guinea Gulf Line Limited
     117476 Palm Line Limited
     239114 United Africa Company Limited
     112584 West African Lighterage and Transport Company Limited

The following files of Dissolved companies are also kept at Companies House, London:

Reference No. 143730 Bromport Steamship Company Limited
     65244 Elders Navigation Collieries Limited
     72110 Imperial Direct West India Mail Service Company Limited
     132775 Alfred L. Jones Trust and Estate Company Limited

The following files of Dissolved companies are now kept at the Public Record Office, London:

Reference No. 61912 Elder Dempster Shipping Limited
     61912 Elder Line Limited
     73475 Elder and Fyffes (Shipping) Limited
     108502 Elder Dempster and Company Limited
     125828 Elder Dempster (Grand Canary) Limited
     125829 Elder Dempster (Tenerife) Limited

The following files of Dissolved companies are kept at the Companies Registration Office, 102, George Street, Edinburgh:

Reference: E.67206 British and African Steam Navigation Company Limited.
    E.67206 British and African Steam Navigation Company (1900) Limited.

3. Unpublished Works

A Short History of the Liverpool Chamber of Commerce
This is a typescript written by Mr Patrick Burford, the present (1972) Secretary of the Liverpool Chamber of Commerce. Also available at the Chamber's offices are the *Annual Reports of the Liverpool Chamber of Commerce*, and these include valuable sections on Liverpool's trade with West Africa.

Reminiscences of one connected with the West African Trade from 1863 to 1910
This typescript was produced by Mr Harry Cotterell, a prominent merchant in the

West African trade, for the guidance of his children. A copy is in the author's possession.

Sir Alfred Jones and the Development of West African Trade
M.A. Thesis by P. N. Davies, University of Liverpool, 1964.

British Shipping and the Growth of the West African Economy, 1910–50
Ph.D. Thesis by P. N. Davies, University of Liverpool, 1967.

A British Merchant in West Africa in the Era of Imperialism
Ph.D. Thesis by Miss Cherry Gertzel, dealing with John Holt. In the Bodleian Library, Oxford.

The Elder Dempster Companies and their Ships
This typescript was written by Mr M. H. Smye, the then Secretary of Elder Dempster Lines Limited in 1957. A copy is in the author's possession.

Glasgow and Africa, Connexions and Attitudes, 1870–1900
Ph.D. Thesis by W. Thompson, University of Strathclyde, 1970.

A Report to Elder Dempster Lines Limited, on the operation and commercial possibilities of an air service in British West Africa
This was produced by Imperial Airways Limited, London, 1935. A copy is in the author's possession.

The History of the United Africa Company Limited, to 1938
This was written anonymously by a senior member of the staff and was based on the recollections of the older employees. A copy is in the author's possession.

b.   *Printed Sources*

1. Government Papers

Committee on the Currency of the West African Colonies, Minutes of Evidence, Cd. 2984, 1899

Royal Commission on Shipping Rings, Cd. 4668–70 and 4685, 1909

Report of the West African Currency Committee, Cd. 6426, 1912

Edible and Oil Producing Nuts and Seeds Committee, Cd. 8248, 1916

Final Report of the Imperial Shipping Committee on the Deferred Rebate System, Cmd. 1802, 1913

Committee on Industry and Trade, (the Balfour Committee) 1924–1927, Cmd. 3282, 1929

Statistical Abstracts for the United Kingdom, for the several British Overseas Dominions and Protectorates, for the British Empire, for the British Commonwealth and the Commonwealth for the relevant years.

Annual Reports for the Gold Coast

Nigeria Handbook, Crown Agents for the Colonies, London, 1953

Debates of the House of Representatives, Lagos, Nigeria

Annual Statements of the Trade of the United Kingdom with Foreign Countries and British Possessions

2. Books

R. G. Albion, *Seaports South of Sahara* (New York: Appleton-Century-Crofts Inc., 1959).

A. Anderson, (D. MacPherson) *Annals of Commerce*, Vol. IV (London: Nichols and Son, 1805).

W. Ashworth, *An Economic History of England, 1870–1939* (London: Methuen, 1960).

W. B. Baikie, *Narrative of an Exploring Voyage up the Rivers Kwo'ra and Bi'nue (commonly known as the Niger and Tsa'dda) in 1854* (London: John Murray, 1956).

P. T. Bauer, *West African Trade* (London: Cambridge University Press, 1954).

C. B. A. Behrens, *Merchant Shipping and the Demands of War,* (London: H.M.S.O., 1955).

J. W. Blake, *European Beginnings in West Africa, 1454–1578* (London: Longmans Green, 1937).

F. C. Bowen, *History of the Canadian Pacific Line* (London: Sampson, Low, Marston & Co., 1928).

C. Brooks, *The Royal Mail Case* (Edinburgh & London: William Hodge & Co., 1933).

Sir A. Burns, *History of Nigeria*, 6th edition (New York: Barnes & Noble, 1963).

H. Burton & D. C. Corner, *Investment and Unit Trusts in Britain and America* (London: Elek. Books, 1968).

T. A. Bushell, *Royal Mail, 1839–1939* (London: Trade & Travel Publications Ltd, 1939).

K. G. Davies, *The Royal African Company* (London: Longmans, Green, 1957).

K. Onwuka Dike, *Trade and Politics in the Niger Delta, 1830–1885* (London: Oxford University Press, 1956).

D. Ellison, (Ed.) *Cox and the Ju Ju Coast* (St Helier: Ellison & Co., 1968).

J. D. Fage, *An Introduction to the History of West Africa* (London: Cambridge University Press, 1955).

C. Ernest Fayle, *Seaborne Trade,* Vol. 1 (London: John Murray, 1920).

C. Ernest Fayle, *The War and the Shipping Industry* (London: Oxford University Press, 1927).

C. Ernest Fayle, *A Short History of the World's Shipping Industry* (London: George Allen & Unwin, 1933).

John E. Flint, *Sir George Goldie and the Making of Nigeria* (London: Oxford University Press, 1960).

C. Fyffe, *A History of Sierra Leone* (London: Oxford University Press, 1962).

J. D. Hargreaves, *Prelude to the Partition of West Africa* (London: MacMillan, 1963).

R. J. Harrison-Church, *West Africa* (London: Longmans, Green, 1966).

A. C. G. Hastings, *The Voyage of the DAYSPRING* (London: John Lane (The Bodley Head, Limited), 1926).

G. K. Helleiner, *Peasant Agriculture, Government, and Economic Growth in Nigeria* (Homewood, Illinois: Richard D. Irwin Inc., 1966).

H. B. Hermon-Hodge, *Gazetteer of Ilorin Province* (London: George Allen and Unwin, 1929).

C. R. Holt, (ed.) *The Diary of John Holt* (Liverpool: Henry Young & Sons, 1948).

B. S. Hoyle and D. Hilling (Eds.) *Seaports and Development in Tropical Africa* (London: MacMillan, 1970).

T. J. Hutchinson, *Narrative of the Niger, Tshadda and Benue Exploration, 1855* (Reprinted by Frank Cass & Co., London, 1966).

F. E. Hyde, *Blue Funnel* (A History of Alfred Holt & Co., Liverpool, 1865–1914) (Liverpool: Liverpool University Press, 1957).

F. E. Hyde, *Shipping Enterprise and Management* (Harrisons of Liverpool, 1830–1939) (Liverpool: Liverpool University Press, 1967).

H. Montgomery Hyde, *Norman Birkett* (London: H. Hamilton, 1964).

D. M. V. Jones, *The Time Shrinkers* (London: David Rendel Ltd, 1971).

Mary Kingsley, *West African Studies* (London: MacMillan, 1899).

A. W. Kirkaldy, *British Shipping* (Its History, Organisation and Importance) (London: Kegan, Paul, Trench, Trubner & Co., 1914).

S. F. Klinghofer, *A Report on a Preliminary Survey of Factors contributing to level of freight rates in the Seaborne Trade of Africa,* U. N. Economic Commission for Africa (New York, 1965).

D. Laird, *Paddy Henderson* (The Story of P. Henderson & Co.) (London & Glasgow: George Outram, 1961).

M. Laird and R. A. K. Oldfield, *Narrative of an expedition into the interior of Africa by the River Niger in the steam vessels QUORRA and ALBURKAH in 1832, 1833 and 1834.* 2 Vols. (London: Richard Bentley, 1837).

Charlotte Leubuscher, *The West African Shipping Trade, 1909–1959* (Leyden: A. W. Sythoff, 1963).

Christopher Lloyd, *The Navy and the Slave Trade* (London: Longmans, Green, 1949).

J. R. McCulloch, *Dictionary of Commerce* (London: Longmans, Green, 1882).

Allister MacMillan, *The Red Book of West Africa* (London: Collingridge, 1920).

Allan McPhee, *The Economic Revolution in British West Africa* (London: George Routledge, 1926).

S. Marriner and F. E. Hyde, *The Senior, John Samuel Swire* (Liverpool: Liverpool University Press, 1967).

E. W. Marwick, *William Balfour Baikie* (Orkney: W. R. MacIntosh, The Kirkwall Press, 1965).

Daniel Marx Junior, *International Shipping Cartels* (New Jersey: Princeton University Press, 1953).

M. F. Maury, *The Physical Geography of the Sea,* 6th Edition (London: Samson, Low, Son & Co., 1856).

G. E. Metcalfe, *Great Britain and Ghana, Documents of Ghana History, 1807–1957* (London: Thomas Nelson, 1964).

A. H. Milne, *Sir Alfred Lewis Jones, K.C.M.G.* (Liverpool: Henry Young & Sons, 1914).

Marischal Murray, *Union Castle Chronicle, 1853–1953* (London: Longmans, Green, 1953).

C. W. Newbury, *British Policy towards West Africa, Selected Documents 1786–1874* (London: Oxford University Press, 1965) and *Selected Documents, 1875–1914* (London: Oxford University Press, 1971).

W. T. Newlyn and D. C. Rowan, *Money and Banking in British Colonial Africa* (London: Oxford University Press, 1954).

S. Daniel Neumark, *Foreign Trade and Economic Development in Africa,* (Stanford: Food Research Institute, 1963).

Roland Oliver and J. D. Fage, *A Short History of Africa* (Harmondsworth: Penguin, 1962).

W. Page, *Commerce and Industry,* (1815–1914) Vol. II (London: Constable & Co., 1919).

Sir F. J. Pedler, *Economic Geography of West Africa* (London: Longmans, Green, 1955).

Sir F. J. Pedler, *The United Africa Company,* to be published in 1973.

Sir Alan Pim, *The Financial and Economic History of the African Tropical Territories* (London: Oxford University Press, 1940).

J. H. Plumb and C. Howard, *West African Explorers* (London: Oxford University Press, 1955).

Howard Robinson, *Carrying British Mails Overseas* (London: George Allen & Unwin, 1964).

R. E. Robinson and J. Gallagher with Alice Denny, *Africa and the Victorians* (London: MacMillan, 1961).

Ronald Ross, *Memoirs* (London: John Murray, 1923).

S. W. Roskill, *A Merchant Fleet in War* (Alfred Holt & Co., 1939–45). (London: Collins, 1962).

J. A. Salter, *Allied Shipping Control* (London: Oxford University Press, 1921).

E. C. Smith, *A Short History of Naval and Marine Engineering* (London: Cambridge University Press, 1937).

J. Russell Smith, *The Ocean Carrier* (London: G. P. Putram, 1908).

J. Russell Smith, *Influence of the Great War upon Shipping* (London: Oxford University Press, 1919).

S. G. Sturmey, *British Shipping and World Competition* (University of London: Athlone Press, 1962).

W. F. Tewson, *The British Cotton Growing Association* (Golden Jubilee, 1904–1954) Issued by the Association, 1954.

R. H. Thornton, *British Shipping* (London: Cambridge University Press, 1959).

Dag Tresselt, *The West African Shipping Range* (Geneva: U.N. Conference on Trade and Development, 1967).

Charles Wilson, *The History of Unilever,* Vols. I and II (London: Cassell, 1954).

C. Wilson and W. Reader, *Men and Machines* (A History of D. Napier and Son, Engineers, Limited) (London: Weidenfeld and Nicolson, 1958).

3. Privately Published Papers

P. N. Davies, *A Short History of the Ships of John Holt and Company (Liverpool) Limited, and the Guinea Gulf Line, Limited.* Published privately by the Company (Liverpool, 1965).

F. Bateman Jones, *Elder Dempster Lines.* Pamphlet published privately by the Company (Liverpool, 1945).

The Elder Dempster Fleet in the War. Published privately by the Company (Liverpool, 1921).

Merchant Adventure. Published privately by John Holt and Company (Liverpool) Limited (Liverpool, 1948).

Compagnie Maritime Belge (Lloyd Royal). House History published by the Company (Antwerp, 1948).

A Short History of the German Africa Lines. Published privately by the Deutsche Afrika-Linien (Hamburg, 1967).

List of Iron, Steel and Wood Vessels built at the Birkenhead Iron Works. (Laird's shipyard) (Birkenhead: Willmer Brothers, 1894).

4. Articles

A. A. Cowan, 'Early Trading Conditions in the Bight of Biafra', *Journal of the Royal African Society* (October, 1935).

P. N. Davies, 'The African Steam Ship Company', *Liverpool and Merseyside* (ed. J. R. Harris) (London: Frank Cass & Co., 1969).

P. N. Davies and A. M. Bourn, 'Lord Kylsant and the Royal Mail', *Business History*, Vol. XIV, No. 2 (July, 1972).

L. C. Fay, 'Elder Dempster Lines, Limited', *Sea Breezes* (September, 1948).

H. S. Goldsmith, C.M.G., 'MacGregor Laird and the Niger', *Journal of the African Society*, Vol. XXXI, No. CXXXV (October, 1932).

R. G. Greenhill, 'The State under Pressure—the West Indian Mail Contract, 1905', *Business History*, Vol. XI, No. 2 (July 1969).

Sir Patrick Hastings, 'The Case of the Royal Mail', *Studies in Accounting Theory*, (ed. W. T. Baxter and S. Davidson) (London: Sweet & Maxwell Limited, 1962).

David Hilling, 'Tema: the Geography of a New Port', *Geography*, Vol. 51, Part 2 (April, 1966).

David Hilling, 'The Evolution of the Major Ports of West Africa', *Geographic Journal*, Vol. 135, Part 3 (September, 1969).

A. G. Hopkins, 'Economic Imperialism in West Africa, Lagos 1880–1892', *Economic History Review*, Vol. 21, No. 3 (December 1968).

R. S. Irving, 'British Railway Investment and Innovation, 1900–1914', Vol. XIII, No. 1 (January, 1971).

A. L. Jones, 'Autobiography', *M.A.P. Magazine* (28 December, 1901).

M. G. Kendall, 'Losses of U.K. Merchant Ships in World War II', *Economica*, n.s., Vol. XV (1948).

W. D. McIntyre, 'British Policy in West Africa—the Ashanti Expedition, 1873-4', *Historical Journal*, Vol. 5, No. 1 (1962).

S. B. Saul, 'The Economic Significance of Constructive Imperialism', *Journal of Economic History*, Vol. 17, No. 2 (June, 1957).

S. B. Saul, 'The British West Indies in Depression, 1880–1914', *Journal of Inter-American Economic Affairs*, Vol. 12, No. 3 (Winter, 1958).

H. P. White, 'Recent Port Developments in the Gold Coast', *Scottish Geographic Magazine*, Vol. 71 (1955).

H. P. White, 'The Ports of West Africa', *Tijdschrift voor Econmoische en Sociale Geographie*, Vol. 50, No. 1 (1959).

5. Works of General Reference

Burke's *Peerage*
Chamber of Shipping of the United Kingdom, *Annual Year Book*
Chamber of Shipping of the United Kingdom, *British Shipping Statistics*
Dictionary of National Biography
Fairplay's Annual Summary of British Shipping Finance
Liverpool Underwriters, Registry for Iron Vessels
Lloyd's Register of Shipping
London and Cambridge Economic Service
Standard Bank, *Annual Economic Review* for Ghana, Nigeria, Sierra Leone and the Gambia
The Times, '300'
West African Directory
Who's Who
Who Was Who

6. Periodicals and Newspapers

African World
Bank of British West Africa, Staff Magazine
Business History
Economica
Economic History Review
The Economist
Elder Dempster Magazine
Fairplay
Financial Times
Geographic Journal
Geography
Great Thoughts
Hansard
Journal of Commerce
Liverpool Courier
Liverpool Daily Post
Liverpool Echo
Liverpool Mercury
Lloyd's List

Manchester City News
M.A.P.
Money Market Review
Motor Trader
Nigerian Daily Express
Nigerline
Ocean
Ocean Mail
Palm Bulletin
Railway News
Sea
Sierra Leone Weekly Review
Standard Bank Review
Statistical and Economic Review
Sunday Strand
The Times
Weekly Courier
West Africa
West African Review
Unilever House Magazine

Index

Index

Abidjan 343

Abonema 244

Accra 43, 58, 75, 119, 290, 298, 300, 342, 347, 363–4

Aden 363

Adjuiah 179

African and Eastern Trade Corporation Ltd 211–13, 221, 224–8; Amalgamation 246–7; Assets 236; Claim against Elder Dempster 262–3; Difficulties 236; Dispute with Elder Dempster 245, 250; Formation 236; Merger with Niger Co 237, 239–40, 242; Results 236

African Association Ltd 16, 88–9, 91, 94–5, 97, 99, 100–2, 105–7, 110–12, 122, 130, 138, 171, 176, 211, 425

African Association (unlimited) 94, 100

African Container Express Ltd 345, 387

African Inland Commercial Co 37

African Oil Mills Co 125

African Steam Ship Co 24, 29, 30, 41, 44–6, 48–53, 55–7, 59–68, 74, 76–8, 80–3, 86–90, 98, 108, 119, 144–5, 149, 173, 199, 230, 253; Financial results 229; Fleet of 50, 65, 82, 89, 158, 405; Liquidation 272–3; Losses 270–1

Africanisation 340–1

Air services 289, 333, 338, 340, 358, 362, 392

Akosombo 364

Albion, R. G. 344

Alsop Stevens & Co 316

Alumina 389, 392

Aluminium 389, 391

American West African Freight Conference 351

American West African Line Inc. 245

Amsinck, Mr 242

Amsterdam 315

Anders, Captain E. C. 304

Anderson, A. 29

Andrew, Captain J. W. 305, 309, 310

Andrews, Mr 300

Anglo-African Steam Ship Co 82

Antwerp 97, 349

Apapa 179, 244, 297, 342, 360, 364, 387

Arriens, Mr 242

Arundell, P. G. H. 337

Ashanti 25–6

Ashworth, William 90

Associated Central West African Lines 184

Astbury, G. G. 14, 239

Atlantic Coaling Co Ltd 253

Atlantic Isles Depot Agreement 183

Australasia 351

Avezathe, G. H. 297, 298, 314, 337

Elder Line Ltd 253, 270-1

Elderpalm Schiffahrts-Agentur G.m.b.h. 363

Elders Colonial Airways Ltd 289, 291, 347; Aircraft used 292-3; Coastal seaplane service 293; Post-war 332-3, 340; Routes followed 292-3

Elders Engineering and Airways Co Ltd 340, 363

Elders Insurance Co Ltd 253

Elders Navigation Colliery Ltd 125-6, 437-8

Elders of South Africa (Proprietary) Ltd 333, 362

Ellerman, Sir John 169

Ellerman Line 169

Ellerton, G. J. 13, 337

Elmina 19-20

Erlebach and Co (ship charterers) 15, 247

Erlebach, D. E. 15, 247

Escardos River 101

Escravos Bar 342

European Economic Community 390

Evans, J. W. 15, 292

Evans, Captain 204

Everton Brow road tests 125

Exley, Captain W. 306

Expatriates employed in West Africa 341, 358

Explorer Class 271, 277

Exports from Canary Islands 127

Exports from West Africa 19, 25, 27, 43, 198, 228, 234, 275, 277, 320-3, 344, 352, 361, 381, 385, 388-9, 390; (see also Appendix:-Tables 1-2 and 4-8)

Fage, J. D. 19

Fairfield Shipbuilding and Engineering Co 53

Far East-West Africa trade 351

Fawcett and Preston 38

Fayle, C. Ernest 187-90, 192-4, 203, 209

Feggetter, H. S. 290

Felixstowe 359, 361

Fernando Po 39, 43, 58, 75

Ferry services 364

Figg Brothers and Sacks 333

Findlay, W. K. 14, 131, 178

Fisher, Benjamin 48

Fletcher, J. T. 52, 64

Fletcher, J. T. & Co 15

Fletcher, J. T. (Shipping) Ltd 69

Fletcher, Parr and Co 53, 56-7, 63, 65-6, 68-9, 76-8, 84, 138, 424; Relations with African S.S. Co 66-8, 80

Flint, J. E. 26, 48, 99, 135

Foreign Office 98-9, 111

Forwood Line 170

Freetown 19, 25, 157, 173, 293, 296, 300, 341, 343, 347, 364

Freight rates 59, 62, 91, 132-3, 135-7, 143, 149, 152-6, 175 (John Holt) 185 (special rates) 237 (U.A.C.), 476-9; Hoegh rate war: 350, 365, 369; Klinghofer conclusions 373; Post-war 209-10, 212-13, 217, 220, 222, 225, 227-8, 232, 316, 323-6, 349, 381-4; Wartime 189, 190-1, 195, 197-8, 202

French Conference 224 (Société Navale de l'Ouest; Chargeurs Réunis; Compagnie de Navigaine)

French interests in West Africa 26, 28

French shipping 223, 280-1; Fraissinet Line 224; Joint service with E.D. 332, 365

Furness, Sir Christopher 105

Furness Withy & Co 105-7, 254

Furness Withy Group 345

Fyffe, Hudson & Co Ltd 128, 184

Gaiser & Co 157

Gallagher, J. 164

Gambia 25, 297, 301, 337-9, 343, 352

Garthorpe 55

Geake, A. C. 14, 247

General Steam Navigation Co 104-5, 107, 139

George, Lloyd 192

World War, Second—*contd.*
to Deep Scheme 297, 298; Ship control 294; Ships Licensing Committee 294; Tonnage Disposal Scheme 320; WALCON ended 348; W.A. Lines co-ordinating committee 301, 315, 322 (*see also* Appendix:- Tables 23-4, for details of E.D. ship losses)

Wyness, A. C. 14, 289, 292

Yapei 364
Yonnibannal 179
Young, Mr 299

Zim Line 338-9
Zinc 389, 391-2
Zochonis, G. B. 121, 140, 156